MI6

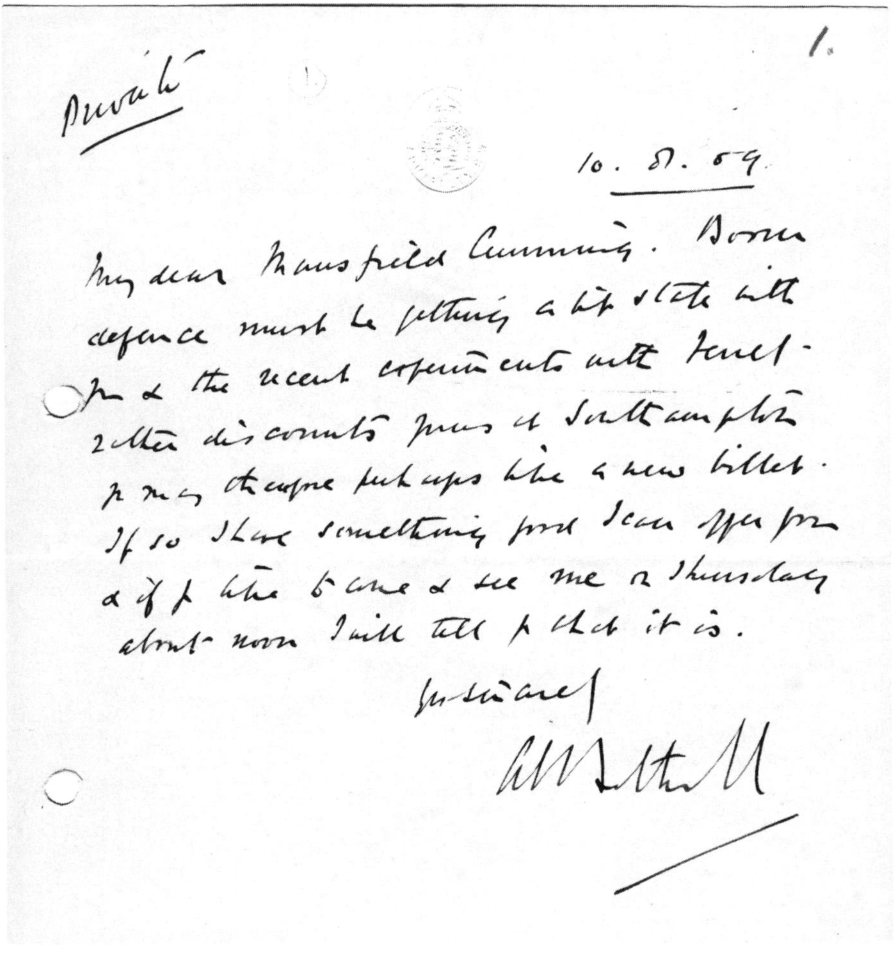

Private

1.

10. 8. 09.

My dear Mansfield Cumming. Boom defence must be getting a bit stale with you & the recent experiments with Ferret & other discomforts from us at Southampton you may therefore perhaps like a new billet. If so I have something good I can offer you & if you like to come & see me on Thursday about noon I will tell you what it is.

Yrs sincerely

A E Bethell

One of SIS's founding documents: the letter of 10 August 1909 from Admiral Alexander Bethell (Director of Naval Intelligence) to Mansfield Cumming offering him 'something good', which turned out to be appointment as Chief of the new Secret Service.

THE SECRET HISTORY OF
MI6

Keith Jeffery

THE PENGUIN PRESS

NEW YORK

2010

THE PENGUIN PRESS
Published by the Penguin Group
Penguin Group (USA) Inc., 375 Hudson Street, New York, New York 10014, U.S.A. •
Penguin Group (Canada), 90 Eglinton Avenue East, Suite 700, Toronto, Ontario, Canada M4P 2Y3 (a division of
Pearson Penguin Canada Inc.) • Penguin Books Ltd, 80 Strand, London WC2R 0RL, England • Penguin Ireland,
25 St. Stephen's Green, Dublin 2, Ireland (a division of Penguin Books Ltd) • Penguin Books Australia Ltd,
250 Camberwell Road, Camberwell, Victoria 3124, Australia (a division of Pearson Australia Group Pty Ltd) •
Penguin Books India Pvt Ltd, 11 Community Centre, Panchsheel Park, New Delhi – 110 017, India •
Penguin Group (NZ), 67 Apollo Drive, Rosedale, North Shore 0632, New Zealand (a division of Pearson
New Zealand Ltd) • Penguin Books (South Africa) (Pty) Ltd, 24 Sturdee Avenue, Rosebank,
Johannesburg 2196, South Africa

Penguin Books Ltd, Registered Offices:
80 Strand, London WC2R 0RL, England

First published in 2010 by The Penguin Press,
a member of Penguin Group (USA) Inc.

10 9 8 7 6 5 4 3 2 1

LIBRARY OF CONGRESS CATALOGING IN PUBLICATION DATA
Jeffery, Keith.
Secret history of MI6 / Keith Jeffery.
p.   cm.
Includes bibliographical references and index.
ISBN 978-1-59420-274-2
1. Great Britain. MI6—History.   2. Intelligence service—Great Britain—History—20th century.   I. Title.
UB251.G7J44 2010
327.1241009—dc22
2010024158

Printed in the United States of America

Contents

Foreword

Keith Jeffery's history of the Secret Intelligence Service 1909–1949 is a landmark in the history of the Service.

At the initiative of my predecessor, John Scarlett, SIS decided in the run up to our centenary to commission an independent and authoritative volume on the history of the Service's first forty years. The aim was to increase public understanding of SIS by explaining our origin and role in a rigorous history, which would be accessible to the widest possible audience but would not damage national security. This is the first time we have given an academic from outside the Service such access to our archives. The Foreign Secretary of the day approved our plans.

Why focus on 1909–1949? Firstly, SIS's first forty years cover a period of vital concern for the United Kingdom. Secondly, 1949 represents a watershed in our professional work with the move to Cold War targets and techniques. Thirdly and most importantly, full details of our history after 1949 are still too sensitive to place in the public domain. Up to 1949 Professor Jeffery has been free to tell a complete story and to put on the public record a well-informed picture of the intelligence contribution to a key period of twentieth-century history. During this time, SIS developed from a small, Europe-focused organisation into a worldwide professional Service ready to take an important role in the Cold War.

Throughout, we have been at pains to provide the necessary openness to enable the author to tell our history definitively. We take very seriously our obligations to protect our agents, our staff and all who assist us. Our policy on the non-release of records themselves, as opposed to information drawn from the archive, remains unchanged. A statement on this policy is outlined below.

Professor Jeffery has had unrestricted access to the Service archive covering the period of this work. He has made his own independent judgements as an experienced academic and scholar. In so doing he has given a detailed account of the challenges, successes and failures faced by the Service and its leadership in our first forty years.

Above all Professor Jeffery's history gives a view of the men and women who, through hard work, dedicated service, character and courage, helped to establish and shape the Service in its difficult and demanding early days. I see these qualities displayed every day in the current Service as SIS staff continue to face danger in far-flung places to protect the United Kingdom and promote the national interest. I know my predecessors would be as proud as I am of the men and women of the Service today.

I am grateful to Keith Jeffery for accepting the appointment to write our history and to Queen's University Belfast for releasing him for this task. It is a fascinating read. I commend it to you.

John Sawers,
Chief of the Secret Intelligence Service

SIS does not disclose the names of agents or of living members of staff and only in exceptional circumstances agrees to waive the anonymity of deceased staff. Exceptionally and in recognition of the Service's aim in publishing the history it has been agreed that there is an overriding justification for making public, within the constraints of what the law permits, some information which ordinarily would be protected.

However, SIS's policy has not restricted the occasional official release of some Service material – we have previously authorised a limited release of SIS information for other biographies of important intelligence figures.

An extensive clearance process with partner-departments and agencies has been implemented to ensure that the history does not compromise national security; is consistent with government policy on "Neither confirm nor deny" and does not damage the public interest. The author, therefore, does not identify by name any previously unnamed agents, only those named already in officially released documents, citations for wartime decorations, or previously approved publications. He also mentions a very small number of agents, who have already identified themselves. He names former staff only when judged essential for historical purposes and to satisfy the Service's aim of informing public understanding of its origin and role.

Preface

The British Secret Intelligence Service – popularly known as MI6 – is the oldest continuously surviving foreign intelligence-gathering organisation in the world. It was founded in October 1909 as the 'Foreign Section' of a new Secret Service Bureau, and over its first forty years grew from modest beginnings to a point in the early Cold War years when it had become a valued and permanent branch of the British state, established on a recognisably modern and professional basis. Although for most of this period SIS supervised British signals intelligence operations (most notably the Second World War triumphs at Bletchley Park over the German 'Enigma' cyphers), it is primarily a human intelligence agency.[1] While this history traces the organisational development of SIS and its relations with government – essential aspects for an understanding of how and why it operated – its story is essentially one of *people*, from the brilliant and idiosyncratic first Chief, Mansfield Cumming, and his two successors, Hugh Sinclair and Stewart Menzies, to the staff of the organisation – men and women who served it across the world – and, not least, to its agents, at the sharp end of the work. It is impossible to generalise about this eclectic and cosmopolitan mix of many nationalities. They included aristocrats and factory workers, society ladies and bureaucrats, patriots and traitors. Among them were individuals of high courage, many of whom (especially during the two world wars) paid with their lives for the vital and hazardous intelligence work they did.

SIS did not emerge from a complete intelligence vacuum. For centuries British governments had covertly gathered information on an ad hoc basis. In the seventeenth century successive English Secretaries of State assembled networks of spies when the country was particularly threatened, and from its establishment in 1782 the Foreign Office, using funding from what became known as the 'Secret Service Vote' or the 'Secret Vote', annually approved by parliament, employed a variety of clandestine means to acquire information and warning about Britain's enemies.[2] By the end of the nineteenth century the army and the navy, too, had intelligence-gathering branches, which processed much information acquired relatively openly by naval and military attachés posted to foreign countries.[3] But, after the turn of the twentieth century, with foreign rivals (Germany in particular) posing a growing challenge to national interests, British policy-makers began to look beyond these unsystematic and unco-ordinated methods. As the Foreign Office worried about the possibility of its diplomatic and consular representatives becoming caught up in (and inevitably embarrassed by) intelligence-gathering, the notion of establishing a dedicated, covert and, above all, deniable agency came to find favour.

The Secret Service Bureau, and the subsequent Secret Intelligence Service, remained publicly unacknowledged by the British government for over eighty years and was given a formal legal basis only by the Intelligence Services Act of 1994. The fact that a publicly available history of any sort has been commissioned, let alone one written by an independent professional historian, is an astounding development, bearing in mind the historic British legacy of secrecy and public silence about intelligence matters. It is also an extraordinary once-in-a-lifetime opportunity (and privilege) to be appointed to write this history, though I am well aware that the fact that I have been deemed suitable to undertake it may in some eyes precisely render me *un*suitable to produce an independent account of SIS's history. But of that the reader must judge.

Part of the agreement made on my appointment was that I should have utterly unrestricted access to the Service archives over its first forty years. I am absolutely confident that this has been the case and it has been an unparalleled treat to be let loose in the archive, which is an immensely rich (though in places patchy) treasure-trove of historical materials. In addition to this access, I have also been allowed to read some post-1949 materials bearing on the history of the Service. In general, the SIS attitude to archives was that they should be kept only if they served some clear operational purpose. Certainly, since no one envisaged that a professional history of any sort would be written, let alone one that might be published, there was no imperative to retain materials for historical reasons. When the Service did begin to think historically, which, from the evidence I have seen, was not much before the 1960s, a huge amount of material had already been lost.

Within SIS the practice appears to have been routinely to destroy documents once their immediate relevance or utility had passed. There is plenty of internal evidence indicating this, some of which has occasionally slipped out into the public domain. In a 1935 letter to Valentine Vivian, head of the counter-espionage Section V in SIS, Oswald 'Jasper' Harker of MI5 remarked, 'An old report of yours regarding a Madame Stahl has just come to light – I enclose a copy as I believe your 1920 records have been destroyed.'[4] Reviewing the work of SIS in the early 1920s, one officer observed that the SIS headquarters 'receives from its overseas branches over 13,000 different reports per annum, exclusive of correspondence about these reports and administrative matters'. He noted that 'the mass of papers involved immediately becomes apparent'. In order to keep the volume of material under control, he added that 'every effort is made to destroy all matter . . . not needed for reference'. The practice of clearing out old papers has also been powerfully stimulated by the fact that the organisation has moved house on some six occasions during the last century.

Over the years some documents were recognised as having real historical significance and were preserved. One such is the 'Bethell letter', from the Director of Naval Intelligence to Mansfield Cumming on 10 August 1909 inviting him to become (as it turned out) the first Chief of the Service.[5] There has, nevertheless, been intermittent, methodical and substantial destruction of records which may, or may not, have been of historical value. But I have found no evidence that the destruction was carried out casually or maliciously, as some sort of cover-up to hide embarrassing facts about SIS's past. The destruction has resulted more from a cultural attitude where the retention of documents in general was assessed in the light of their current (and certainly not historical) value to the Service, primarily in operational terms.

The corollary to unrestricted access to the archives has been an extremely painstaking and fastidious disclosure process. From the start (and for obvious reasons) it was laid down that the identity of any agent could not be revealed for the first time in this book. One result of this stipulation is the regrettable need (from the historian's point of view) to omit some significant and important SIS stories, as it would not be possible to include them without providing at least circumstantial details which could potentially help identify agents. Exceptionally, however, some agents' names

do appear in the book, but each case has been subject to the most careful
and rigorous disclosure criteria. Where agents have clearly named themselves (not uncommon for individuals who worked during the world
wars), this has been relatively straightforward, but simply arguing that
an agent's name is 'in the public domain' is not in itself sufficient, as the
'public domain' constitutes a great range of contexts, from unsubstanti-
ated assertions in sensationalist and evanescent publications (what might
be called 'sub-prime intelligence literature') to serious and scholarly
articles by professional historians.

Strict criteria have also been applied to the naming of SIS officers, who
have served both at home and overseas. SIS have acknowledged that I
may include names of officers already released in official histories and
through the transfer to The National Archives of papers from other government departments with whom SIS officers naturally liaised. But I have
been unable to name a number of other Service officers on national security grounds (which in some instances have overrridden the imperatives
of historical scholarship), including some who have previously been identified in reliable and scholarly works. Though to a certain extent this may
depersonalise the history and has limited my wish to give credit to those
who achieved much for the Service, it has not materially undermined
my ability to recount many important stories of officers and agents who
shaped the Service during its first forty years.

Despite the fact that immense quantities of documents were destroyed,
not least through lack of space, especially during the period covering the
headquarters move from Broadway to Century House in the early 1960s,
a substantial archive survives. The first thing to be said, however, is that
(perhaps surprisingly) the archive contains comparatively little actual intelligence. Over the 1909–49 period with which I am concerned SIS was
always primarily a collection agency, responding to specific or general
requests for information from customer departments, principally its parent department, the Foreign Office, and the armed service ministries.
The information requested (if available) was collected and passed on to
the relevant department. Little or no analysis was applied to this material
within SIS, apart from some outline indication about the reliability, or
otherwise, of the source. Once the raw material was passed on to the user
department, they processed it and normally destroyed the original documents. Intelligence assessments were the job of the particular desk in the

Foreign Office, the Directorate of Military Intelligence and so on, not of SIS.

SIS's deployment and work, therefore, was principally defined by the priorities and perceptions of external agencies. Between the wars Soviet Communism remained the chief target, and a particular concern with naval matters in the Mediterranean and Far East clearly reflected Admiralty perceptions and intelligence requirements. During the early and mid-1930s SIS resources, in any case constrained by an acute shortage of funding, were not focused on the developing challenge of Nazi Germany as much as (admittedly with the benefit of hindsight) they might have been. Although the Service was, nevertheless, quick off the mark to report German rearmament, there was evidently little demand in London for secret intelligence about internal German political developments. There is, for example, almost nothing in the SIS archives (both for this period and during the Second World War) about the persecution of Jews generally or the Final Solution. A report from Switzerland in January 1939 is a rare exception. An SIS representative had asked an Austrian-Jewish refugee if he could supply 'any information about people in concentration camps'. The source said that he knew a man in Geneva who had spent nine months in Dachau, 'but he doubted whether he could get this man to talk. He said German refugees were frightened of saying anything against Germany, because European countries were riddled with Nazi agents and they feared reprisals.'

One of the things I had hoped to do in this history was find instances when I could track the process from the acquisition of a specific piece of intelligence to its actual use, but in the absence of much of the raw material I have found this quite difficult (though in some cases not impossible) to achieve. I might remark that the situation is quite different with regard to signals intelligence where a considerable volume of the raw (or rawish) product survives and can readily be used, as in Sir Harry Hinsley's magisterial volumes, to estimate 'its influence on strategy and operations', as his subtitle promises.[6] During the First World War, nevertheless, I have for example been able to trace the use of human intelligence from the 'Dame Blanche' organisation in occupied Belgium, as well as the ready and informative response of the German naval spy TR/16 to requests for details of German losses in the Battle of Jutland in 1916. In the mid-1930s (though it was not always taken as seriously as it should have been)

SIS reporting was used to inform British assessments of German rearmament. In the Second World War, specific SIS intelligence underpinned the important Bruneval raid in February 1942 and provided early indications of the German V-weapons development programme.

But, on the whole, the story of human intelligence is not generally one of fiendishly clever master-spies, or Mata Hari-like seductresses (though in this volume the keen-eyed reader will find one or two possible examples of these types), achieving fantastic, war-winning intelligence coups. It is more like a pointillist painting, containing tiny fragments of information, gathered by many thousands of individual men and women in circumstances fraught with danger, which need to be collected together to provide the big picture. Watchers along the Norwegian coast in the Second World War, for example, provided precious information about enemy ship movements. These individuals had to get to what were inevitably exposed situations; once there they had not only to collect their intelligence unobserved, but also to communicate it quickly back to London; and at each stage of the process the penalty for discovery was almost certain death. In both world wars, ordinary men and women in enemy-occupied Europe ran similar risks, for example train-watching, carefully logging the movements of railway trains and their cargoes and endeavouring to identify the military units they carried. We ought not to pass over in silence the astonishingly brave actions of these numberless, and for the most part nameless, people, few of whom were the kind of spies so beloved of film and fiction, but many of whom contributed to the successes of British intelligence during the first half of the twentieth century.

The material which survives in the SIS archive is more abundant on the process and administration of acquiring intelligence than on the intelligence itself. 'Sources and methods', the most sensitive of all aspects of intelligence work, are embedded in this material: names of officers, agents, sources, helpers, organisations, commercial companies, operational techniques, various sorts of technical expertise and the rest. While some of these no longer pose any security risk – for example there seems little danger that national security may now be jeopardised by revealing 1940s wireless technology – documents relating to agents and their activities have the potential to jeopardise them and their families, even long after they may have ceased working for SIS. A typical agent file, for instance, may, without giving very much detail, note that she (or he) produced 'much valuable intelligence'. The bulk of the documents may thereafter contain details for years afterwards of the agent's address (say in some foreign city), pension payments and perhaps reports of visits by an SIS welfare officer, bearing a Christmas bottle of whiskey or some other suitable gift. This is exactly the kind of material which the Service rightly believes can never be released.

This history, written as it were from headquarters, reflects the surviving SIS documentation upon which it is primarily based. This means that it has sometimes been difficult to recreate the personal relationships between case-officers and agents which lie at the heart of human intelligence work. Busy case-officers did not often have the time to write reflective notes on their agents' personalities or motivations, though some hints of these fascinating matters have, happily, survived, and are included in my narrative. I have in general used memoir material very sparingly. Although often revealing on the personal side, the recollection of events and emotions, sometimes many years after, presents critical problems of interpretation and assessment for the historian, particularly in the matter of espionage and other covert activities, which are not infrequently cloaked about with a melodramatic air of secrecy, conspiracy, conjecture and invention. This is not to say that such things do not exist – indeed examples of each might be found in this book – and I have drawn on secondary sources in cases where they seem to be particularly illuminating. Nevertheless, my primary objective has been to base the narrative as closely as possible on the surviving contemporaneous documentary record. If this approach risks some loss of vividness, then it does so expressly for the purposes of historical accuracy.

As will be apparent from the reference notes, I have also had privileged access to relevant but closed documents held by other British government departments. These have been especially useful in helping place SIS in its wider bureaucratic context. With a very small number of exceptions, all other primary source materials (including some extremely valuable sources in foreign archives) are fully open to the public.

Quotations from documents in closed and open archives are reproduced exactly as originally written with the following exceptions: proper names rendered in most official papers in block capitals have been given in title case, with agent and operation code-names in quotation marks;

numbering or lettering of individual paragraphs in cables and other documents has not been reproduced; in communications where names of people, places and organisations were given letter codes ('A', 'B', 'C' and so on), the key being transmitted separately, the correct name has been substituted for the code-letter. Queried words in deciphered messages are as in the original (for example, '?reliable'). In a few cases punctuation has been silently adjusted for the sake of clarity. Since records from the SIS archive are not released into the public domain, no individual source references are provided to them. In this case I have followed the precedent set by past British official histories. Calculations of current value of historical sums of money are based on the Retail Price Index, as indicated in www.measuringworth.com which has also been used for exchange-rate information.

This account of SIS's history finishes in 1949, at a moment when the Service had moved from being a tiny, one-man outfit to a recognisably modern and professional organisation. After forty years' existence, SIS was on the threshold of four decades when the Cold War challenge of Soviet Communism would dominate its activities. But these are matters which I leave to my successor, if there is one.

Acknowledgements

Despite the fact that only one name may appear on the title page, no work of historical scholarship can be entirely the result of individual and solitary endeavour, even though there may have been plenty of that. We all, and I especially, owe debts to those who taught and inspired us (among whom I include Sir Harry Hinsley); to fellow scholars on whose exertions we have depended; to archivists and librarians who help preserve the precious source materials we use; and to friends and family for their support, and often forbearance, in the face of what might sometimes seem to be an all-consuming scholarly obsession.

My first debt is to Christopher Baxter who has worked on the project as a post-doctoral research fellow for four years during which he has sustained me with a remarkable capacity for hard work, meticulous scholarship, wise counsel and great steadiness under fire. Sally Falk, Mark Seaman and Tessa Stirling at the Cabinet Office provided constant welcome support, and I have benefited greatly from the unstinted assistance and advice of Gill Bennett and Duncan Stuart (respectively, former Chief Historian at the Foreign and Commonwealth Office and SOE Adviser). Valuable research assistance and advice on particular historical events has been provided by Richard Aldrich, Stacey Barker (Ottawa), Jim Beach, Antony Best, Andrew Cook, John Ferris, M. R. D. Foot, the late Peter Freeman, Elspeth Healey (Austin, Texas), Jaroslav Hrbek (Prague), Peter Jackson, Sarah Kinkel (Yale), Ivar Kraglund (Oslo), Sébastien Laurent (Vincennes), Larry McDonald (College Park), Craig McKay, Judith Milburn and John Barter, Alexander Miller, Emmanuel Pénicaut (Vincennes), Keith Robbins, Alan Sharp, Yigal Sheffy, Richard Stoney (Land Registry), Martin Thomas, Phil Tomaselli and the late Thomas Troy. Patrick Salmon and his colleagues at the Foreign and Commonwealth Office have been of continuing help, as have members of the Security Service, the Historian of GCHQ, the staff of the Intelligence Corps Museum and Malcolm Llewellyn-Jones (Naval

Historical Branch). To my great benefit, the late Baroness Park shared memories of the Service in the late 1940s, and I treasure conversations on wartime and post-war matters I had with the late Tony and Lena Brooks. While I have been working on this history I have encountered tremendous enthusiasm within SIS for the project, and invaluable help from many people on all sides of the Service. Necessarily, they must remain anonymous, though I can name Sir John Scarlett, whose inspiration and drive underpinned the project from the start. He has taken a close interest in the research and writing and has offered much valuable advice and criticism, while always assuring me that the balance of the narrative and the final judgments in the book must be mine alone.

Bill Hamilton of A. M. Heath & Co., Literary Agents, has been a cheerful tower of strength, as has his United States associate Michael Carlisle. Michael Fishwick at Bloomsbury and Eamon Dolan at Penguin USA companionably improved the final version and a marvellous team of professionals including Anna Simpson, Peter James, Catherine Best and Christopher Phipps helped me safely through the publication process.

My colleagues and students in the School of History and Anthropology at Queen's University Belfast have been gratifyingly accommodating about my constant absences from Belfast. The Head of School, David Hayton, has been unstintingly supportive from the start and colleagues, especially on the MA programme (in particular Paul Corthorn, Peter Gray, Andrew Holmes, Sean O'Connell and Emma Reisz), uncomplainingly shouldered extra burdens on my behalf. Many other friends have helped along the way, including Christopher Andrew, Tamsin and Guy Beach, Robert Blyth, Griselda Brook, Colin Cohen, John Dancy, John Fox, Nathalie Genet-Rouffiac, John Gooch, Peter Hennessy, Nicholas Hiley, Peter Martland, Alan Megahey, Eunan O'Halpin, David Robarge, Wesley Wark, and Eva and Charles Woollcombe. At a late stage in the project I got superb care from many in the National Health Service, especially Dr Seamus McAleer, Mr Harry Lewis and Mr Kieran McManus. My closest friends and family, above all Sally, Ben and Alex, should know how much I have appreciated their loving support and understanding, especially over the past year or so, but it does no harm to acknowledge again that most utterly unrepayable of all the many debts I have incurred in the research and writing of this history.

K.J., May 2010

List of Abbreviations

ACSS	Assistant Chief of the Secret Service
AIOC	Anglo-Iranian Oil Company
BCRA	Bureau Central de Renseignements et d'Action
BLAO	Bureau Liaison Armée Occupée (later renamed BOX)
BSC	British Security Co-ordination
C	Chief of the Secret Service
CCU	Civil Control Unit
CE	Counter-espionage
CIA	Central Intelligence Agency
CID	Committee of Imperial Defence
CIGS	Chief of the Imperial General Staff
CIS	Combined Intelligence Section
COI	Co-ordinator of Information
CPGB	Communist Party of Great Britain
CSC	Controller Special Communications
CSS	Chief of the Secret Service
DBFP	*Documents on British Foreign Policy*
DCSS	Deputy Chief of the Secret Service
DD	Deputy Director
DID	Director of Intelligence Division (Admiralty)
DMI	Director of Military Intelligence
DMO	Director of Military Operations
DNI	Director of Naval Intelligence
DSO	Distinguished Service Order
EDES	Ethnikos Dimokratikos Ellinikos Syndesmos (National Democratic Hellenic League)
EMSIB	Eastern Mediterranean Special Intelligence Bureau
FBI	Federal Bureau of Investigation
FECB	Far East Combined Bureau
FO	Foreign Office
GC&CS	Government Code & Cypher School

GOC   General Officer Commanding
GHQ   General Headquarters
GRU   Glavnoye Razvedyvatelnoye Upravleniye (Soviet Military
               Intelligence)
HMG   His Majesty's Government
IIC   Industrial Intelligence Centre
IMT   International Mining Trust
IPI   Indian Political Intelligence
IRA   Irish Republican Army
ISLD   Inter-Services Liaison Department
ISOS   Intelligence Service, Oliver Strachey (decrypts and translations
               of German intelligence messages)
JIC   Joint Intelligence Sub-Committee/Committee
KPD   Kommunistisches Partei Deutschlands (German
               Communist Party)
LRDG   Long Range Desert Group
MA   Military Attaché
MCO   Military Control Officer
MEW   Ministry of Economic Warfare
MI1(c)   Secret Intelligence Service cover, First World War
MI5   Security Service
MI6   Secret Intelligence Service
MIR   Military Intelligence Research
MP   Member of Parliament
NATO   North Atlantic Treaty Organisation
NIA   National Intelligence Authority
NKVD   Narodnyi Kommissariat Vnutrennikh Del (People's
               Commissariat for Internal Affairs) (incorporated state
               security, 1922–3, 1934–43)
OGPU   Obyedinennoye Gosudarstvennoye Politicheskoye
               Upravleniye (Soviet security and intelligence
               service, 1923–34)
OSS   Office of Strategic Services
PCO   Passport Control Officer
PID   Political Intelligence Department
PUSD   Permanent Under Secretary's Department
RAF   Royal Air Force

RII	Resources Investigation Institute
SCU	Special Communication Unit
SD	Sicherheitsdienst
SHAEF	Supreme Headquarters Allied Expeditionary Force
SIM	Servizio Informazione Militare
SIME	Security Intelligence Middle East
SIS	Secret Intelligence Service
SLC	Special Liaison Controllerate
SOE	Special Operations Executive
SS	Secret Service; Schutzstaffel
TNA	The National Archives
VC	Victoria Cross
VCSS	Vice Chief of the Secret Service
WO	War Office
W/T	Wireless telegraphy

PART ONE
EARLY DAYS

I

The beginnings of the Service

SIS began in a curiously understated way. On 7 October 1909 Commander Mansfield Cumming, the founding Chief of the Service, spent his first full day at work. 'Went to the office', he wrote in his diary, 'and remained all day, but saw no one, nor was there anything to do there.'[1] Indeed, for about a month Cumming had little to do, until he and Captain Vernon Kell, who together had been appointed to run a Secret Service Bureau, were able to sort out the duties of their new organisation. Part of the delay in getting started stemmed from the very novelty of the enterprise. Its interdepartmental nature also held things up, entailing some delicate manoeuvres over the relative roles of the sponsoring departments – Foreign Office, Admiralty and War Office – a problem which was intermittently to recur during SIS's first forty years. The profound secrecy of the new Bureau – another continuing feature – also made it difficult for Cumming to get going as quickly as he wished. By the end of 1909, nevertheless, he had successfully established an embryonic organisation devoted to the clandestine collection of foreign intelligence, which in form and function was recognisably the forebear of the Secret Intelligence Service, as it was eventually to become known.

Foreign threats, spy fever and the Secret Service Bureau

The Secret Service Bureau was established at a time of heightened and intensifying international rivalries when British strategic policy-makers were becoming especially concerned about the challenge of an aggressive, ambitious, imperial Germany. For most of the nineteenth century, the United Kingdom had been by far the most powerful country in the world, possessing the greatest empire ever seen, and Britain's leaders had been able to pursue a policy of so-called splendid isolation, largely impervious to any serious threat from other countries. But by the end of the century Britain's economic lead over the rest of the world was beginning to be eroded, and as rival countries started to catch up, the very extent of British power – what the historian Paul Kennedy has called 'imperial overstretch' – came to be regarded as a potential weakness. In 1906 a Foreign Office official characterised the British Empire as being like 'some gouty giant', with fingers and toes spread across the world, which could not be approached 'without eliciting a scream'. In a series of strategic reassessments in the first decade of the twentieth century Britain sought to ease its international position by coming to terms with potential Great Power rivals. Over a five-year period between 1902 and 1907 agreements were made with Japan, France and Russia which eased British naval commitments in the Pacific and Mediterranean, and (temporarily at least) removed the appalling prospect of having to defend the great British imperial possessions in the Indian subcontinent against Russian aggression. At the same time it was effectively assumed in London that there would never now be a war against the United States, thus further easing the burden of defending Britain's worldwide empire.[2]

One major challenge remained, that of imperial Germany, which, not apparently content with being the strongest economic and military power in Continental Europe, by the early 1900s, in evident emulation of Great Britain, had begun to construct a first-class navy and seemed set on carving out a global imperial role. With Britain aligned to Germany's Continental rivals, France and Russia, in what became known as the Triple Entente, policy-makers and public opinion began to worry about the direct threat that might be posed by Germany. Sensational stories of German spies and underground organisations ready to spring into action in the event of a German attack (or 'bolt from the blue') were fuelled by alarmist 'invasion scare' books such as William Le Queux's bestsellers, *The Invasion of 1910* (1906) and *Spies of the Kaiser* (1909), which reinforced widespread concerns about British vulnerability among public and government alike. In the War Office department responsible for army intelligence matters, the Director of Military Operations himself, General John Spencer Ewart, and his colleagues Colonel James Edmonds and Colonel George Macdonogh were all convinced that their opposite numbers in the German General Staff were actively targeting Britain. As

Nicholas Hiley and Christopher Andrew have shown, however, the fears of German clandestine networks in Britain were wildly overblown – fantastic even; there were no legions of German spies and saboteurs. Yet they seemed to hit a Zeitgeist in Britain where generalised (and well-founded) concerns about a growing *relative* international weakness readily fuelled fevered speculations about foreign agents flooding the country and working towards its destruction.[3]

Such was the strength of public opinion that in March 1909 the Prime Minister, Herbert Asquith, responded to the spy fever by appointing a high-powered sub-committee of the Committee of Imperial Defence (the main British defence policy-making body) to consider 'the question of foreign espionage in the United Kingdom'. Chaired by Richard Burdon Haldane, Secretary of State for War, the committee included the First Lord of the Admiralty, the Home Secretary and representatives of the Foreign Office and Treasury, along with Spencer Ewart and his Admiralty counterpart, Admiral Alexander Bethell (Director of Naval Intelligence). As well as assessing the danger arising from espionage in Britain, the sub-committee was charged with considering whether any alteration was 'desirable in the system at present in force in the Admiralty and War Office for obtaining information from abroad'.

'System' was in fact putting it rather strongly, since the existing arrangements for acquiring foreign intelligence were notably haphazard and unsystematic. British army and navy requirements fell into two clear categories: first was primarily technical information about new weapons developments and German military capabilities generally; second was the establishment of some reliable system to give early warning of a German attack. In 1903 William Melville, the Kerry-born former head of the Special Branch in the Metropolitan Police, had been taken on by the Directorate of Military Operations primarily to tackle German espionage in Britain, but he also sent his assistant, Henry Dale Long, on missions to Germany under commercial cover apparently to investigate naval construction. From time to time foreign nationals offered to sell information to the British. Army officers also did some of their own intelligence work. In 1905 James Grierson, Ewart's predecessor as Director of Military Operations, himself visited the Franco-Belgian frontier, and between 1908 and 1911 Ewart's successor, Henry Wilson, accompanied by fellow officers, cycled up and down both sides of France's eastern frontier with Belgium and Germany, exploring possible lines of attack for a German invasion as well as noting (among other things) German railway construction close to the Belgian border.[4]

Between March and July 1909 the Committee of Imperial Defence sub-committee met three times. It heard Edmonds describe how both the French and the Germans had well-organised secret services. His evidence 'left no doubt in the minds of the Sub-Committee that an extensive system of German espionage exists in this country' and that Britain had 'no organisation for keeping in touch with that espionage and for accurately determining its extent or objectives'. The committee were also told that Britain's organisation for acquiring information about developments in foreign ports and dockyards was 'defective', particularly regarding Germany, 'where it is difficult to obtain accurate information'. Both the Admiralty and the War Office observed that they were 'in a difficult position when dealing with foreign spies who may have information to sell, since their dealings have to be direct and not through intermediaries'. At the committee's second meeting (on 20 April) Ewart asked 'whether a small secret service bureau could not be established', and a further sub-committee, chaired by Sir Charles Hardinge (Permanent Under-Secretary at the Foreign Office) and comprising Ewart, Bethell, Sir Edward Henry (Commissioner of the Metropolitan Police) and Archibald Murray (Director of Military Training) was deputed to look into the matter.

On 28 April 1909 Hardinge's sub-committee submitted a report which 'in order to ensure secrecy' was not printed 'and only one copy was in existence'. Their proposals effectively constitute the founding charter of the modern British intelligence community. They recommended that an independent 'secret service bureau' be established which 'must at the same time be in close touch with the Admiralty, the War Office and the Home Office'. It should have three objects. It would first 'serve as a screen between the Admiralty and the War Office and foreign spies who may have information that they wish to sell to the Government'. Second, it would 'send agents to various parts of Great Britain and keep [in] touch with the country police with a view to ascertaining the nature and scope of the espionage that is being carried on by foreign agents'; and third, it would 'act as an intermediate agent between the Admiralty and the War Office and a permanent foreign agent who should be established abroad, with

the view of obtaining information in foreign countries'. The committee thought that this individual could be located at the Belgian capital,
Brussels, and could be 'the medium through which other British foreign
agents sent in their reports, such a course being less likely to excite suspicion than if these agents communicated with Great Britain direct'. It was
proposed that the Bureau should include 'two ex-naval and military officers', with 'a knowledge of foreign languages'. On the recommendation of
Sir Edward Henry, it was agreed both to employ a firm of private detec-
tives for the work and 'that a specially competent agent should be sent
out . . . to get in touch with men in various German ports who would be
willing to send us information particularly in time of strained relations'.
The overall cost of the Bureau was estimated at something over £2,000 a
year (the equivalent of about £150,000 in current money), to be met, at
least in part, out of 'the present secret service vote'.

An interesting feature of these recommendations (which were entirely
accepted by the main sub-committee at their final meeting on 12 July
1909) is the marked bias towards foreign intelligence-gathering contained in the proposed 'objects' of the Bureau, a contrast with the original
focus on domestic counter-intelligence. It is tempting to ascribe this to the
chairmanship of Sir Charles Hardinge, responsible, among other things,
for disbursing Secret Vote money. Under Foreign Office control, the Secret
Vote had for many years been used for a wide variety of purposes, including payments to both the War Office and the Admiralty for the intermittent employment of spies, and, although the service ministries had clearly
positioned themselves as the primary customers for the proposed new
Bureau, we might see Hardinge's hand both in the 'external' emphasis of
his sub-committee's proposals and in the explicit acknowledgement that
funding would be provided from the Secret Vote.[5] Whatever the explanation, the pattern of armed service engagement with, and Foreign Office
control over, the secret service was one that persisted for the next forty
years. Another aspect of the proposal was the extreme secrecy within which
it was made, and the official 'deniability' under which the new Bureau
would operate. A précis of the sub-committee's findings, prepared at the
time the first staff were appointed, noted that 'by means of the Bureau,
our N[aval] and M[ilitary] attachés and Government officials would not
only be freed from the necessity of dealing with spies, but it would also be
impossible to obtain direct evidence that we had any dealings with them at

all'. This, too, was to be a central and lasting feature of the Service.

Once the formation of a Secret Service Bureau had been approved by the main Committee of Imperial Defence on 24 July, a group met on 26 August to work out the details. Sir Edward Henry and Ewart attended, along with Edmonds and Macdonogh. Bethell sent a staff officer, Captain Reginald Temple. The meeting accepted Henry's recommendation that Edward Drew, a former police chief inspector and now a private detective, should be engaged and that the Bureau should begin work as soon as possible in offices leased by him at 64 Victoria Street in Westminster. It was agreed that Long, who had been employed 'for some years' by the War Office, should be the foreign agent based on the Continent. Evidently, Long had already been approached as he was 'willing to accept the appointment' and had agreed to 'obtain a commercial agency in Brussels to cloak his activities'. It was further noted that an agent had been 'employed in Germany by the Admiralty' to cover German ports as suggested by Hardinge's sub-committee. The 26 August meeting was also told that the War Office and Admiralty had officers in mind to staff the Bureau. The War Office proposed Captain Vernon Kell, 'an exceptionally good linguist . . . qualified in French, German, Russian and Chinese' (and who had previously worked in the War Office as Edmonds's 'right-hand man in the Far East section'), while the Admiralty nominated Commander Mansfield Smith-Cumming, 'who is now in charge of the Southampton Boom defence, and who possesses special qualifications for the appointment'. Confirming the continuing senior role of the Foreign Office in the new organisation, on a note of the meeting it was added that the Director of Military Operations (Ewart) 'spoke to Sir C. Harding[e] on 14 September, and he concurred in the above arrangements'.[6]

Sorting out practicalities

The selection of Mansfield Cumming (he tended not to use the 'Smith') as the Admiralty's nominee for the new Bureau was a classic and pioneering example of the informal way in which for a long time the Secret Intelligence Service treated the important subject of recruitment. The fifty-year-old Cumming (born on 1 April 1859) had no apparent intelligence experience. Unlike the War Office's nominee, Vernon Kell (who, in fact, was to take over the domestic side of things), he was not a linguist, and it is not at all clear what 'special qualifications' Cumming actually possessed for the work, nor do we know if he was the only candidate considered.

Cumming, whose original name was Mansfield George Smith, came from a moderately prosperous landed and professional family (his father was a distinguished engineer) and entered the navy after going to the Royal Naval College, Dartmouth, at the age of twelve in 1872. He enjoyed an apparently successful, but not especially outstanding, career at sea and in various shore appointments (including a spell at the Royal Naval College Greenwich at the same time as the future King George V), before retiring in December 1885 'on Active Half Pay' due to unspecified ill-health. Over the next decade or so he worked as private secretary to the Earl of Meath, serving for a time as his agent in Ireland. During these years he married twice: first in 1885 to a South African, Dora Cloete, who died in 1887, and secondly to May Cumming (when he adopted her family name), an independently wealthy woman whose family had estates in Morayshire, Scotland. In April 1898 he returned to the navy to 'superintend the working of the Boom defence at Southampton'. Cumming was a practical man, much enthused by the latest mechanical devices. A keen pioneer motorist, and a hair-raisingly fast driver, he joined the Royal Automobile Club in 1902, and three years later was a founder member (and first Rear Commodore) of its offshoot the Motor Yacht Club (also 'Royal' from 1910). In 1906 he was a founder member of the Royal Aero Club, acquiring a pilot's licence at the age of fifty-four in November 1913.[7]

There are some hints that Cumming's involvement with motor-yachting (which he shared with many other naval officers) may have helped put him in the frame for the new venture. In the early years of the century the Admiralty, intensely interested in the potential of new types of marine engines, was kept fully informed about the activities of the Motor Yacht Club, which ran international racing competitions and encouraged the development of high-performance motor boats. Its concern was by no means confined to British developments. According to the memoirs of another motor-yachting pioneer, Montague Grahame-White, in the spring of 1905 Cumming was sent 'on a tour to study the development of motor propulsion in fishing fleets in Sweden and Holland', in order to ascertain 'the reliability of internal combustion engines running on paraffin'.[8] Perhaps referring to this mission, Cumming wrote in his diary in late October 1909 that he would 'like to get in touch with certain Danes and Swedes – with some of whom I made acquaintance when sent abroad recently by the F.O. [Foreign Office] in connection with Marine Motors'.

UNCONVENTIONAL PORTRAITS OF LEADERS IN MOTORISM.

XLIII.—COMMANDER MANSFIELD CUMMING, R.N.
"Motor Yacht Club."

With his infectious enthusiasm for high-powered cars and motor boats, Mansfield Cumming was celebrated as a pioneer in 'motorism'.

So it was that by the time he was selected for his new job, he appears to have had some experience of information-gathering abroad. All we know for certain, however, is that a month after the Committee of Imperial Defence sub-committee agreed on the formation of a Secret Service Bureau, Alexander Bethell wrote on 10 August 1909 to Cumming observing that 'Boom defence must be getting a bit stale with you' and that he might 'therefore perhaps like a new billet'. Bethell had 'something good' to offer and he invited Cumming up to London to discuss it. Two days later (as Cumming recorded in his diary), Bethell told him 'that the appointment he had to offer was that of Chief of the S.S. Service [*sic*] for the Navy – a new Department about to be formed at the insistence of the I[mperial] D[efence] C[ommittee]'. The work 'was to be the obtaining and collecting of all information required by his Department. I was to work under him and should have charge of all the Agents employed by him and by the W[ar] D[epartment].' Bethell also told him that he would have a 'junior' colleague (Kell was fourteen years younger and of lower equivalent rank), and that the new service was being set up with the agreement of the Director of Military Operations.[9]

While little in Cumming's background seemed particularly suited to secret service matters, he undoubtedly grew into the work, and was certainly attracted by the prospect from the start. 'The offer of the work is most tempting,' he wrote to Bethell on 17 August, 'and I should like very much to undertake it,' but he also made it clear that he was by no means tired of boom defence, and during August and early September managed to establish that he could continue nominally to be in charge of that work while taking on his new duties. Since Hardinge wanted the Bureau to come into existence on 1 October, Drew's office was rented from that date and towards the end of September there was a flurry of activity sorting out arrangements. On 23 September, highlighting difficulties about the precise division of responsibilities which were to bedevil the early months of the organisation, Cumming was 'disappointed' to learn from Bethell that he was 'not to be Chief of the whole Bureau', but that Kell 'was to work with me on equal terms'. Bethell also told him that 'no recognition of our work would be possible, as we were to be dissociated from the authorities entirely, and not recognised by them except secretly'. More positively, however, Cumming learned that Hardinge 'had promised that there should be no stint of money to pay our own Agents &c'.

The first formal meeting of the Secret Service Bureau took place in the War Office on the morning of Monday 4 October 1909 when Edmonds and Macdonogh briefed Cumming and Kell about their new responsibilities. They said that they were going to keep Melville ('the best man we have at present') in 'an office of his own', and that Long, 'another good

man' who spoke German and French, would be sent to Brussels 'to act
as chief agent there'. Edmonds also referred to some other individuals
who had done intelligence work and might be kept on. He gave Kell and
Cumming their first instructions about what would become known as
'tradecraft'. He 'told us never to keep names and addresses on the same
paper' and 'never to use paper with a water mark in it'. They should never
'see any of these scallywags for the first time without M[elville] or someone present', or use the office as a rendezvous. A private room elsewhere
should be rented for the purpose. 'We were not to address letters from
the office or receive letters there, and we were to assume other names.'
Cumming noted in his diary (perhaps this was a joke), 'K[ell] added a
Y to his present name,' but carefully did not commit his own proposed
sobriquet to paper, though he later used the names 'Captain Currey' and
'Captain Spencer'. At the end of the meeting it was settled that as Kell
'was not free for a fortnight, I should commence work by copying out
all the records in M[acdonogh]'s office – as soon as I had procured a Safe
in which to keep them . . . I lunched with K and we had a yarn over the
future, and agreed to work together for the success of the cause.'

For some time, in fact, Cumming remained underemployed. Even before the 4 October meeting he had sketched out plans, but had not as yet
shared them with anyone else. The main focus was on Germany and he
considered that he ought to have agents in the major German naval ports
(such as Wilhelmshaven, Hamburg and Kiel) 'who could be thoroughly
trusted to report extraordinary activity'. He also wanted 'at least one travelling agent'. 'Cover' for the Bureau and its activities was a problem from
the start. Cumming argued that he should have 'some Official nominal
post – for such instance as "work in the N[aval] I[ntelligence] Dept in
connection with suspected persons in the Dockyards". Such a post (not
publicly announced)', he thought, 'would give me some pretext for trying to get help outside.' Meanwhile he found it difficult even to get the
Bureau started. Finding himself sitting in the new Victoria Street office
with nothing to do, he began to learn German to fill the time. When he
went to the War Office 'to take away the first batch of Records to copy',
Macdonogh 'would not allow them to be taken out of the place', and later
wrote to Cumming to say that he 'proposed to hand all the W[ar] O[ffice]
work over to K[ell] and to communicate with him alone on such matters'.

Frustrated, Cumming complained to Bethell he had been told 'that I am not to have letters addressed to the office, am not to see anyone there, nor address letters from there, so that I can not see what possible use it will be . . . Surely', he continued, 'we can not be expected to sit in the office month by month doing absolutely nothing.' His 'only object' was 'to make a first class success out of a new thing'. Noting that Macdonogh wanted to work through Kell alone, Cumming felt 'that any exclusion of myself in favour of K would be fatal to my success'. He argued that it would be 'best to keep the WO and Naval work separate'. He would be 'quite content to have charge of the latter and leave all the former to K, but I must have an equal chance to carry out my part and I can only secure that by being put au courant with all that has been done and with the organisation at our disposal up to the present time'. Cumming also grumbled about what he regarded as the excessive degree of secrecy surrounding the new organisation. It was, he thought, 'only necessary for us to keep our connection with those who pay us a secret'. He wanted to be able to 'let it be known' that he was 'open to receive information', while his own identity would be carefully concealed – 'a matter easily arranged' – and that any 'connection at all with any authority that could be traced in any way' should be suppressed. 'Half the secrecy that we are maintaining', he wrote, 'is of no practical good.'

At last, on 21 October, at a meeting held at the War Office to sort out the working of the Bureau, the separate functions of what became the Security Service and SIS were first formally established. Macdonogh proposed that Kell 'should undertake the whole of the Home work – both Naval and Military, "espionage and contre espionage"', and that Cumming 'should have charge of all the foreign – both N & M'. As Cumming noted in his diary, the 'S.S. Bureau' was to have four 'duties': '1. Act as screens to Ad[miralty] & W.O. [War Office]. 2. Conduct investigations. 3. Correspond with all paid agents and persons desirous of selling secrets. 4. Act as representatives of Ad. & W.O.' Cumming's 'espionage' task was to 'Organise an efficient system by which German progress in Armaments and Naval construction can be watched, being careful in doing so that every thing which would point to concentration should be reported', while Kell's 'contre espionage' was to 'counteract all measures hostile to G.B. taken by foreign Governments'. Kell was to have Melville and Drew, though, in answer to a direct question, Macdonogh said he was to 'avoid employing' the latter if possible. The existing foreign agents were to be kept on, 'and there would be about £2700 for them'. The first 'object' of the Bureau was to 'obtain information of any movement indicating an attack upon this country'. Other tasks were to 'watch all suspected persons – such as foreigners residing in British territory' and 'counteract' the 'formation of demolition centres' in Britain. Finally, the Bureau had to 'organise a scheme of permanent correspondents both at home and abroad, who will furnish information from within the enemies [sic] lines in time of war'. Cumming felt that he was at last making progress, though he thought his was 'the most difficult part' and that since Macdonogh proposed to hand both Melville and Long over to Kell, he would be left with 'no one of any tried value'.

On 28 October a meeting (to which neither Cumming nor Kell was invited) chaired by Hardinge at the Foreign Office confirmed the division of responsibilities within the Bureau. Bethell afterwards told Cumming that the foreign agents were to 'remain as at present', but that there was 'no more money' and that Cumming was to see what he could 'get done voluntarily'. With his actual duties defined, Cumming now turned to the practical arrangements. He thought that there were 'several disadvantages' in sharing an office with Kell and Drew. Although it was 'a large place' it was of 'very little use' and for his purposes quite insecure. He did not think that he could 'create and develop the elaborate organization of which I am to be given charge, from the Office, as I am not to address letters from there, receive them there or see anyone there'. He therefore proposed renting a flat, which would include an office, where he would be available at all times of the day and night. 'A separate Office – such as the present one – ', he remarked, 'immediately suggests a business, and invites interest and curiosity, but a private dwelling calls for no comment.' At home he could organise his work without raising suspicion or attracting attention, and he could meet agents and others in rooms hired for the purpose elsewhere. He would also set up a 'photographic copying plant' at the flat, where it could be 'arranged so that no one will know of its existence'.

Reflecting on the sorts of people he would have to deal with in order to get information (and demonstrating that he had been thinking productively about the whole business of intelligence), Cumming contrasted his position with that of Kell. In Britain, he observed, 'every third man one meets would be glad to help his country', but 'abroad the case is entirely different'. The Consular Service of official British representatives overseas was 'expressly barred', and it was 'useless as a rule to approach natives and invite them to betray their country. Some of the lowest class may consent, but they will of course in turn betray us without scruple if it serves their purpose, and cannot be relied upon for the more important work.' As to 'Englishmen living abroad', they would be 'reluctant to do anything to damage the country they are living in' and would 'be fully aware of the risk they will run – to their business, or even their liberty – if found out'. Cumming wanted 'free scope to make enquiries, sound every person likely to be of use' and 'be able to offer substantial retaining fees and rewards for valuable information'. While he had not so far 'had time to think out any scheme for forming a system of look outs who will give us instant warning of the movements of ships, transports, concentration of foods and stores &c', this was 'the most important work of all', and 'the agents selected must be of reliable character and position, and will have to be paid in proportion to these advantages'.

But Cumming still worried about his prospects. On 3 November he jotted down some despondent reflections: 'cannot do any work in Office. Been there 5 weeks, not yet signed my name. Absolutely cut off from everyone while there, as can not give my address, or be telephoned to under own name.' Kell had 'done more in one day than I have in the whole time'. The system had been 'organized by the Military, who have just had control of my destinies long enough to take away all the work I could do, hand me over by far the most difficult part of the work (for which their own man [Kell] is obviously better suited) and take away all the facilities for doing it. Am firmly convinced that K will oust me altogether before long.' Bethell came to the rescue. After Cumming had poured his heart out over dinner, Bethell assured him 'that I need not do anything to justify my appointment. I must wait patiently for work to come. That I need not sit idle in the Office, but could go about and learn. That I should not be watched, and that he had every confidence.' Bethell told Cumming he could say he was employed in the Naval Intelligence Department, but 'must use great discretion in doing this', and that he could rent a flat ('at my own expense of course') and work there. If the experiment was successful, the Foreign Office might take on the cost. Bethell finally told Cumming that the War Office was 'to have nothing to say to my work, which is to be managed entirely by me, under him (the D.N.I.)'.

Although Bethell's assertion was not strictly true, since from the start the Bureau had been conceived as an interdepartmental service (and the War Office was to remain an important 'customer'), his confidence in Cumming and the reassurance of Admiralty backing was very welcome, and had practical effect three weeks later when arrangements were being made for Cumming to take over 'B', an existing War Office agent based on the Continent. The plan was for Cumming to use him to run agents at Hamburg and Wilhelmshaven and 'one Travelling man', but when Kell insisted that he would come to the first meeting between Cumming and B in order to pay B's salary, Cumming put his foot down. With Bethell's backing he got Ewart and Macdonogh to prevent this and they instructed Kell to hand over the money to Cumming to pay B himself. The meeting with B on 26 November 1909 was Cumming's first encounter with a real spy. He was introduced by Edmonds, who had previously been running him but told B that henceforth Cumming would 'deal entirely with him'. Bethell's staff officer, Reginald Temple, attended the meeting to help with German translation as B (an Austrian) did not speak English. Cumming, who had been taking German lessons at the Berlitz Language School, could 'follow what was said; but not enough to understand all his [B's] ideas and opinions'.

The meeting went well. B 'seemed to think that he should have no difficulty in getting us the information we wanted, as he said all the TRs [Cumming's diary term for Germans – short for 'Tariff Reformers']¹⁰ were open to bribes and could not resist the sight of a gold piece'. It was settled that there should be 'one man in Hanover – to attend primarily to Military matters, one in Wilhelmshaven and one who should travel about, making his headquarters in Stendal or Wittenburg, and visiting all the big [ship] Yards at least once in every three months'. When Cumming raised the question of 'the 4 Dreadnoughts [battleships], supposed to be about to commence building at Pola and elsewhere in Austria', B 'jibbed at this immediately and said he was an Austrian and could do nothing that could hurt his native country'. Cumming thought him 'an intelligent and bold man' and that he would 'probably prove my best aide, but', he added, 'the difficulty about his patriotic feeling for Austria will have to be considered'. Bethell was pleased when Cumming reported these arrangements to him. He believed the War Office 'had evidently recognised that they had made a tactical mistake in dividing the work in the way they had done, and that I [Cumming] had really secured the more important part. He thought all would come right when we had settled down.'

Although Cumming did not finally hand in his keys to the Victoria Street office until March 1910, by the end of November 1909 he had moved into a flat in Ashley Mansions, 254 Vauxhall Bridge Road, and established an independent base there for his section of the Bureau. Early in the New Year he arranged a bogus 'cover address' with the Post Office – 'Messrs Rasen, Falcon Ltd, Box 400, General Post Office, London' – an alleged firm of 'Shippers and Exporters', thus establishing a precedent for the classic 'import and export' espionage cover. He had two telegraphic addresses, 'Sunbonnet, London' for 'general use' and 'Autumn, London' for 'special use'. All correspondence to these addresses was to be redirected to Cumming at Ashley Mansions, any important 'Autumn, London' cables 'by special messenger under a double cover'. Cumming stayed at Ashley Mansions until 1911 when he moved both his flat and his office to 2 Whitehall Court, between Whitehall and Victoria Embankment, adjacent to the War Office and not far from the Admiralty.

The War Office, having conceded responsibility for foreign work, handed over their 'whole German Intelligence system', including B (who had been 'found valuable in Russia and might be required to work there again'), along with 'the names and addresses of the 5 assistants'. By the end of 1909 Cumming had himself begun to run other sources. On 9 December he met 'WK' who had been an Admiralty agent, apparently reporting on German guns. Just before Christmas he briefed 'FRS', who was going to Fiume in Austria-Hungary 'to find out what progress has been made in laying down slips for D[readnought]s'. On New Year's Eve at the Royal Automobile Club in Piccadilly he met 'D', who was based in Hamburg and was one of three agents engaged to warn of likely war. Cumming 'promised him £500 [an astonishing 25 per cent of his then entire budget] if he could send me accurate news of the imminence of war before any other agent, and at least 24 hours before any declaration or overt act'. Although 'the best of the three "passive" agents', D was 'evidently timid and accepts as a foregone conclusion that at the outbreak of war he will fly (and bring his message with him)'. Cumming felt sure 'that he has little resource, and would not risk anything at all to get his warning to us'.

Targeting Germany and running agents

In an exchange of notes with Bethell during January 1910 Cumming formally established his responsibilities vis-à-vis the Admiralty. Bethell laid down that Cumming was to hold himself 'directly responsible to me for all matters connected with your duties' and was 'to assume charge of the entire S.S. Intelligence system outside the United Kingdom, the Military Officer who has been appointed as your colleague being responsible for the work at home'. His 'principal duty' was 'to obtain early and reliable information of all important movements of Naval and Military forces' in order to provide 'timely warning of impending hostilities against this country on the part of any foreign state within the range of your information'. Cumming was also to meet requests for 'special items of information required by the Naval and Military authorities'. For his part, Cumming confirmed that providing advance warning of war was 'by far the most important part of the work', but he also suggested 'that a plan of action should be devised which will ensure the sending of information after hostilities have commenced and whilst the war is actually going on'. He recognised that this was a much more difficult task. Any agent (working, say, in Germany), 'especially if of foreign birth, or if suspected in the smallest degree', would inevitably be closely shadowed, and it would be 'extremely difficult for him to get any information through. If caught, he will certainly be shot.' Cumming also maintained that, while Germany was the principal target, he would like to have agents in neighbouring countries, arguing perceptively that it would 'often be possible to get information about Germany through another country, and secrets that may be carefully guarded from us [in Germany] may be more readily accessible elsewhere'. Wisely, he also observed that political conditions in different European countries could rapidly change and that he needed back-up systems for the supply of information.

At this very early stage Cumming was already thinking sensibly about the problems of foreign intelligence work, but much of this was ambitiously optimistic, and would remain so for years. Even thirty years on in the Second World War, after dramatic advances in wireless technology, establishing reliable and secure agent communications from behind enemy lines proved very difficult indeed. In the meantime, Cumming's progress in establishing the new 'S.S. Bureau' was embodied in a report he prepared in April 1910 covering its first six months of existence. After a slow start, he said that since December 1909 the work had 'increased rapidly until at the present time I have as much as I can tackle'. He described how his 'staff of agents' was 'of two kinds'. In the first place were those watching Germany who were simply 'expected to keep a good look out for any unusual or significant movements or changes – either Naval or Military – and report them. From these agents', he added, '"no news is good news" and in the absence of any evidence to the contrary, it is to be believed that they are doing their duty and are earning the pay they receive.' The other agents were 'those who in addition to giving warning of extraordinary activity on the part of those they are deputed to watch, are expected to collect information of all kinds and forward it to me at stated intervals'. As yet, he was unable to make any firm judgment about these men 'as sufficient time has not elapsed since their appointment to enable me to form an opinion'. The 'principal Agent', B, was paid nearly £1,500 (equivalent in modern terms to about £110,000) for himself and three sub-agents, about whom Cumming knew nothing whatsoever. 'I have never seen them', he remarked, 'or heard their names, and I am not by any means certain that they exist at all.' In April, after a trip to Paris to meet B, Cumming (revealing that the peculiar world of intelligence was beginning to affect his thinking) confided to his diary doubts about the existence of B's sub-agents: 'I could not feel absolutely sure that he had three men in his employment at all, although perhaps this is only the suspicion that grows upon one after the first few months of this work.'

B was a problematic asset in other ways too. As Cumming noted in his April 1910 report, he was 'a foreigner, a potential enemy (for he is an Austrian) and a professional spy'. On the other hand, he was 'intelligent' and had evidently 'rendered good service in the past'. In February he had supplied detailed dimensions of the new 25,000-ton German battleship *Thüringen*, which B had acquired from a naval engineer in Bremen, and which the Naval Intelligence Department was pleased to have. But, on the whole, the reports supplied from B's network were 'very meagre' and did 'not up to the present justify the large salaries paid – more than is paid to all the other Agents put together'. B, argued Cumming, had 'no incentive to send in good reports, as he is paid the same whether they are good or bad', and he wanted to change the system to one whereby the agent would still be paid 'a fairly large retaining fee for himself' (though clearly less than he was currently receiving) with further sums 'on a liberal scale for all information supplied and approved'.

Reviewing his other agents, Cumming recommended that WK should be retained at a salary of £200 (equivalent to £15,000), 'to rise to £240, if he gives satisfaction'. Normally based in Germany, WK had reported in December 1909 about torpedo-boat trials in the Baltic and off Wilhelmshaven, and on naval construction, including submarine work of which there had been a particular concentration so that 'this branch of the Navy' might 'render valuable service in time of war'. In April 1910 Cumming sent him to the Austro-Hungarian ports of Trieste and Pola (now Pula) to investigate naval shipbuilding. WK's report, limited somewhat by the fact that he had 'no technical knowledge' of warships and 'had been much troubled by the police at P[ola]', nevertheless partially confirmed a report which the agent FRS had delivered in January of clandestine warship construction for the Austro-Hungarian navy, which had provoked great interest in the Admiralty and which Bethell asserted was the best job of intelligence work done 'since he came to the office'. Possibly with FRS's report in mind, Cumming declared that his 'most valuable information' had been 'procured by a man who was sent abroad to ascertain certain definite facts'. This contrasted with his three 'passive agents' on whom he depended for 'early information of war' and whose performance was 'difficult to appraise as to their value, as they send in no reports'. Indeed, one of these agents, 'U', seemed particularly feeble. Although he lived for part of the year in Kiel and socialised constantly with German naval officers, he told Cumming that 'he never asked any of them any questions, for fear of arousing suspicion – in fact, when the conversation turned upon Armaments &c, he always asked them to change it'. He assured Cumming, however, that should he 'smell war in the air', he would 'at once hurry across the Dutch frontier and send us a telegram', and even 'if necessary follow it himself'.

For Cumming, a more valuable source, and 'one which it is hoped will be greatly extended', was that of 'voluntary help' provided by British people 'whose business or profession gives them special facilities for finding out what is going on abroad'. One such individual (called 'Mr Queer' in the diary) was a director of a British armaments company and reported that the German firm Krupp were buying up stocks of nickel-tungsten steel for the manufacture of small guns. On returning in January

1910 from a business trip to an unnamed foreign government, he gave Cumming the specification of a heavy gun ('to throw a projectile weighing over 500 kilos') which the government in question had themselves got from Krupp. Among other things this revealed that 'for their larger guns' Krupp were using 'Nickel-Chrome steel, entirely Oil-hardened and tempered'. Queer, who was evidently very well plugged into the European armaments industry, also reported that the Skoda Works in Bohemia had received orders from the Austrian government to manufacture big guns 'for two ships of the "Dreadnought" class'. Cumming concluded his first report by stressing how little he and Kell had in common, and on security grounds urged that the home and foreign sides of the work should be completely autonomous. He further thought it a 'pity that the S.S. Agent [that is, himself] should be obliged to tell even his Chiefs what he is doing – certainly he should not tell more than one person'. Indeed, he concluded that 'it would be far better if he could keep his work, his methods and all knowledge of his assistants entirely to himself'.

One thing which Cumming omitted in his report was any mention of his own intelligence-gathering role. Over five days in February 1910, accompanied by Captain Cyrus H. 'Roy' Regnart, a Royal Marine who was Bethell's assistant in the Naval Intelligence Department, he went twice to Antwerp to meet an agent who failed to appear. He had a more adventurous time in April when (again with Regnart) he went first to Paris to meet his agent B, then on to Liège where they were to meet 'JR', who had promised to provide intelligence on German airship construction and show them a new type of portable weapon he was to smuggle out of Germany. A firearms expert was brought from London, and Cumming organised a professional photographer to join them en route in Brussels. Unfortunately these elaborate – perhaps over-elaborate – plans broke down. Although JR arrived from Berlin, Cumming and the photographer got separated from Regnart and the expert, neither of whom made the rendezvous. JR (who perhaps had more experience than Cumming in these matters) altered the arrangements at the last minute, not bringing the weapon to Liège but keeping it at a previously undisclosed location about an hour's drive away. Cumming and the photographer got there in mid-afternoon, and in failing light quickly had to set to work. JR produced the device only after Cumming had paid him 'the 25 [pounds] agreed on, and also a further 10 for the answers to the questions sent by the airship people'. As JR claimed he was in a hurry to get away and take the weapon back to Germany, Cumming 'had only a few minutes in which to handle the thing, make such measurements as I could, and make a thumbnail sketch. I did my best, but was surprised afterwards to find how much I had managed to leave out.' All he could ascertain was that it had sights 'marked from 100 to 700 M and from 800 to 1900 on the raised part' and that it 'fired 5 shots'. It all seems to have been in vain. Back in London, both the weapons expert and Macdonogh concluded that the device was of no special interest, and Cumming even offered to pay back the £25 he had given to JR. Macdonogh reasonably 'said that it was not fair to make me responsible for all the failures – a certain proportion of which must occur – and that not many offices could afford to make good such losses'. Cumming, who was still at this stage meeting the rent for his combined flat and office out of his own pocket, mused 'that no officer who had not private means could take my work at all, as I reckoned it cost me the whole of my pay to keep it going'.

On 9 May 1910 Cumming's report was considered at a meeting of himself, Kell, Bethell, Ewart and Macdonogh. The division of the work into two quite separate offices was confirmed and the private detective Drew's services dispensed with. On Macdonogh's suggestion it was agreed that the budget (now £6,200) would in future be divided equally between Cumming and Kell. Two days later these proposals were broadly approved by Sir Charles Hardinge. When Macdonogh declared that the money allowed for the Bureau's work was 'not nearly enough for the purpose', Hardinge said 'that if the work required it, the amount must be increased'. Cumming was allowed to lay off some non-producing agents, reduce B's retainer and pay him by results in future. Hardinge further agreed to cover the cost of Cumming's separate office and increase the budget for his necessary travelling expenses, once again assuring him (and Kell) that 'there was no wish to restrict the work in any way, and if the money already granted was not sufficient, more would have to be found from elsewhere. All he wanted was to make sure that it was spent wisely.'

The work of the Bureau

The typescript version of Mansfield Cumming's diary, the most important single source for the early days of the Secret Service Bureau, is tantalisingly incomplete from the end of August 1910 until the beginning of 1914. There are no entries from 1 September to 21 November 1910. Only 6–18 January survives for 1911, and 1912 contains only a few days in January, March and December. For 1913 we have 1 January to 27 May; 26–27 June; 31 July and 10–31 December. From 1 January 1914 the original, handwritten desk diaries are available, though even these have frustrating gaps when Cumming, without any particular explanation, simply seems to have stopped writing it up. We know, for example, from Vernon Kell's diary (itself a pretty sketchy document which covers only June 1910 to July 1911) that there were meetings to review the first year's work of the Bureau in November 1910, and that Kell and Cumming both submitted formal reports, but neither appears to have survived.[11] The growth and development of the Secret Service, however, can be followed in outline from the scanty minutes of five meetings of the committee which supervised the Bureau's work, which met at six-monthly intervals from November 1910 to May 1913, chaired by Sir Arthur Nicolson, who succeeded Hardinge as Permanent Under-Secretary at the Foreign Office in November 1910.

Recognising that the Bureau's work was growing rapidly, the first of these meetings (on 16 November) agreed the appointment of full-time assistants for both Cumming and Kell. Backed by the War Office, Cumming also asked for funds to base an 'officer-agent' (Macdonogh's term) at Copenhagen who would develop a network of sources in Germany, primarily to report on 'German naval construction and armaments', and, if war became a possibility, provide information on 'German naval mobilization & concentration, & the assembly of transports in German harbours & also regarding the movement of troops, especially either towards the north coast or towards Holland & Belgium'. Copenhagen was suggested not only because it was especially well located 'for receiving information from the German Baltic & North Sea ports', but also (as Macdonogh argued, though without providing any specific evidence) because 'Danes in many ways make the best S.S. agents for employment'. Nicolson recognised that the decision to appoint a British intelligence officer permanently in a foreign country (who, in later SIS parlance, would have been the first overseas 'head of station') was not one to be taken lightly. This was as much a new departure as establishing a permanent Secret Service Bureau in the first place, and as General Wilson, who had become Director of Military Operations in August (and was to be very supportive of Cumming), noted, the intention was that 'this appointment should be merely the start of a wider system', with further 'Branch agents' appointed elsewhere if 'this one proved a success'. Nevertheless, since from the start one of the chief purposes of the Bureau had been to distance the British government from the problematic business of secret intelligence-gathering, the Foreign Office clearly wanted to be reassured that no hint of official involvement might accompany this new development. Nicolson insisted that the matter be submitted to the Foreign Secretary, Sir Edward Grey, himself. Grey approved the proposal 'in principle', but wanted 'a great deal more detailed information' about both the circumstances and the individual suggested for the post.

Cumming's candidate was Regnart, 'an excellent linguist, speaking Danish, German & other languages & . . . very keen on S.S. work'. Interviewed about the appointment by Nicolson's private secretary, Lord Errington, Cumming told him that Regnart had private means (which because of the poor rates of pay offered to full-time members of the Bureau was widely thought to be essential), 'did not care for Society' and 'was prepared to sink his identity altogether – even to the extent of taking a shop under a trade name and working it as a bona fide business, to cover his real objects'. Errington 'said that the FO did not wish to place themselves under any obligation to the officer, so that he could come to them in a year or twos time and say that he had lost say £5000, and want it good'. He was also most anxious about maintaining the secrecy of the matter and ensuring that there should not be the remotest possibility of the government being associated with the proposed intelligence work. How was the officer to 'sink his identity', he asked? 'Did the attaches know him? If his letters went astray or were intercepted would he not be traced as having been at his present office?' After Cumming had 'reassured him on all these points', Errington 'appeared satisfied on the whole', though he continued to quiz Cumming about the chances of disclosure. Cumming's carefully prepared scheme was upset in November 1910 by the trial for espionage in Germany of two British officers, Lieutenant

Vivian Brandon and Captain Bernard Trench, who had been caught red-handed in August with maps, notes and photographs of defence and naval installations on the German North Sea coast and along the Kiel Canal. The two men had been working primarily for Regnart (though Cumming had agreed to provide £10 for any 'extra expenses'), and there were fears that his involvement might become known to the Germans.

In the end the appointment was not made and Regnart remained in the Admiralty. In May 1911 the next six-monthly Secret Service Bureau meeting agreed to reallocate 'the £700 for a man at Copenhagen, who had been approved but never appointed', in order to pay for work in Brussels. Reflecting continuing uncertainty about which department was actually in charge, together with a slight misapprehension about how Cumming's organisation would work, Sir Arthur Nicolson referred to this as 'an Admiralty agency in Brussels'. Nicolson had some sense of the interdepartmental nature of the Bureau and also 'understood' that 'both the Admiralty and War Office would be directly under C who would arrange co-ordination of their work'. The committee were very satisfied with its work as a whole. On Wilson's proposal they approved salary increases (from £500 to £600) for Cumming and Kell, for having 'done excellent work'. Bethell also 'spoke in high terms of their work' and remarked that Cumming 'had spent considerable sums out of his own pocket . . . and that he was most economical, travelling second class though he was entitled to first'.[12]

Six months on, the committee thought Cumming and Kell were still doing well: 'Sir A. Nicolson, Admiral Bethell and General Wilson concurring, expressed satisfaction at the excellent work being done by both branches.' Yet the evidence of the intelligence agency's performance during the Agadir Crisis over the summer of 1911 is rather mixed. The crisis was set off by the arrival of the German gunboat *Panther* at the Moroccan port of Agadir which the French regarded as being within their own exclusive sphere of influence, and a sharp deterioration in Franco-German relations for a while seemed to threaten a war between the two countries into which Britain might be drawn. The Secret Service Bureau had been formed to provide intelligence during precisely this kind of situation. Towards the end of July, *The Times* reported that the German High Sea Fleet had begun its 'annual summer cruise' and that one of the German squadrons had passed through the Kiel Canal to the

North Sea, demonstrating that the canal was 'ready for war'. In London there were worries about the location of the German warships, and even that the British fleet might be attacked. During the evening of 26 July Macdonogh sought out Henry Wilson and told him 'that our Admiralty have lost the German Fleet & have asked us to find them. Macdonogh sent [Bertrand] Stewart off to Brussels to see L. [probably Long] & send him round the German Ports.' The whole thing', wrote Wilson in his diary, 'is a Pantomime.'[13]

The 'pantomime' turned into a disaster when a week later Stewart was arrested in Bremen and charged with espionage. By one account he was arrested 'in bed at 1 a.m.'; by another he was in a public lavatory, attempting to destroy a code-book planted on him by a German double-agent. 'The Hun police broke open the door of the privy, [and] he was arrested with the corpus delicti on him.' Stewart, a thirty-nine-year-old London solicitor and officer in the part-time West Kent Yeomanry, was an enthusiastic amateur, who (perhaps disingenuously) claimed during his subsequent prosecution that he 'only knew enough German to obtain his meals and to make himself understood in hotels and on railways'. On Macdonogh's orders, in fact, Stewart was working directly under Cumming, who had sent him in the first instance to Nijmegen in the Netherlands to contact an agent called Verrue who was working in Germany. Inadvisedly accompanying Verrue across the frontier, Stewart had visited Hamburg, Cuxhaven and Bremerhaven before being arrested. When he returned to England after more than two years in a German prison, Stewart claimed £12,500 compensation, blaming Cumming, Macdonogh and Wilson for his predicament.[14] Cumming hazarded that Stewart had been shopped to the Germans by his 'passive' agent 'U' (evidently Verrue), whom Bethell, with the wisdom of hindsight, argued might have 'been a decoy all through'. It is 'annoying', he told Cumming, 'but we must expect drawbacks such as these in this kind of business'.

During September 1911 Cumming's 'early-warning system' also brought reports of threatening developments in Germany. On 4 September Wilson noted a report from an agent in Belgium that two German divisions were concentrating in Malmédy, just across the frontier, which, combined with other indications, seemed so 'ominous' that he briefed Winston Churchill (Home Secretary since February 1910) and Sir Edward Grey personally about the matter. Later in the month Wilson recorded several similar warnings, including on 18 September alone 'no less than four reports of our S.S. from the frontier saying German troops were massing along Belgian frontier'. Alarmist reports of German preparations were circulated to senior ministers, including the Prime Minister himself, and, although they all came to nothing, this did not appear in any way to affect the reputation of Cumming's Bureau (as the minutes of the November 1911 committee meeting confirm, and when it was given a 'special grant' of £500 'because of the crisis').[15]

The minutes of the Secret Service Bureau committee meetings for November 1912 and May 1913 show continued support for Cumming's expanding work. At the latter meeting a combined estimate was approved of £16,212 for both branches, as was Cumming's scheme to develop a network of agents in Norway and Denmark reporting on German naval matters, especially ship movements through the entrance to the Baltic Sea. Sir Arthur Nicolson asked that a proposal in November 1912 to station permanent agents 'in four continental ports' (at a total annual cost of £1,600) be included on the 1913–14 estimates 'and he would then consider it favourably'. Six months later, a slightly scaled-down scheme, costing £1,200, was approved.[16] Late in 1912 Lord Onslow (who had succeeded Errington as Nicolson's private secretary in May 1911) allowed £1,000 'for miscellaneous payments and contingencies', which Cumming called 'my special fund'.

Cumming also secured permission to expand his operations in Belgium, and he proposed that Regnart should be appointed as 'Branch Agent' in Brussels. This led to an extraordinary public disagreement between Cumming and Captain Thomas Jackson, who had succeeded Bethell as Director of Naval Intelligence (but with the new title, which prevailed for the next six years, of Director of the Intelligence Division) in January 1912. When Cumming explained to the May 1913 committee meeting that he wanted 'to employ a certain Marine officer, who possessed special qualifications', Jackson interjected that 'he personally did not consider the man whom C wanted was suitable. He did not consider him either hardworking, clever or tactful, nor that he would be loyal to C, but that was C's affair.' Cumming persevered, asserting that 'the officer in question was well fitted'. Henry Wilson supported him. 'It was', he said, 'impossible to get a perfect man for the appointment, but he knew the officer referred to was keen on his work, a good linguist, and an artist in Secret

Service.' Jackson then changed tack and argued 'that no officer should
be selected for this work while still on the active list. In fact he should
not even be offered it until he had retired and it should not be possible
for him to say that he had left the service [the Royal Navy] in order to
take up the job and thus establish a claim for compensation in case of
discharge.' No one disagreed with this, and in the end Cumming got his
man.[17] Nicolson 'finally said that if & as soon as Roy [Regnart] retired,
I could have him. McJ [Jackson] said we should all regret it, but it was
decided that as I had to work with him, I should be allowed to try him.'
Cumming had no illusions that Regnart would make a congenial colleague. When considering him for the Copenhagen job he had reflected
in his diary that he was 'a very difficult man to work with, as he plays
an independent game and will not submit to control – I shall find him
a constant thorn in my side'. Yet he also believed that he was 'the best
man for the post', and 'I would rather risk a certain amount of personal
discomfort and worry than have a secondrate man as my Chief Branch
Agent'.

The disagreement over Regnart's appointment illustrates both
Cumming's increasing confidence in his own judgment and a preparedness not to defer automatically to higher authority, as well as a shrewd
appreciation of the variable range of personalities he had to deal with in
intelligence work. One such was 'Major H.L.B.' whom he met in January
1911. He was 'a curious looking man with a large hawk like nose, brown
eyes and brown hair. Medium height – about 5.8 – rather showy dressed,
with an enormous pearl pin.' He had 'a shifty look about him' and his nationality was 'very difficult to fix'. He claimed to speak many languages,
but always travelled 'on the Continent as a Spaniard speaking Spanish
and Portuguese'. HLB told Cumming that he had enjoyed a cosmopolitan career as a soldier in Africa, Chief of the Secret Police in Bolivia, a
French secret service agent and an arms dealer. He added that 'the smart-
est Agents in the German service' were in Britain, and one of them, called
von Gessler, 'may be known anywhere by his having 4 rows of teeth'. He
said he (HLB) had a Peruvian ring which contained 'an Indian poison'
that would 'knock a man down in three seconds'. It was 'a bit "risky" to
use, as a microscopic overdose would make a strong man a hopeless idiot
for life and beyond any chance of cure'. Cumming thought the man was
'no doubt a blackguard, but is probably a clever one, and I should like

to get something out of him. All my staff are blackguards,' he continued, 'but they are incapable ones, and a man with a little ingenuity and brains would be a change, even if not an agreeable one.'

Another thing which struck Cumming was the consistently high expectations of potential agents. In August 1910, one man whom he wanted to send on a tour of Germany told him that 'he must have an allowance for Champagne'. In December 1910 the part-Russian, Dutch and English divorced wife of a German officer (whose conduct 'had certainly been reprehensible') offered to get information from a male admirer on the German Naval Staff. She said 'she was not going to do this work for money, but to revenge the slight upon her honour and for the sake of her children'. She agreed, however, to accept £20 a month for 'expenses' and 'was rather insistent upon a "guarantie" [sic] which', noted Cumming with the benefit of not much more than a year in the job and an air of tired cynicism, 'all spies ask for. They explain that it is a guarantee of good faith which is due to them in exchange for the compromising gift of their names and addresses, but my experience teaches me that it means an advance of payment followed by an unbroken silence.' Later the same day Bethell told Cumming about a man who had 'access to Krupps Yard' and might be worth cultivating. Cumming thought that the only way of getting hold of him was 'to ask him to eat and drink, and that all these people without exception make a strong point of doing this in the best style at the most expensive restaurants'. Two Danes who turned up in London, also at the end of 1910, offered Cumming an abundant selection of material, including enlarged maps of German naval bases, sketches of a torpedo mechanism and several signal codes as 'used by Searchlights, Wireless from Submarines &c'. They asked for £5,000 (equivalent to £350,000 in modern prices) which in Cumming's opinion 'was not to be thought of'. Even 'if we had accepted their plans as genuine, we should have offered £200 for the lot'. In the end he paid them nothing other than £10 between them for their travelling expenses, although in conversation (and reflecting his longstanding interest in harbour defences) he had obtained 'a good deal of information' about underground tunnels in the various harbours and the existence of 'land mines laid from a central firing station to different salient points'.

Over the first few years of the Bureau, we can see Cumming working on tradecraft. He appears to have enjoyed using disguise when meeting agents. For a rendezvous in Paris in July 1910 he 'was slightly disguised (toupee & moustache) and had on a rather peculiar costume'. In preparation for meeting (in January 1911) a man he called 'Ironmould', an engineer who was offering to go to Trieste to report on Austrian naval shipbuilding, Cumming was made up at William Berry Clarkson's famous theatrical costume shop in Wardour Street in Soho.[18] The disguise was 'perfect . . . its existence not being noticeable even in a good light'. Cumming 'then went to a photographer and had a photograph taken of the disguise as it is necessary to give the dresser something to go by, if it is desired to repeat a disguise exactly – as in my case'. Cumming also developed other techniques to avoid being identified. In January 1913, meeting a contact called 'Ruffian' – 'a plausible chap, but rather oily looking' who claimed his brother-in-law worked as a foreman in a German gun factory – Cumming arrived by taxi, using a method which he claimed was 'the best I have tried, as it is almost impossible for the man – if a rascal – to point you out to his friends, who may be waiting with a camera &c.'. The trick was to 'drive past the rendezvous on the opposite side' and when the target was spotted, 'drive up close to him, open the door and invite him in. I lean back the moment I have caught his eye, and from then onwards do not show myself at all.' After the conversation was finished the contact was deposited 'at some point well away from the place of meeting . . . Of course,' added Cumming, 'this plan is too expensive for a prolonged meeting, but for a short one it is very good.'

Cumming brought his enthusiasm for the latest technology to bear on some of the intelligence challenges he had to face. Although wireless communications technology was in its infancy, he thought it offered a possible solution to the problem of getting rapid messages through during the period of political tension which it was assumed would precede any German invasion. In the spring of 1912 he discussed with French intelligence colleagues the development of a 'mobile wireless station' in a motor car, with a range of 250 miles, which would be based in Belgium. Although the French thought the Belgian authorities would not allow such a thing, they offered to see if 'the Car &c' could be purchased 'thro' a Belgian Agent (a Govt. official whom they knew of)', but Cumming had his doubts about 'the soundness of the idea'. Contemplating a scheme in January 1913 for a father-and-son team to gather information along the Danish and Norwegian coast using a thirty-ton motor pilot boat,

Cumming reflected that 'the knotty point about the transmission of news remains unsolved'. Late in 1913 Cumming was working on a scheme to base an aeroplane in France, which could be used to keep watch along the country's eastern border, but Macdonogh baulked at the prospective cost – Cumming thought £1,700, the air experts £3,000 or more – and Wilson said it could be done only in co-operation with the French, which he promised to help with.

The approach of war

General Wilson as Director of Military Operations was a particularly active promoter of close Anglo-French relations, and his championing of the alliance with France was part of a wider and growing closeness between the two countries which was reflected in the intelligence world. In January 1910 Wilson's predecessor, John Spencer Ewart, had told Cumming that he 'did not wish any espionnage [*sic*] work done in France just now, as our present excellent relations might be disturbed thereby'. Cumming's earliest liaison contacts with a foreign intelligence service came in March 1912 when he met officers of French Military Intelligence to discuss matters of common interest, inevitably concentrating on gathering information about German capabilities and intentions. The most senior French officer involved, Colonel Charles-Édouard Dupont (head of the Deuxième Bureau of the French General Staff from 1913 to 1918), 'was quite disposed to be frank and friendly and so were the other officers we met subsequently', but it was evident that they were 'a little nervous about telling to strangers of another nation the matters they have kept secret for so long'. Dupont, however, was 'very strong indeed as to the vital necessity of our meeting each other and deciding now at once upon a plan of concerted action to be taken when the crisis came'.

By 1913 the French and British were exchanging intelligence material and Macdonogh was directing requests to the French for specific information through Cumming. In January, for example, he asked about the composition of German armies on their western frontier and 'a new powder for smallarms'. On 6 March Cumming noted that 'a large packet of valuable stuff came in from our friends', which he brought to Wilson, 'who thought it extremely valuable and is to show it to Sir J[ohn] F[rench], the Chief of the Imperial General Staff] at once'. Wilson 'talked to me about the state of affairs and said that it was an extremely good move to get hold of these people, and hoped that we were doing something for them'. Liaison with the French remained close. There is a hint in Cumming's diary that by January 1914 he had an officer actually posted to the French headquarters. In July, on Macdonogh's recommendation, Cumming took on Captain Edward Louis Spiers ('a very good man & interpreter Fr., Ger. & Ital.') and toyed with the idea of sending him to Paris.[19] In February, with Henry Wilson's help, he got French agreement for the aeroplane scheme. He purchased a machine and was making arrangements for its base in France in July, but the declaration of war at the beginning of August seems to have come before any practical use had been made of it.

During discussions with French opposite numbers in 1912 Cumming had discovered that the two services had some agents in common. One, 'HCJ', went to Russia and with Cumming's permission submitted the same reports to both organisations. In April 1913 Cumming learned that HCJ was also working for the Russians. Over lunch at the Savoy Café in London, he told Cumming that he had been engaged by them to help overhaul their 'heavy and clumsy' intelligence organisation. On the same occasion he declared that 'war was very probable between Russia and Austria as the Russians were prepared in a way we did not expect and would require only the slightest pretext to attack the Austrians', a prediction which came to pass the following year. In the spring of 1914 Cumming raised the possibility with Admiral Henry Oliver (who, replacing Jackson, had been Director of the Intelligence Division at the Admiralty since November 1913) of working with the Russian secret service to co-operate in running a Danish network to report on Germany. Even if the Russians would not collaborate officially, Cumming thought of placing an agent in St Petersburg 'to receive & forward telegrams'.

Cumming remained keen to develop official relations with the Russians. In June 1914 a French intelligence officer told him that 'the new Chief of the Russ. SS' was coming to Paris '& as soon as he knows of his arrival he will let me know & will introduce me to him', adding (with that avoidance of official channels which characterises much intelligence work), 'we need not trouble our Attaché in the matter'. The Russian, in fact, came to London, and Cumming met him (apparently along with the

Russian military attaché in Paris, Count Ignatieff). No detailed record survives of what was discussed. A scribbled note in Cumming's hand preserved in his diary says 'Mobilisation Plan in 8 days. We to photograph', though whose plan it was and where it came from is not revealed. But the French were involved too. A few days later Cumming noted a conversation with Admiral Oliver, 'discussing SS matters & the new scheme with Fr. & Russians'. On 2 July Cumming interviewed a potential agent, a 'good Russian – interpreter – speaks French, German, some Spanish & Hindustani'. He was the 'agent for [a] patent motor car wheel' and 'could live in St. P[etersburg] on 400 [pounds]'. Cumming told him he 'could promise nothing, but if Russ scheme went through, he might do as Agent there'. Russia was by no means the limit of Cumming's ambition. During the spring of 1914 Oliver proposed basing an agent in China, at Kiaochow (Jiaozhou) near Tsingtao (Qingdao), where there was a German naval base, and the six-monthly meeting of the Secret Service Bureau committee in May 1914 allotted £200 for the purpose.

Over the first half of 1914 Cumming seems to have spent most of his time working on the deployment of agents along Germany's western frontier, intended both to give early warning of a German attack and to provide the basis for intelligence reporting after war had started. There were two main networks based in Belgium. The first was run by Roy Regnart in Brussels and concentrated on the eastern frontier with Germany, the 'Maastricht appendix' (that part of the Netherlands which protruded south into Belgium and through which the strategists thought a German attack might come), and up into the Netherlands to Venlo and Nijmegen. From here he aimed to watch German 'military centres' such as Cologne, Münster and Oldenburg. The second network was run by 'AC' with a base at Lille in France and primary responsibility for southern Belgium approximately from Liège eastwards to the Channel coast. Reporting to AC was a local agent, 'DB', based at Dinant, south of Namur, who had his own network of sub-agents. Most of the reporting from these networks was practical. In January AC was asked to investigate Dutch railways in the Maastricht appendix and 'to look out for possible Bridge sites (connected with roads) on the banks of the Meuse' just north of Liège. In February DB submitted a report on the railway line between Roermond and Maaseik at the northern end of the appendix. Roy Regnart, troublesome as ever, complained to Cumming that he could 'do nothing without more £ [money]' and said it was 'useless to try & get agents at the Ports & elsewhere' unless he could 'retain them at once and pay them'. He thought 'he ought to have at least £500 a year & a free hand'.

Cumming's networks in Belgium and the Netherlands, as well as shipping-reporting agents based in Denmark, failed completely to provide any advance warning for the assault on France which the Germans launched through Belgium in August 1914. While the broad location of the advance was pretty well predicted (though the Germans avoided the Maastricht appendix), the timing was a complete surprise. The real prewar successes for Cumming's organisation were in technical reporting, especially on German naval construction. One of Cumming's best agents (and the highest paid), Hector Bywater, whom he named 'H2O', produced a regular series of reports in 1913 and 1914. Details are sparse, but in April 1913 Captain Jackson in the Admiralty 'remarked that H2O sent a lot of good stuff'. During 1914 one report on German naval guns was thought so significant that H2O was quizzed in person in London on its contents by Admiral Reginald Tupper, who had commanded the naval gunnery school at Plymouth. H2O also reported on aeronautical matters, another Admiralty priority. In January 1914 another agent supplied 'a big report' on dirigibles (airships). Macdonogh told Cumming that the Director of the Air Department in the Admiralty, Captain Murray Sueter, thought highly of the agent's plans '& said we ought to pay him all we could afford'. Traces of the technical reporting from Cumming's agents have survived in Naval Intelligence Division logbooks written up by the head of the German section, Fleet Paymaster Charles Rotter, collating information on German submarine and battleship construction. That Cumming was able to supply the navy with valued intelligence is reflected by an entry in the diary in March 1914: 'Rotter asked me to get him information about secret building of Submarines. He says they speak of U.21 but may possibly be U.31. He says they have about 50 built & projected.' Despite the success of Cumming's agents in collecting technical intelligence, the impact of this work was less than might have been hoped. Nicholas Hiley has remarked on the resistance which much of this reporting encountered in the Admiralty where the preconceived ideas of some experts led them to question intelligence which stressed the great importance of German developments in torpedoes, submarines, mines and aircraft.[20]

The growth of the Secret Service Bureau over its first five years is reflect-ed in an Account Book for both branches of the Bureau covering April 1912 until September 1914. Its budget, estimated at £2,000 in 1909, had grown to nearly £11,000 by 1912. Although it was originally envis-aged that the money would be divided equally between Kell's Home and Cumming's Foreign branch, in December 1912 Kell's side cost £472 and Cumming's £810, although this included two months' payments of £125 to H2O. Cumming's salary and that of his five home-based staff came to just under £200 a month, less than half the cost of overseas agents. By December 1913 the annual budget for both branches had risen to £15,572, and the proportion of expenditure going to Cumming's side had increased slightly with Foreign getting £841 per month and Home £428. Although spending on Kell's branch increased a little during 1914, on the eve of war it was still significantly less than that for Cumming's. All this was about to change. Over the war years the size of both branches and their budgets would grow exponentially, as perhaps could have been predicted, even in 1914. But how well Cumming's side would respond to the challenges of the next few years, and even whether it would survive as an autonomous institution at all, remained to be seen.

During the early summer of 1914 there is no sense of the imminence of war in Mansfield Cumming's diary. The assassination of the Archduke Franz Ferdinand in Sarajevo on 28 June, and the ensuing July Crisis, pass unremarked. Only from the very last day of July is there an impression of unusual activity. That day Cumming had a meeting with a new recruit, Major Cecil Cameron, the agent AC and two others. Taking codes pro-vided by Cumming, Cameron was to cross the Channel that night, meet a contact in Paris and go on to Dinant at once, before basing himself at Givet on the Franco-Belgian frontier. On 2 August he gave more codes to another colleague, who having borrowed a car and driver 'started off for Brux[elles], via Dover & Ostend'. Intelligence from inside Germany inevitably continued to be a high priority. At the end of July Cumming got Admiral Oliver's sanction to send a woman agent to Berlin and agreed to pay her £100 for a month's work there. What precisely she was to do is not recorded, but the mere fact that Cumming was contemplating such an operation at such a time confirms the suddenness with which the First World War came upon Britain. On 3 August the prospective agent assured Cumming that she could get the correct papers to enable her to travel to Germany, but the next day he had to put her off 'as she cd show no passport'. The last diary entry for that day, 4 August 1914, was 'War declared against Germany – midnt'.

PART TWO

THE FIRST WORLD WAR

2

Status, organisation and expertise

Just over a fortnight after the declaration of war with Germany, a British Expeditionary Force of some forty thousand men had been deployed in northern France. It was an astonishingly successful logistical performance and a tribute to the completeness of the plans which the Directorate of Military Operations had been working on for the previous three years or so. Little thought, however, had been given to the higher direction of this force, beyond the appointment of Field Marshal Sir John French as Commander-in-Chief, and the assumption that, subject to some general instructions concerning relations with Allied forces (principally the French), he would have complete freedom of command in the field. Few people anticipated that from the autumn of 1914 the opposing forces would get bogged down in a costly four-year war of attrition along a line of more or less fixed positions from the English Channel to the Swiss frontier. As the British military commitment escalated into a mass, conscript army, and the 'butcher's bill' of trench warfare mounted, the autonomy of Sir John French and his successor, Sir Douglas Haig, came to be questioned in London where civilian politicians (especially David Lloyd George after he became Prime Minister in December 1916) increasingly sought to assert control over war strategy. For civil–military relations in Britain, the consequence of 'total war' and the necessary mobilisation of all national resources was to shift the wartime balance of power away from the armed services (especially the army) and to the political leadership of the country.

The experience of Mansfield Cumming's infant organisation during the First World War reflected these wider developments. From August 1914 the military authorities' chief intelligence requirement – from whatever source – was operationally useful information for the Expeditionary

Force in the field. Increasingly, both General Headquarters (GHQ) in France and the War Office in London asserted exclusive rights – and control – over the Secret Service. But Cumming argued that he had wider responsibilities beyond the purely military demands of the armies in France and Flanders. As a sailor himself, he was sharply aware of the Admiralty's intelligence needs, which he actively sought to meet. With Foreign Office support, moreover, he managed to retain his institutional autonomy, seeing off successive military attempts to annex his Service and, by the end of the war, he had conclusively established the independent basis and interdepartmental character of an organisation that was to emerge in the early 1920s as the Secret Intelligence Service.

Serving three masters

Cumming's relationship with each of the three departments he served – the Foreign Office, the Admiralty and the War Office – inevitably changed in August 1914 with the service ministries' growing demands for immediate operational intelligence. This was especially true of the War Office. The staffing of British Military Intelligence was immediately affected by the outbreak of war. General Henry Wilson, the Director of Military Operations, who had been very supportive of Cumming, went off to be sub-chief of staff in the expeditionary force and was replaced at the War Office by another Irishman, General Charles Callwell, a fifty-five-year-old 'Dug Out', a retired officer brought back (like so many others) to fill a wartime job. He had been Assistant Director of Military Operations in the early 1900s, but had no direct experience of either Cumming's or Kell's relatively new organisations. George Macdonogh, who as head of 'M.O.5' in the War Office had 'been responsible for all Secret Service work', went to France to take charge of intelligence at GHQ, and was succeeded first by Colonel Douglas MacEwan, who stayed two months before also heading for the front, and in October 1914 by Colonel George Cockerill. For the next eighteen months or so, Callwell and Cockerill were Cumming's principal military masters.[1] There were fewer changes on the naval side. Henry Oliver, in charge of Naval Intelligence since November 1913, moved on to be Chief of the Admiralty War Staff at the beginning of November 1914. He was succeeded by William Reginald

Hall. Widely known as 'Blinker' (because of his nervous twitch), Hall remained Director of the Intelligence Division in the Admiralty for the rest of the war.

From the beginning there were problems of status and hierarchy. No one was very clear who precisely was in charge of the Secret Service, though this ambiguity evidently gave Cumming some useful room for manoeuvre. From the evidence of his diary, between 4 August and 30 September 1914 Cumming visited the War Office and the Admiralty nearly every day, both to brief them about his work and to get approval for spending money. On Sunday 9 August, for example, he 'called on Col. McE[wan] with last night's telegrams'. The following Thursday he saw both MacEwan and 'Roland' [Admiral Oliver], bringing reports to the former and getting his approval to take on two more officers. On 25 August Cumming noted in his diary: 'Called on McE & on Roland, with cipher messages'. Over the first three weeks of the war Cumming also visited the Foreign Office five times (generally seeing Ronald Campbell, the Permanent Under-Secretary's private secretary), but on 26 August Colonel Macdonogh told him that he was 'not to call at F.O. any more'. During September Cumming had three further meetings with Campbell but on each occasion he was accompanying an officer from the War Office or the Admiralty. Further reflecting War Office concerns about Cumming's evident refusal to operate within what they regarded as the proper channels, on 25 September, after he had gone to General Callwell about a staffing matter, MacEwan's replacement, George Cockerill, 'told him off' and instructed him that he was 'not to see Genl. direct'. At this stage, however, there was no attempt to compel Cumming to report exclusively through the War Office and, indeed (perhaps reflecting his own naval background), his regular contact in the Admiralty remained Admiral Oliver, Callwell's director-level opposite number.

The wartime situation of Cumming's organisation involved not just the allocation of duties between the War Office and the Admiralty (not to mention the Foreign Office), but also the question of how it would relate to George Macdonogh's new intelligence branch at GHQ in France, as well as any future liaison with Britain's French, Belgian and Russian allies. During the first two months of the war Cumming made three trips to the Continent, each time taking his own car, which had to be hoisted on and off the cross-Channel ferry. He went to Brussels on 15 August following an angry complaint from Colonel Fairholme, the British military attaché, to the Foreign Office about Cumming's man Henry Dale Long, who had 'made a fool of himself over a "suspect" cyclist'. Here was another potential problem of line-crossing, between the more overt intelligence duties of a military attaché (enhanced by the fact that Britain and Belgium were now wartime allies) and those of the Secret Service. While in Belgium, Cumming and a colleague drove south-east from Brussels towards Wavre where they found the Belgians 'throwing up entrenchments against expected attack', and German Uhlans (cavalry) were reported to be in woods close by. Driving on towards Namur, they were turned back by French troops who 'thought we were TR [German] spies'. At the end of August Cumming motored to Paris for talks with Colonel Wallner and other French Deuxième Bureau officers. At lunch in the Hôtel Grande Bretagne Cumming met an American journalist. Never one to miss an intelligence-gathering opportunity, he offered him $6 a week for German news, but made 'no arrangement for transmission'.

At the end of September Cumming travelled over to France to consult with Macdonogh. At about nine o'clock in the evening on Friday 2 October, motoring east of Paris in country through which the British Expeditionary Force had passed at the beginning of September on the 'retreat from Mons' (before subsequently fighting its way back north), Cumming suffered a serious accident in which his twenty-four-year-old only son, Alistair, was killed and Cumming badly hurt. A telegram from France conveyed the news to May Cumming: 'Deeply regret to inform you that Lieut. A. Smith-Cumming, Seaforth Highlanders, died the result of motor accident on 3rd October, his father Commander Cumming was severely injured and is in French Hospl at Meaux. Lord Kitchener expresses his sympathy.' The laconic entry in Cumming's diary for 3 October reads: 'Poor old Ally died.' The drivers in the Intelligence Corps, which had been formed only with the outbreak of hostilities mainly to provide auxiliary assistance for unit intelligence officers, had gained a reputation for risky, high-speed driving. Macdonogh's deputy at GHQ, Major Walter Kirke, wrote to his wife that 'last night young Cumming went off to Paris with Commander Cumming in the 60 h.p. Fiat of which I told you before as having given me some hairy rides, & piled it up against a tree. Young Cumming was killed, & the old man has had one foot amputated . . . & he is in a [ghastly?] bad way, so we are all rather sick.'[2]

The army telegram sent to May Cumming bearing the grim news of her son's death.

The story of Cumming's misfortune inevitably grew with the telling and it became part of Service mythology, as demonstrated by the vivid version given by the novelist Compton Mackenzie in his 1932 book *Greek Memories*. During the First World War Mackenzie worked for Cumming in Greece, where he was told the story by Commander William Sells, the British naval attaché in Athens, who had heard it at a conference in Malta (attended by Cumming, who had by then been promoted to captain) in March 1916:

In the autumn of 1914 his son, a subaltern in the Seaforths, had been driving him in a fast car on some urgent Intelligence mission in the area of operations. The car going at full speed had crashed into a tree and overturned, pinning Captain Cumming by the leg and flinging his son out on his head. The boy was fatally injured, and his father, hearing him moan something about the cold, tried to extricate himself from the wreck of the car to put a coat over him; but struggle as he might he could not free his smashed leg. Thereupon he had taken out a penknife and hacked away at his smashed leg until he had cut it off, after which he had crawled over to his son and spread a coat over him, being found later lying unconscious by the dead body.

'That's the sort of old chap C is,' said Sells.

However it happened, Cumming certainly lost part of his leg as a result of the accident, as confirmed by the rather less dramatic summary in his service record: '3.10.14: injured in motor accident in France; both legs broken – left foot amputated'.[3]

Subsequent telegrams charted his recovery. On 7 October his condition was 'serious', but the following day it was 'satisfactory', confirmed by 'report progress satisfactory' on 2 November. On 12 October Kirke went to visit him and noted that Cumming was 'out of danger now, I am glad to say, though minus a foot, but the life and soul of the hospital – wonderful fellow!' For six weeks from the beginning of October there are only very sporadic entries in Cumming's diary, among other things listing fellow patients in the hospital as well as nursing staff 'to remember'. But suddenly, on 11 November, Cumming resumed writing up the journal: 'Arrived at home about 3 & commenced work at once.' He had a 'long interview' with Captain Thomas Laycock, his second-in-command who had held the fort in his absence. Being temporarily immobile, for a time people came to him: on 11 November, 'Cockerill came over & stayed an hour'; next day the new Director of Intelligence in the Admiralty, Blinker Hall, came '& stayed over an hour discussing various matters'. His first venture out (to the War Office) was not until 8 December. On 10 December Callwell reported that Cumming 'had just been in to see me, wheeling himself in an invalid chair. He is wonderful all things considered and as keen as ever.'[4] Cumming's enforced immobility may have done some good for the organisation at a time when it was expanding rapidly. Obliged to delegate duties which hitherto he had carried out himself – Laycock, for example, was 'constantly backwards & forwards to Admty & WO' – Cumming had a chance to get to grips with Service administration. On 23 November he recorded in his diary that the monthly expenditure was £4,310, already four and a half times greater than the prewar figure of some £950. Over three-quarters of this was spent on intelligence-gathering networks in Continental Europe and the remainder on the thirteen-strong Head Office staff, which, he reported to Cockerill on 6 December, comprised himself and three officers, four clerks, two female typists, a messenger and '2 outside men' (one of whom was Ernest Bailey, Cumming's chauffeur and servant).

According to an in-house history of British Military Intelligence drawn up after the war, Cumming's accident (which, it asserted, 'incapacitated him for some months', an allegation which Cumming would have challenged) had two main consequences. In the first place it meant that the Secret Service organisation was brought more closely under War Office control; and, second, it led to GHQ in France instituting 'its own independent service'. While this second development reflected the immediate needs of an army in the field for operational intelligence, later in the war it was to provoke disputes about how intelligence-gathering in the battle-zone should be organised and controlled. The intensification of War Office control in London was combined with the incorporation of Kell's security and counter-espionage branch fully into the Directorate of Military Operations organisation (as 'M.O.5(g)'), and these developments underpinned successive attempts by the military to take over Cumming's organisation entirely.[5] In the meantime, however, a version of the pre-war arrangement temporarily continued whereby an interdepartmental committee meeting every six months oversaw Cumming's work. The last peacetime meeting had been in May 1914; the next was in January 1915. Perhaps indicating Cumming's perceived lowly status, Colonel Cockerill only told him about the meeting just before it occurred. It was held in the Foreign Office, which was represented by the Permanent Under-Secretary, Sir Arthur Nicolson. Callwell, Cockerill and two other officers were there for the army, while Sir Graham Greene (Permanent Under-Secretary) and Blinker Hall attended for the Admiralty. 'Finance was discussed,' wrote Cumming in his diary, '& I am to limit myself to 5000 a month, with 1000 in addition as margin.'

Although the location and constitution of the January meeting suggests that the Foreign Office retained overall control, Cumming's day-to-day direction was in the hands of Admiralty and War Office personnel, who themselves did not necessarily follow a common line. The day after the Foreign Office meeting, Cumming had 'a long yarn' with Hall at the Admiralty about the position of an officer in Petrograd (as St Petersburg was renamed for patriotic reasons in 1914) over whom the army and the navy evidently disagreed. Hall 'will back me up if necessary', noted

Cumming, 'but I dont wish to start friction between Army & Navy & so asked him to do nothing until I came to him for help'. Cockerill's deputy, Major C. N. French, who from early 1915 was the principal point of contact between Cumming and the War Office (and remained so for the rest of the war), increasingly seems to have conceived his role as one of command, rather than mere liaison. In March, when there was a difference of opinion over the control of agents in Norway, Hall bluntly assured Cumming that he was 'not in any sense under CF's orders'. Another complication was that, since the outbreak of war, service attachés across Europe had begun to take a more active part in secret intelligence work. Cumming's growing deployment of officers and agents in neutral countries such as the Netherlands and in Scandinavia, moreover, ensured that the Foreign Office took a close interest in his work. At the end of January Ronald Campbell informed Cumming not only that the Admiralty was 'against further extension in Sweden & Denmark at present', but that 'the Norway & Sweden organisations' should be under him (Cumming) rather than Captain Consett, the British naval attaché based in Stockholm. In April 1915, with the increasing volume of General Staff work, the Directorate of Military Operations was reorganised. Colonel Cockerill was promoted brigadier-general and given the title Director of Special Intelligence with overall responsibility for counter-espionage, economic warfare and propaganda, as well as postal, cable and press censorship. Along with the 'Collation of War Intelligence', and the 'investigation of enemy ciphers', 'Liaison with Espionage Service' was given to a new branch, 'M.O.6', under the newly promoted Colonel French.[6]

Scattered through Cumming's 1915 diary are indications of interdepartmental tensions over intelligence matters, though the Foreign Office remained supportive. On 18 June Cumming had an hour's talk with Sir Arthur Nicolson: 'He was very kind & said I might come to him whenever I was in difficulty.' In August Blinker Hall of Naval Intelligence suggested that Cumming should be 'independent of Admty & WO'. Ronald Campbell in the Foreign Office did 'not entirely concur' but 'would like to see me more independent'. The following month, faced with GHQ attempting to expand their intelligence operations, Nicolson proposed 'limiting G.H.Q.'s zones & handing K[ell] & me our £ [money] direct'. Colonel French agreed to the financial arrangement, but did 'not like limitation of areas'. During the late autumn the issue of War Office control came to a head when, on an attempt by the army to take over his Dutch network, Cumming finally lost patience with the persistent incursions of other departments on his organisation. 'Ever since the war started,' he wrote to Nicolson in a long and evidently heartfelt letter, 'my Bureau has been subjected to attacks which have disorganised and almost destroyed it and which have entirely prevented me from devoting my whole energies to the difficult work I have to do.' He asserted that, on the outbreak of war, 'nearly the whole of my existing agents were taken away from their stations and I was left without a staff and with my systems completely dislocated'. Since then his people 'have been attacked by our own authorities in Belgium, Holland, Denmark & Russia'. The War Office had taken over his 'admirable organisation' in Holland, where his work had been 'completely ruined by the interference of other and rival organisations – controlled by officers who have no experience of Secret Service work and who are apparently not influenced by any consideration for the views of the Foreign Office or the need for tact and diplomacy in so delicate a situation'.

For Cumming, the main threat to his position, and indeed to the whole existence of his Service, came from the army. 'I am of course an outsider in the War Office,' he told Nicolson, 'and since the war I have been put under a sub-section of a Department, with a position so subordinate that I am unable to raise my voice in protest against this or any other action affecting my work . . . I remain', he continued, 'outside the pale of the circle in which my duties lie.' It was 'apparently only necessary for an officer (junior to myself) to express a wish, and large portions of my work are taken away from me and given to others'. He argued that when he had first been appointed, his 'duties and limitations were clearly laid down and defined', but no attention was now paid to them. He believed that his Bureau was 'being gradually "side tracked" out of its appointed sphere', and that he would 'presently find' that he had 'nothing left to do but to deal with the degraded individuals who sell their services at such times, while all my work, training and experience of years will go to others who step in to seize the structure built up with so much care'. Cumming asserted that 'if these changes resulted in better work being done or a better organisation being secured' he would 'not have a word to say' and 'would cheerfully retire from a task that had obviously proved too much for my capacity'. Naturally he did not believe that was the case.

In particular, to maintain the secrecy which he regarded as so vital for his work, he asked that he might be 'dissociated from personal connection with the Admiralty or War Office and may be allowed to run my own service independently'. As an important initial step he wanted funds to be paid to him direct and that he should have discretion to pay them out as he wished, under a general authority from the service ministries. He said that there were 'items which it is undesirable should be known to anyone besides those who authorise them' and reasonably argued that it was impossible to keep them 'secret if the accounts pass through both departments'. Besides, if money was paid directly to Cumming, 'my agents would remain unknown and would be able to work safely and secretly and without interference from out side'.

We do not know if Cumming actually sent this long and powerful letter to Sir Arthur Nicolson, as the original top copy has not been found in either the SIS or Foreign Office archives. All that survives is a partial draft annotated in Cumming's handwriting, along with an undated typescript carbon copy of the entire text. Cumming appears to have shown the letter to the Director of Military Operations, General Callwell, for he wrote in his diary on 2 November: 'Saw Genl. C. re my letter to Sir A. which he wished me not to send.' Over the next week Cumming noted that Callwell had 'written a long minute to French defining my duties' and he himself had had 'a long yarn' at the Foreign Office about 'Gen C's letter'. Captain Hall at the Admiralty 'had seen Genl C. re his minute' and said 'that I am to dissociate myself from W.O. command'. Cumming then drew up a short paper embodying the general principles of secret service organisation and function as they seemed to him after some six years of experience. On 10 November he saw Nicolson, who 'said he was quite in accord with the principles laid down in my minute' and was 'very encouraging'. He was 'writing to the General' – an annotation in the diary indicates that this was Macdonogh in France – 'to say that he wishes all S.S. work in neutral countries' to be under Cumming. This was 'to apply also to C.E. [counter-espionage] work'.

On 17 November Nicolson signed a statement confirming that the 'Chief of the Secret Service' would have 'sole control' of 'all espionage and counter-espionage agents abroad'. When 'special information' was required by the Admiralty or the War Office 'he alone' was to be 'responsible for the manner by which it is to be obtained'. Cumming was also to have exclusive responsibility for his own staff and the funds placed at his disposal. He was to 'keep in constant touch with the War Office and Admiralty' who were 'to inform him of their requirements as occasion demands and furnish him with criticisms of his reports in a manner to help towards their improvement where necessary'. Finally, Cumming was to provide Nicolson (as Permanent Under-Secretary of State for Foreign Affairs) with 'a monthly statement of all his disbursements' and was to be subject to Nicolson's 'sole control . . . in all matters connected with the expenditure of Secret Service funds'.

Fending off the War Office

Nicolson's statement was an extremely important document, which Cumming rightly regarded as a 'charter' for his Service. Indeed, the exchanges of late 1915 mark a significant moment in confirming the institutional autonomy of the Service and consolidating the interdepartmental role, under Foreign Office supervision, which was to remain a central characteristic of the organisation as it developed during its first forty years. Securing exclusive control of staff and agents, moreover, meant that Cumming was well placed to maintain that deep secrecy of Service activities upon which he put such great store. Although the Director of Military Operations himself approved the charter, in the battle zone itself GHQ in France continued to assert priority for their own intelligence organisation. At a conference on 29 November about arrangements in France, Walter Kirke 'adopted a very high tone in saying that G.H.Q. was paramount & F.O. had nothing to say in the matter'.

The following month, to cope with the further wartime increase in business, the General Staff in London was again reorganised and a separate Directorate of Military Intelligence established in the War Office. On 23 December Callwell became Director of Military Intelligence (DMI), but he was merely filling in until 3 January 1916 when George Macdonogh, brought back from France, took over the position, which he held until September 1918. In the new structure Colonel French's MO6 branch was retitled MI1 and became the secretarial section of the Directorate, with responsibility, among other things, for the distribution of military intelligence as well as for secret service. In April 1916 MI1 was divided into four sub-sections, with the Secret Service Bureau going to MI1(c), an arrangement which lasted for the rest of the war.[7] Although the title made it look as though Cumming's Bureau was a sub-section of Military Intelligence, at the time the name was given 'it was expressly declared that it had no significance of that nature, but was merely a convenient "nom de guerre"'. From this point on, however, MI1(c) was increasingly used as the cover-name for Cumming's Bureau. At this time, too, Kell's organisation (which had been part of MO5 since 1910) became MI5.

During December 1915 someone in the army, possibly Kirke – who may not have been aware of the charter Cumming had secured from Nicolson (though the evidence of Kirke's diary confirms that he was certainly aware of the Foreign Office's protective attitude towards Cumming's organisation) – took the opportunity of these changes to float a plan for the 'Reorganisation of S.S. in the War Office'. Although in the wake of Nicolson's minute there was no possibility of these proposals being implemented, they are worth quoting as they embody what might be characterised as the 'extreme' army conception of the proper position and role of Cumming's Service, and provide strong evidence of the kinds of military attitudes Cumming and his colleagues came up against. The plan proposed that the new Director of Military Intelligence should take over the Secret Service entirely: 'The F.O. should be eliminated, and in any case "C" must have no direct access to it.' The Naval Intelligence authorities similarly would have to work through the War Office; an arrangement should be made with the Director of the Intelligence Division, whereby he 'entrusts his interests to the D.M.I., it being understood that the latter is the head of the S.S., and that C is his servant'. C's functions were described as 'purely executive', and 'consist in obtaining information from S.S. organisations under his control'. He was *not* responsible for 'distributing any information', which was to be the task of the MI1 section in the War Office. C, in any case, would be 'very fully employed in developing new organisations and keeping existing ones up to the mark by constant correspondence'. C's 'sole channel of communication' with the Director of Military Intelligence was to be through one of the DMI's staff officers, and the MI1 section was to be the only 'channel of communication between the S.S. Bureau and all other Government Offices, British or Foreign, other than foreign S.S. Bureaus'.[8] Thus was Cumming to be relegated to the position of a glorified secretary and extremely subordinate bureaucrat.

Cumming continued to assert a degree of autonomy, but it was in the face of continual challenge from army officers, especially Macdonogh and Colonel French, who both saw the relationship between the War Office and Cumming's Bureau purely in terms of *military* intelligence. In late September 1916 French had written a long letter to Cumming reflecting on the question of secret service and how best it might be organised 'in the event of any future war'. 'Any re-organisation or change', he urged, 'should be thought out now, while we are all filled with the actual and practical experience of what war may demand of S.S., and not postponed until the end of the war.' French argued that there should be a single Secret Service responsible for both naval and military intelligence, 'otherwise we shall always be working at cross purposes, and in almost every area we should have at least two services working, if not against one another, at least in rivalry with one another'. He thought the separation of espionage and counter-espionage was a weakness, and that the position of Cumming and Kell as 'the servants of at least 3 Government Departments and which is indefinite as regards limitations' was 'bad organisation'. French, therefore, proposed that the Secret Service should be controlled by a small joint section of army and navy officers, 'either under the D.M.I. or the D.I.D. [Director of the Intelligence Division]', which would 'settle all matters of policy, and . . . carry out all negotiations with the Foreign Office'. He went on to consider 'the limitation of secret service espionage'. This, he thought, should deal only with naval or military information. 'Where we have dabbled in pseudo-diplomatic action [which he did not define] our information has suffered', and for military missions to deal with 'questions of war trade and various other points unconnected with secret service' had been 'a grievous [*sic*] mistake'. French further maintained that 'when naval or military operations are being carried out in any area, the secret service in that area should be handed over to, absorbed and controlled by the local military or naval headquarters'. 'Secret service based on other parts of the Empire', he added, should 'as a general rule . . . not be under you, but under the local intelligence officers, who in their turn are under the local military or naval authority, and not under the D.M.I. or D.I.D.'.

Although French maintained that he was writing in a personal capacity and simply 'with a view to providing food for discussion', Cumming reacted very badly, resenting the impertinence of a junior officer writing to him in such terms and evidently perceiving in the letter another direct threat to the existence of his organisation. He sent Sir Arthur Nicolson a copy of the letter, with a sharp covering note, trusting 'that the authorities who have the power to control the Secret Service will take such steps as will prevent me while in charge of it, from being constantly interfered with and disturbed by such letters as the attached'. Cumming bluntly claimed that the adoption of the proposals which French had 'sprung upon me' would 'mean the wreck of the whole system'. If the Secret Service were controlled by the suggested 'hybrid' section it would 'still have the same three masters to obey'. From Cumming's point of view, the 'greatest defect of the present Service' was 'the lack of support given to its Chief by the military authorities', who, ever since his appointment, had 'permitted constant interference with my work, have undermined my authority and have treated me as an outsider . . . My instructions from the Foreign Office under whose authority I was appointed, have been ignored, and I have been placed in a false and difficult position in consequence.' Cumming begged, 'for the sake of the efficient working of this important Service which costs a vast sum of money', that his 'present position in relation to the War Office may be put on a more reasonable basis'. Perhaps aware that he himself might be thought to have overstepped the mark with such an openly bitter letter, Cumming concluded by assuring Nicolson that 'my relations with General Macdonogh and Colonel French have always been of a most friendly nature, and I have much to thank them for. In the security of their recognised positions and support which they receive as a matter of course, they do not realise the great difficulties with which I have to contend.'

In this last sentence Cumming identified a crucial problem about the institutional status of the Secret Service which affected it during its early years (and to a certain extent remained a difficulty for some years to come). It was both a strength and a weakness that the Service did not legally exist, or easily fit into the established hierarchies of the armed services or the government as a whole. Its corporate invisibility, or deniability, was part of the reason it had been established in the first place, so that secret intelligence work could be kept quite separate (or apparently so) from the Foreign Office and the service ministries. Yet in wartime, when the supply of military and naval intelligence became an especially high priority, there were strong arguments for fully (or substantially) incorporating the

Secret Service into the inevitably greatly expanded Naval and/or Military Intelligence organisations. For Cumming, more perhaps than his successors as Chief, a further factor was the unproven nature of his Bureau, for which the First World War was undoubtedly a baptism of fire. Of course, one sure way of ensuring that the strongest possible case was made for the survival of an autonomous Secret Service was not just to assemble theoretical arguments about ideal institutional arrangements, but to demonstrate the Service's actual capabilities by successfully providing the type and volume of intelligence its customers required. In the grand British tradition of muddling through, a pragmatic test of viability was always likely to carry great weight. Cumming was no doubt well aware of this, but his appeals to the Foreign Office demonstrate that he knew, too (as his successors also learned), that institutional rivalries within Whitehall could work to the advantage of his Service.

The anomalous situation of Cumming's Bureau underlay an effort by Macdonogh in early 1917 once again to assert War Office control, though the Director of Military Intelligence also stressed the importance of the contribution which the Bureau made to the war effort as a whole. Writing to Cumming on 18 February 1917, Macdonogh wanted to 'make it clear' that he had 'never admitted at any time that you were under the Foreign Office. I consider & always have considered that for all military intelligence you are directly under me, &, as I told you a year ago, I have no intention of allowing your theory of F.O. control to come between myself & you.' Macdonogh was responding to a letter from Cumming (which has not survived) claiming some degree of autonomy for his organisation, and which Macdonogh thought raised two questions: '(1) whether I am director of military intelligence, & (2) whether you are under my orders. The answer to the first question is, I think, obvious, & that being so the answer to the second is equally plain.' Implicitly (and unjustly) taxing Cumming with 'empire-building', Macdonogh wrote that 'the value of any organization does not depend upon its size, the number of subjects it deals with, nor on the extent of its pay list, but on the manner in which it assists the working of the whole machine'. It therefore followed that it was 'much better to be the head of a section which everyone praises both for the quality of its work & for the absence of friction with which it is performed, rather than that of a much larger one which is a perpetual cause of strife to all connected with it'. So that there should be 'no further doubt about the matter', Macdonogh wanted Cumming 'definitely' to inform him 'that you accept the status of being under my orders in all military intelligence matters, unqualified by any control, nominal or otherwise, of any other authority'. If Cumming could not do this, Macdonogh said that he would have to 'inform the F.O. that I have no further use for your branch & that I propose that the W.O. shall in future conduct its own S.S., War Trade, counter-espionage & identification business abroad without you as its intermediary'. A further result of this would be the withdrawal of 'all military officers now employed by you', which was a real threat since a sizeable proportion of Cumming's staff were seconded from either the army or the navy.

No specific response to Macdonogh's ultimatum appears to have survived, though evidently matters did not come to a head. Sporadic evidence from his diary indicates that, while Cumming stayed within the ambit of the Directorate of Military Intelligence, demarcation disputes continued concerning what exactly he was to do and with whom he was permitted to deal. In early June 1917, for example, Cumming noted that Colonel Buchan – John Buchan, the novelist, who headed one of the government's propaganda arms – 'made an appointment to see me to-morrow but the D.M.I. positively forbade me to see him'. Cumming (or Buchan) appealed to the Foreign Office, for a few days later Cumming received 'definite instructions' from Lord Hardinge (who had succeeded Nicolson as Permanent Under-Secretary) 'to supply J.B. with any information he requires without passing it thro' W.O.'. On 26 June Buchan came to Cumming's office where he had 'a long yarn with me re co-operation which we settled on the lines laid down'. Whatever the joint action was, it was surely not military intelligence, and probably closer to Colonel French's category of 'pseudo-diplomatic action', but what the affair demonstrated was that, with Foreign Office support, Cumming could still sidestep direct instructions issued to him by the Director of Military Intelligence.

During the autumn of 1917, in fact, Cumming's relations with the War Office improved, while those with the Admiralty worsened. At what was evidently an irritable meeting with the recently promoted Rear Admiral Hall (Director of the Intelligence Division), the notoriously tetchy Hall queried an arrangement Cumming had for Captain Norman Thwaites (who worked for him in New York) and asked whether Cumming was 'serving the Bureau or the Nation'. Clearly taken aback, Cumming wrote in his diary: 'I should have replied "the <u>nation</u> <u>through</u> the Bureau – my only means of serving it"'. Hall then introduced Cumming to the new naval attaché for Copenhagen, Captain Dix, but refused to allow Cumming 'to speak to him about my [Cumming's] people & work'. Cumming appears to have told Macdonogh about his difficulties with Hall, for the following day he noted that the Director of Military Intelligence had been 'very heartening about my position & hinted definitely that if sacked by Navy he would take me on with pleasure'. Underpinning the improvement in relations with the War Office (and, in the end, also with the Admiralty) was an internal reorganisation of Cumming's Head Office, which had been first mooted in August 1917 and came into effect at the end of the year.

Staffing and organisation

Securing staff posed some problems for Cumming at a time when all young men (or nearly all) wanted to do their bit at the battle front. The notion of working in secret service was as likely to put potential recruits off as encourage them to join up. From the start, indeed, Cumming had been faced with the problem that many of the people who most wanted to be involved were among the least attractive prospects from his point of view. In a memoir written in the 1950s, Frank Stagg, a naval lieutenant who transferred from Blinker Hall's staff in the Admiralty to Cumming in September 1915, recalled that it was 'difficult to get officers released unless they had been gassed or wounded'. Other individuals, such as Thomas Merton, the celebrated physicist, had been rejected for active service on grounds of health, but he was engaged by Cumming in June 1916 as the Service's first-ever scientist. He was granted a commission in the Royal Naval Volunteer Reserve and, being independently wealthy, was taken on 'without pay'.[9]

Cumming's early wartime recruits were typically not career soldiers or sailors. When Frank Stagg joined, three of Cumming's five main staff were Royal Naval Volunteer Reserve officers. One, Lieutenant F. C. Newnum, was an engineer 'from the Colombia emerald mines'; another, Guy Standing, had been an actor in America before the war; the third, Sub-Lieutenant Jolly, worked for the *Tatler*, the society magazine. There was a high turnover of personnel. Apart from Cumming himself, Newnum, who had been taken on in November 1914, was the only senior person to remain continuously in Head Office from 1914 to the end of the war. Stagg, for example, returned to naval duties in June 1917 and Standing left for the Ministry of Information in December 1917. Some people, however, stayed on. Paymaster Percy Sykes, who took charge of the Service accounts in November 1915, continued to do essentially the same job for over a quarter of a century.

From the autumn of 1914 Cumming's expanding Head Office was organised broadly on a geographical basis, reflecting that of the Military Operations directorate. In September 1915, for example, Stagg handled information coming in from Scandinavia, the Baltic and Russia; Newnum took Greece and the Mediterranean; Standing the Americas; and Captain L. N. Cockerell (another mining engineer) was responsible for Belgium and Holland. Later sections were formed for Italy and Switzerland, and South America. A specific Code Section was created in April 1915. In April 1917, Lieutenant H. Brickwood, a volunteer naval officer whose family brewing business was based in Portsmouth and who had been working on coding, was put in charge of a new section formed 'to assist British Prisoners of War to escape from Germany by sending maps, compasses etc., to them by secret means'. Head Office also began to spread beyond 2 Whitehall Court. An office where prospective officers and agents could be interviewed was established at Central House, Kingsway. It had a 'fictitious name' so that the actual work for which candidates were being considered did not have to be revealed 'until their probity and probable usefulness had been discovered', and a 'very secret' Air Section was formed at 11 Park Mansions, South Lambeth Road. A postwar report surmised that the section existed 'to work out the course taken by German air raiders from the interception of their wireless signals to one another', though a couple of MI1(c) 'Air Reports' have survived from March 1918, one of which merely contains quotations on aviation matters from the German press.[10]

At the beginning of December 1915 Cumming took on Colonel Freddie Browning, who had been working in the Ministry of Munitions. The forty-five-year-old Browning, who became Cumming's de facto deputy, was a celebrated cricketer and one of the best amateur squash-racket players in England. By the time he came to work for Cumming he was also a well-known man-about-town and successful businessman, being, among other things, a director of the Savoy Hotel in London. 'He lived his life', recalled Sir Samuel Hoare (who also worked for Cumming during the war), 'as he played his games – with style, with temperament, and with boundless courage.' Hoare described him as 'the most inspiring force behind the most secret branch of our Military Intelligence'.[11] Frank Stagg also remembered him fondly: his 'hospitality was unbounded' and his 'relations with "C" were inimitable, he brought happy evenings to the old man by having gay parties with all the stage beauties that he had at call – and in more serious ways [though here Stagg expressed himself rather ambiguously] he was the perfect link, seldom doing anything himself but linking up with those who knew what was what in any particular line'.[12]

Cumming's Bureau grew steadily throughout the war. By the summer of 1915 he had over thirty Head Office staff, including seven officers, eight clerks and twelve female typists. The women were obviously an important part of the team, though in November one of Cumming's subordinates accused him of 'partiality with the typists – particularly Miss C., instanced my taking her & 4 others to Westminster Bridge one Sunday dinner hour', and alleged that he 'chose the typists on account of their social position'. Although most of Cumming's female staff were unmarried, he seems to have had no prejudice against employing married women, nor even of sending them abroad, though this may have reflected a preference only to send more mature women to foreign posts. It was, nevertheless, in sharp contrast with practice elsewhere in the civil service. In the Foreign Office, for example, women were obliged to resign on marrying. In May 1916 Cumming noted 'Miss [. . .] for Malta; Mrs [. . .] for Alexandria'; in June, 'Mrs [. . .] (did'nt like her!) taken on for Switzerland'; and in February 1917, 'Mrs [. . .] & Miss [. . .] left for Italy.' Cumming, the ace motorist himself, also employed women as drivers. On 28 June 1916 he engaged 'Miss [. . .]' to be a 'chauffeuse'. Evidently she was very capable, for just over a fortnight later she was taking the 'Merc' (Cumming apparently having no objection to a German car) from London to Paris. Perhaps reflecting his reputation as a bit of a ladies' man (and with a penchant for old-world courtesy), he also took an interest in their dress, even to the extent of going to see the Quartermaster-General of the army in November 1917 're lady drivers' uniform'. He recorded in his diary that a secretary going to Egypt in January 1916 was not only to be paid £20 a month but also to receive an 'outfit' grant of £30. Freddie Browning, 'distressed at the way the female element on the staff had [only] buns for lunch . . . got a canteen built on top of Whitehall Court, extracted a chef from the army – an old savoyard – and used the buying agencies of the Savoy to secure cheap food at a time of food stringency'. Perhaps he overdid it, for in February 1918 Cumming was reprimanded by a representative of the Food Controller for holding excessive 'Staff Mess stocks'.

By 1917 the geographical organisation of the Head Office was coming under increasing criticism from the army and the navy. As a 1919 review of wartime naval secret service noted, although the officer in charge of a particular section was, 'as far as possible, conversant with the language and affairs of the country to be dealt with', this officer 'had not, as a rule, any technical knowledge whatever of Naval, Military, or Aeronautical affairs (though fairly able to deal with Political and Economical questions)'. In many cases, moreover, he 'was not even an officer of the Fighting services before the War'. Nevertheless, 'according to the best of his understanding', he 'separated out the Intelligence coming in, en masse, from abroad, and passed it on to the Admiralty, War Office, etc, through its liaison officer'. He was, however, 'quite unable to provide the requisite direction of enquiry on technical matters, professional advice, criticism, or commendation to the Agents abroad, all of which are supremely necessary to success in the provision of Naval or any other special Intelligence'. In fact, it was 'little more than chance that produced anything really useful' to the Naval Intelligence Division.[13]

During the late summer of 1917 Freddie Browning started to work on a scheme to reorganise the Service, which he and Cumming discussed on 23 August with a new member of staff, Major Claude Marjoribanks Dansey. The forty-one-year-old Dansey, who came from a family of English country squires, had an unusually wide range of experience. As a youth he had been moved for health reasons from a conventional English public school (Wellington) to a British boys' school in Bruges, Belgium, and had been seduced by 'Robbie' Ross (who later claimed to have been Oscar Wilde's first lover). Dansey went on to serve in the British South Africa Police during the Matabele Rebellion of 1896, as a colonial policemen fighting bandits in Borneo, and as a British army lieutenant in the South African War of 1899–1902. Between 1904 and 1909 he was a colonial political officer in Somaliland, after which he travelled in Africa and was later employed as resident secretary of a country club in upstate New York. When Dansey worked for Vernon Kell's organisation in the early years of the war, Cumming had had regular dealings (and lunches) with him, and the two men had discussed the possibility of Dansey coming to work for him, which he finally did on 20 August 1917.[14]

Cumming was clearly anxious to accommodate the needs of the armed services, in part perhaps to forestall the possibility of their building up separate secret intelligence services (as to some extent the army had already done), and he began to improve the links between his organisation and them. On 14 September 1917 he saw General Sir David Henderson, the Director-General of Military Aeronautics, and 'discussed with him the question of a liaison officer to take charge of my Aviation Section'. Henderson also agreed that the proposed new independent air force 'should not attempt to set up a rival S.S. organisation but should set tasks to ours'. Admiralty liaison was secured by the appointment on 15 October of the first career naval officer to the Secret Service, Captain Boyle Somerville, who was to head a new Naval Section. Somerville came from a famous Irish family (his sister was one half of Somerville and Ross, authors of the 'Irish R.M.' stories) and was an expert hydrographer, linguist and astronomer. Nearly twenty years after he retired to live back home in County Cork he was murdered by the IRA for helping local lads join the Royal Navy.

As for the army, Macdonogh, the Director of Military Intelligence, once again asserted his control over the Secret Service. On 22 October 1917 he peremptorily summoned Cumming '& told me he was holding a Conference of his Military Staff re my reorganisation which I could attend but not take part in'. He said that he was going to General Headquarters in France the next day 'to tell them he was going to take over the whole S.S. & before doing this he must make sure that he could assure Sir D. Haig [the Commander-in-Chief of the British Expeditionary Force] that he had absolute control over the Military part of the S.S. Bureau'. Macdonogh, therefore, 'proposed to do away with divisions Geographical, & substitute Subject divisions, so that the Military would be self contained & his Military Staff would be able to control more directly the Agents (Head) in the Field'. He also 'said we particularly lacked a good organisation Section resembling that in M.I.5'. Cumming, who also learned on

26 October of Colonel French's plans to take over the Allied Intelligence Mission which had been established in Italy, clearly felt that a positive response was the best way to fight his ground and retain his authority, telling Browning (who was all for appealing to the Prime Minister) that 'to bring about a difference between my 2 Chiefs' was 'the greatest disservice he could render his country at the present time'. After some negotiation Cumming worked out a scheme which Macdonogh explained on 12 November to Admiral Hall. Each of the main customer departments was to have representatives on Cumming's staff. Subject to his 'co-ordination and direction', they would 'send instructions to head agents regarding such information as is required by their respective departments'.

As it emerged at the end of November, the new Head Office structure was divided into six sections. Section I, Economics, was put under Colonel Browning, who nominally remained Cumming's second-in-command. Sections II and III covered Aviation and Naval respectively. Section IV, Military, was headed by Major Dansey, through whom Macdonogh said he would issue instructions to Cumming. This was the largest section, and Dansey not only became responsible for the preparation of military reports and liaison with MI5 and Scotland Yard on counter-espionage and counter-revolutionary matters, but he was also put in charge of the Political Section V, headed by Colonel Rhys Samson, a 'secret service expert', experienced in dealing with agents, who had served in Athens and on various liaison duties with the French. Section VI, Organisation, encompassed administration and technical matters, such as coding, which were grouped together, as much (it appears) for convenience as for any other reason. Smaller Prisoners-of-War and Circulation sections remained separate. The latter existed to distribute material to customer departments and other organisations. By the beginning of 1918 the core Head Office staff (not including administrative and clerical support personnel) comprised some forty officers, more than five times the 1915 total.

While Cumming had clearly fallen in with the Director of Military Intelligence's wishes, he also managed to secure continuing support from Hardinge, who wrote to Macdonogh that the Foreign Office 'should have been disappointed if we had looked for success from any scheme which diminished the authority of the man at the top . . . Much will depend', he continued, 'on the extent to which C asserts himself, but he must be given a fair start. Provided it is clear that he is intended to be master in his own house, he ought to be able to make a success of things.' But first Cumming had to implement the Head Office changes. 'This office', he wrote in his diary at the end of November, 'is much upset at the new organisation & I have had to reply to a lot of objection and criticism.' He hoped that the new arrangement, wherein 'each section officer [would] specialise on his own subject & stick to it', while he was 'to control the whole – run the office & co-ordinate the lot', ought to 'improve the present system', which allowed agents abroad merely to 'send in anything' so long as there was 'plenty of it'. This had resulted in predominantly economic reporting 'with a little second rate C.E. work'. By the time the new system was formally implemented in December 1917, the complaints seem to have evaporated. In the opinion of Boyle Somerville, indeed, the change was a striking success, though the numbers of reports must also have been boosted by the time it inevitably took to build up productive human intelligence sources. In a postwar review of 'Naval Intelligence secret service', he recorded that in the three years to October 1917 the 'total number of Naval reports' had been 260, while 'during the 16 months following reorganisation, namely to February 1919, the number was 8,900. From October 1917 [the month he joined the Bureau], the average per month gradually rose to about 700; and in October 1918, when the number of documents dealt with was the highest, the total for the month was 865.'

Professionalism and expertise

In his postwar review of February 1919, Boyle Somerville observed that an important limitation on the ability of the Secret Service to gather and process the most useful information was the dearth of 'Naval officers, technically qualified to deal with Intelligence'. There were hardly enough of them to provide the staff in Cumming's Head Office, let alone supply specialist assistance in the foreign stations which directed and debriefed the agents who actually collected the information. 'Unfortunately,' he remarked, 'specialists in Naval Intelligence can scarcely be said to have existed before the war, and in any case, those at all competent to deal with it were required either at the Admiralty, or for Active Service afloat.'

The result of this was that 'officers for S.S. abroad – sometimes not even sailors – had to be instructed, somewhat hurriedly, in a bare outline of the requirements, and sent out to do their best'. Somerville argued that until intelligence became a specialism in the navy, 'like Gunnery or Torpedo', there would never be a proper cadre of officers to 'supply the needs of the Admiralty Intelligence Division, and of the Secret Service'. These were perennial problems, concerning both Military and Naval Intelligence. The services themselves had so few first-class intelligence officers that, despite a frequently expressed desire to populate, if not actually control, all the intelligence-gathering agencies, they were reluctant to lose them to the Secret Service. Career army and naval officers, for their part, hesitated to opt for secondment lest association with such an apparently dubious specialism might damage their own career prospects.

Well aware of the equivocal position which Cumming's organisation occupied in what might be described as the British defence community – meeting important needs, while not readily fitting into orthodox armed service hierarchies – but also convinced that the Service had done well during the war, Somerville, as the first ever 'officer in charge of the Naval Section in the Secret Service Bureau', considered it his 'duty' to record 'the means and methods that have proved successful during the War; so that my successors may not find themselves on entirely unknown and untried ground, in following up and improving these methods'. Reflecting grow-ing professionalism on the part of the Service and its officers, Somerville's review not only provides an instructive summary of how Cumming's organisation coped with its first great test, but also set out a rationale for its very existence. Somerville argued that the procurement of naval and military intelligence (which he defined as 'Information upon which Action can be taken') involved two 'mutually dependent' main objects: first, 'Intelligence respecting the affairs of the Enemy, or <u>Espionage</u>'; and, second, 'the prevention of the Enemy from obtaining Intelligence of our affairs, or <u>Counter-Espionage</u>'. Information of the first sort could either be acquired 'openly, or directly in the face of, or in defiance of the Enemy; and, if necessary, forcibly'; or it could be 'obtained by outwitting the Enemy; by entering his country and penetrating his counter-espionage devices; by bribing of traitors; and by any other means (but usually by cunning rather than by force), discovering his affairs and activities. This', he said, 'is known as Secret Service or "S.S.".' Somerville observed that, while during the war counter-espionage had been 'relegated to a special division of the Military Intelligence Directorate (M.I.5)', the armed services and some other government departments (such as the Foreign Office and the Department of Overseas Trade) had maintained their own intelligence branches whose secret service arms were 'collected under one roof, with one Chief; each having its own Sectional Officer'. The 'necessity of having just one main Bureau', he asserted, came first of all from 'the importance of keeping secret, so far as possible, the very existence of any such Bureau, and even of its location as an office', but it also reflected the need for co-ordination and the indivisibility of intelligence-gathering. '"Intelligence", generally speaking', he declared, was 'not an affair of water-tight compartments' and all sections 'should be inter-dependent'. It frequently happened, moreover, 'that a report sent in by an agent abroad under the heading of one particular Section, contains information important to another'. The 'sailing of Transports', for example, was 'both a Naval and a Military affair'.

Illustrating the positive experience that had been gained during the First World War, Somerville set down a number of basic principles which held good for the Service in future years. 'It is a fundamental rule of Secret Service', he wrote, 'that its agents must never interfere in the affairs of the country that is giving them its hospitality.' This was for obvious reasons: apart from 'fouling one's own nest', it was 'difficult enough . . . to "dodge" the enemy counter-espionage, and still to obtain Intelligence about him', but it would only add to 'the difficulty to incur the resentment and enmity of the neutral police, as well'. He stipulated that agents were 'never known by their proper names. Either they adopt some "nom de guerre", or, more usually, are designated by a letter and a figure, e.g., "B.90".' No individual could 'set forth on S.S. without "cover", that is to say, a fictitious cloak for his real activities; – some open and legitimate pursuit, business, or calling under which he can operate without detection'. Potential agents should be approached only by 'intermediaries'. Indeed, it was 'desirable that a (non-British) agent should never know who his Employer or Paymaster really is'. Somerville declared that 'experience shows that for Secret Service generally, much the best results are obtained by employing as agents of both sexes, those whose sense of honour is of as high an order as the courage, acumen, brains, audacity, and presence of mind which are the other essentials of success'. Perhaps a little superfluously (though this was probably a counsel of perfection), he added that 'unscrupulous persons, merely out for large fees, and the rascals who so often offer their services, should be avoided, no matter how tempting their offers'.

By the end of the war the Bureau had developed a system for processing and evaluating information. Somerville described how 'when any report from abroad' was received in London, it was typed in duplicate and sent to the Naval Intelligence Department, 'one of the copies being marked "Criticism Copy"'. The relevant officer in the Admiralty then annotated the copy with one of an eight-point scale, from 'A – Believed to be correct', through 'E – Too vague to be of any value', to 'G – Of no interest' and 'H – Too old to check'. There was also a four-point grading of the report 'as a whole' from 'Z.1' ('Good') to 'Z.4' ('Bad'). But the assessment of reports was itself problematic on security grounds. Somerville wisely observed that it was 'often impossible, without giving away intelligence which should be kept absolutely secret, even from S.S. agents, to say more than is contained in one of these brief, and usually destructive "criticisms"'. In the case of operational reports, moreover, it was 'obviously undesirable to give any criticisms whatever'. Nevertheless, 'when a <u>reasoned</u> criticism can be given, its value to the officer abroad . . . is very great'. Not only would it 'indicate to him the future lines on which it is best to work, but it also informs him as to the value, and above all, as to the reliability of the sub-agent who procured the Intelligence in question'. But there were informal channels for criticism as well. On 16 January 1918 the newly appointed Director of Air Intelligence, Colonel Davidson, came to see Cumming. 'He said that our reports to G.H.Q. often mentioned monoplanes,' wrote Cumming in his diary, 'but the enemy had none of these etc. I urged that criticism was vital to us & he promised to help in this & other matters.'

When Sir Samuel Hoare was taken on at the end of 1915 he was given 'an intensive course in the various war Intelligence departments' over several weeks. 'One day, it would be espionage or contre-espionage, another coding and cyphering, another war trade and contraband, a fourth, postal and telegraphic censorship.'[15] The increasing professional and technical competence of the Service is also illustrated by a 135-page document, 'Notes on Instruction and Recruiting of Agents', compiled at the end of 1918. This included such matters as the use of codes, secret inks, letter boxes (locations where secret messages could be left), sabotage, cover and agents provocateurs. Among the 'few points which cannot be drilled into an agent too soon nor too forcibly' (and evincing much common sense) were 'Don't get cold feet, but if you do get caught keep your mouth shut and don't give anybody away'; 'In writing or wiring to sub-agents don't use your own handwriting or name. Always type'; 'Destroy carbons after typing incriminating matter. An officer [who was working for the Germans] recently blew his brains out to avoid arrest, having been traced by a carbon found in the rooms of a German chief agent who had been arrested'; 'Think as much of the safety of your colleagues as of your own.' It was remarked in the notes that 'no hard and fast rule' could be laid down as to the best cover for an agent, but that 'in the long run' there was 'nothing to beat <u>sound commercial cover</u>'. While among 'the best schemes for good cover' was that of 'commercial traveller', this was 'a hopeless business unless the agent really knows & understands the article he is supposed to sell and also really transacts business in such article'. Agents were advised to have at hand 'an efficient highly technical expert burglar'. With commendable understatement it was conceded that 'the difficulty is to recruit the necessary man for the job. He must be reliable, willing to undergo imprisonment if caught, without giving the show away and if obtainable should be handsomely rewarded.' But the potential results 'might well repay all the trouble', and the notes cited a successful operation involving 'the emptying of the safes in the Austrian Consulate and S.S. in Zurich'.

Forged German bread tickets prepared for MI1(c) to be used by agents working out of Switzerland.

In a section on counter-espionage, the notes considered the use of agents provocateurs targeting enemy secret services, 'one of the most fascinating branches of S.S. work', but also to be indulged in only sparingly, 'as whilst the results are tangible the risk involved to other units of the organisation is considerable'. Successful operations 'by clever agents', however, could 'lead to the complete disorganisation of the service against which they are working' (though 'equally the danger to our own service is a very real one'). An example was given of a successful operation against a German organisation in a neutral country where an attractive 'Belgian woman of good family, who for various reasons had good cause to hate the Boche', was employed to seduce a German agent. She agreed that 'nothing, either of a personal or moral nature, was to be shirked in order to obtain a successful issue'. After 'two months preliminary work', the agent was 'recruited' by her victim and 'engaged by the German S.S. to make a trip to France for them'. Given contact addresses in Paris, she was also supplied with 'several articles of underclothing impregnated with secret ink', partly for 'delivery to a certain address in France and partly for her own use'. Once in France the agent made a full report to the French authorities and, using a police officer in the neutral country 'who was working for us', the entire enemy organisation was destroyed.

The quest for a perfect secret ink was a constant preoccupation for the Bureau. In June 1915 Walter Kirke noted in his diary that Cumming was 'now making enquiries for invisible inks at the London University'. In October he 'heard from C that the best invisible ink is semen', which did not react to the main detection methods.[16] Frank Stagg recalled that 'all were anxious' to obtain secret ink 'which came from a natural source of supply'. He said that he would 'never forget "C's" delight when the Deputy Chief Censor, F. V. Worthington, came one day with the announcement that one of his staff had found out that "semen" would not react to iodine vapour, and told the old man that he had had to remove the discoverer from the office immediately as his colleagues were making life intolerable by accusations of masturbation'. 'We thought', wrote Stagg, 'we had solved a great problem.' But 'our man in Copenhagen . . . evidently stocked it in a bottle – for his letters stank to high heaven and we had to tell him that a fresh operation was necessary for each letter'. One of Thomas Merton's first discoveries after his appointment in June 1916 was the method of secret writing used by German agents, who soaked an article of clothing in the requisite chemicals from which the invisible ink could later be reconstituted. Merton also invented a secret-writing method for Cumming: 'Write on glass or on any hard material with a silver point. The trace will be entirely invisible, but it can be made visible as follows. Make up two solutions A and B. A: Metol 5 grs, citric acid 5 grs, acetic acid 15 grs, water 100 cc. B: Silver nitrate 10 grs, water 100cc. Mix 10 parts of A with one part of B and with 100 parts of water. This is the developer. It can be used only for 10–20 minutes after mixing.'[17]

In one account of the wartime Bureau, a note by Merton's name says 'worked at secret inks, bombs, &c', and it is clear that Cumming warmly encouraged scientific and technical research. It is clear, too, from Merton's experience that this research was shared with MI5 for counter-intelligence work. On Christmas Eve 1914 and early in the New Year Cumming was discussing the recruitment of technicians and the possible establishment of a wireless school, though it seems not to have been for the use of agents as the technology was not yet sufficiently well advanced to allow this. But an important coding section was developed, both to ensure secure lines of communication with representatives abroad by telegraph and to work on deciphering enemy signals. In Head Office Cumming was always ready to try out new gadgets. In March 1915 he drove out to the Sterling Telephone Company in Dagenham, Essex, to inspect a new type of soundproof door. In July two officers came 'to explain & try the Detectophone', evidently a covert listening device. More prosaically (though no doubt useful for office work, and also demonstrating how private-sector business practices could be introduced), in December 'Browning brought a Dictaphone & installed it'. In October 1918, knowing Cumming's predilection for mechanical devices and perhaps concerned about his mobility, Sir William Wiseman, the head of station in New York, sent him a state-of-the-art motorised scooter manufactured by the Autoped Company of Long Island City.[18]

3

Operations in the West

The expansion of Mansfield Cumming's secret service operations initially developed out of his prewar networks in Belgium, the Netherlands and Denmark. But from almost the very beginning he contemplated wider deployments: in Scandinavia, Switzerland, Russia and further afield. Over the first year or so of the war, both on his own behalf and as instructed by the Admiralty and War Office Directorates of Intelligence, he organised networks in the Mediterranean and sent representatives to Spain, Italy, Egypt, the Balkans and Near East, South America and the USA. On a Sunday in October 1916 – perhaps it was a quiet day in the office – he noted in his diary that he had 1,024 'staff & agents' spread across the world. There were sixty at headquarters. The largest number overseas was in Alexandria: '300? [*sic*]'; next came Holland (250), Athens (100), Denmark (80) and Spain ('abt 50'); with smaller numbers in Salonika, Romania, France, Switzerland, Russia, Norway, Sweden, Malta, Italy, New York, South Africa and Portugal. 'S. America' was listed, but with only '?' beside it. In 1914–15, however, as had been the case before the outbreak of war, Cumming's main concentration was in Belgium and the Netherlands.

Secret service in the Low Countries

Although none of Cumming's agents had predicted the German declaration of war in August 1914, it was evident that his Belgian and Dutch networks ought still to have been in a position to report on the timing, strength and direction of the expected German assault on France. Before Macdonogh went to France with the expeditionary force, he arranged that the British army's intelligence-gathering should be divided into two parts. The first would comprise a section based in France at General Headquarters. This 'would endeavour to secure agents in the territory occupied by the enemy north of Luxemburg and convey the information by them either through the line, or round the flanks of the army'. Macdonogh anticipated that this intelligence would chiefly be 'concerned with the strength, composition and movements of the force on our immediate front'. The second section would deal with 'all information from the interior of Germany'. This was 'to be got, if at all, by the S.S. Bureau in London', whose chief – Cumming – was to 'remain in direct communication' with Macdonogh.

The GHQ section took over Cumming's man Roy Regnart in Brussels, as well as Major Cecil Cameron, who had been engaged by Cumming and deployed to Givet scarcely a week before the outbreak of war. GHQ travelled over to France on 14 August 1914. Cumming went to Brussels the following day to attempt to place his agents on a war footing, as well as to regularise Cameron's position vis-à-vis the British embassy and smooth ruffled feathers over some indiscretion committed by Henry Dale Long. But by this stage German troops had penetrated deep into the country, disrupting both Cumming's and Macdonogh's arrangements (such as they were). Their networks were swamped and the post at Givet was withdrawn. Cameron joined Macdonogh at GHQ and was instructed 'to work round our left flank and try to get in rear of the enemy'. He 'showed marked ability and was able to obtain a certain amount of information' before the opposing lines solidified into 'a continuous line of entrenchments from the sea to Switzerland. By November 1914', reported Macdonogh, 'it had become practically impossible to get anything through the front and there were no flanks round which to work.'

Cumming meanwhile endeavoured to develop reporting from the Netherlands. Asked by the Director of Naval Intelligence about 'arrangements on Dutch coast', on 5 August he asked the London manager of a Dutch shipping company, W. H. Müller & Co., to put agents at six points along the coast 'to report Tr [German] warship movements'. Two days later he agreed to pay a representative £30 a month to 'get in touch with friends in Amsterdam'. Cumming was not the only one looking to gather intelligence in the Netherlands. On 19 August the British consul-general at Rotterdam, Ernest Maxse, informed his masters in the Foreign

Office that, in collaboration with Captain Wilfred Henderson (naval attaché in Berlin from October 1913 until withdrawn on the outbreak of war), he had organised a 'complete' intelligence organisation 'on the frontiers of Holland'. It was worked by a Captain Richard Tinsley and Maxse assured London that his office was 'not traceable in it'. Maxse believed that he could 'guarantee correct information on points required by Naval Intelligence Department of the Admiralty and by the Foreign Office . . . Our men and intermediaries', he cabled, were 'reliable'. In London, Foreign Office officials were appalled at diplomats undertaking espionage, however discreetly. Henderson and Maxse had 'acted in defiance of all our repeated and categorical instructions'. Since this was exactly what Cumming's Bureau had been set up to do, Tinsley was transferred to him. Ronald Campbell of the Foreign Office carefully instructed Cumming 'to keep Maxse quite clear of S[ecret] S[ervice]'.[1]

The thirty-eight-year-old Tinsley, who proved to be a difficult character, played an important role in Cumming's Dutch organisation. He was a former merchant navy officer (and an officer in the Royal Naval Reserve) who had been working in Rotterdam since 1909, first as agent for the Cunard Line and subsequently as local manager of the Uranium Steamship Company, a Canadian concern which ran cut-price emigrant ships across the Atlantic. In 1911 he had briefly been expelled by the Dutch government for allowing some returning Russian emigrants to land without authorisation. Tinsley struck Walter Kirke (who met him in November 1915) 'as being a smart fellow, but not a man for whom any really high class agent would work'. With Tinsley 'it is a matter of business', and Kirke doubted 'his imparting patriotic enthusiasm to agents', thus missing 'the best people'. Tinsley, indeed, seemed to fit Cumming's category of 'scallywag'. Ivone Kirkpatrick, who worked for GHQ intelligence in Holland during the latter part of the war, described him as 'a liar and a first-class intriguer with few scruples', while another colleague, Sigismund Payne Best (who was later to serve in SIS), claimed – albeit with the benefit of considerable hindsight – that Cumming himself had told him Tinsley was 'an absolute scoundrel'. Best also reported that Tinsley 'was said to have made something like 200,000 pounds by blackmailing firms in Holland', threatening to have them placed on the British 'Black Book' of companies who were 'dealing with the Germans and who, consequently, were debarred from any commercial dealing with

England'. But Tinsley had admirers, too, including Henry Landau, who worked for him in 1917–18. Landau described him as 'a shrewd executive', with 'a great number of powerful friends', who 'helped to keep the various branches of the Service under him in close co-operation. His chief function, the handling of the Dutch authorities, he carried out admirably.'[2] In September 1918, Major Laurie 'Oppy' Oppenheim, who had been the British military attaché at The Hague since January 1915, gave Cumming 'a good account of T whom he considers perfectly honest & conscientious'.

As the front line stabilised, and opportunities for running agents from France into enemy-occupied territory disappeared, Macdonogh thought of exploiting the thousands of Belgian refugees who were pouring into England, both 'to find out what they knew of the enemy, and, if possible, to recruit from among them agents who would return to their own country'. This was work which 'could have been left to the S.S. Bureau in London', but with Cumming temporarily out of action following his motor accident at the beginning of October 1914, his subordinates, 'though very energetic, had no proper guidance' and, in Macdonogh's opinion, 'were incapable of doing what was required of them'. Macdonogh therefore appointed Major Cameron to work in the Channel port of Folkestone, where, in co-operation with French and Belgian officers, he developed a very extensive intelligence organisation. While he made a success of his job, Cameron was another man with a slightly murky background. He was the son of a distinguished soldier who had won a VC in India and had been head of the War Office Intelligence Department in the 1880s. In 1911 he and his wife (who was a morphine addict) had been convicted of fraud over a bogus insurance claim for a valuable pearl necklace. Cameron had served a jail sentence, but was widely believed to have sacrificed himself by loyally standing by his wife, who had submitted the claim. As a disgraced (though personally well-regarded) ex-officer, unable easily to rejoin the army at the beginning of the war, he was perhaps an ideal candidate for secret service, and this helps explain why Cumming had taken him on at the end of July 1914. But potential revelations about his past remained a liability. Late in 1915 Walter Kirke worried that Lieutenant O'Caffrey, who worked under Cumming running agents through the Netherlands into Belgium targeting aviation intelligence for the Admiralty, had been told of Cameron's history. Since Cameron's agents had complained about O'Caffrey's activities, Kirke feared he might use his knowledge 'to damage Cam's prestige in Holland. In fact', he wrote, 'O'C is likely to be at the root of any trouble, being a Jesuit priest, & not having our ideas of what is correct.'[3]

Cameron's Folkestone bureau soon established an organisation in German-occupied Belgium which concentrated mainly on train-watching. 'It met with considerable success,' noted Macdonogh, 'and we were able to check to a considerable extent enemy movements between Germany and Belgium and thus to prove the falsity of many reports which reached us from London of enormous concentrations of troops in Belgium.' Macdonogh concluded that these reports (which were sent in to the Foreign Office by consular officers in the Netherlands) had all been spread by German propagandists with the deliberate intention of misleading the British. During the autumn and winter of 1914, Cumming's Dutch organisation provided very little useful intelligence, which Macdonogh put down to the fact that Cumming's officers 'had no experience either of war or of S.S.'. Cumming's (and Kell's) prewar man in Brussels, Henry Dale Long, was also a disappointment. Although Cumming paid him money in August and took him on for a further six months in September 1914, by December doubts were beginning to emerge and Cumming noted in his diary a 'warm discussion' of Long's 'merits'. In March 1915 he told Kirke that Long was a 'stumer' (failure), and his contract does not seem to have been renewed.[4]

Responding to growing demands for information, Macdonogh set up an additional organisation, based in London under Major Ernest Wallinger, an artilleryman who had lost a foot at the Battle of Le Cateau in August 1914. Thus by early 1915 three distinct British clandestine intelligence organisations were operating in the Low Countries. Two of them, Cameron's at Folkestone (known as 'CF') and Wallinger's in London ('WL'), came directly under Macdonogh at GHQ, by now situated at Saint-Omer in northern France. The third, run by Tinsley in the Netherlands (and known as the 'T Service'), reported to Cumming in London. At this stage Tinsley's organisation was Cumming's largest single commitment by far, at least in financial terms. In a list of (apparently) monthly payments for intelligence networks drawn up in April 1915, some £3,000 for 'Tin' was nearly half of the total outgoings of £6,313. The next largest expenditure was £1,000 for Colonel Rhys Samson's office in Athens. By November 1915 (according to Kirke) Tinsley's 'show' was costing £5,000 a month.[5] In his diary the same month Cumming recorded an annotated list of 'R.B.T.'s staff', which was twenty-six strong (including two women, one a typist). The list appears to comprise both office assistants and actual agents. Against two names are 'contraband, political' and 'naval questionnaire'. Three others are marked 'Russian', 'Hungarian' and 'Ruthenian' respectively. Nine individuals are identified as 'Belgian' (one 'in Germany'); and there are four Germans, including 'Krupp works', 'Koln' and 'Augsburg'.

What did these agents do? A postwar history of British Military Intelligence in France during the latter part of the war written by Colonel Reginald Drake (Walter Kirke's successor at GHQ) noted that 'the bulk of the work of Secret Service in occupied territory was devoted to train watching', in order to trace the movements of enemy units – information 'of vital importance in drawing up the enemy's order of battle'. This 'had a direct effect on the operations and movements of our own forces, and became therefore the first objective of our Secret Service system'. Drake added that 'subsidiary efforts' were devoted to reports on defensive works, shipping movements from the Belgian ports of Zeebrugge and Ostend, and 'technical details as to artillery, aviation, aerodromes and similar matters', as well as 'the acquisition by theft or purchase of German military compilations, and all military information generally'. Tinsley's organisation also kept an eye out for enemy agents seeking to get to the United Kingdom or travel further afield. Information from Cumming's Rotterdam station contributed to the detection of five German agents in 1915 and one in 1916. In June 1916 Tinsley identified a German intelligence cover-address in The Hague, from where a number of United States journalists had been recruited by the Germans. One of these men, George Bacon, was arrested in England, court-martialled and in March 1917 sentenced to death. This was later commuted to life imprisonment and Bacon was deported to the United States where he provided evidence leading to the conviction in New York of the network's two leaders.[6]

Little raw intelligence from Cumming's agents during the first two years of the war has survived in the SIS archive, but there are some fragments of information from an agent code-named 'Horse' who was based in Maastricht in 1916. A message dated 31 August (circulated by London on 9 September) reported that the Germans were building a new railway line to improve communications between Visé in eastern Belgium and Aix-la-Chapelle (Aachen). A week later Horse told London that 'all available barges' had been requisitioned in Belgium, 'filled with gravel and sent in direction of S. Quentin about front present line of trenches'. Another agent, '20017', was a Continental European who had lived in England before the war, but had been deported following a conviction for 'obtaining credit by fraud from London boarding house keepers'. In 1916, having deserted (he said) from a German air force unit on the Eastern Front, he made contact with Cumming's representative at The Hague and handed over documents signed by General von Linsingen, head of the Militär Luftstreitkräfte (army air corps). According to a report from 1927 (when he once again offered his services to SIS) he was 'taken on by the Military Section of the "T" Organisation and was sent back to Germany 5 or 6 times, coming out each time with useful material, particularly on his last visit when he brought back part of the contents of von Linsingen's safe'. His information, however, was 'considered too good to be genuine (although later it proved to be absolutely correct)', so he was not permitted to return to Germany. He remained in the Netherlands and was 'reduced to recruiting deserters, for whom he was paid according to their value'. Early in 1917 he unwisely attempted to re-enter Germany, was arrested at the frontier, court-martialled by the Germans and sentenced to fifteen years' penal servitude.

Drake observed that the two GHQ organisations – Cameron's CF and Wallinger's WL – 'were, in fact, not only in actual if unconscious competition with each other, but also with parallel systems controlled by the War Office [Cumming] and our French and Belgian Allies'. Inter-service rivalry, moreover, was unhealthy, and in some cases 'disastrous', as it led to 'denunciations, buying up of other services' agents, duplication of reports, and collaboration between agents of the various Allied systems', so that 'information arrived at the various Headquarters in a manner which was not only confusing but sometimes unreliable and apt to be dangerous'. Double reporting was a particular problem, in that there could be 'an apparent confirmation of news really originating from the same source', owing to its having being received from 'what appeared to be different and independent places of origin'.[7]

Attempts to systematise the position were reflected in the War Office's successive efforts to take over all or part of Cumming's organisation.

Cumming was himself conscious of the problems, not least because Cameron's and Wallinger's organisations initially enjoyed greater success than his did. 'During the summer of 1915', wrote Macdonogh, 'the G.H.Q. system of train watching was brought to a high pitch of perfection, while the War Office system [Cumming's, though we can see here Macdonogh asserting his control over it] owing to difficulties with the Dutch police got little information of value.' On 22 July 1915 (recording in his diary a conference of War Office and Foreign Office representatives) Cumming 'protested against divided control & many organisations & suggested handing over the whole system in Holland to G.H.Q.'. But this apparently applied only to the military side of his reporting. A few months later, with the army again encroaching, when Cumming drafted his complaint about this to Sir Arthur Nicolson, he noted that in Holland he had 'created and built up an admirable organisation which has – alone among several rivals – kept clear of arrest or "fusillade"'. The 'military part of this' had been handed over to Major Oppenheim, military attaché at The Hague, who had 'sent in as his own, the reports collected by my agents'. Oppenheim, 'being on the spot', had 'gradually absorbed all my best men for his part of the work and left me the indifferent ones'. Furthermore, it was now proposed that Oppenheim himself should be put under Cameron in Folkestone: 'in fact one of my most valuable organisations is to be taken away from my control and handed over to my former subordinate [Cameron] – who himself was robbed from me since the war began. My bureau', added Cumming acidly, 'is to continue to supply the funds!' Cumming was prepared to acquiesce in the new arrangement only because his work in Holland had been 'completely ruined by the interference of other and rival organisations', but he claimed he was now faced with 'a similar invasion in other countries' and feared that being 'under no adequate control' this would 'bring trouble and disorganisation'.[8]

With Foreign Office backing, Cumming managed to resist some of the army's more predatory ambitions. Despite concerns about the Dutch government's attitude, in view of wartime priorities the Foreign Office relaxed its ban on the involvement of diplomatic personnel in intelligence-gathering sufficiently to allow Oppenheim to act as a 'clearing-house' and 'sift' all military information obtained by Tinsley's organisation before sending it on to Cumming in London. This arrangement worked increasingly well and improved the quality and reliability of the information coming out of the Low Countries. In November 1915 Macdonogh established a system of 'zones' for the rival services, with Cumming broadly given freedom to work in Belgium east of Brussels, while the two GHQ organisations were restricted to the western part of the country. But, as Drake observed, such an artificial arrangement was 'fundamentally unsound' and could severely limit the ability of a particular network to collect valuable intelligence. The inevitable overlapping and line-crossing resulting from the rival networks also made for poor security, and disaster struck in 1916 when the Germans arrested a large number of British agents, 'with the result that our train watching services (both those of G.H.Q. and of the War Office) almost ceased to exist'.[9]

In May Tinsley was exposed in the Dutch press as a 'British agent', and Kirke considered that subsequent, though unsuccessful, efforts to expel him were due to German pressure. The Dutch, in fact, were well aware of both the Allied and enemy intelligence organisations operating on their soil, and it is clear from Walter Kirke's diary that part of the price the British paid to ensure that their presence continued to be tolerated was the sharing of information with the Dutch authorities. In June reports from Tinsley's organisation which Oppenheim was forwarding to Cumming were seized by the Germans when they captured the Great Eastern Railway Company's steamer *Brussels*, operating the cross-Channel ferry from the Hook of Holland to Tilbury. This was followed by the unravelling of Tinsley's train-watching network, comprising over forty posts, and the arrest of 'nearly all' his agents. It appeared that his man in Maastricht, one Frankignoul, had over-centralised the organisation, consistently channelled its reports out along a single route (a tram which ran across the Belgian frontier) and also allowed his agents to know each other's identities. Thus, after the Germans had intercepted a batch of reports, they were able to roll up most of the network, executing a group of eleven members at Hasselt on 16 December 1916. As early as August, however, the flow of information from Tinsley's organisation had dried up and Kirke saw no sign of it reviving.[10]

Over the next six months the situation improved markedly, following the appointment of Captain Henry Landau to take charge of the military side of Tinsley's operation. Just twenty-two years old when the war started, Landau had been born in South Africa to an Afrikaner mother and English father. Educated in South Africa, as well as at public school in England (Dulwich College), he was intellectually very able. He studied at Caius College, Cambridge, and graduated with first-class honours in Natural Sciences. An accomplished linguist – he had fluent Dutch, French and German – he went to France in August 1914 with a volunteer hospital unit, later gaining a commission in the Royal Artillery. When he was delayed on leave in London with measles, a female acquaintance recommended him to the Secret Service Bureau. Interviewed (according to Cumming's diary) on 8 June 1916, Landau claimed in his 1934 memoirs that Cumming told him, 'You are just the man we want,' and said that he was to 'join T in Rotterdam', reorganise the train-watching service and be 'in complete charge of the Military Section'. He was instructed to leave immediately and 'at eight-thirty that evening I was on my way to Harwich'.[11] The archives tell a slightly different story. A week after the interview, Landau wrote to Colonel Browning saying that his artillery unit was posting him back to France and asking if MI1(c) still wanted him. 'I shall be very grateful indeed if you will do your best for me,' he wrote. 'I have told you already how very keen I am on the work.' Three days later, having consulted Tinsley, Browning replied that 'our people in Rotterdam have asked us to send you over on a month's trial'. After some more administrative delays, and a possible further meeting with Cumming, Landau left for Rotterdam some time in July 1916.

Whatever the precise circumstances of his appointment, once Landau got to Rotterdam it turned out that he had a real gift for intelligence work. A postwar assessment recorded that he had been 'employed during the war as 2nd in command to T[insley] in Rotterdam and was undoubtedly the brains of the institution', before adding that he was 'foreign in appearance', could 'mix in any class of society, but that some people take a great dislike to him owing to his somewhat furtive manner'. During the war itself this seems not to have been a handicap and, indeed, a certain degree of stealthiness may have been of assistance while Landau endeavoured to rebuild Tinsley's organisation. Over the autumn and winter of 1916 he was able to repair some of the damage, so much so that in February 1917 Colonel Edgar Cox, head of MI3 in the War Office (responsible for the analysis of all German military information), told the Director of Military Intelligence that 'information received through "C" during the past four months' had been 'invaluable'. He noted that, although comparing the value of material coming from the different systems in Belgium 'was impossible owing to the fact that they dealt with different areas', a 'certain amount of information' was 'received only through "C"', and that 'Major Cameron's train-watching reports would not have been complete without the corroboration of "C"'. As to the 'form in which the reports were presented', moreover, '"C's" organisation was undoubtedly superior, having the advantage of the expert knowledge of the military attaché at The Hague [Oppenheim] to edit and control.'[12]

'La Dame Blanche' and others

Weaknesses in Cameron's organisation brought Landau a particular piece of good fortune in the summer of 1917 when (as he recounted in his memoirs) 'an emissary from Belgium under the assumed name of St. Lambert' came to offer the service of 'a large group of patriots . . . desirous of organizing an espionage service in the occupied territory'. In fact the 'espionage service' already existed. Based in Liège and led by two electrical engineers, Walthère Dewé and Herman Chauvin, the network (which became known as 'La Dame Blanche', a mythical female figure whose appearance was supposed to herald the downfall of the imperial German Hohenzollern dynasty) had been supplying information for Cameron's organisation. But they had become unsettled by the 'contradictory' instructions issued by one of Cameron's agents, and had completely lost confidence in him after a security breach had betrayed some of their members to the Germans. While offering their services to Landau, they did so only on condition that they would be 'recognised as soldiers of the Allied armies'. This was a fundamental requirement for the civilian men and women involved. They did not want to be 'vulgar spies'. Indeed, the leaders of the organisation forbade the use of the terms 'espionage' or 'spy', preferring 'agent' or 'soldier' to indicate their military role as intelligence-gatherers. As Chauvin asserted: 'for the new recruit the status of a soldier was certain proof of the value of the work asked of him' and represented the prospect after the war of official recognition of the services he had rendered. Crucially, it also let him be 'seen as a brother in arms by the valiant soldiers at the Front to whom all thoughts were turned'.[13]

Over the last fifteen months of the war the organisation grew to more than 800-strong, a large number of whom were women. All members took a military oath of allegiance and after the war they were eventually recognised formally as the Corps d'Observation Anglais, a 'Volunteer Service attached to the British Army in France'. By September 1918 there were some eighty train-watching posts, 'and in addition a great number of "Promeneur Posts"' which reported on any German military units in their immediate area. The network covered much of occupied Belgium and reached as far as Hirson and Mézières (both important railway centres) across the French frontier. La Dame Blanche was organised along military lines into three 'battalions'. An analysis by Tammy Proctor of Battalion III, which was centred on Brussels, gives an idea of the kinds of people involved. About a third of the 190 battalion members were women, and the unit was led by an unmarried female schoolteacher in her forties, Laure Tandel. The ages of members ranged from sixteen to eighty-one years, though the majority fell between twenty and forty-two. Observing that 60 per cent of the women were single (and 7 per cent widowed), Proctor concluded that 'independent, older women were more likely than younger women to work as formal soldiers' in the organisation.

INFANTRY UNIT

Officers   Soldiers   Horses   Carts

ARTILLERY UNIT

Officers   Soldiers   Horses   Guns   Ammunition Wagons

CAVALRY UNIT

Officers   Soldiers   Horses   Carts

BRIDGE TRAIN

Officers   Soldiers   Horses   Pontoons and Carts

Silhouettes showing composition of trains conveying constituted units.
Multiply all wagons and flat trucks by three to get requisite numbers
Retain one officer coach per train

LANDAU, *ALL'S FAIR*, P.61

Guidance for train-watchers in German-occupied Belgium.

Tandel's unit contained a diverse range of occupations: the men included labourers, civil servants, engineers and railway workers; the women, schoolteachers, shop assistants and a significant number 'without profession'. The organisation had a strong religious element, in terms both of personnel and of motivation. One list of British awards contains the names of forty-four priests, as well as one nun and a reverend mother. Volunteers clustered by both occupation and family, the latter an especially important factor. Anna Kesseler, a Brussels widow in her mid-fifties, who had lost her only son in battle in 1914, joined up with her four daughters, acting as couriers, transcribers and letter boxes, holding reports for onward transmission. Three unmarried sisters called Weimerskirch ran a Catholic bookshop in Liège which provided another reliable letter box. Inevitably, these networks suffered casualties, though La Dame Blanche's security was notably good. Two brothers from Tintigny in south-eastern Belgium, Antony and Louis Collard, were caught with intelligence reports in their possession and subsequently executed. Their father and two sisters were also in La Dame Blanche, one of the latter dying shortly after the war from an illness contracted following imprisonment by the Germans.[14]

Getting information out of occupied territory was relatively easy in the early days before the lines of trenches settled down along the Western Front. The Belgian–Dutch frontier remained relatively porous, too, until 1916 when the Germans tightened up security and erected a high-voltage electrified fence along the border. Experienced smugglers were engaged and various devices developed to cross this fence, including rubber gloves and boots as well as an insulated climbing frame. Landau noted two other methods: employing the boatmen who were permitted to ply barges between Rotterdam and Antwerp (though under close German surveillance); and using farm labourers working fields adjacent to the border, who could simply 'toss messages across the wire when the sentry was not looking' (though this was considerably more dangerous than it might seem). Over the last two years of the war, Landau aimed to have at least six separate 'tuyaux' (pipes) available for communications between occupied Belgium and the Netherlands. 'When one broke down, we had the other five in reserve, and others were continuously being established.' One of La Dame Blanche's greatest successes was the establishment in the autumn of 1917 of an effective train-watching operation in Hirson, monitoring a strategically important railway running parallel to the German lines. With the help of a Hirson-born trainee French priest, Landau was able to contact a former railwayman who lived at Fourmies alongside the line and who agreed to help. It was a real family endeavour. 'Every one in this humble household', wrote Landau, 'did their share of watching.' During the day it was the man's fourteen- and thirteen-year-old sisters; at night he and his wife took over. 'The composition of the trains was jotted down in terms of comestibles: beans for soldiers, chicory for horses, coffee for cannons, and so on.' Reports were 'hidden in the hollow handle of a kitchen broom, which was left innocently in its place in the corner'. From 23 September 1917, when this post began operating, Landau reckoned that 'not a single troop train was missed'. Getting the reports across the frontier involved the usual sleight-of-hand including a Belgian midwife whose job allowed her to travel around the countryside and whose 'special vocation' was 'the delivery of deadly spy reports, cunningly wrapped around the whale-bones of her corset'.[15]

La Dame Blanche was the most successful single British human intelligence operation of the First World War. Learning from the painful experience of 1914–16, guided by Landau and Dewé's sharp sense of security, and sustained, above all, by the patriotic devotion of the brave Belgian and French men and women who collected the precious information and brought the reports to Cumming's Rotterdam headquarters, by the last year of the war it was producing military intelligence in copious quantities. 'Il n'y a aucun doute qu'en ce moment critique', wrote Landau to the leaders of the organisation in January 1918, 'votre organisation représente de loin la source la plus fertile que les Alliés possèdent et que vous obtenez des résultats dont l'importance ne peut être estimé.'[16] Much of this intelligence was shared through the Bureau Central Interallié (Allied Central Office), created in the autumn of 1915, which comprised military missions from the French, British, Belgian, Russian, Portuguese and subsequently the United States governments. By July 1916 Cumming noted in his diary that he had twelve staff seconded to the headquarters of the Bureau on the Boulevard Saint-Germain in Paris.[17]

No complete archive of British reporting from the Netherlands has survived, but a broad indication of the type, volume and distribution of material produced can be gained from the 2,500 or so intelligence reports sent by MI1(c) to the British Intelligence Mission at the French General Headquarters between March 1917 and July 1918. The great majority of these comprised train-watching reports, in the first instance telegraphed to London (and to British GHQ in France) by the British military attaché at The Hague. Between March and September 1917 most of these reports were ascribed to CF and WL agents, but from October 1917 there was an increasing number of railway 'traffic returns' from clusters of sources coded 'T' – 'TB', 'TH', 'TO' and 'TQ'. Each was also marked with a 'C.X.' number, a prefix which Cumming had adopted in October 1915 to indicate cable traffic from his representatives. Plausibly, therefore, these reports came from Tinsley's networks, including La Dame Blanche. The growing importance of both train-watching and Tinsley's organisation is confirmed by a comparison of the reports for the first weeks of April in 1917 and 1918. Of the thirty-six reports sent to the French GHQ between 1 and 6 April 1917, twenty-eight concerned 'movements of troops', of which eight were derived from railway observation, six each from enemy deserters and unidentified 'agents', four from 'refugees', three from Belgian workmen and one from an intercepted postcard sent by a German soldier. Over the equivalent period in 1918 there were thirty-four reports, thirty-one dealing with troop movements. Twenty-nine of these were train-watching returns, the vast majority (twenty-five) deriving from T sources.[18]

Information on railway traffic was supplemented by a wide range of other material. During June 1917 a particularly productive head agent, 'B.9' (Cumming's agents were letter-coded according to their country, 'B' for Belgium, 'H' for Holland, 'D' for Denmark and so on), reported that a new single-track railway had been built between Heist, Knokke and Westkappelle in northern Belgium. Citing 'a local inhabitant' who had just left the district, he reported improved fortifications at the strategically important port of Zeebrugge, including 'a great number of very deep concrete shelters', newly constructed along the sea wall. He also sent in a detailed plan of a large ammunition factory at Grossenbaum, between Düsseldorf and Duisburg in western Germany, which had been provided by 'a deported Belgian' who had been working there. From an anonymous source Oppenheim got a detailed sketch-map of a new railway at Kinkempois, allowing traffic from Aachen to Brussels and Namur to bypass neighbouring Liège. Some of these reports could clearly inform military action. Zeebrugge, which was a valuable naval base for German units deployed to disrupt British communications across the Channel, was under constant attack, most notably in the famous St George's Day raid in 1918 when concrete-filled ships were sunk, blocking the entrance to the harbour. Although the Grossenbaum munitions works was just out of range to be bombed from the air, the Kinkempois 'railway triangle' was attacked by eleven British bombers on 22 May 1918.[19]

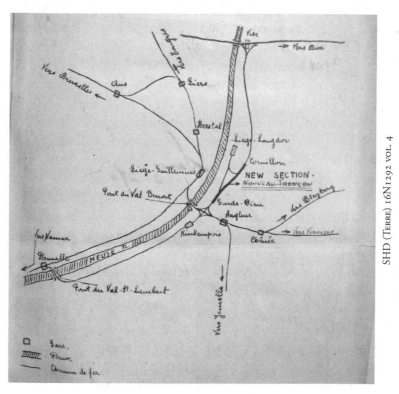

SHD (TERRE) 16N1292 VOL. 4

Sketch map of a new railway line at Kinkempois, near Liège, supplied to British Intelligence in June 1917.

In addition to the occasional low-level reporting on factories and railways in Germany, Cumming's Rotterdam station had one exceptional, high-grade agent, known variously as 'Agent VII', 'H.16' or, most commonly, 'TR/16' (indicating 'Tinsley-Rotterdam', akin to 'Cameron-Folkestone' and 'Wallinger-London'). Henry Landau devoted a whole chapter of his 1934 memoirs to this man, whom he described as 'the greatest of the Allied war-time spies'. Although Landau asserted that he had met him 'several times', the agent denied this when the Service mounted an urgent inquiry to see if the German authorities might be able to identify him from the account in Landau's book. TR/16 had 'no recollection of anyone named Landau' but thought it 'possible that he may have known him by sight and been known to him through visits to "T"'s office in Rotterdam'. Aged about forty at the beginning of the war, TR/16 (Dr Karl Krüger) was a naval engineer who had worked successfully in the German ship-building industry. He was a 'walk-in', who, apparently fired by a mixture of resentment and greed, had offered his services at the British legation in The Hague in November 1914. At the time he represented himself to Tinsley as a Dane, but it later emerged that he was actually a German, who, while serving in the German navy and having 'insulted a relative of the Kaiser while at one of the northern sea ports', had been 'court-martialled and degraded, thereby becoming very embittered against his country'. As a postwar SIS minute observed, moreover, he worked 'for very large sums of money, for which he is still always greedy'. But the information he supplied about German submarine and naval construction 'was always accurate, up to date and of the very greatest possible value'. Over fifty of TR/16's reports have survived in the Admiralty papers where it is noted that he 'made complete tours of the German shipyards approximately every month from May 1915 to January 1919. Considerable value was attached to his information.' There is an accurate sketch he made of the new German battleship *Bayern* at dock in March 1916. Later the same year he was asked to report on German losses at the Battle of Jutland (31 May 1916), the only engagement between the main British and German fleets during the war. The battle itself was inconclusive, with heavy losses on both sides, and the Admiralty badly needed to know how much damage the German fleet had suffered and how soon it might be able to fight again. On 2 June London told Tinsley in Rotterdam that 'reliable information' on the subject was 'urgently required'. The same day Tinsley passed on the instruction to TR/16. Between 3 and 20 June he visited ten German dockyards, including Kiel, Bremen, Rostock and Danzig and on 27 June delivered a comprehensive five-page report which the Admiralty Director of the Intelligence Division praised as '100%'. From the British point of view, the most reassuring aspect of the report was confirmation that the Germans had sustained more serious damage than they had admitted. TR/16 reported, for example, that eight capital ships would be out of service for at least three months.[20] The principal result of Jutland, indeed, was that for the rest of the war the German fleet never again ventured out to battle.

Agent TR/16's March 1916 drawing of the new German battleship Bayern.

In July 1918 London calculated that Tinsley's operation accounted for '70% of the total intelligence obtained by all the Allied armies not only through the Netherlands but also through other neutral states' and remarked on the 'rôle unique et merveilleux' of their work collecting information about enemy movements in the zone immediately behind the front line. Although this statement was undoubtedly intended to boost morale and may have overestimated the position somewhat, by this stage Cumming's operation was so successful that the British authorities were considering placing all the Dutch–Belgian military intelligence organisations under Tinsley, though the war ended before this could be implemented.[21] But intelligence is only as good as the use to which it is put. Over the early spring of 1918 MI1(c)'s reports (among many others) confirmed that the Germans were preparing for a push on the Western

Front. The fact of a German attack was not in doubt; Brigadier Cox at General Headquarters predicted the moment and strength of the enemy quite accurately. But the British high command underestimated its intensity and the Commander-in-Chief, Sir Douglas Haig, remained absurdly over-optimistic. When the offensive came, on 21 March, the Germans advanced forty miles in a few days, and two further waves of the offensive in April and May kept the Allies on the defensive. Once the Germans had run out of steam by the early summer, however, the Allies, better supplied with matériel and men (especially the thousands of fresh American troops arriving at the front) and sustained by their excellent intelligence, gained the upper hand. They began from August onwards to push their opponents back, so much so that their retreat (and a weakening domestic situation) drove the Germans to sue for an armistice on 11 November 1918.[22]

After the war, individuals who had assisted British intelligence organisations pressed for and obtained public recognition of their war service. The British government published long lists of agents who had worked for Cameron's and Wallinger's networks, as well as La Dame Blanche. In August 1919 Walthère Dewé, Herman Chauvin and 727 other Belgians (including 210 women) were listed as 'mentioned in despatches', ten posthumously. During January 1920 the Director of Military Intelligence, General Sir William Thwaites (accompanied by Landau and Wallinger), awarded over seven hundred orders and medals to Belgian and French citizens in a series of public investitures at Ghent, Lille, Brussels and Liège.[23] For these people their wartime secret intelligence work was a matter of great pride, as well as a demonstration that on the so-called home front they had also done their bit, and they were glad for it to receive such public notice. It represented, moreover, a further important dimension of the human intelligence work of Cumming's Bureau, moving beyond the engagement of foreign citizens – often from crude financial motives – to spy in foreign states and sometimes against their own country. Those Belgians and French who worked in occupied territory during the First World War saw themselves as working not only for the British but also on behalf of their own country against a common enemy. This was a crucial distinction and made the engagement of such people a very different exercise from that of finding agents in peacetime. In meeting this desire for public recognition, however, the British authorities jeopardised the future safety of such civilians taking part in intelligence work (though no one at the time anticipated that this might be a problem).

Scandinavia

In contrast to the Low Countries, where much of the information gathered was military, Cumming's initial focus in Scandinavia concerned naval intelligence. Prewar efforts to follow German warship movements were renewed, and with the imposition of a wartime blockade on the enemy powers his Bureau was also deployed to monitor this and help plug gaps which the Germans might exploit. Evidence is scanty as to Cumming's precise deployments, but there is enough to demonstrate a fair range of activity. Some of his prewar ship-reporting arrangements appear to have survived. On 22 August 1914 he noted in his diary that 'Norseman' left for Esbjerg (on the west coast of Denmark). On 2 January 1915 Norseman was included on an 'Agents pay list' for a sizeable monthly payment of £300, while Cumming's representative in Copenhagen had a total budget of only £250. The following March Blinker Hall in the Admiralty agreed 'to a trial of Norseman's fishing boat temporarily'. In July, by which time he had been included in the Copenhagen budget, Norseman came to London where Cumming met him in the Metropole Hotel and 'agreed to pay him £50 a month to include everything except rail fares'. He featured on the Copenhagen estimate (which by now totalled £1,080) in November 1915 and thereafter disappears from the record. Another agent in Denmark was a Danish naval officer, Captain Walter Christmas, who had been Naval Officer in Charge at the Skaw, on the northernmost tip of the country. According to Frank Stagg, who between September 1915 and June 1917 handled all naval reporting in Head Office, Christmas 'gave us all his navy's coastwatching reports'. The agent apparently stipulated 'that a pretty girl was always at a Skaw hotel as go-between'. But late in 1915 one of these 'inadvertently gave him away' and he had to be evacuated to London. Cumming's man in Copenhagen, too, was rumbled by the Danish authorities and, although convicted of espionage against Germany, was allowed to leave the country in November 1915. A postwar account of 'Naval Intelligence by Secret Service methods' noted that 'along the Danish coasts, on both east and west sides of the peninsula' there had been 'several groups' of coast-watchers, 'usually mutually ignorant of each other's existence, so that some sort of check could be maintained'. There were also 'organisations on the Swedish western coast, particularly on The Sound, opposite Copenhagen, and at Malmo'. The watch here was 'very close and effective'. In places the channel was barely half a mile wide, 'and even submarines were thus clearly visible, except on dark nights or very thick weather'. No trace of these reports, or further assessment of their value, has apparently survived.

As everywhere else, Cumming was under pressure to provide intelligence from his Danish operation. Denmark was most useful as a base from which to target Germany. 'D.1' had contacts in German munitions circles and reported in November 1915 that he knew one particular Dutch firm had been 'shipping ore for Krupps'. In May 1916 'D.10' delivered a long and detailed account of 'internal conditions' in Germany which (no doubt to its readers' satisfaction) highlighted the many shortages caused by the Allied blockade. Lack of wheat flour had led to the manufacture of 'Straw Bread' using 15–20 per cent of straw flour: 'Tastes unpleasantly sour and bitter, and . . . irritates the intestines'. Rubber was so scarce that copper wire was now 'insulated with a sort of paper'. Substitutes for cotton and jute were hard to find. 'As an auxiliary there is now manufactured woven paper stuff mixed with yarn.'

'D.2' was a head agent with a productive subordinate in Vamdrup in southern Denmark who in March 1917 reported details of the extensive help Danish State Railways was giving to the Germans. In January 1918 he cited a German soldier on leave reporting 'thousands of troops daily passing through Hamburg [and] Hanover from Russia', which was probably part of the build-up for the German spring offensive. Reflecting the higher society gossip which also came the way of Cumming's men, 'D.5', quoting the wife of a 'highly placed' official in the Danish Foreign Office, reported that the German minister in Copenhagen was proposing a close alliance between Germany and Denmark, with the 'Danish speaking part [of] Schleswig to go to Denmark as compensation'. In April 1918, 'D.62' returned from Germany with some high-level military gossip from a staff officer on General von Gallwitz's staff. Hindenburg and Ludendorff (the effective military dictators of Germany) 'had ordered [an] offensive between Verdun and the Vosges, in Duke Albrecht of Württemberg's army group. It was expected in April but delayed owing to disputes between Generals Gallwitz and Bothmer. Gallwitz wishes to attack but Bothmer does not, as he states losses would be too heavy. Duke has no control over them.'[24]

Smaller-scale operations in Sweden and Norway produced similar kinds of material. Asked by the War Trade Intelligence Department in London to investigate the suspiciously large volume of honey being imported into Sweden, one of Cumming's men 'tapped the casks on the quays at Gothenburg' and discovered that 'more than 80% of it was pure rubber', apparently bound for Germany. In April 1917 a report came from 'S.50' in Stockholm that a 'lady governess returned from Hamburg states that food riots occur there weekly'. The following month he reported that he had attended 'a big private dinner' with 'nearly all the big Jewish bankers and financiers here in Stockholm' and had canvassed their opinion about German and Russian politics. They thought that the new liberal-democratic Menshevik government in Russia, installed following the February Revolution, had 'now succeeded in making its position secure, particularly from the very violent ultra-socialist party' (the Bolsheviks). Several of the bankers who had recently visited Germany said that the position was 'going from bad to worse, and that Austria in particular' was 'shouting for peace'. Both these opinions were over-sanguine. The Russian Bolsheviks overthrew the Mensheviks in the October Revolution, while the Germans were far from beaten, even though war enthusiasm was waning in Austria. As intelligence, moreover, S.50's reports did not go much beyond the regular kind of reporting which London might expect diplomats to pick up in their normal course of work. Many of the surviving reports emanating from Cumming's First World War networks covered similar ground, though occasionally some harder, more 'military' information was supplied. In January 1918, 'N.20' reported from Christiania (Oslo) information from 'a German commercial traveller' that factories in Flanders, Aachen, Hanover and Cassel had been 'hurriedly emptied recently and made into hospitals'. The following month 'S.8' quoted a Swede who had 'served with distinction in the German army' as saying that the planned offensive 'probably takes place in about 4 weeks'. The 'almost universal opinion in Germany' was that this was the 'last card and if it fails game is absolutely up because of shortage of men, disorganization, and desperate condition of civil population'.[25]

Other neutrals

Like Scandinavia, neutral Switzerland appeared to be another handy spot from which enemy countries might be targeted, as is clear from Cumming's desire to get an operation established there from very early in the war. In August 1914 he appointed a good linguist with business cover working for a 'firm of shippers' as his representative and by late November there were four staff in Switzerland. By the beginning of 1915 this man was being given £250 a month for agents, and in March Cumming 'agreed to let him expand to 300'. But the return was poor. On a visit to London in July 1915, Cumming told the representative 'that his 6 telegrams in March had cost £50 apiece & were not worth 50/- [£2.50] the lot'. Cumming insisted that payment could thenceforth only be 'by results'. This seems to have had some effect, as in September the representative told Cumming that he 'may expect about 15 reports a month from 4 travellers in Tr [Germany] & others, costing about £110 a month'. During March 1915 Cumming had already been considering reinforcing his Swiss operation and in April he sent Major L. G. Campbell out to the French border town of Annemasse, near Geneva, to establish another network, and Major Hans Vischer, a Swiss-born Cambridge graduate and former missionary who had been working in the Colonial Office, to work from a base in Berne. The same month, noting that 'C's Swiss system' was 'not as extensive as it might be', Walter Kirke at General Headquarters decided with Cecil Cameron that they should develop their own intelligence organisation in Switzerland, with the result that they sponsored two networks, one headed by Captain John Wallinger of the Indian Police, elder brother of Ernest Wallinger, who ran the WL intelligence organisation out of London.[26]

None of these ventures was very successful. The Swiss resented the use of their country as a kind of intelligence clearing-house where spies from every belligerent power engaged in an espionage free-for-all. From the autumn of 1915 the British networks in Switzerland began to unravel. In September Cumming noted that '7 or 8' of Wallinger's 'bridge watchers' had been 'jugged in Switzerland' and he also closed down Vischer's operation. In November 1915, after an Englishman called Peter Wright had been jailed on a charge of spying, it was reported as being the sixty-eighth such conviction since the beginning of the war. One network of German spies had 'involved 112 persons of various nationalities'. Press reports suggested that the Swiss police were watching a further four hundred people, that the prisons were overcrowded and even that 'a concentration camp may be formed'.[27] The GHQ networks suffered a further series of reverses and even Wallinger's imaginative engagement of the author Somerset Maugham (who fictionalised his experiences in a collection of short stories, *Ashenden: or the British Agent*) failed to revive his organisation. In January 1916 Kirke learned that most of Cumming's agents had been detained, and that Campbell had escaped only because the Swiss police had apparently arrested the wrong man.[28]

As British intelligence officers in the Netherlands, Scandinavia and Switzerland discovered, running operations in neutral countries potentially raised difficulties, not only with the host authorities, but also with the Foreign Office and the British diplomats in the country concerned. Although the prewar line that consular officials, and even service attachés, should have nothing to do with secret intelligence was in some places (notably the Netherlands) modified somewhat once hostilities had commenced, problems continued elsewhere. In March 1915 Kirke wrung some concessions from Ronald Campbell of the Foreign Office. Consuls, he agreed, could be used for the transmission of messages and would be permitted to recommend individuals as possible agents, but they 'must have no direct relations with agents'. Discussing the situation in Switzerland in November 1915, Campbell told Kirke that Nicolson would not let the military attaché 'have anything to do with Intelligence'. Kirke countered that 'if he did not help in Intelligence the M.A. was useless' and that anyone who was sent out to work in Switzerland had to have some 'official position' or he could not stay in the country 'without becoming an object of suspicion & embarrassing the F.O.'. 'It is clear', grumbled Kirke to his diary, 'that the prejudices of peace time still exist very strongly, and that we are much hampered as compared with the Germans or even the French.'[29]

Part of the perennial Foreign Office worry about mixing diplomacy with espionage concerned cover. Giving intelligence personnel positions as diplomats might, if they were discovered, jeopardise the status of the entire mission. But for the intelligence agencies 'natural' cover, for example as a businessman or journalist, might not provide a secure enough situation especially (as Kirke argued) in wartime.[30] Much also depended on the particular diplomats concerned. The attitudes of ambassadors and heads of mission varied. Sir Horace Rumbold proved to be more accommodating than most after he became minister at Berne in September 1916, allowing the appointment of Cumming's man Captain Edward Harran as assistant military attaché and other individuals to consular posts. Harran had been working since December 1915 as a Military Permit Officer, which, with the title Military Control Officer (MCO), emerged as the most plausible cover adopted during the First World War. Working in Military Control Offices set up under Kell's counter-espionage Bureau during 1915 (initially in London, Paris, Rome and New York), these officers issued permits for people to travel to and from the United Kingdom and into British military zones. It was a role which usefully involved an overt information-gathering function, licensing the officers, for example, to question individuals, to enquire into their background and reasons for wishing to travel, and (perhaps most importantly) to liaise with local police and security agencies. It was, it seemed, almost perfect cover for anyone wanting to run an intelligence network. In due course Cumming was given the job of administering the MCOs in foreign countries, but this did not come cheap. In July 1916 he requested from the Foreign Office, and received, '£5000 more per month' (approximately £243,000 at current values) to fund eleven additional officers, for Petrograd, Paris, Madrid, Lisbon, Rome, Athens, Alexandria, Stockholm, Oslo, Copenhagen and New York.

In June 1916 Harran replaced Campbell as Cumming's chief representative in Switzerland and by the end of the year had a core staff of four: one doing the travel permit work; one liaising with the local French secret service, as well as recruiting and training agents; and one (under civilian cover) focusing on information from Austria, while Harran himself concentrated on Germany 'and information from behind German lines'. During 1917 officers were also sent to Geneva, Zurich, Basle and Lausanne. Not all these were successful, and the representative in Zurich was 'relieved from his post on account of drink'. Although the hope was to get agents into both Germany and Austria, a review of the Swiss reports suggests that the operation did little more than retail a fair bit of gossip, report on the domestic political situation and provide some economic intelligence on German embargo-breaking operations. There was a smattering of reports from diplomats and other sources with Near

Eastern connections about the Ottoman empire, which had come into the war on Germany's side in October 1914. The Swiss reports, however, are notable for a handful of MI1(c) comments indicating that, in a few cases at least, some evaluation was applied to material before it was circulated to customer departments. A report about Hungarian politics from Geneva on 30 November 1917 entitled 'The views of Dr. Oscar Jaszi of the University of Budapest' had a 'prefatory note by M.I.1.c.': 'Dr. Oscar Jaszi is a man of high character and is probably the most honest and straightforward of the Magyar political leaders.'[31] A qualified meteorologist was attached to Cumming's Berne office. His sole function was to ascend 'to a certain height up a mountain twice a day' and telegraph to London 'the direction and force of the wind'. It was reported that 'the purpose of this was intended partly to work out the possibility of gas attacks and partly for the information of the Air Force'. Rather to Harran's dismay (though perhaps reflecting a comparative lack of productivity), in January 1918 Cumming brought Vischer back to take over in Berne, and he remained in charge until the end of the war.

Cumming exploited the Military Control Office system for both cover and intelligence generally. His Bureau, moreover, was evidently a convenient mechanism through which the offices could be funded. A similar system appears to have obtained regarding the Naval Intelligence Division's existing organisation in Spain, which as a maritime country with many overseas trading interests was an important target for blockade-watching. Although in his diary Cumming noted sending men to Spain in August 1914 and April 1915, these do not appear to have been part of a network. In July 1915 Blinker Hall told Cumming that he was 'to link up with the Spanish organisation' and provide a car for Hall's man in Vigo. In 1916, Cumming proposed, with Hall's approval, to set up a 'military intelligence mission' in Lisbon. In September Cumming was more expansive. He told Hall 'of our proposal to start a C.E. [counter-espionage] branch for Spain with headquarters at Hendaye, & that this would include a nucleus for recruiting men to go into Germany'. Hans Vischer was put in charge as Military Control Officer. A postwar report noted that he had been instructed 'not to do any S.S. work' since 'during the whole of the war the Admiralty conducted S.S. work in Spain and Portugal'. By February 1917 Vischer had a staff of eight with offices in Madrid, Seville, Bilbao, Vigo and Barcelona. As in the

Low Countries, military intelligence tried to muscle in on the territory. In January 1917 Cumming asked Wallinger 'to cut out recruiting in Spain altogether as far as my work is concerned', and in February 1918 he noted that Colonel French in the War Office was 'making arrangements' with an army officer in Gibraltar 'to carry out some form of S.S. in Spain!'. In May 1917 an apparent proposal that Cumming might take over the Admiralty operation there (which he did not in any case wish to do) left Admiral Hall 'very angry'.

The position in Iberia reflected the ambiguous relationships the Secret Service Bureau had with other British intelligence organisations during the First World War. Cumming's uncertainty in October 1916 as to the exact number of his 'staff and agents' in Spain ('abt 50') suggests that this may principally have been the Admiralty's network, paid through Cumming's budget, but over which in practice he had no control. Cumming's management, however, of the Military Control organisation – which primarily reported to MI5 – reflected his determination to keep charge of all clandestine intelligence and security work in foreign countries. He was not entirely successful in this, having to concede that MI5 could have stations in some Allied countries (such as those in Paris and Rome), though their posts in Washington and New York came partly under his supervision. In February 1918 the Director of Military Intelligence proposed that MI5 take over all Cumming's 'organisations in Allied countries'. Although Campbell at the Foreign Office said he 'ought not to accept this', Cumming felt that 'he could not but obey orders'. Neutral countries were a different matter, however, and Cumming kept control of the Military Control Offices in such places as Copenhagen, Oslo, Stockholm, Berne and Madrid.[32]

Commercial and economic intelligence

At the beginning of 1915 Campbell of the Foreign Office congratulated Cumming on the excellence of 'our commercial intelligence'. The Bureau's reporting on economic and blockade matters, which constituted an important part of its work during the First World War, was useful to Cumming's military customers, as well as to the War Trade Intelligence Department and the Ministry of Munitions. From about the beginning of 1917 MI1(c) circulated a digest on 'Economic Conditions (Enemy Countries)', 'based exclusively on information received from agents and other confidential sources'. These summaries came out two or three times a month, and drew on reports from Berne, Rotterdam, Italy, from escaped British prisoners-of-war and even from Central America. As Colonel French of the War Office warned a colleague in the Ministry of Munitions in August 1915, information from within the enemy countries themselves was especially hard to obtain. French remarked on 'the great difficulty of getting anyone into Germany or Austria'. Apparently unaware of the agent TR/16's existence (though this may reflect a simple lack of communication between Naval and Military Intelligence), French said that such agents 'as we did succeed in getting there, were people without technical knowledge, only capable of reporting in general terms'. To help remedy this deficiency, the Munitions official agreed to draw up a questionnaire 'to indicate to the agents employed what they should look for'. French asked that it 'be of as simple a character as possible as questions of too minute technical a nature would only lead to misleading replies'. In January 1917 a request from Sir Douglas Haig in France for a compilation of 'the latest information' concerning German munitions production was prepared in the Ministry of Munitions using a fair proportion of MI1(c) material. Among reports received 'from the Director of Military Intelligence' were ones from Copenhagen about Krupp gun production, from Stockholm on Swedish high-explosives manufacture, and a third containing details about working arrangements in the Krupp works. 'Tiger' in Stockholm had got the information from 'a Swedish engineer' who had 'just returned from Essen and sold iron to Krupps'.[33]

Frank Stagg, who handled Russian information at Head Office, had great ambitions for the new economic work. 'We are', he told Samuel Hoare, 'now throwing a network of Commercial Intelligence Systems all over the world and are in a fair way to becoming the Intelligence Service of the new Ministry of Commerce [which he predicted would emerge after the war], which means that we are about to replace the Consular Service and the Board of Trade Representatives in the Colonies.' Stagg hoped that the Bureau could 'replace the antiquated hidebound methods of the old Consular Service by such as will give British Traders confidence and pluck to launch out into foreign enterprises with as much vigour as the Germans displayed before the war'. Above all it was necessary to 'get

*A caricature by H. F. Crowther Smith of Frank Stagg,
the officer at Head Office responsible for Russian
information. Here we see him inspecting a Bolshevik.*

a firm footing' in Russia, and he hoped Hoare would be able to produce 'sufficient information to serve up some tempting dishes not merely to the British Govt but to big financial and commercial interests in the City'. He suggested that Hoare contact 'respectable pushing British firms in such towns as Moscow, Kiev, Odessa, Nijni, Batoum &c who would gladly send you reports on openings for British Finance and . . . Trade'. This was a global challenge. 'We are doing it in South America and getting excellent results,' wrote Stagg, 'are just getting our toes in Africa, have correspondents in the Far East and of course the European neutrals are being sucked dry of all the information within their frontiers.' Perhaps a little over-excited by the possibilities (yet also aware of the sensitivities in Moscow), Stagg told Hoare that if he saw 'a favourable opportunity' to go ahead with what Stagg called 'the Russo-British Economic Problem Solution', he should do so, 'whilst keeping all the time within the instructions the Chief has given you (or if you do go beyond them to take good care that you are not found out, more especially by the Embassy)'. He was 'quite certain' that any positive result would leave the War Trade Intelligence Department 'in raptures'; the Foreign Office would 'make no demur'; and 'the Chief will give you all the funds and assistance you ask for'.[34]

The acquisition of economic and commercial information demonstrates that the contribution of Cumming's organisation to intelligence generally during the First World War has to be seen as part of a range of organisations and sources. The same applies to naval and military intelligence. Beyond TR/16's extremely impressive reporting on German naval matters, on balance MI1(c)'s most significant contribution in the western theatre of operations during 1914–18 was through Tinsley's train-watching and other networks in the Low Countries, which, while they improved steadily in the last year or so of the conflict, were to the very end complemented by the army's own networks. Despite successive attempts by the War Office to take over Cumming's operations, that there was a proposal in the last months of the war to place all this reporting under MI1(c) strongly suggests that the wartime performance of the Bureau had been sufficiently successful to ensure its survival as an independent agency.

4

Working further afield

Although the British intelligence effort, like the war effort generally, was more focused on the Western Front than anywhere else, the world-wide ramifications of the conflict meant that Cumming's organisation took on ever expanding responsibilities. From early in the war liaison with the Russians was underpinned by the establishment of a mission in Petrograd. While in the west 'gallant little Belgium' had become a rallying-cry for Allied opposition to German militarism, in south-central Europe 'gallant little Serbia' seemed equally threatened by Germany's ally Austria-Hungary. Vienna's desire to crush Serbia, and Russia's equal determination to resist it, meant that the Balkans became another important theatre of operations. The entry into the war on the enemy side at the end of October 1914 of the Ottoman empire, which stretched from European Turkey through the Middle East and Arabia, widened the conflict even further and required the Allies to deploy forces in the Mediterranean and across the region. In the western hemisphere, while the traditionally isolationist United States at first remained neutral, it too became a focus for Allied and enemy activities. The Allies and the Central Powers (Germany, Austria and Turkey) mounted propaganda campaigns to mobilise American opinion behind their causes, and both sides worked actively to cut off American economic support from the other. As the United States moved closer and closer to the Allies – eventually declaring war on Germany in April 1917 – this developed into a struggle mainly between the British, endeavouring to plug any American gaps in their blockade against the enemy, and the Germans, themselves determined to cut the vital transatlantic supply routes, by means of both surface and submarine attacks on merchant ships, as well as by means of subversion and actual sabotage of Allied cargoes in the United States itself. Here, too, with an office in New York from 1915, Cumming's Bureau had a role to play.

Russian allies

Although Cumming's prewar plans to establish a representative in Russia were interrupted by the outbreak of the war, the new situation in which Britain, Russia and France were now active co-belligerents against Germany and Austria-Hungary underpinned the establishment of formal liaison arrangements between their intelligence agencies. During September 1914 Cumming had several meetings with General Yermaloff, the Russian military attaché in London, prepared himself to visit Russia and selected Captain Archibald Campbell to be his representative in Petrograd. There is no clue in Cumming's diary to why he chose Campbell, whom he engaged on 13 August – 'K. [possibly Kell] called & brought him.' Reflecting in 1917 on the wartime development of intelligence work in Russia, General Macdonogh, the Director of Military Intelligence, described Campbell as 'an officer of considerable ingenuity, ability and push, but of singularly unattractive personality'. But this was with the benefit of hindsight and followed the painful experience of a difficult posting in Russia during which Campbell had ruffled feathers among both diplomats and other military liaison officers serving in the country, among whom were Colonel Alfred 'Flurry' Knox, a prickly Ulsterman who had been military attaché since May 1914, and General Sir John Hanbury-Williams, who had been sent out by the Secretary of State for War, Lord Kitchener, to head a mission at the Russian General Headquarters and 'to report to him direct'.

The War Office had approved Cumming's planned visit to Russia, but at the last moment Admiral Oliver at the Admiralty prohibited him from going. So it was that Campbell, accompanied by (among others) Lieutenant Stephen Alley (who had been born and brought up in Russia), set off for Petrograd on 26 September 1914. The duty of the mission was 'to get in touch with the officers of the Russian General Staff dealing with Secret service, and so to obtain information from the Russian Intelligence Department about the enemy'. One of the advantages of placing the mission under Cumming was (as a wartime account of the

'British Intelligence Organisation in Russia' rather delicately put it) 'that it involved no reference to the finance branches of the War Office and that it admitted of great elasticity as regards both numbers and classes of person employed'. Although working under the Secret Service Bureau and charged with liaising on secret service matters, Campbell's mission was scarcely clandestine and had no direct involvement with espionage. The officers all wore uniform and were given a room in the Russian War Office where they had 'somewhat exceptional facilities as regards access to the Russian military authorities'. As a postwar report recorded, their main function was simply to pass on to London Russian-acquired intelligence about the enemy. Alley, for example, 'held no written communication with C, but telegraphed identifications of German forces and situation reports at great length. He employed no agents.'[1]

The history of Cumming's intelligence mission in Russia confirms the sometimes very difficult relationships between secret service personnel and orthodox diplomatic and military representatives, even within the context of a wartime alliance. Here, too, clashes of personality exacerbated the problems, as Knox's touchy *amour propre* collided with Campbell's blunter and more unsubtle approach. The ad-hoc nature of Campbell's mission, its indeterminate responsibilities and, above all, its embedding in the Russian War Office had the result that Russian General Staff officers began to approach him with matters which properly should have been communicated through Knox or Hanbury-Williams. These included a request for technically qualified signals personnel and a scheme to send Cossacks to the Western Front. Campbell had scarcely arrived in Petrograd before the British naval and military attachés began to complain about him. Leaving Alley to hold the fort, Campbell was summoned back to London. He arrived with evidently welcome reports of the situation in Russia. Cumming took him to see General Callwell (Director of Military Operations) who during a long interview 'quite abandoned' his hitherto hostile attitude. Callwell told Henry Wilson that Campbell had provided 'much interesting information' about 'the condition of things in the Russian Army', especially regarding 'their deficiency in electric communications in all forms, and the ignorance of their use. He says that the disaster which happened earlier in the war to General Samsonov [killed at the Battle of Tannenberg in August 1914] was entirely due to all their messages being sent by wireless and en clair, to these being taken up by

the Germans, and to the Germans actually sending them orders in reply.'²
With the DMO's approval, Cumming's officers began interviewing and
selecting a 'corps of telegraphists' to go to Russia. Cumming (and perhaps
Callwell too) had ambitions for Campbell's mission beyond mere secret
service liaison. Among the topics noted in his diary for a War Office
meeting on 14 December about Petrograd was the 'influencing of plans
to conform to our desires. Russia', he added, 'will be the most important
country for us in future & we shd sow seed & strike roots now.'

Meanwhile both Sir George Buchanan, the ambassador in Petrograd,
and Colonel Knox had written to the Foreign Office to complain about
Campbell's mission. The arrangement put Knox in an 'anomalous and
very unpleasant position', as he was 'unaware' of the scope of the mission's
work, yet its members were in British uniform and subordinate to him in
rank. Campbell's methods, moreover, had been 'the reverse of tactful'. The
ambassador asserted that much of the information sent back was common knowledge and not worth the 'unnecessary expense' of maintaining
the mission. Besides, they had also provided unreliable 'political gossip'
which Buchanan himself had been obliged to refute. Faced with these
criticisms, Callwell accepted that Campbell had 'not been a success' and
would be allowed to return to Russia only in order to get the proposed
'corps of telegraphists' up and running. While all information regarding
the enemy was to be transmitted in consultation with the military attaché (with whom he was to 'work on terms of the closest co-operation')
Campbell would continue to 'work directly under the orders of "C" and
communicate through him, and would obtain from him instructions as
to the special points on which information was required'.³

Inevitably this rather Byzantine arrangement failed to work. Part of
Campbell's raison d'être was removed when the Russians decided that they
did not, after all, want the telegraphists, and in March 1915 Buchanan
complained again about Campbell's ill-defined position, noting that he
was failing to submit his telegrams through him. He proposed that the
mission be reconstituted or placed entirely under the military attaché.
This was firmly resisted by the War Office on the grounds that 'if the ambassador were to be placed in full control of the Mission (a course which
was strongly to be deprecated) it was for him to devise a practical scheme;
but', they added trenchantly, 'Secret Service was not a matter with which
amateurs could be entrusted, and in addition the fact that "C" provided

the necessary funds made it seem inadvisable that the Mission should be cut off from direct communication with him'. Understandably, the Foreign Office did not pass on these views to Petrograd, but merely offered to withdraw Campbell and his mission as a last resort, while observing that to do so would deprive the Admiralty and the War Office 'of much useful information which was conveyed to them through "C"'. They did concede, however, that the complaints about Campbell 'were not just confined to his personal bearing, which had given constant offence, but also to his indiscretion both in advertising his "secret mission" and in assuming unwarrantable authority'.[4]

In May 1915 Campbell was replaced by Major Cudbert Thornhill, an Indian Army officer, 'first class Russian scholar' and 'a good shot with rifle, catapult, shot-gun and blow-pipe'.[5] Relations improved in Petrograd. Although 'at first somewhat grudgingly accepted by Knox', as Thornhill 'confined himself strictly to his duties and proved himself a very good intelligence officer', he 'succeeded in placing the Mission on thoroughly good terms with the Embassy, and everything went perfectly smoothly'. Over the succeeding twelve months or so, however, and for reasons that are unclear, relations between Thornhill and Cumming became 'somewhat strained'. Macdonogh thought it was 'mainly owing . . . to injudicious letters written by both of them'. In any case, the continuing pressure to take over the mission, both from Knox at the embassy and from the War Office, made Thornhill's job something of a poisoned chalice. The fact that the actual work was hardly clandestine made it difficult for Cumming to defend his control over it. In February 1916, after a visit to Petrograd, General Callwell proposed (though this was not acted on) that the mission be placed under Knox. Cumming was 'much upset', but, as Walter Kirke argued, 'his man was doing no S.S. work in Russia, and was merely transmitting information from the Russian Int. Branch . . . If he worked his own agents into Germany from Russia that was another matter, but apparently he did not.' Reflecting in May 1916 on the 'stormy times' of his Bureau's Russian experience, Cumming mused that his people had been 'alternately kicked and caressed by the M.A. and Embassy'.[6]

During 1916 there was another change in personnel when Thornhill was transferred to the embassy as assistant military attaché (where he was given special responsibility for 'enemy identifications') and Sir Samuel Hoare (with the rank of lieutenant-colonel) was appointed in his place. The thirty-six-year-old Hoare came from a wealthy banking family and had been a Conservative MP since 1910. Commissioned into the Norfolk Yeomanry at the beginning of the war, following serious ill-health at the end of 1914 which prevented him going to the front, he had been languishing as a recruiting officer in Norwich. Here he started to learn Russian (he was a talented linguist) in the hope of finding work with one of the various military missions in Russia. Early in 1916 a fellow Conservative MP and former diplomat, John Baird (later Viscount Stonehaven), who was working in the Secret Service Bureau, put him in touch with Cumming, who initially engaged him to develop war trade information and also report on the general situation of the Russian mission. Hoare did this so satisfactorily that in May 1916 Cumming told him that he was to take over the mission from Thornhill. Cumming wanted him to work on a 'new branch of our business' – 'Enemy Trading' – which he conceived as more than just reporting on blockade and general economic matters, but as also involving 'questions affecting the improvement of our own trade, which would otherwise be taken by the enemy'.[7]

Cumming's formal instructions to Hoare emphasised that he was to supply information to the Admiralty and the War Office, as well as the War Trade Intelligence Department, and was also to be in charge of the Military Control Office, issuing passport visas for travel to the United Kingdom. He would be directly responsible to the Chief of the Secret Service – 'C.S.S.' – and as far as he could, 'without risk of causing annoyance to our Ally', was to 'obtain information from Russian unofficial sources, taking care that you shall never appear to be doing anything prejudicial to their interests or that could be in any way mistaken for espionage'. Privately, Cumming hoped Hoare would 'succeed in keeping on friendly terms with the M.A.' (Knox) but would 'resist attempts on anyone's part to absorb the Mission, which, as you will understand, is an integral and essential part of a complex and far-reaching system'. This was easier said than done, though for a while after Hoare took over in July 1916 things went well. 'Identifications', namely the supply from London of Western Front identifications and their distribution to the Russian General Staff and, conversely, the transmission of Russian identifications to London, were considered 'most satisfactory', and, reported Macdonogh, 'Hoare obtained for us most valuable information regarding war trade.' Hoare's own recollection of the work was that the greater part

was 'of a routine character, the signalling of suspected persons, the holding up of contraband, the transmission of [Russian] agents' reports, and
the exchange of departmental memoranda'. 'For days', however, Hoare
would wonder 'what good the office was doing, and then, unexpectedly, some piece of Intelligence would come into my hands that would
compensate me for all my previous waste of time. Now and again, I
would obtain a really important report upon the internal condition of
Germany.' He was, for example, given the confidential statistics provided
for a ministerial statement on food supply and manpower to be made in
a secret sitting of the Reichstag (parliament). 'Sometimes, also, though
not often, I obtained valuable information about the movements of the
German Fleet in the Baltic.'[8]

By the autumn of 1916, however, Knox had launched another bid to
take over all Hoare's military work and a rather arid bureaucratic argument commenced over who should have the room in the Russian War
Office. While Knox evidently coveted it, Hoare maintained that he
could not continue his work if he lost it, since the official position that it
provided gave him an important and essential status vis-à-vis the Russians.
Both men appealed to London where Macdonogh ruled in Hoare's
favour regarding the room, but laid down that Knox was to decide on
the distribution of the information produced and Thornhill was to be
liaison officer between the two teams. When in January 1917 the mission
and the embassy were required to send officers to Romania, which left
them both short-handed, Knox returned to the charge and asked that Sir
Henry Wilson, who was about to visit Russia with a high-powered Allied
mission led by Lord Milner, should be given authority during his stay to
decide on the organisation of intelligence in Russia. 'I think', remarked
Macdonogh to Wilson, 'the trouble is that we have two very difficult
people to deal with. They both have considerable ability and are accus-
tomed to be independent.'[9]

Wilson's visit gave Hoare the opportunity to report on the work of
MI1(c)'s operation in Russia. By February 1917 it had eighteen staff
(including Hoare): nine commissioned officers and nine civilians (including one female, Miss W. V. Spink). The main duties of the Military Section,
under Captain John Dymoke Scale, concerned identifications and the
distribution of military information, while the Military Control Section,
under Alley (now promoted captain), dealt with 'the control of all

passengers travelling from Russia to England or France, contre-espionage of every kind, and the co-ordination of our Secret Service with the Russian Secret Service'. Alley was also responsible for the exchange of naval intelligence, on occasions receiving from the Russian Admiralty 'information of the greatest importance as to the movements of enemy ships'. The War Trade Section worked directly under Hoare himself and handled the forwarding of statistics of all sorts and assisted with the Russian 'Black List' of blockade-breakers. This section, Hoare asserted, had 'been extremely useful both to London and Petrograd'. He claimed, for example, that a report which he had written had 'materially altered the conduct of the Blockade and . . . smoothed the trade relations between Russia and England'. Hoare concluded his report by strongly arguing that the work of both the Military Section and the intelligence mission would be seriously damaged if responsibility for the former were given to the military attaché. He stressed the interdepartmental nature of his mission, and that, whatever happened on the military side, the naval and war trade work could not be handed over. 'It will be remembered', he wrote, 'that M.I.1(c), the section under which I directly work, is the organisation into which our Secret Service has developed.' With words which might be borne in mind for the future, when Hoare himself served successively as Foreign Secretary and as British ambassador to Spain, he added that 'both as a matter of policy and a necessity of organisation, it has always been found necessary to keep the Secret Service as a unit working in harmony with, but quite independent of the staffs of Embassies and Legations'.[10]

Very few explicit records have survived of reporting from Hoare's mission, though a letter from Cumming to Hoare not long after he had arrived in Petrograd thanked him for letters he had written to Frank Stagg: 'They were extremely interesting and just what I wanted.' In December 1916 Hoare began sending 'weekly notes' on the situation in Russia. 'Personally,' he wrote presciently on Boxing Day, 'I am convinced that Russia will never fight through another winter.' Among the handful of Russian reports sent in 'by our agents abroad through "C"', which have been preserved in the SIS archives, is a transcript ('from the Speaker's own notes') of Professor Pavel Miliukov's famous speech to the Duma (parliament) on 1 November 1916 when he fiercely attacked the Prime Minister, Boris Sturmer, as incompetent and pro-German. Miliukov raised the spectre of 'dark forces fighting for Germany and attempting to destroy popular

1st January, 1917.

THE DEATH OF RASPUTIN.

In the early morning of Saturday, December 30th, there was
enacted in Petrograd one of those crimes which by their magnitude
blurr the well-defined rules of ethics and by their results change
the history of a generation.

GREGORY EPHEMICH NOVICH - for RASPUTIN, "the rake", was only
the nickname that his excesses gained him in his village - had
governed Russia since the day, four years ago, when first he
showed in the Imperial Palace in Poland, his healing powers over
the Tsarevitch.   To describe the influence that he possessed,
the scandals that surrounded his life, the tragedies that followed
in his path, is to rewrite a Dumas romance.

Three times he was within an inch of being murdered.   Once
an outraged peasant girl from his native Siberia stabbed him -
the wound did not prove fatal.   Next, the monk Heliodor seemed
to have him at his mercy in the Petrograd cell of the Metropolitan of Kieff - Rasputin's great strength and the arrival of help
saved his life.   Again, only ten months ago in a cabinet of
one of the best Petrograd restaurants - the 'Bear' - certain
officers of the Chevaliers Gardes would have killed him if his
familiars of the secret police had not appeared in time.   The
papers said nothing of these things - indeed to mention his name
brought a fine of 3000 roubles.   Day and night the secret police
were near him.   Because he withdrew them, Chvostoff, the Minister
of the Interior was dismissed.   Only from time to time the
moujik's uncontrollable appetite for debauch left him defenceless
before his enemies.   There is in Moscow a former officer of the
Guards, now relegated to the Gendarmes, who boasts that the
achievement of his career was the beating he gave Rasputin during
some wild orgie.   There are others who have seen him madly drunk
in the streets and public places.   Of one of these incidents
there is a photograph, and a photograph which is said to have
been shown to the Emperor.   True to his nickname it was at an
orgie that Rasputin met his death.

*The first page of Samuel Hoare's dramatic account of the death of
Rasputin. Because of its sensational nature, he admitted to writing
it in 'the style of the "Daily Mail"'.*

unity', accused Sturmer of being in collusion with the influential monk Rasputin and concluded with a sharp series of criticisms, asking each time, 'is this stupidity or treachery?'. The notorious Rasputin, who was widely believed to exercise evil political influence over the Empress Alexandra, was murdered in the early morning of Saturday 30 December. On New Year's Eve Hoare cabled Cumming, who was the first person to get the news confirmed in London. On 2 January 1917 Hoare despatched a ten-page report of the event to Freddie Browning, which he suggested Cumming might show to the King, George V. It was, he wrote, 'one of those crimes which by their magnitude blur the well-defined rules of ethics and by their results change the history of a generation'. 'If it is written in the style of the "Daily Mail",' he told Browning, 'my answer is that the whole question is so sensational that one cannot describe it as one would if it were an ordinary episode of the war.'[11]

The Milner Mission had been sent out to assess the situation in Russia and bolster up its war effort, especially in order to tie down German forces on the Eastern Front. But by the start of 1917 the Russian state was so enfeebled and the political and military leadership so apparently out of touch with popular opinion that little could be done to save the imperial regime. According to his memoirs, Hoare sought to persuade Milner of 'the gravity of the internal crisis through which Russia was passing' and, indeed, Milner returned to England with very gloomy predictions about the future of the country. On the military side, Wilson, unwisely attaching 'more weight to Knox's opinion on any matter affecting the Russian Army' than he did to the opinion 'of any other man in Russia', reported mistakenly on the essential 'soundness' of the Russian army. But Milner was better informed than Wilson (or Knox). The Russian imperial monarchy was swept away in the February Revolution of 1917 and replaced by a social democratic government under Prince Lvov, who was succeeded in May by the socialist Alexander Kerensky. At first there were hopes in the West that a more constitutional regime, promising democratic reform, might actually strengthen the Russian war effort. Reporting from London (where he had returned on sick leave) in late March 1917 on 'Secret Service in Russia', Hoare asserted that 'no doubt one of the first actions of the new Government will be to sweep away the whole system of innumerable separate agencies and concentrate the attention of the Secret Service upon obtaining enemy information'. Each of the new ministers running relevant departments was 'a strong Anglophile' and there was 'now for the first time a chance of close and effective co-operation between the British Secret Service and the Intelligence organisations of Russia'.[12]

This was over-optimistic. Russian revolutionary forces were being strengthened, as confirmed by reports circulated through MI1(c). In April a cable reported that the principal figure at a series of émigré meetings in New York had been 'Leon Trotzki', a 'pretended Russian socialist who, it is believed, is in reality a German' (here 'No' was written in the margin). He was reported as advocating the overthrow of the new government in Russia and 'the starting of revolutions in England and Germany'. Trotsky 'and various other socialists' had left New York for Russia on 27 March. Trotsky was interned at Halifax, Nova Scotia, for a month, apparently on orders from the Naval Intelligence Division in London, but was allowed to proceed early in May.[13] At almost exactly the same time agent 'SW5' reported from Berne that '40 Russian revolutionaries, fanatical followers of Lenin, including Lenin himself, [had] left for Russia via Germany' – this was the famous 'sealed train' which conveyed the Bolshevik leader to Petrograd. Permission to travel had been granted by the German government only after receiving Lenin's personal guarantee 'that every one of his 40 followers' favoured 'an immediate peace'. SW5 argued, however, that the members of Lenin's party were 'in the minority among the Russians in Switzerland', and that their beliefs were 'held to be of a fanatical and narrow-minded nature. My own view is that these people would be absolutely harmless if, which unfortunately is not the case, other Russians had been allowed to return.' He considered it 'highly expedient' that visas should immediately be given to 'followers of the patriotic Russian revolutionary movement to visit Russia via France and England'. It must, he declared, 'at all costs be avoided' that Lenin's group 'be allowed to represent the opinions of those Russians living in Switzerland, who on account of their so-called martyrdom and exile have attained a certain prestige in this country'. They had, he added, been sought out by enemy spies 'to play the game of Germany'.

Neither Lenin nor Trotsky was a German agent, and they 'played the game of Germany' only in so far as they wished to take Russia out of what they thought was a costly and unnecessary war. As Russia staggered from political crisis to political crisis during 1917, and disaffection began to spread through its armed forces, the Allied governments (joined by the United States when it declared war on Germany on 6 April 1917) strove to keep Russia in the war. One part of this effort involved an intelligence operation initiated by Cumming's representative in the United States, Sir William Wiseman.

Secret service in the USA

There is very little evidence indeed about the early work of the Secret Service Bureau in the United States. Before the war British intelligence activities in North America had been confined to sporadic operations run by the Home Office, the Irish Office and the India Office, targeting Irish

Crowther Smith's caricature of Sir William Wiseman, Cumming's influential representative in the USA, 1916–18.

and Indian revolutionaries based in emigrant communities across the country.[14] The first mention of United States work in Cumming's diary was in March 1915 when he interviewed an agent to 'act as N.Y. correspondent'. In July a 'new agent' was despatched to New York, and a note about the processing of telegrams sent from America, which mentioned a well-known firm of United States bankers and information of interest to the Director of Army Contracts, suggests that the main priority was blockade and commercial intelligence. Supporting this was the suggestion the following month that an organisation might be based in two Canadian banks and an international accountancy firm with 'many agencies in USA, all Scotch'. Confirming that there were also security and counter-intelligence interests in the United States, Kell proposed on 5 August 'a scheme for a Bureau in N.Y. to be run jointly'.

On 15 September Cumming engaged the thirty-year-old Captain Sir William Wiseman, who was to become one of the most significant British intelligence officers during the First World War. Wiseman was a baronet – a title first awarded to an ancestor in 1628, to which he had succeeded in 1893. He was educated at Winchester College and Jesus College, Cambridge (where he won a boxing Blue for representing the university against Oxford), though he left without taking a degree. He then worked first as a journalist and later as a businessman in Mexico and Canada. At the beginning of the war he returned to England to join the army, but was incapacitated for further active service after being gassed and temporarily blinded near Ypres in July 1915. Later that year, seeking employment in the War Office, he ran into Cumming, who had served alongside his father in the Royal Navy. 'Willie' Wiseman evidently impressed sufficiently to be taken on 'for general work'. By the end of September, Cumming had earmarked Wiseman and an older man to be his representatives in North America. He brought them both round to be briefed in the Admiralty and War Office and on 20 October 1915 the two men departed for New York. It seems that Wiseman's forty-four-year-old colleague, who was promised an allowance of £500 a year and for whom Cumming arranged a diplomatic passport, was to be the senior partner of the two. Since Cumming had initially taken the older man to see Blinker Hall at the Admiralty (and had only afterwards taken Wiseman too), it is most likely that his primary duty was naval intelligence concerning the security of war supplies from east-coast United States ports.[15]

Following their arrival in New York on 28 October, however, Cumming's men encountered a familiar problem of co-ordination with the Admiralty's existing information-gathering arrangements. Captain Guy Gaunt, British naval attaché to the United States since January 1914, had already established a network of agents to collect intelligence in North America and also to counter enemy activities such as sabotage and propaganda. Although his diplomatic status made this work potentially very problematic with the American authorities, Gaunt felt he had matters well in hand and clearly objected to Wiseman and his companion muscling in on his territory. Wiseman remained in New York for less than three weeks. His colleague stayed on for another month before returning to London. There Hall decided that he was not now needed in New York and Cumming redeployed him for counter-espionage work in the Eastern Mediterranean. Wiseman, however, was retained to head Cumming's North American organisation, along with a newly recruited assistant, Captain Norman Thwaites. Thwaites (who had been wounded and invalided out of active service at the front) had worked before the war as a journalist in the United States, and not only spoke fluent German but, having been private secretary to the newspaper publisher Joseph Pulitzer for ten years, was also very well connected in American press and political circles. From January 1916 the two men established themselves in New York, ostensibly as part of the Transport Department of the Ministry of Munitions, where Thwaites took on Military Control duties.

While the USA remained neutral, Wiseman and his colleagues managed to keep their work largely hidden from the authorities, though they liaised with American officers on an individual basis, including Thwaites's friend Captain Thomas J. Tunney, head of the New York Police Department bomb squad. Tunney came from Irish Protestant stock and had a brother in the Royal Irish Constabulary. Items of information were passed to the Americans through the head of the Canadian Government Police, Colonel Percy Sherwood. Wiseman remained in charge of MI1(c)'s operations in North America for the rest of the war, and, reflecting the semi-public roles which some of Cumming's other wartime representatives enjoyed, his position became progressively less clandestine. When he first landed in October 1915, he described himself to the United States immigration authorities as a 'merchant'. In January 1916 he had become a 'soldier', and in November a 'courier'. In November 1917, by which time the USA had entered the war, he arrived (with, among others, the economist John Maynard Keynes) in New York as part of Lord Reading's high-level mission to the United States, sent to reinforce the relationship between the wartime allies. By now he was 'on official business to U.S. government'. Thwaites (who had described himself as an 'author' in January 1916), also travelled with the Reading Mission, and by then was openly 'on Captain Wiseman's staff'.[16]

Wiseman's instructions from Cumming were to concentrate on 'Contre-Espionage', including 'the investigation of suspects about whom the authorities at home required information', 'a general watch on the Irish movement in the United States' and 'investigation into Hindu Sedition in America'. Once established in New York, he was also given some propaganda work, and Wiseman found that his office 'soon became a general information bureau for all Britishers', called on to serve the needs of the embassy, consulates and other British missions. Work on Indian seditionists was shared with the India Office, whose representative Sir Robert Nathan was based in Vancouver from May 1916. In the summer of 1916 Wiseman's office was strengthened by the addition of a naval officer, Lieutenant Henry Fitzroy, as Permit Officer (who carried out the Military Control work), though his arrival was followed by a dispute over whether he was responsible to Captain Gaunt, the consul-general in New York, or Wiseman. In the event Fitzroy's 'unfortunate manner' in dealing with Americans led to his being recalled. Wiseman held on to the Military Control work. Before Fitzroy went, however, he had managed to extend the surveillance of passenger traffic through New York by roping in 'every would-be traveller who desired to go to South American ports . . . even when a British visa was not absolutely necessary'. In October 1916 Cumming noted eight 'staff and agents' in New York. By January 1918 MI1(c) had ten regular officers, plus an office staff, as well as a 'Western Organization' of ten full-time and some part-time agents (of whom two were German), the entire operation costing $8,816 ($121,400 in current prices) a month.[17]

Cumming's organisation in the USA had some successes. In the spring of 1916 information from an agent helped thwart a German plan to sabotage the important Welland Canal in Ontario, and Thwaites headed investigations leading to the discovery of a bomb factory in New

York harbour set up by the German saboteur Franz von Kleist Rintelen. Wiseman was able to help Robert Nathan cripple an émigré Indian seditionist organisation, the Ghadr ('revolt') Party, operating on the west coast of the United States. Supported by locally based German agents, the conspirators planned to send a ship loaded with arms to India to foment rebellion. But, with information supplied by Nathan and others, the authorities rounded up and tried nearly a hundred individuals in San Francisco between November 1917 and July 1918. With his press contacts and experience Norman Thwaites was able to do much on the propaganda side. One unusual coup occurred after he and Wiseman had been entertained to dinner by an anglophile millionaire industrialist, Oscar Lewisohn, at his Long Island mansion. During the evening their host passed round some holiday photographs in one of which Thwaites recognised the German ambassador Count Johann von Bernsdorff in a swimming costume with his arms round two similarly dressed young women, neither of whom was his wife. Without Lewisohn's knowledge Thwaites managed to extract the picture, get it copied and then have it distributed to the press where it appeared, much to Bernsdorff's embarrassment.[18]

Wiseman's greatest achievement lay in the access and influence he was able to secure at the very highest levels of the United States administration, making him the most successful 'agent of influence' in the first forty years of SIS. Thwaites provided a link to an old friend, Frank Polk, who was appointed Counselor to Secretary of State Robert Lansing in 1915 and was effectively the second-in-command in the State Department. Polk became responsible for intelligence matters, supervising the counter-espionage work of various departments and co-ordinating the activities of United States agencies involved in gathering intelligence from foreign sources. But a more important contact was Colonel Edward House, President Woodrow Wilson's confidant and principal adviser, who was the focus of constant attention from those who wished to communicate with the President.[19]

Wiseman's first meeting with House occurred quite fortuitously when in December 1916 the British ambassador, Sir Cecil Spring Rice, employed him to deliver a message to the colonel. Wiseman made an immediate and extremely favourable impression. House thought him 'the most imp[ortan]t caller I have had for some time' and the two men met frequently thereafter. Sir William's arrival on the scene came at a time when Wilson and House had been losing confidence in the ailing Spring Rice, whose Republican political attitudes and unsympathetic manner had alienated them. On 6 December there was also a change of government in London, when David Lloyd George replaced Herbert Asquith as Prime Minister. Sir Edward Grey, Foreign Secretary in Asquith's government, and with whom House had regularly communicated directly, was left out of the new Cabinet; thus House had lost his high-level entrée into the British administration and was perhaps especially susceptible to the possibilities of close communication being re-established through Wiseman. Sir William so charmed and impressed House that the latter thought Britain would be 'far better' represented by him than by Spring Rice. Enticingly, Wiseman told House 'in the gravest confidence' that he was 'in direct communication with the Foreign Office', and that neither the ambassador nor other members of the embassy were aware of it. This was, in fact, only half true. While Wiseman certainly had independent communications with London which the embassy knew nothing about, the principal line he had to the Foreign Office was through Cumming at MI1(c). House was not to know this, and, evidently won over by both Wiseman's discretion and his apparently privileged position, told President Wilson he judged that Wiseman 'reflects the views of his government'.[20]

Wiseman was well aware that in assuming a position as intermediary between the American and British governments he was moving beyond a mere intelligence role. According to Arthur Willert, American correspondent of *The Times*, Wiseman told London in January 1917 that he was taking 'a more active interest in politics than he would ordinarily have considered his duty because the Ambassador and his staff have practically all their friends among the leaders of the Republican Party'. This had 'produced an unfortunate situation' in that President Wilson's administration had 'come to regard the British officials as Republican partisans'. Yet, once Spring Rice became aware of Wiseman's newly privileged position, he sought to exploit the information-gathering possibilities and asked Wiseman to let him know 'at once any political information which you may receive or give in order that I may check it against other information'.[21]

The crucial subject about which the British were interested, of course, was that of the United States entering the war. Both British overt and covert publicity and propaganda efforts were focused on marshalling American political and public opinion behind the Allies, while a whole range of information-gathering resources – again, both overt and covert – was devoted to ascertaining the views of policy-makers and opinion-formers in Washington and elsewhere. Cumming's organisation played its part, as did Room 40, the Admiralty's signals intelligence department, which by 1916 was successfully deciphering American diplomatic telegrams as well as enemy ones. Maurice Hankey, Secretary to the Committee of Imperial Defence, described information from Berlin–Washington traffic as 'priceless'. British intelligence expertise underpinned the dissemination of the famous Zimmermann Telegram of 16 January 1917, in which the German Foreign Minister, Arthur Zimmermann, informed his ambassador in Mexico that Germany intended to begin unrestricted submarine warfare on 1 February. If as a result of this the USA ceased to be neutral, Germany offered the Mexican government an alliance, a joint declaration of war on the USA and help for Mexico to recover the states of Texas, New Mexico and Arizona, which it had lost in the mid-nineteenth century. Aware that their cable communications were vulnerable to attack, the German Foreign Ministry had arranged with the American embassy in Berlin to send telegrams on their behalf, but since these cables passed through British territory they, too, were intercepted for Room 40 to decrypt. So it was with the Zimmermann telegram. Admiralty Intelligence, indeed, had a partial decode of it even before the original had reached its intended recipient in Mexico City. The British (naturally suppressing the fact that they had acquired the telegram by intercepting American diplomatic communications) provided Washington with a copy, which was subsequently released to the press. The German decision to extend submarine warfare (which put American ships in the front line) had already caused Washington to break off diplomatic relations on 3 February, and the publication of the telegram on 1 March gave a further powerful boost to anti-German feeling in the USA.[22]

At this crucial juncture Wiseman played a central role in providing an insight into both presidential and public opinion in the USA. In time for an Imperial War Conference scheduled to be held in London at the end of March, Wiseman and House together prepared a memorandum on American attitudes towards Britain and the war. House told Wiseman 'that the President had read it and thought it a just statement', though in forwarding it for transmission to London Wiseman warned Spring Rice that it was not an official American document. While the paper conceded that Americans were 'beginning to realise that it may not be possible for them to remain at peace with Germany', it noted that the mass of the people were not particularly pro-British or pro-Ally. Americans, for example, were deeply concerned about British policy in Ireland (where the 1916 Easter Rising had been sharply suppressed and its leaders court-martialled and executed) and British blockade policies were widely resented. There was, wrote Wiseman and House, 'a feeling among the Americans that if they tolerate too much they will lose their prestige and authority as a world power'. Thus any decision to enter the conflict would be based on considerations of America's own national interest: 'If the United States goes to war with Germany – which she probably will – it will be to uphold American rights and assert her dignity as a nation.'[23]

This remarkable document, jointly drafted by the British intelligence chief in North America and President Wilson's closest confidential adviser, and validated by the President of the United States himself, encapsulates the high quality of Wiseman's influence and political reporting, which continued after the USA declared war on Germany on 6 April 1917, and which from late 1917 was channelled through the Political Section V at Cumming's Head Office in London. Wiseman's friendship with House brought him unprecedented (for a Briton) access to the President – they met regularly and he spent a week's vacation with him and the colonel in August 1918. Over the last nineteen months of the war Wiseman played a pivotal role in articulating American views on such matters as war finance, representation in Allied organisations, the deployment of troops in the battle zone, policy towards Russia and the plans for peace. In this he did much to assist the development of Allied co-operation in 1917–18. W. B. Fowler, historian of the Anglo-American wartime partnership, places Wiseman in the 'front rank', giving him much of the credit for helping keep in check many of the inevitable animosities and conflicts which threatened to upset relations between these two powerful, ambitious and competitive Great Powers, whose essential national interests would never wholly coincide, no matter how close their relationship was claimed to be.[24]

Whatever their long-term potential differences might have been, during 1917 both states wanted to keep the Russians in the war. On 7 April

1917, the British Foreign Secretary, Arthur Balfour, worrying that 'revolutionary pacifists' were becoming dangerously influential in Russia, cabled Spring Rice to organise, as a matter of the 'highest importance', the despatch of 'messages from labour leaders, from Russian Americans, and from prominent men in the U.S. emphasising necessity of continuing the war in order to secure triumph of principles of freedom and democracy'.[25] Given the task of implementing this, Wiseman organised some appeals to be sent, but there is no evidence that they had the slightest effect in Russia. In order to counter the impact of allegedly pro-German returning exiles – Leon Trotsky, for example – Wiseman also proposed an ambitious plan to send to Russia parties of pro-Ally émigrés – Czech, Slovak and Polish, as well as Russian – who had 'made good' in America, to be 'lecturers and propagandists'. They would 'carry with them details of the German intrigues in America and warn their Russian comrades against similar traps'. They would emphasise 'the necessity for the two great republics working together for the freedom of the World', and 'persuade the Russians to attack the Germans with all their might, and thus accomplish the overthrow of the Hohenzollern dynasty and autocracy in Berlin'. Wiseman argued that the operation 'has to be entirely unofficial, and very secretly organised, as any idea of Government support would ruin the scheme'. It was, in fact, precisely the kind of deniable operation for which the Secret Service was ideally suited.

Wiseman put the plan to both Colonel House and the Foreign Office in London. Having indicated to House that the scheme was based on reliable British intelligence from within Russia, and to London that he was working on information gathered by the United States government, Wiseman got both sides to agree. While approving the plan, Balfour's private secretary, Sir Eric Drummond, indicated that London would prefer the Americans to run it on their own, but Wiseman told him that the Americans had no means of dealing with the émigré groups upon which the scheme depended, except through himself. Besides, there was a glittering intelligence prize to be won. 'It is possible', cabled Wiseman, 'that by acting practically as a confidential agent for the United States Government I might strengthen the understanding with House so that in future he will keep us informed of steps taken by the United States Government in their foreign affairs, which would ordinarily not be a matter of common knowledge to the Governments of the two countries.'[26]

Wiseman got London and Washington each to allocate $75,000 (approximately $1.2 million in modern prices) to his scheme and recruited the British author Somerset Maugham (to whom he was related by marriage) to go to Russia.

Maugham, who had gained intelligence experience in Switzerland in 1915–16, spoke Russian and could use his existing good cover as a writer and journalist. Although he afterwards wrote that his instructions were 'to get in touch with parties hostile to the government and devise a scheme that would keep Russia in the war and prevent the Bolsheviks, supported by the Central Powers, from seizing power', the surviving evidence suggests something slightly less ambitious. A review of Maugham's mission after it had finished said that it had been part of a broad plan 'to start an Intelligence and Propaganda service in Russia'. The intelligence side was to expose 'German political intrigues', and Maugham was to help supply material for propaganda purposes. Wiseman's agents were also to 'ascertain whether it was possible to support the more responsible elements in Russia. No attempt was to be made to support any reactionary movement, but it was thought it might be possible, to some extent, to "guide the storm".' Given the parlous internal condition of Russia, even this was over-sanguine. Supplied with $21,000 (approximately $350,000 today) for expenses and travelling from the west coast of the United States, through Japan and Vladivostok, Maugham reached Petrograd in early September 1917.[27]

While the ambassador, Sir George Buchanan, was informed of his presence (though not his precise mission), Maugham made no formal contact with Cumming's remaining personnel in Russia. Accompanied by Emanuel Voska, a Czech émigré leader long resident in the USA, he contacted Tomáš Masaryk in the hope of mobilising Czech and Slovak elements in Russia to work for the Allied cause. Using the cover-name 'Somerville' for Maugham, Wiseman supplied the State Department with his reports, which have been credited with providing the best political intelligence the Americans had about Russia at the time. They were, for example, among the very few accurately to assess the weakness of Alexander Kerensky's administration and the strength of the Bolshevik movement, as well as indicating the possibilities of mobilising Polish and other nationalists against Germany. Having reported in late September that Kerensky's government was losing support and would probably not last very much longer, Maugham secured an interview with Kerensky himself on 30 October in which the Russian asked him to tell Lloyd George that with Germany offering peace and the winter coming on he did not think his government could continue. By the time Maugham's report of this interview reached the Foreign Office on 18 November, Kerensky had indeed been toppled and Maugham summoned back to London.[28] The Bolsheviks seized power on 7 November. Because Russia was still using the old Julian calendar, which was thirteen days behind the West, it was frequently called the 'October Revolution'. They immediately sued for peace. After a ceasefire was agreed on 16 December, peace talks led to the harsh Treaty of Brest-Litovsk on 3 March 1918, by which the Russian government had to give up control over former imperial territories in Poland, Finland, Latvia, Lithuania and Estonia.

These developments vitiated Wiseman's scheme and Maugham (who suffered ill-health) never returned to Russia, though his suggestion that secret subsidies should be paid to national self-determination groups within Russia, including Cossacks, was one which intermittently attracted successive decision-makers in both London and Washington. Wiseman remained close to Colonel House and President Wilson, though the growing formalisation of Anglo-American relations affected his situation. General Macdonogh's insistence that intelligence liaison with Allied states should be through orthodox military channels undermined Wiseman's position as part of Cumming's organisation and reinforced Vernon Kell's desire to establish a Military Control Office in the USA under direct MI5 control. Wiseman told Cumming in December 1917 that he wanted to continue as his representative 'for S.S. & Political work'. Presumably alluding to the Somerset Maugham operation in Russia, he said that part of the 'S.I.' (secret intelligence) work could be handed over to the Americans, with the rest under Major Thwaites, who should also be appointed Military Control Officer and made responsible to the military attaché. In March 1918 Thwaites became head of the MI5 office in New York while remaining part of Cumming's organisation. But the loss of counter-intelligence work to MI5 (which the Director of Military Intelligence specifically ordered) left Cumming 'very much hurt'. Charles Ascherson at Head Office in London told Wiseman that he 'certainly sympathize[d] with him, as it does seem rough that, after his organization has built up the business and carried it on so satisfactorily for over two years, it should now be taken away from him bodily and I think he feels it very much'.[29]

Lloyd George, meanwhile, had appointed Wiseman 'liaison officer between the War Cabinet and any special representative they might send out to represent them in the United States'. Colonel House understood that Wiseman was 'now acting as liaison officer between me personally and the British Government'. Lloyd George was rather inclined to seek policy advice and assistance outside the 'usual channels' and this development did not go down very well among established civil servants. When Wiseman asked Cumming for copies of MI1(c)'s political reports 'for Col. H.', the answer from Ronald Campbell in the Foreign Office was a blunt 'No'. Cumming, too, thought that passing raw secret service papers 'to show to Colonel H. for the P[resident]' was 'far too dangerous'. Lord Reading, who replaced Spring Rice as ambassador in January 1918, nevertheless regularly used Wiseman for liaison with the Americans. On a trip back to London in April 1918, Sir William told Cumming 'many interesting things about his work in America, especially his personal relations with the President, Lord Reading & Col. H.'. For the rest of the war, while retaining some secret service responsibilities, Wiseman's time was mostly taken up with liaison duties. In October 1918 he returned to Europe, leaving Thwaites in charge in New York. During the Paris Peace Conference he served as A. J. Balfour's special adviser on Anglo-American affairs, and in March 1919 he provided General Marlborough Churchill, the Chief of United States Military Intelligence, with a personal introduction to Cumming. But with President Wilson and Colonel House in Paris, too, and able to deal directly with their Allied counterparts, Wiseman's usefulness as a go-between declined sharply, and although they occasionally met during the spring of 1919, he appears to have left Cumming's organisation by the end of May.[30]

The Mediterranean and beyond

Since the late eighteenth century Britain's interests in the Mediterranean and Middle East had been reinforced by its imperial presence in India. A paramount requirement was to prevent any other Great Power – particularly France or Russia – from dominating the region and threatening to interrupt imperial communications with the East, especially after the opening of the Suez Canal in 1877. Agreements with France and Russia in the early twentieth century had eased the problem, but, from the early 1900s, increasing German involvement in the Ottoman Turkish empire, which stretched to Persia (Iran) in the east, included the Arabian lands of Syria, Lebanon and the Arabian peninsula, and even technically encompassed Egypt, raised new fears for Britain's regional security. From at least 1912 (and through to the end of the war) Secret Service funds had been used by the Foreign Office to purchase a major shareholding in the Constantinople Quays Company, aiming to give the British government covert commercial influence in Turkey.[31] Further south, Britain had in practice controlled Egypt since the 1880s, and a series of 'fortress colonies' – such as Gibraltar, Malta and Aden – secured its position, but with the outbreak of war in August 1914 nothing could be taken for granted. At the end of October Turkey entered the war on the side of the Central Powers. Britain responded by imposing a protectorate on Egypt, which rapidly became an important military base and remained so for the rest of the war, and by sending troops to Mesopotamia (now Iraq), which turned into a major theatre of operations. Italy, which had been a member of the Triple Alliance with Germany and Austria-Hungary since 1882, was also a concern. Although it declared neutrality on the outbreak of the war, and appeared thereafter to be leaning more towards the Allies, German diplomatic overtures meant that its support could not necessarily be relied on.

The first indication that Cumming was developing work against Turkey comes at the end of 1914. On 29 December, his deputy, Captain Laycock, interviewed an Englishman formerly resident in Constantinople (Istanbul) and on New Year's Eve there was a flurry of activity relating to a new organisation in the Aegean Sea at the entrance to the strategically important Dardanelles. Deposits of five and eight thousand francs respectively were arranged for banks in Corfu and Salonika. Supplies were to be sent to an island off the Turkish coast near Smyrna (İzmir), and a Libyan from Tripoli was earmarked to go to Constantinople itself to make contacts there. During January 1915 Cumming was instructed by Blinker Hall at the Admiralty to provide back-up for a scheme (proposed by Maurice Hankey) to bribe Turkey out of the war. Hall, typically without referring to any higher authority, authorised that up to four million pounds be offered to the Turks, selecting Edwin Whittall and George

Griffin Eady to negotiate with the Turks. Whittall came from a family long resident in the Near East and Eady was a civil engineer who had been engaged in railway construction in Turkey before the war. Cumming provided funds and administrative support and arranged secure communications to Dedeagach (Alexandroupolis) in north-eastern Greece near the Turkish frontier. Whittall, however, told Cumming in January that the project was a 'forlorn hope', and so it turned out. Whatever prospects there might have been were swept away by the Allied naval bombardments launched in February 1915 on Gallipoli which it was hoped would force the Dardanelles and open the way to Constantinople. When Eady returned in April he reported to Cumming that 'the day he opened nego[tiatio]ns we bombarded Dardanelles. The day his man landed at Smyrna we bombarded it! Money no use.' Eady thought that he might be able to get an agreement if Constantinople was 'internationalised – ie left in nominal Turkish possession under international control', but the landings at Gallipoli on 25 April and the subsequent fierce campaign, which lasted until the ignominious Allied withdrawal in January 1916, destroyed any hope of a negotiated agreement.[32]

The Turkish venture illustrates the extent to which, at this stage of the war (and evidently so far as Hall was concerned), Cumming's main function appears simply to have been to provide operational support. This is further illustrated by a scheme mounted in the spring of 1915 to track German efforts to supply submarines. On 22 February Hall showed Cumming a signal 'stating that a vessel known to be in the Balearics may be supplying Tr [German] Subs'. Cumming acquired the 1,300-ton yacht *Beryl* to investigate this and it set off on a cruise from San Sebastián in north-west Spain, along the Iberian coast and to the Balearic Islands in the Mediterranean, before reaching Barcelona. Cumming lent the yacht's skipper, Captain Cullen, his 'telephoto camera in two cases', a 'Battery of Lenses' and 'two pairs Zeiss glasses' and 'promised him [a] Ross telescope'. When Hall told Cumming that he was in search of some tugs, Cumming organised their purchase. In April 1915 Cumming sent the keen yachtsman Shelley Scarlett (Lord Abinger) and his yacht *St George* to Gibraltar to work with the *Beryl*. Before he went Scarlett was provided with a code, a safe and a pair of Zeiss glasses. No evidence has survived in the SIS archive of what intelligence (if any) these ventures may have produced. Intelligence-gathering efforts in other parts of the Mediterranean are indicated by Cumming's diary notes of individuals being despatched from London. On 9 March 1915, Colonel Callwell 'approved idea of sending a good man to Genoa'. In May Hall introduced Cumming to a husband-and-wife team, who within four days had been taken on for some unspecified purpose 'at 400 [pounds] between them' and had departed for Venice. In July they returned, called on Cumming and 'were dismissed with thanks'.

Italy came into the war in stages. Following the Treaty of London in April 1915, when the Allies offered substantial military and financial aid and granted Italian claims to territory in the South Tyrol, along the Adriatic coast, in North Africa and western Turkey, Italy declared war on Austria-Hungary (23 May) and Turkey (20 August), though it did not go to war against Germany until 28 August 1916. Allied intelligence co-operation in the Mediterranean (mostly relating to counterespionage) was explored at an Anglo-French–Italian conference attended by Cumming in Malta in early March 1916. Afterwards it was reported that 'our several Intelligence Bureaux are now very much clearer about their share of the special work discussed, and a much closer co-operation with the Italians will result'. Liaison between the British and the French 'was already close', and Captain Smith-Cumming had 'been able to get into much closer contact with the allied work in the Mediterranean generally and its special needs'.[33]

From June 1916 a formal intelligence mission was established in Italy in which Kell's organisation had an interest. In July 1917, Sir Samuel Hoare, who had done a similar job in Russia, was appointed by Cumming to head 'the Special Intelligence Section of the British Mission with the Italian General Staff', an appointment representing both MI1(c) and Vernon Kell's MI5. Put in charge of offices at Rome, Milan and Genoa, Hoare was to 'maintain close touch with the Information Branch of the Italian General Staff' and 'co-operate closely with the head of the "Field Intelligence Section" of the British Mission' (responsible for operational military information). Hoare did not at first run any agents, though he did report on political matters. In December 1917 Macdonogh in London approved Hoare's proposal to obtain political information through *The Times*'s correspondent, 'as it is of course his proper business'. Hoare also dabbled in what became known as 'special operations', telling Macdonogh in January 1918 that he had given £100 to help fund a 'big

pro-war demonstration' being organised to coincide with the opening of
the Italian parliament. By this stage Hoare and his colleagues were reporting directly to the Directorate of Military Intelligence in the War Office
and Cumming had been cut out of the work altogether. In March 1918,
indeed, Cumming had met the Italian head of Naval Intelligence and had
'had to admit with some shame that I had now no organisation in Italy'.[34]

Reviewing his work overall in August 1918, he noted that the 'Italian
Military Intelligence service, upon which we have had to depend, is from
the point of view of personnel and influence entirely inadequate'. Rivalries
between different Italian agencies, moreover, gravely handicapped security and counter-espionage work. From the spring of 1918 officers in
Hoare's mission began exploring the possibility of sending agents into
Austria and Turkey. Liaison was established with Czechoslovak elements
who already had train-watching agents in enemy territory. It was also
hoped to recruit 'Southern Slavs', such as Istrians, Croats and Dalmatians,
though their employment raised difficulties with the Italians, who heartily distrusted them. 'None the less,' wrote Hoare, 'it is hoped in course of
time to develop a Jugo-Slav service for Croatia and Dalmatia.' Writing as
he was just three months before the unexpectedly rapid end of the war,
however, it is unlikely that Hoare's team were able to make much progress
on this front.[35]

Cumming's most extensive commitments in the Mediterranean region focused on Greece and Turkey. Concerned about information from
'Asia', in January 1915 Callwell told Cumming that he was 'starting an
organisation in Athens'. It would have to be squared with the British army
commander in Egypt, but Cumming noted that Callwell would 'hand his
people over to me when organised'. Callwell agreed that Cumming should
send out Major Rhys Samson (hitherto working on liaison duties with
the French) to set up a joint espionage and counter-espionage operation
in Athens. From February 1915 Samson, with cover as assistant military
attaché, started to work on gathering Turkish military information. Two
fellow countrymen, who had lived in the region before the war, were engaged. Using a humanitarian relief agency as cover, they began recruiting
agents, mainly Asiatic Greeks, to work in Turkey itself. One example of
their work has survived: an eight-page report from Keşan in European
Turkey, on one of the main supply routes to the Gallipoli peninsula, dated
13 May, sent on by Athens on 24 May and received in London on 4 June

1915. The report noted the movement of Turkish reinforcements (some under German command) to Gallipoli and described how 'the moral[e] of all the troops is gone'. One German officer, it alleged, 'shot thirteen Turkish officers during the recent fighting'. There were shortages of food and military supplies. The report asserted that the region around Keşan close to the Turco-Greek frontier could be captured by '10,000 soldiers': 'All the Christians and Pomaks (Bulgarian speaking Moslems) would flock to the Allies' colours.' Christians in the Turkish forces had been disarmed and 'were employed in digging trenches, doing spade-work, etc', but 'would do good work as guides and soldiers. All the local Christians ask is 24 hours' grace to pay off old scores on the Moslem population.'

A despatch from Athens on 17 July with 'Extracts from Dedeagatch letter of 8th July 1915' contained reports from agents numbers '2', '4' and '5', again reporting low morale: 'The Turks were much dispirited as a result of the last battle on the peninsula. They expect to be driven out of their positions at the next attack.' A Greek who had visited Chanak (Çanakkale) on the Asian shore reported that there were wounded 'everywhere'. There were reports of Turkish officers deserting and 'at Uzun Keupri [Uzunköprü, north of Keşan] 24 Turkish officers and soldiers were killed by four German officers for desertion. Comrades of the Turks killed the four German officers.' A third report from Athens, on 16 September, said that, because of chronic shortages of ammunition, 'a sustained attack by the Allies' was 'the thing which is most dreaded by the Turkish general staff'. The Greek minister at Constantinople had learned 'that if continuous pressure was brought to bear by the Allies, the Turks could not last a month'. These three reports were each circulated only to the Admiralty Director of Intelligence and Colonel French in the War Office. There is no indication of what influence they may have had on decision-making, though they corroborate the over-optimism which permeated the early days of the Gallipoli campaign, and the widely held assumption that the Turks would not put up stiff resistance. The first two reports, indeed, may have contributed to the decision to launch a new assault at Suvla Bay during the first week of August, but by the time of the third report that offensive had petered out into a costly stalemate.

Espionage was also run from Mytilene on the island of Lesbos where the main agent, Clifford Heathcote-Smith, a Briton long resident in the region, had over a period of eighteen months in 1915–16 produced results which the General Officer Commanding in Egypt, Sir Archibald Murray, described as 'exceptionally valuable'. The reports submitted included a plan of the Smyrna batteries and defences upon which the Royal Navy had largely based their bombardments in February 1916; early information concerning the Turks' second campaign against Egypt (1916), which had easily been repulsed, and the despatch of Turkish troops to the Galician front; daily statistics of troop trains and the transport of munitions from Constantinople into Asia Minor; and the distribution of Turkish divisions throughout the Ottoman empire. 'It is beyond discussion', wrote Heathcote-Smith in January 1917, that his agent 'at daily and ever-present personal risk has rendered Great Britain and the Allies service of very real worth – that incidentally may have saved us many lives'.

By the late summer of 1915, Samson's organisation, by now known as the Bureau of Military Information, was also focusing on economic and blockade intelligence, and had begun to take on some counter-espionage work, to investigate both German political intrigues in Greece and arrangements for the supply of enemy submarines operating in the Eastern Mediterranean. Towards the end of 1915 Captain Compton Mackenzie, who had been serving as an intelligence officer at Gallipoli, was sent on sick leave to Athens and ended up being seconded to work under Samson. The thirty-two-year-old Mackenzie was already a well-known novelist who over the next two years brought a creative writer's sensibility to his duties in Cumming's Bureau. After the war he wrote entertainingly about his intelligence experiences in three volumes of memoirs, *First Athenian Memories*, *Greek Memories* and *Ægean Memories*, the second of which was banned for contravening the Official Secrets Act. During the war he was reputed to have sent in some reports in blank verse, which 'pleased the old man'. 'We like your poetical reports immensely,' wrote Cumming in February 1917. 'Please send us some more.'[36] Not everyone was so admiring. Commenting on a report submitted in the summer of 1916, Colonel French of MI1 declared that, 'as a soldier', he was 'perhaps prejudiced in favour of a simpler and less melodramatic literary style'.

Whatever the literary merits of his reports, after Samson (now promoted to colonel) had moved on at the end of 1915 to head the Eastern Mediterranean Special Intelligence Bureau (EMSIB) in Alexandria – established as a joint MI1(c)–MI5 headquarters[37] – and Mackenzie had taken charge, he built up rather a successful operation, on both the intelligence and counter-intelligence sides. Mackenzie was operating in a very unstable political environment. While the Greek King Constantine I was strongly pro-German, the Prime Minister, Eleftherios Venizelos, was equally pro-Ally. After the latter won an election in June 1915 he allowed the Allies to base substantial forces at Salonika to help with the defence of Serbia and attack Bulgaria, which joined the Central Powers in October. With British forces in Greece, counter-intelligence work (which came to take up most of Mackenzie's time and part of which developed into a full-scale Military Control Office) naturally became of direct interest to Vernon Kell's organisation. In August 1916, while deprecating Mackenzie's 'well known extravagant verbiage', Eric Holt-Wilson of MI5 noted operations in which Mackenzie had foiled the escape from Greece of some 'dangerous Germans' and also prevented 'coastal contraband work'. He thought that there was no doubt at all 'that, however flamboyant his methods, they irritate and unsettle the painstaking local Boche' to such an extent that he thought they might 'shortly assassinate him, if we do not'. Kell and Macdonogh agreed, the former remarking that Mackenzie was 'a thorn in the Boche's flesh', and since 'he gets apparently all the information the Minister and the M.A. [military attaché] require', he should be left where he was.

Mackenzie was closely identified with the Venizelists and when in December 1916 the political situation deteriorated in Athens he had to move his headquarters to the island of Syra (Siros) in the Cyclades, south-east of the capital. Here for a few months he led an exciting if unorthodox intelligence life. Provided with an effective blank cheque from Cumming, by the early summer of 1917 Mackenzie had created a lavishly resourced Aegean Intelligence Service, with a staff of thirty-nine officers, a 200-ton ex-royal yacht and a budget of £5,000 (equivalent to something over £200,000 today) per month. He had ambitious plans for his organisation. In March he told Cumming that two of his officers, Machray and Dewhurst, would go to Volo (Volos) 'and while nominally controlling passports (more or less a sinecure at Volo) would run an active espionage and contre-espionage organisation from Volo to Yannina [Ioannina]'. Another officer was to concentrate on air force intelligence, and Asia Minor as a whole was to be targeted from a series of bases in the Dodecanese Islands. Mackenzie's office at Syra would 'occupy itself solely with information about the interior of Greece'. Much of this derived from Military Control, passport and visa work. By the summer of 1917 Mackenzie's 'so-called passport records' included some '20,000 names on cards', comprising 'a general index of every kind of activity out here', which, with associated records, formed 'a complete history of Greece from the beginning of the Dardanelles expedition to the present time'. Mackenzie appears to have run a very effective outfit, but he did so in an idiosyncratic and individualistic fashion which did not suit more conventionally minded colleagues. There was also the more general difficulty, which afflicted Cumming's officers in a number of places, of where (and how) they fitted into orthodox military and diplomatic hierarchies. Mackenzie's operation served both Cumming's and Kell's departments, and, as such, was 'a branch of the E.M.S.I.B.', based in Cairo. Meanwhile Mackenzie submitted regular reports on political matters to the British minister at Athens; Turkish intelligence was sent directly to the Military Intelligence department at General Headquarters in Cairo; and naval information was given to the Vice Admiral Commanding the Eastern Mediterranean Squadron, at Mudros on the island of Lemnos. In July 1917 the vice admiral took over the operation and began to break it up. Mackenzie's adventure ended when Cumming recalled him at the end of the following month.[38]

Cumming retained some residual interests in Greece, which had come into the war on the Allied side in June 1917 after King Constantine was forced to abdicate and Venizelos formed a new government. Lieutenant Commander John Myres, who had been in Mackenzie's organisation,[39] stayed on in Athens working on counter-intelligence. Reflecting how confused the situation was, however, in September 1917 Blinker Hall told Cumming he 'now wanted Myres to be under the Admiral', while the British minister in Athens, Lord Granville, disagreed. In February 1918 Cumming raised the matter of Myres's status with Hall, but could record only that 'no one knows under whom he is serving'. In March the Director of Military Intelligence raised the possibility that MI5 should take over work in Greece (which was now almost entirely counter-intelligence under Military Control Office cover), but nothing came of this and in June Hall told Cumming that he had to keep Myres on 'as he was persona grata to Venizelos'.

One of Mackenzie's proposals to Cumming in July 1917 was that 'good information' from Turkey could be obtained by sending agents in 'via Switzerland and get them out by our own routes in Asia Minor'.[40] Cumming was not very keen on this. In April he had told Mackenzie to 'drop Turkish and Syrian matters as part of your main objective', since 'we are getting Turkish information through Switzerland', which was dealt with by 'a large Bureau in Paris' (presumably the Bureau Central Interallié). A few relevant reports have survived. In December 1916 Berne forwarded an assessment of the Turkish situation 'from a new Agent, who has gathered this information from friends in Constantinople'. The government's financial position was precarious, agricultural production 'mediocre' and food supplies unreliable. Volatile public opinion was increasingly antagonistic towards the Germans: 'sacrificed to the interests of foreign allies, whose names they can neither pronounce nor remember, their [the people's] resignation of the beginning is now giving place little by little to complaints against the much detested Germans'. In August 1917 Geneva provided a thirty-two-page update, based on interviews with 'some 20 prominent and well-known Ottomans' in Switzerland and a similar number of Greeks and Americans 'lately arrived here from many parts of Asia Minor'. This covered such topics as Turkish military intentions in Mesopotamia, Palestine and Arabia; agricultural production; reported attacks on 'Non-Turkish races in Syria and Asia Minor' (including the removal of Greek Christians from coastal areas); and the political situation in Constantinople. The general conclusion was that, with German support, there was 'going to be a strong Turkish Offensive in Mesopotamia', with a 'violent preliminary attack in Palestine preceding an, if necessary, vigorous defence of Jerusalem'. In October 1917 'G.23' reported that the Kaiser, on a visit to Constantinople, had reviewed a German division said to be en route to Mesopotamia. This information tied in with other reports which the War Office had received regarding a possible Turco-German offensive and informed a modest (though generally successful) British push in Mesopotamia and a renewed advance in Palestine, where Jerusalem was captured in December.[41]

Romania, which occupied a pivotal geographical position in the Balkans, had been an important intelligence target from the start of the war. Courted by both sides, and ruled by a royal family with significant Austro-German connections, Romania remained neutral in August 1914. Under the liberal, francophile Prime Minister, Ion Brătianu, however, the country increasingly leaned towards the Allies. In December 1915

Cumming hired an Englishman called Bertie Maw, who had been in the Romanian oil business before the war, to go out to collect military and economic intelligence. According to a postwar account prepared in SIS, he drew on his own knowledge of the country, exploited prewar contacts and built up a useful network of agents from Romanian railway and customs personnel, who provided 'reports about goods passing into Austria-Hungary'. In February 1916 Cumming also sent Captain Laycock (who had acted as his deputy in 1914) to Bucharest 'where he commenced operations parallel to Mr Maw', though evidently concentrating on military information. In April 1916, however, Cumming told Samuel Hoare in Petrograd that the Director of Military Intelligence was 'very disappointed with the quality and quantity of news received from Roumania'. The DMI had been hoping for intelligence on 'troop movements in and out of Bulgaria and military information from Servia', but hitherto the results had been poor. Laycock, wrote Cumming, 'is a very able man and from his long service in this Office he knows exactly what is required'. But both Maw's and Laycock's work was overtaken by events. After Romania entered the war on the Allied side in August 1916 it was quickly overrun by the Central Powers. Maw's network collapsed and Laycock's organisation, which had become an overt military mission linked to the British military attaché, had to withdraw with the Romanian government to Jassy (Iaşi) in the north-east of the country where they clung on with Russian support.

Laycock stayed with the Romanians at least until the spring of 1918. Little evidence survives of his work, though his ambiguous position in the British Military Mission to the Romanian army evidently caused some problems. A colleague reported to Cumming in January 1918 about 'the difficulties put in Laycock's way in Roumania & the antagonism shown by our own people to the office there'. In December 1917 Admiral Hall ('decidedly seedy and irritable') scolded Cumming 'about lack of information from Roumania & was not satisfied with my reply that Laycock was Chef de Mission to the M.A. for a long time & his S.S. work spoiled'. Cumming 'refrained from saying that my N.E. [Near East] organisation had been broken up & taken away by Adml Aegean'. From September 1917 to March 1918 Laycock had some sort of subsidiary operation at Galatz (Galaţi), south of Jassy, under a colleague who spoke six languages (including Romanian) and had enlisted as a trooper in the Imperial

Russian Horse Artillery in June 1915. Granted an honorary commission in the British army in February 1918, he got into trouble for telling his bank that he was paid by the 'Secret Service Department'. This provoked a sharp letter from the head of Section VI (Personnel), telling him that it was 'a very irregular proceeding to mention the words "Secret Service Department" etc., to anybody, and it is even worse to put it in writing. Please be more careful in future.' In 1918 a Canadian, Colonel Joseph Boyle, purported to do great work in Romania. He claimed that he had 'got into touch with an organisation of Jews whom he bribed to destroy the Russian Black Sea Fleet', which it was feared might fall into enemy hands. Boyle promised the saboteurs 'so much per ton sunk', and after some ships had been attacked, claiming Cumming's authority, he wrote IOUs to the tune of £2 million. A memorandum addressed to the Chief of the Service in 1924, however, noted that none of the bonds had by then been redeemed.

Cumming's organisation had only a tenuous involvement with the Middle East. Like some of the work he did for Naval Intelligence, it appears that he provided administrative and financial support for operations actually run by other departments. Formally, once Egypt had become a British protectorate in December 1914, MI1(c) could have no direct responsibilities there. Nevertheless, Rhys Samson, who became head of the newly created Eastern Mediterranean Special Intelligence Bureau in March 1916, was indisputably a Cumming appointee. In April 1916 Walter Kirke noted that the Mediterranean was 'all run by Samson, the best man C has', and Captain Gilbert Clayton, Director of Intelligence at the British military headquarters in Cairo, favoured making Samson's organisation into a permanent fixture, writing warmly about it to Cumming.[42]

An espionage operation based in Alexandria which came under the EMSIB ran agents in Palestine and Syria, though the return was patchy. A recent analysis of British intelligence in the Middle East by Yigal Sheffy has concluded that the best information came from signals and air intelligence methods. 'Human sources', states Sheffy, 'generally provided traditional field information,' derived from train- and road-watching, and 'they hardly ever obtained reliable or relevant information on high-level policy or intentions' (though there is no evidence that they were ever asked to do this). There were also problems of getting information out in time to be useful. One network, however, called NILI (an acronym of a Hebrew biblical phrase meaning 'Eternal One of Isra'el Will Not Lie') did collect 'abundant military information through Palestine and south Syria'. Hoping to influence the British into supporting Jewish interests, the group was organised by 'Mack' (Aaron Aaronsohn), a fervent Zionist who ran an agricultural experimental station near Haifa, conveniently located for sea pick-ups of couriers and agents. Although Aaronsohn worked for what was then MI1(c)'s Alexandria office from early in the war, the peak period of productivity seems to have come in 1917.[43] In May an unidentified intelligence officer in Paris wrote to the Director of EMSIB: 'You certainly seem to be getting good stuff through Mack.' In June Cumming noted that 'they consider him [Aaronsohn] very valuable in Cairo'. Twenty years afterwards, Colonel Walter Gribbon, who had been in charge of Near Eastern Intelligence in the War Office at the time, suggested that it was 'largely owing to the information' provided by the Aaronsohn network that General Allenby 'was able to conduct his campaign in Palestine so successfully'. Unfortunately, in the autumn of 1917, 'after a very successful period', one of their couriers 'was arrested by the Turks and after various tortures gave away some 60 names'. Among these was Aaronsohn's sister, Sarah, who committed suicide, having been tortured by the Turks. Aaronsohn had attempted to free his man by bribing his Turkish captors with funds supplied by the British. In early October he asked for £5,000 'with which to procure the release of this man'. Cumming responded by pointing out that while 'we did not on principle pay money for the release of agents', he had sent the still considerable sum of £2,000 'to Cairo for Aaronsohn's people as payment in consideration for past services rendered'. Though reluctant on intelligence grounds to pay any further money, Cumming recognised that there might be a strong political justification for such an action. In the end, EMSIB in Cairo agreed to advance £4,000 'to buy off Turkish torturers', but 'it was found impossible to hand over this money'.

In October 1917 Cumming's contacts with the Aaronsohns also provided the British government with back-channel communications to Jewish groups in Palestine. In November 1917 Aaron Aaronsohn's brother Samuel (who was then in London) was given an advance copy of the Balfour Declaration (in which the British government stated that they viewed 'with favour the establishment in Palestine of a national home for the Jewish people') for him to smuggle into Palestine in order to encourage Jews with their work in support of the Allied war effort. Cumming, too, liaised with the Zionist leader Chaim Weizmann, meeting him several times in 1917 and 1918 to discuss Jewish affairs. The advance of Allenby's forces northwards into Palestine in 1917 and 1918 overran whatever remained of Cumming's operations there. On 18 September 1918, by which stage British forces had reached Syria and some six weeks before Turkey signed an armistice, Cumming noted in his diary that his organisation in Palestine had now been 'transferred to [the] military'.

There is very little evidence of activity by MI1(c) in further-flung areas such as South America and the Far East. In February 1915 Blinker Hall instructed him 'to send a good man to Santiago & Punta Arenas' in Chile for an unspecified 'certain purpose' and with a generous budget of 'up to £2000'. The Admiralty were concerned about German commerce raiders operating in the seas around South America, and there was need, too, for economic intelligence in support of the Allied blockade of the Central Powers. Cumming noted another 'S. American scheme' in his diary in October 1915, and in 1916–17 several officers (some by the specific request of Admiralty Intelligence) were despatched to the Continent. From May 1917 A. H. A. Knox-Little took charge of South America in Head Office. He was described as a 'member of an important firm trading in that continent', and had sole charge of 'a large agency which he worked entirely on his own until the end of the war'. Although there was British intelligence activity in the Far East during the war (mainly keeping track of covert German intrigues), most of this was handled by the military and naval authorities on the spot, in collaboration with Indian agencies and the local colonial police.[44] In January 1917 Cumming was consulted about a scheme to develop work in China proposed by General Dudley Ridout, the senior army officer at Singapore. Cumming was evidently not averse to expanding into the Far East. When in November 1917 a candidate approached him 'wanting a job connected with Japan', Cumming rejected him on the grounds that he was 'too old & set'. During 1918, however, a number of possible officers were interviewed to work in China, and one was actually sent out under business cover, but was recalled by telegram immediately on his arrival at Shanghai 'since it had been reported that he had been indiscreet on board ship so that his mission was known'. In July 1918 Cumming sent out another individual, with cover as a furniture-dealer. He was recalled after a month when it was 'discovered that he had merely obtained a passage to the Far East for his own purposes and did not intend to work'. No further efforts to start an organisation in the Far East were made until 1920.

Russian enemies

SIS's coverage of Russia during the revolutionary period is illustrated in a collection of documents which Captain William James, Assistant Director of Naval Intelligence under Blinker Hall during the war, assembled in March 1919. He had the Naval Intelligence Department collect together 'all the reports sent in from 1914 to 1919 by our agents through "C", which appear to be of historical value'. It was noted that there was 'a complete file at "C's" office'. This no longer exists, but part of the Naval Intelligence selection, comprising 101 'political' reports, has been preserved in the SIS archives. Eleven concern Russia between October 1916 and December 1918, and, of these, just three are from MI1(c) sources in Russia itself between the time of the Bolshevik revolution in the late autumn of 1917 and the end of 1918. On 5 October 1917 Petrograd reported on a 'democratic conference' which confirmed that the Bolshevik leaders were 'the ablest men in Party tactics' and that Party cohesion was weak 'except on the extreme "Left"'. On 21 November (received in London on 14 December) a six-page despatch was sent containing 'Notes on the November (Bolshevik) Revolution in Russia', from 'a reliable source'. This contained a potted history of events in Russia from the summer of 1917 and described the central role which the Military-Revolutionary Committee, ably mobilised by Trotsky, had played in the coup and how the Bolsheviks were attacking the last remaining pockets of support for Kerensky. The third CX report, on 'affairs in Russia', dates from July 1918, and was from 'our representative in Moscow'. It contains eighteen pages of miscellaneous material, mainly relating to the politico-military situation in the Ukraine, and including letters to and from the anti-Bolshevik, 'White' Russian General Anton Denikin. MI1(c) conceded that 'while some passages are a little obscure', it had 'been thought better in view of the scarcity of news from Russia to leave them entire, and let them speak for themselves'.

Assuming that the Naval Intelligence Department's 1919 definition of 'historical value' was not so restricted as to exclude a great number of reports (and the inclusion of the July 1918 despatch with its ragbag of material suggests otherwise), and that the reports which have survived are broadly representative of what was being provided through 'C', it appears that in the confused days of the October Revolution and after Cumming's representatives (who in any case had never been organised for political intelligence gathering) were not contributing very much to whatever information London was getting about the situation in Russia. Samuel Hoare, who came home on sick leave in February 1917, was never replaced. Major John Scale, an Indian Army officer who had qualified as a Russian interpreter before the war and had fought with distinction on the Western Front before being posted to Petrograd, seems to have acted thereafter as head of the mission which, following the Bolshevik seizure of power, had to leave the Russian War Office and was given accommodation in the British embassy. The change of regime and the withdrawal of the country from the war not only meant that Russia became a target for British intelligence but also left Tsarist Russian officers stranded in the West by the revolutionary events back home. In December 1917 Cumming went to the Admiralty 'to meet Admiral Volkov and Lt. Okerlund of Russian Service', who wanted the British to 'say that their S.S. is worth the £15,000 monthly that it costs. If we state this, our Treasury will advance them the money.' There is no indication whether this offer was taken up, though in the ensuing years British intelligence agencies (among many others) employed numerous former Tsarist officers and agents. Knox (now a general and back in London) told Cumming in January 1918 that 'Russian S.S. officers are to be trusted & would work loyally for us as they are penniless.' The following month General Macdonogh, the Director of Military Intelligence, said he was not against employing Russians, but warned Cumming that he should 'choose our men very carefully as Russia is divided into Bolsheviks & pro-Germans (the latter being better class folks who would welcome any power that would maintain order)'.

Cumming, meanwhile, began to work on 'an entirely new S.S. Service [sic] in Russia'. In January 1918 he proposed to Macdonogh that this might be organised from Stockholm or Oslo. Major Scale was named to run it and, as SIS's Baltic area Inspector (or co-ordinator), he began to build up a team, using officers who had, like him, served in Hoare's mission. Scale told Cumming that he was sending Leo Steveni (a fluent Russian-speaker whose father had been a timber merchant in the country) to Canada 'to enlist & instruct agents for Russia'. In March 1918 they discussed trying to exploit some of the estimated twenty thousand sailors on sequestered Russian ships who were about to be repatriated. On 15 March he 'introduced Mr. Reilly who is willing to go to Russia for us' to Cumming, who noted in his diary that Reilly was 'very clever – very doubtful – has been everywhere & done everything'. Reilly was to 'take out £500 in notes & £750 in diamonds', but Cumming felt it 'a great gamble as he is to visit all our men in Vologda, Kief [sic], Moscow &c'. Reilly, the so-called 'ace of spies' – brilliant, audacious and uncontrollable – was to work for Cumming over the next few years. He had been born Shlomo Rosenblum in (or near) Odessa in the early 1870s. In the late 1890s, having moved to England, he married an Irishwoman and reinvented himself as 'Sidney George Reilly'. By 1918 he had travelled extensively in Asia, made money in various business ventures and lived in France, England, Russia and the USA, where in 1917 he met Norman Thwaites, who appears to have provided the link to Scale and the opportunity to work for MI1(c). He did not, however, come particularly well recommended from New York, whence a series of cables described him as 'untrustworthy and unsuitable'; 'a shrewd businessman of undoubted ability but without patriotism or principles and therefore not to be recommended for any position which requires loyalty as he would not hesitate to use it to further his own commercial interests'; and a 'Greek Jew; very clever; entirely unscrupulous'. He was, indeed, another of Cumming's scallywags.[45]

Employing Reilly was perhaps a high-risk strategy, but, with the code-name 'ST/1', he set off for north Russia before the end of March 1918. On 16 April, having gone to Petrograd, he reported that the Bolsheviks were 'the only real power in Russia', and that some sort of agreement would have to be made with them in order, for example, to secure the Allied bases at Murmansk and Archangel and to prevent 'the [Russian] Baltic fleet from passing to the Germans by their destruction or rendering it unserviceable'. At the same time, opposition to the Bolsheviks was 'constantly growing and, if suitably supported', would 'finally lead' to their overthrow. Between October 1917 and the spring of 1918 attempts had been made by the remaining British diplomatic representatives in Russia, notably Robert Bruce Lockhart, to broker some sort of modus vivendi with the new regime. But opinion in London (and other Allied capitals) had been hardening against the Bolsheviks and increasingly moving towards active intervention in the country, providing political and military support for anti-revolutionary elements. Reilly's report, therefore, provided useful ammunition for the hard-line interventionists, whose views came to dominate British policy in 1918 and 1919. Moving on to Moscow in early May, Reilly first courted the Bolshevik leaders (claiming to have marched directly up to the Kremlin in British uniform) and then their opponents, in particular Boris Savinkov, who had already moved from political opposition to plotting a coup. Reilly, though working under several aliases and moving his lodging frequently thanks to the complaisance of various mistresses, was soon marked by the Cheka (the Bolshevik secret police), who correctly identified him as a prime mover in what became known as the 'Lockhart plot' to overthrow the regime, though Lockhart himself was not one of the conspirators.[46]

Cumming's Russian dispositions in 1918 reflect the growing commitment to intervention, though there is little hard evidence of the extent to which intelligence was actually gathered, or how it may have informed British policy. In April Cumming and colleagues had a 'long talk' about sending men to Central Asia where they could watch the Trans-Siberian Railway '& report any military preparations on it'. In May the Director of Military Intelligence summoned Cumming to see General Frederick Poole, commanding the British troops in Archangel, who wanted him to send Colonel Boyle out to 'take charge of the Russian part of Scale's organisation'. In June Cumming noted that there were still a dozen British intelligence officers (not all of whom were working for him), some in uniform, stationed in Russia. But there was clandestine work too. On 27 July he interviewed a man who was aiming to 'travel in Russia in peasants dress'. Two days later he noted that 'Mr Dukes arrived from Russia unexpectedly.' He seemed 'a first rate man for our job 'tho a little independent in spirit'. A talented musician, Paul Dukes, who was to become 'ST/25' and work undercover for Cumming in 1918–19, had been living in Russia since 1908 and had been an assistant conductor with the Imperial Mariinsky Opera at the outbreak of the war. During the first half of 1918, ostensibly serving as a King's Messenger (an official British government courier), he had been reporting back to the Foreign Office on internal conditions in Russia.[47]

On 31 August 1918, responding to the murder of Moisei Uritsky, head of the Petrograd Cheka, and the attempted murder of Lenin, both of which were falsely blamed on Allied intrigues, the Cheka stormed the British embassy in Petrograd, killing the naval attaché, Captain Cromie, in the process. Lockhart was arrested and briefly held at the Lubyanka prison in Moscow, while Reilly evaded arrest by going underground and eventually escaping in disguise through Petrograd, German-occupied Estonia and Finland. The attack on the British embassy marked the final breakdown of diplomatic relations between the two countries. For the next eighteen months or so, with direct military intervention in Russia and sustained support for White Russian forces in the Russian Civil War, Britain and Soviet Russia were openly at war. For much longer afterwards, and with varying intensity over the succeeding seven decades, the perceived threat of Soviet Communism powerfully coloured the attitudes of Britain's policy-makers in general and its intelligence community in particular.

PART THREE
THE INTERWAR YEARS

5

The emergence of SIS

In 1917 Mansfield Cumming famously remarked to Compton Mackenzie that after the war he should come to work with him in the Secret Service. He told him the business was 'capital sport' and 'much more fun in peacetime than in war-time'.[1] Perhaps so, and no doubt Cumming was not the only person during those sombre wartime days to hark nostalgically back to some idyllic prewar existence which, they hoped, might return in the future, but for the Secret Service the actuality of the transition from war to peace, and the troubled years which followed, was not much 'fun'. As had been the case during the war, the independent existence of the Service was threatened, and, although the Foreign Office was confirmed as the Service's parent department, relations between the diplomats and their clandestine colleagues were sometimes difficult, especially over the question of cover. Above all, for almost two decades financial stringency dominated the Service's work and meant that it had to operate on a shoestring at a time when the new revolutionary regime in Soviet Russia appeared to pose a major threat, and, in the 1930s, when the rise of aggressive and ambitious governments in Italy, Germany and Japan further challenged Britain's worldwide interests.

Postwar reorganisation schemes

With the end of the shooting war in 1918, Cumming had to face a more insidious, though less lethal, battle in Whitehall for the independent survival of his Bureau. Crucial (and enduring) issues relating to the nature and organisation of British secret intelligence were fiercely debated, and although Cumming ultimately achieved his aim of keeping Whitehall

departments – especially the service ministries – at arm's length and securing autonomy for what became known as the Secret Intelligence Service,
during the early days of peace this outcome was by no means certain.

Three days after the Armistice, General William Thwaites, who had
been George Macdonogh's successor as Director of Military Intelligence
for barely a month, proposed amalgamating Cumming's and Kell's organisations into a Special Intelligence Service under a single chief. He
further proposed that a significant number of army, navy and air force
officers should be seconded to the Service to avoid stagnation and a loss
of touch with realities. Liaison between the new SIS and the armed service Directorates of Intelligence would be provided by the 'formation
of a joint naval, military and air intelligence section to consist of three
or six officers from the three services'. Clearly envisaging a supervisory
role for this section over the amalgamated Secret Service, Thwaites said
that it 'would consider and work out in conjunction with that Service
any developments in its organization'. Writing to the Director of Naval
Intelligence, Admiral Blinker Hall, Thwaites also proposed that 'our two
cryptographic branches' (the War Office's MI1(b) and the Admiralty's
Room 40) should 'be amalgamated and placed under this section'.

Lord Hardinge, Permanent Under-Secretary at the Foreign Office, responded cautiously. 'The present system', he wrote on 25 November, 'has
had all the defects of every condominium; but it has worked, and all
things considered has survived the test of four years of war with a fair
measure of success.' He agreed that 'some change will be necessary', but
he felt that now was not the time. 'It would', he argued, 'be premature
to make any alteration until Peace is signed and we can see our way a
little clearer.' Hall, too, wanted to wait. 'I should like more time to think
it over,' he told Thwaites. While he agreed that 'amalgamation should
eventually take place . . . at the present moment when all the Heads of
the Government are full of peace resolutions and the coming [Peace]
Conference', he did not think that there was 'much chance of putting a
big scheme through successfully'. Cumming initially kept his opinion to
himself. On 30 November Thwaites complained to him that he 'had not
replied to his Minute re amalgamation', but (as Cumming noted in his
diary), when he 'asked my opinion on the scheme', he 'did not appear
to give consideration to what I did say'. What he said would have been
negative. An unsigned internal memorandum, 'Personal for "C"', on

15 November had dismissed Thwaites's scheme on three grounds. First: 'that the methods, personnel and venue for the two services are entirely different' – counter-espionage work 'is done in England . . . Espionage is conducted abroad.' Second was 'a practical consideration', since it seemed 'impossible that MI5 should continue as a strictly military organisation'. In peacetime its work 'will be police work'; the Home Office would certainly be involved and 'obviously the Home Office could not touch espionage'. The third argument was that the Foreign Office 'must remain the only department that can be responsible for the espionage side of Secret Service'. As it 'involves operations abroad, and though the F.O. will always disavow them, for that very reason (paradoxical as it may seem) they must have full cognisance of what is being done, and power to check it, so that at the very least they may know what they are to disavow'.

In January 1919 Cumming combined these points in a forcefully argued paper against the amalgamation proposal. Sensing that financial retrenchment was in the air, he smartly argued that the scheme appeared 'to be far too extravagant and expensive for acceptance as a practical measure'. Whereas before the war the central Secret Service staff had 'consisted of three persons', the new proposal provided 'for six or twelve officers for the Naval, Military and Air Services alone'. He reaffirmed the principle that the Chief of the Service 'must be in supreme control', and noted that the scheme dealt with the 'Army, Navy and Air Service only', ignoring 'the Political and Economic Sections of my Bureau', which, he asserted, would 'become the most important of all and must be provided for on equal terms with the rest'. If this were done, the cost of the headquarters staff would 'amount to almost as much as we were allowed for the whole of the Secret Service all over the world before the war'. Moving on to the offensive, he argued that Military Intelligence were not 'in any sense competent to say what is required for S.S. in peace time. They have', he declared, 'no knowledge or experience of the matter at all and are competent only to say what the military requirements will be.' While Cumming asserted that 'S.S. should be separate and apart from other Government departments', implicit in his paper (which appears to have been prepared for Hardinge) was the assumption that the Foreign Office should remain in charge of the Bureau.

Bitter wartime experience meant that Cumming wanted as little to do with the War Office as possible. During the war, he wrote, the War Office

had 'country by country destroyed my Organisation'. If an efficient secret service was to be built up 'for the much more severe conditions of
Peace', it 'must be kept clear of War Office interference or there will be
no chance of securing efficiency or of maintaining the Secrecy which is an
essential of its success or even of its continuance'. Cumming went on to
complain about 'the constant robbery' of his staff during the war. It was
'scarcely an exaggeration to say that whenever one of my men displayed
unusual capacity he was taken away from me and I was left stranded'. He
'earnestly' begged to be allowed to 're-organise the S.S. for peace time
without the interference of the Military authorities'. Harking back to the
arrangement laid down by Sir Arthur Nicolson in November 1915, he
asked that the departments concerned should merely inform him of their
requirements 'and leave him to carry them out free from their hindrance'.
If, he concluded (and putting his own position on the line), he were not
reasonably successful 'then he should be discharged, but he should be
given a fair chance to do his work'.

Inevitably, the debate about intelligence organisation was going to
surface at ministerial level. In a general election in December 1918, the
Prime Minister, David Lloyd George, widely regarded as 'the man who
won the war', secured a landslide victory and a powerful new mandate for
his coalition government. Ultimately, however, he depended for survival
on Conservative and Unionist MPs, whose natural disposition towards
financial orthodoxy, social conservatism and 'small government' limited
the extent to which he could follow his own liberal and radical inclina-
tions, especially on the domestic front. Beyond the negotiation of an
international settlement at the Paris Peace Conference, which absorbed
him for the first half of 1919, was the matter of domestic reconstruction. In Britain, as elsewhere in the world, attitudes to both issues were
powerfully coloured by widespread fears of revolution, both at home and
abroad. Not only had the Bolsheviks seized power in Russia (preaching,
moreover, a gospel of international revolution), but the end of the war
had seen the collapse of the Central Powers' empires – Germany, Austria-
Hungary and Turkey – as well as a wave of revolutionary unrest across the
world. Even in the United Kingdom there were worrying portents. There
was a sharp rise in industrial unrest (even among the police); revolutionary demonstrations occurred in 'Red Clydeside' and other industrial
centres; in Dublin Irish republicans met in the first Dáil (parliament)

and declared independence; and in army camps in Britain and abroad war-weary soldiers agitated mutinously for quicker demobilisation.[2]

In January 1919, within a week of his appointment as First Lord of the Admiralty, Walter Long (a senior Conservative politician) circulated a paper on the 'Secret Service'. During the last year of the war, Long (who had been Colonial Secretary between 1916 and 1919) increasingly nursed concerns about Bolshevik, trade union and German-fomented subversion in Britain. He shared these with a friend, Basil Thomson, Assistant Commissioner of the Metropolitan Police and head of the Special Branch, whose remit was political crime. Thomson, an enthusiastic empire-builder who wanted to concentrate all domestic security work into a Directorate of Intelligence, in turn encouraged Long's ideas for an expanded and co-ordinated domestic intelligence organisation which might combine Special Branch and MI5 (and clearly could be led by Thomson himself).[3] Disturbed by 'elements of unrest', and manifestations of Bolshevism, Long told his Cabinet colleagues that 'we must be vigilant, and, above all, have an efficient, well-paid Secret Service on the civil side'. His memorandum prompted one from the Home Secretary, Edward Shortt, who agreed 'that the question of the Secret Service is of very great importance' and worried about 'serious attempts to disseminate Bolshevist doctrines in this country'. These were 'exceedingly dangerous, requiring most careful watching and strong anti-Bolshevist propaganda'.[4]

While the primary concern of both ministers was domestic security, when the matter came before the Cabinet on 24 January, the discussion widened out to include the organisation of secret service in general. It was noted that, apart from the Home Office, several other departments had an interest, and Long stressed the need for some sort of co-ordinating authority. 'The matter', he insisted, 'was of urgent importance in view of the danger of Bolshevism', which he was 'sure was on the increase.' It was decided to set up a committee under the chairmanship of Lord Curzon to find out 'what was being done at present by the Secret Service branches of the several Departments' and ascertain 'how that work could best be co-ordinated with a view to the necessary action being taken with the utmost promptitude'.[5] Curzon, acting Foreign Secretary while Arthur Balfour was at the peace conference in Paris (and who was to succeed him at the end of October 1919), was a toweringly grand British imperial proconsul. As a former Viceroy of India and long-time observer of the 'Great Game' between Britain and Russia over influence in Central Asia, Curzon was likely to appreciate the critical importance of foreign intelligence.

Following the appointment of the committee (which, apart from Curzon, comprised Shortt, Long, Winston Churchill (Secretary of State for War) and Ian MacPherson (Chief Secretary for Ireland)), Cumming, evidently concerned about the position of his Bureau, went to see Long, who he noted had 'confused "Secret Service" with Secret Police', but felt he had been able to put him right on this, and wrote that he 'appeared quite sound as regards my work'. He also saw Hardinge, who had prepared a 'very satisfactory' letter to Curzon embodying Cumming's views on the matter. Hardinge was concerned, as he telegraphed to Curzon on 28 January, that if Curzon's committee was going to discuss the 'Foreign Secret Service' (which was 'quite distinct from [the] Home Office and Irish Office organisations'), the control hitherto exercised by the Foreign Office should be maintained.

Usefully describing the position of Cumming's Bureau as it was in early 1919, and reiterating principles which underlay the Foreign Office's relationship with SIS over its first forty years, in a letter of 7 February Hardinge impressed on Curzon that 'the Secret Service run by the Foreign Office deals with foreign countries alone'. It had 'nothing to do with information to be obtained in Great Britain, Ireland or the Colonies', and it was 'essential that the control of secret service operations in foreign countries should be in the hands of the Foreign Office', which was 'the only Government Department in a position to decide whether such operations may or may not conflict with the general foreign policy of H.M. Government, and to consider whether they may not create serious difficulties with foreign Governments if discovered'. This, he added, was 'even more important in peace time than in war, for in war time acts are committed and measures taken in neutral countries that would hardly be tolerated in times of peace'. Foreign Office control, he wrote, was 'secured by holding the purse strings'. Glossing over Cumming's bitter opinions about his wartime relations with the service ministries, Hardinge asserted that the Foreign Office had kept in 'the closest possible touch with the Directors of Naval and Military Intelligence' and that during the war 'the operations of the Secret Service, thanks to the most able co-operation of General Macdonogh and Admiral Hall', had 'been worked with very happy results', and he believed 'it may truly be said that its success has been second to none'. Hardinge finally put in a word on behalf of Cumming himself, whose work and duties were 'exceedingly technical, requiring very special qualities which are not easy to find'. The Foreign Office had 'been extremely fortunate in securing the services of the present Chief' who had now served 'for nearly ten years' and had 'a unique experience of Secret Service both in peace and war'.

These representations had the intended effect, at least in delaying any decision about the future of Cumming's organisation. When Curzon's committee met, while it reviewed the recent history of covert intelligence work (mentioning in particular the success of the 'Foreign Office service' during the war), it focused mainly on domestic, civil intelligence, endorsing Long's recommendation for an amalgamated Secret Service Department to be formed with Basil Thomson as head. This had more serious implications for Kell than for Cumming, as, despite the fact that MI5 remained responsible for counter-espionage and *military* security, Thomson's expanding department threatened to take over any wider duties on the counter-subversion side. Cumming, for his part, managed to block any ambitions Thomson had to operate overseas, securing agreement that 'all anti-Bolshevik work abroad' would be his responsibility alone. As for 'the military and naval branches of the secret service', Curzon's committee thought that the question of reorganisation should be left for consideration by the Committee of Imperial Defence (or some similar body) until after the peace treaty had been signed. While the committee thought 'that it would be desirable to co-ordinate all intelligence for military purposes and to establish one organization which will serve alike the War Office, Admiralty and Air Force', crucially, however, they suggested that it would 'probably be found convenient to maintain the distinction between military and civil intelligence', which appeared to leave the option open for Cumming's 'Foreign Office' Bureau to continue as a separate entity.[6]

But the War Office snake was only scotched, not killed. Towards the end of February 1919 Cumming reported that the Director of Military Intelligence was 'still firmly set upon the idea of amalgamation between my department and MI5'. Appalled by the prospect of combining domestic and foreign intelligence-gathering, Cumming deployed a fresh argument against the idea. Raising 'the prospect of a Labour Government in the near future' (a striking prediction, since at this stage Labour had fewer than seventy out of 700 MPs in the House of Commons and the first British Labour government was as yet five years away), and revealing a shrewd appreciation of how secret service matters might be interpreted by both politicians and the general public, he argued that this made it 'necessary that the S. of S. for Foreign Affairs, with his hand on his heart, should be able to declare that the Secret Service has no connection with the control of labour unrest'. Since it had 'been clearly proved that money from these strikes' had been 'supplied by Bolsheviks', MI5 would inevitably 'be connected with labour and Bolshevik troubles'. In April 1919 he prepared a further series of criticisms on specific aspects of the War Office amalgamation scheme. The proposal focused purely on military intelligence and entirely ignored 'the important Sections which deal with Politics and Trade'; the Chief of the Secret Service would have 'no authority whatever'; and, because they would all be seconded from the armed services, 'his so-called staff would not be his subordinates but would owe allegiance to their respective chiefs'. Overall, he dismissed the scheme as 'utterly unworkable from the points of view of Efficiency and Economy and most important of all – Secrecy'. For good measure, he also objected to the suggested name for the new agency: the Special Intelligence Service. 'The Secret Service', he wrote, 'is a good enough title for my organisation and is the name of the Service I was appointed to command.'

Whatever his organisation was called, Cumming had not seen the last amalgamation scheme. Towards the end of 1919 Thwaites returned to the attack, enlisting the support of Commodore Hugh Sinclair (who had succeeded Blinker Hall as Director of Naval Intelligence in January 1919). This time the scheme was not to integrate the 'Espionage and Counter Espionage Services' but to join them 'under one head' and administer them as one Secret Intelligence Service. The head of this service would be superior to both Cumming and Kell, and would himself be answerable to a committee comprising the Permanent Under-Secretary at the Foreign Office and the three armed service Directors of Intelligence. Efficiency savings could be made by combining 'administrative, secretarial, record, legal and technical services', as well as 'fusion of records'. While he had 'an open mind on the subject', Sinclair allowed himself to be associated with the proposal, and pressed Hardinge to override Cumming's hitherto obstructive attitude. 'I hope', he urged, 'you will see your way to order C— to explore the possibilities in close co-operation with K— .'

Cumming was no more enamoured of this scheme than the last. Writing to Hardinge's private secretary, Nevile Bland (a man who was intermittently to play an important role in the development of SIS over the next twenty-five years), Cumming bluntly said that there were no further administrative economies to be made and 'no records to fuse', since 'the C.E. [counter-espionage] service is not concerned with the obtaining of knowledge and information (if it is obeying the rules laid down)'. Above all he resented being superseded by any other individual. 'Unless the authorities are dissatisfied with the present C.S.S.,' he wrote, 'some considerable gain ought to be indicated to make up for putting him under some unknown person who cannot have equal experience, and whose interference therefore will in all probability be prejudicial both to efficiency and economy, to say nothing of secrecy and safety.' If Hardinge insisted, he would 'of course, co-operate with Colonel Kell as suggested', but he protested 'against disclosing the details of my secret organisation to anyone'. He worried lest the scheme was merely a device to save MI5, arguing that 'from the time Sir Basil Thomson was given charge of anti-Bolshevik and undesirable-alien control in this country the work of MI5 practically ceased'. These 'persistent proposals' were, he suggested, 'intended to enable the very expensive staff of M.I.5 to find new spheres of activity in my office where they are not required. This', he continued, 'would be unwise and an unfair burden to me, and prejudicial to my staff who are highly trained and experienced.' Cumming also hoped that Hardinge might 'consider the proposals in the light of the position that would arise when the present C.S.S. retires', after which 'a determined effort would be made to put Colonel Kell into the position, to the prejudice of the present loyal and trained staff and the lasting detriment of the S.S. whose ten years experience would be entirely lost'. In a separate minute to Bland, Cumming observed that it was 'the third scheme put forward since the Armistice', each of which had been 'aimed at diminishing the authority & command of the C.S.S.', and he acidly commented that the proposed date for implementing the scheme – 1 April 1920 – 'seems suitable'.

Various other intelligence reorganisation schemes circulated during 1920. One envisaged amalgamating 'the S.S. with M.I.5 under the Assistant Commissioner of Police' (Basil Thomson). Another proposed that 'all British Governmental S.S. Organisations', including Cumming's and Kell's departments, signals intelligence, Indian Political Intelligence and parts of the police Special Branch, as well as the 'Post Office Officials concerned in the examination of correspondence', should be 'placed under one executive Chief'. In the end, departmental interests (it was never likely that the Foreign Office would willingly relinquish control of Cumming's Bureau) and personal factors (Basil Thomson, for example, was widely regarded as being dangerously over-mighty), together with the clear practical difficulties of imposing any significant reorganisation, meant that nothing much was done.

For Cumming, meanwhile, the debate prompted him to think hard about the purpose of his organisation and, drawing on his ten years' experience, in early 1920 he noted down some thoughts about 'the essentials of the Secret Service'. The 'first, last and most necessary essential of a S.S.', he wrote, 'is that it should be SECRET'. This, he lamented, 'is the first thing to be forgotten in any scheme and the last thing to be remembered in putting it into practice'. The second essential was that 'the S.S. at home must be small and self-contained and its personnel must be independent of any control other than that of its Chief. No one should have power to take away his trained staff or to give them orders.' The third requirement was the reiteration of Nicolson's minute of November 1915 confirming the functional autonomy of the Chief of the Secret Service, and giving him sole control of 'all espionage and Counter-espionage agents abroad'. While he would be independent of the War Office and the Admiralty, he would 'keep in constant touch' with those departments, who would 'inform him of their requirements as occasion demands and furnish him with criticisms of his reports in a manner to help towards their improvement where necessary'. Finally, the 'C.S.S.' would provide a monthly financial report to the Permanent Under-Secretary at the Foreign Office, and would be subject to his sole control 'in all matters connected with the expenditure of Secret Service funds'. In a supplementary paper, clearly reflecting on his recent wartime experience, Cumming allowed that the Service should be organised in peacetime so that the personnel and records in any particular district could be handed over 'complete as a going concern' when that area fell 'within the zone of Military operations'. Nevertheless, 'in Neutral countries or Allied countries not in a fighting zone, the S.S. should be left to do its work without interference'.

By the end of 1920 Cumming had secured – at least in the medium term – the survival of the Secret Service as an autonomous department under the Foreign Office. Briefing Sir Eyre Crowe about his work on 17 October, just before Crowe succeeded Hardinge as Permanent Under-Secretary, Cumming assured him that, 'in the accepted meaning of the words Secret Service', there was 'no such thing in this country'. He maintained that 'we have never practised any of the black arts usually ascribed to S.S. and which have been adopted elsewhere', and he asserted the value of his organisation for the Foreign Office. It dealt, he said, 'with classes of society which the Embassies cannot touch', and the Service's reports represented 'a valuable supplement to those obtained from official sources', as well as 'the main source of information of the great social conspiracies which are rife throughout the world'. Although there is no hint of it in Cumming's diary, Crowe's initial response to the reports he received from the Secret Service was not at all favourable. In a note to his private secretary, Nevile Bland, who was evidently away from the office, Crowe complained that he was 'snowed under! Also daily irritated by your S.S. reports, which are a mass of rubbishy tittle tattle. It is a scandal that I should be required to read such stuff.'[7]

Cumming, nevertheless, evidently found an ally in Crowe, who early in 1921 moved to clarify the close relationship of the Foreign Office with the Service. For some time reports from Cumming's Bureau had been handled by the Political Intelligence Department (PID) of the Foreign Office, which had been established in March 1918. As part of a general departmental reorganisation (and in response to expenditure cuts), however, Crowe abolished it in late 1920. In January 1921, concerned that political information was being requested by (and supplied to) the War Office, liaison between the Secret Service and the Foreign Office was formalised on two levels. It was decided that, in countries where there were Service representatives, a senior member of each British diplomatic mission 'should be appointed to confer regularly with the chief representative of the Secret Service' in that country, who would supply him with 'all political reports obtained by him and his agents'. At the London end, the Secret Service would no longer copy and distribute substantially raw intelligence reports, 'approximately in the form in which they are received', but daily summaries would be prepared, to which 'reports of special interest should be attached'. These would be sent 'only to the Foreign Office and Sir B. Thomson'. It was decided that the War Office and Admiralty (which would continue to receive specific technical information) would henceforward not be supplied directly with political reports. They 'should be informed of as much as is necessary of the revised arrangements, and told that such political information as may concern them will in future be supplied from the Foreign Office'. As Cumming recorded in his diary, Sir Robert Nathan, who headed the Political Section V, was to be the Service's 'liaison officer with the Heads of Depts of the F.O. & to have access to them'. He would 'summarise the reports and send in a daily [later altered to 'periodic'] epitome'.

These decisions in January 1921, which clearly positioned the Secret Service closer to the Foreign Office than to any other government department, as a corollary distanced it from the service ministries. They reflected the new, peacetime situation, and an understanding that political intelligence was now especially at a premium. A February 1921 Foreign Office circular to diplomatic missions in Europe claimed that 'to-day the old type of Secret Service' had disappeared and 'melodrama has given place to a more sober style of enquiry from which the diplomat need no longer, as he was very properly required to do before, withdraw the hem of his garment'. Intelligence was now 'largely concerned with subterranean revolutionary movements and individuals', and 'instead of spying on the military defences of individual countries', it devoted itself 'principally to detecting tendencies subversive of the established order of things, irrespective of whether these are directed against the United Kingdom or are International in character'. Be that as it may, a parallel Secret Service circular in March 1921 to representatives abroad, which summarised the enhanced liaison arrangements with embassies and legations (and pointed out that the very existence of the 'branch' might 'depend on your usefulness' to the minister), also indicated that the collection of intelligence for the armed services remained a Service responsibility. 'For the present,' it instructed, 'your reports on Naval and Military matters will be dealt with by you as heretofore.'

Finance and economy

Running parallel to the various reorganisation schemes was the constant pressure to reduce spending which Cumming's Bureau shared with every British government department during the years following the First World War. Yet alongside the demands for economy were continuing high expectations of what the Secret Service Bureau might still do. Typical of this was a meeting at the Foreign Office on 28 December 1918 at which Lord Hardinge told Cumming he could continue 'our organisation in Russia @ £3000+ [a] month until 31st March', while also agreeing to Cumming 'going ahead & arranging for a Peace[time] S.S. on the basis of £30,000 a year'. On New Year's Eve 1918 he held a meeting at Head Office on the 'question of cutting down organisations'. This was followed by an interview with the Director of Military Intelligence who 'asked what we were doing in the way of *increasing* our organ[isatio]n in Germany [emphasis added]'. Cumming presented Thwaites with 'a draft Peace Estimate showing a budget of £2000 for Germany & Austria, but he told me we should require £30,000 for these countries alone & that he would fight for this amount'.

In fact, the unsettled conditions across the postwar world intensified demands for good intelligence. On 7 April 1919 a conference called by Hardinge of Cumming, Kell and the Directors of Military and Naval Intelligence agreed to ask the Treasury for a 'special allowance of £18,000 a month' for Cumming's 'War Office' work, which, 'with his normal annual expenditure of £30,000, would bring the cost of his branch alone to approximately £250,000 for the year'. By contrast Kell needed only £60,000. Reporting on a visit to London the same month to discuss the future of the New York organisation, William Wiseman wrote to his colleague Norman Thwaites that, although Cumming had 'been reduced financially to a peace basis', the Foreign Office 'was already beginning to find this is an impracticable position'. Information was being requested 'by various departments as to enemy activity in all parts of the world, and the authorities are realising that a good Intelligence service is more than ever necessary at the present juncture'. In May 1919 Cumming told Compton Mackenzie that 'far from closing down – as we thought we should have to do after the war – we are actually expanding, and we have any amount of work to do in the immediate future'.[8]

In mid-1919 Cumming and his colleagues began work on a scheme to use the Military Control Organisation both as a means of providing cover for intelligence work and as a source of income. During May it was proposed to give Cumming's Military Control Officers in foreign countries the status of vice consuls and allocate responsibility to Cumming for the 'Anti-Bolshevik' Secret Service (providing reports for Basil Thomson) as well as 'Passport Control'. It was calculated that the cost of these two functions of some £75,000 a year could be met by 'a 5/- [25 pence] rate' (presumably for each visa issued).[9] In September the arrangements were hammered out between Cumming and Lord Curzon's private secretary, Ronald Campbell. Cumming promised Campbell that 'all political reports sent home by my P.C. man' would 'go through the Minister' and that 'my man should not deal directly with agents', thus reassuring Campbell that there would be no risk of the regular diplomats being mixed up directly with 'secret service work'. Cumming secured an agreement from Campbell that reports could be cabled back to London 'over the Minister's signature', thus giving them privileged protection over the public cable or mail. It was settled that Cumming's representatives would be given the title of Passport Control Officer and Major Herbert Spencer from Cumming's staff was appointed first Director of Passport Control Department.

The vital financial contribution which Passport Control made to Cumming's organisation is illustrated by a set of accounts he drew up at the end of October 1919. This detailed twenty-four officers and twenty-five clerical and support staff at Head Office, along with five officers under Major Spencer running the Passport Control section. Abroad there were thirty Passport Control Offices, most of which had only two or three staff, and a total overseas staff of some eighty or so. Of his total expenditure of £295,256 (some £9.7 million in current terms), £235,700 was devoted to 'S.S.', of which £45,500 was 'PC SS', presumably the anti-Bolshevik reporting conducted for Basil Thomson. Passport Control itself cost £56,690 and the remaining £2,866 was for unspecified 'A. B.' (Anti-Bolshevik) work of some sort. On the revenue side, £132,000 was ascribed to the Secret Service Vote; £5,000 to the 'P.I.D.' (the Foreign Office's Political Intelligence Department); £56,690 for overt Passport Control work (balancing the equivalent sum on the expenditure side); and £103,700 for 'PC SS'. There are three significant features of these accounts. First, Cumming's core overseas office costs, amounting to nearly £57,000 a year, were covered by the Passport Control budget. Second, a substantial proportion (35 per cent) of his income (the proportion not covered by the Secret Service Vote – passed annually by parliament – and the PID money) came from apparently unattributable (and unexplained) 'PC SS' sources. Third, the £58,200 surplus of this income over 'PC SS' expenditure appears to have been available to fund secret service work generally.

The cross-subsidy from the Passport Control Organisation was to remain an important component of Secret Service funding throughout the interwar years. Among other advantages, it could help ease pressure on the Secret Service Vote, the single most public acknowledgement of British covert intelligence work, and which both ministers and officials felt could be a hostage to fortune for critics of the security and intelligence services.[10] Fears in the autumn of 1918 that parliament might not 'continue to vote an adequate sum for Secret Services after the war, more especially if a Labour Government comes into power', led to the remarkable suggestion that 'a capital sum, say of £1,000,000, should be invested in War Loan in the name of trustees, and the interest used for maintaining the [Secret] Services'. This idea of providing an endowment so that secret agencies would no longer be dependent on (or accountable to) parliament found its way into the February 1919 Secret Service Committee report, where the suggestion was commended 'to the favourable consideration of the Treasury and the Cabinet'.[11]

But the real challenge to the postwar intelligence community came less from critical Labour politicians than from the Prime Minister and the Chancellor of the Exchequer urging retrenchment. British public finances were further affected by a sharp decline in the country's economic situation. From the winter of 1919–20, inflation, pay cuts, a fall in industrial production and rising unemployment came to dominate the scene and reinforced the pressure for government spending cuts. On his return from Paris after the Treaty of Versailles had been signed with Germany on 28 June 1919, Lloyd George initiated a wide-ranging review of government policy, telling the Cabinet on 5 August that scarce resources had to be diverted away from military spending and towards social and industrial reconstruction. British forces, he observed, 'had destroyed the only enemy we had in Europe', but if the country now 'maintained a larger Army and Navy and Air Force than we had before we entered the War, people would say, either that the War had been a failure, or that we were making provision to fight an imaginary foe'. The consequent reassessment of national priorities led to massive budget cuts for the armed services and the definition of the famous 'ten-year rule', by which the service ministries in framing their estimates were to assume that 'the British Empire will not be engaged in any great war during the next ten years'.[12]

Cumming was well aware of the economic realities. As early as 8 March 1919 he reported that he had reduced his 'expenditure from the £80,000 at the time of the Armistice to £40,000 a month'. Lord Hardinge responded by noting that the Treasury 'will press strongly for a stringent retrenchment' and that Cumming would have to budget for a figure of £60,000 a year. In July 1919 Lord Drogheda of the Foreign Office told Cumming of Lord Curzon's opinion that 'he considered S.S. a luxury we could not afford in the present state of our finances as it did not produce value for the money spent on it'. During the second half of 1919 Cumming continued to economise. A meeting in mid-August discussed the reduction of staff 'to post war limits'; the closure of the Head Office 'from noon Sats to 10 Mondays'; and the acquisition of new premises. Removal to a new location was desirable both to save money and for security reasons. Cumming was certain that, following the experience of the war which had 'resulted in the existence of the office and its activities being known to hundreds', it would be impossible to 'maintain any semblance of secrecy' about Whitehall Court, and he obtained Lord Hardinge's approval to 'take a small house on a lease' for his main headquarters building.

Cumming acquired a substantial Victorian villa, West House, at 1 Melbury Road in Holland Park in west London, whither headquarters moved on 23 December 1919. This was some distance from Whitehall, but evidently security considerations were uppermost. 'No one to know of address,' wrote Cumming in his diary and he even considered (perhaps a bit maliciously) not revealing it to the Director of Military Intelligence. A letter to an individual summoned to Melbury Road shows that the information was too secret to be put on paper. The individual concerned was to report to 1 Adam Street (off the Strand) where he would be given the Head Office address. 'It is about half an hours underground ride . . . [on] the other side of London,' he was told, 'but as we do not make the address public I am afraid this is the only way I can tell it to you.' In another move to enhance secrecy, Cumming asked that his staff 'whose salaries were paid out of S.S. funds could have them paid free of Income Tax . . . It was', he wrote, 'undesirable that their names & connection with S.S. should be known to anyone.' This privilege, agreed to by the Foreign Office, was jealously guarded by the Service for decades to come.

The pressure for economy was relentless. At the beginning of 1920 Nevile Bland told Cumming that the Chancellor of the Exchequer had asked for his estimate to 'be reduced to half'. In February Bland revealed that the Secret Service's income 'should be cut down to £65,000'. On 2 March Cumming learned that Hardinge had confirmed the £65,000 figure, but had added that 'the matter was to be put up to the Cabinet'. On the plus side, Hardinge was to raise Passport Control fees by 50 per cent, 'thus providing a good income'. A fortnight later Bland confirmed to Cumming 'categorically' that 'Passport Control with its cover & funds were an integral part of our financial scheme', which was just as well as Robert Nathan calculated that, without it, the Service would 'require an additional £100,000'.

The proposed budget cut to £65,000 greatly alarmed Winston Churchill, the Secretary of State for War, who protested about it to his senior Cabinet colleagues. 'With the world in its present condition of extreme unrest and changing friendships and antagonisms, and with our greatly reduced and weak military forces,' he argued, 'it is more than ever vital for us to have good and timely information.' Setting up a Secret Service organisation was a slow business; 'five or ten years' were 'required to create a good system', which could be 'swept away by a stroke of the pen'. It would, he wrote, 'be an act of the utmost imprudence to cripple our arrangements at the present most critical time'. Churchill circulated a table prepared by Cumming showing proposed expenditure both under the original 1920–1 estimate of £125,000 and under the new estimate of £65,000. In each case allocations of £15,000 for 'Headquarters', £1,000 for 'Technical' and £10,000 for 'Contingent' remained the same, but in the reduced scheme there were deep cuts abroad. The stations in Vladivostok, Prague, Warsaw, Italy, Spain and Portugal were abolished (saving £7,000), and £4,000 earmarked 'for the inauguration of a service of information from Berlin, Munich and Hamburg' was cut. Spending reductions elsewhere, however, suggested a slightly greater emphasis on work against Germany than Russia. 'Helsingfors (for North Russia)' was cut from £20,000 to £8,000, and 'Holland (for Germany &c)' from £30,000 to £18,000. Representation at a reduced level was maintained for Switzerland (£3,000); 'Vienna and Prague' (£2,000); and Copenhagen, South Russia and France

(£1,000 each). The USA was reduced from £9,000 to £4,000; but the biggest cut of all was the Far East, from £15,000 to £1,000.[13]

The bleak prospect presented by Cumming's £65,000 scheme (as well as Churchill's powerful support) had the desired effect. Cumming kept his budget of £125,000 and on 24 March Hardinge told him that he could withdraw the notices closing down stations. But it was just a stay of execution. The following spring, Otto Niemeyer of the Treasury thought a total Secret Service vote for 1921–2 (of which Cumming's organisation formed just a part) 'of £475,000 against this year's £400,000 . . . and a prewar £50,000 does not look at all pretty'. Believing that this 'would arouse determined opposition' in the House of Commons 'and a demand for details which it would be most undesirable to grant', the Treasury again wanted significant reductions. A high-level official committee, chaired by Sir Warren Fisher (Permanent Secretary to the Treasury and Head of the Home Civil Service) and comprising Sir Eyre Crowe (Foreign Office) and Sir Maurice Hankey (Cabinet Secretary), was appointed by the Cabinet to make recommendations 'for reducing expenditure and avoiding overlapping'. Nevile Bland was appointed secretary. 'He is', wrote Crowe, 'the only person besides myself who is acquainted with each of the three main subheads of "Foreign Secret Service"' ('Foreign Intelligence', 'Contre-Espionage' and 'Miscellaneous').[14]

During May and June 1921 this powerful triumvirate painstakingly investigated the whole range of British Secret Service and its cost. The total Secret Service Vote was divided between different departments, of which the largest allocations went to the Foreign Office (£185,000), the Irish government (£160,000) and the War Office (£90,000). Crowe told the committee that £126,000 of the Foreign Office's £185,000 'was needed for C', £31,000 'for the requirements of M.I.5' and £28,000 for 'Foreign Office purposes'. Illustrating the rather miscellaneous nature of Secret Service spending, this £28,000 included £5,000 'for propaganda', £10,000 'for contingencies' and 'a considerable [though unspecified] allocation to His Majesty's Legation at Tehran'. Crowe told the committee that Cumming's 'espionage service' provided information 'for the naval, military and air authorities, as well as the Foreign Office, India Office and Sir Basil Thomson'. After he explained that the Foreign Office 'would be content with a considerable [sic] smaller volume of Foreign secret intelligence than that received at present, provided that certain features such as Asia Minor and the Caucasus, Bolshevism, and the activities of the German Socialist Party were still adequately covered', the committee wondered if some contraction in the War Office demands for information might provide a basis for 'a reduction of the £126,000 allocated to C'. By the time the committee subsequently interviewed Cumming, the War Office had said that while they particularly needed military information on Germany, Russia, Japan, the USA and Turkey, they were prepared to do without it from other countries. Cumming himself thought that with these reductions he could 'effect savings' bringing down his estimate to some £87,500.[15]

The 1921 Secret Service Committee reported favourably on the work of Cumming's organisation, finding little or no overlap between it and other branches. They noted the importance of the Passport Control system for its funding and that 'by prevailing upon the military authorities to moderate their demands' the estimate could be reduced to '£100,000, with hope of a further substantial drop next year'. Across the board, however, they could find little scope for 'the actual saving of money', but by transferring as many charges as possible from the Secret Vote to 'public accounts', they were able to propose a reduction of over £100,000 in the overall Secret Vote. For Vernon Kell, the report was a great relief. At first the committee had been 'sceptical as to the necessity at the present juncture of maintaining a counter-espionage organisation', but, advised 'that the agents of at least four Powers are already showing activity in this country' and, alerted to 'the new factor of bolshevism in the navy and army', the committee concluded that there was 'justification for the continuance of M.I.5', albeit with a reduced budget. For Basil Thomson the outcome was not so good. The committee suggested that his Directorate of Intelligence should lose its independent existence and be incorporated into 'the general organisation of the Metropolitan Police'. Facing sharp criticism from his titular superior, the Commissioner of the Metropolitan Police, and having lost the confidence of the Prime Minister, Thomson was forced out of office. 'I did not resign,' he told his friend Hugh Sinclair, the Director of Naval Intelligence, 'but was the victim of the usual intrigue with which I[ntelligence] O[fficer]s are familiar.'[16]

Cumming's organisation faced further pressure for economies in the next financial year. At the beginning of 1922 the Treasury proposed cutting his budget to £65,000 for 1922–3, rehearsing a familiar series of arguments against the necessity for a continued high level of Secret Service expenditure. All government departments were being required to economise and 'on general grounds' it was 'essential that economies should be effected on Secret Service as on other Services'. Bearing this in mind, it was 'not reasonable to ask that every risk should be guarded against'. It was equally unreasonable 'to maintain 3½ years after the Armistice an organisation far more elaborate than was found sufficient in pre-war days'. Finally, the increasing difficulty was noted of defending in parliament 'the present large provision for Secret Service', as well as the 'considerable danger that if reductions cannot be made the House will press for details of expenditure, and thus make it exceedingly difficult for Departments to preserve the necessary secrecy for such work'.[17] The Secretary of State for War, Sir Laming Worthington-Evans (who had succeeded Churchill in February 1921), sprang to the defence of 'S.I.S.'. Even before the proposed cut it had not been 'possible to maintain a S.I.S. service in all countries'; though 'war no longer exists the situations all over the world are so complex that greater vigilance on the part of S.I.S. is required than in 1914'; and if the grant were reduced to £65,000, it would mean 'that the whole of the system will have to be re-cast' and 'the spade work already put in will be completely lost and the money previously spent on it thus wasted'. Worthington-Evans estimated that 'to produce the military and political information demanded' SIS would need a total of £150,000, comprising the £125,000 he asserted it had actually received in 1921–2, plus £25,000 due to the absorption of work previously done by Army Intelligence in Constantinople, Egypt and Germany. His figures were in fact an overestimate, since the entire Foreign Office portion of the Secret Service Vote had been £125,000, of which Cumming had been advanced £100,000.[18]

Deciding that total secret service spending should be just £200,000, the Cabinet once again asked Fisher, Crowe and Hankey to look into the matter. With the continual struggle for funding since the end of the war understandably beginning to take its toll, at their first meeting Crowe stressed 'the disadvantages of the present hand-to-mouth arrangements'. The 'absolute uncertainty prevailing from year to year as to future Secret Service votes made it impossible to offer any security of tenure to agents so that the better class of man fought shy of taking service in this capacity'. His colleagues agreed in principle that 'some guarantee of permanency' was required, but conceded that this was a matter for the Cabinet to decide. Nevile Bland (again serving as secretary) drew up budget projections for Cumming's organisation on a £65,000, £85,000 and £150,000 basis. When quizzed on these, Cumming said that at the £65,000 level 'two agents paid from Headquarters would have to be dismissed, and the Political section would be abolished'. Cumming was accompanied by Colonel Stewart Menzies, who provided liaison between the Secret Service and the War Office. Employing a careful double negative Menzies conceded that 'the £85,000 basis would probably be not unsatisfactory', though it would leave coverage stretched in the Near and Middle East, as well as the USA. Depending on reductions in other parts of the secret service estimate (for example from the Irish and Home Offices, the former as a result of the Anglo-Irish agreement of December 1921 bringing an end to the Irish War of Independence), the committee thought that £5,000 extra could be found for Cumming.[19]

At the beginning of April 1922, the committee reported to the Cabinet that one of their objects had been 'to *augment* so far as might be requisite the sum designated to foreign intelligence' (emphasis added). This was a remarkable assertion, in sharp contrast to the unvarying demands for reductions which had dominated the debate about finance since the end of the war. Naturally, the reduced overall figure of £200,000 was sacrosanct, but, with savings from other budgets, the committee suggested that Cumming be given £90,000 for the year 1922–3. They were 'satisfied that for £90,000 a foreign intelligence organisation' could be provided which, 'while necessarily of a less elaborate character', would cover all the essential countries and would 'involve neither the abandonment, nor unduly drastic curtailment, of any essential services'.[20] While financial stringency was to continue to affect the Service and its work in the 1920s and 1930s, the deep spending cuts of 1919–22 were not repeated. Indeed, in the mid-1920s, although overall secret service expenditure declined, the Foreign Office share saw a modest increase.[21] The report of Sir Warren Fisher's committee in the spring of 1922 marked an important moment for the survival of the Secret Intelligence Service, for, underpinning the committee's reversal – albeit modest – of the budget reductions which had applied unremittingly since the end of the war, there was an acceptance of Cumming's organisation as an important and autonomous government agency devoted to the clandestine collection of foreign information.

Staffing and structure

The establishment of a more or less settled budget not only confirmed the institutional value of the Secret Service to the government, but also reflected the fact that the immediate threat to its independent existence had passed. The replacement as Prime Minister of Lloyd George by Andrew Bonar Law, who headed a majority Conservative administration after winning a general election in November 1922, also reduced the likelihood (for the meantime) of any major change to the government's overall security and intelligence organisation. Cumming himself must take much of the credit for successfully steering his organisation through the choppy waters of the Great War and the troubled years that followed. One measure of his achievement is a comprehensive appreciation of the Service, describing its function, its relations with other government departments and its 'internal organisation', which would have scarcely been possible to produce while the Bureau had been under continuous pressure, its future and even perhaps its very existence uncertain. The review was apparently prepared some time between the fall of Lloyd George's government on 23 October 1922 (which is mentioned in the text) and Cumming's death on 14 June 1923 (for the document has marginal annotations by him). One comment concerned the title of the organisation. The appreciation began with the statement: 'The S.I.S. (Special Intelligence Service) is the offspring and successor of the pre-war "Secret Service", developed and altered to suit post-war conditions . . . Both the name S.I.S.', it stated, 'and the definition of that Service's functions, which date from 1919, are self invented.' 'This is not correct,' noted Cumming in his characteristic green ink. 'My appointment in 1909 was "Chief of the Secret Service" & I have always been so styled in official papers. I have never authorised any change in my title.' By late 1922, although the name 'MI1(c)' was still widely employed (and was used right up to the beginning of the Second World War), 'SIS' had also been employed for some time. In February 1920 a report from Geneva about Bolshevik conspirators was marked as being circulated from 'S.I.S.'. (A report in the same file, circulated the previous month, was marked 'M.I.1.c', suggesting that there might have been a change in practice at this time.) The abbreviation also occurred abroad. An intelligence summary from 'S.I.S. (Constantinople Branch)', for example, appears on a document from December 1920.[22] But whether

'S.I.S.' stood for *Special* or *Secret* Intelligence Service is not clear, though Cumming's evident irritation with the former (first expressed in April 1919) might suggest both that 'Special' was quite commonly used and that 'Secret' might therefore have been more readily adopted by colleagues and subordinates. Although the title Secret Intelligence Service was suggested for the amalgamated intelligence organisation proposed by the War Office at the end of 1919, there is no evidence of it being used generally at that time.

The SIS appreciation defined the term 'Secret Service' as 'the gathering of information by means of individuals secretly paid for the purpose, that is to say, through "spies"'. But the anonymous writer went on to complain that 'the words "spy" and "secret service" have acquired a limited and unpleasant meaning through public misconception due to sensational literature', and that the terms 'agent' and 'special intelligence' were to be preferred. The paper contended that the class of 'agent' employed was, 'as a general rule, high socially and morally – anyhow, infinitely higher than the uninitiated would ever expect', and that there was 'nothing in the duties of an S.I.S. Representative which can call for censure, or cause a gentleman to think twice before enlisting in the service'. These views were clearly aspirational (and perhaps part of a necessary seizing of the moral high ground by intelligence officers themselves), a fact reinforced by the improbable assertions that 'no agent is recruited for the purpose of betraying his own country or ideals', that 'an individual's vices are not played upon in order to obtain a hold upon him', and that 'certain conventions such as the Red Cross, religious bodies, etc are not used for the purpose of cover or agents', all of which (though not specifically the Red Cross) had been done (or contemplated) during the 1914–18 war.

SIS's relations with government were succinctly outlined. It reported to the three armed service ministries, the Foreign, Home, Colonial and India Offices and the Department of Overseas Trade. Marking a significant change, it was noted that under Lloyd George's government 'copies of more important reports were also circulated to the Prime Minister and certain members of the Cabinet'. This had now been 'discontinued' under a ruling from the Foreign Secretary, confirmed by the Prime Minister, 'whereby he decided to receive his advice and information through constitutional channels', that is to say from the particular government department concerned. Close relations with the armed forces departments were secured by each service intelligence staff having 'a separate liaison section actually forming part of the S.I.S. H.Q. staff'. Although relations were naturally also very close with the Foreign Office, it was felt that both the functions and limitations of 'the S.I.S. work' were 'not as fully realised' by other civil departments. Partly this was a result of the necessary secrecy under which SIS operated, but this could sometimes be taken too far. One (unspecified) department 'authorised to receive reports' had considered them all so secret 'that they were immediately placed in a locked box after being read by one individual and never again referred to'.

The paper also summarised liaison with the other security and intelligence agencies. The 'S.S. Branch' of the police at Scotland Yard was 'to all intents and purposes the complement of the S.I.S.', while MI5 was responsible for 'special intelligence' in 'all countries under the British Flag' and was 'concerned solely in the tracking of Foreign Military (and Naval &c) agents working in British territory, and with the moral security of the Armed Forces of the Crown', another complementary function. MI5, moreover, had 'no right to maintain agents of any kind in any Foreign Country without the knowledge and consent of S.I.S.'. The third analogous British organisation was Indian Political Intelligence (IPI), directed from Simla in India, though it had its headquarters in London. IPI's function was 'the watching of subjects of the Indian Empire in all countries save India itself and certain neighbouring States'. This involved working in foreign countries, but potential overlap with SIS was monitored by careful liaison and co-operation between the two services.

The outline of the Service's 'internal organisation' reflected changes introduced by Cumming since the end of the war. As part of his postwar cost-cutting he told Ronald Campbell of the Foreign Office in March 1919 that he would have to give up the 'Organisation by Departments' – with separate sections for each customer department – which had been imposed on him in November 1917 and replace it with a 'system on a "Geographical" Basis', rather as had been the case earlier in the war. What in fact emerged was a combination of the two, with a Production side, primarily responsible for the overseas deployment of the Service, and a Circulation side, which provided the link with the customer departments, both 'transmitting all information obtained' and generally 'acting as a liaison between the S.I.S. and the said Departments'. Reflecting the two-way process involved, this section later became known as Requirements. By early 1923, the Production side was envisaged as containing nine groups, covering different geographical regions, with a supervising Inspector over each, but, while seven groups covering Europe, the Near East and the Far East had been organised, the North American one was not yet operational and the South American Group was 'definitely still only theoretical'. A diagram showing the budget figures for SIS's overseas stations prepared later in 1923 shows that a New York station was in existence and indicates the share of expenditure met by Passport Control. It suggests that the £90,000 budget recommended by the Secret Service Committee in 1922 represented only part of the funds required for the Service. Out of a total budget of £170,800, 'Headquarters' was allocated £26,000 and £20,000 was earmarked for 'Contingent', leaving £124,800 for overseas operations. The income side showed four sources of revenue: an 'S.S. Grant' of £112,000; 'Passport Control', £44,000; 'Far East Res[erve]', £14,000; and 'Scotland Yard', £800.[23]

On the Circulation side, the armed service branches (Sections II–IV in the November 1917 arrangement) remained. Reflecting postwar priorities, Section V, Political, was the largest (with two officers and five secretaries in January 1923), and Section I, Economics (which had primarily been devoted to wartime blockade work), had disappeared altogether. In order to help maintain the secrecy of the organisation, Cumming and Nevile Bland agreed in February 1922 that requests for information from (and responses to) departments other than the armed services should all pass through the Permanent Under-Secretary at the Foreign Office. Apart from Section V, there is not much evidence from the early 1920s, however, that the section numbers were widely used in Head Office. This, too, presumably reflected postwar realities: the elaborate 1917 (and, as Cumming had observed in 1919, expensive) structure for a Head Office of up to a hundred staff was not necessary in the evidently more informal postwar circumstances when the office had shrunk to less than half its wartime size. What had in 1917 been Section VI, Organisation, survived (though not as a formal section) in the central administration of the Service, categorised at the start of 1923 as 'Chief's Staff' (which sounded grander than it was: Cumming, 'Pay' Sykes and two secretaries); Registry (eight staff); Coding (two); Typing (four); Main Office (two); and 'Miscellaneous', including 'translations etc' (four).

During the war the Secret Service had suffered from a considerable turnover of personnel, and Cumming had complained about the armed services' propensity to pinch valuable officers from him just as they were settling into their jobs. Over the postwar years, however, despite the vicissitudes of finance, there was greater stability and continuity of staff, and Cumming managed to assemble a core group of officers, many of whom were to play important roles in the history of the Service up to and during the Second World War. Among his closest colleagues was Paymaster Percy Stanley Sykes, who joined in November 1915 at the age of thirty-seven. A qualified accountant, 'Pay' Sykes was to manage the finances of the Service for thirty years. When he finally retired in 1946, the Director of Naval Intelligence wrote that he was a 'specialist' with 'exceptional experience and qualifications for his present post' who had 'carried out his professional duties of a specialised nature with zeal and ability'.[24] In April 1919 Cumming appointed Major Desmond Morton to be his head of Production. Born in 1891, Morton came from a prosperous landed and professional background and had been educated at Eton and the Royal Military Academy, Woolwich, before embarking on a military career in the Royal Field Artillery. After the outbreak of war in August 1914 he served on the Western Front almost continuously for three years, winning a Military Cross in 1916. Wounded and invalided home in 1917, he returned to France and saw out the war as an aide-de-camp to the British Commander-in-Chief, Field Marshal Sir Douglas Haig. Morton served in SIS for over fifteen years, and continued to have an important intelligence role in Whitehall thereafter, serving as Winston Churchill's liaison officer with SIS for much of the Second World War.[25]

Another significant appointment was Colonel Stewart Menzies, an Old Etonian cavalryman from a very privileged social background. He was a career soldier who had served with the Life Guards on the Western Front and been decorated for gallantry before being gassed, after which he was appointed to a security intelligence position at General Headquarters. By 1918 he was a liaison officer between the Directorate of Military Intelligence and MI1(c). Although employed (and paid for) by the army, he was primarily located in Cumming's organisation. After a spell in Paris in early 1919 on Basil Thomson's security staff attached to the British delegation at the peace conference, he succeeded Claude Dansey as head of Cumming's Military Section IV, although he did not transfer from the War Office to the SIS payroll until 1 April 1923. He remained on it, however, for nearly thirty years and was to be Chief from 1939 to 1952. In January 1921 Cumming appointed Major Malcolm 'Woolly' Woollcombe to work in Sir Robert Nathan's section. Cumming had initially thought to employ Nathan, an old India hand who had worked very successfully against Indian subversives in North America during the war, to take over MI1(c)'s work in the USA, focusing now on Irish and Irish-American revolutionaries,[26] but he kept him at home and put him in charge of the Political Section V. For two years before his early death in June 1921, Nathan, who was plagued by ill-health, was the second most important officer in SIS. According to Woollcombe family tradition, Nathan had offered Woollcombe a job in MI1(c) following a lecture which Nathan had given at the army Staff College. Barely six months after joining the Service, Woollcombe was put in charge of the Political Section, which he continued to superintend (with some distinction) until his own health broke down and he retired in 1944.[27]

In addition to the cadre of long-serving Head Office staff, recruited during the war or shortly afterwards, a significant number of overseas representatives, who joined at much the same time, also had lengthy careers in the Service. One such was Major (later Colonel) Valentine Vivian – widely known in SIS by his initials, 'V.V.', and sometimes as 'Val'. Vivian, born in 1886, son of the successful portrait painter Comley Vivian, was educated at St Paul's School, where he was a classical scholar. Although he apparently had ambitions to work at the Victoria and Albert Museum, in 1906 he joined the Indian Police, rising by 1914 to be assistant director of the criminal intelligence department. After war service with the Indian Army in the Middle East he became Indian Political Intelligence's representative in (and later headed) the jointly funded MI1(c)/IPI Constantinople operation. By the spring of 1922, when the Indian government wanted to recall Vivian to India, Eyre Crowe of the Foreign Office declared that 'the utility of the existing organisation in Constantinople depended very much on its chief'.[28] Vivian came to Head Office in London for the first six months of 1923 before going abroad again, to the British army of occupation in Germany. He spent the rest of his working life in SIS, rising to be Deputy Chief and not retiring until well after the Second World War. Knowledgeable, thoughtful and personally kind, towards the end of his career he acquired a reputation for ineffectual fastidiousness.

The importance of individuals, and their personalities, was accentuated by the smallness of the Service. In the autumn of 1919, Head Office had fewer than fifty staff, while overseas there were seventy-two officers and an indeterminate number of support staff. By 1923, successive budget cuts had had their effect. At home there were sixteen officers, thirty secretaries (all female) and twenty weekly paid staff, including drivers, 'chars' (charwomen – that is, cleaners), messengers and (a typical Cumming requirement) one 'car washer'. No provision is made for technical and scientific staff in the surviving account books for 1921–3, although in July 1919 Cumming took on a Dr S. Dawson 'as chemist', and renewed his contract (at a slightly reduced level) in July 1921. It seems that, at this stage, scientific assistance was provided on a consultancy basis. In any case, SIS could also call for assistance from the technical branches of the armed services. Abroad, there were forty-eight officers and clerks (distributed among thirty-three stations) and approximately seventy-seven ancillary staff. These figures, of course, did not include agents. In the 1920s the British Secret Service, with a worldwide remit, had a total complement of fewer than two hundred people, sixty-odd at home and approximately twice that number abroad.

From Cumming to Sinclair

The travails of the immediate postwar years (not to mention those of the war itself) seem to have taken a considerable physical toll on Cumming. According to Frank Stagg, he became a 'martyr to angina', and, fifty-nine years old at the end of the war, clearly could not go on for ever. In the autumn of 1919, though he had 'no intention of retiring' unless he was 'asked to do so', he raised the question of his pension with Lord Hardinge at the Foreign Office. Although he had the substantive rank of a naval captain, neither his time on boom defence nor his years as Chief of the Secret Service counted towards his pension, and so the Foreign Secretary approved the purchase out of public funds of an annuity to make up his prospective pension to that of a captain. Prepared to retire or not, there is some evidence that Cumming had thought about the future. Compton Mackenzie claimed that when he returned to London in 1917 Cumming had proposed that Mackenzie come to Head Office as his number two. 'I'll go through the war,' he allegedly told Mackenzie, 'and I'll stick on for a couple of years after it's over, and when I go you'll step into my place.'[29] There was never any likelihood of this happening, not least because Mackenzie was appalled at the prospect. At the beginning of 1921 Cumming, evidently with retirement in the not-too-distant future in mind, was worried about the possibility of Kell replacing him, but there appears to have been no serious discussion about the subject until February 1922 when he had a conversation with Nevile Bland about 'a successor for me'. Bland said that 'neither D.M. [Desmond Morton] nor S.M. [Stewart Menzies] would be acceptable & thinks a naval man would be preferred anyway'. 'R.' (probably Commander E. H. Russell, who worked in the Naval Section in SIS Head Office) was 'a bit young' and 'R.R.S.' (unidentified) was 'too old'.

In the end it was to be 'a naval man', and some time in late 1922 or early 1923 Rear Admiral Hugh 'Quex' Sinclair was selected to be the second Chief. Writing in January 1923, Cumming told Sir Samuel Hoare that he was pleased Sinclair had been chosen and that he thought him 'in every way qualified & suitable' to take over the Service. 'I feel sure', he wrote, 'that in his capable hands this org[anisatio]n will grow to be v. useful – it is not too much to say – essential – to the Govt. Departments we serve.'[30] The forty-nine-year-old Sinclair was a career sailor who had been educated at the Britannia Naval College at Dartmouth and entered the navy as a midshipman in 1888. From his service record it is clear that he was an exceptional officer. From the start his ability and professional knowledge were described as 'very good'. The record is characterised by positive comments: 'steady and trustworthy'; 'zealous & capable'; 'Excellent tact & temper. Very discreet & loyal'; 'exceptional powers of administration'.[31] During the First World War he had served in the Mobilisation Division of the Admiralty and finished up as chief of staff of the battle-cruiser force. In January 1919 he succeeded Blinker Hall as Director of Naval Intelligence, a move which the notoriously hard-to-please Hall warmly welcomed. Hall was 'delighted', and told Sinclair that it was 'not often given to men that they see their job filled by the only man who can do it'.[32] He stayed in Naval Intelligence for only eighteen months and in August 1921 was appointed to a three-year stint as 'Rear Admiral "S"' (commander of the Submarine Service). This would have taken him to August 1924, but by the late spring of 1923, with Cumming's health failing, it had evidently been decided that he would take over as Chief of SIS in September that year.[33]

There is some suggestion that even this timetable might have been accelerated as Frank Stagg recorded a 'farewell' dinner for Cumming at about this time. '"Blinker"', he recalled, 'eulogised him [Cumming] magnificently for his wonderful work. In his reply "C" said ". . . you've come to bury 'C' Sir – not to praise him"'. Cumming died – 'suddenly', according to the death notice in *The Times* – on 14 June 1923 at 1 Melbury Road, which was both the Service headquarters and his London home. In his autobiography, the journalist and thriller-writer Valentine Williams, whom Cumming had befriended during the war, claimed to have been the last person to see him alive. Hearing that he was retiring and about to leave London, Williams called to return some books he had borrowed and 'spent the afternoon with him, chatting about old times'. When Williams left at about six o'clock, Cumming was 'comfortably in-stalled in a corner of the sofa. When his secretary went in to see him soon after she found him dead.'[34]

The appointment of Hugh Sinclair to head the Secret Service – he actually commenced work on 3 September 1923 – illustrates the extent to which the status of the Service had risen during Cumming's time as Chief. Far from the Director of Naval Intelligence appointing some evidently junior officer to the post, a former DNI himself took it over. There were other differences, too. Sinclair was socially very well connected (he had been appointed a naval aide-de-camp to the King in February 1920) and, along with his flag rank as an admiral, this helped give him greater Whitehall clout than his predecessor. Unlike Cumming, on the other hand, Sinclair was a noted bon vivant, and had a stormy private life, being divorced in 1920. His nickname 'Quex' had been bestowed on him as a young man, and was derived from Arthur Pinero's play *The Gay Lord Quex*, in which the hero was described as having been 'the wickedest man in London', though he had subsequently become a reformed character.[35] While one of his obituarists claimed that he 'was intolerant of any sort of slackness or inefficiency, which he was likely to castigate with an astonishing flow of forcible language, such as was traditional in an earlier generation of sea officers', he was also 'one of the most imperturbable of men', and it was claimed that 'no emergency ever saw him "rattled"'. In addition he was 'always appreciative of good service in a subordinate', and he appears to have been a very popular commanding officer (he was captain of HMS *Renown* in 1916–17). Judging from an account of the 'annual submarine dinner' in 1921, he was very affectionately regarded by his subordinates in the Submarine Service.[36] Whatever his qualities of leadership, which in the early summer of 1923 were yet to be proved for SIS, those of his predecessor had ensured that the Service had a future for him to preside over.

6

From Boche to Bolsheviks

At the end of the First World War, Sir Henry Wilson, the Chief of the Imperial General Staff, declared that 'our real danger now is not the Boch[e] but Bolshevism'. This became an underlying consideration for much British policy-making during the years that followed. Indeed, this perceived threat was intermittently to dominate British foreign (and some domestic) policy perceptions for much of the twentieth century. In December 1926, reflecting on the events of the British General Strike that year and of supposed Soviet agitation in the Far East, Sir William Tyrrell, Permanent Under-Secretary at the Foreign Office, told the Foreign Secretary that 'Russian interference in our coal strike and Russian proceedings in China might justify us in assuming that we are virtually at war.'[1] These attitudes had an impact on SIS. In the years following the First World War the Service was mainly preoccupied with the challenge of international Communism, powerfully backed by Soviet Russia. In the post-revolutionary Russian turmoil, the Service sponsored a number of adventurous operations in an effort find out what was going on and forged links with various anti-Bolshevik White Russian and ethnic-minority groups. As well as operating within the Soviet Union itself, SIS took responsibility for identifying Communist front organisations and tracking revolutionaries and subversives across Europe and the wider world.

Targeting Bolshevik Russia

On 28 December 1918 Cumming called on Lord Hardinge at the Foreign Office and secured his permission 'to our continuing our organisation in

Russia' at £3,000 a month 'until 31st March'. Cumming's own accounts the following autumn included £6,600 for 'Russia', but also £50,000 for 'Scandinavia', most, if not all, of which was earmarked for Russian intelligence work. The Service's 1922–3 in-house review made it clear that 'the actual location of an S.I.S. office' had 'but little bearing on the nature of the information emanating from that office', and specifically noted that, for example, an office in Norway ('a country never likely to be of itself of any interest to Great Britain') could 'really be the chief centre of information concerning Russia, or some important international movement with ramifications in every civilised country'. The 'first principle of the S.I.S. overseas organisation', it stated, was 'to gather news about the countries bordering on the one in which the local headquarters is situated, the more so, since generally speaking, Representatives are warned not to attempt to acquire information of a nature likely to be actively resented by the country affording asylum'. That this was substantially the case is confirmed by the 1920–1 estimates Cumming prepared for an annual budget of either £125,000 or £65,000. Under the higher budget £24,000 was allocated for 'Russia' under the following three headings: 'Vladivostock', £2,000; 'South', £2,000; and 'Helsingfors [Helsinki] (for North Russia)', £20,000. On the £65,000 basis, the Russian share fell to £9,000: £8,000 for Helsinki, and the other thousand for the 'South'. Vladivostok was omitted altogether. In both schemes, 'Russia' was the second largest SIS commitment, after 'Holland (for Germany, &c)' – £18,000 on the lower budget – which also inevitably included much anti-Bolshevik work.[2]

'Intervention' in Russia began as an effort to shore up Russian forces fighting against the Central Powers, but after the Soviet government signed a peace treaty in the spring of 1918, British and Allied forces found themselves aligned with counter-revolutionary White Russian elements in an escalating Russian civil war.[3] This meant that any SIS activities in Russia, however carefully designed for purely information-gathering purposes, could inevitably become identified with direct anti-Soviet operations of one sort or another.

Over the autumn and winter of 1918 one intelligence source was the left-leaning writer and journalist Arthur Ransome. Working as the Petrograd correspondent of the *Daily News*, Ransome had become friendly with Lenin and other Bolshevik leaders. His mistress, Yevgeniya Petrovna Shelepina (who became his second wife in 1924), was Trotsky's secretary.

As Robert Bruce Lockhart observed to the Foreign Office in May 1919, Shelepina had been 'working with Ransome in connexion with MI1c and was incidentally instrumental in getting out of Russia the numerous Bolshevik papers and literature which Ransome sent on to you'.[4] In December 1918 an officer in MI1(c) told MI5 that Ransome (who was known as 'S.76') had 'done quite good work for us'. The same month Ransome and Major John Scale, the head of station in Stockholm (and SIS Inspector co-ordinating work in the Baltic area), devised a scheme whereby Ransome would leave the *Daily News* and return to Russia as a representative of the British Museum, with a 'private mandate' to 'collect all the available documents (published and otherwise) bearing on Bolshevism'. Ransome thought that 'such a request would enormously flatter the Bolsheviks, and enable him to go everywhere and get anything of this sort'. Ransome's closeness to the Bolsheviks had made him suspect in the eyes of some, but Cumming shrewdly argued that his socialist political sympathies might actually boost his intelligence-gathering potential. Putting the plan to William Tyrrell at the Foreign Office on 19 December 1918, Cumming recognised that he could not 'expect an unbiassed account of affairs from him. But', he continued, 'allowances can be made for his prejudices (and it has to be said that, making this allowance, the information he has provided us with during the last month has been satisfactory)'. Besides, Ransome was 'probably the one person available to go openly to Moscow and Petrograd, and to give us first-hand information of the condition of things, and at any rate the ostensible policies that are being pursued there'.

Tyrrell approved the scheme, and Ransome spent six weeks in Russia in February–March 1919, but there is no evidence that he was able to supply much – or any – useful intelligence during this period. His main concern seems to have been his eventually successful efforts to get Shelepina out of Russia and into England. Perhaps in the end his political leanings did undermine his value as an intelligence agent. The opinion of one officer in the Stockholm station was that 'S.76 may be regarded as absolutely honest,' and that his reports about Russia could 'be relied upon absolutely with only the proviso that his view tends to be coloured by his personal sympathies with men like Litvinov and Radek [respectively the Soviet envoy in London and a member of the Bolshevik Central Executive Committee]'. Although he would 'report what he sees . . . he does not see quite straight'.

While Ransome operated in Russia openly under his own name, others working for Cumming did not. One such was agent ST/25, Paul Dukes. When he was recruited in the summer of 1918, Dukes recalled that he had been told: 'we want someone to remain there [in Russia] to keep us informed of the march of events'. Sir Robert Nathan instructed him to 'report on changes of policy, the attitude of the population, military and naval matters, what possibilities there might be for an alteration of regime, and what part Germany was playing'. Briefed in Stockholm by Major Scale, and with forged documents cheekily identifying himself as 'Joseph Ilitch Afirenko', a Ukrainian clerk of the Cheka, Dukes returned to Petrograd through Finland in December 1918.

Displaying great courage and a real gift for undercover work, for most of a year he based himself in Russia under a number of disguises. For a while he was a post office clerk named 'Alexander Markovitch'. With the help of a doctor friend he posed as an epileptic, and later he became 'Comrade Alexander Bankau', a soldier in the 'Automobile Section of the VIIIth Army'. Dukes reported mostly low-level, though accurate, information about conditions in Russia which he managed to send out by courier. In March 1919 the Naval Intelligence Department described him as 'the only reliable & regular source of information about happenings in [the] Baltic Fleet, and everyone who knows [the] conditions under which he works can have nothing but admiration for him'. One of his reports, from the end of April 1919, had been 'written on tissue paper' and 'carried out of the country by a Russian officer who hid it in his boot'. It described factory strikes, disturbances in the Russian fleet, inflation and the desperate food situation. Predicting 'coming inevitable change', it asserted that there was 'little hope of any lasting settlement, or comfort other than that any system of administration will be less intolerable than the present'.[5]

In order to keep in touch with Dukes, Cumming personally organised two high-performance shallow-draft motor boats under Lieutenant Augustus Agar ('ST/34') to be stationed (with the permission of the Finnish authorities) at the Terijoki Yacht Club on the Gulf of Finland close to the then Russian frontier, only some twenty-five miles from Petrograd and the adjoining island naval base at Kronstadt. The twenty-nine-year-old Agar, who had served aboard HMS *Iphigenia* in north Russia in 1917 and 1918, was a brave and independent-minded man of action who took enthusiastically to 'special operations'. Admiral Walter Cowan, commanding the British naval forces in the Baltic whose task was to prevent Soviet domination of the sea, was out of the same mould as Agar, and, by allowing the vessels to be equipped with torpedoes, evidently contemplated something more than just ferrying couriers in and out of Russia. It took Agar and the motor boats some time to reach Finland, as they were held up for a while by Swedish customs, who questioned their implausible cover story that the vessels were the latest type of pleasure boats and the crews (in plain clothes) were actually salesmen. The Finns were more accommodating, and within three days of his arrival at Terijoki in mid-June Agar had successfully negotiated his forty-knot vessel through the minefield of the Kronstadt defences, landed a courier near Petrograd and made it back safely to his base.[6]

Because of the short nights of the northern summer, Dukes himself sent instructions not to attempt another sortie until mid-July. Meanwhile an anti-Bolshevik demonstration in one of the garrisons on the Russian shore of the Gulf of Finland was being crushed by a Soviet naval bombardment and Agar resolved to take what action he could. According to his memoirs, Agar signalled Cumming in London asking permission to attack the Soviet fleet. The reply, 'Boats to be used for Intelligence purposes only – stop – Take no action unless specially directed by S.N.O. [Senior Naval Officer] Baltic',[7] was enough for Agar, who without waiting to hear from Cowan, correctly assumed that retrospective permission would be given. On 16 June a first attempt was abandoned after one of the motor boats broke down and had to be towed back to base. The next night, despite problems with the torpedo mechanism, which had to be repaired as they approached the Soviet naval base, Agar again penetrated the Kronstadt defences, sank the heavy cruiser *Oleg* and under heavy fire got safely away. Following this, two attempts by Agar to get Dukes out failed: one when Dukes's courier was spotted by a Soviet patrol, and the second when their rowing boat foundered near the rendezvous point. On 17–18 August, Agar, with a flotilla of seven motor boats, launched another attack on Kronstadt in which two Soviet battleships were sunk, thus securing Allied naval command of the Baltic. On 25 August he made a final effort to exfiltrate Dukes, but in attempting to evade the Kronstadt searchlights at full speed he rammed his boat into a breakwater and had to nurse his badly damaged vessel back without completing the mission.[8]

Scale evidently disapproved of Agar's actions. The attacks on the Soviet fleet, although (and perhaps because) they were so spectacular and successful, by alerting the enemy to the presence of British units made it much more difficult for a motor boat to slip past the port defences to deliver a courier or pick up an agent. In August 1919 Scale described Agar to Cumming as 'very "difficile"', and asked Admiral Cowan to replace him. The potential conflict demonstrated here between 'special operations' and 'secret intelligence' was a constant concern for intelligence practitioners. It was an issue, moreover, which was to crop up during the Second World War, especially in the relations between SIS and its sibling service, SOE (Special Operations Executive).

Dukes eventually escaped through Latvia and, on his return to England, was rewarded with a knighthood – the only member of the Service during its first forty years to be thus rewarded for work in the field. Although, apparently, 'sufficient evidence [was] available to justify ST/25 being recommended for V.C.' he was found, 'as a civilian', not to be eligible for a military decoration. Agar, however, brought home at about the same time, was awarded the VC for his part in sinking the *Oleg* and a DSO for the second attack. Dukes's vivid eyewitness accounts of conditions in Soviet Russia were much in demand after he got back to London on 17 September, and this surely helped to secure Cumming's reputation as the country's most important intelligence chief. On 18 September Dukes reported in person to both the Director of Military Intelligence and Sir Basil Thomson. Cumming also took him to see the Secretary for War, Winston Churchill, who gave him a 'long interview over 1½ hours'. On 20 September Cumming brought him to meet Lord Curzon at his private residence, 1 Carlton House Terrace.

Dukes left the Service the following year, but he was obviously very taken with his experience, and he stayed involved on an occasional basis. In May 1920, when the Foreign Office official Rex Leeper, who had been working in the Political Intelligence Department, was going to Poland on a 'fact-finding' mission, as well as to review the work of Cumming's representative at Warsaw 'and make suggestions for the future', Dukes was to accompany him on behalf of SIS, ostensibly as his secretary, and offered to work only 'for bare expenses'. In the end Dukes went out independently, and stayed in Poland for six months, attempting (without apparently much success) to establish a network of agents to work on

Russia, but nevertheless sending back what Nathan described as 'very interesting' reports about the anti-Bolshevik side in the Russian Civil War.[9] He got back to England in November 1920, and over the next few years evidently nursed ambitions to return to Russia as an agent. But his high profile as a 'Russian expert' (for example, he toured the United States giving lectures on the topic), his contacts with increasingly unreliable White Russians, and the Bolsheviks' keen interest in his movements meant that it was practically impossible for him to enter Russia clandestinely.

Sidney Reilly

When Paul Dukes was in Poland in the autumn of 1920, he was joined there by Sidney Reilly. 'They are', reported the head of station in Warsaw, 'as happy as a pair of "sand boys" constructing a perfectly good new Russia'. One of the problems with Reilly, which was to do for him in the

Sidney Reilly, the so-called 'Ace of Spies',
caught by Crowther Smith in RAF uniform.

end, was his dangerous fusion of espionage with a dedicated personal mission to bring down the Bolshevik government. Not only did the latter generally involve him with counter-revolutionary groups who were (as it turned out) increasingly penetrated by the Communists, but it also appears to have undermined his judgment on matters of security: that essential quality which the successful spy must have of knowing whom to trust and whom not.

After his return from Petrograd in October 1918, Reilly had spent some time in south Russia, where the British were actively supporting White Russian forces under General Anton Denikin. Accompanied by Captain George Hill, another MI1(c) Moscow veteran, and ostensibly attached to the Commercial Department of the Foreign Office, Reilly had been instructed by Cumming to collect political information which was 'urgently needed from the whole of South Russia'. Reflecting the scarcity of intelligence about Russia in general, Cumming added that if 'sufficient information' had been procured about the region by the end of February, the two men might move in the direction of 'Moscow and the North'. In the event Hill returned home in early February and Reilly stayed only a few weeks longer. But between late December 1918 and late February 1919 he supplied fifteen despatches which were described in the Foreign Office as containing 'a fund of useful information on the subject of the whole situation in South Russia'.[10] The reports were not politically neutral. Reilly strongly favoured Allied backing for Denikin, and, observing that 'the Bolshevik armies will not stand up to regular troops', felt that the White forces could defeat their Red adversaries. Reporting that Allied equipment and economic help was not sufficient, but that actual troops were needed too, he was also very critical of the Cossack leader, General Krasnoff, who had only grudgingly accepted Denikin's supreme command. Reilly remarked, nevertheless, that 'the trump cards are in our hands and it should not be difficult to persuade Krasnoff that above all we look to him to carry out the agreement with Denikin not only in the letter but also in the spirit'.

Cumming had other representatives in South Russia. Lieutenant Commander Malcolm Maclaren ('RS/1') was a Russian (and Polish) expert who had arrived in Odessa via Bucharest in early 1919 by a roundabout route from Archangel. Having previously worked in Petrograd, he was 'wanted by the Bolsheviks'. Maclaren was accompanied by another

Petrograd veteran, Harold Gibson, who was to have a long and varied career in SIS. When Maclaren arrived in Odessa in March 1919 he telegraphed Cumming that Reilly was already there, 'evidently working for you'. Since he appeared to have 'established himself very well', had 'good agents' and was 'obtaining very satisfactory results', Maclaren offered to resign, but he was instead told to stay in the region, where he settled down to gathering intelligence for about a year before moving to Sevastopol in April 1920. By August he was back in London. Gibson, who was bilingual in Russian (having been brought up partly in Moscow where his father had managed a chemical works), and a qualified interpreter in French, German and Czech, travelled through south Russia and Bessarabia before being posted in mid-October 1919 to the SIS station in Constantinople (later known as Istanbul), where he remained for three years.

During 1919 (and while he pursued his own multifarious business interests) Reilly continued to work intermittently for Cumming. Between September and December 1919 he moved between London and Paris 'on special duty for M.I.1.c'. By the end of the year he was in Prague, supplying 'much appreciated' (though unspecified) information for London. Writing to Nathan from Paris in March 1920, Reilly reflected that the 'counter-revolution in Germany' (the abortive, reactionary Kapp Putsch, which briefly threatened to bring down the newly established Weimar Republic) would, if successful, have enormous repercussions in Russia and, he predicted, mean 'a rapid termination of the Bolshevik régime'. He had an agent, well regarded in right-wing monarchist circles, whom he could send to Berlin (which was 'to-day the navel of the world'), though he advised London that he should not go until the situation in Germany was clearer. But Nathan wanted the agent to be despatched at once and to be paid £300 (£8,600 in current money). Revealing that, towards the end of the financial year, even SIS was prey to British civil service accounting practices, his 'first and foremost' reason was that 'we can afford the money this year and probably shall not be able to do so after the 1st April'. Besides, Head Office was 'very anxious . . . to find out the inwards of what is going on in Berlin'. But Reilly (perhaps demonstrating a finer sense of priorities than Nathan) successfully counselled delay, 'being guided mainly by the desire to obtain the most useful results for us and not in any way to waste the limited funds at our disposal for this purpose'.

Although Reilly was himself passionately opposed to the Soviet regime, he had no illusions about the unreliability of some of the anti-Bolshevik groups with whom he associated. He told Cumming that 'from experience' he had 'no faith . . . in the capabilities of the Russian Monarchists', who were thought to have been involved with the Kapp Putsch. He thought that significant 'Russian–German activities' were only possible either with Communists in both countries combining to foment revolution or (and here, remarkably, he anticipated the Nazi–Soviet Pact of 1939) in the form of an 'alliance between German militarists and Russian Bolsheviks mainly with the object of attacking Poland'. Reilly's main value for SIS was his knowledge of Russian affairs. Towards the end of March 1920 he sent Nathan 'an initial list of 58 Bolsheviks'. Much of the intelligence collected by him was handed on to Sir Basil Thomson at Scotland Yard, including 'Portraits of Bolshevik Missionaries', a 'Card Index of agents of Reds' and a 'Map showing location of resident Soviet agents in Europe'.

In the summer of 1920 Cumming launched an ambitious operation suggested by Reilly to form an international 'anti-Bolshevik intelligence service' by sending Vladimir Gregorievich Orlov, alias Orbanski, to recruit collaborators across Europe. Orlov had been a Tsarist intelligence officer and general criminal investigator under the Soviet regime before escaping from Russia. With Malcolm Maclaren, whom Cumming had summoned home from Istanbul in April 1920 'to take complete charge of our affairs in North Europe', Reilly, Orlov and Dukes toured east-central Europe spotting potential anti-Bolshevik agents, and signing them either for nothing, or for a regular stipend, or for an exchange of information. In Warsaw they recruited five; in Riga their haul was eleven; in Reval (now Tallinn), four; in Helsinki, three; in Terijoki, two; in Stockholm, ten; in Berlin, fourteen; in Prague, three; and in Kovno (Kaunas), two. Most of these collaborators were exiled Russian former military and intelligence officers, but there was also a selection of officials of the various host countries' intelligence services, including some based in Berlin. Reporting to Desmond Morton at Head Office in December 1920, Reilly wrote that Maclaren and Orlov had 'done a tremendous amount of spadework and that everything now depends upon how it will be utilized'. Reilly believed that Orlov, who would be in charge of the new organisation, should be 'very well supported' by the British.

Although in the autumn of 1920 Cumming had described Reilly's work as 'highly important', there were some indications that the 'ace of spies' was starting to prove troublesome for the Service. Reporting that Reilly had been 'boasting of being in close touch with the Secretary of State for War', the Admiralty complained that he had been 'wearing Naval Uniform in Paris'. He upset the Foreign Office by sending a telegram from Warsaw through the British legation, an impropriety which threatened to implicate the regular diplomats with intelligence work. His flourishing contacts with White Russian émigrés, such as Boris Savinkov, who promoted an anti-Bolshevik congress in Warsaw in June 1921 and who constantly needed funds to support his grandiose plans for bringing down the Soviet regime, threatened to leave Reilly (and potentially his British Secret Service associates) politically exposed. Towards the end of 1921, when Reilly wanted to bring Savinkov to London, proposing that he should meet Winston Churchill (at this time Colonial Secretary) and the Prime Minister's private secretary, Sir Edward Grigg, among others, Cumming declined to help organise a visa for him after the Foreign Office had refused to issue one.[11] Changes at Head Office following the unexpected death of Sir Robert Nathan in June 1921, the constant pressure to reduce expenditure and, most important of all, the British government's efforts to normalise relations with the Soviet Union, marked by the Anglo-Soviet negotiations culminating in the trade agreement of 16 March 1921, powerfully combined to restrict any enthusiasm Cumming and his colleagues might have had for ambitious, expansionist and expensive anti-Bolshevik schemes with the capacity to develop from straightforward intelligence-gathering exercises to full-scale political operations aimed at bringing down the Soviet government.

At the end of July 1921 Maclaren in Warsaw was instructed by London to close down his operation, although for some years a few of the contacts he and Orlov had made remained in touch with SIS through the Baltic stations. In the meantime, Orlov, Savinkov and Reilly continued their anti-Bolshevik crusade throughout Europe, but their links to SIS grew less close. In January 1922 the SIS head of station in Vienna asked Bertie Maw in London whether 'Reilly, who occasionally blows into this office, and says he is part of our London show, is really your representative and should be talked to in all confidence'. Remarking that 'personally' he thought Reilly 'knows far too much about our show', Maw passed the enquiry on to Desmond Morton whose response indicated that Reilly's time with SIS was coming to an end. Vienna was to 'give Reilly no more information than is absolutely necessary' and Maw was instructed to tell Vienna 'that Reilly is not a member of our office and does not serve C. in that he is not receiving any pay from us'. Morton added, however, that Reilly had 'worked at one time during the war for C's organisation' and was 'now undoubtedly of a certain use to us'. Nevertheless, 'we do not altogether know what to make of him'. Since Reilly was 'a political intriguer of no mean class' (and Boris Savinkov's 'right hand man'), Morton argued that it was 'infinitely better for us to keep in with him, whereby he tells us a great deal of what he is doing, than to quarrel with him when we should hear nothing of his activities'. 'Whatever may be Reilly's faults,' added Morton, 'I personally would stake my reputation that he is not anti-British, at the moment at any rate, and never has been. He is an astute commercial man out for himself, and really genuinely hates the Bolsheviks.'

Although SIS kept track of Reilly over the next couple of years, there is no evidence that the Service made any real efforts even 'to keep in with him' as Morton had suggested. Increasingly involved with Savinkov's machinations, Reilly was to suffer the same fate. In August 1924 Savinkov was lured back to Russia, convicted of 'counter-revolution' (among other crimes), and in May the following year died in prison – perhaps having committed suicide. Reilly, for his part, was enticed back to his death in the Soviet Union in September 1925 by the Trust, a bogus Russian monarchist organisation based in Paris and set up by the Soviet secret police (the OGPU since July 1923) precisely to penetrate and neutralise their anti-Bolshevik opponents. It was an extremely successful operation which also seems to have duped the experienced SIS officer Ernest Boyce, who in the summer of 1918 had briefly been the main Service representative in Moscow, and from 1920 served as head of station in Helsinki and Tallinn in Estonia. From early 1922 SIS had been aware of the Trust, and an agent, '21028', had been deputed to keep an eye on it, with the aim of ascertaining its activities and, potentially, exploiting it for intelligence on the Soviet Union. In 1925 Boyce had the idea of employing Reilly, an old friend, to penetrate the organisation and, evidently without clearing the scheme with his superiors in London, he got 21028 to arrange meetings for Reilly with White Russians in Paris and Trust representatives in Finland. At the latter, on 25 September 1925, Reilly was lured across the Soviet frontier. He never returned, but was imprisoned by the OGPU, interrogated and shot on 5 November. Boyce had to take some of the blame for the tragedy. Back in London, as recalled by Harry Carr, his assistant in Helsinki, he was 'carpeted by the "Chief" for the role he had played in this unfortunate affair'.[12]

The Baltic stations

As the political situation in the Soviet Union stabilised in the early 1920s, the stations in the capitals of Finland, Estonia and Latvia (Helsinki, Tallinn and Riga) worked together on the Soviet target. These three stations comprised SIS's Baltic Group. In July 1920 Scale was replaced as the Group Inspector by Colonel Ronald Meiklejohn, who had served as an intelligence officer with the British intervention force at Murmansk the previous year. From April 1921 Meiklejohn based himself at Tallinn. Helsinki's main priority was naval intelligence, since it was best placed to cover the Russian Baltic Fleet; Tallinn concentrated more on military intelligence; while Riga was mainly engaged on political and economic targets. The three stations exchanged copies of the reports they sent to London, but nearly all the military intelligence they produced was sent first to Tallinn for co-ordination. Britain also wanted to keep track of the Communist threat to the security and internal stability of the United Kingdom, especially as represented by the Comintern – the Third Communist International – established by Lenin in March 1919 to promote world revolution. Cumming having established SIS as the primary agency for overseas intelligence-gathering, a fair amount of this work was done for MI5 and the Special Branch. In May 1920, for example, Scotland House (Special Branch) asked SIS to keep an eye on a prominent Communist British journalist, Francis Meynell, who was proposing to visit Rotterdam and Berlin as correspondent of the left-wing *Daily Herald*. Demonstrating that Sir Basil Thomson wanted information which could be used for counter-propaganda purposes, the brief to SIS observed that Meynell 'is known to be free with champagne suppers, and any striking contrasts between his way of living and the simplicity enjoined by Socialist principle would be of interest to us'. From the early 1920s a series of roughly biannual 'Most Secret' memoranda entitled 'Review of the Communist Movement' were compiled for the Foreign

Office by Section I of SIS, summarising developments across the world in impressive detail.

The Baltic and other European stations depended almost entirely for Russian intelligence on émigrés, and their most important head agents (for example Vladimir Orlov) were usually former Tsarist officers. Many had fallen on hard times, such as the part-time office cleaner in a Passport Control Office in the Balkans who had been a Russian army colonel. Many of these exiles appeared to remain in contact with informants inside the country and to find it relatively easy to recruit fellow refugees. Their evidently sincere dedication to the destruction of Bolshevism, along with the fact that SIS had also recruited a number of Anglo-Russian case officers who were like-minded and thus predisposed to trust them, contributed to an initially rather uncritical acceptance of their product. Their dependence on the pay of Western intelligence services, however, combined with the steady erosion of their access, led inevitably to the fabrication of reports which neither Head Office nor customer departments were initially able to validate with confidence against other comparable Russian material, although it is clear that the existence of the problem was recognised by SIS from the early 1920s onwards. In April 1921, for example, Orlov reported from Berlin that 'a band of adventurers' had 'sprung up' who were 'fabricating forged documents supposed to be of Soviet official origin and are selling these forgeries to various papers and "White" organisations'. In August, another report from Orlov named an individual who supplied forged documents 'to the French Government who would seem to swallow them wholesale. We could', he added, 'send you tons of them.' Passing the report on to Special Branch, Desmond Morton noted that SIS had recently 'sent out a stiffener to our people abroad to the effect that they must give something definite about the origin of any documents they get hold of'. Reflecting a persistent problem with potentially forged documents, this sensible warning was repeated in a circular Sinclair sent out to all stations in May 1925, instructing them to 'use every precaution in accepting as genuine any alleged Communist document that may be offered to you . . . The only facts which can be considered in future as in any way proof of authenticity is the complete story of the manner in which the alleged document has been obtained, and the hands through which it has passed between those of the alleged writer and the S.I.S. representative.'

In due course some of these agents began to work for several services simultaneously, including German Military Intelligence (the Abwehr), and they also became channels for double-agent operations. As the White Russian diaspora settled down into communities in Warsaw, Berlin and Paris, in addition to the Baltic states, they formed inter-communicating centres of counter-revolutionary plotting, propaganda and intelligence. They consequently became easily identifiable targets for penetration and disinformation by the Cheka and its successor, the OGPU. They also began to produce mutually corroborative fabrications, which purported to be from different sources but all too often were not. SIS assisted this process after Cumming in 1921 helped Orlov to set himself up in Berlin as an anti-Bolshevik propagandist working partly for the German police and partly on his own behalf. He soon became well known throughout European intelligence circles for running a 'factory' for creating and circulating reports, which, if not forged, were mostly from dubious sources. He was paid off by Cumming in the spring of 1922, though the Service continued informal contact. In 1924 Morton described him to Sinclair as a 'born intriguer and ambitious', and warned that a document produced by Orlov alone could 'never be accepted' without corroboration from a separate source. In April 1927 a Constantinople agent who had recently visited Berlin and contacted Orlov reported that his organisation was 'completely controlled by the [O.]G.P.U. and with the consent and cooperation of the German S.S. [Secret Service]'. Orlov had 'an elaborate machinery for forging documents' and, 'with information supplied by the G.P.U.', his organisation wrote up 'numerous reports for various Intelligence services throughout Europe'. The agent provided a list of twenty-one Russians used by Orlov to distribute material, three of whom (based in three different countries) were existing SIS contacts. By December 1937 Orlov had been written off completely. 'We cannot lay it down too strongly', instructed London, 'that our experience of this individual is that no reliance whatsoever can be placed on anything he says or does.'

Nineteen-twenties Europe was full of dubious White Russian characters representing themselves as secret agents. One of Orlov's associates in Berlin, for example, was Count Alexander Nelidov who, having offered his services to SIS in Istanbul in 1925 and been turned down, was arrested and deported by the Turks the following year and reappeared in Berlin in 1927, working with Orlov and claiming to be a British agent.

By 1928 he was in the pay of the Germans, though he was suspected by them of working for the French and the Poles, and was already renowned as a purveyor of faked intelligence. In 1929 the Germans arrested and expelled him, apparently for paying a senior official of the Interior Ministry with forged £100 Bank of England notes for information allegedly for the British. He then moved to Brussels where he continued to work with Orlov. In 1940, after the Soviet Military Intelligence officer Walter Krivitsky had defected to the Americans and been debriefed by MI5, SIS learned that Nelidov had also been working in Berlin for the Russians. At least one of these people came to a sticky end. Orlov, who moved to Brussels after the Nazis came to power in Germany, was arrested by the Germans and died after being tortured in December 1940.[13]

This toxic state of affairs led to a major embarrassment for SIS in 1921 when Lord Curzon, ignoring the reservations of some of his Foreign Office advisers, as well as Sir Robert Nathan and Sir Basil Thomson, sent a protest note to the Soviet government about their alleged interference in Ireland and India. This was based on SIS reports from two documentary sources: agent 'BP/11' based in Estonia, and another allegedly well-placed source in Berlin. The station chief in Tallinn, Meiklejohn, assured London that BP/11 had penetrated the Estonian office of Litvinov (at the time Soviet Deputy Commissar for Foreign Affairs) and was 'an agent whose reliability has been proved on many occasions'. The agent had supplied over two hundred 'summaries and paraphrases' of cables between Litvinov in Tallinn, Moscow and the Soviet Trade Delegation in London during the spring of 1921, which revealed Soviet aid for Sinn Fein 'germ cells' in Ireland. Although both Nathan and Thomson individually expressed some concerns about the material and its source, SIS argued that it was 'hardly possible that the long series of telegrams could be a forgery'. In the summer of 1921, SIS provided the newly established interdepartmental committee on Bolshevism with a selection of documents, said to have been obtained from the Soviet representative's office in Berlin, which detailed Soviet subversion against India. The Soviets responded to Curzon's protest based on this material with a disconcertingly cool dismissal, which convincingly exposed the reports for the elementary fabrications they were. This naturally enraged Curzon, who was 'positively appalled' and dismayed that SIS should have relied on discredited 'German sources of information'.[14]

One result was a tightening up of procedures in SIS, reinforcing Desmond Morton's introduction of more systematic methods into the Production Department (which was also known as the Production Section or Production Branch). A memorandum on the 'classification of reports' issued in May 1922 laid down that all information should be 'submitted to careful consideration, both as regards reliability and value'. Reports were to be given one of three gradings: 'A1', 'A2' and 'B'. The highest category included 'those whose subject matter suggests their being regarded as of primary importance', and which were based either on 'original documents actually in the possession of S.I.S. or to which a representative of S.I.S. has had access', or 'statements by agents of exceptional reliability in which the S.I.S. repose especial confidence for peculiar reasons'. The second category included reports 'which, for various reasons, cannot be classified as 'A.1'', but which are of significance, both as regards subject matter and reliability'. The third category, 'B', included reports 'of less importance, but the interest and reliability of which are such as to justify their being issued'. Customer departments, however, were additionally reminded that SIS reports should not be accepted in isolation but 'should, of course, be considered in conjunction with reports from official sources'.[15] Despite this sensible reform, implying as it did that SIS should be extremely sceptical about *all* reports, the problem of bogus documents was to dog SIS for some time, as the Zinoviev Letter affair in 1924 was to demonstrate all too dramatically.

Of all the SIS stations in the Baltic, Riga was the most productive. It was opened in February 1921 when Rafael Farina came out from London to be head of station with cover as British Passport Control Officer. Farina, whose mother was British and father Italian, had been born in Switzerland in 1877. Educated at Cheltenham College, he trained at Camborne School of Mines and then worked as a mining engineer in Siberia. Excluded from military service because of a damaged left foot, he worked in the Ministry of Munitions during the First World War and had been in charge of the Russian Section of MI5 before joining SIS. With an assistant (who had been working in Warsaw and Helsinki and was 'fully acquainted with Intelligence work') and two secretaries, apart from his Passport Control duties Farina 'was also to be responsible for the collection of special intelligence concerning Latvia and Lithuania', and would be 'the sole representative of the S.I.S. for these two countries, directly under the orders of the Head Office in London and nobody else'.

On his appointment Farina was extensively briefed by the Production Section, a development which marked the increasing professionalisation of the Service and clearly reflected Desmond Morton's desire to ensure greater order and rigour in its procedures. There were instructions on the 'numbering of agents' and the correct form for submitting reports. For the latter, Farina was to 'allot numbers to every source from which you obtain information, whether that source is a paid, unpaid agent or even an unconscious source which you constantly tap'. Farina was to be 'FR/1', his assistant 'FR/2', and other sources given subsequent numbers in the FR series. He was to provide Head Office with 'full particulars' of any agent or source he made use of 'in order that we may card them up for reference in PROD'. This should include 'the name of the individual, his [sic] nationality, social position, abbreviated past history, probably [sic] qualifications for employment, what lines he may be likely to be best on, and why, etc'. Any particulars 'likely to lead to the identification of the individual in case your letter got into the wrong hand should be put into code'. It was important that Farina supplied his list of sources 'at the very earliest opportunity' so that when an FR report came into Head Office 'we shall at once understand who the author or authors are'. There were also 'brief hints on the form of reports' which confirmed that every report and letter to Head Office should be identified 'with lettered prefix and a serial number'. Three copies of all reports, 'except political reports', of which '2 will be ample', were to be submitted. 'As a rule', agents' reports should not be sent in unedited; 'Read the agent's report yourself and if it is faultless send it on, but usually it is infinitely better to re-write it in the light of your own greater knowledge.' Farina was also advised to 'try to collate news as much as possible' and not send in the same bag 'more than one report dealing with the same subject'.[16]

While the initial instructions given to Farina were quite detailed, there is no evidence that he was given much, if any, preliminary training. After going directly to Riga, however, he was instructed once he had settled in to go to Tallinn and 'spend 10 days or a fortnight there with BP/1 [Ernest Boyce], seeing how he does Intelligence work, and picking up as much information as he can give you on the spot'. Farina remained at Riga for ten years, during which he developed an impressive-looking organisation for work against the Soviet target, mainly due to the efforts of his assistants 'FR/3' and 'FR/4'. The former group, comprising eleven sub-sources, seems to have been run through a Russian head agent, a journalist based in Riga, who was known as 'FR/3/Riga'. Strikingly few of the sub-agents' names were known, which raises the question whether they ever existed at all. The anonymous star source of the group, resident in Moscow and recruited before May 1923, was run through an equally anonymous cut-out (a trusted middleman providing a deniable link with an agent) in Riga. The agent, designated 'FR/3/Moscow' (also 'FR/3/K') and said to be employed in the Comintern Secretariat with access to documents, was a prolific producer, with over fifty reports from him remaining on file. But he is also credited with having supplied the Zinoviev Letter in October 1924. Since this was later adjudged to be a forgery, it may well be that his existence was fabricated as well as his reports. On the other hand, a sub-source introduced in late 1924 by FR/3/Moscow, whose name was known and who was said to be a fully conscious and paid agent, provided minutes of Sovnarkom (the Soviet of People's Commissars) meetings. Regarded as particularly valuable by SIS and its customers, Head Office Circulating sections subjected them to careful scrutiny and concluded they were probably genuine.

The FR/4 group included twenty-four sub-agents allegedly overseen by 'FR/4/Riga', whose main sub-source was said to be his brother-in-law (name unknown), who lived in Moscow. Initially designated 'FR/4.V/Moscow', he later became '31004/V'. FR/4 never explained to an incurious Head Office how he had met FR/4/Riga, nor what steps (if any) he had taken to confirm the existence of 31004/V, who transmitted reports from some fifteen other anonymous sub-agents in Russia, allegedly based in a wide range of Soviet civilian and military organisations. In March 1928 Desmond Morton initiated a thoroughgoing analysis of the group. While some of the sub-sources were believed to have provided genuine information, the investigation concluded that most reports were bogus. One sub-agent, 'an alleged airman friend who could supply reports in Persian from the Persian Embassy at Moscow . . . supplied one complete fake which turned out to be a Turkish translation of a portion of the Koran'. Intelligence about a Russian 'death ray' from another sub-agent 'proved to be feats of imagination'. Morton concluded that there was 'something very wrong indeed with the group'. While there was (he argued) some evidence that FR/4/Riga was honest and that he had 'certain genuine contacts', the same 'could not be said' about the Moscow agent 31004/V, whose sources were 'supplemented in a very large degree by [forged] reports received from a "club" source in Berlin, probably Orlov'. After it had emerged that the French in Riga were also being supplied with many identical reports, which they also doubted, in April 1928 Sinclair declared, 'All this is most unsatisfactory & unless there are strong reasons to the contrary, 31004/V's agency must be closed down,' which it was.

Across the region SIS appointed representatives with some Russian experience. In November 1926 Ernest Boyce, Passport Control Officer at Helsinki as well as Tallinn, and who had worked in the Russian mining industry before the war, was replaced as head of station at Tallinn by a Cambridge graduate, son of a British shipbuilder and a Russian mother. He had served with army intelligence in Salonika and the Caucasus in 1916–19, spoke Russian and French fluently and had 'moderate' Bulgarian. In March 1930, he was replaced as Passport Control Officer by an Oxford man who had served with the British Military Mission in south Russia in 1918–19 and had 'considerable experience of producing amateur dramatics'. Afterwards described as 'an eccentric individual who flies off at a tangent and is difficult to pin down', he remained at Tallinn until the entire British diplomatic mission had to withdraw in September 1940.

Harry Carr, born in Archangel in 1899 where his father managed a sawmill, spoke Russian like a native. At Haileybury School in England he captained the rugby XV. Commissioned into the army too late to serve during the war, he was sent to north Russia as an interpreter in 1919 and on demobilisation back in England towards the end of the year was given a temporary posting by MI1(c) as a Russian translator in Helsinki. Soon made a permanent member of staff, initially as Assistant Passport Control Officer (PCO), he stayed with the Service for the rest of his working life. When Ernest Boyce left the Service in the summer of 1928, Carr became first acting head, then head of the Helsinki station, where he remained until July 1941. At Riga, Farina was succeeded in March 1931 by Harold Gibson, who was followed in 1934 by Captain Leslie Nicholson, a regular army officer who had worked in the intelligence section of the British occupation forces in the Rhineland in the early 1920s. In 1930 he had been taken on by SIS and initially posted to Prague as PCO.[17]

The pattern of activity at Riga was to a very great extent repeated elsewhere in the Baltic. The Tallinn station was in direct or indirect touch with some forty significant contacts from the early to mid-1920s. It is difficult, however, to discern any reporting sources among them who were both regular and reliable. Some had multiple intelligence relationships and haunted the whole region, like '31017', resident in Finland from 1918, in Tallinn from 1920 and in Danzig in the late 1930s. He had been a member of the Petrograd Secret Police before the war and from 1918 onwards worked successively, and sometimes simultaneously, for exiled White Russian intelligence organisations in Finland, Estonia, Latvia, Poland, Berlin and Paris; and also for the Estonians in Tallinn, the Germans in Berlin and the French in Paris.

The most important and trustworthy contacts in Tallinn were among those from local intelligence organisations. An Estonian signals intelligence agency, for example, provided intercepts of Soviet wireless messages between 1931 and 1939 which contained order-of-battle information 'of great value' to the War Office. Liaison relationships also involved information from the British side, though this had to be transmitted with some care. Towards the end of 1930, the representative at Tallinn told Head Office that a contact in the Estonian counter-intelligence organisation 'would be extremely grateful' if he could obtain for them 'photographs of OGPU and Comintern agents and other Russian Communists', who had been expelled from the United Kingdom 'on account of espionage, or propaganda, and other underground and disruptive activities'. Passing the request to Special Branch at Scotland Yard, Valentine Vivian noted that SIS's man in Tallinn 'would be more than obliged since the Estonian authorities give him much useful local information and he would be glad of a quid pro quo to give them'. In due course material was provided, but Scotland Yard warned SIS that there could be 'most unpleasant complications' if the source of the information was ever publicly revealed. In turn Sinclair (briefed by Vivian) told Tallinn 'that any indiscretion of the part of the local authorities in respect of this information or the source from which it emanated would create the greatest embarrassment and effectually prevent any further co-operation'.

Liaison services themselves were by no means immune to the inherent problems of reporting on Russia. Baltic agent 'BP/42', who was resident in Moscow and had 'connections in Soviet institutions', agreed for a retainer of £50 a month to 'send information three times monthly' about political matters and 'on subject of propaganda'. After his own involvement with the OGPU (who blackmailed him over gambling debts) was discovered he was charged with treason but escaped to Austria, where he continued to peddle intelligence on Russia until the early 1930s. There he was reported to be employed by the Nazi Intelligence Office in Berlin and was offering reports to SIS through a mutual contact in Finland. By 1934 (as SIS discovered in 1946 from captured German documents) he had graduated to the Abwehr, was reporting to them on Russia and into the bargain had passed them an SIS questionnaire on Russia received from his Finnish contact.

Western and Central Europe

During the early 1920s SIS overseas deployments settled down into a pattern which continued until the mid-1930s. In the spring 1923 budget £27,000 was allocated for the Baltic and Scandinavian stations; £22,000 to the German Group (£8,000 of which was earmarked for Holland and £3,000 for Belgium); £16,000 for the Swiss Group, which also included France, Italy, Spain and Portugal; and £10,000 for the Central European Group of Austria, Czechoslovakia, Hungary, Bulgaria, Yugoslavia and Romania. Further afield, £20,000 was allocated for the Near East; £18,000 for the Far East; and £9,000 for New York.

In October 1919 Henry Landau, who had done so well in the Netherlands during the war, was sent to Germany to be the Service representative there. Cumming, as Landau recalled in a memoir, assured him that Berlin was 'the best of his appointments abroad'. In addition to his Secret Service work, Landau was to be the chief Passport Control Officer, but when he arrived he found that, as a result of much 'competition and overlapping' between different Allied missions on the intelligence side, there was little such work for him to do. In what was effectively a one-man station he also encountered administrative problems, and he was perhaps not best suited for the bureaucratic demands of peacetime intelligence work.[18] Although 'brilliant in conception', wrote an SIS colleague, he required 'a practical man with him to work anything out'. In Berlin, he got into financial difficulties and had to leave the Service in 1920. London subsequently had some difficulty in satisfactorily filling the Berlin post. After two officers had followed in quick succession, Captain Frank Foley was installed as head of station in 1923, where he remained until the outbreak of war in 1939. Foley, born in 1884, was a studious youth who had hoped for an academic career and studied philosophy in France and Germany before the war. In August 1914 he was in Hamburg and, 'disguised as a German', managed to escape through the Netherlands to England, where he joined the army in 1915. Wounded on the Western Front in March 1918, he transferred to the Intelligence Corps, who posted him to the British occupation forces in Cologne, whence he was appointed, initially as an assistant, to the Berlin Passport Control Office.[19]

From its inception until the mid-1930s the Berlin station concentrated on the Bolshevik target. With the establishment of a Soviet mission there in early 1920, Berlin, as reports in late 1920 asserted, was seen as a 'centre for International Bolshevism' where the Western European Secretariat, or Bureau, of the Comintern was based, dedicated to 'the spreading of Communist ideas throughout Western Europe'. Soviet personnel in Berlin were believed to be employing 'the usual Bolshevik tactics, viz. camouflaging espionage and propaganda under a veneer of respectability and sincerity'. Some reports tracking the travel movements of individual Soviet and Comintern officials appear to have been reliable and were circulated to Scotland Yard, who found them helpful in their study of the Bolshevik threat to the United Kingdom, but it is evident that the mostly White Russian sources (who included Vladimir Orlov) were frequently unreliable and many of the documents they supplied were forgeries. In 1922, one female agent, 'BN/61', supplied purported records of Western European Secretariat meetings, but after investigation Berlin had to report, with 'regret', that, although 'the majority of the facts' were genuine, most of the documents themselves were forged. Told by her case officer that he would pay only for actual minutes, 'in order to earn her money' the agent 'either invented entirely the protocols of the meetings, or faked them from bits of gossip which she heard'.

In October 1923 Charles Howard (known as 'Dick') Ellis was sent out to work under Foley on the Soviet target. Australian-born (in 1895), of British parents, Ellis joined the army in 1915 and served on the Western Front and in the Middle East, ending up with the British forces in

Transcaspia and the Caucasus in 1918–19. In October 1921 he abandoned an undergraduate course at Oxford (St Edmund Hall) and was taken on by the Service to work in Istanbul. There he married a Russian woman and became the contact for a number of Russian agents. Long afterwards Ellis reflected on the over-close relationships between SIS's Russian-speaking officers, using their own names, and their Russian agents, and the socialising between both groups which led to a most unprofessional level of interconsciousness. As these individuals spread out over Central and Eastern Europe, the Russian cadre of SIS case-officers and their head agents became far too well known to the White Russian communities, and thus, in turn, to the OGPU. While Ellis knew no German (though as a talented linguist he soon added it to his fluent Russian), in October 1923 he was posted to Berlin, where he was given a list of Russian agents to run and was himself approached by several White Russians who had heard of his transfer from friends in Turkey. Provided with little specific briefing or preliminary training – a typical experience for the time – Ellis was largely left to fend for himself and learn on the job. Afterwards he complained that desk officers at Head Office, who had no agent-running experience and seldom visited stations, knew very little about the realities of work in the field and frequently nursed unrealistic expectations of what could be achieved. Ellis applied to be moved away from Berlin in 1926, and he settled under journalist cover, first in Vienna and then in Geneva, where he continued to work on German and Russian targets principally through his Berlin-based Russian agents, some of whom clearly were also working (at least) for German intelligence. Reflecting after the war on one agent, whom he believed also to be working for both the Poles and the Estonians (but who told him he had refused to work for the Germans), Ellis described him as 'no fool and, like most Russians of his type, played both ends against the middle'. Nevertheless, he 'served me well, and on the whole his information was sound. He kept me well informed about "phoney" agents and was useful in that respect.'

Switzerland was a significant intelligence centre and, as during the First World War, continued to be an important base for Near and Middle Eastern work. The India Office intelligence agency, Indian Political Intelligence (IPI), had representatives in the country who liaised closely with Cumming's men. In March 1920 Cumming agreed with Charles

Tegart, a charismatic Irishman who had been seconded to IPI from the Calcutta Police, that MI1(c) would fund the IPI representative in Geneva to the tune of £1,500 a year and 'get from him all his non-Indian stuff in exchange'. In June, Rhys Samson proposed that he should be based in Switzerland to co-ordinate 'Pan-Islamic Intelligence in Western Europe' and from there run 'a certain Turkish Nationalist who would be in a position to get inside information on Turkish affairs'. By the end of the year, however, with the pressure for economy beginning to bite, a 'conference of Swiss affairs' at Head Office agreed to cut the payment to IPI to £500. On the other hand, the finances for Swiss work were for a couple of years boosted by funding of £2,500 from the British military authorities in Turkey, brought in with Samson, who was transferred from Istanbul in September 1920 to be Inspector of the Swiss Group and (briefly) head of station at Geneva.

Examples of SIS reporting survive in an 'Eastern Summary' circulated to the Foreign, India, Colonial and War Offices. In January 1923, for example, there was intelligence about the Egyptian nationalist leader Abdul Hamid Said, and the alleged formation of 'a new terrorist organisation', provided from 'a highly reliable agent' in Lausanne 'who has been in a position to obtain this information at first hand'. SIS's informant, moreover, confirmed the prevailing assumption that most nationalist groups working against British imperial interests (wherever in the world they might be) were supported by Moscow gold. The funds for the new terrorist organisation, he reported, 'will be provided by the Soviet authorities, through the medium of the Soviet representative in Rome'. Both human and signals intelligence were extremely valuable for informing British negotiating tactics at the Lausanne conference between November 1922 and July 1923, which finally secured a lasting peace settlement with Turkey. So much so that the senior British negotiator, Sir Horace Rumbold, observed that 'the information we obtained at the psychological moments from secret sources was invaluable to us, and put us in the position of a man who is playing Bridge and knows the cards in his adversary's hand'.[20]

Although between the wars (as Vivian observed to Vernon Kell in October 1937) the Swiss security authorities were prepared to share information with SIS 'regarding Communism or other international subversive movements of mutual interest', Switzerland's traditional policy of neutrality meant that the Service had to be especially careful where other intelligence work was concerned. With former allies from the Great War, such as France and Belgium, the situation was slightly different. The experience of working closely together in organisations like the Bureau Central Interallié left a useful legacy of co-operation and personal contacts. One example of this was the Bureau Liaison Armée Occupée (BLAO, which in 1930, 'as a precautionary measure', changed its name to BOX), an Anglo-French–Belgian organisation established in December 1921 principally on Stewart Menzies's initiative and based in Paris. Formed to share information on Communist subversion, its work was later extended to German military intelligence. By the early 1930s it was focusing almost entirely on Germany and had 'about ten agents', of which four were 'first class, and all very cheap'. SIS found it tremendously useful being 'allowed to run an organisation in Paris' which underpinned close secret service relations with the French. In May 1931, when the Belgians, fearing that their neutrality might be compromised by it, threatened to close BOX down, SIS reckoned that the organisation provided valuable Russian, Turkish, Balkan and Hungarian information; that it replied 'to any military questions on Italy'; that there was exchange of intelligence on Germany ('the French maintain about six times our staff'); and that information was 'occasionally obtained regarding French matters which would certainly not be given to our M.A. [military attaché]'.

Another useful supply of information came from officer 'KL/2', whose role illustrates the importance of personal contacts and the establishment of trust between case-officer and agent – an absolutely key issue when handling agents. He had served with military liaison in France during the war. In 1919 he was sent by Basil Thomson to liaise 'semi-officially' with the French police, but unknown to them was also working for Cumming and reporting 'on internal conditions in France, socialist and labour troubles etc.'. In the mid-1920s a problem arose when Scotland Yard wanted to post KL/2 back to London. Maurice Jeffes, SIS head of station in Paris since October 1922, explained to Sinclair that this would, he feared, 'frighten these people [KL/2's agents] badly'. They were all 'police officials of good standing, who have been persuaded by KL/2, after some years of acquaintance dating back to the war, to take money in exchange for information useful to S.I.S.'. It was 'very doubtful if they would now be willing to place their careers unreservedly in fresh hands'. In the event they did not need to, as KL/2 stayed on for several years, though it is not clear whether his network remained very productive. During the 1920s Paris supplied London with a steady stream of reports on Communism in France. On the whole Jeffes's evaluation of the Communist threat was quite measured. Commenting in November 1926 on an apparently alarmist report sent to him from London, he observed that although the total number of Communists was, 'at first glance, somewhat disquieting, when viewed in perspective with the remainder of the population they are in a considerable minority'. He asserted that unless the situation developed 'unexpectedly in such a way as to give the Communists an unlooked for opportunity', it seemed to him 'that they have a very long way to go indeed before they can hope to carry through successfully a serious revolutionary movement in France'.

There is ample evidence in the French intelligence records of the productively close and continuous liaison between SIS and its French opposite numbers between the wars. On the SIS side, from the early 1920s the main people involved were Jeffes (who stayed as representative in Paris until 1937, when he returned to London to be Director of the Passport Control Organisation) and Stewart Menzies. Since the principal French intelligence agency, the Deuxième Bureau, was a branch of Military Intelligence, Menzies, as head of the Military Section IV (he also had fluent French), was the appropriate contact in London. A sample of the exchanges between Menzies and Colonel Robert Lainey in Paris during 1925 gives a flavour of the relationship. In March Menzies asked Lainey for information about 'a certain Muneyuki', who was believed to be a Japanese naval intelligence agent working under the assistant naval attaché at the Japanese embassy in Paris and working on British as well as French targets. In June there was an enquiry from Lainey about a Japanese aviation expert in London believed to be involved in espionage. The same month Menzies raised the case of two Japanese officers who had got into trouble for taking photographs of fortifications at Calais. 'I should be greatly obliged', he wrote, 'if you could give me any particulars of the incident, especially the names of the two officers concerned, in case they ever attempt the same thing in this country.' In 1926 the two services exchanged information about alleged Italian intelligence agents.[21]

Since the French were world leaders in aviation technology, the Air Ministry particularly desired information about developments and capabilities. In May 1925 the SIS Air Section II noted that the 'collection of aeronautical intelligence' was 'undoubtedly quite a different proposition to the collection of naval or military intelligence'. There was 'a wide and ill-defined gap between pure S.S. work, i.e. the purloining of documents, etc. and the work of an Air Attaché who has always to be thinking of his official position'. As the Air Ministry (unlike the other two service ministries) was responsible for both civil and military matters it needed to be 'well-informed about all aeronautical development'. And because of the 'very vague distinction' between civil and military aeroplanes, an agent, 'while collecting civil aviation information', could 'easily find himself in the position to obtain military information of great value'. Arising from this, journalistic cover was arranged for a British aviation expert based in Paris, who toured the Continent in 1925 allegedly to research a series of articles on the development of civil aviation. He supplied information about aerodromes which was 'new' and 'of interest', and both the Air Ministry and the Admiralty hoped that he would be able to investigate the important question of oil reserves for aviation fuel. The Air Ministry, too, wanted information on the Dornier aircraft factory at Romanshorn in Switzerland, where it was understood that prototype aircraft were tested, but there is no evidence that the agent did any further work for the Service.

From the mid-1920s two separate SIS organisations operated in Paris. The original station (coded '27000' and headed by Jeffes) existed under Passport Control Office cover and liaised with the French security service primarily on counter-espionage matters. In 1926 a second station ('45000') was set up under Wilfred Dunderdale, to deal with the Deuxième Bureau principally on Soviet and German armed forces intelligence. Dunderdale, known both as Bill and 'Biffy', the latter apparently from his prowess as a boxer in the navy at the end of the First World War, was born on Christmas Eve 1899, the son of a British naval engineer based in Odessa. Fluent in Russian, he was employed by Naval Intelligence as an interpreter for the British Senior Naval Officer in Sevastopol in 1919, and also on 'special intelligence duties', the latter involving reporting on the military and political situation generally in south Russia. A man of great charm and savoir-faire, in old age he became an incorrigible raconteur. He liked to tell the story of how, while still in his teens, as interpreter for a White Russian general, he found himself translating outside a railway sleeping compartment where the general and his British mistress were seducing each other. He was a great friend of Ian Fleming, and claimed that he found parts of his own stories in the James Bond novels. When head of the SIS Paris station in the 1930s, he had a penchant for pretty women and fast cars, and has been proposed as one of the possible models for Bond.[22]

Dunderdale was involved in the debriefing of the first high-level Soviet Party official to defect to the West after the revolution, Boris Georgievitch Bajanov, a Politburo secretary who had been an assistant to Stalin in 1923. In early 1928, along with a Russian cavalry officer, Arkady Maximov, he arrived in India, claiming to have important information on the organisation of the Central Committee of the Communist Party, on the Comintern budget and on the working of the OGPU in the Soviet Union and abroad. Alerted to their arrival by IPI, Sinclair declared himself 'strongly opposed' to their coming to England, seeing it merely as 'a transparent ruse to effect their desire to make their way to Europe'. But it was arranged with the Deuxième Bureau to bring the two men to France, where Dunderdale (who concealed his connection with SIS) ran their interrogation. He reported that Maximov was of 'absolutely no interest to us as he is a typical low-class post-revolutionary officer', but Bajanov was 'an exceptionally intelligent man', from whom he had 'extracted 140 pages of information'. We are, he told Menzies, 'producing a whole book mainly on the Polit Bureau and the [O.]G.P.U.', which he hoped would 'be a very important guide'. The material included a 'description of the Government mechanism' and lively pen-portraits of some two dozen 'Bolshevist leaders'. While the former was described as 'very accurate', London was advised that the latter were less reliable, being 'the somewhat prejudiced views of an unsuccessful Communist who now has leanings towards Fascism'. Dunderdale also thought that Bajanov (who quickly settled into the Russian émigré community in Paris) 'considerably exaggerates the strength of the anti-Bolsheviks and the results attained by them in their secret anti-Soviet work abroad'. Towards the end of 1928 an agent in Denmark reported that the OGPU, finding that Bajanov had 'taken very important documents with him', had 'given very urgent instructions to its agents in Paris, London, Berlin, etc. to endeavour to render him innocuous'. Valentine Vivian thought that by now the Soviets had 'missed the bus', but in any case he understood Bajanov to be ill and 'that Tuberculosis is likely to save the G.P.U. agents the expense of a cartridge'. Bajanov, in fact, survived to recount a version of his story to a British journalist in Paris in the 1970s.[23]

During the war Cumming's representatives in Iberia – by the end of 1917 he had men in both Madrid and Lisbon – had played second fiddle to Blinker Hall's Naval Intelligence Department. By 1919–20, however, SIS was established in both Madrid and Barcelona, but in 1922 with the abolition of visas between Spain and the United Kingdom the Passport Control Office in the Spanish capital was closed down and the Service's resources were concentrated in Barcelona. This office was run from Geneva until it, too, was wound up in December 1923. For the rest of the 1920s a skeleton network was maintained mostly under business cover, with agents communicating in a variety of ways. One, who worked for a Liverpool-based shipping company, was to receive messages written inside the postal wrappers for copies of the *Observer* newspaper mailed from England. Another, a merchant in Valencia, was instructed to use three envelopes. The inner one was to be 'addressed only to X/O' (the appropriate person at Head Office). This was to be placed in one marked 'for "C"', which in turn went into one addressed to 'G. N. Bland Esq', the whole package being given to the British consul in Valencia for transmission to London in a diplomatic bag. Reflecting an increasingly professional approach to intelligence work, in February 1924 this agent was specifically told that 'information from public sources, from the press or of historical interest only' was 'not required'. Bearing in mind the growing discontent in Spain and the apparently precarious position of the military regime of General Primo de Rivera (who had seized power in September 1923), the main priority was for political intelligence, including 'inside and advance information of a violent upheaval against the Military Régime'. London was also interested in 'relations between Spain and Italy, which may affect the strategical situation in the Mediterranean', the 'policy of Spain with regard to Gibraltar', and the political and military situation of Spanish Morocco. With this agent, at least, London expressed no interest at all in Communists.

After the Armistice in 1918 Major Hans Vischer, who was based in Berne, was instructed to open stations in the capitals of countries emerging from the ruins of the Austro-Hungarian empire: Vienna, Prague and Budapest. Captain Ernan Forbes-Dennis was Passport Control Officer and head of station at Vienna from December 1919 to October 1922.

Many years afterwards he recalled that he had been given no specific instructions and that 'the diplomats at the Legation were still very much of the old school who cultivated the members of the old aristocratic families' rather than establishing any contacts with the circles now controlling the country. Forbes-Dennis managed to establish 'a firm relationship' with the social-democrat head of the Vienna police, Dr Johannes Schober, founder of the International Criminal Police Association, later Interpol. But he did not run agents, had no covert sources and had his hands full with Passport Control work. One acquaintance who passed through Vienna in the summer of 1920 told Desmond Morton he was 'very sorry for Forbes-Dennis here. He is having a devil of a time with no help and surrounded by what appear to be thousands of seekers after passport visas.' In 1922 Forbes-Dennis resigned. He and his wife, the novelist Phyllis Bottome, set up a finishing school in Kitzbühel, Austria, where Ian Fleming was later a pupil.[24] He was replaced by his assistant, whom Forbes-Dennis dismissed as having 'decidedly leftish views' and alleged had been 'constantly catching VD and having to have medical treatment'. He was succeeded by Captain Thomas J. Kendrick in December 1925. Kendrick, a South African who had served in Field Intelligence Security during the war, and with MI1(c) in Cologne after the war, remained head of station until he was arrested by the Gestapo in August 1938.

In the interwar years, Kendrick was regarded by London as one of their best heads of station. Leaving the bulk of the Passport Control duties to assistants, he concentrated on Communist groups in Austria, as well as developing networks working on Czechoslovakia. One of these was run by an ex-officer of the Imperial Austrian Army, who worked in the Czechoslovak Ministry of Defence. Designated '44084', he was an ethnic German who, although rabidly anti-Czech, had automatically become a Czechoslovak national on the collapse of the Habsburg empire. Among his agents was an electrical engineer doing military service, who provided information on call signs, military codes and details of wireless sets. Another worked in the army General Staff and supplied mobilisation maps. A third worked for Skoda and provided details of the firm's aircraft production. Agent 44084 also had useful contacts in banking and industrial circles, as well as acquaintances in the gendarmerie and civil service. He took on a sub-agent who allegedly had a friend in the President's

Private Office, but by the early 1930s London had begun to mistrust the source and suspect that his reports had been fabricated.

The Near and Middle East

SIS's organisation in Turkey emerged from the intelligence branch of the British occupation forces which remained in the former Ottoman empire until after the Treaty of Lausanne of 23 August 1923. For well over a century the Near and Middle East had been important for Britain. Apart from wide-ranging economic and commercial interests, the sea route from the Mediterranean to the Indian Ocean through the Suez Canal was a vital imperial line of communications, to be protected against other Great Powers, especially France and Russia, the latter also constantly seeking to control the passage from the Black Sea through the Straits at Constantinople (Istanbul). In the aftermath of the First World War, two new factors, nationalism and Communism, which British policy-makers and officials often (mistakenly) assumed to be the same thing, emerged to challenge imperial interests across the region. Among the most threatening was the nationalist movement under Kemal Atatürk, who from early 1920 sought to depose the Sultan (who had been kept in power by the victorious Allies), establish an independent Turkish republic and drive the British-backed Greeks from Asia Minor.[25] From 1919 until the autumn of 1922 intelligence was at a premium as there was a real possibility of British forces in the region having to resume active operations. During the Chanak Crisis of September–October 1922 Lloyd George threatened to go to war against the Turkish nationalists, but his Conservative coalition partners had little stomach for such a fight and turned him out of office. The ensuing general election brought in a fervently anti-Communist right-wing Tory government under Bonar Law. In May 1923 Law was succeeded as Prime Minister by Stanley Baldwin, whose dedication to financial orthodoxy meant that government spending continued to be kept under very strict control.

During the immediate postwar years Cumming regarded the Constantinople operation as 'one of the most important, if not the most important, of all my agencies' and a colleague at Head Office asserted that 'a better service of information has never been organised regarding events in the Near East'. Much of this came from a very productive signals intelligence unit working under army cover within the occupation forces. When in early 1922 to save money it was proposed to maintain this but cut human intelligence work, the head of station responded sharply with a reflection on the limitations of 'sigint' (signals intelligence). Acknowledging the British ability to read Turkey's (and other countries') diplomatic communications, he noted that signals intelligence 'gets most valuable information regarding existing foreign relations, but it cannot hope to touch but very lightly all the movements of subversion & intrigue which go on behind the scenes, for the latter are seldom if ever mentioned even in cypher cables'. There were practical difficulties, too. Ready access to the actual cable traffic would last only for as long as the occupation forces remained. Thereafter the intercept operation could only 'be worked with the greatest difficulty & danger', and, in case it were 'caught out', an 'ordinary S.I.S organisation' should be maintained to 'fall back upon' and prevent a 'complete break' in intelligence work, 'a contingency which must be avoided'.[26]

The station, too, proved to be an important nursery of officers who were to serve in SIS until the Second World War and beyond. Valentine Vivian, Rhys Samson's deputy in 1919 (and successor as head of station from 1920 to 1923), was one. Among other colleagues who worked for the Service in early postwar Turkey were Harold Gibson and Wilfred Dunderdale. Gibson – 'Gibbie' – worked in Istanbul from October 1919 until 1922, when he was posted to Sofia in September and Bucharest (where he became head of station) in December. In Istanbul both Dunderdale and Gibson recruited networks of Russian anti-Communist agents. It was not unusual for agents and their case-officers to strike up close relationships and the two SIS men continued to run some of these agents when they moved on to other stations. One former Tsarist officer (whose motives were described as 'finance, anti-Bolshevik, pro-British'), 'HV/109', moved with Gibson to Bucharest, from where he ran a large group of sub-agents in the Ukraine and Bessarabia. But he also forged links with other foreign intelligence services, including the Romanians and Bulgarians. By November 1930 it was thought likely that the OGPU had become aware of him. SIS also worked on the Turkish target, though this was not without risk. One successful agent, 'RV/5', gathered information in his men's outfitting shop, which was patronised by officers associated with the reformist Committee of Union and Progress. But one of the tailor's sub-agents in the Turkish Foreign Ministry was caught red-handed, following which RV/5 himself was transferred to Egypt 'because his position in Constantinople was endangered'.

SIS's efforts to collect intelligence on Kemal and the Nationalist movement met with varying success. During 1921 Vivian submitted weekly situation reports which Woollcombe in London thought were 'of immense value'. At the Turkish end, however (and demonstrating how problematic SIS's relations with customers could be), Vivian complained in December that Colonel Gribbon of Army Intelligence had tried to persuade him to 'recant on one of my Situation Reports, not on the grounds that the information was not well supported, but on the grounds that he would like it to have a different twist in order to help a policy which he favoured . . . Of course I refused,' wrote Vivian, though 'tactfully enough not to offend him.' One 'very reliable' agent, 'JQ/6', a 'Turkman of European appearance', Russian education and a former Russian cavalry officer who spoke 'Turkman, Tartar, Turkish, Russian, Rumanian and fair English and German', with good contacts in Turkmeni, Caucasian and Azerbaijani circles, set up a coffee shop in Istanbul which became a centre of Kemalist political gatherings. But by January 1923, having become known to many 'Azerbaijanis now working for Turks', he had to be got quickly out of Istanbul. SIS 'bought him a perfectly genuine Polish passport . . . with all the necessary visas' and moved him to Romania. Vivian described him as 'one of the very best agents we have got'. He was 'ardently Anglophile, and being still young I have great hopes of his future usefulness'. JQ/6 went on to Berlin, where SIS remained in contact. In 1929 he was sent to Baghdad (masquerading as an Iranian, but also carrying a German passport) to work on Soviet activity in the region. There he was to set up a transport business, for which SIS would provide a modest amount of capital, optimistically hoping that 'in time' the business 'should pay for itself and even make a profit'. But the agent (who was perhaps not so reliable after all) disappeared without trace between Marseilles and Baghdad and was never heard of again.

In the immediate postwar years, an Indian, who went under the pseudonym 'Parsifal', was run by Vivian, who asserted long afterwards that he had penetrated Kemalist circles and, until discovered in 1921, had provided most of SIS's information on Kemal's intentions and activities. An early SIS report from agent 'MS/1' in December 1920 quoted Dimitri

Atchkoff, a Bulgarian parliamentarian and close friend of Kemal, as asserting that the Turkish leader was primarily a nationalist, whose main interest was to clear Asia Minor of the Greeks. If Britain were to back Turkey rather than Greece (as Lloyd George preferred), he argued that this would at once 'put a stop to the unnatural collaboration between the Turks and the Bolsheviks'. In his study of British intelligence during the Chanak Crisis, John Ferris has argued that SIS accurately identified the differences between Ankara (which became the capital of Turkey in 1923) and Moscow, demonstrating that the Turkish nationalists were not in any way Bolshevik pawns. In January 1923, for example, SIS reported that Kemal was reluctant to fall in with Soviet plans to form a bloc consisting of 'Russia, Turkey, Persia, Afghanistan and other Moslem States'. SIS's analysis suggested that the Turks were more than happy to intrigue behind the backs of the Soviets in order to create a 'Moslem Federation' which would exclude Moscow's involvement.[27] Although SIS's principal preoccupation in Turkey, as in other places, was Soviet diplomatic and subversive activity, the Service's clear-sighted assessment of the integrity of Turkish nationalism suggests that it could at times move beyond that limited world-view which, in the 1920s and after, saw every threat and adverse shift in international relations as being in some way caused by the evil machinations of Communists.

SIS was similarly unalarmist about Communism in Egypt. In September 1921 Major G. W. Courtney, an MI5 officer who had been head of the Eastern Mediterranean Special Intelligence Bureau, was appointed to be head of a new SIS Cairo station, a post he was to hold until 1938. Courtney was also instructed to collect intelligence from Palestine and Syria, though Head Office appreciated that this might take some time, and (according to Courtney) declared that they would treat him 'as a bride and expect nothing for nine months'. In fact the new station was not finally established until early 1923. From then until 1937, when its strength was increased by one officer, it consisted of just Courtney and a single secretary. While little evidence of work during the 1920s in Syria and Palestine survives, the Cairo station reported regularly on Bolshevism in Egypt. When London was alarmed by reports of strong Communist agitation among the Jewish and Arab population in Alexandria, Courtney expressed the opinion that the significance of the Communist movement was liable to be 'greatly exaggerated'. Reflecting the general attitude of the Istanbul station, Cairo asserted that there was no evidence that the nationalist leader Sa'ad Zaghloul 'and the Extremists' were 'enlisting bolshevik support to gain their ends. Rather the reverse is the case. All parties here, whatever their differences, are intensely national at the present moment, and will not entertain the idea of any foreign interference.' In the mid-1920s, partly because of robust police work against the movement, Courtney likened Communism in Egypt to 'a pulled up weed, which has still part of its roots in the soil', and he noted evidence of contacts between Communists in Egypt, Syria, Palestine and the Sudan. In the summer of 1926 he characterised attempts by Communist agitators to make inroads in Egypt as 'somewhat feeble efforts'. In June 1928, Courtney dismissed as 'journalistic licence' sensationalist reports in *The Times* (published on 6 and 7 May) describing the growth of Communism in Egypt, and denied that there was any 'new and dangerous complexion to the prospects of Communism in Egypt'.

The limited scale of SIS's deployment in the Middle East did not result from any strategic choice on the part of the Service, but was dictated by its tiny budget. It is clear that, had funding been available, the Service would have expanded its reach in many parts of the world. This is illustrated by a detailed report prepared in 1927 by Valentine Vivian on the prospects of secret service work 'in Arabia and the Red Sea area generally'. After leaving Istanbul in 1923, Vivian had served as Regional Inspector for Western Europe (the German Group), based first in Cologne and later in London. At the end of 1925 he became head of a new Section V at Head Office, devoted to counter-intelligence and counter-Communist work. Sinclair also used him to think strategically about the Service, as with this Arabia report, following a four-month tour between December 1926 and April 1927, during which Vivian visited Egypt, the Sudan, Palestine, Transjordan, Aden and India. En route he happily discovered that SIS was better received in the field than at home. 'The element of reserve perceptible in the attitude of Departments at home towards S.I.S. expansion in Arabia', he wrote, found 'no echo in the attitude of the local British administrations'. Because of the 'vastness and backwardness' of Arabia, there was 'no one centre or nodal point from which the country as a whole' could be 'worked'. Cairo, in fact, was the only possible place for a representative (who would be additional to the existing head of station). But he also proposed that three 'advanced bases', under a 'chief local agent', be established: at Jeddah in Saudi Arabia itself; at Port Sudan on the Red Sea coast of Sudan; and at Bushire (Bushehr) in Iran on the Persian Gulf (where the work could be handled by the existing British–Indian Political Agent). Jeddah would be used 'for collecting information from the Hejaz and Ibn Saud's dominions'; Bushire for central Arabia; and Port Sudan for 'Southern Arabia and Eritrea'. Vivian drew up quite an elaborate plan with projected costs of £3,500 a year for 'a minimum practical beginning'. This, he hazarded, would be sufficient for 'a nucleus from which an organisation of a more permanent nature' might be expected to grow. But, however strong the theoretical case might have been for SIS expansion in the 1920s, there were no available funds to support it, so the scheme was still-born.

One aspect of the scheme on which Vivian focused particular attention was that of the chief local agents. Although they 'need not be British or European', he argued that 'they should be selected from among persons already established on the spot'. He observed that Jeddah posed a particular problem due to the presence there 'of a very intelligent, potentially hostile element in the person of Mr. H. St. J. Philby'. Philby was 'the one individual in Jeddah, who, if he were otherwise than he is, could solve our difficulties', being 'second to few Englishmen . . . in his knowledge of modern Arabia'. Unfortunately, however, he had become 'seriously disgruntled on account of his disagreements with the Government on Arabian policy', and 'whether sincere or merely posing (as I suspect), now pretends to champion the interests of Ibn Saoud [*sic*] against "exploitation by British Imperialism"'. Vivian had encountered the self-opinionated Philby as an assistant commissioner in the Punjab before the war, and Vivan's wife Mary had been a childhood friend of Philby's wife, Dora. It is curious that, while in the 1920s St John Philby (whom Valentine Vivian thought was admirably qualified to be an SIS agent) was widely but wrongly suspected in Arabia of being a British spy, twenty years later no one, let alone Vivian, had the slightest suspicion of his son, Kim. When Kim joined SIS in the 1940s, Vivian took a personal interest in his progress and was in later life sharply criticised for fostering his career in the Service. It was a cruel irony indeed that the Service's anti-Communist expert should have taken under his avuncular wing the Service's worst Communist traitor.

7

Domestic matters

During the 1920s the modern title of the Service gradually became established. Although the report of the 1925 Cabinet Secret Service Committee spoke of the 'Secret Intelligence Service, commonly known as S.I.S.',[1] an abbreviated version of the report (in the SIS archives) used the term 'Special Intelligence Service', which suggests that even in SIS itself some uncertainty remained about what the Service was called. In October 1928 a police Special Branch memorandum described SIS as 'the Special Intelligence section of the Foreign Office'. From a security perspective this was not necessarily a bad thing for a deeply secret organisation, though it had the potential to be unnecessarily confusing. Usage within both Whitehall and SIS varied considerably. 'C's organisation' was quite common, and MI1(c) was still being employed in August 1939, by an SIS officer for a communication with the War Office. Early in the Second World War a new cover name, MI6, was adopted, superseding MI1(c) and becoming very widely used thereafter.

SIS and signals intelligence

When he became Chief of SIS, Hugh Sinclair was also made non-operational director of the Government Code and Cypher School (GC&CS), Britain's unified signals intelligence agency created out of the remnants of the wartime Admiralty and War Office cryptographic branches, NID25 (popularly known as Room 40) and MI1(b) respectively.[2] In November 1918, along with his scheme for an amalgamated secret service, the Director of Military Intelligence, William Thwaites, had proposed to his naval counterpart, Blinker Hall, that the two signals intelligence sections should be united in a single 'School' (so called to provide cover by stressing the organisation's positive side, for example in studying ways to achieve secure communications). Hall agreed, deftly offering 'housing room' in the Admiralty 'for the military side, so that all their joint knowledge and brains might be combined with the least possible over-lapping'. But Colonel C. N. French, Thwaites's chief staff officer in MI1, opposed a rapid amalgamation. The War Office had been particularly successful with foreign diplomatic traffic. By 1918 they claimed to have solved fifty-two diplomatic codes, including those of France and the United States.[3] French argued that 'during the Peace negotiations' the information produced by MI1(b) would 'be as, or perhaps more, important than it has ever been during the time of hostilities'. Furthermore, since cryptographers were 'somewhat kittle-cattle to deal with and all of them, if they are any good, have somewhat peculiar temperaments', their work might suffer if they were 'shifted from their present quarters in Cork Street [in Mayfair] to the Admiralty'.

French was not the only person with definite opinions on the subject. In January 1919 Lord Curzon (acting Foreign Secretary while Lord Balfour was at the Paris Peace Conference) declared that the Foreign Office was 'the proper place for the new school to be housed'. Sinclair (at this stage Director of Naval Intelligence) disagreed. The School, he argued, should be located in the Admiralty, since the fighting services possessed the required expertise and 'all the arrangements as regards deciphering messages' were 'already in existence in the Admiralty building'. This was not just a matter of convenience. 'Without wishing to disparage the Foreign Office in the least,' he continued, 'it is considered that the atmosphere of calm deliberation which characterizes that department is not suited to an organisation such as the proposed Code and Cypher School, which, above all things, must be a "live" undertaking, especially in connection with the "breaking" of codes and cyphers.' The matter was settled on 29 April 1919 at a conference chaired by Curzon, along with the First Lord (Walter Long) and the Secretary for War and Air (Winston Churchill), which decided that the new School should be placed in the Admiralty (albeit under civilian administration). Curzon, nevertheless, arguing that in peacetime its work would be almost entirely political, secured for the Foreign Office the valuable power of controlling the information produced. It was decided that he (as acting Foreign Secretary) should receive all intercepted telegrams and be responsible for passing them on 'to the

Prime Minister or other Cabinet Ministers concerned when they were of sufficient importance'.[4]

It is evident from the discussions in early 1919 that the Foreign Office, and Lord Curzon in particular, recognised the high potential value of the diplomatic decrypts produced by the Code and Cypher School. In mid-1921 (by which time he had succeeded Balfour as Foreign Secretary) Curzon unequivocally described the School as 'by far the most important branch of our confidential work'. The 'deciphered telegrams of foreign Govts.', he wrote, 'are without doubt the most valuable source of our secret information respecting their policy and actions. They provide the most accurate and, withal, intrinsically the cheapest, means of obtaining secret political information that exists.'[5] By this stage, taking advantage of the fact that in February 1921 Walter Long, who was interested in intelligence matters, was replaced at the Admiralty by Arthur Lee, who was not, Curzon had already begun to press for the administrative transfer of the School to the Foreign Office. In May Lee agreed (Sinclair does not appear to have objected) and from 1 April 1922 the Foreign Office assumed direct responsibility for the School (while agreeing to return five named individuals to the Admiralty in the event of a war).[6] But this arrangement did not suit the service ministries, who lodged a vigorous complaint in April 1923, claiming that the School had 'entirely lost its interdepartmental character' since the Foreign Office had taken over 'complete control'. The row simmered on until November when Sir Eyre Crowe, Permanent Under-Secretary at the Foreign Office, devised a compromise whereby the School was placed under the general authority of Sinclair, by now Chief of SIS. Personally acceptable to the armed service intelligence chiefs, Sinclair nevertheless remained answerable to the Foreign Office.[7]

This is not to say that Sinclair was necessarily the best man for the job. Although as Director of Naval Intelligence he had been involved in the creation of the GC&CS in 1919, and clearly appreciated how valuable signals intelligence could be, his role as a customer for sigint in the summer of 1920, when the service intelligence chiefs wanted to publicise the details of intercepted Soviet telegrams, suggests that he did not at this time fully understand how the injudicious use of signals intelligence could risk the precious source itself. From May 1920 GC&CS succeeded in reading the communications of the Soviet Trade Delegation in London. These revealed that the Soviets were indulging in secret political work, including providing a subsidy to the left-wing *Daily Herald*, and contemplating ways of 'arming the British "proletariat"'. Some intercepts were leaked to the press on 17 August, and the evidence of Soviet perfidy mightily enraged senior military and naval officers, including the Chief of the Imperial General Staff, Field Marshal Sir Henry Wilson, who was shocked at the extent to which the government was apparently prepared to ignore the Soviet behaviour. He told his political master, Winston Churchill, that 'our (soldier) loyalty to the Cabinet' was being put under 'severe strain' and (with a hint of political blackmail) that 'we had a still higher loyalty to our King and to England'. Churchill, in fact, agreed and urged Lloyd George to publish more intercepts. But aware of the accompanying risk to the source of the intelligence, Churchill asked the service intelligence chiefs (including Sinclair) 'to report to what extent the incriminating telegrams can be published without undue damage to the permanent interests of the cipher school'. The servicemen (as well as Basil Thomson) concluded that the threat posed by the Soviet delegation justified disclosure. The Cabinet sensibly decided otherwise, although a few intercepts were leaked to the press, presumably by members of the intelligence community.[8]

As it happened, the Soviets missed the significance of the published intercepts and did not apparently realise that their communications were being deciphered until December, but the episode reveals how Sinclair and his colleagues let their patriotic (and right-wing) political hearts override their intelligence chiefs' heads, as well, perhaps, as their constitutional duty to serve the government in power. For them, the evidence of Bolshevik duplicity overwhelmed any other consideration, not only the future ability of GC&CS to decipher foreign governments' communications, but also the broader political context and the policy being pursued by the government of the day. Wilson's claim about servicemen's loyalties being strained, and so on, and the alarmist accusations of Communist subversion were part of a grotesque overreaction to the actual threat posed by the tiny Soviet delegation and the manifest reluctance (well understood by Lloyd George) of the British working class to indulge in violent revolution. Yet during the 1920s Sinclair was implicated in a tendency within the intelligence community which moved beyond the simple process of collecting intelligence and from time to time trespassed into its use as well.

The arrangement whereby the Chief of SIS was simultaneously Director of the Government Code and Cypher School lasted for more than twenty years. Although the armed services kept some residual expertise in the field, SIS effectively acquired monopoly control over British signals intelligence, a fact which was to prove extremely important in the future. This branch of the British intelligence community was notably successful. John Ferris has estimated that 'the GC&CS was one of the world's largest code-breaking agencies, perhaps the biggest; as effective as any other, better than most, possibly the best on earth between 1919 and 1935'. It provided Whitehall with a steady stream of intercepted and decrypted telegrams of foreign governments. It had sustained success throughout the interwar years against French, United States and Japanese traffic, and that of many smaller powers. Up to 1930 or so, it also had 'near mastery' of Italian diplomatic systems. It was less successful against Soviet traffic in Europe, especially from late 1920, though it continued to be able to read a fair proportion of Asian material. Germany, a low priority in the 1920s, was a blind spot, and continued to be so in the 1930s, though success against Japanese traffic helped illuminate British understanding of the forces behind the German–Japanese–Italian Anti-Comintern Pact of 1936–7.[9]

From the beginning of his time as Chief, as well as stiffening up the Service's internal organisation, Sinclair sought to expand its reach over the British intelligence community as a whole. At the end of 1923 he told Crowe at the Foreign Office that he wanted 'to undertake a certain re-organisation of this Service, which should be more efficient, and what is more important, should provide a basis for a war organisation'.[10] Archival evidence from the start of 1924 confirms that, on the Circulation side, the Political Section V had become Section I (in place of the defunct Economic Section) and the geographically arranged Production sections had been concentrated into four groupings: G.1 (the Baltic Group), G.2 (Scandinavian Group), G.3–5 (Western and Central Europe Groups), and G.6–7 (Near and Far Eastern Groups). There was no indication of any provision for the envisaged North and South American Groups. Within six months G.1 and G.2 had been amalgamated.

In January 1924, too, Sinclair held a meeting with the head of the Code and Cypher School confirming the integration of its work with that of SIS. It was 'accepted that G.C. & C.S. was responsible for cryptography, and S.I.S. for the distribution of intelligence derived from this source as well as supplying intelligence and criticism to G.C. & C.S. to assist cryptography'. Section I of SIS was to 'supply G.C. & C.S. with list of general subjects on which to concentrate . . . Armed Forces Sections of S.I.S. to collaborate'. The Code and Cypher School, moreover, was to 'have full access to S.I.S. records'. By June 1924, however, and perhaps reflecting the considerable volume of intercept material produced, GC&CS was instructed to distribute decrypts directly to its customer departments, though copies of all material were also to be sent to Sinclair. There were some practical difficulties with this, since the two organisations were located in separate places. SIS was in Melbury Road, while GC&CS (also for money-saving reasons) had been exiled to Queen's Gate in Kensington, which one cryptanalyst afterwards described as 'more comfortable' than its previous premises but 'rather remote from other departments'.[11] Concerned about this issue, Sinclair was to raise it with the Cabinet's Secret Service Committee in 1925.

The Zinoviev Letter

Although the 1921 Secret Service Committee had clearly distinguished between domestic and foreign intelligence (with SIS primarily responsible for the latter) and had found little or no overlap between the different agencies, absolute separation of activities was impossible to achieve in practice. SIS's role in monitoring revolutionary activities of various sorts, especially those of international Communism, meant that no hard-and-fast rule could consistently be applied against working within the United Kingdom. If, say, a suspected Communist agent was being tracked by SIS across Continental Europe and came to Britain, it might not be feasible or, indeed, desirable suddenly to hand over the operation to MI5 or Special Branch at the moment the suspect entered the country. During the 1920s and early 1930s SIS also ran some agents exclusively within Great Britain. Foreign diplomats and businessmen presented another range of both threats and opportunities in which SIS might have a legitimate interest. In particular (and complementing GC&CS's work on diplomatic cable traffic in and out of London), embassies (and their staff) themselves could constitute a source of 'foreign intelligence from foreign sources'.

In the interwar years, too, a number of shadowy organisations, mostly organised and funded by right-wing businessmen, worked alongside the formal British security and intelligence agencies. Some were exploited by Basil Thomson in the immediate postwar years, but it is clear that SIS also had direct contact with them. One such was the Committee to Collect Information on Russia, with which Sidney Reilly had links and which in 1921 produced a 'Who's Who in Russia' that both SIS and the Foreign Office found useful. Another was the Makgill Organisation, an 'industrial intelligence service' set up after the Russian revolution by a wealthy baronet, Sir George Makgill, with backing from the Federation of British Industries and the Coal Owners' and Shipowners' Associations. In 1920 or 1921, after Vernon Kell of MI5 had introduced Makgill to Desmond Morton of SIS, the two men collaborated by exchanging information and pooling two of Makgill's sources in particular. One (who was used up to 1923) 'reported on Communist affairs in [the] U.K. and, with increasing vividness of imagination, on international and continental communism'. The other, Kenneth A. Stott, employed by SIS in 1924–5, was 'wholly UK based', 'had a long previous communist connection' and reported on 'some international communist matters as they affected U.K.'.[12]

Right-wing fears about the onward march of Communism were reinforced by a change of government in Britain. Seeking a mandate from the electorate to back a new policy of economic protectionism, the Conservative Stanley Baldwin, who had succeeded Andrew Bonar Law as Prime Minister in May 1923, called a general election at the end of the year. Although the Conservatives won the largest number of seats, they failed to secure an overall majority, and in January 1924 Labour, the second largest party in parliament, with Liberal Party support unexpectedly formed their first-ever government with Ramsay MacDonald as Prime Minister and Foreign Secretary. Conscious of their minority position, the new administration proved both moderate and capable. Although the Labour Cabinet included idealistic internationalists like C. P. Trevelyan, who favoured dismantling the security and intelligence services, there is no evidence that this had any practical effect. According to one new Cabinet minister, Josiah Wedgwood, the government's slogan was 'we must not annoy the Civil Service', and this seems to have applied to SIS as much as any other department.[13] While distancing Labour politically from Communism (for example barring Communists from being members

of the Labour Party), MacDonald sought to normalise Anglo-Soviet relations, exciting Conservative critics by quickly granting formal British
recognition to the Soviet Union and opening negotiations for a comprehensive treaty to settle all outstanding questions between the two states. A
draft treaty was initialled on 8 August 1924. All this was accompanied by
a constant stream of Conservative criticism in parliament and the press,
accusing the government of falling increasingly under left-wing influence.

   MacDonald's political position was gravely undermined when over the
summer of 1924 the government clumsily mishandled the Campbell
Case. John Ross Campbell, a Scottish Communist and acting editor of
the fiercely left-wing *Workers Weekly*, had published 'An Open Letter to
the Fighting Forces' calling on servicemen 'not merely to refuse to go to
war' but also 'to go forward in a common attack on the capitalists and
smash capitalism for ever'. Campbell was arrested and charged under the
1797 Incitement to Mutiny Act. This was accompanied by political uproar: right-wingers called for this revolutionary to be locked up, while
left-wingers complained about the suppression of free speech. When the
government dropped the prosecution, ostensibly for technical reasons,
the Liberals, asserting that this had been done under left-wing pressure,
withdrew their support. MacDonald lost a vote of censure in parliament
and called an election for 29 October.

   On 24 October the right-wing *Daily Mail* published the leaked text of
a letter purporting to be from the Soviet leader Grigori Zinoviev to the
Communist Party of Great Britain urging them to rouse the British proletariat in advance of armed insurrection and class war.[14] The same day, as
the rest of the British press reported on 25 October (a 'Bombshell' and
'The truth at last', declared *The Times*), the Foreign Office released the
text with that of a strongly worded protest to the Soviet chargé d'affaires
in London.[15] Although it has been claimed that the Zinoviev Letter decisively contributed to Labour losing the election, their vote in fact went
up, and the Conservatives under Baldwin won an absolute majority due
to the collapse of the Liberal vote. The suspicion remains, nevertheless,
that right-wing elements, with the connivance of allies in the security and
intelligence services, deliberately used the letter (and perhaps even manufactured it) to ensure a Labour defeat. SIS was certainly involved, as the
letter had been obtained by the Riga station, who had forwarded an
English text to Head Office on 2 October. The source cited was FR/3/K,

S O V I E T   R U S S I A.

Letter to ...(...)
...
... Latvia,
L/3900
...
2.10.24.

Instructions to British Communist Party. *9/10/24*

Executive Committee,
Third
Communist International.

Presidium.

Sept.15th,1924.

Moscow.

VERY SECRET.

To the Central Committee,
British Communist Party,

Dear Comrades,

The time is approaching for the Parliament of
England to consider the Treaty concluded between the
Governments of Great Britain and the SSSR for the
purpose of ratification. The fierce campaign raised
by the British bourgeoisie around the question shows
that the majority of the same, together with reaction-
-ary circles, are against the Treaty for the purpose
of breaking off an agreement consolidating the ties
between the proletariats of the two countries lead-
-ing to the restoration of normal relations between
England and the SSSR.

The proletariat of Great Britain, which pronounced
its weighty word when danger threatened of a break-off
of the past negotiations and compelled the Government
of MACDONALD to conclude the Treaty, must show the
greatest possible energy in the further struggle for
ratification and against the endeavours of British
capitalists to compel Parliament to annul it.

It is indispensable to stir up the masses of the
British proletariat, to bring into movement the army
of unemployed proletarians, whose position can be im-
-proved only after a loan has been granted to the SSSR
for the restoration of her economics and when business
collaboration between the British and Russian prolet-
-ariats has been put in order. It is imperative that
the group in the Labour Party sympathising with the
Treaty should bring increased pressure to bear upon
the Government and parliamentary circles in favour of
the ratification of the Treaty.

Keep close observation over the leaders of the Labour
Party, because these may easily be found in the lead-
ingstrings of the bourgeoisie. The foreign policy of
the Labour Party as it is already represents an inferior
copy of the policy of the Curzon Government. Organise
a campaign of disclosures of the foreign policy of
MACDONALD.

The IKKI will willingly place at your disposal the
wide material in its possession regarding the activities
of British imperialism in the Middle and Far East. In
the meanwhile, however, strain every nerve in the
struggle for the /

*The first page of the notorious Zinoviev Letter, showing its despatch
from Latvia on 2 October 1924 and its circulation to British government
departments a week later.*

Riga's star agent in Moscow. It took about a week to reach London and, having been evaluated by Desmond Morton, was circulated by SIS on 9 October to the Foreign Office and other departments.[16] A covering note said that the document contained 'strong incitement to armed revolution' and 'evidence of intention to contaminate the Armed Forces', and was 'a flagrant violation' of 'the Anglo-Russian Treaty signed on the 8th August'. Though, apparently, no systematic checks had been made, SIS also categorically vouched that 'the authenticity of the document is undoubted'.[17]

The Foreign Office, nevertheless, carefully sought further corroboration from SIS. This was provided by Desmond Morton on 11 October based (he maintained) on information received from 'Jim Finney' (code-named 'Furniture Dealer'), one of the agents jointly run with Makgill's organisation, who had been infiltrated into the Communist Party of Great Britain. According to Morton, Finney reported that the Party Central Committee had recently received a letter of instruction from Moscow concerning 'action which the C.P.G.B. was to take with regard to making the proletariat force Parliament to ratify the Anglo-Soviet Treaty' and that 'particular efforts were to be made to permeate the Armed Forces of the Crown with Communist agents'. This, concluded Morton, 'seems undoubtedly confirmation of the receipt by the C.P.G.B. of Zinoviev's letter'. But the original report contained no reference to any particular communication from Moscow, and Morton said he had ascertained details of a *specific* letter only during a subsequent meeting with the agent. Reflecting how curious it was that the agent had not mentioned so apparently significant a directive from Moscow in the original report, Milicent Bagot, a retired MI5 officer who spent three years in the late 1960s exhaustively investigating the affair, suggested that the agent had been 'asked "loaded" questions by Morton, who is known to have been working on the Riga report and had no doubt put the two together in his mind'.[18]

On 13 October SIS assured Sir Eyre Crowe that Morton's information provided 'strong confirmation of the genuineness of our document [the Zinoviev Letter]'. This was interpreted by Crowe as 'absolutely reliable authority that the Russian letter was received and discussed at a recent meeting of the Central Committee of the Communist Party of Great Britain', and on this basis he recommended to MacDonald that a formal note of protest be submitted and full information be given to the press.[19] Morton's 'strong confirmation', therefore, already perhaps more than the evidence supported, became 'absolutely reliable authority', and the basis for explicit government action. It was only after the Soviet chargé, Christian Rakovsky, had dismissed the letter as 'a gross forgery' (which it almost certainly was) that on 27 October Crowe asked Malcolm Woollcombe for further information. Had, for example, the text been received in English or Russian and could an SIS officer explain things personally to the Prime Minister, who in the meantime had himself begun to wonder if the letter were bogus? Riga told Head Office that their original version had been in Russian, which had been translated by a secretary in the station before transmission to London, thus revealing that the English text was not quite as 'authentic' as had at first been claimed.[20]

The Cabinet met to discuss the case on 31 October. Some ministers, including Trevelyan and Lord Parmoor, were very critical of 'Foreign Office officials', suspecting that some had 'stooped to a mean political trick to damage the Labour Party'. Parmoor, who over a thirty-year political career moved from being a quintessential establishment man and Conservative MP to an international socialist and senior Labour leader, favoured an inquiry which would (as the assistant Cabinet Secretary Thomas Jones recorded) 'table all the available evidence and expose our Secret Service', and a committee was deputed 'to examine at once the authenticity of the Zinovieff letter'.[21] Responding to more questions from MacDonald about the text and provenance of the letter, SIS declared that it was 'highly important' that 'definite proof be obtained for our own satisfaction and for that of the Foreign Office'. Perhaps appreciating that this could be interpreted as back-pedalling on the assurances already given, SIS added that this did 'not, of course, imply that either we or the Foreign Office doubt the authenticity of the document in any way'. But, despite further exchanges with Riga, SIS could add nothing more conclusive. Reflecting a perhaps over-fastidious attitude towards the Secret Service, MacDonald was noticeably reluctant during the whole affair to question any SIS officer in person. On one occasion Crowe took Malcolm Woollcombe of SIS's Section I with him to the Prime Minister, but (according to Woollcombe's son) the intelligence officer had to remain 'out of sight in an adjoining room with a communicating door, and the Prime Minister's questions were put to him by Crowe, who relayed the substance of my father's answers'.[22] Sir Wyndham Childs (the Assistant Commissioner at

Scotland Yard, responsible for the Special Branch), whom the committee also interviewed, was unable to add anything more about the alleged reception of the letter by the CPGB, and when the committee reported to the Cabinet on 4 November they 'found it impossible on the evidence before them to come to a positive conclusion on the subject'.[23]

MacDonald resigned the same day and the matter passed to Baldwin's new Conservative government. On 12 November another committee, chaired by the new Foreign Secretary, Austen Chamberlain, and including Lord Curzon, was formed to investigate the matter. A week later, 'after hearing all the necessary witnesses', they 'were unanimously of the opinion that there was no doubt as to the authenticity of the letter'.[24] We do not know who constituted 'all the necessary witnesses' (there is no written report of their deliberations), but they do not seem to have included anyone from SIS. Sinclair had evidently been ready to give evidence, for he provided Crowe with a note of 'five very good reasons' why the letter was considered genuine which he had prepared in the event of being called before the committee. Sinclair declared, wrongly, that the letter had come 'direct from an agent <u>in Moscow</u> for a long time in our service, and of proved reliability. He is an official in the Secretariat of the 3rd International, who works directly under Zinoviev and has access to his secret files.' Though Sinclair may have believed this to be so, it was not precisely the case, as the claimed source was one of FR/3's sub-agents, about whom much was alleged but little definite was known. In his second and third reasons, Sinclair repeated some circumstantial corroboration, including the highly suspect assertion that the letter had been received by the Communist Party of Great Britain. Two further reasons turned round the possibility of the letter being a forgery. On the one hand, Sinclair baldly stated that 'if it was a forgery, by this time we should have proof of it', which was more a matter of faith than evidence, and, on the other, he declared that 'the possibility of being taken in by "White Russians"' had been 'entirely excluded'. SIS 'made it our special business to be acquainted to the methods and personnel of the various "White Russian" and other forging organisations, especially the main one in Berlin [Orlov], with the object of preventing ourselves from having forgeries planted on us'. In this particular case, moreover, he stated categorically that SIS was 'aware of the identity of every person who handled the document on its journey from Zinoviev's files to our hands'.

We might allow that Sinclair (or whichever SIS subordinate drafted the paper) had in mind some rather fine distinction between being 'aware of' and 'knowing' an identity, but in the sense which the assertion was clearly meant to convey to Crowe or the Foreign Secretary (or whoever), it was simply untrue, as FR/3 never revealed the specific identity of his alleged Comintern source. Only one of Sinclair's reasons, his fifth – 'because of the subject matter' – was actually any good at all, though this was still essentially circumstantial evidence. Sinclair correctly argued that the letter 'was entirely consistent with all that the Communists have been enunciating and putting into effect', though he ignored other evidence which suggested that, at least temporarily, the Comintern had been anxious to avoid any action which would undermine MacDonald's minority Labour government.[25] In the spring of 1924, for example, the Riga station had sent London a copy of a letter from the Comintern to the CPGB stating that overt anti-government action 'was only permissible should the Government commit some grave infringement of the rights of the working classes'.

SIS's resolute validation of the Zinoviev Letter, and its suppression of any evidence to the contrary, underpinned the consistent Foreign Office position for the next fifty years (at least) that the letter was genuine. Since the general content of the letter was never in doubt – the Soviets were indeed keen on fomenting revolution in Britain – and bearing in mind the broadly (and sometimes fiercely) anti-Bolshevik views held by SIS officers, among many other public servants, the Service attitude appears to have combined an element of wish-fulfilment with an understandable, if unattractive, desire not to admit to having made a mistake. SIS, and the security and intelligence agencies in general, have also been accused of leaking the letter both to the press and to Conservative Central Office in a deliberate effort to discredit the Labour government. 'As you know the civil service has no politics,' wrote one official in November 1924 to Lord Derby, a former Conservative Secretary for War, 'but I fancy they would contribute heavily to a statue to Zinovieff & Mr. Campbell, for the effect they had on the election.'[26]

So it may well have been in SIS, whose officers had numerous contacts and acquaintances in Conservative political and business circles. It is highly likely that some talk of the letter, if not the text itself, was shared beyond Whitehall. In April 1969 Desmond Morton even claimed that

Stewart Menzies had sent a copy of the letter to the *Daily Mail* through the post, an assertion greeted with 'amazement and disbelief' inside SIS.[27] On 21 October 1924, however, three days before the letter's publication and because of its particular encouragement of subversion within the armed services, complete copies of the text were circulated to the home military commands in Great Britain, and it was reported that the Admiralty were considering similar action. With such a wide distribution it was surely only a matter of time before the document became public. Whoever leaked the letter, SIS's role was less than glorious, and the whole affair shows how an almost obsessive and blinkered concentration on one target can dangerously influence the exercise of sensible critical judgment.

The 1925 Secret Service Committee

The Zinoviev Letter affair exposed weaknesses in the co-ordination of work between SIS and Special Branch in particular, and in February 1925 Stanley Baldwin reconvened the Secret Service Committee of Sir Warren Fisher, Sir Eyre Crowe and Sir Maurice Hankey to report 'on the existing organisations and their relationship to one another', and to make recommendations 'as to any changes which in their opinion would conduce to the greater efficiency of the system'. At their first meeting the committee decided that in reviewing SIS, MI5 and the Special Branch at Scotland Yard 'their broad aim should be to secure greater concentration, both administrative and geographical'. They also agreed to consider 'whether the ideal of placing the three branches under one chief is attainable'. Their first evidence was from Sinclair who bluntly described the 'whole organisation of British Secret service' as being 'fundamentally wrong'. The continuation of Indian Political Intelligence (IPI) 'as a separate entity was a farce'. MI5 'contained several vested interests due to the length of time which certain officers had served the department'. 'With proper reorganisation', he thought that MI5's staff of thirty could be reduced to about five. Overall, he argued strongly for amalgamating SIS, the Government Code and Cypher School, IPI and MI5 'under one head and one roof in the neighbourhood of Whitehall'. All work 'concerning communism and similar movements' should be transferred from Scotland Yard to the new organisation. The Passport and Passport Control Offices could be 'housed on the ground floor of the same building as cover, as well as for convenience'.[28]

Over three weeks in March 1925, the committee interviewed all the other relevant agency heads, and on 19 March brought Sinclair and Sir Wyndham Childs together to discuss a list provided by Sinclair of 'recent examples of lack of co-operation between this Organisation [SIS], Scotland Yard and the Home Office'. They showed 'the inefficiency and waste of time, money and labour now involved in S.S. work in general, owing to C's Organisation, Passport Control Department, G.C.&C.S., M.I.5, I.P.I. and Scotland Yard not being under the same roof or housed so close to one another that it is possible for the Officers in each Department constantly to have personal conversations with Officers in any other'. Sinclair argued that the Zinoviev Letter 'was a classic illustration of the overlapping inevitable under the present system'. It had been discovered abroad, was addressed to the Communist Party in England, and 'enjoined revolutionary action both in civil and military spheres'. Thus, 'under the present arrangement of divided responsibility in the British secret service', it concerned SIS, Special Branch and MI5. Childs had already told the committee that 'he had never seen C in connection with the Zinoviev letter'. Sinclair 'had not told him that he proposed to employ an agent in this country for this purpose, and the result of such employment had not been reported to him'. Sinclair's agent, moreover, had 'claimed to be in a position to report the proceedings at the meeting of the Central Executive Committee of the communist party at which the Zinoviev letter was considered'. But Childs firmly asserted that he 'could prove through agents that such a meeting had never been held'.[29] In this respect, Childs was right and Sinclair was wrong.

On 24 March the committee met to 'take stock' of the evidence so far submitted. The secretary, Nevile Bland, minuted 'that unified direction was the ideal towards which we ought to work' and that 'the first step to this end was to associate the various branches in one building', though both Sinclair and Kell strongly objected to being housed in Scotland Yard. In a subsequent note, Sir Maurice Hankey objected to the first of these conclusions, on the grounds that the connection with government departments 'for whose benefit they were respectively established' – Foreign Office, Home Office and so on – was more important than those between agencies. His 'present inclination' was 'not, even as an ideal in the distant future, to go beyond doing everything we can to secure the closest co-ordination without altering the present balance of Ministerial and Departmental responsibility'. The committee's pace of work slowed down over the summer of 1925. Sir John Anderson, Permanent Under-Secretary at the Home Office, who had attended all the meetings so far, was formally added to the committee in June, as was Sir William Tyrrell, who had succeeded Sir Eyre Crowe as Permanent Under-Secretary at the Foreign Office after the latter's early death at the end of April. Evidence was taken from the service Directors of Intelligence, who expressed 'general satisfaction with both S.I.S. and M.I.5'. While General Sir John Burnett-Stuart, Director of Military Operations and Intelligence (the Directorates of Military Operations and Intelligence having been amalgamated in 1922), declared that while 'S.I.S. had improved enormously under "C"', he was 'quite content with things as they were'. He 'would hesitate to put too much power into the hands of so energetic and capable an officer as "C"'. There was also 'the advantage of the check which three separate organizations automatically provided on each other's results'.[30]

Having commissioned a report on the Special Branch (which concluded that it required some internal reorganisation) the Secret Service Committee delivered their report in December 1925. They had 'no hesitation in saying that if there were to-day no British secret service of any kind' and they had been called upon to organise one from scratch, they 'should not adopt the existing system as our model', but would have endeavoured 'to create a single department'. Yet 'the heterogeneous interests, liaisons, traditions and responsibilities of the different services', as well as the 'marked reluctance of the majority of those concerned to advocate any drastic change', left the committee with 'a strong impression that an attempt to form a coalition would, if it were not an actual failure, at any rate lead to no great improvement'. Hankey's argument about maintaining existing departmental responsibilities was accepted (for example: 'Place the head of the Indian Political Intelligence under the chief of a combined secret service, and what becomes of the authority of the Government of India?'). 'With all the divers aspects of our present day secret service', moreover (and using a Gilbert and Sullivan analogy), 'the head of a combined organisation would have to be more than a Pooh Bah – he would have to be the Lord High Executioner as well.' While this was a defeat for Sinclair and the Foreign Office, which had championed the single-agency option, the committee commended Sinclair as 'a zealous, intelligent and exceptionally competent officer'. It recommended 'that someone, preferably "C", who has a peculiar flair for such things, should be made responsible for keeping a look-out for a suitable building, or buildings, in the neighbourhood of Whitehall, to which the outlying branches could be transferred'. This, it was believed, would facilitate the closer liaison between SIS, its fellow agencies and customers which everyone thought was desirable. The committee also thought that the 'relations between what are probably the two most important sections, namely the Secret Intelligence Service and Scotland Yard', could be improved, and that SS1, the liaison department between Scotland Yard and SIS, should either (like the service ministries) second a representative to work 'on "C"'s staff', or 'transfer itself bodily' to SIS.[31]

Sinclair acted swiftly to find a new combined headquarters closer to Whitehall. In the spring of 1926 he moved both SIS and GC&CS into offices in Broadway Buildings, a two-year-old nine-storey office block opposite St James's Park Underground station, conveniently located between the headquarters of the London Missionary Society and the Old Star and Crown pub. At the end of September 1926, the Passport Control head office moved into 21 Queen Anne's Gate, adjoining Broadway Buildings, and an internal passageway was constructed linking the two buildings. Since it was 'essential that the connection between the P.C. Office and the S.I.S. Office be kept secret', Sinclair instructed that SIS staff should 'in no circumstances use the Queen Anne's Gate entrance'. Initially SIS and GC&CS occupied only the third, fourth and fifth floors, though they steadily expanded until, shortly before the Second World War, they took over the whole building.

Sinclair, too, had a flat in Queen Anne's Gate with a link to SIS so that he could move unobserved between his residence and his office on the fourth floor of Broadway Buildings. Here visitors were required to knock on a hatch, after which they might be admitted to the Chief's outer office by one of his secretaries. A green light over the door of the inner office indicated whether Sinclair was engaged or not. For the ordinary visitor, the experience had an ineffable air of mystery. The interwar Chairman of the Conservative Party, J. C. C. Davidson, long afterwards recalled (and perhaps embellished) one such occasion. Sinclair's secretary, the formidable Miss Pettigrew, had asked him to come to see the Chief. 'When I enquired how I should come, she told me through the office of the sanitary engineer. I went to that entrance and passed through the rooms with lavatory pans and baths etc., and through a double door.' Met by Miss Pettigrew, Davidson was ushered 'into a room that was quite out of this world . . . There was a mother-of-pearl handled pistol on a round table in the middle, a cigar box, a Turkish carpet with so deep a pile that you nearly got lost in it, and a handsome desk behind which sat "C".'[32]

Relations with other agencies

One issue which surfaced during the 1925 Secret Service Committee proceedings was that of SIS's domestic activities. Reinforcing his argument for the creation of a unified secret service, Sinclair told the committee that it was 'impossible to draw the line between espionage and contre-espionage, for both were concerned solely with foreign activities'. MI5, for example, 'looked to him to obtain abroad information relating to spies working in the United Kingdom and were then supposed to follow it up in this country; but they had no "agents" and had to rely on informers and the interception of letters in the post'. Following this statement, Sir John Anderson asked did SIS 'at present employ any agents in the United Kingdom?' With a slight air of evasion, Sinclair replied 'that as neither M.I.5 nor Scotland Yard were prepared to do so, he had been compelled to make his own arrangements in this respect for checking information received from abroad and had done so successfully'. At the committee session devoted to examining co-operation (or otherwise) between SIS and Special Branch, Wyndham Childs had complained about Sinclair's unilateral employment of an agent in England who in Childs's view, moreover, had provided unreliable information. At a subsequent meeting, Anderson once again 'expressed concern at C's activities in this country, which he thought, if not curtailed, might sooner or later lead to trouble'.[33] So it did.

Towards the end of 1925 Valentine Vivian's new Section V began to handle counter-intelligence and counter-Communist work. Liaison with the India Office and Scotland Yard was transferred from Section I (which continued to process work for the Foreign Office). The new section took over the running of what became known as the 'Casuals': United Kingdom-based sources, including Desmond Morton's existing network acquired through Sir George Makgill and other contacts. Morton, indeed, as head of Production, retained a close interest in the work of the section, which overlapped with that of both Scotland Yard and MI5. Following the recommendations of the 1925 Secret Service Committee, SIS endeavoured to improve liaison particularly with the counter-subversion experts, Captains Hugh Miller and Guy Liddell, in Scotland Yard's semi-autonomous section SS1, which was loosely part of the Special Branch. In April 1926 Sinclair proposed to Childs that Vivian should actually be seconded to SS1, though nothing came of the suggestion. The following month the British General Strike conclusively demonstrated to Sinclair's satisfaction the sinister links between international Communism and domestic labour unrest. On 13 May, the day after the nine-day stoppage had been called off by the trade union leadership, Sinclair sent a draft memorandum to Childs 'showing the connection of the Soviet Government with the Trades Unions'. Linking Soviet statements about labour activism, British trade union attendance at international workers' conferences and organisations such as the Anglo-Russian Trade Union Unity Committee, the evidence gathered by SIS proved 'beyond doubt' that the idea for the General Strike had been 'conceived many months ago at Moscow'; that the Soviet 'directors of the movement' had 'found facile accomplices' in British trade unionism; and that 'through the combined efforts of these unscrupulous people, the responsible Trade Union leaders have been exploited and swept along'.

Sinclair (who copied the paper to Bland at the Foreign Office) told Childs that he hoped the occasion would not arise which would 'necessitate' it 'being made use of'. He advised him that, if it were to be used, Foreign Office permission would first have to be obtained as, in his opinion, 'its publication in any form would entail a severance of diplomatic relations with the Soviet Government'. Since Sinclair described his document as having been 'set out in a popular and elementary form' (evidently suitable for publication), and he appears also to have volunteered its transmission to Childs, it is not clear how seriously we should take his hope that the necessity for using it would 'not arise'. But it is obvious that he was well aware of the potential political ramifications which intelligence-based revelations from anti-Communist operations might provoke. So was the government. In March 1927, the Prime Minister, Stanley Baldwin, reconvened the Secret Service Committee to examine 'the state of affairs at Scotland Yard'. At the first meeting Sir William Tyrrell explained that Baldwin's 'principal source' of concern 'was the fear that the political work at Scotland Yard might at any moment give rise to a scandal, owing to the Labour Party obtaining some plausible pretext to complain that a government department was being employed for party politics'. Tyrrell further suggested that 'Scotland Yard's anti-red activities' might be 'handed over to somebody who was not "on the books"'. In a subsequent letter he was more explicit, recommending 'the transfer to S.I.S.' of all the relevant 'members of the staff of Scotland Yard'. Tyrrell clearly shared the desire for an amalgamated intelligence organisation, and, as he assured Sinclair in May 1927, he 'never missed an opportunity . . . of taking advantage of any opening in order to bring it about'. Over the first two meetings, however, Sir John Anderson, defending his departmental interests (and backed up by Hankey and Fisher), argued against Tyrrell, emphasising 'the necessity for retaining in the hands of the Home Secretary the control of any civil measures for the internal security of the country'. Rather than SIS taking over the 'political work' of Special Branch, he suggested that it might be concentrated in MI5.[34]

By the time the committee met again, the Arcos raid on 12 May 1927 had once more highlighted the problems of intelligence co-ordination as well as the considerable costs of its political fall-out. Arcos, the All-Russian Co-operative Society Limited, through which all Soviet businesses operated in the United Kingdom, was widely (and rightly) regarded as a front for Soviet propaganda and subversion. From the early 1920s both SIS and MI5 had taken a close interest in the company and its headquarters at 49 Moorgate in the City of London. From October 1926 an Arcos employee ('a British subject of undoubted loyalty') had passed information to SIS's Bertie Maw, who worked in Morton's Production branch. In March 1927 the informant provided evidence that a British army signals training manual had been copied in the Moorgate office.[35] Since (as Sinclair reported later) this 'concerned an act of espionage against the Armed Forces', SIS passed the evidence over to MI5 who, having satisfied themselves that the evidence was genuine, on 11 May set it before the uncompromisingly anti-Communist Home Secretary, Sir William Joynson-Hicks. He, in turn, persuaded the Prime Minister to authorise a raid on the Arcos offices, which, hastily organised and poorly executed, took place the following afternoon.[36]

No significant evidence of Soviet espionage was discovered. At SIS Sinclair and Morton were furious about the raid, which, apart from anything else, ruined Section V's continuing operations against Arcos. On 23 May the Cabinet resolved to break off diplomatic relations with the USSR, and, in the absence of any bona fide evidence from the Arcos offices, decided to use signals intercept evidence to justify the break. There was a stormy debate in the House of Commons on 26 May, during which Vivian, rather like Woollcombe three years earlier, sat in Sir Austen Chamberlain's room 'writing answers to scribbled questions on which the Foreign Secretary required information'. In Christopher Andrew's words, the debate on the affair 'developed into an orgy of governmental indiscretion about secret intelligence for which there is no parallel in modern parliamentary history'. Alerted to the vulnerability of its diplomatic communications by these revelations and the publication of six intercepted telegrams in a subsequent White Paper, Moscow adopted the much more secure 'one-time pad' method of encryption and robbed Britain of one of its most valuable intelligence assets.[37]

Sinclair as Director of GC&CS in 1927 took a rather different view of the public use of intercept evidence than he had done as Director of Naval Intelligence in 1920. On the day of the Commons debate he sent a 'personal & urgent' note to Tyrrell stating that there was a document from the Arcos offices which provided 'direct proof of the participation of members of the Soviet Legation in revolutionary activities in this country'. But it was too late to stop the revelations. Sinclair complained afterwards that 'had the existence of this document been known in time, and especially if there had still been a possibility of obtaining additional evidence through further searches', the publication of the decrypted telegrams could have been avoided. As it was, their publication had been 'authorised only as a measure of desperation to bolster up a case vital to Government'. Sinclair observed that the whole affair demonstrated 'the danger which is caused by the absence of any central control or authority'. While 'The Secret Service' was 'spoken of as though it were one body', in reality it was three separate organisations (SIS, MI5 and Special Branch), 'each with its peculiar objectives, prejudices, methods and limitations'. The remedy, he asserted, 'lies in the unification of these three bodies'. Sinclair repeated this opinion to the Secret Service Committee. Although both Tyrrell and Fisher took the view that co-operation between the agencies had broken down, Anderson 'did not think the episode strengthened the claim for any radical alteration of existing arrangements' and the committee adjourned in June 1927 without making any recommendations at all.[38]

But the problem of overlap and inter-agency relations remained, especially as SIS continued to monitor Communist activity at home as well as abroad. During 1927 Desmond Morton was heavily involved in a lengthy operation which contributed to the conviction in January 1928 of Wilfred Macartney and a German Communist, Georg Hansen, for offences under the Official Secrets Act. Macartney, who had worked for MI1(c) under Compton Mackenzie during the war, was as much an inept petty criminal and confidence trickster as a spy. Indeed, Mackenzie afterwards referred to him as being in jail for 'comic opera espionage'. But the evidence against him, especially as detailed by Morton (who appeared before the court as 'Peter Hamilton'), linked him through Hansen to Arcos and Soviet intelligence.[39] Morton's interest in the Macartney case was heightened by his position, in addition to his Production role, as head of another new SIS department, Section VI, formed during 1926–7 to gather intelligence on the economic preparations for war of potential enemies including Germany and the Soviet Union.[40]

Like Section V, Section VI was closely concerned with Communist activities at home as well as overseas, and Morton was also involved in a collaborative operation run by SIS and MI5 from 1925 investigating William Norman Ewer, the foreign editor of the *Daily Herald*, who was suspected of running a Communist espionage network. While SIS kept watch on the group abroad, MI5 ran postal and telephone surveillance at home. In the spring of 1929 Sinclair told the Foreign Office that the operation conclusively proved that Ewer's group 'were conducting Secret service activities on behalf of, and with money supplied by, the Soviet Government and the Communist Party of Great Britain'. In 1928 Albert Allen (an ex-policeman whose real name was Arthur Francis Lakey) told MI5 that two Special Branch men had been working for Ewer since 1922, which led to the arrest in April 1929 of Inspector Ginhoven and Sergeant Jane, along with an ex-policeman, Walter E. Dale. Among the evidence seized was a diary kept by Dale which revealed that between 1922 and 1927 'unremitting surveillance' had been 'maintained by Dale and his friends upon the premises and personnel of S.I.S and of the Code and Cipher School', that 'laborious efforts were made to identify and trace to their homes officers and members of the secretarial staff' of both organisations, 'and that the move of both offices . . . to joint premises at Broadway Buildings under a common style was accurately observed and recorded'. One result of this was the removal from the publicly available *Post Office London Directory* of the anodyne entry 'Government Communications Ltd' among the tenants of Broadway Buildings which had appeared in the 1928 and 1929 edition listings.

Allen also reported to MI5 that in 1923 a secretary at SIS's Melbury Road headquarters, Mrs Moon, had been targeted by Ewer's agent, Rose Edwardes, who approached the woman 'representing herself to be a member of the American Intelligence Service'. She offered Moon £5 a week to work for her, 'and a good bonus for any useful pieces of information she might be able to obtain'. But the SIS secretary 'apparently got nervous and eventually refused to take up the work', although over 'a number of conversations' Edwardes had apparently been 'able to find out a good deal of what went on at Melbury Road so far as it was known to Mrs Moon'. Moon had at the time reported the approach to the authorities but, reflected Jasper Harker of MI5, she had 'suppressed a good deal' and had not been 'anxious to give such information as would put us on the track of the mysterious lady from the American Secret Service who was supposed to have approached her'.[41]

This was by no means the only suspected Communist targeting of SIS. Another intriguing case concerned the four Lunn sisters, all born in Russia of an English expatriate family, whom Desmond Morton asked MI5 to report on in August 1925. Edith, the eldest, regarded as a committed Bolshevik, had worked as a secretary for the Comintern in 1919 and, by 1925, was travelling about Britain with a known Soviet agent, Andrew Rothstein, 'as husband and wife'. The next sister, Lucy, was said to have been working as a secretary for SIS's Near Eastern organisation since 1919. Helen, the third sister, had worked as a 'lady translator' at the Government Code and Cypher School since about 1920, while the youngest, Margaret, had briefly worked as an SIS secretary in Helsinki, before being dismissed for suspected espionage based on Communist sympathies. But she, too, afterwards got a job for a while as a translator with GC&CS. In this unusual case, guilt by association was evidently not assumed. In March 1926 Morton told MI5 that he had consulted Sinclair, who wanted no further action to be taken. He was, it seems, satisfied that both 'Lunn girls . . . employed under S.I.S.' (Lucy and Helen) were 'quite sound from a security standpoint'.[42]

The revelations about Ginhoven and Jane intensified Sinclair's desire for the rationalisation of British intelligence, including (as he caustically observed in May 1929 to Sir Ronald Lindsay, Permanent Under-Secretary at the Foreign Office) 'the radical reorganisation of the Special Branch on a basis allowing for a proper realisation of the intricacy, delicacy and secrecy of the subjects dealt with'. Exchanges between SIS and Special Branch in early 1929, following the appointment of a new police Assistant Commissioner, Trevor Bigham, indicate their respective roles. SS1 in Scotland Yard performed 'the civil work of a Home Intelligence Service' (while MI5 covered the military side). Sinclair told Bigham that during 1928 SIS had supplied 908 reports to the Special Branch, including 412 about individuals, 299 about organisations, seventy-eight about 'arms traffic' and eight concerning the 'forgery of British currency'. Reviewing the Special Branch for Sinclair in January 1929, Vivian observed that it existed to combat a 'special type of crime', which 'may be described as one vast conspiracy to subvert the existing social order and the Constitution by violent means'. He told Sinclair that SS1 not only possessed 'an almost unequalled knowledge of the subject in all its ramifications, but the cordial co-operation of S.I.S.'. But serious practical difficulties arose from the attitude of Colonel J. F. C. Carter, the Deputy Assistant Commissioner directly responsible for Special Branch, who in Vivian's opinion was 'hardly competent for the task' and 'lived in a mental atmosphere narrowly circumscribed by the exigencies of local information and concrete Police action'. Carter, in fact, had more counter-intelligence experience than Vivian, having worked with both Hoare (in Rome) during the war and Sir Robert Nathan in 1921. Some progress towards co-ordination was made in April 1929 when an SIS officer was appointed joint head of the SIS and Special Branch Registries with the aim of forming 'a "common pool" of information on the various aspects of the one subject (Communism)' and facilitating the efficient and secure exchange of 'secret papers'.

Carter, meanwhile, became extremely suspicious of SIS's growing domestic network of Casuals, which was expanded during 1929 by

Morton's recruitment of Maxwell Knight, a fervent anti-Communist, mildly eccentric jazz musician and keen naturalist who had worked for Sir George Makgill. According to Morton, Knight had 'a small amateur detective or secret service in London, consisting of about 100 individuals in all walks of life, many of whom speak foreign languages'. He also claimed that, 'when required to for his previous masters', Knight 'and two friends burgled, three nights running', the offices of Communist and Labour Party organisations in Scotland. Knight was taken on, initially for a three-month trial, but after Morton had sent him around the country to gather information on Communist organisations he reported that 'with every passing month MK has got his agents nearer and nearer the centre of affairs' and Sinclair approved his continued employment. Carter, however, soon got wind of this expanded operation and was understandably aggrieved at SIS muscling in on his territory. Indeed, if a report by Knight of a meeting over lunch with the Deputy Assistant Commissioner on 23 July 1930, as passed on by Morton, is anything to go by, Carter was incandescent with fury about the development. He accused Morton (whom he called a 'worm') of 'exceeding his duties'. The policeman declared that he would make Morton 'go on his knees to him on the carpet at Scotland Yard before he has done'. Carter, whose political sympathies appear to have been rather more left-wing than those of either Knight or Morton, contended that Morton was 'doing the whole of this thing for the Conservative Party'. He observed that Ramsay MacDonald's second Labour government (which had come into power after Labour won the most seats, though not an absolute majority, in the May 1929 general election) were 'against this sort of work' and he had 'to carry out their policy'.

Although a meeting was held in October between Vivian and Carter at which (according to Vivian's record of it) it was agreed that SIS should continue to collect information through domestic sources, 'in consultation' with Scotland Yard, the dispute ground on until Sir John Anderson (whose department was administratively responsible for the police) intervened and summoned Sinclair to the Home Office in January 1931 to what turned out to be a very uncomfortable meeting about the Casual organisation. Recalling Sinclair's evidence to the 1925 Secret Service Committee, Anderson noted that when the organisation had been started 'it had been represented as a small one designed for the purpose of checking certain items of C's information from abroad'. It now appeared that it 'was expanding and as such was proving a source of grave embarrassment to the Home Office'. Anderson complained that 'endeavours had been made to recruit Civil Servants', a procedure 'that he could not possibly countenance'. One of the 'principals in the organisation [evidently Maxwell Knight] was, or had been, connected with the British Fascisti and was under suspicion of working for political organisations, such as the Conservative Party'. Anderson further 'pointed out the danger of a Government organisation such as S.I.S. being in any way associated with such undertakings'. Sinclair, on the defensive (and presumably briefed by Morton), said that the 'organisation at present consisted of only five individuals including the principal referred to. The latter had not been connected with the British Fascisti for the last three years, and documentary proof could be produced to support this. Neither was he connected with any of the political secret organisations.' On the matter of using civil servants, Sinclair admitted that two officials 'had been recruited temporarily to assist in pursuing certain lines of enquiry but that their services had long since been dispensed with'. Both Scotland Yard and MI5, he insisted, 'were fully aware of the existence and objects of the organisation and Scotland Yard had agreed in the arrangements, which for some months past had been working smoothly'. Anderson does not seem to have been reassured, and, a little ominously, concluded by saying that while 'he did not wish to appear obstructive' he proposed to convene a further meeting with Sir Robert Vansittart (Permanent Under-Secretary at the Foreign Office since January 1930), Kell, Trevor Bigham and Sinclair, 'in order that there might be no misunderstanding in regard to this matter'.

Back at SIS Sinclair circulated a summary of the meeting to Menzies, Morton and Vivian. Vivian minuted, 'we are up against bare faced distortions of the truth', and Morton provided a series of comments on Anderson's charges, broadly backing up Sinclair's points, though he contradicted the assertion that two civil servants had been temporarily employed. 'No endeavour', he wrote, 'has ever been made to recruit a Civil Servant.' A 'private friend' of the 'Intermediary' (Knight) had 'volunteered in his spare time to collect certain information quite unconnected with his Department', but this 'was stopped' and orders had been 'given that no Civil Servant should be employed'. He confirmed that the organisation comprised only the 'Intermediary' and four agents, 'and all efforts to obtain information' were 'confined to these five, with the negligible exception that occasionally the Intermediary hears certain scraps of information in social talk, supplementing what had already been received from the four agents'. Morton also confirmed Sinclair's answer about Knight's alleged membership of the British Fascisti, though the detail of the answer is open to question and perhaps Morton himself had been misled on this point. Knight had certainly been a member of the British Fascists, serving as Assistant Chief of Staff of the organisation as well as its Director of Intelligence. Whatever political views he had held at the time, in the early 1950s Knight claimed that he had joined the Fascists at Makgill's request in 1924, merely 'for the purposes of obtaining information', and had remained a member until 1930 'when it more or less became ineffectual'.[43]

Relations between SIS and Special Branch took another dip in the spring of 1931 when Bigham unilaterally decided to dispense with the services of the officer who had jointly run the two agencies' registries for the previous two years. Sinclair thought this 'a retrograde step calculated to destroy a valuable system, built up, not without difficulty, for the purpose of implementing the recommendations of the Cabinet Secret Service Committee'. After Bigham had refused to reconsider his action, Sinclair complained to Vansittart, noting that he would 'endeavour to continue to co-operate with Scotland Yard, but if trouble arises in connection with any failure of such co-operation, I must decline to be held responsible for it'. In the light of this serious breakdown in relations, the Secret Service Committee (now comprising Anderson, Fisher, Hankey and Vansittart) was reconvened 'to discuss the difficulties which had arisen in the inter-relation between C's organisation and Scotland Yard'. Bigham and Carter told the committee 'that S.S.1 (Captains Miller and Liddell) was superfluous and their work in so far as it was necessary could be done by Colonel Carter himself'. They also regarded the section 'as being an outpost of C's organisation and liable to involve Scotland Yard in difficulties'.[44]

After the committee's first meeting, Vansittart bravely organised a party for its members, as well as Scotland Yard and SIS people, which Sinclair afterwards thought had succeeded 'in clearing the air a bit'. Bigham and Carter, however, remained adamant that Miller and Liddell had to go. Sinclair, who saw them as 'experts in considering foreign subversive movements in relation to affairs at home and on a much broader and more important basis than that open to the Police side of Special Branch', could not employ them himself. There would be nothing for them to do, since SIS's liaison with Special Branch was satisfactorily handled by Vivian and would continue to be so. He proposed, therefore, that they might be placed directly under the Home Office.

In the end it was Sir John Anderson who came up with the solution by reviving his 1927 suggestion that Colonel Kell and MI5 took over 'S.S.1 and all its duties'. Since MI5 was 'already responsible for counter espionage not only for the fighting services but for all government departments', this was 'a logical extension of its duties'. Thus there would 'be only two organisations dealing with secret service work, C covering foreign countries, and M.I.5 the Empire'.[45] Although this ignored Indian Political Intelligence, which continued to serve its specialist function, so it was to be. SIS was stripped of its domestic operations, and the Casuals were transferred to MI5, which ceased to be a branch of the War Office and adopted its modern title of the Security Service. Guy Liddell and Maxwell Knight went on to have very distinguished careers in MI5, while Section V under Vivian provided liaison between the two agencies. The new arrangement came into force on 1 October 1931.[46] Thus, exactly twenty-two years after their creation, the Foreign and Home branches of the Secret Service Bureau, now the Secret Intelligence Service and the Security Service, took on their modern form and distinct spheres of responsibility which were to survive for at least the next eighty years.

Spilling the beans

One way of cashing in on secret work was to write or lecture about it for money. A perhaps predictable consequence of British secret service successes during the First World War was the desire by some of those involved, both officers and agents, to tell their stories to a wider public. In March 1919 Norman Thwaites, acting head of station in New York, told Sir William Wiseman (who was in Europe) there were 'signs that we are going to have an influx of "British Secret Service" agents who propose to lecture on their experiences'. One Nicolas Everitt, who had apparently

worked for Naval Intelligence, had already arrived, but Thwaites assured
Wiseman that the New York office had already 'cramped his style' by
planting stories in the *World* newspaper ridiculing him. Thwaites thought
Everitt was 'quite harmless and a good patriot who needs the money, but
his boastful talks' were 'in bad taste'. Everitt's excuse was that Blinker
Hall, who had successfully stood as a Conservative MP in the 1918
general election, had 'set the example by telling tall stories during his
election campaign of the wonders performed'.[47] Cumming's own addic-
tion to secrecy meant that he had offered no such encouragement to his
subordinates. Years afterwards, Pay Sykes wrote that Cumming 'took a
poor view' of Hall's action. One day, he recalled, sitting in a traffic jam
outside the National Gallery, Cumming 'turned to me & said "Sykes, I
am going to publish my memoirs." "Really, Sir," I queried. "Yes" he said.
"The book will be quarto size, bound in red, top-edge gilt, subtitled 'The
Indiscretions of the CSS.' It will have four hundred pages, all blank."'[48]

In 1928 Somerset Maugham's *Ashenden, or the British Agent* was
published, 'founded', he wrote, 'on my experiences in the Intelligence
Department during the war, but rearranged for the purposes of fiction'.[49]
This was another way of exploiting clandestine government work, and, by
turning it into fiction, perhaps hoping to evade accusations of revealing
too much about the structure and workings of British intelligence. The
book seemed clearly autobiographical. The central character, Ashenden,
was, like Maugham, a novelist and dramatist based in Switzerland.
Subsequent commentators, moreover, have endeavoured to link characters in the book with actual people. Ashenden's superior, R (the single-
letter title itself echoing Secret Service practice), for example, has been
identified as John Wallinger, who took Maugham on for his War Office
intelligence network in 1915. Maugham observed that the work of an
agent was 'on the whole extremely monotonous'. Much of it was 'uncom-
monly useless' and, since the material it offered for stories was 'scrappy
and pointless', the author himself had 'to make it coherent, dramatic and
probable'.[50] One unsympathetic reviewer, Orlo Williams (a clerk of the
House of Commons with some intelligence experience), wanly thought
Maugham had undoubtedly captured the monotony of the work. He
noted that Ashenden 'was not a spy, but an agent, and nobody who read
agents' reports during the War will be surprised that his work was as
dreary as these reports'. Maugham had 'done something' to 'get what

excitement there might have been out of such experiences', but the result was 'only moderately entertaining'.[51]

Sir Paul Dukes, an enthusiastic self-publicist, in part supported himself through lecturing and journalism, much of which recycled the same basic material. In 1922, describing himself on the title page as 'Formerly Chief of the British Secret Intelligence Service in Soviet Russia', his first book of Russian reminiscences, *Red Dusk and the Morrow: Adventures and Investigations in Soviet Russia*, was published. Despite accusations from the Soviet government that he had plotted to overthrow it, Dukes claimed that he 'went to Russia not to conspire but to inquire'. In the book he recounted how he had been recruited by the Secret Service, but was careful to disguise some details of MI1(c). Taken to a building 'in a side street in the vicinity of Trafalgar Square', he had been 'whisked' in an 'elevator' to 'the top floor, above which additional superstructures had been built for war-emergency offices' – a description which more or less fitted Cumming's wartime Head Office at Whitehall Court. He described being taken to see the Chief, but dramatically broke off his narrative as he entered Cumming's office. 'There are still things', he wrote, 'I may not divulge.' By 1930, when the *Tatler* published an eight-part 'thrilling series of experiences' about 'Secret Service in Red Russia' by Dukes, he divulged a little more. Again he recounted being 'whisked in a lift to a pile of offices built on top of the roof'. There, 'in a dark office with a low ceiling, the light behind him, sat an officer in admiral's uniform'. Thus promoting Cumming to the rank of his successor, Dukes added that 'the Chief was known to those who knew him by the cryptic sign of a single letter of the alphabet'.[52] Although Vivian thought Dukes's articles 'appear to be sailing pretty near the wind', no action was taken about his revelations.

In May 1937, when Dukes was 'writing further reminiscences of the year 1919', he told Vivian that 'in 1920 and 1921' Cumming had allowed him 'to consult the files of my reports from Russia of that year for articles' he was 'writing at the time'. Now he wanted to 'consult them again' as it 'would be a great convenience . . . in establishing certain events and dates'. Illustrating what would be a continuing problem for historians of SIS, Vivian told him that a search had been made for the documents, 'but without any result I am afraid. All records prior to the year 1920 have, as I think you know, been destroyed, and, as regards those of 1920 and 1921 relating to your case, I am told that either they have been summarised and destroyed or that they are so lost in general files that it is impossible to dig them out.'

Dukes's reassembled and expanded reminiscences were published in *The Story of 'ST 25'*, dedicated (in 1938) 'To the memory of the Chief'. Again, he recounted being taken by lift to a 'roof-labyrinth' to meet Cumming, and, though he still did not name him, he lifted the veil of secrecy yet a little further than before. 'To his subordinates and associates,' he wrote, 'he was invariably known and signed himself by a single letter of the alphabet in ink of a particular hue'. Cumming, asserted Dukes, had 'read and approved of these pages', including all the information 'here related about him and the roof-labyrinth, but I never received permission to mention his name, which probably would have been little known to the general public anyway'.[53] Wisely he submitted a draft of chapter one of the book (covering his appointment and briefing in London) to SIS and had it returned with no redactions requested. 'I cannot imagine any of it doing any harm', wrote Vivian, 'in view of the original book "Red Dust" [*sic*].' Dukes's writings, however, illustrate a perennial feature of the memoir problem which we might call 'revelation-creep', whereby successive versions of secret service stories incrementally reveal more and more, but at each stage not quite enough to provoke official action.

Dukes's careful submission of material prior to publication probably owed something to the difficulties Compton Mackenzie had incurred in 1932 with his book *Greek Memories*. This was Mackenzie's third volume of wartime memoirs, in the second of which, *First Athenian Memories* (1931), he had recounted his first few months in late 1915 working for Mansfield Cumming's Bureau. Although he revealed that 'the real object of C's organization' was 'to obtain information about the enemy', he did not provide much detail or further identify Cumming. 'The initial of C', he wrote, 'was invoked to justify everything, but who C was and where C was and what C was and why C was we were not told.'[54] Although livelier and more personal than Somerset Maugham's fictionalised account, the book does not appear to have caused the authorities any concern, though chapter five, 'Early absurdities of secret-service', cannot have endeared him to all of his former colleagues in the Service. Trouble came with the much more informative *Greek Memories*, published in October 1932, which provoked the first (and by no means the last) prosecution under the Official Secrets Act through which the British government sought to suppress the publication of a memoir about the security and intelligence services.

The press reaction to *Greek Memories* focused on the revelations about Cumming. 'Mystery Chief of the Secret Service', 'Capt "C's" identity disclosed', trumpeted the *Daily Telegraph* on the day of publication, 27 October. Reporting on the book, Hector Bywater, Cumming's very successful prewar agent (a fact he did not disclose) and now the *Telegraph*'s naval correspondent, announced that 'the identity of this remarkable man, who before and during the war probed the naval and military secrets of the Central Powers', had been 'revealed in print for the first time'.[55] This sensational disclosure prompted Sinclair to get MI5 to initiate moves to have the book banned. By three o'clock that afternoon the Director of Public Prosecutions had himself telephoned the publishers and 'suggested to them that they might like to withdraw the book, pointing out however that he was merely giving them friendly advice'.[56] The same day Sinclair sent Sir Robert Vansittart at the Foreign Office 'a list of some points' which were 'considered objectionable from the point of view of national interest', and which rehearsed the kinds of arguments which would be deployed again in similar future prosecutions. The volume blew SIS's cover, a perennially important concern for the Service. It 'blazons the connection between the Passport Control Department and the S.S.'. While conceding that 'this is already known in some quarters', the manner in which it was now explained and emphasised was 'highly undesirable'. Mackenzie had also betrayed 'the fact that the Section known as "M.I.1.c" in the War Office' was 'a cover of the S.S., thereby disclosing the identity of certain present officers of the service', whose names were printed in the publicly available *War Office List*. He had given 'the full names and particulars of a number of individuals previously employed in the S.S.', some of whom were 'earmarked for re-employment in case of future war, and some of whom unofficially assist the present S.S. It thereby renders both classes useless and renders those living in foreign countries liable to dangerous interference.' Finally, the book established 'a very dangerous precedent for present employees on leaving the Service and also for journalists, with whom the Service is of necessity in touch for various reasons'.

A memorandum prepared by SIS for the Director of Public Prosecutions listed a series of passages in the book 'held to be objectionable on the ground that they prevent and endanger the present and future practice of the Secret Service', the 'whole foundation' of which was its 'secrecy'. The 'lengthy and detailed statements of organisation, which may appear dull to the general reader, afford valuable links to an officer of a Foreign Secret Service endeavouring to piece together our system of working'. Personal details, 'recorded and carefully collated by the Secret services of foreign countries' might 'cause the persons mentioned to become objects of retribution' and render them useless for 'effective service' in the future. Sir Reginald Lane Poole, one of Mackenzie's lawyers, asserted that the government wanted to make an example of him 'in order to warn Lloyd George and Winston Churchill' against using unreleased official documents in their memoirs. Someone else told Mackenzie 'that there had been a Cabinet meeting at which the Attorney-General had announced I had destroyed the whole Secret Service . . . and that it was going to cost the country at least two million pounds to undo the harm I had done'. Whatever the reason, Mackenzie was prosecuted under the technical provision of the Official Secrets Act of 'communicating to unauthorised persons . . . information which he obtained while holding office under his Majesty'. Mackenzie, in fact, was legally sunk by the way in which he had assembled the book, cutting and pasting lengthy passages from official documents and telegrams. He afterwards jocularly blamed his wartime secretary for suggesting making 'a third copy' of any documents which he 'might one day find useful'. Without these 'testifying documents', *Greek Memories* 'would never have been accepted as anything more than the embroidery, or even the deliberate invention, of a novelist'.[57]

At the committal proceedings Valentine Vivian appeared in camera and gave detailed evidence of the passages 'to which grave objection can be taken on Secret Service grounds', naming sixteen individuals who as officers or agents had connections with SIS.[58] He was quite roughly cross-examined by one of Mackenzie's barristers, St John Hutchinson, so much so that Vivian prepared a ten-page expansion of his arguments for the subsequent trial. In open court Hutchinson had extracted admissions from a Foreign Office official that, although the publication of official documents was prohibited by the Official Secrets Act, he did not think 'the public interest' had been 'prejudiced' by the actual contents of the material which Mackenzie had used and that 'the publication of these documents' could 'do no harm to anyone'. Evidently sensing that adverse publicity – always a problem in cases of this sort – might outweigh the exemplary value of the prosecution, the government moved to come to an arrangement with Mackenzie's lawyers. After a conference had been held at the Foreign Office between Vansittart, the Director of Public Prosecutions, Sir Vernon Kell and Vivian, 'at which it was decided on certain conditions not to press for imprisonment', Mackenzie was offered a deal that if he pleaded guilty it would 'only be a fine not exceeding £500 and £500 costs'.[59]

When the case went to trial in January 1933 Mackenzie duly pleaded guilty. Extremely good character references for him were produced in court and the judge was persuaded that Mackenzie was 'an honourable man' who believed he was 'doing no harm' in publishing the documents. The judge also hoped that the case might 'do something' to 'warn those who are urged to write similar books that they are offences'. Declaring that he had 'thought deeply over the matter' and (in the circumstances rather improbably since the matter had been settled in advance) 'hesitated very much whether I ought to send you to prison', he imposed a comparatively light fine of only £100, as well as ordering Mackenzie to pay £100 towards the costs of the prosecution. For *The Times*, the lesson from the case was that the Official Secrets Act did not exist only to restrain 'sinister machinations' such as 'espionage and other felonies', but its scope was 'much wider'. Lending weight to Mackenzie's supposition that the prosecution might have been aimed against political memoirs as much as secret service ones, the newspaper reckoned that it might have 'something of a message for the authors, and in particular the autobiographers, of our own time'. It had an effect on Mackenzie. In his final volume of wartime memoirs, published eight years later, he 'suppressed a certain amount of interesting material about espionage because, although the publication of it twenty-two years later could do no harm to anybody or anything', he could not 'be bothered with any more arguments about Intelligence work'.[60]

In the meantime Mackenzie got his revenge with a novel, *Water on the Brain* ('a deliberate caricature of Intelligence'), which savagely satirised the whole world of secret service. N, the chief of M.Q.99(E), the Directorate of Extraordinary Intelligence, warns his new recruit, Arthur Blenkinsop, that their work did not 'consist entirely of meeting mysterious Polish countesses in old castles'. The 'greater part of the work' was 'routine stuff. Card-indexing, filing, making out lists, putting agents' reports into proper English'. The headquarters of the organisation is a detached house, Pomona Lodge, in north London which, abandoned by the service after a security lapse, was to become a home 'for the servants of bureaucracy who have been driven mad in the service of their country'. At the time of Mackenzie's novel, however, it was 'not yet officially a lunatic asylum'. Here N, using 'that green ink which is reserved for the correspondence of high officials in the Secret Service', kept a strict eye on security. The archives, for example, had been protected by a band of 'muscular deaf-mutes', who had had to be dismissed 'after the man-handling of a high official in the Home Office who had not taken the precaution to arrange beforehand with N that he was going to call and who in consequence had been suspected of being a foreign agent by these worthy fellows'.[61]

Another hazard for the Service lay in the overseas publication of espionage memoirs. In 1934 the reputable New York firm of G. P. Putnam's Sons published *All's Fair: The Story of the British Secret Service behind the German Lines*, by Henry Landau, who had been part of Cumming's organisation in the Netherlands and, among other things, had helped run the Dame Blanche network. The book sold extremely well, going into seven impressions by the end of the year. 'One of my chief objects' in writing it, claimed Landau, was 'to place on record the splendid services which the Secret Service agents of Belgian and French nationality rendered the Allied cause during the War'. Recognising the problem of naming agents, he asserted that he had 'only mentioned such names as were known to the Germans through the arrests they made; others I have either changed, or not mentioned at all'. He had done this 'in order to protect former agents in the event of another invasion of Belgium and France during their lifetime' and maintained that he was 'the best judge of what information would compromise them'. Since he had 'protected their lives during the War', he was, 'therefore, competent now to know what can be divulged'.[62] SIS was not so sure. One reader at the Rotterdam station considered that, with only one exception, 'its perusal by interested German authorities' could have 'no repercussion on the activities of this post'. But that exception was a Dutch agent whose 'connections with this post' had 'for the last ten years' been 'forgotten', and it was 'regrettable that Landau should have chosen him by name for mention in his book'. An officer in London also worried that the important agent TR/16 (whom Landau called 'the Dane') might be identifiable. When consulted in August 1934, however, TR/16 felt that he was at no risk at all.

In November 1934 Eric Holt-Wilson of MI5 told Stewart Menzies that Landau, apparently seeking a British publisher for his book, had approached the British literary agents Curtis Brown. Menzies wanted them warned off, 'bearing in mind our main purpose is to prevent the publication of the newest version of the book over here'. Landau, who by now had become an American citizen, was thought to be travelling to England and, 'in view of his close association with this office', Menzies was 'considering whether it would not be a good move if I interviewed him and warned him that he is running a grave risk of being prosecuted for infringement of the Official Secrets Act'. Although Landau did not then return to England, there was no British edition of his memoirs until in 1938 Jarrolds published a rather anodyne autobiography, *Spreading the Spy Net: The Story of a British Spy Director*, which covered his early life and wartime experiences, including a short account of 'the Dane'. He also repeated word for word from *All's Fair* how he had met Cumming for the first time. Taken to an office at the top of Whitehall Court, he 'was confronted with a kindly man who immediately put me at my ease. It was the Chief, Captain C., a captain in the Navy. He swung around in a swivel chair to look at me – a grey-haired man of about sixty, in naval uniform and short of stature.'[63]

The designation of 'C' was information which Vivian in October 1932 had judged 'objectionable' in Compton Mackenzie's book. 'The agreed impersonal term ("C"), by which the head of S.I.S. is still known in Government Departments', he wrote, was among the details by which 'interested persons' could 'identify Sir Mansfield Cumming's successor'. By 1934 this was evidently old news and no action was taken against Landau or his British publishers. In any case, Cumming's successor had already passed judgment on this ex-Service officer at the time his first book had been published. In a circular to all SIS's European and Middle Eastern stations, while placing him on 'the Report list' (to keep track of his movements), Sinclair effectively excommunicated the former officer. 'Landau', read the message, 'was once employed in this organisation. His conduct has since been unsatisfactory and contact or communication with him should be avoided.'

8

Existing on a shoestring

Between the wars SIS's limited resources were thinly spread across the world. It was, moreover, never a very large organisation. Of the thirty-three overseas stations in the early 1920s, most were one-man operations (there were no female station heads until after the Second World War), with one or perhaps two secretaries (usually women) for administrative support. By 1938–9, there were sixty-nine officers and 134 ancillary staff in thirty-four overseas stations, and the overseas deployment of the Service amounted only to some 200 personnel, though there was, of course, also an uncountable number of agents. The expansion of the Service reflected the increasing demands being made of it, though this was constantly limited by the lack of funds. In November 1929 Valentine Vivian prepared a memorandum for the Foreign Office highlighting the rather modest resources devoted to secret service in Britain as compared to other countries, observing, moreover, that 'No Government, except that of Great Britain, would seem to be so ingenuous as openly to budget for, and accurately to publish, the amount annually intended for Secret Service expenditure.'[1] The Italian invasion of Ethiopia in October 1935 inevitably stimulated a sharp rise in demands for information from SIS which, in turn, led Sinclair on 9 October to sign off a strongly worded 'memorandum on Secret Service funds', in which the evident frustrations of his dozen years as Chief, trying to meet incessant demands with inadequate resources, fuelled a *cri de coeur* for increased funding. 'Since the War,' he began, 'the British Secret Intelligence Service has been constantly hampered, by lack of funds, in the performance of its duties.' The 'want of money' had been 'increasingly felt in recent years, during which other Nations have turned Great Britain's gesture in unilateral disarmament [under the ten-year rule] to account by seizing the opportunity to re-arm secretly'. In these circumstances, he argued, 'official sources of information have proved even worse than useless', with governments routinely dissembling on the issue. 'The most glaring case in point', he wrote, 'has been that of Germany.' Until the German government had 'themselves made the facts public, practically the only sources of information on her re-armament were those available to the Secret Service'. It was, moreover, 'a melancholy fact that the march of events has proved their information correct'.

Sinclair argued that 'a great deal more could, and would, have been accomplished had the Service been in possession of adequate Funds'. Drawing a characteristically naval analogy, he said that his budget, which was meant to cover the whole world other than the United Kingdom, India and the colonies, 'only equals that spent every year on the main-tenance (not the cost) of one of H.M. Destroyers in Home Waters', and was much less than the money devoted to secret services by Britain's foreign rivals. Sinclair asserted that 'a satisfactory Secret Service' depended 'essentially upon maintaining a complete and interwoven scheme of work', with as wide a geographical presence and coverage as possible. But, 'owing to lack of funds', it was 'not possible to maintain any Service in such countries as Switzerland, Spain, Yugoslavia, Albania and Arabia, and, in consequence, a great deal of information about other and neighbouring countries, which could be obtained in these countries, escapes us'. The 'necessity for spreading the butter thin', he observed, 'has proved particularly unfortunate in the present Italian crisis'. For years, since Italy had 'been regarded as a friend and ally, intensive S.S. work was not pursued against that country, the main effort being directed against Germany' (an observation which made sense only when the targeting of Comintern operations emanating from Berlin was taken into account). The crisis had obliged the Service not only to divert funds from other work, but also to spend lavishly 'on obtaining intelligence of a nature which S.I.S. is not normally expected to supply in peace time' (tracking, for example, the movements of Italian warships).

Nor was Italy the only problem. Sinclair also remarked on the 'unsatisfactory position' regarding the Far East, 'especially in regard to Japan'. Even 'by diverting sums being spent, with valuable results, on other countries', the amount available for recent efforts in the region was 'wholly insufficient, and only suffices to maintain a skeleton organisation'. Sinclair stressed that, even when adequate funds were available, it took 'at least 2–3 years, under the most favourable circumstances, to establish a satisfactory S.S. in any country'. Meanwhile SIS, 'living, as it does, a hand to mouth existence, with vast areas to cover', was able only 'to scratch the surface'. To 'obtain really inside information', he wrote, 'means spending big money'. He claimed that opportunities frequently occurred 'of dealing with individuals in responsible positions', but 'the offer to them of the few hundreds a year, which represents the amount usually available, is naturally treated by them with contempt'. 'Whatever may be the outcome of the present crisis,' he concluded, 'it is plainly apparent that, in the future, Germany, Japan and Italy will have to be regarded as potential enemies from without, as well as Soviet Russia from within.' The situation 'cannot possibly be covered by the existing S.I.S. Organisation, depending, as it does, upon a limited number of Passport Control Officers and representatives anchored to their posts in the capital, and possessing neither the means nor the mobility for covering the many industrial and strategic posts from which essential information can alone be obtained'. Sinclair asserted that a 'complete plan' had 'been worked out for the establishment of a network of permanent resident agents at the vital points' in Germany, Italy and Japan, but 'to put this plan into execution' would 'necessitate a large increase in S.S. funds'. The precise amount was unspecified, but, without it, 'no guarantees' could be given 'that the S.I.S. will be able to meet the demands of the Armed Forces Departments in times of crisis'.

Having sent copies of his paper to Hankey, Fisher, Vansittart and the Chiefs of Staff (he was clearly not taking any chances), Sinclair secured an increase in funding. From £180,000 in 1935 (at which level it had been since the late 1920s), the Secret Service Vote (covering MI5 as well as SIS) was increased to £350,000 for both 1936 and 1937, to £450,000 in 1938 and £500,000 in 1939.[2] No evidence of the 'complete plan' for 'permanent resident agents' has survived in the Service archives (though this may have been the genesis of the Z Organisation created in 1936), and the expansion of SIS activity, especially in Western Europe, was incremental rather than dramatic. And while the budget increased very markedly in the later 1930s, there were still limitations on what could be done. Reflecting in November 1939 on SIS work since 1935, Commander Reginald 'Rex' Howard concluded that the Service had been 'handicapped very considerably by lack of money'. Howard, a sailor who had served on submarines before the First World War, had joined the Service in November 1931 and became Sinclair's chief staff officer in September 1935. Even as late as 1 June 1939, he had been 'informed by C.S.S. that our activities had been considerably curtailed owing to lack of money, and later, towards the end of July, C.S.S. informed me that the position was even worse, and it was practically impossible to obtain further supplies'. Recruitment, too, was seriously affected 'owing to lack of money', wrote Howard, 'and also to the fact that employment in S.I.S. is non-pensionable'. These grumbles about lack of resources, as well as (from the service departments) the inadequate supply of information demonstrate twin permanent and unchanging truths about intelligence: that, no matter what the circumstances, there is never enough money; and, equally, no matter how much information is provided, there is never enough of it.

Working in the USA

SIS retained a small but active presence under Passport Control cover in New York during the interwar years. From October 1919 until March 1922 Maurice Jeffes was Passport Control Officer, and was succeeded as Cumming's representative by J. P. Maine. Captain Herbert Bardsley Taylor, who joined SIS directly from the Royal Navy, took over in June 1929 and held the position (symbolised in SIS as '48000') until August 1937, when he was brought back to London to be assistant to G.2, who headed the Americas section. From then until the war Captain Sir James Paget was head of station. The forty-nine-year-old Paget was not an intelligence specialist. A baronet, thanks to his grandfather having been an extremely distinguished doctor, he had been a career naval officer before retiring in 1937. That he had no particular qualifications for the job (though his mother was American) rather confirms the comparative unimportance of the station by the late 1930s. Between the wars, however, part of the work was for the armed services. In June 1921 the War Office asked for information on American 'inventions of war material, chemical warfare and aircraft developments'. In March 1922 Stewart Menzies told Sir Warren Fisher's Secret Service Committee that both 'the Air Ministry and the Admiralty considered it extremely important to keep a close eye on naval and aeronautical developments in the United States'. Indeed, the £85,000 annual budget under discussion, which was otherwise thought more or less acceptable, 'would not give adequate scope for such work in America. To do properly what was required in that sphere,' continued Menzies, 'from £3,000 to £4,000 extra would be needed.'[3] It seems that the committee accepted this point, since they found another £5,000 for SIS, but little enough of this appears to have been spent in the USA. The £8,520 allocated to the New York station in April 1923 (of which none was set aside for agents) all came from the Passport Control budget, as did the £5,507 earmarked for 1932–3. In that year, six agents were on the New York books, two unpaid and four paid, and of the latter only one was on a regular retainer (of $100 a month). By 1934–5 his retainer had been increased to $200 a month; one other agent was on $100; and a total of £900 per annum of secret service money was allocated for 'Agents'.[4]

Substantial evidence of somewhat uneven reporting from New York on Communist and radical groups in North America has survived in the archive, but there is only a little relating to armed forces intelligence. In 1930–1 an employee in a firm of consulting engineers with American naval contacts was taken on as a 'paid conscious agent' who knew that he was working for the British. But the Admiralty was unimpressed with the result. One report, about solidifying gasoline, was described as 'absolute nonsense', and another, on steel density, was 'obvious nonsense, and informant appears to be unacquainted with subject'. By 1932 the agent had been dropped. An undated report sent by New York in the early 1930s indicates the kind of naval intelligence sought (though not, alas, whether any was actually acquired). A British ex-Royal Navy sailor had two American brothers-in-law who were 'working on one of the new cruisers' being constructed in Philadelphia. Taylor was assured that the Briton could obtain from them 'any information required'. In May 1934 London noted that if figures 'giving the reserve ammunition for the United States Army' could be acquired, 'they would be of considerable interest'.

As in the latter years of the First World War, SIS's North American operation continued to concentrate on the activities of Irish republicans and Indian radicals. These were reported to Indian Political Intelligence, Scotland Yard and MI5. Wiseman, Nathan and their associates had been so successful that in a February 1921 report on 'British espionage in the United States', the future long-serving director of the Federal Bureau of Investigation, J. Edgar Hoover, claimed that at the end of the war 'the English were much better informed on radical activities in this country, at least in New York, than the United States Government'. By 1921, he asserted that the British were still very active and 'must have a very efficient force in operation'. Hoover appended a 'list of known British agents', evidently based on extremely circumstantial evidence. It included such improbable characters as the Jamaican-born black activist Marcus Garvey, the Irish labour radical James Larkin and a 'P. S. Irwin', the 'active head of an organization at Miami known as the "Overseas Club"', an 'international British Society with headquarters in London'. Irwin's guilt was apparently due to his being 'the only white man connected with the branch at Miami all the others being negroes', and the fact that he appeared 'to be greatly interested in collecting data concerning both the black and white races, which will interest the British Government'.[5]

The United States authorities regarded British intelligence activities with some ambivalence and revelations had the potential to be very embarrassing. In June 1921 Jeffes cabled that a former confidential secretary had 'become violently mad. Detained in public hospital. Talking freely of secret service affairs.' 'Do you wish anything done?' he asked. Cumming gave Jeffes 'a free hand in the matter', but little was possible. Warning Norman Thwaites, Desmond Morton remarked: 'As a matter of fact, presumably so far as you are concerned, all that she can say is ancient history, and as awkward for the Americans as for ourselves,' a consideration which 'really applies to our show at large'. In March 1920 Frank L. Polk in the State Department, who had worked closely with Wiseman during the war, asked that the 'British Secret Service office in New York' restrict their activities as it 'had been too well advertised in the past'. Yet, reflecting his passionately anglophile outlook, Polk does not appear to have demanded that SIS cease spying in the USA entirely, merely (as he wrote in his diary) 'that they try to cover it up as the Irish and others were sure to make trouble'. American records also reveal that in 1925 the State Department certainly knew that British 'officials' in New York were targeting Indian nationalists in the USA.[6]

Much reporting, however, concerned left-wing subversives. In June 1927 Captain Hugh Miller of Scotland Yard forwarded a request from the United States embassy in London for information about a named American citizen who was suspected of having been involved 'in the transmission of funds for Soviet propaganda in the Philippines' (then under United States rule). Vivian reported 'No Trace', but added that a similarly named person was involved in a 'reported Communist Centre in Macao'. SIS also volunteered information. In April 1928 Vivian told Miller that the SIS representative in Peking (Beijing) had obtained information from a source in Harbin that the Comintern had 'ordered the despatch of six agitators from the Far East to the United States, with instructions to work among employees in the textile industries'. They were to be supplied with American passports and 'chosen from graduates of the Lenin Institute for Propaganda'. Vivian said that the information could be passed on to the Americans 'provided the source is carefully concealed and no indication whatever' was given that it 'emanates from Harbin'.

The SIS representatives in New York supplied a steady stream of reports on Communist activities in the USA, drawn from police and Military Intelligence contacts, as well as their own sources. While SIS regularly circulated this material, there were periodic doubts about its quality. In autumn 1928 Vivian complained that Jeffes's successor J. P. Maine's 'style is peculiar, his views are exaggerated and his perspective is extremely doubtful'. When in June 1930 Maine's successor, Taylor, asserted that there were 'at least two million persons enrolled in Communist or Communist-affiliated organisations', Captain Miller thought the figure was 'very much exaggerated'. Even after Taylor had defended the figure, quoting an American journalist, Walter S. Steele, Miller still doubted it. Steele, he thought, was 'a journalist of the excitable order, who is inclined to lump all Radicals as Communists', and it was 'quite improbable that a vast organisation as carefully and systematically articulated as that which he describes can exist in the U.S.A.'.

In March 1932, Vivian, responding to a report on the left-leaning League for Independent Political Action, charged Taylor with being too unselective in his reporting. 'The U.S.A.', minuted Vivian, 'is the home of crank societies – most of them semi-social and semi-political – but practically <u>all</u> devoted to the generation and release of hot-air.' Unless they had 'a <u>real connexion</u> with international subversion movements', reports about them could 'serve no possible purpose here but fill up space in the registry'. Taylor had claimed that the League's aims were 'merely the Communist programme re-written', but Vivian said that was 'not in itself sufficient' to identify the organisation 'with subversive Communist propaganda or organisation to make the report worth recording. After all,' he added sarcastically, 'some of J. M. Keynes' tenets coincide with Communist tenets, but we don't keep a file of his students of Economics.' The Chief himself instructed Taylor to be more discriminating. Before he sent a report 'on any of these unimportant societies', insisted Sinclair, 'the test should be applied – "Is there any proof of any connection whatso-ever between the Society concerned and organised Communism?" If the answer is "No" the report is not required.' There were other criticisms, too. In May 1934 London told Taylor (who had been asked in August 1930 to 'keep a sharp look-out for personnel suitable for the penetration of Japan') that 'the information concerning Japan' in a recent report was 'hopelessly inaccurate', and that 'concerning the United States' had 'obvi-ously been taken from public speeches'.[7]

There were limitations to what SIS could achieve in the USA. In May 1935 Kathleen 'Jane' Sissmore of MI5 raised with Valentine Vivian 'the poverty of your information with regard to the progress of Communism in the United States', with one notable exception, a network run by Jay Lovestone in New York, which had been comprehensively penetrated by SIS. Lovestone, who led the anti-Stalin Communist Party (Opposition), had worldwide contacts, and London was particularly interested in in-formation about those in Britain and the empire. Canadian names were passed on to the Ottawa authorities, while others, including the Indian Communist M. N. Roy, the Trinidadian 'rabid Trotskyite' C. L. R. James and the liberal-Marxist British intellectual Harold Laski (who could hardly be described as a 'subversive'), were passed on to Scotland Yard, MI5 and Indian Political Intelligence. Flatteringly for SIS, an October 1935 report quoted Lovestone (who was planning a trip to Europe) as saying 'that the British Intelligence Service was the only thing he had ever been afraid of' and he was very fearful of being arrested if he went to England.[8]

On 30 December 1936, Sinclair, taking a Christmas holiday trip across the Atlantic, inspected the New York office himself. The books and card index, he reported, 'were well kept and up to date', but the office, 'though clean, presents a somewhat dingy appearance, owing to the furni-ture and fittings being completely worn out, having been in use for over

twenty years'. He immediately ordered Taylor to arrange 'the complete re-
furnishing of the office' and interviewed the four members of staff 'most
of whom are elderly married men [who] appeared rather down at heel'.
Having satisfied himself that, 'owing to the extremely high cost of living
in New York, they had not really enough to live on', and in a gesture that
showed why his staff liked him so, he ordered supplementary payments
to be made to them out of the secret service 'Other Moneys'.

Generally the British and United States authorities co-operated well,
particularly concerning the Bolshevik target, and their intelligence repre-
sentatives in the Baltic states pooled reports. Between the wars, however,
US–UK intelligence liaison was principally handled through the United
States embassy in London, originally with Basil Thomson and Scotland
Yard and more latterly with MI5. In October 1937, observing that the
British had 'for some time been seriously worried by the development of
German Nazi and Italian Fascist organisations within the British Empire',
Guy Liddell (writing from MI5 on behalf of Vernon Kell) proposed to
N. D. Borum at the United States embassy that 'the official exchange of
information that has operated between us so successfully over a period of
eighteen years on Comintern affairs' should be extended to cover German
and Italian matters. Washington was not keen, distinguishing between
the activities of the Comintern, with which the Soviet government had
consistently denied any link, and those of German Nazi and Italian Fascist
political organisations which were 'admittedly connected with the political parties controlling the governments of Germany and Italy respectively'. Reflecting that this position was not in practice utterly inflexible,
the State Department official John Hickerson nevertheless allowed 'the
possibility of exchanges of information in specific instances where such
exchanges appear to be mutually appropriate and advantageous'.[9]

But Liddell wanted something more formal, to build on MI5's success
in helping the FBI round up an important German spy ring operating in
the USA which had been communicating with Germany through a Mrs
Jessie Jordan in Perth, Scotland.[10] In the spring of 1938 he visited the
USA and determined that both the military authorities and the FBI were
'more than anxious to establish a liaison with us, which could cover not
only Soviet, German and Italian activities, but also those of the Japanese'.
The difficulty, he observed, was how to do so 'without causing offence
to the State Department, with whom we have been in touch via the

Counsellor of the American Embassy here ever since the war'.[11] Liddell thought that there was now 'a unique opportunity' to capitalise on the 'existing good relations and reinforce cooperation which might prove of vital importance' if the liaison developed 'in future emergency or war'.

SIS was keen, also, to improve 48000's position, as he had hitherto 'never had a really good working arrangement with the U.S. authorities'. But, as Vivian explained to his colleagues in London, Liddell's own contacts had been 'based on the assumption that Great Britain has clean hands, so far as the U.S.A. is concerned, and that we indulge in no espionage activities whatever in the U.S.A., which, if discovered, would undoubtedly destroy mutual confidence and put an end to such liaison'. Before proceeding (and naming 48000 – by now Sir James Paget – as the primary link with the United States authorities), Liddell wanted SIS 'to make a frank avowal of the Rutland business', which had preoccupied both SIS and MI5 for some time. Since 1933 it had been known that Frederick Joseph Rutland, a former RAF officer and expert in naval aviation, had been working as a spy for the Japanese. Although he had been based in the USA and was working against American aviation targets, no word of this had been breathed to the Americans.[12]

The Rutland case was one thing, but what Liddell did not know was that SIS was currently 'actually engaged in air and naval espionage against the U.S.A.'. When Vivian told him this, it appears to have shocked him rigid (Liddell, Vivian noted with considerable understatement, 'was definitely not happy'). It clearly jeopardised his existing contacts and also made it 'quite impossible for him to sponsor 48000 as the local representative of British–American Intelligence liaison in the United States'. For SIS, therefore, as Vivian put it to his colleagues in May 1938, 'it is for us to consider whether our Air and Naval work against the U.S.A. is of sufficient importance to maintain against the potential advantages of a satisfactory liaison'. The issue went round to the various sections in Head Office, who (though in some cases slightly grudgingly) agreed that active espionage in the USA might be stopped. The Air Section, for example, reported the Air Ministry's opinion that collaboration had improved recently and the United States air attaché had been 'considerably more open'. As a result, they considered that they could obtain through the attaché 'any information which we should otherwise have got'. They additionally expressed the hope that the enhanced MI5 liaison on counter-intelligence matters might desirably develop into 'collaboration with the Americans in obtaining information on Germany and Japan'.

With assurances from all the sections that, in effect, it was more productive to be friends with the United States than continue to treat it as an intelligence target, on 7 June 1938 Sinclair ordered that 'work against America is to cease as soon as possible'. 'We hope', wrote Vivian to Liddell, 'that this will finally clear the way for a valuable liaison, which will not stop at the exchange of information regarding international subversive movements, but will expand into a solid Anglo-American liaison on the German and Japanese activities which threaten the interests of both countries equally.' In fact matters moved rather slowly thereafter. During 1939 Paget began making direct contacts with the FBI and both the Army and Navy Departments, but as the international situation deteriorated, and especially after the outbreak of war on 3 September, the State Department became, as Liddell put it, 'anxious to bottleneck everything and not to let the soldiers and policemen get loose on their own'. Accordingly, 'in view of the delicate political situation', Paget was ordered to restrict his contacts to the State Department. 'At the same time, using all your tact', he was asked if he could 'see if there is any likelihood of [James] Dunn [head of the Political Relations Department and Paget's contact at State] receding from the position he has taken up regarding any of the other departments'. Before very long, indeed, there would be a massive expansion of SIS work in North America and greatly enhanced Anglo-American intelligence liaison, managed, however, not by Paget but by William Stephenson, his successor as 48000.

The Far East

During the early twentieth century the United Kingdom had very extensive commercial, imperial and strategic interests across South-East and East Asia. Flanked by Britain's imperial possessions of India and Burma, and with garrison outposts at Hong Kong in the south and Weihaiwei (Weihei) in the north (the latter held until 1930), China was especially important for British trade and investment. With its weak central government and perennial internal divisions, China presented more of an opportunity than a threat to British interests, while Japan, from the late nineteenth century a rapidly industrialising and ambitious maritime power, represented a very serious potential challenge. While this had been alleviated by the Anglo-Japanese Alliance of 1902, and Japan had fought (though fairly half-heartedly) on the Allied side in the First World War, some British policy-makers continued to regard it as a real threat, particularly after the alliance lapsed in 1923. In London, too, there was an increasing appreciation in the 1920s and 1930s that Britain's imperial resources were scarcely adequate to meet its responsibilities to defend its widely scattered Far Eastern interests. In such circumstances good and timely intelligence could be of vital assistance.[13]

From a very early stage Cumming had intentions to develop secret service work in the Far East, but while his postwar plans for the region were quite expansive, they appear to have been of comparatively marginal importance. When in 1920 Winston Churchill presented his Cabinet colleagues with schemes for £125,000 and £65,000 Secret Service budgets, the biggest cut Cumming proposed for the latter was the Far East, from £15,000 to £1,000.[14] Bearing in mind the Admiralty's interest in the region, however, this may have been a tactical suggestion on Cumming's part. If so, it seems to have been successful, since in 1923 (even after the Secret Service allocation had been reduced to £90,000) the Far Eastern Group retained a total budget of £18,200, of which only £1,200 was Passport Control money. But the reductions which affected all aspects of SIS work had their impact here too. In 1934–5, the next year for which we have reliable figures, only £6,460 was devoted to both China and Japan.

As elsewhere, SIS's Far Eastern dispositions in the 1920s were primarily directed against the Bolshevik target. In December 1920 Cumming agreed with the India Office jointly to send out Godfrey Denham, who had been Deputy Director of the Delhi Intelligence Bureau (which monitored subversive activities within India), to be 'head of the organisation' in the Far East, the India Office 'paying him his salary & office fund', and Cumming 'providing £10,000 a year for 3 years of our work'. The following February Denham went out to Shanghai 'with a mandate to be in charge of all our work in Japan, China, Tibet and Siberia and Southern Asia'. In June 1921 he produced a forty-five-page paper on 'Bolshevism and Chinese Communism and Anarchism' which pulled together all the available information on left-wing personalities, organisations and activities in China. His conclusion was one of balanced gloom: 'Thus with Bolshevik activity in the North and a growing Chinese Anarchist party in the South, both of which are extremely anti-British in their propaganda, there is every need for care in the future.' In 1921–2 Denham reported extensively (and expansively) on the political situation in both China and Japan. Had he confined himself to the collection and circulation of secret intelligence he might have ruffled fewer feathers, but his mixture of intelligence and assessment inevitably trespassed on the role which the regular diplomats saw as theirs alone. A long paper, entitled '"Dangerous thoughts" in Japan', warning about the spread of anarchism, was particularly ill received in the Tokyo embassy. Denham's 'account of socialistic and other revolutionary movements in this country', complained the ambassador to the Foreign Secretary in September 1922, 'does not agree with the other information in my possession'. Denham, for example, had estimated membership of revolutionary societies at some 57,000, while the embassy thought the figure was nearer 7,000.

After the Indian government had withdrawn their support (for reasons of economy), and SIS had proposed reducing his pay, Denham left China in 1923 to become Inspector-General of the Straits Settlements Police in Malaya (and later a successful businessman). At some point in early 1923 a vice consul at Shanghai, Harry Nathaniel Steptoe, was recruited to help plug the gap left by Denham's departure. The thirty-one-year-old Steptoe had first gone to China in 1912, served in the West African Frontier Force during the First World War and, exploiting a facility for languages, joined the Consular Service in China in 1919.[15] Initially given the designation 'C/33', he began well and, over nearly twenty years with SIS, embodied both the strengths and, increasingly, the weaknesses of the Service's Far Eastern work. In October 1923, the SIS representative in Singapore, who seems to have assumed some of the supervisory functions formerly exercised by Denham, hoped Morton would let the Chief know 'how deeply we are indebted to C/33 for keeping Shanghai going during the last very difficult period of over half a year . . . In fact had it not been for his almost superhuman energy the whole show there would have dwindled to a dangerous degree.'

The Singapore representative's proposals for what he called the 'Shanghai Agency' envisaged a junior role for Steptoe with a view to his eventual long-term employment in SIS. In the meantime Steptoe was fitting in

SIS work with his ordinary consular passport and visa duties and, as yet, was not 'sufficiently qualified to enable him to be a fully satisfactory whole time representative for S.I.S.'. These reservations throw light both on Steptoe and on some of the qualities thought necessary for a 'whole time' SIS officer. It was thought that Steptoe was a bit 'young' and 'does not always perhaps control his indignation or his zeal when, for example, hostile criticisms are directed against the S.I.S.'. The Singapore represent-ative had spoken to Steptoe about this, 'saying that it was only the bitter pangs of experience which had caused me to become a hypocrite when I deemed it necessary, thereby, at times, being able to turn an unfriendly critic into a friendly patron!'. He felt that Steptoe would be able to take over the Shanghai station in about two years and that in the meantime another member of the Consular Service could take Denham's place.

There were some delays before this individual's secondment to SIS could be finalised in June 1924. Meanwhile Steptoe, who continued to fill in, was 'far from fit' and beginning to show signs of the chronic ill-health that was increasingly to plague him. In January 1924 it was noted that Steptoe was 'very fully occupied as Passport Officer, etc. all day, and his work for us is done at nights, on Saturdays and on Sundays'. Despite these concerns, and after he had gone home on sick leave, in July Singapore again reported on Steptoe in glowing terms: 'He has a natural flair for our work, and I hope you will keep your eye on him for future work.' Once Denham's successor was installed in Shanghai (where he remained only until August 1925), Steptoe was posted to Peking, with cover as a local vice consul. In June 1925 SIS provided the British min-ister, Charles Palairet, with evidence that the Soviets were fomenting un-rest in China. This was a photograph of a letter signed by the Russian ambassador, 'procured from a very secret source', which instructed 'local committee in Shanghai to prevent strikers from returning to work and to "incite labouring masses by meetings"'. Palairet, in turn, passed it on 'privately' to the Chinese government.

The so-called 30 May Massacre at the International Settlement in Shanghai in 1925, when Chinese demonstrators were shot by British and British-Indian police, was followed by a wave of strikes and anti-British protests in southern China and Hong Kong. Perhaps slightly defensively (but also evidently to flag up SIS's capabilities in the region), Sinclair told Nevile Bland at the Foreign Office that 'in view of the present trouble at Shanghai, it may be of interest to recall that we gave advance information of this in April last, which has already been confirmed up to the hilt by what has actually happened'. In April, for example, SIS had circulated 'a translation of a very secret despatch dated <u>26 February, 1925</u>, from the Executive Committee of the 3rd International to its centre at Vladivostock', containing 'clear proof of the implication of the 3rd International in the present strike movement in Shanghai'. On 25 June Sinclair sent Tyrrell at the Foreign Office a three-page 'recapitulation of information, mainly documentary, and obtained from a number of sources', which 'clearly shows that the unrest is very largely due to the intrigues of the Soviet Government, and has been very cleverly organised by them'. SIS also acquired copies of the correspondence of the Soviet ambassador, L. M. Karakhan, through an employee of the Soviet consulate-general in Shanghai, despatches which were so inflammatory that they thought 'he must have been drunk when he wrote them'.

Steptoe had other interests, too. In an intriguing signal to London in June 1928 he proposed paying $2,000 to an American naval rating stationed on the Philippines 'to supply detailed information on Corregidor defences'. In July 1929 he took on a Chinese man in Shanghai (for '$100 a month, plus reasonable expenses'). 'In addition to knowing the leading Chinese, both bankers, officials and merchants, he also knows the leading members of the present Nanking [Nanjing] Government.' Unusually, Steptoe had arranged to see this agent personally, 'since it must be remembered that Chinese agents are very [?often] in possession of information which they will not, repeat not, commit to paper, and which can only be abstracted from them by careful cross-questioning'. But, he reassured Sinclair, 'I have taken reasonable precautions to see that this agent does not know my real identity either personally, or in my official capacity'. Another target was Formosa (Taiwan), then a Japanese possession. Steptoe found a British merchant in Amoy (Xiamen) on the south-east China coast who undertook 'to find suitable man either in Amoy or Formosa for penetration Pescadores', a strategically important group of fortified islands off Formosa's west coast where there was a Japanese naval base.

By 1930 Steptoe had become '28,000', the senior SIS representative in China, but something of a one-man band. Not only were there no funds for any extensive organisation, but his own success in developing intelligence work in the late 1920s was accompanied by a conviction of the need for a personal relationship with his Chinese agents, which made it very difficult to find even a temporary replacement for him. In dealing with agents, he told London, 'especially when they are orientals, it is necessary not only to use tact but above all to exercise considerable ingenuity in putting to them certain questions in order to draw from them more information than they are usually disposed to put on paper'. The need for back-up intensified as his health became more precarious. In 1926 he contracted amoebic dysentery, which necessitated six months' home leave. In July 1930, after another health scare, Sinclair approved his immediate return to England, while instructing that it was 'imperative that reports should continue on the Chinese political situation not only in the North, but in the Centre and South China'. Steptoe found a temporary local replacement, though Sinclair still warned that he 'should not leave for home' until he was 'satisfied that the existing Chinese agents will work for him, as it is most important that there is no decrease of information during your absence'. It is clear from this signal that Steptoe was producing intelligence which at SIS headquarters, at least, was considered sufficiently useful for the prospect of a diminished flow to be viewed with concern. The following year Steptoe assisted with the intelligence exploitation of a vast haul of Comintern documents recovered by the Shanghai Municipal Police after the arrest of Hilaire Noulens of the Comintern's clandestine Far East Bureau in June 1931. Although Noulens's capture was a worldwide sensation, Vivian in London cautiously concluded that it did 'little more than administer a temporary and partial check to Communist-inspired centres of revolt or disaffection'.[16]

During 1931, however, things began to go wrong. Steptoe, always rather a difficult character, became more opinionated and started, dangerously, to luxuriate in his secret service role. One sympathetic observer described him in September 1931 as 'an interesting and quite pleasant sort of fellow', but one who had struck him as 'being afflicted with a weakness that I have noticed in so many other "hush hush" men. He loves to weave a veil of mystery over his doings and whisper strange warnings. No doubt he has to be careful of what he does and says, but this pose is apt to defeat its purpose.'[17] He also began to offend British diplomats in China. When he accused the editor of the English-language *North China Daily News* of being 'rather too subservient to the wishes of the legation', the offended editor complained to Sir Miles Lampson (later Lord Killearn), the British minister. In December 1931 Lampson wrote to Vansittart at the Foreign Office suggesting that Steptoe (and hence SIS) was a waste of resources: 'In these days of strict economy are Steptoe's elaborate telegraphic reports justified?. . . Much that he sends is to my mind unnecessary. Indeed we could abolish him altogether so far as Legation is concerned without impairment of efficiency of our Service.' Steptoe defended himself to Sinclair, but, once again, his health was breaking down. 'It appears', he wrote alarmingly in January 1932, 'that the whole of my internal mechanism is functioning at a high rate of speed: no digestion takes place but merely fermentation with all its attendant discomfort.' He was again advised to take sick leave.

Sinclair was sympathetic, telling Steptoe that Vansittart had 'just expressed his appreciation of your work during crisis' (the Japanese invasion of Manchuria in September 1931, during which Steptoe had been posted to Peking 'on special duty'). But he was also very concerned about the Service's work in what he rightly regarded as a vitally important theatre. 'There is no intention of replacing you', he cabled in February 1932, 'as long as you can stand the strain, but you must realise the serious danger of your organisation breaking down if there is no-one trained and immediately available to take your place if your health gives way. Understudy will take months to train and must be found, as Far East will be of paramount importance for years.' The breakdown of relations with the British mission, exacerbated by Steptoe's overstepping of the mark, and the way in which he had evidently begun to report widely on political matters (admittedly following the pattern set by Denham), highlighted a perennial tension between diplomats and secret intelligence personnel. The former, whose legitimate role was to report on the situation in their host country, were often apprehensive about the presence of the latter, whose rather more specialised function of supplying secret intelligence secretly acquired could, if discovered, at the least cause diplomatic embarrassment and, at the worst, a serious international incident. Some ambassadors and ministers, too, were especially jealous of their position and insisted on a strict control over what was reported home. Even Steptoe recognised that Lampson was 'absolutely opposed to any expression of opinion on the China situation unless he is the spokesman for that opinion', and 'that while he may agree with most of the opinions I hold concerning the situation in this country, he does <u>not</u> approve of my expressing them to you [Sinclair] & the Foreign Office'.

One matter increasingly of concern to SIS in the 1930s was that of communications. In general the Service favoured supplying stations with wireless sets which would provide secure (given that reliable cyphers were employed), autonomous communications, not dependent on the world-wide (albeit British-dominated) cable network. But wireless sets could not be introduced without the permission of the British diplomatic mission in the country concerned. When SIS proposed to install a set in the Shanghai consulate-general in July 1933, Lampson turned it down flat, taking the opportunity again to complain about the Service in general (and presumably Steptoe in particular). They should keep 'to their own province' and report 'on such things as communist activities, Indian movements, drug traffic etc instead of encroaching on the political side'. Sinclair thought Lampson's attitude 'extremely unfair' and that he had 'completely misunderstood the functions of S.I.S.', which were 'primarily to supply information to the Foreign Office and the Fighting Forces which cannot be obtained through official channels'. The British government, he added, was 'hardly likely to expend some £100,000 a year on obtaining information solely about such comparatively unimportant matters as drug traffic, or even Communism'.

The clear priority which Sinclair gave here to 'Foreign Office' and 'Fighting Force' information echoed a paper on SIS's position in the Far East which he had circulated to the three armed service Intelligence Directors in March 1928. The 'primary Far East intelligence target', he said, was Japan. After five years of repeated failures and the expenditure of large sums of money, all that had been achieved was the establishment of a skeleton organisation which aimed to give warning of Japanese mobilisation. In April 1923 Cumming had sent out a representative, 'CT/60', working under business cover to report on Japanese naval and air matters. After two years he had a network of some dozen contacts located in several locations, including Tokyo, Kobe and Nagasaki, but claimed that he could only proceed very slowly because of 'the complete mistrust that these people (from the highest to the lowest) have of their fellow beings'. Evidently frustrated by the continued lack of progress (and having spent some £5,000 on the organisation), in April 1928 Sinclair bluntly asked the service intelligence chiefs if they considered further expenditure on the Japanese intelligence target was justified. The Admiralty said 'No', the War Office and Air Ministry 'Yes', but the Foreign Office decided against any further expenditure, noting that 'valuable information' was already provided from time to time from an unspecified 'Japanese source', though this was presumably signals intelligence from GC&CS, which had had some success with Japanese codes.

The arrival in May 1933 of a new naval Commander-in-Chief, Far East Station, Admiral Sir Frederic Dreyer, stirred things up. The forceful and ambitious Dreyer had been Deputy Chief of the Naval Staff and had been expected to rise to the very top of the navy, but his career had been cut short by the Invergordon Mutiny of 1931 for which the Staff had to take some collective responsibility, and so he had to be content with the China station. Convinced that war with Japan was inevitable, he complained to Sinclair in September about the attitude of Admiral Gerald Dickens, the Director of Naval Intelligence: 'How in the name of hell can he expect the powers that be <u>to put their shoulders to the wheel</u> and give me the ships, men, harbour defence gear, etc., of which I am so lamentably short, if he, the D.N.I., tells me that such a war is "<u>REMOTE</u>"!!' Dreyer formed a good first impression of Steptoe ('I like him very much and think he is very intelligent'), but the navy's relations with SIS in the Far East began to sour towards the end of 1933 over the Service's lack of progress in obtaining intelligence on Japan. Tasked by Sinclair on the matter, Steptoe explained the particular problems presented by the Japanese target. 'Every effort', he claimed, had been made 'to find a person who will take over our Organization in [Japan] as a whole time job'. But 'to do the work successfully' it was 'imperative' that the person had fluent Japanese and, in any case, the growing climate of xenophobia and suspicion in Japan made any initiative extremely risky: 'to attempt to build up an organisation now, when every foreigner is so closely watched, and the spy scare so prevalent is, if not an impossible task, an exceedingly delicate one'. A further difficulty was the attitude of the British ambassador, Sir Francis Lindley, who strongly opposed the use of the embassy for SIS work or communications.

The navy's dissatisfaction with SIS was reinforced by Captain W. E. C. Tait, the Deputy Director of Naval Intelligence, who, in the light of Japan's increasingly aggressive 'policy of expansion in the Far East', had been sent out at the end of 1933 to report on the naval intelligence position. Tait, who proposed that a new regional inter-service intelligence office be established in Hong Kong (which later emerged as the Far East Combined Bureau), was very critical of SIS, especially in relation to the lack of information supplied on Japan, Formosa and the Pescadores. He complained about Steptoe's apparently cultivated air of secretiveness, which had served to undermine his reputation. 'Secretiveness and mystery', wrote Tait, 'are accepted only as long as people are ready to believe there is something behind them. Once there creeps a doubt into this frame of mind, the very secretive precautions that are taken only increase suspicions, until it is honestly believed by some that there is a lot of mystery about C.X. [Steptoe] and very little else.' Steptoe, as a result, was 'to a certain extent discredited'.[18]

By April 1934 Dreyer, too, had lost confidence in Steptoe. While he conceded that Steptoe was 'an adept' and had 'considerable flair' for 'Chinese political forecasts', what Dreyer wanted was 'actual facts concerning fortifications' and 'warnings of definite preparations for hostilities in Japan or any of her possessions'. Steptoe 'talks too much', Dreyer told Sinclair, and his 'indiscreet and boastful talk has left no doubt on people's minds generally as to what his real functions are. Perhaps', he added facetiously, 'Steptoe is only a dummy and you have a real S.I.S. working quite independent of him.' Dreyer suggested that, so well known was Steptoe's real role, his 'presence alone would be quite enough to destroy any S.I.S. organisation which may be built up, just when we need it most. Or perhaps our little yellow friends will push him into the Whangpoa [Huangpu River, which runs through Shanghai] without further ado when their time comes.'

Having become aware of Dreyer's criticisms, Steptoe offered to resign, but Sinclair loyally backed his man. 'You still retain my complete confidence and the fact that you do not agree with senior officials belonging to other departments is no reason for your resigning from the S.I.S. If this were so,' he continued, 'I should have to resign from my position several times every week.' All the same, the Service's failure to obtain 'Japanese Naval and Military information' was recognised in Broadway and, on Vivian's suggestion, in June 1934 Sinclair decided to appoint a new representative to be based at Hong Kong to take over the Japanese target from Steptoe.

The failure of SIS and Steptoe in Japan in the early 1930s stemmed from a combination of scarce resources, which (among other reasons) obliged

SIS to persevere with 28000's one-man-band operation; progressively increasing demands for information, especially from the armed services in the face of a growing threat from Japan; and personality problems, particularly as they affected the unfortunate and chronically unwell Steptoe. Even if he had been better placed in his relationships with his military, naval and diplomatic colleagues, it is doubtful that Steptoe's progress in gathering intelligence on Japan would have been any better. It was unrealistic to expect him, however well versed in Communism and Chinese politics, to take on a very different target and one that lay at geographical arm's length. Sinclair was right when he wrote to Dreyer in July 1934: 'I do not think that, even now, you or the G.O.C. realise the extreme difficulty of obtaining secret information about Japan or Formosa.' Sinclair was sending out a fresh individual 'to take over the Naval and Military Intelligence', but he also remarked 'that there appears to be no prospect whatsoever of obtaining any additional funds with which to finance this undertaking, which makes the task even more difficult than it otherwise would be'. A note by a source who had assisted Steptoe since 1928 addressed the fighting services' criticism about the lack of Japanese information. 'If they require plans stolen,' he wrote in August 1934, 'serving officers bribed etc (which unquestionably is the most efficient method of obtaining what they require) they must provide far greater sums of money than are at present available.'

SIS's new man in Hong Kong was Charles Drage, a retired naval lieutenant commander who had served in China in 1923–6 aboard the sloop HMS *Bluebell*. Working under business cover, he had to begin from scratch as the embryonic network established in the 1920s had completely collapsed by the early 1930s. Drage was assisted by a South African who had been recruited by the Berlin station in 1923 and had later served in Mukden (Shenyang). This assistant had a flair for recruiting what was called the 'mechanised type of agent': Chinese seamen who visited ports in Japan and Formosa. At the beginning of 1936 it was reported in Broadway that four ports in Japan (Yokosuka, Kobe, Asaka and Hiroshima) and two in Formosa (Keelung and Taiku) were being watched. Formosa was an easier nut to crack than Japan itself and in October 1938 Drage boasted that he controlled 'the only secret intelligence organization in Formosa' and therefore had 'a monopoly of reliable information from that Island'. But the return was not very great. In April 1938 after Naval Intelligence had complained about the paucity of intelligence from the Far East, Sinclair was supplied with a list of seventy-two SIS agents and contacts working in the region, of whom twenty-nine were thought 'likely to obtain Japanese Naval information'. Though this represented a fair spread of assets, a lack of ability to communicate rapidly severely limited the timeliness with which any information could be delivered. In 1935 SIS agents in Osaka and Tokyo had experimented with sending coded messages through regular telegraph channels and a courier service had been tried from Kobe. It was not altogether reliable and in September 1936 Sinclair, when reaffirming SIS's responsibility 'for maintaining a Coast Watching Organisation, in order to give advance information of troop movements or possible mobilisation', went on to grumble to Drage that 'the breakdowns which are frequently occurring with this organisation coupled with misleading reports such as you have furnished on this matter, give rise to the gravest anxiety here'. There were losses of agents, too. Early in 1937 an agent was arrested and tortured 'shortly after handing in coded troop movement telegram for Hong Kong'. Fortunately a fellow sub-agent secretly engaged a lawyer and at a cost of $500 secured his colleague's release.

By the late 1930s SIS was still having difficulties in meeting the increasing requirements of the armed services, though there were occasional successes, such as Sinclair's report in January 1938, 'from an unimpeachable source' (which may have been signals intelligence), 'that the new Japanese battleships are to be of 46,000 tons (gross) with an armament of twelve 16" guns'. Hankey was sufficiently impressed to congratulate him warmly 'on obtaining such an important and remarkable piece of information'. Drage, apparently producing some good information from Formosa, was much less successful with Japan. Steptoe continued to report primarily on political matters from Shanghai, while Frank Liot Hill, appointed head of station in Peking in the early 1930s with an ambitious brief to penetrate eastern Siberia, Manchuria and Korea, as well as north China, does not seem to have been producing very much. Hill was still endeavouring to establish viable networks in late 1939, and his list of agents shows that some of his reporting was based on one or two Chinese sources strategically placed at the important Fengtai railway junction just south-west of Peking. In theory they should have been able to provide detailed intelligence on Japanese order of battle as troop trains moved through the junction from the coast and onwards to central China.

The Jonny Case

The case of Johann ('Jonny') Heinrich de Graff, a German Communist and agent of both the Comintern and the Fourth Department of the Red Army Staff (later the GRU, Soviet Military Intelligence), was one of the most striking SIS successes of the 1930s. It provided, through a rare penetration lasting for five years, a unique insight into the working practices and personalities of the Comintern. It enabled SIS to forestall a planned Communist revolution in Brazil and was thus an early case of clandestine political action by the Service in Britain's interests. Geographically, the case spanned Moscow, the United Kingdom, Germany, China and Latin America, and it provided a fuller understanding than hitherto of the extent of Soviet policies and methods of interference in other countries in pursuit of both its political revolutionary and its paramilitary aims. The information from de Graff was confirmed and complemented by two additional sources: another early Soviet defector, an NKVD agent who also started talking to SIS in 1933; and 'Mask' intercept material from Comintern communications provided by GC&CS.[19]

In modern parlance de Graff was a walk-in. The first contact with him was made by Frank Foley, SIS head of station in Berlin since 1923. On 13 February 1933 Foley reported to Sinclair that he was in touch with one Ludwig Dinkelmeyer (de Graff's alias), 'German born May 11th '94', a 'Member of Executive of Communist International and Secretary General of illegal Red Front Fighters Union here'. The German, who said he had visited England twice in 1931–2 'to report to Moscow on Communist Party of Great Britain', had, Foley's signal continued, 'offered to become agent for me. He states he can give me complete information about Communist propaganda amongst British Armed Forces and continue to keep me informed of most Communist work in England arranged from here.' De Graff wanted money: 2,000 Reichsmarks down and 500 per month (about £144 and £36; in modern prices something over £7,300 and £1,800 respectively). 'Consider this most important contact I have yet made and convinced his genuineness. May I continue negotiations?' asked Foley.

The 'Jonny Case', as it became known in SIS, entered the Service folklore, and the story – certainly a good one – undoubtedly grew with the telling. Years afterwards, Vivian said that, after he had been urgently summoned to his office by Sinclair and shown Foley's telegram, the Chief said he was immediately to go to Berlin. When Vivian protested that he had no overnight luggage, Sinclair said, 'I've done all that, your wife will be up at 11.00 with a suitcase packed for a week and here are your reservations.' The archive record more prosaically shows, rather, that Sinclair sent a signal to Berlin summoning Foley home at once. While Foley, and others, helped run the agent, Vivian became Jonny's principal case-officer, writing up the reports and providing information against which Jonny's reporting was checked. But Sinclair also took an extremely close interest, so much so that the matter was described on Head Office documents as 'a CSS only case'.

Jonny's first report (delivered in March 1933) was a twenty-eight-page description of 'Communist disintegration work among H.M. [His Majesty's] Forces', which Sinclair (after checking corroborative details with MI5) judged to be 'genuine and of the utmost value'. Communication with Jonny was problematic. SIS had no way of contacting him and, after Vivian had provided him with a 'dead letterbox' address, it was left that he could meet his SIS handlers only (as Vivian recalled) 'if he was able to give us an address where he could meet him in comparative safety'. In March 1933 Nazi pressure forced Jonny out of Germany and Foley had to meet him in Prague. Three months later Jonny was sent under business cover as a 'soybean merchant' to review a clandestine Soviet mission in Manchuria (then occupied by the Japanese and known as Manchukuo). On his return to Europe in December he was debriefed by Vivian in Copenhagen over a period of several days. Jonny's next Comintern assignment was to Shanghai in February–July 1934 to revive their Far East organisation, which had been disrupted in the wake of Hilaire Noulens's arrest. There he was handled by Harry Steptoe, who transmitted reports back to London on the weakness of the Comintern presence in China and stating, reassuringly, that the subversive threat to British forces stationed in Shanghai was negligible, a conclusion the War Office described as 'quite interesting'. A later report from Jonny after his return from Shanghai in autumn 1934 stressed that the connection between Comintern activities and Soviet foreign policy was so close that it was impossible to imagine them apart from one another.

The main value of Jonny's reporting, however, lay not so much in the political aspects of Comintern activity as in what Vivian called the 'technical aspects': the aliases, passport details, physical descriptions and travel plans of other Comintern agents that Jonny met, about which Vivian commented extensively. In this respect the damage done to the Comintern by Jonny was considerable, and he was right to be mindful of his own security and to remind SIS, as he did, of evidence of Communist penetration of Scotland Yard.[20] What was Jonny's motivation? Although financial considerations remained important, by late 1934 Vivian thought there were additional personal factors. Foley, for example, was able to help with the welfare of his wife while Jonny was away. What is clear is that Jonny was brilliantly exploited and handled by Foley, Vivian and even the much maligned Steptoe.

The most dramatic part of the Jonny case was the role he played in disrupting a planned Communist revolution in South America. Briefed in Paris in November 1934, Vivian learned that Jonny was being sent to Brazil. With special operations and explosives training, his task was to assist a Comintern operation in support of Luís Carlos Prestes's revolutionary movement which aimed to topple the right-wing government of President Getúlio Vargas, who had seized power in 1930. There was no SIS station in Brazil, and thus no one to handle Jonny, or to provide communications, or to deal with the embassy in a situation which might develop disastrously for British interests – at a time, moreover, when the United Kingdom had very substantial investments there. Vivian, therefore, with a warm recommendation provided by Vansittart at the Foreign Office to the ambassador, Sir William Seeds, went out himself to make the appropriate arrangements. By the time he arrived in Rio de Janeiro on 11 February 1935, Vivian had an address for Jonny but no rendezvous. In his version of the story he found the house and rang the doorbell: 'a negro servant opened the door, screamed and shut it in my face'. Vivian rang again, but there was no answer, so he went round the side and found an open, though high, window. 'As I scrambled in and fell down the other side, an enormous arm protruded from a curtain levelling a 500 automatic Colt [sic] at me.' The arm belonged to Jonny, who had expected less friendly visitors.

Matters improved thereafter, and Vivian had several meetings with Jonny, though one, on Copacabana beach, left him badly sunburned. The ambassador, meanwhile, was typically difficult. Seeds told Vivian that he 'would do a great deal for Sir Robert Vansittart', but would not let any of his officials 'act as an intermediary'. Nor would he 'take the part that Vansittart thinks I can of warning the Brazilian Government if and when a revolution is to take place. They will think we have got spies in the country and I won't do it.' Before he returned to London, Vivian found a local British businessman to provide a link with Jonny, who over the next few months reported regularly on the progress of the conspiracy. By June things appeared to be coming to a head. Sinclair told Vansittart on 12 June that the plot had 'made alarming progress'. The 'first act' of the revolutionary government, he warned, 'would be to take possession of all the British undertakings in Brazil, and to deport all British subjects connected with them'. He told the Director of Naval Intelligence that it was 'almost certain that a revolution will break out before the end of the year, which may necessitate naval action being taken in order to protect British interests'. Faced with this intelligence, Vansittart decided to instruct Seeds to warn President Vargas, which he did on 20 June, though, 'as zero hour of plot is still distant', Seeds was 'anxious that Brazilian authorities should not take precipitate action'.

Vargas (who had been 'grateful and interested' in response to Seeds's warning) applied some counter-measures, but the Comintern conspirators remained at large, and a distinct possibility remained that some leftist army units might mutiny, which indeed occurred four months later. Alerted by Jonny on the evening of 25 November that things would happen in Rio within twenty-four to forty-eight hours, SIS's local businessman contact in turn warned the ambassador. At 10 p.m. on 26 November, the businessman was called to a rendezvous by Jonny and told that Prestes and his military friends were going to strike that night. At 3 a.m. the SIS man told the ambassador, but, more effectively, he also warned the general manager of the Canadian-owned Brazilian Traction, Light and Power Company (colloquially known as the Light), the principal Rio utilities company, who was able to hinder and frustrate the revolutionaries by cutting off the 'power supply from revolting barracks, who were thus without light and could not operate their radio stations'. After some heavy fighting, the rising collapsed. Further information from Jonny led the Brazilian authorities to the chief Comintern representative and a mass of incriminating documents, which subsequently enabled the destruction of the revolutionaries' South American apparatus.

During the general round-up of conspirators in January 1936 Jonny himself was arrested, but, with the businessman's help, was released and escaped to the Argentine. He was eventually recalled to Moscow in December and, despite Vivian's misgivings, insisted on going. He survived a Comintern inquiry and was sent back to Brazil to assemble a team intended to take over a Communist military network in Japan. After his wireless operator failed to turn up, this appears to have been abandoned and Jonny stayed on, enjoying the (by now very considerable) financial fruits of his espionage endeavours. From 1938 SIS had a representative in the region (based in Montevideo) who employed Jonny 'as a sort of Nazi agent-provocateur', a role he was not very good at playing. As Vivian recalled, 'after the very sensational work that he had done for years it was a small meat'. In November 1939 he was arrested for 'espionage' and very roughly handled by the Brazilian police. After the businessman managed to alert London, the Foreign Office protested to the Brazilian ambassador, and Jonny was released. He was brought back to Britain and later settled in Canada, where some years later he told stories of his work as a British intelligence agent to the press.[21]

Opportunities and difficulties in Europe

Under Harold Gibson, head of station in Bucharest from December 1922, Romania was regarded as an important location for work on the Soviet Union. Gibson had originally gone to Romania as a correspondent for the *Morning Post*, and from 1924, assisted by his younger brother Archie (who also operated under journalistic cover) and drawing extensively on White Russian contacts from his time in Turkey (including his agent HV/109), he assembled a sizeable network of sources. During the 1920s he ran some seventy individuals, though not all necessarily at the same time, on the Romanian and Soviet sides of the frontier. One of Gibson's groups was run by a clerk ('313') in the Sevastopol naval base. He worked for a Romanian secret service officer who was also passing information to Gibson. Agent 313 had sub-sources who provided an 'abundance of useful material' on the Soviet Black Sea Fleet, before one of them betrayed him in 1930. There were also Red Army sources in the Ukraine and as far afield as Irkutsk in Central Asia. In 1930, the heads of both the Naval and Military Sections at Broadway – Russell and

Menzies respectively – commented favourably on the reports produced (none of which has survived). Menzies declared that they 'have proved accurate time after time'. After Harold Gibson's departure for Riga in March 1931 (taking HV/109 with him), his successor, Major Montagu 'Monty' Chidson, and Archie Gibson established new networks, based in part on Ukrainian nationalist groups with sources in Soviet military and industrial organisations. Although SIS forged quite close relations with both the Romanian security police and military intelligence – with the latter greatly facilitating the movement of agents and couriers across the Romanian–Soviet frontier – Archie Gibson claimed afterwards that (unlike the position in the Baltic states) nearly all of the Bucharest station's Soviet reports came from its own sources.

Maintaining independent lines of information like this was valued in London. In January 1936 Menzies's deputy at Head Office insisted that it was 'most important' that SIS's organisation in Romania 'should be maintained in one form or another; otherwise we shall be entirely dependent on the S.I.S. posts in the Baltic states, which are themselves practically dependent on information provided by the General Staffs of those states'. But by this stage SIS's Romanian operations had been fatally compromised by the Flemmer affair. In October 1935 the head of the Romanian Military Secret Service, Major Mihail Muruzov, informed Chidson that he had arrested two brothers, Mikhail and Alexander Flemmer, who had been working both for the Romanians and for Harold Gibson's agent 109 (though not for SIS). Muruzov had discovered that the Flemmers were OGPU agents. He said that any public trial would be most undesirable – especially as it might reveal the close association between the Romanians and SIS – and that he planned to shoot the two men, having first interrogated them. Chidson strongly agreed with the need for secrecy and accepted Muruzov's offer to question the Flemmers himself in order to ascertain the extent to which SIS's organisation in Romania and its courier lines in the Soviet Union might have been compromised. After interrogating the unfortunate brothers and 109, Muruzov concluded that the latter was innocent, but that the OGPU had thoroughly penetrated both the Romanian and SIS anti-Soviet networks. Chidson, while conceding the possibility of some damage, refused to panic and wanted to carry on as usual until he had firm evidence to the contrary. As it turned out, this was a serious error of judgment.

Muruzov, meanwhile, had arrested one of 109's sub-agents, '109/18', and satisfied himself that he, too, was working for the Soviets, though he admitted to Chidson in December 1935 that it 'was difficult to pin anything definite on him'. Nevertheless, as with the Flemmers, he proposed arranging his 'quiet disposal'. Chidson, vehemently opposed to the killing of one of his own agents, got Muruzov to release him, but (presumably to be on the safe side) had him dismissed from SIS employment. The affair clearly rocked the Service. Reviewing the situation at Broadway in January 1936, some officers felt that the Bucharest station could no longer be relied upon for Soviet information. Menzies was 'profoundly disturbed' about the extent of OGPU penetration in the Romanian networks, but he also maintained that SIS could not prove 109/18's guilt. His impression, indeed, was that 'much valuable material' had come 'from this station during the regime of the present 14000 [Chidson]'. The War Office had cast no serious doubt upon the reliability of SIS's sources and (straining perhaps to make the best of the situation) he felt it 'almost impossible that the O.G.P.U. should have fed us with genuine material for years'. In Bucharest Chidson was equally reluctant to accept that his entire operation was compromised. During February, in an effort to contact two of 313's sources and resume work, he sent a trusted agent into the Soviet Union. Neither he nor 313's contacts were heard of again. Presumed betrayed to the OGPU through 109/18, by April 1936 they had been reported as casualties. This was, in effect, the end of SIS's Soviet operations in Romania.

Chidson was subsequently transferred to The Hague, and in August 1936 Archie Gibson took over as head of station at Bucharest. Shortly afterwards he reported Muruzov's annoyance at SIS's attempts to try to sustain an organisation in Romania, which the latter correctly presumed could not operate against the Soviet Union and which he therefore assumed was either working or preparing to work against Romania. Muruzov, wrote Gibson, had in fact been very helpful to the British, 'putting his own men at our disposal', providing facilities for frontier-crossing, 'to say nothing of information which came from his sources and many other favours. From us,' reported Gibson, 'he has had a gold cigarette case, an occasional gift of cigarettes and, from time to time, some information.' But the Bucharest station (and the Anglo-Romanian intelligence relationship as a whole) never recovered from the Flemmer debacle. The whole affair amply demonstrated a recurring dilemma whereby continuing and apparently well-founded intelligence operations are suddenly undermined by the discovery of possible treachery. Perhaps hoping against hope and clearly reluctant to abandon years of careful intelligence work, neither Chidson nor Menzies was initially willing to concede that SIS's Romania operations might have been thoroughly compromised. While in one sense (and in marked contrast to Muruzov's much more hard-nosed and ruthless attitude) this embodied a commendable faith in their existing agents, if not also (and less admirably) in their own good judgment, in the end it appears to have had fatal consequences for the network Chidson tried to revive in the spring of 1936. Chidson's perhaps overly trusting attitude was also to have disastrous consequences at his next posting, where Folkert van Koutrik, the assistant to SIS's head agent at The Hague station, was turned by the Abwehr and betrayed leading German agents of both SIS and MI5.

In contrast to Romania, which had taken the Allied side during the First World War, Bulgaria had been an enemy power, and between the wars the SIS station in Sofia had little or no official contact with the local security services. Here, indeed, the generally applied prohibition on working against the country of residence did not apply and at the start the station concentrated on looking out for breaches of the Neuilly peace treaty, which the Bulgarians had signed in November 1919. Subversive activities of Communists and the Internal Macedonian Revolutionary Organisation (a violent extreme nationalist group with ambitions to add Greek and Yugoslav territory to Bulgaria) were important targets. Throughout the interwar years Sofia set its net wider and began to gather intelligence on Yugoslavia, Romania, Turkey, Italy, the Soviet Union and, as the Second World War approached, Germany. The head agent of one SIS network, a journalist with good contacts among top Yugoslav officials, supplied political and economic information on Yugoslavia, Italy and Germany. Another head agent, based in Belgrade, had a source who supplied weekly lists of goods carried on Danube barges between Yugoslavia, Germany, Romania and Bulgaria. A third, a White Russian living in Sofia, ran sub-groups which supplied Bulgarian military material information on arms shipments to Bulgaria and illegal immigrants to Palestine. One of his agents, who had sources in the Turkish army and naval dockyards, was described as having 'pro-Communist leanings', being 'against the Kemalist regime' and also needing 'money for his mistress'.

Between the wars the Sofia station ('11000') had an unusually high turnover of staff. From 1920 until the war there were six heads of station, all of whom operated under Passport Control cover. They included an ex-actor, three sailors, including Lieutenant Commander Leonard Hamilton Stokes (April 1924 to December 1929) and Engineer Captain Charles Limpenny (1933 to July 1935), one soldier, Captain (later Major) William Mackinnon Gray (August 1935 to September 1937), and an airman. The most intriguing of these appointments was that of the fifty-one-year-old Limpenny, a submariner and presumably longstanding acquaintance of Sinclair's. One of a talented and creative West Country family – the concert pianist Moura Lympany was his niece – he had been appointed an ADC to the King in December 1932, and on his formal retirement from the Royal Navy in April 1933 was promoted rear admiral.[22] What the diplomatic corps in a small Balkan capital (let alone the local security authorities) made of such a distinguished personage occupying the comparatively modest position of Passport Control Officer is anyone's guess.

Limpenny evidently made a success of his posting because, after brief sojourns in Athens and Stockholm, he was brought back to Broadway in December 1936 to take over as head of the Economic Section, where he stayed until June 1946. The same could not be said of his successor, Mackinnon Gray, who had been introduced to SIS in 1932, and had spent some time as a 'learner' at Istanbul and an assistant at Jerusalem before his appointment to Sofia. Gray had a problematic personal life. In 1936 his wife sued for divorce, and there was concern that his SIS appointment might get mentioned in the proceedings. Situations like this, when crises in the private lives of officers (and, indeed, agents) might jeopardise cover or security generally, were not uncommon, though in this instance – and to his evident relief – Gray's real role in Sofia remained secret.[23] During 1937, however, concerns were raised about financial irregularities in the payment of an agent. Sinclair ordered an inspection of the Sofia office and sent Limpenny out to investigate the matter. The results of these enquiries revealed Gray to have been guilty of carelessness and slipshod record-keeping rather than peculation, but they also throw revealing light on the mechanisms by which a local SIS station ran its finances. While there were strict rules that any local expenditure had to be approved from London (which Gray had failed to follow), funds appear routinely to have been transferred from Head Office to the head of station's personal bank account and from there to a second offshore account. In Sofia local currency for paying agents was acquired clandestinely on the 'Black Bourse' by the wife of a junior member of the Passport Office staff.

In September 1937 Gray simply abandoned his post, returned home without authorisation and resigned from the Service. In Sofia Limpenny made good some bounced cheques and reported that there was no cause for anxiety regarding the functioning of the local SIS organisation. Thus the SIS senior management might have hoped that the Mackinnon Gray case was closed. In 1941, however, after he murdered his second wife and attempted suicide in Chilcompton, near Bath in Somerset, there was a fresh alarm that his secret service work might be exposed. This time Valentine Vivian was despatched for damage limitation and successfully arranged with the Somerset Chief Constable to leave any reference to Passport Control out of the legal proceedings. Gray, who recovered from his self-inflicted wound, was sentenced to death at Winchester in July 1941, but was reprieved and subsequently jailed for life.[24] He evidently had a difficult and troubled private life. There is no way of estimating the extent to which (if at all) the pressures of secret intelligence work may have exacerbated his personal problems, though one may reasonably suppose that the strains of having to maintain a secret professional existence may not have helped. What is clear from this case, however, is that domestic crises, of whatever sort, had an unsettling potential to go public and endanger operations. Thus the Service took these kinds of problems very seriously indeed.

Even though Sinclair and Pay Sykes (in charge of SIS finance) tried to keep close tabs on Service expenditure, the realities of funding intelligence work at station level, regularly requiring untraceable payments in cash or precious goods of various sorts, inevitably meant that officers and agents, the former of whom were not particularly well paid, could be faced with considerable temptations. Not everyone was able to resist. In the early 1920s one of the Riga station's staff decamped with the Passport Control Officer's seal, a month's advance salary and £500 (equivalent to £20,000 today) in diamonds and gold, stolen from a dealer who had smuggled it out of the Soviet Union. During the following decade the sharp increase in the numbers of Jewish refugees seeking to travel to Palestine underpinned the development of a black market in the necessary British visas. During the 1930s there were three cases of visa-trafficking in the Warsaw Passport Control Office. The most serious, in July 1936, threatened to expose SIS's role in the Passport Control organisation and the British ambassador wanted to prevent Major Shelley, the Passport Control Officer (and SIS head of station in Warsaw), and other diplomats from having to appear in court lest 'they might be asked questions about the internal affairs of the Passport Control Office which it would be inexpedient for them to answer'.[25]

The worst financial scandal of the 1930s occurred in the Netherlands. Here Major Ernest Dalton, a First World War MI1(c) veteran, had been head of station since April 1924. But his time at The Hague was overshadowed by the revelation in the mid-1930s that he had got into financial difficulties and embezzled several thousand pounds' worth of visa fees.[26] Dalton's wife was seriously ill and he himself suffered from 'blood poisoning'. Efforts to recoup the money through gambling having failed, he collapsed under the strain and committed suicide in July 1936. 'I have got myself into such a mess', he wrote, 'that this is the only way out.' Sent out to deal with the situation, Rex Howard vetoed a suggestion by one of Dalton's assistants that his death should be put down to 'heart failure'. The ambassador sensibly argued that 'it was better to be quite frank in the first instance, as otherwise it would be thought that there was something to hide'. Traces of the Dalton tragedy remained at the station. Officers subsequently posted to The Hague were solemnly taken to what had been his bedroom and shown the badly repaired mark in the wall caused by the bullet with which he had killed himself.

Further investigation and suspicions of connivance among the station staff in Dalton's 'defalcations' led to some dismissals and the Dutch-speaking Monty Chidson (his wife was Dutch), urgently summoned from Bucharest, became head of station with instructions 'to take such steps as he may think fit to ensure that all matters in the office are systematised & regularised as soon as possible'. That Chidson's attitude to security was not all that might have been desired became evident to Howard at dinner one evening. Chidson wanted to introduce his Rotterdam-resident brother-in-law as he 'had good connections' and 'might be useful'. Reporting on the occasion, Howard wrote that 'about half way through dinner, I remarked to the b-in-law that I supposed he knew from Chidson that the latter had now become P.C.O.'. The brother-in-law replied 'that he did not know there was such a post & understood Chidson was in the Secret Service & that was all he knew he did'. He went on to talk 'quite openly & loudly to Chidson about the Secret Service & his connection with it. The people at the next table', recorded Howard, 'were obviously taking a great interest in the conversation & I abruptly changed it.'

As in the Low Countries, during the 1930s SIS's operations in Scandinavia gradually moved away from the Soviet target to focus on Germany. Here, too, local sensitivities about their neutral status, and well-founded fears of antagonising the Germans, influenced the extent of co-operation with local security and intelligence authorities. In Stockholm, sources in Swedish Military Intelligence were prepared to share information about suspected Communist activities in the late 1920s and early 1930s, but were markedly less forthcoming about Germany. Lieutenant-Commander John Martin, who became head of station in October 1937, made sustained efforts to recruit locally based Britons and Swedes whose business connections with Germany offered the possibility of intelligence which might survive the outbreak of war. A Norwegian clerk in a shipping company in Oslo, for example, was taken on in 1939 to report on arms shipments. He in turn recruited a sub-source to visit German ports, but no evidence survives that they produced intelligence of any great value.

The situation in Denmark was rather similar. In January 1927 London had given the longstanding head of station in Copenhagen (in post since 1920) four main objectives in order of priority: Germany, Russia, 'Norwegian & Swedish air' and 'Arms Traffic'. He reported considerable endeavours, but not much substantive progress in any of these areas. He was followed by a retired RAF officer, appointed to Copenhagen in August 1928 after less than a year in the Service, including three months as a learner on the Athens station. His departure from the Service in mid-1936 reflects the continuing hand-to-mouth financial basis on which the interwar organisation was run, depending to a great extent on representatives having a private income to supplement the hairshirt salaries SIS for the most part offered. He resigned after the brusque rejection of a plaintive appeal to the Chief that, after twenty-two years in government service and at the age of forty-six with growing family responsibilities, he might be given established status, perhaps in the RAF, with some pension entitlement.

Both the Copenhagen head of station from 1936 until early 1940 and his predecessor put a good deal of effort into acquiring assets in Schleswig-Holstein, where they hoped ethnic Danes resident on the German side of the frontier could be recruited as agents. In January 1938 Sinclair observed that 'by its geographical position' Copenhagen was 'very favourably situated' for obtaining information on Germany. The head of station was, therefore, to concentrate almost exclusively on that target, to 'make every endeavour' to acquire information on the German armed forces, and especially to try to recruit a naval officer. But Copenhagen was a one-man station, and, with no operational assistants (though he did have two secretaries), this was much easier instructed than implemented. Although there were Danes in Germany who could cross the frontier and report low-level eyewitness information on the German forces in the area, contact with them was necessarily cautious; the Germans were alert, their counter-espionage measures active, and they could easily close the border, as they did at the time of the Munich crisis. No wireless sets were yet available to overcome such a simple but effective break in contact. None of the station's resident agents had sufficient access to contemplate recruiting a German officer, naval or not. Danish businessmen with reasons to travel to Germany tended to be understandably unwilling to jeopardise their interests by taking more than minimal risks. The traditional Danish neutrality was widely felt to be good for Denmark and vulnerable to German displeasure. Under these circumstances, it was quite creditable that in 1934–7 the station delivered between four and five hundred reports a year, even if most of them were rather run of the mill. But London inevitably wanted more and better information, especially on economic and political matters. In late 1938 Broadway sent Copenhagen the Circulating sections' collective comments on the station's recent reporting: no political information of value; 'slight improvement' in air reporting; military reporting 'disappointing'; the 'location of the German fleet in German harbours efficiently carried out'. It was hardly a ringing endorsement of the station's efforts.

During most of the interwar years, SIS had only a minimal operation in Norway. Between October 1924 and September 1938 there was no full-time representative. For much of this time, indeed, Biffy Dunderdale, while based in Paris, was also nominally head of the Oslo station, though the SIS representative in Stockholm, John Martin, also had a watching brief. In fact, for much of this period quite a lot of local work was handled, and a very productive liaison maintained with the Norwegian authorities, by one of the unsung heroes of the Service, an extremely capable multilingual female secretary. In the late 1930s the likely importance of Norway (especially on the naval side) brought a reinforcement of the station, though this was not initially without difficulties. Late in 1938 Sinclair decided to appoint a permanent representative to Oslo 'to obtain information on all types of German activities, particularly naval movements, and the reactions of his neighbouring Scandinavian countries thereto'. The individual selected, Lieutenant Commander Joseph Newill, a retired sailor and fluent Norwegian-speaker, was appointed from 1 January 1939. Although he seemed ideally suited for the job, on 8 May he told Rex Howard at Head Office that he was 'in a constant state of perplexity', had made no progress since his arrival and wondered 'whether I shall ever do so. I doubt', he added, 'whether I have the natural guile so essential for this work!' Later the same month John Martin from Stockholm delivered a savagely damning judgment on Newill, whom he rated 'a complete flop', 'never likely to do any good or be of any use' and 'should be got rid of'. Newill had told him that the job was not what he had thought it would be and was 'far more hard work' than he was prepared to do. 'I am 52,' he had told Martin, 'and I am not going to work myself to death at my time of life.' He had, in any case, no need to work, since he had a private income far in excess of his salary (at the time, of course, normally a positive attribute for work in SIS). Being plunged in on his own had clearly unsettled Newill, but he slowly got to grips with the work. When Sinclair sent Frank Foley to Oslo in August 1939 to review the situation there he reported that Newill was 'a good man in the right place'. And after Foley had been installed at Oslo to oversee all the Scandinavian stations, he was able to manage Newill closely and professionally, so that by October 1939 he was functioning satisfactorily and confidently, especially on the naval reporting and maritime front.

In the 1930s independent Ireland became an intelligence target for SIS. After the separatist nationalist, Eamon de Valera, came to power at the head of a Fianna Fáil government in March 1932, he set about dismantling the remaining links with the British empire, and in the new 1937 constitution abolished the role of the British monarch as head of state. Hesitating to declare Eire a republic, however, he devised the concept of Ireland's 'external association' with the British Commonwealth. The government in London was anxious to keep tabs on Irish political opinion and MI5 was asked to set up an organisation to report on Eire. Kell, recalled Vivian some years later, 'refused point blank on the grounds that such a project was too dangerous and that, moreover, he had no suitable personnel or means to carry it out'. The Prime Minister then sent for Sinclair, told him that now Eire had to be regarded as a 'foreign country', SIS would have 'to do what Kell had refused to do'. Sinclair deputed Vivian to provide 'a periodical survey of the situation in Ireland, with particular reference to extremist republican opinion, the I.R.A. and German penetration'. This task, reflected Vivian, was 'not within our regular range of duties', and was 'undertaken reluctantly as no other Department was willing to take the risk'. Because of the 'extraordinary delicacy and dangers' of the operation, he was instructed to report only to Sinclair and not to mention the matter to anyone inside or outside the Service, unless directly involved. Essentially, this was not an intelligence operation, and there was no real network of agents, but, in the words of an MI5 review of its wartime activities in Ireland, it constituted a 'very restricted information service', in which Vivian, using Southern Irish contacts principally secured through the Royal Ulster Constabulary, provided 'a limited cross section of private opinion of current events of political or public interest in Eire'.[27] After the outbreak of war, when Ireland remained neutral, there were heightened worries, especially in the Admiralty, that German submarines might re-provision in Ireland or the country be used for intelligence activities against the United Kingdom. There was a modest expansion of SIS's work but, after MI5 finally engaged with Eire, Britain's security requirements in this area were met by an eventually close liaison between the Security Service and the Irish authorities.[28]

9

Approaching war

In the spring of 1932 the British Cabinet abandoned the ten-year rule it had adopted in 1919, though, because of the desperate economic circumstances of the time, this was not taken to be a signal that defence expenditure might immediately be increased. Nevertheless, in the mid-1930s the government's purse-strings began slowly to be loosened, as Britain started to rearm in the face of mounting international challenges. The occupation of Manchuria by an aggressive, expansionist Japan in 1931 challenged British interests in the Far East. In the 1930s, too, the Italian Fascist dictator Benito Mussolini began to pursue an increasingly assertive foreign policy, seeking to establish a new Roman empire across the Mediterranean and in Africa. With a modern, powerful navy under construction, Italian ambitions threatened Britain's vital imperial communications and trade across the Mediterranean, Red Sea and Indian Ocean. Adolf Hitler's ascent to power in Germany in 1933 was accompanied by heightened German aspirations, as his militaristic Nazi government set about righting the wrongs (as they saw it) of the punitive Versailles peace settlement. Germany's militarism unsettled and alarmed its neighbours, especially the newly independent, post-1919 states of Czechoslovakia and Poland in Central Europe.

Crises in the 1930s

From the start the new Nazi government in Germany began persecuting Jews and implementing increasingly restrictive and draconian policies which were to culminate in the Final Solution. Anti-Semitism, indeed, was rife throughout interwar Europe and had stimulated a growing stream of refugees to Palestine, where Zionists endeavoured to establish a Jewish National Home. In Palestine, which the British ruled as a League of Nations Mandate under the Versailles treaty, the growing numbers of Jewish settlers helped to destabilise an already difficult communal situation and contributed to the outbreak of an Arab rebellion against the Jews and the British which lasted from April to October 1936, and erupted again from November 1937 to November 1938. Backed by the RAF, who took the leading role in 'imperial policing' through the Middle East, SIS had established a station in Jerusalem in 1933. The representative had cover as Military Liaison Officer in Air Headquarters, and the air force paid the greater part of the station's expenses. Major John Shelley, a fluent Arabic-speaker who had been a Military Intelligence officer in Shanghai, was the first head of station, but was not a great success and was replaced early in 1936 by ex-Indian Army Major John Teague, who by 1939 had two assistants. One tiny indicator of the Service's refocusing on Germany in the mid-1930s occurs in the records relating to an officer, talent-spotted by Shelley in 1934. He was interviewed by Rex Howard, who judged him 'to be of a superior type & eminently suitable' for appointment in the Middle East. Having been approved for employment in the Service, but waiting for a vacancy to occur, the candidate wrote to Howard arguing that he could increase his usefulness 'by learning another language'. What would be the most suitable one for him to learn? Having consulted Shelley on the matter, Howard noted: 'German suggested.'

Palestine became an increasingly heavy commitment for the army and RAF as internecine strife intensified and the Arab revolt simmered on. In the later 1930s troubles in Palestine kept some twenty thousand British troops pinned down 'in peace-keeping operations which showed no sign of ever coming to an end'.[1] Although the work of the Jerusalem station had originally been intended to cover the Arab Middle East generally, under Teague it tended to concentrate on Palestine and the help that neighbouring countries were giving to the rebellion. Teague himself recalled that political intelligence from Iraq 'was only generally second grade', though information was 'quite good about the clandestine support that the Iraq Government was giving to the Mufti of Jerusalem, as the spear head of the Palestine revolt'. Syria and Lebanon, he thought, were 'not too bad', but 'Persia [Iran] remained naked and unashamed'. Another task was monitoring illegal Jewish immigration, as the Mandate authorities had placed a limit on Jewish settlement in the country. Drawing on SIS's resources in Turkey and the Balkans, Teague reported that SIS tracked the departure of ships from Black Sea countries and their movement through the Dardanelles. 'The fact', he added (embodying a shrewd participant's observation about the acquisition and use of intelligence), 'that the British could do nothing to prevent these derelict hulks from reaching the shores of Palestine did not make the information in itself less excellent.'

The Ethiopian Crisis of 1935–6 epitomised Mussolini's new imperialistic foreign policy. Seeking to expand its African possessions, which already included Libya, Eritrea and Italian Somaliland, Italy invaded Ethiopia in October 1935 and in seven months had conquered the country. As with Japan in Manchuria, the aggressor power simply ignored international protests, a lesson not lost on Hitler later in the decade. During the crisis the perennial problem of SIS finance was illustrated by work in Malta. As tension rose in the autumn of 1935 Biffy Dunderdale was put in charge of a new organisation to develop intelligence operations from the island and co-ordinate it with the armed service authorities there. One early venture was a disinformation scheme whereby SIS set about circulating a rumour among Italian agents and 'unreliable' Maltese that a special installation with 'shattering interference apparatus' to bring down aircraft was being erected on the RAF station at Kalafrana in the south-east of the island. But Malta had hardly got started before operations were checked. 'Until further funds are forthcoming,' instructed Sinclair on 25 October, 'no more commitments of any sort are to be entered into in connection with the Mediterranean situation.'

Another crisis bringing work for SIS was the Spanish Civil War, which broke out in July 1936 between the left-wing Republican government and Nationalist forces led by General Francisco Franco. Although Britain and France brokered a widely supported, though largely ineffectual, Non-Intervention Agreement in August 1936, Germany and Italy (especially the latter) provided men and matériel for the Nationalists; and the Soviet Union intervened on the Republican side, which was also boosted by volunteers from many countries in the International Brigades. SIS's existing, if rather haphazard, monitoring of Communist activity in Spain meant that the Service was initially better equipped to report on Soviet involvement, though some of this was frustratingly imprecise. In April 1936 a report from a Moroccan-based agent (communicating through Gibraltar) stated that in March an unnamed Soviet ship had landed 'two large boxes containing rifles and small arms at Algeciras'. The report added that at about the same time the Soviets had provided 'a few million pounds' to Communist organisations in Spain. The Political Section in Broadway thought the whole thing 'of little value' as the agent did not 'appear to have checked up his information'. SIS, however, as it informed French Deuxième Bureau colleagues in April, had 'not the slightest doubt that the Communist International, through its centre in Paris, is financing and controlling overt and subterranean activities in Spain'. French opinions were solicited on the matter, since 'the establishment of a Soviet regime in the Iberian Peninsula is hardly a happening which anyone can view with equanimity for military, political or economic reasons'.[2]

SIS was less well positioned to get information on the Nationalist side, but after a fiercely anti-Communist Englishman, Major Hugh Pollard, assisted the Nationalists in July 1936 by flying Franco from the Canary Islands to Morocco, allowing the general to kick-start the armed challenge to the Republic, the Service thought that he might be able to help. Pollard, sporting editor of the magazine *Country Life*, was a fervent, Fascist-sympathising Catholic with a colourful past, including time as a 'police adviser' in Dublin Castle during the Anglo-Irish War of 1919–21.[3] In November 1936 Frederick Winterbotham, head of the Air Section, approached Pollard and asked him if he would be prepared to go to Spain and personally put a long series of questions to Franco about his military plans, the external aid he was receiving and how he intended to use his air force. But Pollard asked for too much in return – a diplomatic passport, 'pay and allowances on the full scale' and expenses to cover the cost of his horses – he planned to do some hunting while in Spain – and the scheme did not proceed (though during the war Pollard later served in SOE).

The following spring, by which time the Nationalists had been making advances in the north of the country, the Directorate of Military Intelligence (responding to a complaint passed on by the Cabinet Secretary, Sir Maurice Hankey that there was not enough 'red-hot information from Spain') noted on 9 March that, owing to the 'sudden outbreak' of the war, SIS had 'unavoidably been somewhat slow in developing their organisation' in the country. Sinclair was well aware of the problem, though he observed that it was a matter which 'cannot be done on the spur of the moment'. David Footman of the Political Section remarked on the 'violent spy hysteria on both sides' and defined the ideal as 'agents who can talk freely to the men at the top'. He proposed various possibilities, including liaison with the French through Dunderdale, placing someone at the headquarters of General Eoin O'Duffy (who commanded a ramshackle collection of Irish Fascist Blueshirts), and getting an agent into an ambulance or relief organisation on either side. By the end of March some progress had been made. Dunderdale found a man to report on the flow of foreign volunteers into Spain, and Leonard Hamilton Stokes, a sailor who had first been employed by the Service in the Balkans, began developing some sources from Gibraltar in the south. Aware that the government side was better covered, Sinclair ordered a special effort 'regarding General Franco's position, policy and prospects'. There was evidently not much progress on this front as six months later Footman minuted that it should be impressed upon Hamilton Stokes 'that General Franco's position and policy, his relations with Italy, and Germany, the Italian intentions, military support and naval co-operation together form the most urgent European problem of today', and he 'should spare no effort in developing his organisation to cover them'.

Despite the lack of success in Spain itself, Sinclair was evidently getting good intelligence on Mussolini and his intentions concerning the conflict, for on 19 October 1937 he wrote a well-informed note for Sir Warren Fisher on the subject. 'The main point of the present situation to my mind', wrote Sinclair, 'is that Mussolini has simply got to go on in Spain, and that as we are not in a position to go to War, it is far better to let him exhaust himself <u>in</u> Spain rather than he should "run amok" <u>outside</u> Spain.' Sinclair argued that if 'we are cautious' Mussolini might 'dish himself': 'Taking the long view, time seems to be more on our side than his and nothing is to be gained by rushing matters.' He thought that Germany might egg the Italians on to challenge Britain and France, but was itself likely to remain neutral and 'profit by the occasion to achieve her aims as regards Austria and Czechoslovakia'. If there was some useful political intelligence, the same could not be said on the technical side. Also in October 1937, London told the two SIS stations in Paris that War Office requirements were not being met for technical data on new German and Russian weapons being used in Spain. Over the succeeding months Dunderdale recruited an agent who had contacts among Francoist interrogators of Russian International Brigade prisoners-of-war and provided photographs of a new quick-firing Soviet machine gun, as well as information about Soviet high-speed fighters and the arrival of a Soviet air brigade of bombers.

This was evidently not enough for the Air Ministry, who complained bitterly on 1 November 1938 that 'after more than 2 years of civil war in Spain in which the latest equipment of the Italian Air Force (German, Russian and French also) has been employed', they had 'received practically nothing of concrete value from the technical and tactical points of view in the way of secret intelligence'. SIS had provided 'virtually no information about guns, bombs, anti-aircraft, nor any statistics which would enable us to determine the relative advantages of the different types of weapon in use'. Air Intelligence 'should have expected by now that we should have quite a museum of guns, bombs, fuses, shells and other technical equipment delivered to our armament research people through the efforts of S.I.S.'. It was conceded that 'the organisation of secret intelligence work is no doubt difficult but the conditions for obtaining such information could hardly be easier than they are in a civil war in Spain where in both sides there must be very large numbers of traitors at large, and a very large proportion of them sorely in need of cash'.

Sinclair was appalled by this devastating critique. 'Why has this not been drawn to my notice before?' he asked, prompting an understandably defensive response from 'IIa' of the Air Section. Specific requests for technical equipment had apparently been made in July 1937 and July 1938, but without significant response, and telegrams reiterating the requirements had been 'immediately despatched' to the relevant stations. Representatives had been offered 'an additional £500' for 'obtaining samples of technical equipment'. The official admitted that little information had been provided 'on guns, bombs or anti-aircraft statistics during 1937/8 and only one fragment of bomb and no technical equipment whatsoever' had been received 'since the beginning of the Civil War in Spain'. He suggested rather lamely that part of the explanation lay in 'the difficulty of contacting German XA [Air Force] personnel serving in nationalist Spain', as they were 'unapproachable by reason of being isolated in aerodromes under German control'.

In April 1937 Sinclair had told Hamilton Stokes in Gibraltar that gathering intelligence on the Italian armed forces was 'of the highest importance'. On 2 June he assured Hankey that, 'in my opinion, Italy should occupy the position of Public Enemy No. 1, as far as this country is concerned', and, fearing a crisis in Anglo-Italian relations (which did not in the end occur), London sent out questionnaires on Italian naval and military matters to the heads of station at Sofia, Brussels, Cairo, Rome, Athens, Vienna and Paris. For nearly three years, up to August 1938, a network targeting the Italian navy in Trieste and Genoa had operated quite successfully out of Austria, but after the Anschluss which united Germany and Austria in March 1938, arrests by the Gestapo broke up the organisation.

By the time Franco and the Nationalists had won the Spanish Civil War in the spring of 1939, there is little evidence that SIS had been able to produce very much of value in political or technical military information. At this stage, however, the Service's chief focus had turned to Italy and Germany. In February 1937 Captain E. H. Russell, head of SIS's Naval Section, told Sinclair that 'for many years to come the Mediterranean will be one of the chief centres of activity during strained relations or war'. It was therefore 'essential to obtain a resident agent both in Sardinia and Sicily . . . to report on naval concentrations and coast defences, air concentrations, aerodromes and military subjects'. On 10 March a circular went out to all the SIS stations in Europe and North Africa to find suitable candidates. Within a month Biffy Dunderdale in Paris believed he had discovered the very man, a French commercial traveller, already working as an agent for the French navy. Dunderdale said that his motivation to work for the British too was that 'he believes our two countries should stand together whilst he is also desirous of adding to his income'. This agent's brief relationship with SIS demonstrates some of the practical difficulties of expanding operations. Dunderdale paid him quite generously to visit the strategically important island of Pantellaria (a particular target, west of Malta between Sicily and Tunisia). When his report went to London, Winterbotham of the Air Section cast doubt on details of the Italian aircraft carrier *Miragli*, allegedly in the island harbour, while the Naval Section maintained more of an open mind. Although Rex Howard thought it 'extremely doubtful' that the agent had been to Pantellaria at all, the report was passed on to the Admiralty and Air Ministry for comment. Dunderdale began to get cold feet about employing a man who had been 'doing this kind of work far too long under too many masters', and claimed that 'in normal circumstances I should never employ such

an individual but in view of the present situation I thought I would give
him a trial'. Even after the Admiralty and Air Ministry commented favourably on his intelligence (which suggests that in this case their critical
faculties might have been blunter than those of SIS), the risk of running
an existing French agent seems to have been too great for Dunderdale,
who appears to have dropped him shortly thereafter.

Anglo-French liaison

The fact that SIS stations operated in France from the mid-1920s onwards
reflects the importance of liaison with the French security and intelligence authorities. At the start, Biffy Dunderdale's station focused mostly
on the Soviet target, using (among others) some White Russian contacts
first established in postwar Istanbul. Dunderdale was very protective of
these men, a number of whom supplied information from within the
Soviet Union, though a proportion of this could hardly be described as
espionage. In 1934 he described one Paris-based émigré, who had been
employed by SIS for seven years, as being particularly useful in obtaining
official handbooks from the Russian Military Publishing Office, in which
he had 'a friend to whom he frequently sent presents'. He also supplied
'reports on Russian naval matters based on personal knowledge, press &
casual sources', as well as obtaining 'newspapers prohibited for exporta-
tion'. Another of Dunderdale's old Istanbul contacts worked in a Soviet
army office in Tiflis and sent information about military movements and
some technical material on weapons and equipment to Paris enclosed in
local newspapers. There was also a network in south Russia based round
a railway official, whose reports on railway traffic in the 'central Asian
Military District' Menzies described in November 1930 as 'very valuable'.
Eighteen months later, however, this agent and his group were dropped
for being too costly.

The French authorities were aware of at least some of Dunderdale's
activities, and there had been direct co-operation, for example, in debriefing the Soviet defector Boris Bajanov in 1928. During the 1930s,
moreover, it is clear that the French not only condoned Dunderdale's
work but also collaborated with SIS in targeting Germany.[4] In November
1933, based partly on information evidently provided by official French

sources, Menzies circulated a detailed review of the state of French intelligence. As in Britain, money was an issue and Menzies observed that the French equivalent of SIS (the Service de Renseignements) had recently been obliged to reduce some operations due to budget cuts. He noted the close relations between the French and Polish Secret Services and that the French were obtaining valuable results on Italy from a network based in Algiers. Several French agents had been placed in Germany, but they were 'definitely forbidden to send in any reports at present', as they were intended solely for use in time of war. Menzies also thought it worth remarking that the French were employing a number of 'high class female agents'.

From the mid-1930s Dunderdale forged increasingly close relations with French colleagues. Lieutenant Paul Paillole of the counter-espionage Service de Centralisation des Renseignements met him in 1937, and afterwards recalled that he was a most agreeable and charming colleague ('un camarade séduisant, d'une elegance raffinée') whose efforts to foster friendly relations were greatly appreciated on the French side. By the late 1930s both sides were sharing information about the Abwehr (Military Intelligence) and the Sicherheitsdienst (the Schutzstaffel (SS) security service), as well as the methods and propaganda of the Nazi regime generally.[5] On a visit to Colonel Rivet, head of the Service de Renseignements, in October 1937, Menzies (described by the French as the 'Chief' of the British Intelligence Service) said that he was interested in three broad topics: German military information; Italian activities in the Mediterranean generally, as well as specific details of Italian and German military equipment being used in the Spanish Civil War; and political opinion in France, especially about possible Anglo-French action regarding Spain. Menzies admitted to the French that there were many shortcomings in his intelligence on the German army, but that he was much better informed about Italian matters and military developments in Spain. Reflecting on German ambitions in Central Europe, he predicted that German forces might occupy Austria within three weeks (it was in fact five months before this happened), and Germany would certainly put similar pressure on Czechoslovakia. He thought that neither French nor British public opinion would favour going to war over Czechoslovakia. The British, he insisted, were not ready for military action, nor would they be for some time. In his view, therefore, the only option for the moment was to wait. The French considered that this unusually frank political opinion was 'certainly a personal opinion', but not a 'negligible' one, bearing in mind the significant role they assumed Menzies played in the British War Office.[6]

In July 1938, through Rivet, Menzies arranged a meeting with French intelligence officers for Major Richard Stevens, head of station-designate at The Hague.[7] Stevens subsequently spent some time at the Deuxième Bureau (the intelligence branch of the French War Ministry), where the French shared information with him about German agents they believed were run from the Netherlands to work in France. Stevens confirmed to London that the French were most anxious to establish closer liaison with the Netherlands SIS station for both secret intelligence and counter-intelligence matters. He reported that he had been received by the French with the 'utmost kindness and frankness' and that their 'offer of reciprocal co-operation' was 'an absolutely genuine one and without arrière pensée of any sort'. Thanking Rivet personally for the 'extraordinarily kind reception which you gave to Stevens during his few days in Paris', Sinclair asserted that he had 'come back more French than British, and you certainly have a good Representative in my Service! I trust', he added, 'that the collaboration which will be arranged in Holland will prove of value to both our services.'

Over the next few months there were further reciprocal visits between the French and British services. In December 1938 David Footman (of the Head Office Political Section) went to Paris to build collaboration on political intelligence matters especially relating to the Soviet Union, the Far East and the Mediterranean. On his return to London he reported that a meeting with a French Colonial Intelligence officer had passed off 'very happily', largely due 'to the excellent personal relations which 45000 [Dunderdale] has already established with his French friends'. In January 1939 Dunderdale was involved in a visit to Paris by Captain John Godfrey, the Director of Naval Intelligence-designate. On 12 January Godfrey came to Dunderdale's office to be shown SIS's methods of work, security, production of maps, reports and plans, including aerial photographs. Dunderdale afterwards learned from a mutual friend that Godfrey was satisfied with the visit, as were the French. 'Their impression of Capt. Godfrey was a very good one,' he reported, 'and I am sure that they will do everything for us after his visit.' At the end of

January a French intelligence mission came to London for talks involving Menzies and Stevens of SIS, along with Kell and other MI5 officers. Menzies told the French he believed the Germans were not seriously preparing for military action against the West. Further afield, he noted that the British were extremely concerned about Japanese activities in the Far East. The Middle East was also a problem, and he hoped that there could be improved liaison between SIS and French intelligence in Syria and Egypt. Stevens, who worried that some of his predecessor's agents might have been turned by the Germans (how right he was), reported that he had established very good links with the security authorities in the Netherlands and was developing a twenty-strong network to work against the Germans. This, added Menzies, would be entirely at the service of the French and he proposed that while SIS focused on developing anti-German work in the Netherlands, the French should concentrate on doing so in Belgium and Luxembourg.[8] About this time, too, on SIS initiative, the Dame Blanche organisation was being reactivated.

Among the topics raised during the French visit to London in January 1939 was that of the two services collaborating with anti-German double agents based in the Low Countries. One such was a Belgian, 'Li 270', who had been recruited by both French intelligence and the German Abwehr in 1934. He provided his French case-officer with German questionnaires on the French aircraft industry (together with his replies), and in January 1939 supplied another document indicating intelligence requirements on Britain. This also focused on air power and revealed German suspicions that the British wanted to establish airbases in the Netherlands. Menzies was sufficiently interested to press his French counterparts in March 1939 for any further information from the agent. There was nothing more from the German side, but in June 1939 Li 270 was approached by the Italians to spy on England. While the return from this agent was not great, Olivier Forcade has observed that it illustrates the 'prudent partnership' of the two intelligence services, and their increasing co-operation, 'independent of staff talks and diplomacy', on the eve of war.[9] This early SIS engagement with double agents was one of the origins of the Double-Cross System which produced such valuable returns during the Second World War.

Over the spring of 1939 Dunderdale began to work with the French on arrangements for mobilisation in the event of war with Germany or

Italy, and he got Menzies to invite Rivet to London for informal discussions regarding arrangements should a British Expeditionary Force again be deployed in France. During their visit (in early June), Rivet, Captain Henri Navarre (of the German Section of the Service de Renseignements) and Commandant Brun (their mobilisation officer) were given red-carpet treatment, being put up at the Dorchester Hotel and dined at the Savoy, as well as having discussions with Menzies, Hubert Hatton-Hall (of the Army Section) and Rex Howard. With the scale and intensity of Anglo-French co-operation stepping up markedly over the summer of 1939, Sinclair worried about the burden Dunderdale was carrying. While recognising that he was the principal link with the French, Sinclair felt it was 'impossible' for him 'to carry out all aspects of this liaison contact' without interfering with his 'most important work', which was obtaining intelligence. Sinclair therefore told Dunderdale to confine himself to work connected with agents, 'agent doubles' and French General Staff duties, while the head of station (now Major Geoffrey W. Courtney, who had replaced Jeffes in late 1937) would deal with counter-espionage, field security, censorship, passports 'and any kindred matters'.

One cost of the burgeoning Anglo-French intelligence relationship was an increasing British reliance on what turned out to be inflated French estimates of German strength and capabilities. Douglas Porch has argued that the Deuxième Bureau's low status and limited budget had 'serious consequences on the quality of intelligence passed on to the high command . . . Annoyed that their message was not striking home, intelligence officers raised the tone of their reports, [and] exaggerated the numbers of German soldiers, tanks and aircraft.' Lieutenant Colonel Kenneth Strong, who had been assistant military attaché in Berlin until the outbreak of war and then served in the Military Intelligence German Section in the War Office, recalled that French estimates were sometimes 20 per cent higher than British figures. This phenomenon continued into 1940, when (according to F. H. Hinsley) it 'led Whitehall into over-estimating the total number of German divisions', though this, he asserted, 'had no unfortunate strategic consequences'.[10]

Of all Dunderdale's French liaisons built up during the 1930s, the most important turned out to be that with Captain Gustave Bertrand, head of the French cryptanalytical department, the Section des Examens. Between 1931 and 1938 an exceptionally valuable French spy in the communications section of the German army, Hans-Thilo Schmidt (known as 'Asché') supplied information about the Enigma cypher machine. Bertrand passed some of this material to the Poles and the British, helping the former both to build replicas of the machine and to decrypt some Enigma traffic from 1933 until December 1938, when the Germans introduced improvements. By Hinsley's account, the British initially 'showed no great interest in collaborating' with the French (or, indeed, the Poles).[11] By the autumn of 1938, however, the situation had changed significantly and at the start of October Commander Alastair Denniston, the head of the Government Code and Cypher School (GC&CS), told Sinclair that documents supplied by Bertrand were 'of assistance to our researches on the Enigma machine'. Indeed, Captain Tiltman of GC&CS's Military Section described the documents as 'of first importance and the saving of time and labour resulting from their possession is quite incalculable'. Dunderdale brought Bertrand to London to liaise personally with colleagues in GC&CS and from October 1938 the French handed over a wealth of signals intelligence material to the British through Dunderdale.

Although in January 1939 Bertrand organised a meeting between French, British and Polish experts, British willingness to co-operate with the Poles (and the Poles' readiness to share their work on Enigma) did not really develop until after Neville Chamberlain's public guarantee at the end of March to side with Poland in the event of a German attack. Late in July a second, and much more productive, Anglo-French–Polish meeting was held near Warsaw, following which the Poles supplied replica Enigma machines for both the British and the French. On 16 August Bertrand, accompanied by Dunderdale, delivered one of these to London. According to Bertrand, they were given a 'triumphant welcome' at Victoria Station by Stewart Menzies, dressed for dinner with the rosette of the Légion d'Honneur (which he had received for service in the First World War) in his buttonhole.[12] Although Menzies clearly appreciated the significance of this occasion, and the importance of the French and, especially, the Polish contributions to GC&CS's work on Enigma, he can scarcely have anticipated just how momentous and vital the wartime breaking of Enigma would be. This astounding breakthrough was not by itself a war-winning achievement, but F. H. Hinsley afterwards calculated that it shortened the war – and saved countless Allied lives – by perhaps three or even four years.[13]

Penetrating Germany

By the spring of 1938 it was no longer primarily finance which constrained SIS's work. In April 1938 Sinclair told the Deputy Chief of the Air Staff that it was not 'a question of money, as we have now ample funds with which to take advantage of an opportunity which offers, or any circumstances that may arise, in which money might help'. 'No one', he said, was 'more fully alive to the importance of obtaining information as to German Air Rearmament than the S.I.S., but the fact of the matter is that during the last twelve months or so, things have become very difficult indeed in Germany.' Ever since the Nazi assumption of power in March 1933 Sinclair had been worried about Germany. In October that year he told Ernest Dalton, head of station at The Hague, that 'unless a miracle intervened' there would be war between France and Germany in a very few years. With Sinclair evidently assuming that (as in 1914–18) the Netherlands would remain neutral, Dalton was instructed to ensure that '(i), our communications and (ii), information about the German Armed Forces shall be maintained in the event of war'. In the early 1930s SIS had few sources within Germany itself. The most important was a Balt, Baron William de Ropp, born in Lithuania (then part of the Russian empire) in the 1880s. He was naturalised British, having served with the British forces in the First World War. After the war he had offered his services to British intelligence, and was first seen by Menzies on 30 April 1919, after which he was taken on as an agent. He worked as a journalist in Germany and the Baltic states, and during the 1920s, coded '821', he reported regularly on German political matters. Although there were concerns in Head Office about just how valuable he was (especially as he was being paid £1,000 a year), the pressing need for intelligence following Hitler's rise to power gave him a rarity value. 'He is putting out some good stuff at the moment,' wrote Rex Howard in February 1934, 'and is our almost only [sic] resource in Germany.'

One of de Ropp's high-level Berlin contacts arranged for the head of SIS's Air Section, Frederick Winterbotham (posing as a 'member of the Air Staff'), to visit Germany in March 1934, during which he had an interview with Hitler, made his number with several senior Nazis, met young Luftwaffe pilots and successfully established himself with them as a friendly face. On his return Winterbotham reported on the Germans' unmistakable plans to develop a first-class, modern air force.[14] De Ropp himself built up relationships with the Reichswehr, the Luftwaffe and the Schutzstaffel (SS). In September 1934, at Hitler's personal invitation and with a select party of British guests, he attended the Nuremberg rally, and reported to SIS on the occasion. He received subsequent invitations to Nuremberg and in October 1937 met the Gestapo leader Reinhard Heydrich, whom he proposed to cultivate through liaison against 'Bolshevik personalities and intrigues'. Worried that the Germans might themselves manipulate the contact, Vivian turned down the suggestion as too risky. 'I would have nothing to do with this tortuous scheme,' he minuted. 'ACHTUNG!'

De Ropp was mainly briefed and debriefed by Woollcombe during visits to London, but he also reported discreetly in Berlin, met by Foley or a colleague from the Berlin station. This, though, became increasingly hazardous. There exists on file a copy of some extremely detailed security instructions laid down by Sinclair personally to Foley in October 1933 for meeting de Ropp and handling his reports so as to avoid the slightest risk of compromise. No papers relating to the agent were to be kept in Foley's office or typed there; no meetings held in apartments or in the PCO's office; de Ropp's reports were to be written on the day fixed for a meeting and at the last minute before the meeting, 'so that he walks straight out to the meeting with them, and they are in his possession, or in his flat, for as short a time as possible'; meetings to take place on the last day before bag day (when the diplomatic bag was sent to London) 'according to a pre-arranged roster of varying rendezvous. This in order to avoid telephone messages about meetings.' These instructions are a clear indication of the importance attached to the case, and of Sinclair's own close attention to detail. In August 1938, following the Anschluss and increased Gestapo surveillance of foreigners, de Ropp began to get edgy and asked to be moved away from Germany, but Sinclair did not approve. 'If de Ropp is to be of any use,' he wrote, 'he must work between here and Germany.' The agent, however, relocated to Switzerland that August and, although he continued to report for the next seven years, his work was increasingly discounted at Head Office. By July 1944 Claude Dansey, then Vice Chief of the Service, decided that all de Ropp represented now was 'a vehicle for Nazi propaganda'.

The question remains open as to which side got the greater benefit from the de Ropp case. The Germans evidently thought that they got the British contacts they wanted, although it did them little good in the end. Through Winterbotham, who seems to have played his part well, the British got timely intelligence about the development of the Luftwaffe which they probably would not otherwise have been able to acquire, as well as uniquely close-up observations on the characters and ideas of the Nazi leadership. In June 1938 Woollcombe estimated that 'at least 70%' of SIS's German political intelligence came from one very good source, de Ropp. 'If for any reason we lose him,' he wrote, 'it is obvious that our supply of "XP" [political information] will . . . be very seriously affected.' Whether or not this intelligence was put to good use by its recipients is a different matter.

SIS's best source for German naval matters was the veteran agent Dr Karl Krüger (TR/16) whose continued access to German shipyards informed reports especially about submarines, the construction of which had been prohibited under the Treaty of Versailles. This was of special interest to the Admiralty as the U-boat was (in Wesley Wark's words) 'preeminently an anti-British weapon'. In the spring of 1935 SIS reported that the Germans had begun discreet preparations to rebuild their U-boat force and there were 'strong indications' they were 'already constructing several submarines'. Demonstrating the confused state of contemporary intelligence on this subject, the naval attaché in Berlin, Captain Gerard Muirhead-Gould, while confirming German ambitions to have a submarine arm, erroneously assured London that construction had not yet commenced. Although the Admiralty, it appears, initially placed more weight on Muirhead-Gould's assessment than on SIS's report, the latter was confirmed by a public statement from Berlin the following month. In July 1936, again apparently based on SIS information from Krüger, a detailed paper on German naval construction, jointly prepared by the Naval Intelligence Directorate and the Industrial Intelligence Centre (which had been established by Desmond Morton in 1931), reported German plans for the mass production of submarines.[15] The Admiralty, however, remained unconvinced, though afterwards it turned out to be quite true. In November 1939 the SIS Naval Section grumbled with some justification that they had warned about German submarine construction and had 'continued this warning notwithstanding the incredulity of the Admiralty when the German[s] informed them officially that it was not taking place'.

At the beginning of 1938 Winterbotham affirmed that German air information was 'one of the most vital to the country and no opportunity should be lost to hammer into the heads of the representatives concerned the necessity to obtain some agents of high standing in place of a whole bunch of organisations'. Frank Foley, for example, should be instructed to 'cling on to "Jones" at all costs'. In April 1937 a person signing himself 'B. Jones' had handed a letter into the British consul in Zurich for onward despatch to the 'Officer Commanding the Military Section of the Intelligence Service'. The letter expressed pro-British sentiments and explained that a Luftwaffe officer friend of the writer was willing to supply documents at £100 a time. Copies of five recent German Air Ministry orders were enclosed, which, when the material was forwarded to London, were found to be of the highest importance. The case was controlled by Head Office with Foley in a supporting role, but was extremely difficult to run, mainly because of the problems posed by communicating in a police state with a pseudonymous document-producing agent who refused personal contact. Communication was through poste-restante addresses in Germany and 'Jones' deposited several packets of documents with British consuls in Germany and Switzerland. The agent abruptly ceased activity in February 1938, less than a year after he had made the first contact, when he felt himself coming under suspicion. It was a frustratingly brief run of success, as Winterbotham had estimated the material supplied to be 'worth all the rest of the money spent on German air information put together'.

Four months later Winterbotham sent an RAF officer, '479', on a motoring tour of Germany to obtain eyewitness reports of German airfields. Bringing with him 'a suitable [female] secretary', 479 paused in the Netherlands where he spent two days 'coaching' his companion. For three weeks they toured Germany, but found the going quite hard. As a general rule the Germans, it seemed, did not bring the edges of their airfields right up to the road. In the worst cases there was a belt of cultivation one or two hundred yards deep between the road and the aerodrome, evidently intended to keep interested observers at a distance and 'quite unlike anything in this country'. In too many instances 479 could see only the tails of aircraft and 'seldom got close enough to get numbers'. He was also driving a distinctive vehicle, and 'every time we stopped we were surrounded by small boys all anxious to know the power, speed,

Sir Mansfield Cumming, Chief of the Service from its creation until 1923. This portrait by
H. F. Crowther Smith shows him in the full-dress uniform of a Royal Navy Captain, wearing
British, French, Russian, Belgian and Italian decorations.

Early headquarters buildings:
64 Victoria Street (*top*) where
Cumming shared a cramped office
with Vernon Kell in the autumn of
1909; Ashley Mansions (*bottom*),
254 Vauxhall Bridge Road, a
six-story residential block where
Cumming lived and had his office
from November 1909 until 1911.

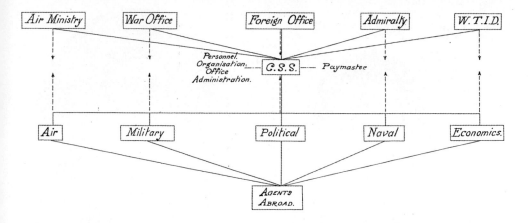

A chart drawn by Colonel C. N. French of the War Office on 7 December 1917, showing the new organisation of Cumming's headquarters.

Christmas Day

Called on D.I.D. , paid my respects
I told him that I regretted very much
that he was not satisfied with our
Naval information & that it he &
my other Chiefs decided that they
could do better with some one else They
must not allow personal considerations
to stand in the way. At the same time
I could assure him that I was doing my best
& believed that the new organisation w⁰.
put fresh blood & energy into the work.

Working on Christmas Day 1917. This page from Cumming's diary records a meeting with the Director of the Admiralty Intelligence Department at which Cumming typically put his position on the line.

Spying in the First World War: Captain Henry Landau (*top left*), based in Rotterdam, was Cumming's link to the 800-strong 'La Dame Blanche' organisation working in enemy-occupied territory; Jeanne Goeseels (*top right*), a respectable middle-aged member of La Dame Blanche, who, when arrested with another agent, sacrificed her reputation but saved his life by persuading the Germans he was her lover; Walthère Dewé (*right*), leader of La Dame Blanche and its successor in the Second World War, during which he was killed by the Nazis. His wife, seen here, also worked in the organisation.

Two of Paul Dukes's many personas: the personable musician, and the Bolshevik secret policeman 'Joseph Afirenko', one of the disguises he assumed when spying in revolutionary Russia.

2 Whitehall Court, a sumptuous apartment block close to the War Office and the Admiralty where Cumming had his headquarters (and residence) from 1911 until 1919. He originally rented apartment number 54 on the top floor, but as the organisation expanded other apartments were acquired.

The more modest premises at West House, 1 Melbury Road, in Holland Park, west London, where SIS had its headquarters from December 1919 to May 1926.

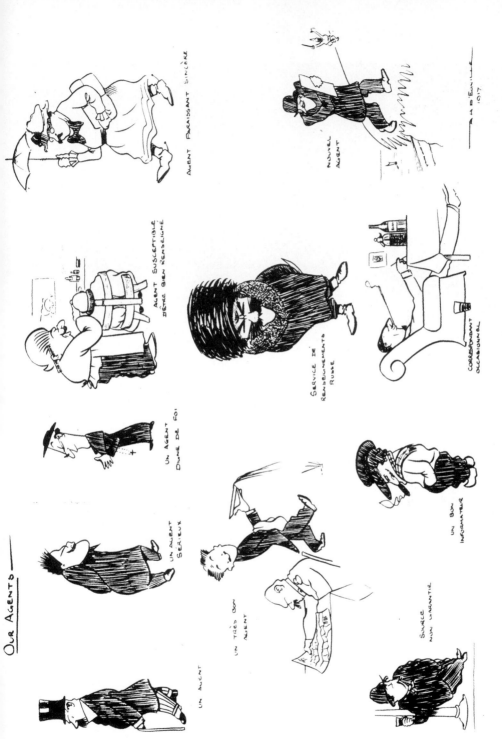

Various espionage 'types', wittily sketched in 1917 by an Intelligence Corps officer A. W. D'Egville.

Mansfield Cumming being knighted by King George V in the Quadrangle of Buckingham Palace, 26 July 1919.

Harry Carr, head of the Helsinki Station, 1928–41, and Controller Northern Area after the war.

Stewart Menzies, then head of the Military Section at headquarters, with his second wife, Pamela, in December 1932.

The agent Jonny de Graff and his wife.

Harry Nathaniel Steptoe, SIS's senior man in China for most of the interwar years.

Radio equipment recovered from a Chinese Communist Party communications centre by the Shanghai Metropolitan Police in October 1934 and passed on to SIS.

Broadway Buildings,
54 Broadway, in 1929: SIS
headquarters from May 1926
to 1964. The Chief's office was
behind the last two windows on
the right of the fourth floor.

Valentine Vivian, the classical
scholar and former Indian
policeman who joined in 1918
and remained for over thirty
years, serving as Deputy Chief
during the Second World War.

Sir Hugh Sinclair, Chief of SIS from September 1923 to November 1939.

The famous interwar Berlin head of station, Frank Foley (*left*), was posted to Oslo in September 1939, where he was photographed with his assistant, Leslie Mitchell.

Maurice Jeffes and Malcolm Woollcombe outside Buckingham Palace on 11 July 1939, after the award of their CMGs. Jeffes (*left*) was SIS representative in New York and Paris before becoming Director of Passport Control in 1938, and Woollcombe (flanked by his wife, Eileen, and 16-year-old son, Robert) headed SIS's Political Section.

Naval intelligence from Nazi Germany. Two photographs taken by agent TR/16 in Kiel on 30 June and 1 July 1937. One shows destroyers being fitted out at the Germania shipyard and the other the foredeck of the S.S. *Windhoek*.

Group Captain F. W. Winterbotham, head of SIS's Air Section (*left*), meeting his agent Baron de Ropp in East Prussia, 1936.

An agent radio transmitter, as supplied to 'Service Clarence' in Belgium in 1939.

Brigadier Richard 'Pop' Gambier-Parry (*left*), SIS's brilliant communications supremo throughout the Second World War.

Bletchley Park in Buckinghamshire was bought in 1938 to be SIS's War Station and became the site of Britain's wartime signals intelligence triumphs.

Hugh Sinclair, the bon viveur, in relaxed mode with an unidentified woman on the transatlantic liner R.M.S. *Berengaria*, Christmas 1936.

make and price of our Wolseley. There can be few small boys in N.W. Germany', he reported, 'who do not remember the strange English couple and their car.' More dangerously, they attracted the attention of Nazi Brown Shirts, who 'turned the car inside out' and followed the couple for several days. The two 'decided to confuse the issue so made wild dashes all over the country' which 'either shook them off or they lost interest'. After covering some 2,400 miles, 479 cut the mission short and returned home, principally because his companion had become 'alarmingly tired and sick with indigestion'. She had nevertheless done 'very good work drawing etc' and deserved 'the highest praise for risking her reputation to help me out of a difficulty' (479 had originally planned to travel with his German-speaking sister, but her husband had refused to allow her to go). Winterbotham considered 479's report to be 'of considerable value', having succeeded in 'discovering the exact positions of concentration aerodromes, which we had previously been unable to get'. He sent the agent to Germany again in September 1938, when he brought back some unspecified, though 'very valuable', information.

On the military side, in February 1938 Sinclair himself cabled Monty Chidson at The Hague suggesting that the recent purge of the German armed forces 'makes available officers who will be antagonistic to the Nazi Party and might succumb to tempting offers from us . . . Funds are available.' Similar wires were sent to Prague, Paris and Brussels. Chidson was asked if Krüger (TR/16) might be asked to find a disaffected officer, for which the Service would be prepared to pay 'a very handsome bonus'. In addition, 'a considerable sum would be available for payment to the officer himself, such sum being dependent on the position he held and the consequent value of his information'. Krüger had been reporting on the Luftschutzbund (the air defence organisation, in which he was employed), and also naval shipbuilding (as he had done for so many years). In June 1937 he supplied secretly taken photographs of destroyers being fitted out at the Germania Werft in Kiel. Towards the end of the year the Economic Section VI in Head Office noted reports and maps, useful 'from a bomb target point of view'.

By the late 1930s, Krüger, now over sixty, was beginning to run out of steam and thinking of retiring. There were increasing comments about the inaccuracy of his reports and security in Germany, too, was tightening. He had a scare in March 1938 when the Gestapo visited him after he

had been spotted near an airfield. Krüger (who by this stage was known
as '016') continued to work on naval matters and coast defences, meeting
his case-officer in Rotterdam every month up to 18 July 1939, when the
next meeting was scheduled for 20 August. 'He failed to arrive,' reported
The Hague on 24 August, but a postcard purporting to be from him had
been received proposing a meeting in Germany. This aroused suspicions
since it was the first time he had ever 'suggested that someone should visit
him in 12-land [Germany]'. The Head Office minuting on the report
was uniformly pessimistic. 'This is one of the agents [Jack] Hooper said
the Germans knew of,' wrote one officer. 'Looks as though he has been
liquidated.' 'He may well have written the post-card under the direction
of the Gestapo,' observed Howard. 'Looks like a trap,' added Vivian. So
it was (and, wisely, no one was sent to meet him in Germany), though
the Service did not discover until after the war that Krüger had been betrayed by a member of The Hague station staff, Folkert van Koutrik, who
had been recruited by the Abwehr in October 1938.[16] A proforma for the
Finance Section on 7 November 1939 laconically records poor Krüger's
fate. By the entry 'To whom payment discontinued' was typed '016'; and
against 'Remarks': 'Agent presumed "dead"'.

   The patchy state of secret intelligence in the period immediately before
the war was revealed in late June 1938 when Rex Howard asked each
of the Head Office sections to report on whether or not their German
requirements were being met. Menzies, head of the Military Section IV,
replied that he was 'satisfied with the efforts although the results are disappointing in that we have no military source of any standing and have
to rely on numerous small fry'. Winterbotham remarked: 'Results are
not very good but I am hopeful.' Rather more encouragingly, Captain
Russell (for whom Krüger was an important source) reported that penetration of German dockyards was satisfactory for peacetime requirements, but he lamented the fact that he did not have either an officer or
a rating serving in the fleet, or a person who could mix freely with naval
officers. Admiral Limpenny, head of the Economic Section VI, reported
'excellent' information on naval construction, but less good for aircraft.
Over the last eighteen months 'very little' had been received 'in regard to
production figures and numbers of hands employed in individual factories'. There was a 'serious lack of information' on 'Land Armaments', and
the only information he had 'on manufacture and outputs of German

gun factories' came from the Anglo-French–Belgian BOX organisation. Finally, Woollcombe offered his opinion on the political intelligence he received. While de Ropp was the most prolific source, he had a fair number of other, occasional agents, including some journalists working in Germany, and stressed the need 'to increase our supply of first class agents who can provide real authoritative information on German high policy, especially so that we should not be so dependent on de Ropp, who may at any time come under the eye of the Gestapo and drop out of the picture'.

Gestapo attention made life very difficult for the Vienna station, which continued to operate after the Anschluss. The Passport Control Office, too, was overwhelmed with work issuing visas for Jews desperate to leave the country. The head of station and PCO, Tommy Kendrick, reported early in August 1938 that his staff were 'so overwrought that they will burst into tears at the slightest provocation'. He apologised to Sinclair that his SIS reports were 'somewhat scrappy and badly collated' because of the pressure of Passport Control work. Meanwhile a number of Kendrick's agents were picked up by the Gestapo, who arrested Kendrick himself on 17 August when he was actually on his way to England for a holiday. He was interrogated for three days before being released and ordered to leave the country, after which all intelligence work ceased. As soon as he had been arrested, an assistant and two female secretaries, 'who did all the secret work, were packed off to London' and Kenneth Benton, who had been working in the station for almost a year, 'burned everything secret'. As the office had no official protection (although attached to a consulate-general the Passport Control staff did not have diplomatic status), Benton 'was afraid that the Gestapo might just come in and search the whole office, so everything that could be burned was destroyed'.[17] This was just as well, and on 19 August Menzies reassured the Foreign Office (who were naturally worried about the possible diplomatic fall-out) that there was 'not the slightest likelihood of any compromising material being found in the shape of documentary evidence'.

Like Vienna, the Passport Control Office in Berlin was swamped by applications from Jews trying to escape the Reich. Frank Foley's significant work in helping many thousands of Jews to get British visas was carried out as part of his duties as Passport Control Officer rather than as SIS head of station.[18] Foley had a particularly difficult balance to strike

between his differing responsibilities. He had developed 'a long standing and officially established liaison' with the German police 'for the
exchange of information about Communism'. This had survived the
establishment of the Nazi regime. In October 1937 Foley's relations
with the Gestapo's 'Communist expert' were described as 'cordial'. By
this stage, however, his refusal (on Sinclair's express orders) 'to satisfy
the Gestapo lust for information on the subject of anti-Nazi Germans
in England on the false grounds that they are Communists' had alienated other senior Gestapo officials. Unfortunately, there are practically no
relevant surviving SIS files, which might have thrown light on the inevitable trade-off which Foley had to make between his Passport Control and
intelligence duties, let alone any covert methods by which he may have
assisted individual Jewish families, or the possible intelligence he might
have obtained from them. What we do know is that he was an extremely
effective and articulate PCO, deeply sympathetic to and reporting with
great clarity and force on the position of the Jews who were trying to
leave Germany (and overloading his office in the process).

Foley, like other Passport Control staff, got caught up in SIS's campaign
to get them diplomatic status, so much so that in March 1939 Sinclair
was prepared to dissemble on his part. After the ambassador in Berlin,
Sir Nevile Henderson, refused to allow this, Sinclair hoped that he might
change his mind if he was 'given a guarantee' that Foley was 'not engaged
in S.I.S. activity'. Sinclair therefore proposed to assure both the Foreign
Office and the ambassador that this was the case on the rather specious
grounds that Foley was 'not employing German nationals' and was 'only
obtaining political information through British nationals' which was 'no
more than the Embassy itself' was doing.[19] In fact Foley had certainly in
the past employed 'German nationals' for espionage purposes, and, if not
precisely so doing at the time of Sinclair's signal, he certainly had assistants for whom Germans worked.

The impact of SIS intelligence and the use to which it was put by the
government are difficult to assess as very few SIS reports, let alone commentary on them, have survived in either closed or open archives. Much
of the most secret material was routinely destroyed after it had been read
(and potentially summarised in other briefing papers). There are sporadic
references to 'secret intelligence', but they are sometimes so general as to
prevent any assessment of SIS's specific part (if any) in its production.

In September 1938, for example, Sir Alexander Cadogan, Permanent Under-Secretary at the Foreign Office, returned from holiday to find that Gladwyn Jebb had left him a 'stack of telegrams & papers, which I started reading. There's certainly enough in the Secret Reports to make one's hair stand on end. But I never swallow all these things, and I am presented with a <u>selection</u>.'[20] Since Jebb, as Cadogan's private secretary, was the link-man between the Foreign Office and SIS, it is highly probable that among that 'stack of telegrams & papers' was SIS-generated material. But how much of it there was and what effect it had, beyond Cadogan's scepticism, is impossible to judge. That SIS reports reached the highest levels, however, is demonstrated by the fortunate survival of one such report, written by Woollcombe, and retained by him, apparently for understandable, if rather touching, emotions of pride. His paper reviewed the political campaign in Germany for the return of overseas colonies lost under the Versailles treaty, and noted that 'one large compact area', probably in West Africa, was thought to be the most desirable objective. In the margin, in Neville Chamberlain's handwriting, indicating his agreement with Woollcombe's assessment, is 'What did I say.'[21]

From Munich to war

The need for good intelligence on high-level German policy-making was amply demonstrated during the Munich Crisis in the autumn of 1938 when it seemed as if war might break out in the face of Hitler's territorial ambitions in Central Europe. After Germany and Austria had been united in the Anschluss of March 1938, Hitler turned his attention to Czechoslovakia. A quarter of the country's twelve million population were ethnic Germans, concentrated in the Sudetenland in the west, along the borders of the now enlarged Germany. Nazi policy was to unite these Germans into the Fatherland, which would effectively destroy the Czechoslovak state. In May there was a 'war scare', and the British government issued a warning against a German attack. 'There is no doubt whatever in my mind', Sinclair told Sir Warren Fisher on 27 May, 'that the Germans intended to try and slip in to Czechoslovakia during the last weekend, but owing to our having found out what they were up to, such an uproar arose that they have now put off their scheme for the present.' But he added that their plan was 'all ready, and on the order "Go" it will be carried out if and when Hitler decides to do so'.²² On 18 July an SIS memorandum for the Committee of Imperial Defence (CID) argued that it was 'impossible to predict with absolute certainty what course the Germans will pursue towards Czechoslovakia, because decisions rest with one man, Hitler, who is to a large extent incalculable, even to his intimates'. Nevertheless, 'matters have many appearances of working up to a crisis, with August and September as the probable danger periods'. How right they were.

On 12 September 1938 Sinclair sent Colonel Hastings 'Pug' Ismay, the CID secretary, a 'summary of certain naval indications' which showed 'that Germany is preparing for world-wide war'. Moreover, 'in the absence of definite signs that these preparations are being suspended or abandoned, the conclusion can only be formed that Hitler intends to attack Czechoslovakia on or about the dates we originally stated, viz: September 24th–28th, and is prepared to support such action by world-wide war if necessary'. For the Czechoslovaks the position was desperate, though not yet perhaps hopeless. While neither of its allies, France and the Soviet Union, was in fact prepared to go to war on its behalf, the British government under Neville Chamberlain seized the diplomatic initiative in an effort to find a peaceful solution to the crisis. Beyond the understandable desire simply to avoid war, the British were also anxious to buy time. Well aware of German rearmament (although there is some evidence that both its progress and German – though not Hitler's – resolve were slightly overestimated), there was a need to let British preparations reach a point where the country and its armed forces were better prepared to fight a war if necessary. On 15 and 22 September, Chamberlain famously flew to Germany to negotiate personally with Hitler, and over these crucial days there were intense discussions in London as to what line Britain should take. It was a difficult choice: should Britain firmly back the Czechoslovaks and risk immediate war with Germany, or should pressure be put on Prague to concede what many people regarded as Germany's legitimate claims for the Sudetenland, but at grievous cost to the Czechoslovak state, accompanied by a perhaps cynical (or realpolitik) concession that force was the only relevant factor?

It is an indicator of how tricky these issues were, and how the government sought advice from all kinds of sources, that, unusually and apparently uniquely for the history of the Service so far, SIS was formally asked to submit a 'policy paper' in the week between Chamberlain's two trips. Whatever advice Sinclair and his colleagues may have provided to government hitherto, it appears always to have been on an informal basis. SIS's specific function was to supply secret intelligence, not policy advice, but in this instance, as Sinclair told Sir Warren Fisher on 19 September, the Foreign Office had 'asked for our remarks . . . as to what course of action should be taken in Foreign Affairs in the present circumstances and with regard to the future'. The result was a paper by Woollcombe entitled 'What should we do?' Woollcombe began by reviewing 'the aims of the Germans', which constituted the 'establishment of general "paramountcy" or "supremacy" in Europe'. This included the 'absorption of at least the Sudeten areas of Czechoslovakia', and the domination of the rest of the country, as well as 'political and economic hegemony over the whole of Central and S.E. Europe, on the "Vassal State" principle'; the 'recovery, sooner or later, of lost territory' in the East; the 'downfall of the Soviet regime'; and 'penetration in the Middle East and the increasing of Britain's difficulties there'. As to 'German methods and principles', 'first and foremost' was '<u>force</u>', and the creation 'of the strongest possible Armed Forces, sufficient to overcome any combination of Powers and emerge victorious in any conflagration'. Woollcombe added that 'the [German] Armed Forces leaders do not consider that this stage is yet reached'.

What, then, was Britain to do? Woollcombe had three proposals for the 'immediate or near future'. First was the '<u>peaceful separation from Czechoslovakia</u>, and joining to Germany, <u>of the Sudeten German areas</u>'. This would 'forestall the inevitable', he argued. Czechoslovak 'security and unity', moreover, could never be maintained in 'any solution which leaves the Sudetens in the State'. Indeed, there was now an opportunity 'to leave intact a State which would be literally Czechoslovak – a compact, homogeneous, neutralised State under international guarantee'. Second, Woollcombe recommended that Britain endeavour to secure an Anglo-Italian agreement in order to weaken 'the Rome–Berlin axis'; and third, he urged a settlement in Palestine, perhaps by partitioning the territory, but 'on lines which went an appreciable way' towards meeting Arab demands. This was 'vital if we are not to risk having the Arab world (to which Germany is devoting increasing attention) against us, let alone the necessity of diminishing our growing military etc. commitments in Palestine'. In the longer term, it was clear that Britain 'should unremittingly build up our armaments . . . Platitudinous though it may be,' he argued, 'our only chance of preserving peace is to be ready for war on any scale, without relying too much on outside support,' though the existing 'defensive alliance' with France should be maintained and consolidated. 'Franco-British strength and absolute solidarity'; friendly relations with Italy and (if possible) Japan, as well as 'smaller States earmarked as "Vassals" of Germany . . . injecting them with resisting power and courage' would all help to ensure 'that Germany's "style is cramped"'. He also proposed that Britain should cultivate friendship with Germany 'as far as we can, and without sacrifice of our principles and vital interests'.

'It may be argued', he concluded, 'that this would be giving in to Germany, strengthening Hitler's position and encouraging him to go to extremes.' It was better, however, 'that realities be faced and that wrongs, if they do exist, be righted, than leave it to Hitler to do the righting in his own way and time – particularly if, concurrently, we and the French unremittingly build up our strength and lessen Germany's potentialities for making trouble'. Sinclair endorsed Woollcombe's paper – the Foreign Office copy is marked 'View of S.I.S.'[23] (and it also echoed the views Menzies had expressed to his French counterparts the previous October) – but it is not clear how influential it may have been, though it evidently accorded with the majority view in government. Replying to Sinclair on 20 September, Warren Fisher thought it 'a most excellent document', which confirmed 'in our own rearming the vital need for rapid & effective strengthening of our air position'. He also believed that it was 'air that must "hold the ring" for us – at all events in the initial months. It is thro' air that the Germans can get at us, & had we used the last few years effectively in that arm, the Germans wd not have been able to override us as they have this present year.'

Over the weekend of 17/18 September both the British Cabinet and the French agreed to allow the annexation of the Sudetenland in exchange for a guarantee of the new borders. But, when Chamberlain returned to Germany on 22 September, he found Hitler had raised his demands. Not only did he now want to occupy the Sudetenland immediately, but he also insisted that Polish and Hungarian claims for Czechoslovak territory be met. This was more than the Cabinet would allow and it was decided to support France if it backed Czechoslovakia. Still seeking to avert war, and with Italy's involvement, Chamberlain agreed to a conference in Munich between Germany, Britain, France and Italy. Here, on 29 September, it was confirmed that neither France nor Britain was prepared to go to war with Germany on behalf of Czechoslovakia and the country's fate was sealed in the Munich Agreement, which effectively met Hitler's raised demands. This was not 'peace at any price'. Even Chamberlain did not subscribe to that absurdity. But it was certainly peace at a higher price than the anti-appeasers would have paid. In October German troops occupied the Sudetenland.

During the crisis the SIS station in Prague had been reporting on Czechoslovak military opinion. In early 1938 Harold Gibson, head of station since February 1934, had been given permission by London to establish liaison with the head of Czechoslovak Military Intelligence, Colonel František Moravec. This was primarily to help Gibson acquire information on German targets, and was quickly very rewarding. In March 1938 Gibson reported that the Czechoslovaks had supplied information on German military movements in Austria 'more detailed and exhaustive than anything I could have hoped to obtain through independent agents'. The liaison developed so well that in the midst of the Munich Crisis one of Gibson's Czechoslovak military contacts, while bitterly critical of France and its betrayal of an ally, assured Gibson that, whatever the politicians may have decided, it would not interfere with 'our collaboration'.

Following the German occupation of the Sudetenland, the survival of the rump of Czechoslovakia as an independent state became increasingly uncertain. When Gibson's assistant, Wilfrid Hindle, posted to Prague in February 1938, asked in January 1939 if he could bring his family out to join him, Rex Howard in London unhelpfully replied: 'I am afraid I cannot possibly tell you how long you will stay in Prague because one does not know from one day to the next what is going to happen in Europe.' He recommended, nevertheless, that Hindle stay in rented furnished accommodation, and 'you should on no account consider the question of getting your furniture out . . . In the present state of Europe', he concluded, 'it is difficult to give any guarantee of anything.' By the early spring of 1939 it was clear, however, that the Germans were preparing to occupy the rest of Czechoslovakia. In his memoirs, Moravec claims that his well-placed agent in the German General Staff, 'A.54', Paul Thümmel, provided advance warning of the invasion, which was scheduled for 15 March. With Gibson's help, Moravec and ten of his most senior officers were flown to London in an SIS-chartered plane on 14 March.[24] No explicit trace of this dramatic operation survives in the SIS archives, although on 14 March Gibson requested London to grant him use of an emergency reserve of $1,000 and £200, and reported the same day that he had taken custody of Moravec's 'most important intelligence archives' in his office. The Germans indeed entered Prague on 15 March, and over the next two weeks, with deft use of King's Messengers and diplomatic bags, Gibson managed to get the Czechoslovak intelligence archive safely to London, from where Moravec and his colleagues were able to run operations during the Second World War. On 30 March, Gibson and the remaining SIS station staff left for London.

The Munich Crisis stimulated a brief flurry of SIS activity in the Mediterranean. Towards the end of September 1938, Captain Russell of the Naval Section noted that the Service might 'be called upon at any time now to report the locations of Italian warships' and a range of stations in Southern Europe were instructed to have 'tip and run' agents ready to deploy at short notice. The stations were authorised to spend up to £500 on this without referring back to London. On 28 September Hamilton Stokes in Gibraltar was told to 'open up the Malta station immediately'. Steps were taken, but on 4 October, after the Munich Agreement had been signed, the work was scaled back 'in view of the present improvement in the international situation'. Even by late 1938 there was no blank cheque for any large-scale expansion of SIS operations. Some decision-makers, apparently, believed with Chamberlain (as he famously declared on his return from Munich) that the agreement had indeed provided 'peace for our time'.

After Munich SIS continued to report on Hitler and his ambitions, although in October 1938 Woollcombe admitted that the political work on Germany rested on a 'very narrow basis', with only two 'solid' sources: de Ropp (who by this stage was proving less reliable) and a high-status Baltic German with social connections across Europe, who was run from London by Dick Ellis and whom Woollcombe described as 'first class', though with 'limitations' as he could not be 'a permanent agent for German information'. Based in Italy (where he was 'our best agent') and Switzerland, in 1938–9 he passed on material gathered from friends and relations in the German army, the Nazi Party and high industrial circles. On 8 November in a circular to European stations arising from his Section I's 'Crisis Stocktaking', Woollcombe urged representatives 'to find more first class alternatives for 12-land [German] "high policy" information'. Recognising that 'sources of this type, having real access to "the goods", are few and far between', he nevertheless wrote that it was 'very desirable that we should be well informed regarding the leadership, strength, resources, methods, aims, real position and prospects, etc., of anti-Nazi movements, for without such information it is very difficult to judge how seriously they are to be taken or whether they contain any appreciable alternative regime potentialities'. He thought especially that (while this 'must involve a lot of speculation') 'we should have lines on the military clique, or cliques, who would like to see a change of régime'.

In a wide-ranging review of 'tendencies and reactions' ('prepared at the request of the Foreign Office' and circulated in November 1938) SIS asserted that the Munich settlement had left Hitler 'in a dissatisfied and spiteful frame of mind', though it remained difficult to predict what he might do: 'Not even Herr Hitler's intimates, according to one of them, knew for certain if he would really risk a world war.' It seemed clear, however, that in the immediate future Nazi attention would 'to a large extent [be] occupied with the furtherance and consolidation of the Eastward trend', as well as 'atomisation' ('a process of creating small States on a racial and self-determination basis'), which SIS suggested contained 'interesting possibilities for countries like Roumania and Poland'. While the Service did not report much anti-war feeling among the population in general, it did identify some opposition to war among the army chiefs, though for the most part only on the grounds of 'Germany's unreadiness to engage in a general war of long duration'.

In December Sinclair provided a further paper on 'Germany: factors, aims, methods, etc', which stressed Hitler's 'incalculability and lightning-like decisions'. 'Among his characteristics are fanaticism, mysticism, ruthlessness, cunning, vanity, moods of exaltation and depression, fits of bitter and self-righteous resentment, and what can only be termed a streak of madness; but with it all there is great tenacity of purpose.' The paper realistically played down the influence of internal opposition: 'Notwithstanding divergencies, internal discontent and widespread

unpopularity of the régime below the surface, Herr Hitler's will is supreme.' Germany's ambitions to dominate east-central Europe were
stressed. The 'general indications' were 'that Poland was "for it" sooner or
later'. In a 'summary of information from secret sources', Gladwyn Jebb
drew on this paper with a stern warning to his colleagues that, if 'any
references' to the remarks of these secret sources leaked out, they would
'be in grave danger of "liquidation" and what is more important, we shall
be deprived of their information'. He included information which now
suggested that Hitler might also be contemplating a westward strike.
The 'present air strength of Germany would enable her easily to "cover"
London and Paris', reported Jebb, 'and no consideration would be paid
to considerations of law and humanity. London, in particular, it was said,
could be destroyed in a couple of days by unceasing bombing attacks.'[25]

During the spring of 1939 there were concerns about the information
on the German armed forces which SIS was able to provide. In March
Rex Howard worried about the inability of stations at short notice to
send agents into Germany to report on specific aerodromes. Just days
before the outbreak of the Second World War, Dick Ellis reported a
rather unconvincing series of steps taken by the Service to warn of an
impending German attack. The highly regarded '22124/X' had 'arranged
with his brother in the VDA [Volksbund für Deutschtum im Ausland –
Society for Germanism Abroad] to let him know by telegram in Rome
if war is certain'. A female agent, whose daughter was 'in daily touch
with the Ribbentrops' (Joachim von Ribbentrop was the German Foreign
Minister), had 'promised to do everything to warn us by telegram'.
Another agent had been sent to Wilhelmshaven 'to warn us about sailings
of warships and indications of impending air-raids'. He had 'made his
own arrangements to get into Holland or Belgium', from where he would
'wire or telephone'. An agent in Basel, Switzerland, was to telephone 'if
he hears from Swiss-Air (in close touch with Lufthansa) of an impending air-attack'. While this was not, perhaps, very encouraging, there was
slightly more hope of identifying key German ship movements at the
outbreak of war. In April 1939 Captain Russell reassured Commander
Frank Slocum (G.3) that he was 'well served' regarding information from
German North Sea ports, 'except that after the frontier is closed we shall
probably not get it out in time unless agents have W/T'. In fact, an 'in-
structional' wireless set had already been sent out to The Hague station

for one of its German-based agents and SIS's Communications Section VIII was prepared to provide more equipment when agents had been trained and 'if C.S.S. gives approval'.

A month before the outbreak of war Menzies wisely suggested that the stations in Copenhagen, The Hague and Brussels ought 'to consider the possibility of their countries being overrun', in which case 'it would be of paramount importance for them to leave behind reliable sources'. Wireless sets, he said, would also need to be provided. Evidently concerned that planning for any kind of 'stay-behind' organisation might appear defeatist, Menzies wanted it emphasised to the representatives that 'they must avoid in any way alarming persons whom they approach, and they should make it clear that we consider that if the situation envisaged occurred, it would only be for a short time as we are absolutely confident of complete victory in the end'.

Following the German occupation of the remainder of Czechoslovakia in March 1939, attention began to focus on the growing threat to Poland, where Germany had particularly begun to target the Free City of Danzig on the Baltic and the Polish Corridor granted to Poland under the Treaty of Versailles which isolated the German territory of East Prussia. In March the Cabinet decided that a public statement should be made to indicate 'our intention to support Poland'. In May the Foreign Office asked the Berlin and Rome embassies to spread the message informally that if Germany invaded Poland both Britain and France would come to its aid. Since a copy of this telegram was sent to Sinclair, it may be assumed that SIS was also to participate in the campaign. On 7 July a bogus Cabinet decision stating that any armed clash between Germany and Poland over Danzig would be regarded by Britain as a *casus belli* was prepared for SIS to communicate to the Germans.[26] A week later SIS circulated a paper on 'Germany and Poland' which said that Hitler was determined to solve the 'Danzig question' during the autumn, with the danger period coming in late August/early September: 'We are sceptical as regards "dates" for action', but it seemed likely that whenever Hitler acted it would be 'a lightning decision within 24 hours of the event'. The paper argued that a lot depended on how seriously Hitler took Anglo-French, and particularly British, determination to honour pledges to Poland. At the moment he still needed to be convinced 'that we meant business and were not bluffing'. SIS also reported that it had 'nothing to show that any political conversations are taking place between Berlin and Moscow' and that the idea of an agreement between Hitler and Stalin was 'very hypothetical'. Thus SIS was quite sensible about Germany's intentions towards Poland, though its observation that Hitler 'certainly wants to avoid a major war if possible', while literally true (he would have been delighted to secure his objectives without war), could provoke over-optimism about any desire for 'peace' he might have.

Like so many others, Broadway was dumbfounded by the Nazi–Soviet non-aggression pact of August 1939. In fact, an SIS agent, code-named the 'Baron', with good contacts among the Junkers of East Prussia and run by Harry Carr from Helsinki, had first reported secret German–Soviet negotiations in the spring of 1939. A further report in June that the talks were making good progress was greeted with incredulity in London, where the desk officer concerned refused even to circulate it to the Foreign Office as he could not understand how the Baron could have had access to such extremely secret matters without high-level contacts in the German Foreign Office. Carr discovered afterwards (and too late) that his agent had got the information from close friends in East Prussia who themselves had been visited by officials involved in the negotiations and had talked freely among such trusted company. The June report arrived just as Sir William Strang of the Foreign Office was visiting Moscow in a last-ditch effort to secure an Anglo-Soviet agreement. Head Office naively commented to Carr that it could not be correct for Molotov (the Soviet Foreign Minister) to have said to Strang the day before 'the exact opposite of statements in the report from your source'. But such was the case, and the Nazi–Soviet Pact paved the way for both Germany and the Soviet Union to invade, and occupy, Poland. The Pact was announced on 22 August. That evening John Darwin of Section VIII wrote in his diary: 'Russo-German pact! Everything very alarming . . . C.S.S. on warpath in view of possibility that we have been accused of letting F.O. down. The usual chase after a scapegoat that can't defend itself. I think this one can.' The implications were obvious and the following day Darwin sent his wife Sibyl a postcard from the Travellers Club in London. 'I don't want to seem alarmist,' he wrote, 'but I really think that the Germans will invade Poland this weekend or early next week,' a prediction that was out by only a day or two.[27]

Creative improvisation

The 1930s saw a considerable expansion in SIS activities, especially as the international situation worsened during the second half of the decade. One important development in 1931 was the creation of an Industrial Intelligence Centre (IIC), headed by Major Desmond Morton and drawing on the expertise he had developed in SIS's Economic Section VI, which had itself been created some time in 1926–7.[28] The Centre began as a 'secret nucleus', and stayed embedded within the Service until 1934. It had a wide sphere of interest, though the principal focus was on industrial capacity for war. One definition of industrial intelligence was 'any information regarding the industrial development of a country which may throw light upon the extent of its potential armed forces effort or plans'.[29] Morton made quite a success of it, but its expanding activities began to eat into SIS's own scarce resources. In May 1932 Sinclair complained to Sir Edward Crowe at the Department of Overseas Trade that the centre had cost almost £3,000 over the last year, at a time when SIS funds were 'already strained to breaking point' owing to the fall in the international value of sterling. Hankey was not very sympathetic to Sinclair, and evidently valued the work of Morton's new outfit. He thought SIS 'ought to fit it in somehow, if necessary by letting something else go'.[30]

Morton's development of industrial intelligence inevitably brought him into contact with commercial firms. One such was the majority state-owned Anglo-Persian Oil Company (forerunner of British Petroleum). In July 1931 Vivian had suggested to Morton that Anglo-Persian, with its global reach, might be a valuable source of information, especially about non-British oil concerns. Colonel H. E. Medlicott, head of Anglo-Persian's Security Branch, agreed in principle that the company might co-operate with Morton, but told Vivian that it would be much easier if 'this was divorced from [the] great secrecy of Secret Service'. Even while it remained part of SIS, Morton's Centre had a very fruitful relationship with Anglo-Persian, over the next three years producing a stream of reports (mostly on Soviet Russia and Germany), which were circulated through a sub-committee of the Committee of Imperial Defence. Under Morton the IIC developed a distinctive and autonomous existence which led Sinclair in October 1934 to separate it from SIS. Morton ceased to be a member of the Service and Major Humphrey Plowden took over as head of Section VI. The IIC became a customer of SIS, and Sinclair laid down that Plowden was 'to work with the I.I.C. along the same lines as other circulating sections work with the government departments which they serve'.

Although the Passport Control cover which SIS representatives enjoyed between the wars had considerable practical benefits, especially in terms of funding, by the early 1930s it was beginning to become threadbare in places. Perhaps surprisingly, Sinclair seems not to have been very concerned about this. Responding in March 1934 to a complaint from the Director of Naval Intelligence about the nature of Steptoe's real duties in China being 'so widely known', Sinclair blandly remarked that he did not think 'this really matters very much, as the activities of our Passport Control Officers all over the world are perfectly well known'. A concern for deniability, nevertheless, seems to have been part of the motivation in the expansion of United Kingdom-based agents, of whom there was a gradual increase during the 1930s, and also the creation of the Z Organisation in 1936. This was an agent-running department for obtaining intelligence on Germany and Italy set up by Sinclair under the able but extremely acerbic Claude Dansey. Dansey, who had worked for Mansfield Cumming between 1917 and 1919, had rejoined the Service to be head of the Rome station in April 1931, where he remained until March 1936. Sinclair's idea with the Z Organisation was to keep it entirely separate from the existing SIS structure, hoping that in the event of war it might have more chance of operating successfully than any of the existing networks.

Dansey set up his headquarters in Bush House, on the Aldwych, with business cover as the Export Department of Geoffrey Duveen & Co. One of his first officers, Lieutenant Commander Kenneth Cohen, a retired naval officer who had specialised in torpedo duties (when he may have come to Sinclair's notice), was a Staff College graduate and spoke good Russian, French and German. In 1937 he was 'interviewed anonymously by arrangement in my car on The Mall', by a 'Mr Mansfield', who turned out to be Dansey. Cohen afterwards described Dansey as 'a "copybook" secret service man. Dapper, establishment, Boodles [Club], poker-playing expression, bitterly cynical, but with unlimited and illogical charm available, particularly for women'.[31] The organisation operated entirely under business cover and Dansey exploited his and Sinclair's contacts in the business and commercial world to infiltrate and/or enlist people to work for them. Although the idea of a new, and more secure, wing of the Service was, perhaps, sound, the execution of the scheme left something to be desired. Recruitment appears to have been done just as haphazardly as for SIS in general, and training was rudimentary. One officer was engaged straight from Cambridge University, given a short briefing on military requirements and sent to Vienna, ostensibly working for a film company but actually to report on German order of battle and other armed service

Claude Dansey, head of station in Rome
(1931–6), who later led the 'Z Organisation'
and was Assistant Chief of SIS during the
Second World War.

targets. With no instructions on how to carry out this work and no background to help him with his cover, he simply toured Germany 'sending back what he noticed, on his travels, of German Army identifications, aircraft, radar and other equipment'.

Cohen recalled that not much was produced. 'We beavered away with various characters – mostly disreputable or impecunious – who had (or professed to have) some pretext for visiting Nazi Germany or Fascist Italy. They brought back little more than low level identifications of troops and planes.' One 'agent', who never left England, managed to send back coded postcards through an associate in Germany, before being unmasked by Dansey. Cohen himself met a couple of higher-level agents, one with contacts to Dr Schacht, 'Germany's "financial wizard"', and another German navy anti-Nazi whom Cohen had to contact in Switzerland.[32] Z Organisation also developed a naval reporting system, using British merchant navy captains on ships sailing to German and Italian ports. Briefed on specific requirements, they were provided with cameras and debriefed by a Z Organisation representative.

The 22000 Organisation was similar to Z Organisation but operated within the main SIS establishment. It started in early 1938 with two officers, the senior being Dick Ellis, and, as with Z, its primary tasks were the penetration of Germany and Italy. Agents were recruited mostly from the business, journalistic and academic world. Over the short period before the war broke out, it does not seem to have made a very great intelligence contribution. One postwar review claimed that '22000 agents produced economic intelligence on the Rhineland and Ruhr, and a certain amount of information on German Order of Battle.' A relative of the Italian Foreign Minister, Count Ciano, was considered by the Foreign Office to be 'a valuable political source'. Sinclair sent Ellis and others abroad on particular missions, including one SIS officer as a tourist to Taranto to report on the harbour's defences. One of Ellis's contacts (with whom Desmond Morton also had dealings) was a wealthy Canadian businessman in his forties, William Stephenson, who had a distinguished First World War record as a fighter pilot. In the mid-1930s, Stephenson, who later played a very significant role in SIS as head of the British Security Co-ordination in New York during the Second World War, had created his own private clandestine industrial intelligence organisation, the services of which he offered to the British government. Put into contact with

SIS (which was initially not very enthusiastic), Stephenson meanwhile set up in Stockholm the International Mining Trust (IMT), 'under cover of which he aimed to develop contacts into Germany and elsewhere to provide industrial and other intelligence'. Closer links were established after Ellis began developing the 22000 network, and up to the outbreak of the war the IMT proved quite useful in providing information on German armament potential. Ellis afterwards served for a time as Stephenson's SIS deputy in New York.[33]

In the mid-1930s a branch (Section X) was set up to tap telephone lines of embassies in London. Much of this was done in close co-operation with MI5. By 1938 the work had expanded so much that a P (or Press) Section was established to distribute the product. Sinclair and Vansittart at the Foreign Office worried about telephone security at British missions abroad and the Service was given responsibility for checking this. But with only one General Post Office telephone specialist available 'and with the general apathy and ignorance that appears to have prevailed abroad, nothing much was achieved'. Section X, nevertheless, successfully listened in to conversations to and from, and within, a large number of foreign embassies. These are variously said to have included, prior to the outbreak of war, those of Germany, Spain, Italy, Japan and the USSR. This produced quite a large volume of political, economic and military information. Conversations, for example, between the German military attachés in London and Berlin appear to have been particularly revealing, and included 'details of a reconnaissance that the former was to carry out of possible landing beaches along the South and West coasts of Ireland'.

During 1937 Sinclair, 'convinced of the inevitability of war', also initiated expansion plans for the Government Code and Cypher School (GC&CS). He instructed the School's operational head, Commander Alastair Denniston, to identify 'the right type of recruit' to reinforce GC&CS *immediately* on the outbreak of war'. Having secured Treasury sanction for '56 seniors, men or women' and '30 girls' with graduate-level knowledge of at least two relevant languages, Denniston discreetly combed British universities and mobilised his network of contacts for potential recruits. A series of courses were arranged for candidates to give them 'even a dim idea of what would be required of them'. As a result, GC&CS was crucially able to expand rapidly in the summer of 1939 to meet wartime signals intelligence demands. Though focusing more on universities, GC&CS's recruitment process was as informal and personalised as that for SIS as a whole. Frank Adcock, Professor of Ancient History at Cambridge, who had worked in the Admiralty's Room 40 during the First World War, was particularly assiduous on Denniston's behalf. One Cambridge colleague, an Italian specialist, recalled being invited to dinner by Adcock and under conditions of great secrecy being offered 'a post in an organisation working under the Foreign Office, but which was so secret that he couldn't tell me anything about it'.[34]

In April 1938 Sinclair recruited a former soldier, Captain Richard Gambier-Parry, from the telecommunications firm Philco Limited, to create SIS's Communication Section VIII. Gambier-Parry claimed that he was given the following oral instructions by Sinclair: 'I get a great deal of valuable information. They drive it round Europe in a "Carrozza" [a coach or carriage] before it reaches me. Your business here will be to do something about it – Good morning.' Section VIII's most difficult task was the provision of wireless sets for agents. Nothing suitable was available commercially, so Gambier-Parry established a small workshop and laboratory at Barnes in west London to research and develop secure portable sets. In October 1938 Head Office recognised that providing agents with wireless sets raised difficult issues about the trustworthiness of the individual, whether he was sufficiently 'intelligent' and 'could be taught Morse [code]', and how the sets would be concealed. The representative in Athens reflected the cautious line taken by several stations. For an agent to be caught with a wireless set, 'and the better the disguise, the more compromising', would be 'equivalent to a death warrant'. Apart from those rare individuals 'actuated by idealistic motives', he could not see 'many candidates coming forward'. After Gambier-Parry had sent a prototype set to Stevens at The Hague in March 1939, Head Office decided that risks now had to be taken with providing sets for agents operating in German ports, especially ones capable of reporting the departure of commerce raiders, since the 'early interception of these vessels will depend on timely warning of their departure'. Commander Russell of the Naval Section dismissed the argument that being caught with a wireless set meant an automatic death penalty as 'they already face the death penalty and I fail to see any reason why the information they obtain should deteriorate in war'. Since the Service failed to recruit *any* successful agents to report from German ports, however, this debate remained purely theoretical.

Wireless equipment for SIS stations abroad was technically less problematic but normally needed the permission of the local British minister, which was not always forthcoming. Nevertheless, good progress was made by September 1939. The first station wireless to prove its worth was that at Prague during the 1938 Czech crisis when it was the only effective means of communication, for both SIS and the Foreign Office, between Prague and London. In August–September 1939 an SIS wireless became the only link through which London received news of the rapidly changing situation until the final collapse of Poland.

Early in 1939 a main SIS communications facility, with a full twenty-four-hour service, some four transmitters and six receiving positions, was set up at the Service's new 'war station', Bletchley Park, a small country house and estate in Buckinghamshire some fifty miles north-west of London. Based on the widely held fears that any war would begin with massive enemy air attacks, contingency plans were made throughout government to relocate office functions in an emergency out of the centre of London. Sinclair bought the property on 9 June 1938 for £6,000 (£275,000 in modern values). This was clearly done on his own initiative, and there is a Service tradition that he paid for it out of his own pocket. Whether this is true is less certain. The relevant property transaction documents show him personally as the sole owner, and after he died in November 1939, apart from legacies of £3,500 to each of his two sons, his sister Evelyn inherited the remainder of his property, with a total value of £21,391. In April 1940 Evelyn (as personal representative of 'Sir Hugh Sinclair deceased') transferred Bletchley Park to William Ridley and Percy Stanley Sykes (the Service's Finance Officer) for ten shillings (fifty pence). In their turn, on 3 March 1947, Ridley and Sykes transferred the property to the Ministry of Works, again for ten shillings, all of which strongly suggests that the original purchase money had come from public, if not also SIS, funds.[35] The initial purchase price was in any case only the start. In November 1938 Sinclair noted that the cost of installing telephone and teleprinter lines to Bletchley Park was likely to cost 'several thousand Pounds'. During the Munich Crisis, partly as a precautionary measure and partly as a mobilisation exercise, Sinclair sent the Government Code and Cypher School and Head Office staff to Bletchley. He claimed afterwards to Sir Warren Fisher that it was 'the only War Station that functioned correctly during the crisis'. After the crisis most of the staff returned to London, but in August 1939 the code-breakers returned. Bletchley Park became their headquarters and the site of their great wartime triumphs.[36]

Also in the first half of 1938 Sinclair decided to set up an organisation 'to plan, prepare and, when necessary, carry out sabotage and other clandestine operations, as opposed to the gathering of intelligence'.[37] This was Section IX or D (allegedly for 'Destruction') Section. A Royal Engineer, Major Laurence Grand, was seconded to be its head. While he had no experience of intelligence work, he was described as 'a man of energy and ideas, to whose personal force tribute is paid by all who worked with him'. Grand wrote his own, wide-ranging brief, a 'preliminary survey of possibilities of sabotage' dated 31 May 1938. This consisted mainly of sabotage targets in Germany, including the electrical supply system, telephone communications, railways, 'adulteration of food supplies' and 'Agriculture, by the introduction of pests to crops or diseases to animals'. There was also a category entitled 'moral sabotage, by means of rumours, remarks causing dissatisfaction with the Nazi Party'. For this, Grand thought all that was required was 'one man in every town with an automatic telephone exchange', and suggested that, 'as the activities of this branch will only be verbal, the Jews might be persuaded to produce an organisation in peace time which will be available for this work in war'. Sinclair accepted the scheme, warning him to exercise extreme caution to avoid diplomatic incidents and to concentrate in the first instance on cutting supplies to Germany of Swedish iron ore and Romanian oil. Menzies explained SIS's thinking on this matter to French opposite numbers in February 1939. He was, he said, convinced of the need to use both propaganda and terrorism against Germany and Italy, just as they were planning to do against France and England. He admitted that there was currently no effective English propaganda in Germany, but that there were plans to distribute twenty thousand anti-Nazi 'tracts' in envelopes mailed in Germany and also to develop a German-language radio service to broadcast truthful news bulletins specially chosen to influence German public opinion. As to sabotage, SIS had been studying the subject for more than a year and Menzies believed that, in time of conflict, 'acts of terrorism' would 'crystallise' opposition to the Nazi regime and profoundly disrupt

MOST SECRET

MEMORANDUM.

For reasons connected with this Department, certain officers have been investigating the possibilities of bacteriological warfare and after reading their report it is thought that the possibilities of this form of warfare may have been under-rated, especially the destruction of our flocks by anthrax or foot and mouth disease, also the contamination of our water and milk supply.

It is understood that this matter is now dealt with by a sub-committee of the C.I.D. known as the "Emergency Public Health Laboratory Services", but, so far as can be traced, their last meeting was on May 31st, 1938, but our information on this matter may not be up-to-date.

It is considered that you might wish to ask this body whether it has considered problems on the following lines:-

A.

(1) What useful area of the British Isles could be infected by, say, 10 aircraft each carrying one ton of anthrax spores?

(2) How soon after this raid would most of our live stock be infected?

(3) What effect will the cessation of most of our milk supply have on Britain in war time?

(4) Have we, or is it necessary to have ready, the requisite stores for passive defence and/or active retaliation to attacks of this nature?

B.   As a further example -

(1) Can, say, one hundred Nazi agents supplied with bacteriological material and operating in the London Underground Railways during the rush hours, start a serious epidemic in London?

(2) Is the Prime Minister's (or any other persons' of national importance) milk boiled before use? (Milk bottles on doorsteps can be tampered with).

(3)/

SIS's concern with enemy special operations led them to consider possible biological attacks on the United Kingdom. Illustrating more innocent days, this paper reveals that in 1939 even the Prime Minister got a doorstep milk delivery.

military and economic life in Germany. Potential targets (such as factories and communications) had already been identified, as had the personnel to mount attacks (for example Communists and anarchists).[38]

SIS's consideration of offensive sabotage operations clearly also informed thinking about the defensive side. In July 1938 Sinclair sent Ismay 'Scheme D', some notes prepared by Section IX 'on the protection against sabotage of power stations and H/T [high-tension] transmission lines'. The following August he sent him a paper on bacteriological warfare, which reflected further work in Grand's section. The 'possibilities of this form of warfare', it asserted, 'may have been under-rated, especially the destruction of our flocks by anthrax or foot and mouth disease, also the contamination of our water and milk supply'. Various scenarios were raised: 'Can, say, one hundred Nazi agents supplied with bacteriological material and operating in the London Underground Railways during the rush hours, start a serious epidemic in London?' Reflecting a more innocent age, when even the prime minister had a conventional, daily doorstep milk delivery, the memorandum asked: 'Is the Prime Minister's (or any other persons' of national importance) milk boiled before use? (Milk bottles on doorsteps can be tampered with.)'

By 1939 Section IX had established a presence at Bletchley to develop sabotage material, including incendiaries, plastic explosives and fuses. Among the various sabotage plans against German targets were the destruction of lock gates on the Kiel Canal and the 'possibility of placing mustard gas on the seats of the [Berlin] Opera House before a major Nazi rally'. Over the summer of 1939 British yachtsmen were sent to reconnoitre beaches for clandestine landings from Trondheim to the Franco-Belgian frontier. D Section's activities abroad, especially contacting and briefing foreign nationals, were sometimes done with scant reference to security, and alarmed a number of British diplomatic missions. There was also a potential overlap between it and the War Office Section GSR (later to become MIR, Military Intelligence Research), which had been created essentially for the same purpose. Both organisations, for example, were planning the sabotage of the Romanian oil route up the Danube. Grand was also keen on propaganda, 'but here again enthusiasm seems to have run away with discretion' and there was overlap with the government's 'official' covert propaganda organ, the Enemy Publicity Section at Electra House on the Victoria Embankment.

SIS played an important part in the development of clandestine air photography. Towards the end of 1938 Winterbotham's Section II set up an Air Photographic Unit. This was an Anglo-French joint SIS–Deuxième Bureau venture with business cover as the Aeronautical Research and Sales Corporation. An American Lockheed plane was purchased by the French, and SIS engaged an Australian pilot, Sidney Cotton. Cotton and his team developed cutting-edge photographic techniques for air reconnaissance which provided better results than ever before. By the end of 1938 clandestine photographs were being taken of Italian bases and airfields. The Air Ministry paid for a second Lockheed and assistance was given by the RAF Experimental Establishment at Farnborough. Cotton proceeded round Europe, flying at very high altitudes over Germany and Italy, photographing large numbers of airfields and other military intelligence targets. Indeed, so successful was he that by mid-1939 there was a bottleneck in the production of this material through a shortage of trained photographic interpreters. Shortly after the outbreak of war Cotton's organisation was taken over by the Air Ministry, but SIS could claim with some justification to have been the initiator of modern high-altitude, high-speed photo-reconnaissance.[39]

PART FOUR
THE IMPACT OF WAR

10

Keeping afloat

The diary of the Section VIII officer John Darwin for 1 September 1939 recounts how the news of war was received by SIS: 'Gambier rang up 7 [a.m]. German troops over the frontier 6.30. Our 77077 (Code Germans invade Poland) worked v. well. F.O. showed "masterly inactivity".' On Sunday 3 September: 'War on Germany declared 11 a.m. B.S.T. [British Summer Time]. Usual row with F.O. asking us to transmit reams of unnecessary messages. 11.15 Air Raid warning – Staff arrived in basement & teleprinters going in 3 mins. Very satisfactory & encouraging. C.S.S. in very good heart.'[1] The declaration of war does not, however, appear to have struck very momentously at the Service's bureaucratic processes. On 4 September an officer in the Registry proposed sending out a message seeking to standardise the size of 'source slips' attached to reports,[2] and the first circular to all stations issued from the Chief after war had been declared laid down that 'applications for the supply of office furniture, office stationery, safes, etc.' should henceforth be addressed to the Accountant Officer.[3]

In keeping with the plans for the evacuation of government departments from the capital on the outbreak of war, a substantial part of the headquarters staff and Section VIII (Communications) moved to the War Station at Bletchley Park, whither the Government Code and Cypher School had gone in August. To facilitate the penetration of Germany, Dansey and most of his Z Organisation moved to Switzerland. As both the Service and GC&CS expanded rapidly in the early months of the war, and with Bletchley Park 'bursting at the seams', other outstations were established. Section VIII moved from Bletchley to Whaddon Hall, about five miles away. Section V and the Registry were subsequently transferred to St Albans. When the expected German air raids did not materialise (and ironically before the London blitz began), there was a drift back, so that by March 1940 the main body of headquarters staff had returned to central London. Even so, significant parts of SIS remained dispersed, bringing bureaucratic and logistical problems for the rest of the war.

Change at the top

The sixty-six-year-old Sinclair, who had been suffering from cancer of the spleen, was taken into hospital in late October. He demonstrated stylish sangfroid to the very end. On the morning of 4 November he sent a message to a friend saying: 'First bulletin: Nearly dead.' So he was, for he died later that day.[4] 'Life has been made even more bloody by the death of our beloved CSS,' wrote John Darwin. 'He died at 4.30 pm. He is quite definitely irreplaceable. There will never be anyone like him.' It had been clear for a while that his days were numbered, and there were evidently concerns within the Service about the succession. On the day Sinclair died, Malcolm Woollcombe, head of the Political Section, which dealt most closely with the Foreign Office, saw the Permanent Under-Secretary, Sir Alexander Cadogan, 'to protest about idea of anyone being brought in from outside to succeed "C"'. There is no evidence Woollcombe had any particular outside individual in mind. He may, however, have pressed the case for Menzies, Sinclair's de facto deputy and the obvious internal candidate, since Cadogan noted in his diary that he was 'not satisfied that Menzies is the man'. On 5 November Cadogan saw Menzies, who handed him a sealed letter which Sinclair had written two days before. 'In the event of my death, or of anything happening to me which will prevent my continuing in my present appointment,' it read, 'I wish to place on record that, in my considered opinion, the most suitable individual, in every respect, to take my place, is Colonel Stewart Graham Menzies, DSO, MC.' Perhaps fearing for the forty-nine-year-old Menzies's chances, Sinclair took care to copy this letter to Sir Horace Wilson at the Treasury and the Chief of the Imperial General Staff, Sir Edmund Ironside.[5]

Despite Sinclair's efforts, the job was no shoe-in. Horace Wilson reported that Hankey (who had been made a member of the War Cabinet in

Written the day before he died, Sir Hugh Sinclair's letter recommending that Stewart Menzies should succeed him.

September 1939) had 'some doubts about Menzies', and suggested that Brigadier Jasper Harker (head of MI5's counter-espionage and counter-subversion division) might have to be considered, as well as Admiral John Godfrey (the Director of Naval Intelligence (DNI)), of whom he had

heard 'some good opinions'. Cadogan, while making it clear both that
the Foreign Secretary would make the final decision and that the post
should be filled 'with the least possible delay', asked the three service ministries for their views. Displaying army solidarity, the War Office backed
Menzies. Air put forward Major Archibald Boyle, currently Deputy
Director of Air Intelligence, who had been engaged 'on intelligence work
at the Air Ministry since the last war'. Winston Churchill, the First Lord
of the Admiralty, proposed Captain Gerard Muirhead-Gould (naval attaché in Berlin, 1933–6). But, in what Cadogan described in his diary as
a 'tiresome' letter, Churchill also waxed eloquent both about the matter
generally and about the deficiencies of SIS. 'According to custom,' he
wrote, 'this appointment should fall to a Naval Officer.' During Sinclair's
'declining years', he asserted, 'very great shortcomings were experienced
by the Admiralty in the service we have received'. Cryptography was 'a
blank so far as we are concerned, and has become mainly political', and
he considered that the condition of naval intelligence was currently 'altogether inferior to what we had in the last war'. Churchill, Cadogan
grumbled, 'ought to have enough of his own to do without butting into
other people's business'.[6]

  Although Churchill told Cadogan that he had 'been thinking a great
deal' about the matter, and that he had been 'most favourably impressed' by
Muirhead-Gould's 'characteristics, as well as by his record', the Admiralty
nomination had its odd aspects. The DNI, Godfrey, appears to have been
ignored completely as a candidate. Muirhead-Gould himself had a 'weak
heart' which disbarred him from a sea command, and in 1940 apparently led him to be posted as Captain-in-Charge at Sydney, Australia.
Cadogan, moreover, received a damning report on him from a Foreign
Office source who said Muirhead-Gould had not been 'a conspicuous
success' as an attaché. He was of 'a suspicious and slightly irascible nature
which leads him to look for insults, real or imaginary'. While captain of
HMS *Devonshire* he had acquired the nickname 'Captain Bligh' (of mutiny on the *Bounty* fame). Unexpectedly, perhaps, he was 'an expert on
petit point, to which he devotes quite a lot of his spare time'. Cadogan
caustically considered this was 'the thing most strongly in his favour'.[7]

  Who else was in the frame? An undated note in Cadogan's handwriting lists five names. There were three generals – Robert Haining,
William Bartholomew and Thomas Humphreys – who had each served

as Director or Deputy Director of Military Operations and Intelligence; Lord Davidson, former chairman of the Conservative Party and a long-time confidant of Stanley Baldwin, who would have been regarded as a safe pair of hands; and Sir William Wiseman, the SIS representative in the USA during the First World War. It has been suggested that Claude Dansey was interested in the job, but Sir Ronald Campbell, the British ambassador in Paris, having spoken to Dansey (whom he had known since 1914 and thought was 'reliable'), told Cadogan that Dansey did '<u>not</u> want the job himself and admits that he is too old for it' (he was sixty-three). Nevertheless, observing that Dansey had 'worked for "C" for 25 years or so' and 'knows the thing inside out', Campbell thought it might be worth while Cadogan speaking to him, which he did on 16 November when he presumably sought his views on the succession. 'I'm sure he's very clever & very subtle,' wrote Cadogan in his diary afterwards, 'but I have no proof of it because I can't hear 10% of what he says.'[8]

After three weeks, Cadogan began to worry about the delay in coming to a decision. Menzies, he thought, 'was in a difficult position, and it's silly of everyone to go on funking Winston'. Finally, on 28 November at a meeting attended by the Prime Minister and the three service ministers, the Foreign Secretary Lord Halifax 'played his hand well and won the trick'. It was unanimously agreed that Menzies should have the job, but also that there should be 'some enquiry' into the organisation of the Service. The next day Halifax saw Menzies, offered him the job, urged him to 'take an early opportunity of having a frank discussion' with both the Air Minister and the First Lord, neither of whom was satisfied with the information their departments were getting from SIS, and told him of the proposal that 'two members of the War Cabinet, Lord Chatfield [a former First Sea Lord, currently Minister for Co-ordination of Defence] and Lord Hankey, might be asked to go into the matter [of SIS organisation] and to give us all the benefit of their great experience'. According to one member of the Service, John Darwin, the appointment of Menzies was 'a tremendous relief to us all. Nothing can replace old Quex but SGM has never really had a chance with such an overwhelming character as his commanding officer, during the past fifteen years.' It is, he added, 'wonderful to think that, after the vicissitudes of the last few weeks, we have got somebody that one can trust at the head of things'.[9]

Responding to customer departments

The Service ministries' criticisms of SIS around the time of Sinclair's death were sharpened by the very embarrassing Venlo incident of 9 November 1939 when two SIS officers, having been enticed into a meeting with what they thought were representatives of German army opposition to Hitler, were captured on the Dutch–German frontier (see chapter 11). Menzies naturally sprang to the Service's defence, but he thought the timing of the complaints was appalling. 'If the Service has lost the confidence of the Departments,' he wrote to Gladwyn Jebb on 14 November, 'it seems monstrous that those in charge have waited the departure of the Chief before launching their criticisms.' He was clearly very anxious about the overall position of SIS and told Guy Liddell of MI5 that 'every sort of intrigue' was 'going on by those who want to take over the organisation' and that criticisms were 'being made from every quarter from ignorant people'.[10]

To defend the Service's recent work, Menzies assembled a twenty-six-page document with reports from section heads. He wished to stress, 'with all possible emphasis, that the S.I.S. work has been carried on in enemy, or potential enemy, countries, under very great difficulties, faced as we have been, by an all-powerful and ruthless enemy contre-espionage service'. He noted that in the 1914–18 war secret service efforts to penetrate Germany had been 'a complete failure' (though the prewar agent TR/16 had continued to transmit reports), whereas 'in this war, in spite of well nigh insuperable obstacles, the flow of information from inside Germany, for all Departments' had been 'maintained unceasingly'. He added that 'one of our chief successes of recent years' had been the penetration of foreign 'Secret Services and the utilisation of their agents'. Perhaps with Venlo in mind, he asserted that this was 'so as to reduce to a minimum the number of misadventures which would otherwise be attributed to, and embarrass, H.M.G. [His Majesty's Government]'. In what appears to be a veiled reference to the cryptological help received from the Poles and the French (which helped GC&CS to crack the Enigma cypher machine), he said that 'we are about to reap the fruits' of liaison with other secret services, 'which should be of inestimable benefit to the Air Ministry within a few weeks, and probably to the Admiralty within a month or two'.[11]

Nor was this the only achievement. Menzies claimed on the economic side that the Service was about 'to obtain complete details of the traffic on the Rhine and Danube, apart from numerous other schemes on behalf of the M.E.W. [Ministry of Economic Warfare], which are rapidly ripening now that funds are available'. He also noted that since its establishment only 'about eighteen months ago' the Communications Section VIII had developed to such an extent that it had 'no rival in the world'. It had been the 'sole means of communication for the Military section during the Polish campaign', and a 'very intricate' wireless scheme was nearing completion 'to ensure a regular flow of information should the Low Countries be invaded'. Rex Howard also emphasised communications. 'In face of considerable difficulty', he wrote, wireless facilities had been developed, so that the Service was now in 'communication with the majority of our representatives abroad'. In addition, 'the use of agents' W/T sets has been developed, and we now have a certain number functioning in enemy territory, and also from neutral countries'. As a sideswipe against captious criticism (and stressing the dangers and difficulties of secret service work was an understandable reaction), Howard went on to suggest that 'if the individual or individuals who are now attacking S.I.S. efficiency, will use their imagination, would they kindly picture themselves in the position of an individual who is operating a set in one of the foregoing countries, with all the penalties likely to ensue if discovered'.

Along with this robust defence of the Service, Howard added a cautionary note about the reporting of German warship movements, which throws instructive light on both the limitations and the ambitions of early wartime espionage. In the 'last war, owing to W/T interception, immediate information was received when ships were raising steam, and their movements when they left harbour'. Because the Germans now maintained wireless silence, this was no longer possible, 'and consequently the Admiralty have appeared to become more dependent on our information, which can only be obtained from resident agents in Germany equipped with W/T sets, or sending agents into Germany, or communicating with agents resident in Germany by means of couriers'. As this presented very considerable difficulties (to put it mildly), Howard considered 'that ship movements must be obtained to a much larger extent by air reconnaissance by day and patrols by night. In spite of repeated endeavours, it has not yet been found possible to establish a reliable agent in one of the

German naval ports who could be equipped with a W/T set in communication with us.'

Other reports by the heads of the Circulating Sections highlighted two perennial problems for the Service. These concerned the nature of the intelligence requested and obtained, and the process through which the intelligence was provided. In the first case there was the contrast between longer-term political and strategic intelligence and much more focused and immediate technical information, together with what might be called tactical intelligence. The former category was generally in most demand from the Foreign Office, while the latter was of greater interest for the armed services. This was especially so in wartime when, for example, intelligence about the likelihood of German offensive operations, or some general estimate of enemy capabilities, was of rather less compelling interest than detailed information about a specific weapon, or timely and accurate warning about an actual attack. But SIS was able to provide this kind of short-term intelligence only if it had a rapid and secure communications system. SIS officers, moreover, also complained that some of the reports they did manage to provide were simply ignored, or apparently disbelieved, by the service ministries.

There were problems, too, with the processing of information. There was a tendency on the part of the Service Liaison Sections simply to pass on raw intelligence to their customer departments, without comment or any assessment of the material's reliability. By contrast, Malcolm Woollcombe and the Political Section collated information before forwarding it to the Foreign Office, and 'made a point of eliminating all items of doubtful credibility or minor importance'. Apart from the fact that SIS was apparently better able to provide the kind of intelligence favoured by the Foreign Office, this procedure also appears to have contributed to the higher reputation the Service maintained with that department. On the other hand, the elimination or discounting of information *believed* to be unreliable or of only secondary importance could contribute to a situation where the Service was providing its customers with information about the world as the customers *believed* it to be, rather than necessarily the real picture. This was the nub of the producer–consumer dilemma which is a constant concern for any intelligence organisation and which for SIS continued throughout the war. It was constantly argued (with reason) that close co-ordination was highly desirable between the producers and the consumers of intelligence. Only then could the intelligence agencies fully understand what was required and thus meet their customers' requirements. But if the relationship were too close, and the understanding too complete, then there was a danger that the intelligence sought and provided might merely reflect the preconceived needs of the consumers.

Whatever the potential dangers of too intimate a relationship between producer and consumer, it was clearly necessary for SIS to maintain close, if not also cordial, relations with the Foreign Office, the service ministries and the Ministry of Economic Warfare. This was also appreciated by the realists in the customer departments. One such was Admiral Godfrey, who contacted Menzies (before he had succeeded as Chief) with what could be interpreted as a conciliatory peace-offering from a potential rival and critic. 'I have been meaning to write to you for some time', he wrote on 18 November, 'about various aspects of intelligence work, which before the war I used to discuss with Admiral Sinclair.' Noting that 'we have a strong advocate in the First Lord' (Churchill since September 1939), Godfrey proposed that the War Cabinet should be pressed to provide greatly increased funding for SIS: 'The whole question is, I suppose, one of money and unless money can be made available in sufficient quantities, I doubt whether we are likely to get our intelligence.'

Having offered his support for SIS, Godfrey then provided Menzies with a list of the Admiralty's six 'primary needs'. First was 'knowledge of the whereabouts of the more important German Naval units in and about German ports'. Godfrey, apparently less well informed (or less optimistic) than Menzies about the signals intelligence possibilities, argued that 'whether or not Cryptography will ever again give us the knowledge we had of German movements in the late war', a special effort should be put into placing agents in German ports as well as 'in the acquisition of documents at their various Naval Headquarters and in Berlin'. Next Godfrey wanted knowledge of German shipping movements through 'the Belts and Sound' (the Danish islands at the entrance to the Baltic Sea) 'and within sight of the Norwegian, Swedish and Danish coasts'. He stressed one particular interest: 'You can well understand that information concerning the passage down the Norwegian coast of ships carrying iron ore to Germany is vital, but without knowledge of these ships' movements, the Navy can do very little.' Godfrey, who noted that 'since the war started only 8 reports of movements through the Sound and Belts have reached me, and 3 only regarding movements on the Norwegian Coast from CX [secret intelligence] sources', quoted a letter from Coastal Command showing that the air force were 'thinking on similar lines'. 'We should', they wrote, 'have Agents at prominent points who will give us information of the passage of any big merchant ships or men of war.'

Godfrey's third priority was for information about German submarine construction, as he was 'still without information whether Germany is embarking on a large U-boat ship building programme, or is going into mass production, or is devoting her resources to other things'. He complained, too, that he found himself 'in great difficulties when asked, as I am, for information on this subject, as it is extremely difficult to say why it cannot be obtained'. The fourth priority was the 'state of readiness of German Naval units', which he recognised was 'a difficult thing to find out'. Fifth was 'the progress and state of completion of the [German battleship] BISMARCK and other ships building and projected'. 'Will the BISMARCK be completed early or late next year? Our own big-ship-building programme is based on the answer to this question. If early, KG5 [the battleship *King George V*] and other ships must be accelerated and work on smaller units correspondingly retarded. These', he added, 'are obviously decisions of the greatest national importance.' Finally he wanted information on German mines. The Germans, he asserted, had 'invented a new and particularly vicious mine, probably on the magnetic principle'. If one of these could be obtained, or drawings of one, 'we could without doubt produce the antidote'. 'Money cannot possibly be any object when approaching this problem, as our daily losses are formidable and show no diminution. The matter is one of the most vital importance and I am constantly being bombarded with demands for information which I cannot satisfy.'

Godfrey's shopping list was a real challenge to SIS, which, alas, was unable to be of much immediate help, though the Naval Section insisted that forty-nine (not three) Norwegian reports had been received and an observation report on the *Bismarck* had been made on 11 November. It is clear that in this respect the loss of TR/16 was a grievous blow. A German magnetic mine was, however, obtained, but not by SIS. On 23 November a mine dropped by a German aircraft off Shoeburyness on the Thames estuary was recovered and dissected, after which effective counter-measures were developed.[12] Even when good intelligence was acquired, it was not always believed. One example cited concerned drawings that were passed to the Admiralty early in 1939 purporting to be a new type of German torpedo. The Admiralty dismissed these as fabrications, but in May 1940 the Director of Naval Intelligence admitted that a captured German torpedo was 'practically the same as that shown on the drawings sent by S.I.S. early last year'.

The Hankey review

In December 1939 the inquiry mooted at the time of Menzies's appointment was entrusted to Lord Hankey with Sir Alexander Cadogan's private secretary, Gladwyn Jebb, as secretary. Like previous private secretaries to the Permanent Under-Secretary, Jebb was a crucial linking figure between the Foreign Office and clandestine agencies. Hankey's son, Christopher, 'took the minutes of all the meetings',[13] and his notes of the evidence from the main customer departments give a vivid picture of how secret intelligence was processed and how SIS was generally regarded in early 1940.

At the beginning of February Hankey interviewed Godfrey, and this in particular allows us to see how matters had advanced over the ten weeks or so since the DNI had written to Menzies. Liaison between the Admiralty and SIS had improved with the secondment of two officers to the Service (including one of Godfrey's deputies). Regarding actual intelligence, however, the Admiralty were still 'in rather a poor way', with Godfrey's requirements of November still being ill provided. There was some progress in Denmark where 'an organisation was being built up under difficulties', and in Norway 'the position of ground intelligence was rather better', but the only area where SIS had been able to provide 'good help' was information about ships in neutral ports. Godfrey followed up his interview with a letter to Hankey and a note on 'sources of information'. Clearly well disposed towards SIS in general, Godfrey made allowances for its deficiencies. 'I should like to say', he wrote, 'that many criticisms in the past have been due to causes beyond the control of the S.I.S., who, <u>if they had had the money</u>, could have provided us with a splendid organisation in existence when the war broke out and capable of rapid expansion.'[14]

In the accompanying paper Godfrey thought about the future: 'I do not know what can be achieved in Germany. Their contra-espionage organisation is extremely good, but abroad there may be a chance of catching up, if we are prepared to spend in neutral countries the same knowledge and money as the Gestapo [*sic*] are credited with doing now.' Godfrey thought that an organisation could be established in South America and the Middle East 'that will bear fruit in the near future and compete on equal terms with the Gestapo. We may', he added, 'have to use their own methods, but I am convinced that in this, as in other realms, we can beat the Germans at their own game and improvise where they rely on years of preparation.' For all the current difficulties, Godfrey remained optimistic. Naval liaison with SIS was 'good' and 'development is being pursued with vigour, and although nothing can make up for lack of money in peace-time, I am still hopeful that, given reasonable luck, improvements may be achieved during the forthcoming year'.[15] Godfrey's observations to Hankey (which he niftily copied to Menzies) must have been welcome indeed to SIS, but, in truth, there was not yet much of substance to rely on: improvisation, 'reasonable luck' and catching up with the Germans. These were scarcely guaranteed to bring victory, even if they fell securely within the fine old British tradition of muddling through.

The army view was similar. The recently appointed Director of Military Intelligence, General 'Paddy' Beaumont-Nesbitt, told Hankey that 'relations between his Department and the Secret Intelligence Service were, generally speaking, admirable and that, so far as he was concerned, the S.I.S. gave fairly good results'. 'Little information', however, was being supplied about Germany 'and the position was not as good as it ought to be in Eastern Germany and Poland'. While 'political information of a general character was good', on the technical side 'this was not the case'. The War Office wanted 'to check up on figures for stores, munitions and implements of war', but, while 'there were plenty of rumours', what 'they really wanted was photostat copies of documents or other positive proof'. Beaumont-Nesbitt confirmed that the army did not want 'interpretation'. In his view 'the S.I.S. should not "interpret" information at all: it should confine itself to producing facts'.

Of the three service departments the air force was by far the least happy. The Director of Air Intelligence, Air Commodore Kenneth Buss, bluntly told Hankey that he was 'generally dissatisfied' with the intelligence received.[16] This was especially so from within Germany itself. Perhaps remembering Frederick Winterbotham's agent 479 driving round Germany trying to spot Luftwaffe airfields, he 'could not understand why there was such a general lack of "ground" information and thought [though he cannot have thought very hard about this] that even under war conditions it would have been comparatively simple to get people to go within sight of an aerodrome and report what aeroplanes were there'. He reported that most of the questionnaires submitted to SIS by the air force 'remained entirely unanswered, more especially when, as was generally the case, technical information was required'. Buss believed that while the current air liaison officer (Winterbotham) was 'regarded as quite good' (though 'entirely "C"'s man'), matters could be improved both by introducing more RAF officers into SIS and by training SIS officers who currently had no 'specialised air knowledge'.

As well as investigating service needs, Hankey also interviewed Desmond Morton, by now Director of Intelligence at the Ministry of Economic Warfare. Morton (a former SIS officer himself) was very negative. SIS, he said, 'was not producing the material required', especially 'definite information', such as 'copies of the customs returns of certain neutral countries' or reports on 'occasional surreptitious cargoes'. Rather reflecting Buss's complaint about the lack of technical expertise on the part of SIS's representatives in the field, Morton thought that they simply 'did not know precisely what sort of information was required'. SIS had 'essentially a military character, with "a strong political adjunct" in the shape of Mr. Woollcombe'. The Economic Section, by contrast, 'was not perhaps very strong and ought to be reinforced'. The problem was 'largely one of liaison', though he admitted that 'there had lately been signs of improvement in this direction'.

While each of the customer departments consulted by Hankey had reservations about what Morton called 'S.I.S. intelligence, strictly speaking' – human intelligence (humint) – the situation regarding signals intelligence was much more favourable. Morton said that commercial intercepts were 'much the brightest side'. By this means his department had 'obtained a very full knowledge of the present state of Russo-German commercial relations' and 'conclusive evidence' that 'the Russians had so far provided nothing of what the Germans required'. Telephone intercepts, which Morton likewise received from SIS, 'were also very useful'.

While Air Intelligence reported that they had obtained 'a great deal of information' from GC&CS, Admiral Godfrey said that 'cryptography' had 'so far not provided any good naval material'. This 'was certainly not due to any shortcoming on the part of the Government Code and Cypher School', who were 'in any case, making very promising progress'. But for Godfrey 'the one really bright spot' was 'the "'Y' side",[17] in particular the intercepted signals and call signs, which the Admiralty found of the greatest possible use. All praise for this state of affairs', he added, 'was due to Colonel Gambier-Parry.'

In addition to investigating SIS's intelligence-gathering activities, Hankey also looked into the more problematic (as was increasingly to be the case) matter of covert action, and in particular Colonel Laurence Grand's special operations Section IX or D. Hankey interviewed Grand 'in the company of Colonel Menzies, with the main object of trying to discover exactly what his activities were'. Grand said that his chief propaganda function was the distribution of material in Germany, and for this 'he employed various channels – Catholics, Junkers, Socialists and the like'. His section made special efforts to ensure 'that the paper and ink should, if possible, resemble German materials'. He said that 'about 70–80,000 "pieces" were now being distributed monthly in Germany' and asserted that there were 'three secret presses run by anti-Nazis in Prague, Hamburg and Berlin', but admitted that he 'had actually no control' over their output. When pressed by Hankey, Grand evasively replied that he 'did not think' these presses had been 'entirely quiescent'.

Grand argued that the dissemination of propaganda in neutral countries was almost as important as that in Germany. His main operation was based in Belgrade where he said he 'managed to reach "large sections of the population by indirect means", notably a private press, a whispering campaign and making use of commercial agents. A press agency had also been established.' Hankey asked Grand how much all this was costing. Grand replied that he 'found it impossible to distinguish between expenditure on propaganda and that on sabotage', but 'until recently he had been spending at the rate of about £11,000 a month on all his activities'. Menzies said that he was 'himself going into Colonel Grand's finances, and would be in a position before long to give a more definite picture'.

Lord Hankey's report, delivered on 11 March 1940, broadly gave SIS a clean bill of health. No fundamental changes were recommended concerning the Service's core human intelligence functions and Hankey specially mentioned 'the strong impression I have derived of the healthy spirit of loyalty, esprit de corps and devotion to duty which animates all ranks of S.S. [the Secret Service]'. This was no doubt a great relief to Menzies, who had evidently been extremely concerned that the very existence of the Service was at risk. On 14 February he had sent Jebb a 'brief historical sketch' of SIS which affirmed 'that success in S.S. work must always be the result of years of patient work, and not of improvisation'. Menzies warned Jebb that 'the machine can be destroyed by a stroke of the pen, lessons can be forgotten overnight, but I can personally conceive of no greater catastrophe from a national point of view'.[18]

Clearly Jebb and Hankey heeded this Cassandra-like warning, and Menzies's own responses to criticisms of SIS were included in the final report. Hankey noted Air Intelligence's desire for 'more information as to the numbers of aircraft present on German aerodromes'. He remarked that 'at first sight' this would 'appear to be relatively easy information to obtain', but he had been informed 'that the Germans exercise the utmost precaution to prevent any approach by strangers to their aerodromes'. Not only was this an unrealistic complaint, therefore, but Hankey thought it largely superfluous. 'As a matter of fact,' he added, 'the Air Intelligence Service is well informed about the location of the German air forces from a source which it is unnecessary to disclose.'[19] To the Air Ministry's complaint about the lack of technical intelligence, Hankey reported SIS's observation that not only was 'a certain amount of information of a detailed character . . . already supplied', but that it took 'years to develop regular and dependable sources' for specific technical information. 'The funds available before the war were not sufficient for this and it is extremely difficult to build up the necessary contacts in time of war.' It would take a long time 'before the machine can be built up afresh in Poland and Czecho-Slovakia and even in Holland, where the Venloo [sic] incident has badly dislocated the organisation'. 'I do not think', commented Hankey, 'that Colonel Menzies' explanations can be contested.'

Despite his broad support for SIS, Hankey appreciated that improvements could be made in the higher co-ordination of intelligence and in liaison with its customers. For the former he proposed that there should be a monthly meeting of the Permanent Under-Secretary at the

Foreign Office, the Directors of Intelligence of the armed services and the Ministry of Economic Warfare, and the Chief of SIS. This body would discuss policy and review the collection and processing of secret intelligence generally. Hankey had originally thought that this should be linked to the Joint Intelligence Sub-Committee (which had been set up before the war to co-ordinate the armed services' intelligence), 'but Colonel Menzies pointed out that from the earliest days S.S. had, for vital reasons of secrecy, deliberately been kept aloof from regular Government Committees such as the Committee of Imperial Defence and the Chiefs of Staffs organisation, and that meetings on a less formal basis . . . would be preferable'. As for liaison, Hankey argued that the development of closer relations between the customer departments and SIS (for example by the secondment of officers) was desirable and 'should create a closer mutual understanding between all concerned'. While the navy and the army were more or less satisfied with the existing arrangements, Hankey recommended 'the temporary introduction into S.S. of new blood from the Air Staff'.

None of Hankey's findings so far was very contentious and his con-clusions regarding signals intelligence were equally uncontroversial. He recommended no changes or developments at all for the cryptographical work of GC&CS, although he did propose that, because there had been an enormous expansion of sigint work, a separate 'Y' Committee should be established to oversee and co-ordinate the technical interception side of things.[20] Covert action (which Hankey called 'subterranean activities') had been 'forced on the Government by the conditions of modern war-fare', and had proved to be 'by far the most difficult of the activities of [the] S.S. to assess correctly'. 'At first sight,' he observed, 'the natural in-stinct of any human person is to recoil from this undesirable business as something he would rather know nothing about.' But he then provided the classic rationale for any kind of dirty tricks: if the enemy do it, so must we. The Germans, he wrote, 'have brought the development of sab-otage and kindred subterranean services to a high pitch of efficiency and it is unavoidable to maintain them ourselves unless we are to be placed at a serious disadvantage'.

Hankey noted that propaganda and sabotage were entrusted to Section IX. So far as 'large scale sabotage' was concerned, it was 'too early to ex-press an opinion as to the efficiency of this Section as, up to the present

time, none of the planned major operations have been put into practice'. Rather ambiguously, he added that 'when called upon to produce
schemes for particular operations at short notice, the Section has displayed ingenuity and resource'. Some 'useful' small-scale sabotage had
been achieved 'on the Danube and on the Polish Railways, particularly in
Galicia', where communications between Germany, Romania and Russia
had been 'hampered to a considerable extent'. He noted, however, the
friction which had arisen between Section IX and MIR in the War Office
and recommended that Menzies and the Director of Military Intelligence
should ensure 'the closest co-operation and pooling of ideas' between the
two organisations. As for propaganda, Hankey found himself 'on much
more delicate ground'. Although both Grand and, apparently, Menzies
had put up a vigorous argument for SIS to continue to produce and distribute material, Hankey felt that the production of propaganda should
be left to the existing Foreign Office organisation and that SIS should be
responsible for its distribution only in 'enemy countries and Russia'. There
was clearly also a worry about Grand's maverick independent-mindedness. In order to ensure 'complete mutual understanding' between the
Foreign Office organisation and SIS, it was proposed that weekly meetings should be held, and that 'if any difficulties arise which cannot be
settled jointly' they should be reported to Hankey himself to sort out.

   One of the problems Hankey had in producing any sort of definitive report was the fact that most of the issues raised – for example that of liaison
with the service ministries – were actually being addressed while he was
conducting the inquiry. Menzies, too, had begun his time as Chief with
some administrative reorganisation. Hankey remarked that on appointment Menzies had been 'considerably overloaded with immediate charge
of the War Station as well as of headquarters', but had 'now carried out
considerable measures of decentralisation'. Colonel Vivian had been confirmed as head of the War Station at Bletchley and 'Deputy Director [sic]',
for which Hankey thought him 'admirably qualified'. Claude Dansey had
'taken over the control of a number of sections which previously reported
direct to Colonel Menzies'. These included all agents run from London,
as well as the Italian and Swiss stations. Dansey, while continuing in
charge of the Z Organisation based in Switzerland, came to London
to be Assistant Chief (ACSS). In February 1940 Rex Howard became
Menzies's chief staff officer. But there was no systematic reorganisation of

the Service and its ramshackle peacetime structure continued essentially unaltered into the war. It reflected a high degree of clumsy ad hoccery, combining individual specialisms and preferences with sections created to meet immediate, short-term requirements, rather than as a result of any cool and logical assessment of the Service needs and functions.

If after the completion of Hankey's report Menzies hoped for a breathing space, during which he could settle down and develop the Service to meet wartime demands, he was to be disappointed, as the dramatic German drive into Scandinavia, the Low Countries and France once more put SIS under severe pressure. On 9 April 1940 German forces invaded Denmark and Norway, swiftly occupying all of the former and much of the latter. On 23 April, Sir Samuel Hoare, the Air Minister, and the only Cabinet minister to have been an SIS officer, wrote to Hankey that he had 'been a good deal worried by the fact that we had no serious warning from S.I.S. or other intelligence sources of the German invasion of Norway'. Hoare said that there had been some Air Intelligence reports indicating 'that something out of the ordinary' was taking place on 6–7 April and that these had 'of course' been passed on to the Admiralty and the War Office. He felt that the Joint Intelligence Sub-Committee should be used to collate 'the various reports received by the Air Ministry and by other Departments' and comment on 'the mass of information which is circulated to the War Cabinet and the Chiefs of Staff'. This raised two issues: the acquisition of intelligence and its processing. Hankey responded quickly on both matters. He asked Menzies to comment on the first and in the meantime told Hoare he agreed that the Joint Intelligence Sub-Committee should produce more complete appreciations. With a deft sideswipe at Hoare's own ministry, however, he added that so far as assessment was concerned it was 'the job of the Intelligence Departments of the Services' to weigh secret service information 'with intelligence from other sources, such as diplomatic channels and air reconnaissance'. He recalled 'that for months past we have been receiving warnings' of German force concentrations in Baltic ports, yet he was afraid 'that our Service Authorities have never taken the possibility of an attack on Denmark and Norway sufficiently seriously'.[21]

The very next day Menzies saw Hankey and gave him a report 'showing the information that had become available and had been sent forward prior to the Scandinavian invasion'. Hankey was 'greatly impressed with the Note', and passed it on to Hoare. 'In my opinion,' he commented, 'S.I.S. present a cast iron case. They have given warnings which, in the aggregate, are as definite as you could expect to receive.' He pointed out that SIS did not take responsibility 'for forming appreciations on the material they submit. That is the job of the Service Departments . . . When S.I.S. have sent the information to the Heads of the Intelligence Departments in the Services they have done their job.' Hankey bluntly observed that the service Directors of Intelligence had 'to see that those responsible for plans and operations get the intelligence in the right form', and he rather suspected 'that that is where the fault lies', thus placing the matter firmly back in Hoare's departmental lap. Hankey, however, was too old a Whitehall dog needlessly to antagonise a fellow minister. 'It may be', he observed, 'that intelligence and operations are not quite sufficiently linked up', and he therefore strongly supported Hoare's 'idea of intelligence appreciations'.[22]

Hankey, nevertheless, was sufficiently concerned about the processing of intelligence that he thought the matter should be taken up with the Prime Minister, Neville Chamberlain. He sent Menzies's report to Sir Horace Wilson, observing that although most of the intelligence had been sent to the Directorate of Naval Intelligence 'we did not get any warnings as far as I can recollect from the Admiralty'. It is, repeated Hankey, 'not the business of S.S. to comment on the facts. They merely furnish them to the Directors of Intelligence of the Service Departments whose business it is to send them to the appropriate authorities. I am not satisfied', he concluded, 'that the Services have done their job very effectively.' Wilson and Hankey discussed the matter with Chamberlain, who agreed that, if possible, the Joint Intelligence Sub-Committee (JIC) should be instructed to maintain 'a running and connected story based upon such Intelligence material as seems to point to the need for action'.[23]

Whatever direction Neville Chamberlain may have been able to give to the work of the JIC, it was overtaken by further events on the Continent after the Germans invaded Holland, Belgium, Luxembourg and France on 10 May. Chamberlain resigned the same day and was replaced by Winston Churchill, whose 'galvanic energy' was to transform the central direction of the British war effort. Churchill's longstanding interest in intelligence matters was underscored by the transfer of Desmond Morton from the Ministry of Economic Warfare to the 10 Downing Street staff and his appointment 'to keep personal liaison' between Churchill and SIS.[24] On 3 June 1940 Morton attended the first meeting of what was called the Secret Service Committee. Also present were Cadogan, Hankey, the three service Intelligence Directors, Menzies, Lord Lloyd (Colonial Secretary) and Gladwyn Jebb. On the agenda was 'the re-organisation of the S.I.S. machine' necessitated by the German occupation of the coast-line from northern Norway to the English Channel, and 'the means of continuing S.I.S. activities' following the anticipated entry of Italy into the war (which actually happened on 10 June). Judging from the rather sketchy record of the meeting, in the event it appears mainly to have involved Menzies defending SIS's wartime performance:

> Colonel Menzies made a statement on the subject of communications with various organisations which he had now established behind the German lines from the extreme north of Norway to Belgium. He also described his organisation in Baltic ports, Finland and Sweden, together with the strengthening of his machine which had been accomplished in the Iberian Peninsula. Some mention was also made of the S.I.S. organisation in Italy, Greece and Turkey.
>
> Various questions were asked of Colonel Menzies, notably in regard to the presentation of reports, the manner in which they reached the authorities concerned, the exact use made of intercepts and the way in which they are linked up with other information, and the functions of the Joint Intelligence Committee. Some discussion also ensued on the part which the S.I.S. might play in the event of an invasion of Great Britain.[25]

The co-ordination and processing of intelligence was clearly an important issue, which Hankey had evidently intended should be addressed by his proposed monthly meetings. But the Secret Service Committee never really got off the ground. It was eight months before a second meeting (in March 1941), and no further meetings were held that year. The scheme failed in the first place because of SIS's traditional reluctance to become involved in any formal reporting structure. This was not just a matter of convenience (though it was undoubtedly that too); it stemmed from a desire to avoid what might readily turn into a mechanism for government departments merely to criticise the Service. There was also a genuine security aspect, in which the integrity and value of SIS was protected by its maintaining the lowest-possible profile, even within government itself. SIS, thus, could best keep up with its customers' requirements by regular, informal meetings and liaison. The problem (as is inevitably the case with any secret intelligence organisation at any time) was how security, with its accompanying lack of institutional and individual definition, could best be reconciled with the efficient and effective integration of the Service and its functions into the wider government bureaucracy.

Concerns about security also contributed to a situation where SIS's role in providing intelligence was not always acknowledged when customer departments used it in their own reports. The issue surfaced early in August 1940, after Anthony Eden (the Secretary of State for War) had complained in Cabinet that he was getting 'no information from France' and Churchill had received a report from General Spears, his personal representative with General Charles de Gaulle, of a Free French agent's visit to Brittany (which had actually been organised by SIS). De Gaulle had escaped to London in June 1940 and assumed leadership of the Free French movement. Churchill sent for Menzies and 'dressed him down roundly for his failure to produce more information from German-occupied territories'. When Menzies retorted that 'a very fair amount of information was in fact obtained', Churchill suggested 'that there was a conspiracy to keep this from him' and directed Menzies to 'send copies of all such reports' directly to Major Morton for submission to him. Menzies responded almost immediately with a batch of reports which Morton appreciatively told him on 18 May were 'exactly the sort of thing I want to see'. More importantly, perhaps, the Prime Minister 'was very grateful for the information'. Menzies also had to keep the Foreign Secretary, Lord Halifax, sweet and, 'in order to avoid the Prime Minister producing some titbit of information at the Cabinet culled from an S.I.S. report which the Foreign Secretary has never heard of', he promised to keep him fully informed as well.[26]

This was the origin of the system whereby for the rest of the war Menzies himself personally supplied Churchill with raw intelligence, while also sending SIS reports to Desmond Morton at No. 10 Downing Street. But, as Menzies recalled afterwards, from now on 'a small red box', of which only he and the Prime Minister had the keys, 'was deposited on the latter's bed each morning, within it all relevant reports, and intercepts obtained by G.C. & C.S., over the previous 24 hours'. A September 1940 note by Churchill's principal private secretary, Eric Seal, more prosaically recorded that the daily boxes 'from "C"' were 'to be put on the Prime Minister's desk and left for him to re-lock'. The boxes were marked '"only to be opened by the Prime Minister in person". This marking', added Seal, 'is not mere camouflage and is to be taken seriously.' However precisely they were supplied, in time these boxes contained material from Britain's single most valuable intelligence source – the German Enigma decrypts – which in turn contributed to the close relationship that built up between Menzies and Churchill and undoubtedly enhanced SIS's reputation at the highest level. In the spring of 1941 Hugh Dalton (Minister of Economic Warfare) noted that Churchill regarded Menzies as 'a wonderful fellow, and was always sending for him'.[27]

Liaison between the services and SIS was not just a one-way street, and SIS's reluctance to be integrated into the central intelligence machinery could have its costs, as demonstrated by the recriminations that followed the disaster at Dakar in September 1940 when a Free French expedition, supported by a British naval flotilla, was driven back by the local French forces. The operation had been compromised by leakages from among the Free French and Poles in London.[28] It had also been assumed that the Dakar garrison, and the Senegal French colonial administration, would readily come over to the Free French side, and SIS was criticised for not warning to the contrary. Menzies indignantly observed that 'as we were not specifically asked to obtain information from the Dakar district', he assumed that 'the requisite data' had been provided by 'other sources'. He suggested that, had he been given a month's warning, it might have been possible to provide more information about local feeling in Dakar, and in any case the Vichy authorities knew all about the plans, owing to their being public knowledge in 'far too wide a circle' in London. He thought it would be 'monstrous if any charge should be levelled against the Intelligence Services, including the S.I.S.'.[29]

Cadogan rather sympathised with Menzies: 'Neither the S.I.S., so far as I know, nor the F.O. were consulted or inf[orme]d when the Dakar affair was first planned.' But evidently the Prime Minister was looking for scapegoats, and Cadogan had his private secretary, Henry Hopkinson, convey the SIS defence to the Cabinet Secretary, Sir Edward Bridges. Bridges, in turn, consulted General Hastings Ismay, Churchill's chief of staff, but Ismay was much less understanding and effectively accused Menzies of being disingenuous. There was, he asserted, 'a standing arrangement whereby every facility is given to S.I.S. to know what is going on. "C" can either come himself, or send people to this Office at all times to discuss matters . . . and to read Papers.' The Joint Intelligence Sub-Committee, he added, 'knew all about the projected Dakar expedition', and the service Directors of Intelligence (who were all members of the committee) each had a representative in SIS. Finally, he observed that SIS had a responsibility to show more initiative in these matters. It was, he said, 'a false assumption that the Intelligence Services should not set about getting information until they are asked to do so'. It was their job 'to keep in touch with plans of likely or pending operations, and to take steps to get information in relation to them without specific orders'. While conceding that 'the relation between the Service Departments and S.I.S.' was not 'my affair', Bridges thought it 'obviously important that there should be no misunderstanding as to where the initiative lies with regard to obtaining information'. Clearly (and realistically) appreciating that Menzies might respond very badly to Ismay's trenchant views, Bridges thought it 'would be better' that the note 'should not be shown to "C"'. He suggested, however, that 'discreet enquiries' should be made 'in order to make certain that the position is clearly understood'.[30]

The debate stimulated by Dakar exposed one of the most problematic aspects of SIS's relations with its customers: that of tasking, and the overall question of who should take the initiative in the crucial matter of intelligence targeting. It also exposed the risk that SIS could run of being hoist with its own petard. Part of the Service's mystique, and arguably an indispensable part of its modus operandi, was for 'C', as the keeper of the deepest secrets, to appear to 'know everything', and the substance of Ismay's criticism was that SIS had not only been in a position to be well informed about the Dakar plans, but also ought to have made sure that it was so. Cadogan, however, sprang to Menzies's defence, arguing that while the theory was all very well, it was a different matter in practice. He accepted that 'C' could 'come himself' to the Cabinet Offices 'to find out what is contemplated', but this 'hardly amounts to that full co-operation' which he 'thought to be eminently desirable'. Ismay's point about the service Directors of Intelligence having representatives in SIS was only 'satisfactory if those officers are kept fully informed by the three

Directors'. While he conceded that it was Menzies's job 'to obtain information without being asked for it', it was 'difficult to pursue intensive
investigations all over the world at all times', and 'if his activities could
be concentrated on the important spots at the right time, I am sure that
would help'. Neither was it all Menzies's fault: 'If it is his duty to keep
enquiring as to what plans may be in hand, I should have thought that, to
make assurance doubly sure, it would equally be the duty of the planners
to take him into their confidence.'[31]

The row in the end appears to have been solved by the informal means
traditionally favoured by SIS. Cadogan spoke to Ismay, evidently soothing
ruffled feathers. Menzies, too, had 'a long talk' with Ismay and assured him
that he now had 'a most excellent liaison' with the Joint Planning Staff. 'At
the end of his talk,' reported Bridges, 'Ismay told "C" that, if at any time
he felt that he was not kept sufficiently in touch with events, he should not
hesitate to let us know.' 'Good,' minuted Hopkinson on Bridges's letter, no
doubt expressing a relieved Foreign Office view of the matter.[32]

Whatever Menzies's improved relations with the Joint Planning Staff
and the War Cabinet Secretariat, the armed services continued to complain about the supply of intelligence from SIS. This was very evident from
the March 1941 Secret Service Committee meeting which Cadogan specifically called 'to ascertain whether the Directors of Intelligence had any
points to make in regard to the operation of the Secret Service'. Inevitably
they had. Their first concern was the likelihood of a German invasion of
Britain. Although information from air reconnaissance and interception
was 'improving', there was 'still a lack of up-to-date information from
agents'. 'A good deal of intelligence of a somewhat vague and general
character' had been provided, but the War Office 'were greatly exercised
over the impossibility of obtaining exact information from ports in regard to the date and hour of the departure of invasion forces'. Menzies
said that the main difficulty concerned communications. In the first place
there was the problem of getting agents into occupied Europe. He reported that the Air Ministry 'were doing their best' and that he was 'in touch
with' the Admiralty regarding 'the provision of suitable craft'. As for the
organisation on the ground, in Belgium it was 'working satisfactorily'
and he hoped 'in a month or two' to have a large number of wireless sets
operating in France. There were problems in Norway 'owing to the indiscretion of Norwegian agents', but good information was coming from

Stockholm. Holland was 'the weakest spot', and there was 'obstruction' from the Dutch government-in-exile. In the Balkans Menzies said that the German occupation of Romania and Bulgaria had severely disrupted the flow of intelligence. Regarding Greece and Albania, 'preparations had been made against an eventual overrunning of those countries', but he warned that it 'was not possible to guarantee that these plans would work in practice'.

Charged with the 'inadequacy' of information from Italy, Menzies said that 'the greatest difficulty arose out of the disappearance of French information', but asserted that his relations with the Vichy French Deuxième Bureau 'were improving and he hoped to get more from that source'. Attention was also drawn to 'the lack of reliable information from American contacts' (presumably from diplomatic missions across German-occupied Europe). For much of the meeting the best Menzies could do was proffer vague promises that the position would get better. Regarding America he was 'hopeful of improvement'. Information 'had hitherto been difficult to obtain from North Africa', but 'the situation was now developing satisfactorily through the installation of W/T sets in Tunis'. Information about troop movements in Russia 'was coming through better', and 'steps had been taken to improve the transmission of information from the Far East, but this again presented very great difficulties'. Responding to criticisms that 'nothing whatever had been received form German ports' about the movements of the German navy, Menzies said this was 'largely' due to the lack of wireless communication, 'which had not been as fully developed before the war as it is now'.

All through the meeting Menzies had clearly been on the defensive, but right at the end he drew attention to the difficulties SIS faced arising from the 'creation and expansion' of special operations whose interests, 'in many respects, ran counter to his own'. There was a question of 'priorities, competition for agents, communication, transport, passages, etc.'. Menzies got the committee to agree that Cadogan should put up a recommendation to the Foreign Secretary and 'if necessary' the Cabinet, urging that intelligence should 'always be given priority' over special operations work.[33] Although in fact no formal decision was extracted from the Foreign Secretary at this stage, Menzies had identified a general problem which, with varying intensity, was to affect SIS's place in the British war effort for the next few years.

Special operations and the creation of SOE

At the beginning of the war special operations, which comprised mostly sabotage and propaganda work, had been organised within SIS by Laurence Grand's Section IX. But as Menzies observed to the Secret Service Committee in March 1941, the practice of 'SO' was frequently quite inimical to that of 'SI' – intelligence. Any spectacular act of sabotage, for example, was likely to provoke an intense security response from the enemy, which in turn could jeopardise the less dramatic and more sustained activities necessary for the acquisition of secret intelligence. Within SIS, moreover, the tension between special operations and intelligence was exacerbated by the personalities involved. Grand, for all his evident imagination and enthusiasm, was markedly better at ideas than administration, and there were worries about the lavish way in which he spent money on his various schemes. While in March 1940 Hankey had given him a qualified benefit of the doubt, in SIS Claude Dansey had raised the question of whether Grand should 'conform and co-operate' with the rest of the Service, or simply 'go on galloping about the world at his own gait'. Cadogan was sufficiently concerned in May–June 1940 to canvass opinions about Grand and his work. Beaumont-Nesbitt, the Director of Military Intelligence, described Grand as 'gifted, enthusiastic and persuasive, but I do not regard him as being well balanced or reliable', and Archie Boyle of Air Intelligence said he was 'an expensive luxury'. Gladwyn Jebb was the most damning of all. Grand's judgment, he wrote with evident relish, 'is almost always wrong, his knowledge wide but alarmingly superficial, his organisation in many respects a laughing stock, and he is a consistent and fluent liar'. Jebb conceded that Grand was 'generous and liked by his staff', but 'to pit such a man against the German General Staff and the German Military Intelligence Service is like arranging an attack on a Panzer Division by an actor mounted on a donkey'.[34]

The whole question was reviewed at a high-level meeting with the Foreign Secretary at the end of June 1940 when Menzies effectively washed his hands of Grand. An informal pencilled note of the meeting gives a flavour of Menzies's exasperation with his unbiddable subordinate: '"C" says responsibility too much for him. "D" [Grand] represents his own views as "C"'s. D's great ideas. Doesn't seek advice before putting out schemes . . . Schemes not weighed sufficiently . . . <u>But</u> C can't control him.'

Over the summer of 1940 the management of British special operations was restructured. A new organisation, which emerged in September as the Special Operations Executive (SOE), was set up under Hugh Dalton, the recently appointed Minister for Economic Warfare, who (according to his memoirs) was instructed by Churchill to 'set Europe ablaze'.[35] Jebb was installed as chief executive officer of the organisation, which took over SIS's Section IX, the rump of MIR (the special operations branch at the War Office) and responsibility for 'subversive propaganda'. The transfer of Section IX to the new organisation was completed with such speed that it had been implemented before SIS had been formally notified. Although complaining about this, on 4 September Menzies assured Jebb that he welcomed the change and had no wish to retain responsibility for sabotage and subversive activities. Presciently, however, he noted 'the grave disadvantage of running two sections of the secret service, with intimately interlocking interest, under two masters'. Sir Frank Nelson, who had worked for SIS in the Z Organisation in Berne, was given charge of special operations with Grand as his deputy, but, when it soon became clear that this would not work, Grand was summarily dismissed and transferred to a staff job in India.

Jebb was well aware of the need for the 'friendly co-operation of C' if special operations were to function efficiently, and he acknowledged potential clashes of interest, observing that 'a project may quite possibly be good for purposes of Subversion, but bad for purposes of Intelligence', and that there might be competition for transport and communications resources. To mitigate these, in an 'Agreement between C [Menzies] and D [Nelson]' (drafted by Jebb on 15 September 1940) he laid down at the start that all of SOE's cypher communications would run through SIS, that intelligence collected by SOE would be passed on to SIS, and that SIS approval would be sought when engaging agents. All of these matters were to cause friction between SIS and SOE over the next few years, exacerbated by the exponential expansion of SOE under the dynamic leadership of Dalton, Jebb, Nelson and Lieutenant Colonel Colin Gubbins (who had been appointed Director of Operations), and at a time, at least initially, when SIS itself had few successes of its own.

During 1940 and early 1941 more or less satisfactory relations between

SIS and SOE were maintained between Menzies's liaison officer, Colonel E. E. Calthrop (a wheelchair-bound multiple sclerosis sufferer who had won a Military Cross in the First World War), and Frank Nelson, who was unfailingly courteous and collegial. SOE, nevertheless, complained about an incident of line-crossing in Lisbon (which was actually Claude Dansey's fault, when in seeking to co-operate with special operations he allowed them to contact an existing SIS agent), while SIS complained of insecure behaviour by an SOE officer in Stockholm, planned sabotage jeopardising liaison relations in Finland and a risk of compromise over signals intelligence. A weekly meeting was organised between Jebb, Nelson and Menzies, but towards the end of April 1941 Admiral Godfrey at Naval Intelligence weighed in with a memorandum on the division of interests between SIS and special operations. He stressed how dependent the navy was on SIS intelligence and asserted that SIS operations in several countries were being damaged by SOE's attempts to create sabotage organisations 'with untrained personnel', and he wanted a Chiefs of Staff directive embodying a general principle that 'the collection of Intelligence in regard to the enemy and the safeguarding of the means of collecting this Intelligence in the future must have priority over other subversive activities'. But Menzies (as was his way), rather than seeking a ruling from supposed higher authority, accepted a solution offered by Claude Dansey to arbitrate between the two services on condition that both Chiefs gave him their 'entire confidence'.

Dansey, who had the reputation of being a poor team player, set the position out in a clear-sighted and perhaps unexpectedly constructive memorandum to Menzies on 1 May 1941. 'We have to face the fact', he wrote, 'that S.O.2 [SOE] lives and grows – at an astonishing rate – seemingly without any governing factor as far as finance goes, and that whether we like it or not they do become in a sense competitors,' for example in the fields of communications, material and transport, and 'above all' in the limited supply of potential agents. 'If we cannot kill [it], and I do not think we can let us for [the] sake of work and war effort try to live on & work on friendly terms. I for one counsel Collaboration.' Menzies and Nelson accepted Dansey's recommendation that the heads of the Geographical sections in both organisations should keep constantly in touch with each other to 'settle questions to mutual satisfaction', and any unresolvable differences should be referred to Dansey for a final decision.[36] Good relations between the two agencies were also assisted by Air Commodore Archie Boyle (the Air Ministry's candidate for Chief of SIS in 1939) who was appointed SOE's Director of Intelligence and Security in June 1941, a job he kept for the rest of the war. In September he and Dansey took charge of the circulation of all information from SIS to SOE. There is ample evidence in SIS files that Boyle was respected and trusted in SIS and got on particularly well with Menzies, Dansey and Vivian, and, importantly, that he was able to defuse numerous incipient conflicts. Some issues, including code-names for operations, seem to have been no problem at all. 'Confirm that the Greek Alphabet, names of motor cars, names of precious stones, big game, fruit and colours are reserved for S.I.S.,' Dansey was told in November 1941. 'I have abandoned fruits for S.O.E. purposes . . . I understand that you will suggest to S.I.S. as additional categories, musicians and poets, and I shall therefore keep off them.'

But it was not all sweetness and light. Late in 1941 SOE proposed that the two services be jointly represented in West Africa under an SOE nominee. Menzies's chief of staff, Rex Howard, did 'not like the proposal at all'. SIS, he wrote, 'is an established organisation whereas S.O.E. is of mushroom growth'. Although SIS officers headed joint representation in the USA and Malta, the converse certainly did not apply: 'I consider the principle of allowing S.O.E. to be in charge of S.I.S. activities in <u>any</u> area would be wrong.' There were also problems with communications, prompting a sharp minute on 8 December from Gambier-Parry, who felt 'most strongly that we must face a complete show-down with S.O.E. that we either <u>absolutely</u> control their communications, including the manufacture and supply of equipment, training, preparation of operations . . . or we cut completely adrift and let them wallow in their own mire!'. Just before Christmas 1941 Dansey, citing the dispute over West Africa and accusing SOE of 'a lack of good faith', withdrew as arbitrator between the two services.[37]

Gambier-Parry returned to the fray in January 1942, complaining about SOE's escalating demands for independent wireless communications. 'It invariably comes back to the point', he wrote, 'where they envisage hundreds upon hundreds of agents equipped with wireless sets all over the face of the world, particularly of Europe.' In February Gambier-Parry described SOE communications plans as 'extravagant, insecure, fatuous and very dangerous'. In the end Menzies, perhaps happy to be rid of this particular poisoned chalice, agreed that SOE should broadly have charge of its own wireless communications. Nelson was clearly delighted, on 27 March sending Menzies a handwritten note along with his formal acceptance of the new arrangement: 'Dear Stuart [sic]. Thank you so much!' Other activities caused alarm in SIS, including 'Pickaxe' operations – whereby SOE planned to infiltrate Soviet agents into Western Europe. Menzies, who first learned of this in February 1942 only after Calthrop got hold of a leaked SOE report on the matter, emphatically reminded SOE that they were obliged to have prior Foreign Office clearance for such proposals and to consult SIS about them.

In February 1942 Hugh Dalton was replaced as Minister for Economic Warfare (with responsibility for SOE) by Lord Selborne, an altogether more emollient character. From the start Selborne was concerned about the friction between SOE and SIS and raised the matter with Anthony Eden (Foreign Secretary since December 1940), who had apparently been unaware of the problem. Selborne sent Eden a paper by Nelson in which he emphasised his own good personal relations with both Menzies and Dansey, but described SIS's overall attitude as 'to delay rather than to expedite the natural expansion of S.O.E.'. He suggested that whereas SIS initially saw SOE as a 'rather ineffective and ridiculous collection of amateurs who might endanger S.I.S. if not kept quiet', they now seemed to regard SOE 'as dangerous rivals who, if not squashed quickly', would 'eventually squash them'. This was because 'we have outstripped them in many directions and proved ourselves in many directions to be a more efficient organisation. It is nonetheless', he added (with perhaps a hint of disingenuousness), 'both foolish and deplorable since the last thing S.O.E. wants is to obstruct S.I.S. in the slightest degree.' Selborne also consulted Gladwyn Jebb, who reinforced Nelson's defence of SOE's professionalism, suggested that SIS was over-addicted to the 'false beard' mentality, stressed the need for genuine two-way co-operation between the two organisations and proposed appointing 'some impartial person of high standing' to act as 'Conciliator'.[38]

Selborne took this proposal to the Cabinet, but Menzies (as before) was firmly opposed to submitting SIS to any external arbitration. What was needed, he argued, was 'a final act of priority, which must be accepted by both services'. He made it clear, however, that such a decision could really only go one way: 'if it is decided that S.O.E. has priority, then it must be realised, without any equivocation, that information will suffer. If I have priority, I do not think it will necessarily interfere much with S.O.E.' At the same time as Selborne was trying to get the Cabinet to adjudicate between SIS and SOE, the Chiefs of Staff came up with a proposal to amalgamate the two organisations, with a single executive head who would be under the 'general direction' of the Chiefs of Staff Committee, but with 'provision for consultation' with the Foreign Office. This was anathema to the Foreign Office where it was argued (with Menzies's support) that differences could be smoothed out in a fortnightly meeting presided over by Sir Alexander Cadogan.[39] The efforts here of both Selborne and the Chiefs of Staff echo the service ministries' attempts during the First World War to prise control of SIS from the Foreign Office. War inevitably sharpened the tensions between the operational military and political information sides of secret service. This was powerfully exacerbated in the early 1940s by the existence of SOE, whose rapid growth and apparent ability to strike against the enemy – at a time when British military successes were especially welcome – tended to eclipse the quieter achievements (such as they were) of SIS.

Even so, in the Whitehall battle for independence and control, SIS and the Foreign Office were able to fend off the challenges of both the military and SOE. In fact, the absence of formal decisions about the precise relationship between SIS and SOE worked markedly to SIS's advantage. The Cabinet never resolved the question and there was no 'final act of priority' such as Menzies had proposed. But the Foreign Office, in a typically effortless assumption of bureaucratic superiority, was able deftly to out manoeuvre attempts by less practised Whitehall warriors to change the status of SIS. Relations with SOE continued on a comparatively amicable basis even after Nelson, who resigned suffering from exhaustion in May 1942, was replaced by the more formal and assertive Charles Hambro. While tensions continued to trouble the relationship, there is evidence that in London at least a serious effort was made on both sides to work together.

When Hambro complained in July 1942 that the information flow from SIS to SOE was insufficient, Menzies demurred. 'Your Regional Sections', he wrote, 'have, for some time past, been sending down officers about once a week to their opposite Sections here and . . . in some cases entire files have been placed at their disposal . . . I do not think under the circumstances any organisation could have behaved in a more generous way than we have.' Although Menzies was (perhaps understandably) being more emphatic on this point than was absolutely necessary, Hambro backed off with quite good grace. Having consulted his people, he found they after all confirmed Menzies's 'impression of an improvement in the contacts between our respective Regional and Country Sections and', he added, 'I am most grateful to you and to the A.C.S.S. [Dansey]'.

Whatever the day-to-day relations between SIS and SOE, by the end of 1942 the Foreign Office had firmly resolved that there was no future for SOE after the war had ended. Essentially this was a further assertion of Foreign Office primacy. 'My Secretary of State', wrote Cadogan to Hambro on 22 December, 'does not consider that there will be room for two secret British organisations in Europe once hostilities have ceased. Nor could he agree that after that date there should be any underground British organisation which is not responsible to the Foreign Secretary.' Cadogan conceded that SOE might not 'necessarily come to an abrupt end as soon as we sign an Armistice', but, 'as and when hostilities terminate in different parts of the world, any S.O.E. representatives who may remain in Government service should be transferred to the War Office if they are to perform any overt duties with the military' or 'to the S.I.S. if they are to perform underground work'. Although SOE was strenuously to resist this conclusion, so, in fact, it was to be.

Section VIII

During the difficult early years of the war, one area of undoubted SIS achievement was that of wireless communications. Much of the credit for this was due to CSC, the Controller Special Communications, Richard Gambier-Parry, who from early 1938 had built up a remarkable team (styling themselves 'plumbers') in his new Communications Section VIII. As is so often the case with committed technical experts, he was something of a monomaniac. Like Laurence Grand, he was a fertile source of ideas and also impatient with what he regarded as pettifogging administrative matters. But, unlike Grand, Gambier-Parry was crucially and manifestly able to convert his inspirations and imagination into practical achievements, so much so that during the war he was asked to take on a considerable amount of work for departments other than SIS. In 1940 Admiral Godfrey singled out Gambier-Parry's section for particular praise and in January 1941 Sir David Petrie (later head of MI5) noted 'the very efficient wireless installation maintained by M.I.6'.[40] Beyond providing for SIS communications at home (for example between headquarters and outstations such as Bletchley Park) and abroad (both to foreign stations and individual agents), as well as those of SOE (to 1942) and various Allied governments-in-exile, Gambier-Parry became responsible for a dedicated secure communications network designed to carry SIS traffic (including the signals intelligence produced by GC&CS) to customer departments in government and the armed services, as well as both King George VI's and the Prime Minister's communications when they were abroad. On Petrie's recommendation, in May 1941 he took on the Radio Security Service, previously run by the General Post Office under War Office and MI5 direction, which had been formed to intercept and collect foreign communications, as well as locating their source – providing some of the vital raw material for the GC&CS code-breakers. After the war, a GC&CS historian remarked that the transfer of the work to SIS 'at last' established it 'on a durable basis', and ensured 'wholehearted technical support'.[41] Gambier-Parry also set up and ran several transmitting stations for the propaganda output of the Ministry of Economic Warfare and the Political Warfare Executive, including what was called Freiheit (Freedom) Radio. Supporting all this was a research and development branch devoted to (among other things) producing robust and reliable wireless sets for use in the field, and a training school at Hans Place in London which processed over 600 operators.[42]

At the start of the war Section VIII, as a non-military organisation, suffered in terms of priority for equipment and personnel. There was also a security aspect, with questions being raised locally as to what the two hundred or so civilians based at Whaddon Hall were actually doing. In common with SIS itself, in July 1940 Section VIII acquired a military cover name and became known as No. 1 Special Signal Unit. Reflecting the difficulties of creating really good cover, the acronym SSU was quickly found to be less than satisfactory, as some inquisitive outsiders interpreted 'SS' as 'Secret Service'. Others did not like the 'SS' echo of the hated German Schutzstaffel, and so in 1941 the designation was changed to SCU: Special Communication Unit.

In July 1941, a volcanic explosion from Gambier-Parry against the long-serving Service head of finance and administration, Commander Percy 'Pay' Sykes, not only illustrates the problems thrown up by Gambier-Parry's rather buccaneering approach to record-keeping (along with his own combative temperament), but also perhaps gives a hint of the war-time strain under which the men were working. Sykes's department had produced a highly critical audit of Section VIII for 1940–1, particularly pinpointing their inadequate paperwork. Gambier-Parry dismissed the report as 'a mass of ill-informed, ill-construed, illogical innuendo' with 'a complete lack of conception of the wide issues at stake', together with what he identified as 'a bitter and underhand personal attack which is as unhelpful as it is fictitious'. With injured pride and withering sarcasm, he warmed to his theme:

> No consideration at all is given to the fact that during this period our annual estimates rose from an original figure of £63,000 to £178,000 and we were working at the highest pressure, forming a military unit, equipping some 60 technical vehicles, putting up two Broadcasting stations and a recording centre, at a speed which many experts would consider impossible, carrying ever-increasing telegraphic traffic, developing the new science of agents communications, coping with S.O.2 communications, carrying an expanding circulation of J.Q. [Polish signals] at home and abroad, and endeavouring to contribute to the process of winning the war. But, then, these auditors wouldn't want to know that we do any of these things. It seems to be of greater importance that one order has become entangled with another.

Sykes, although himself a stickler for correct office procedure, was only doing his job, and arguably a fastidious attention to detail was of particular importance in wartime when administration and expenditure could so easily get out of control. Yet the fact that Gambier-Parry's outbursts (of which there were many) were tolerated, and he remained in charge of communications for the rest of the war and after, suggests that he was sufficiently good at his job for generous allowances to be made for his excitable temperament.

Headquarters changes

The increased tempo of SIS work in 1939–40 put pressure on the United Kingdom organisation and necessitated a reform of the existing head-quarters. By late 1940 this was largely complete. Claude Dansey, back from Switzerland, was installed as Assistant CSS, effectively Menzies's second-in-command, despite Vivian's existing designation as Deputy CSS (which he tried without success to defend).[43] Dansey took charge of two new sections, A and O. A Section, under Frank Foley (ex-head of the Berlin station and latterly in Norway), was charged with rebuild-ing networks in occupied Europe and had sub-sections for Scandinavia, Holland, Belgium and A.5, the Free French. O (for Operations) Section was headed by Commander Frank Slocum (a former regular naval officer who had served with the Grand Fleet in the First World War), whose job was to organise SIS's sea and air communications.[44]

Valentine Vivian, meanwhile, ran the War Station at Bletchley Park, and handled counter-espionage (Section V), including liaison with MI5. The presence of Allied governments-in-exile and large numbers of for-eign servicemen and refugees meant that a great deal of work which would normally have been 'performed by M.I.6 in certain foreign coun-tries' (such as recruiting agents) was now 'automatically transferred to the U.K.', thus trespassing on MI5's territory. In order to 'interlock the functions of M.I.5 and M.I.6', it was arranged in July 1940 that Section V should simultaneously be Section B.26 of MI5 and the SIS officers therein would communicate with the British police and civil authorities as if they were members of MI5.

SIS also made plans against the possibility of a German invasion of Britain itself. A new Section VII was set up which by July had begun to identify potential stay-behind agents. Working jointly with Vivian and David Boyle, Gambier-Parry trained and equipped six agents with wireless sets in Norfolk, Suffolk, Sussex, Somerset, Cornwall and Devon, deployed mobile signals units across home commands and successfully ran a war game code-named 'Plan 333'. This had 'produced good signal-ling and 76% deciphered messages'. The network was eventually extended to include twenty-four 'head agents' with wireless sets. Recruitment was specially restricted to 'people who, by the nature of their occupation, could remain in enemy controlled territory and continue their normal occupations without arousing undue suspicion', such as 'doctors, dentists, chemists, bakers and small shopkeepers', all of whose jobs required them 'either to move around in the course of their professional duties or to receive many visits from other people'. As one of his last acts while head of Section D, Colonel Grand also recruited some eighty saboteurs and supplied them with secret dumps of equipment and devices. Finally, in case the worst came to the worst (and echoing similar arrangements being discussed for the royal family), plans were prepared to relocate a skeleton SIS headquarters to Canada.

Organising potential stay-behind communications was not just a technical matter, but also involved the human problems of recruiting suitable agents. This, in turn, revealed some extraordinary preconceptions. Towards the end of September 1940 the Director of Military Intelligence reported that 'M.I.6' – evidently Gambier-Parry – was very pessimistic about the possibilities in Iceland, the Faroes and Shetland as 'ethnologically, the peoples of all these Islands are far too primitive and unintelligent to master even the simplest methods of handling W/T, and the introduction of alien inhabitants would, of course, attract attention at once'. The Orkneys, he conceded, 'might conceivably be a trial worth making, but my Admiralty contacts give me little hope, even there, of finding the right man'.

There were further headquarters changes in 1942, partly in response to criticism from customer departments. In February 1942 it was agreed that each armed service Director of Intelligence would 'appoint a senior officer' to SIS to act as a Deputy Director, who would 'work in close concert with a Deputy Director to be appointed by "C" from among his existing staff'. Each of these officers was to 'represent the particular needs of his own Service director', and together they would 'formulate plans with a view to improving the S.I.S. Service material, under the direction of "C"'.[45] Menzies implemented this with effect from 6 March, when Colonel John Cordeaux became Deputy Director/Navy, Colonel Edward Beddington DD/Army and Air Commodore Lionel 'Lousy' Payne DD/Air. The intention, as Cadogan recalled three years later, was that Claude Dansey, the Assistant Chief, would 'sit in with them as a Foreign Office Deputy', evidently to ensure that political intelligence requirements were not entirely neglected in the face of the service departments' demands. In order both to keep Foreign Office representation in SIS and to help Menzies with his administrative burdens, Cadogan sent Patrick Reilly (who had been private secretary to Lord Selborne) to Broadway to be his personal assistant.[46]

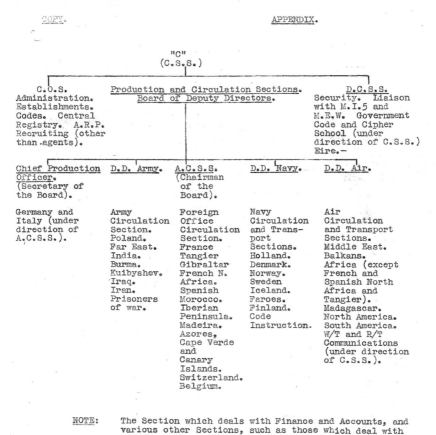

The SIS headquarters reorganisation of March 1942, indicating the way in which Claude Dansey (ACSS) sidelined his rival, Valentine Vivian (DCSS).

Each of these men had intelligence experience. 'Bill' Cordeaux, as he was known, a career Royal Marine and keen amateur footballer, had worked in the Naval Intelligence Division since 1938. Beddington was a wise old bird, an Old Etonian cavalryman who had served in Military Intelligence during the First World War and then pursued a successful business career, ending up in the 1930s as vice chairman of the United Africa Company (later part of Unilever). In September 1940 he had been brought out of retirement by the Chief of the Imperial General Staff, Sir John 'Jack' Dill, an old Staff College chum, to run MI3, responsible for military intelligence on Iberia, Italy and the Balkans. This he did until Dill's successor, Sir Alan Brooke ('Brookie' to Beddington), asked him to take on the job at SIS.[47] Between the wars Payne had intermittently worked in Air Intelligence, but in 1938, threatened with appointment as the Senior Air Staff Officer in Iraq, he had resigned and become air correspondent for the *Daily Telegraph*. Canvassing then for an intelligence job, he had approached Vernon Kell at MI5. Kell passed him on to SIS, who rejected him as 'not thought suitable', though conceding that he had a 'good brain, which he is willing to use if given time'. He also had 'some strange friends, but is often well informed, probably due to the fact that information is more readily obtained in bed'. At the start of the war, however, he had been taken back on to the intelligence strength at the Air Ministry.

The new appointees quickly set to work and by the start of April had sketched out proposals for a headquarters reorganisation. They began by stressing that if SIS's 'primary duty in war-time' was 'the obtaining (excluding intercepting) by clandestine methods information for the Fighting Services and the Foreign Office, then its present organisation needs reconsideration, particularly if it is also accepted that such information is chiefly of use where action can be taken'. They agreed that too much of SIS's time and resources was taken up by work for the security Section V and the economic Section VI. They proposed reducing the latter to a liaison section and curtailing the work of Section V 'to those aspects of C.E. [counter-espionage] work on which it is possible to take action at once or at some readily foreseeable future date, or which provides positive intelligence for S.I.S.'. Another important recommendation was that the Production Branch should be combined under the four Deputy Directors, who would constitute a board with Dansey in the chair. In order to take some of the pressure of work off Menzies they also proposed 'the decentralisation of the work of S.I.S. to Vice "Cs" in Middle East, India, Africa other than N. Africa [and] America'. They also wisely (and perhaps with the hiatus of late 1939 in mind) suggested that Menzies should designate an officer as deputy 'to act for you in the event of your illness, or in case of your death pending a fresh appointment'.

We can, perhaps, see the hand of Dansey in these proposals, which excluded his old adversary Valentine Vivian from the Board of Deputy Directors, likely to become the key executive body in the revamped structure. Yet since there is no evidence that Menzies made any specific decision about nominating a potential successor, Vivian (who was left in charge of liaison with MI5, the Ministry of Economic Warfare, GC&CS and 'Eire') may have been content with his continuing status as Deputy Chief. The rest of the recommendations were implemented at the beginning of May, with each of the Deputy Directors taking responsibility for specific geographical regions, as well as retaining their primary service liaison function. Although this appeared to be a sensible tidying up of the central SIS bureaucracy, some anomalies remained. Responsibility, for example, for links with the Vichy French (Section P.5, 'special lines known to ACSS', under Beddington) was kept separate from the Free French (in Section P.1 under Dansey). It also remains questionable whether combining responsibility for some elements of the production and for circulation of information in individual directors was necessarily a wise move. Moreover, giving responsibility for production matters to the three service Deputy Directors certainly undermined the original intention that 'each officer would represent the particular needs of his own Service director' within SIS.[48]

Indeed, as is so often the case, these outsiders brought into SIS appear to have fallen under the seductive spell of the Service and took to defending it against their home departments. Less than a month after his appointment, Payne, for example, wrote a long and thoughtful memorandum in which he ascribed the intelligence failures of May 1940 as much to the service ministries' misinterpretation of information as to any deficiencies in SIS. 'It is doubtful', he wrote, 'whether the Chiefs of Staff realise how many reports, which are of great value, come from S.I.S. agents.' A week later, noting that SIS primarily circulated 'undigested' information (as the service ministries wanted), he expressed his 'anxiety . . . to ensure that S.I.S. get the credit for accurate information they obtain, and do not get blamed for circulating, <u>on a high level</u>, agents' reports which can be proved, or subsequently turn out, to be inaccurate'.

Recruitment

The war put tremendous pressure on SIS's hitherto rather haphazard recruitment system. There was a very busy buyers' market in which SIS had to compete with the armed services, SOE, GC&CS, governments-in-exile and various other analogous bodies, such as the Ministry of Economic Warfare, for the inevitably limited pool of suitable personnel. SIS was also under pressure to take on increased numbers of foreign nationals, many of whom had escaped occupied Europe and were mustard keen to get back and do their bit. But the security stakes were as high as ever and the Service had to be vigilant against enemy efforts to place their people within its ranks. When recruiting officers or agents, the usual procedure was for the name to be sent to MI5 for checking against their register of suspect persons. This was a negative vetting process, and the reply 'No trace' was generally regarded as sufficient. From the summer of 1940, however, when SIS began intensively to recruit from among those who had fled the Continent, Claude Dansey worried that there should be a more thorough investigation, if only because 'every agent, no matter what his nationality and feelings, may be possessed of some information of importance to the enemy . . . A negative reply from M.I.5', he instructed, 'must not absolve officers from enquiring into the past and family history of all candidates under examination.' From the following spring, a systematic look out for potential agents was kept at MI5's Royal Victoria Patriotic Schools London Reception Centre in Wandsworth where aliens entering the United Kingdom were sent for processing. In April and May 1941 SIS's spotter there reported that he had recruited twenty-eight agents and passed on five further names for special operations. The supply of candidates varied, however. In April he did not recommend anyone for A.3 (the Belgian Section), 'as no Belgians were interesting, and very few arrived in the U.K.'.

SIS cast its net far and wide for recruits. In January 1941, for example, the New York station reported that a Frenchman about to be repatriated to France expected to return to employment with a shipping company at Le Havre where he 'would be able to spy on their business to Paris, Marseilles, Toulon etc'. He also recommended a steward on the French transatlantic liner *Normandie* who was 'extremely intelligent [with] unquestioned patriotism and hostile to present [French] regime' and would 'be able to travel about France on steamship company's business which should afford him excellent cover'. The same month the Cairo station reported that a French engineer about to return home 'felt unable to work as an agent in France for family reasons (and fear)', but had recommended his brother-in-law, who ran a cheese factory in Lorraine. A Czech law student, who had been studying in France but had escaped, was interviewed in Bermuda in June 1942 and 'gave the names of several of his student friends who are reliable de Gaullists . . . anxious to work for the Allies in France'. He stated that 'many of the Czechs frequent a cafe at 59 rue de la Republique in Marseilles and that the Germans plant agents there who pretend to be loyal Czechs, thus catching several of them'. Some 'notes on the recruiting of agents for France' which London sent to New York in December 1943 illustrate the kinds of people SIS wished to employ, though the specification was a counsel of perfection. Agents, it affirmed, should be courageous, observant, meticulous, quick-witted, resourceful, persevering and self-confident. An individual's 'motives and integrity should be beyond doubt' and 'checked by reference to his past history and, where possible, by the testimony of persons who know him'. Men without dependants were preferred: 'The fact that a man has a wife or children in France is a definite disadvantage. Experience has shown that they are a source of danger to him and that the enemy do not hesitate to use them as hostages.'

One example of how swift and informal the recruitment process could be (especially when the Service was responding to urgent wartime needs) is that of Commander Roy Kendall in December 1941. As a result of the Japanese offensive in South-East Asia which followed the attack on Pearl Harbor, there was suddenly a much heightened need for intelligence in the region. Kendall, a very experienced sailor who had been serving as Commodore of Convoys in the Channel and North Sea, was selected to be SIS representative in Australia 'for the purpose of penetrating the Japanese Mandated Islands or other areas in the Pacific'. He was clearly well qualified for this. In the 1930s, based at Rabaul in New Britain, he had served as a master mariner in the Papua New Guinea inter-island trade. Although born in London, his family were in Australia. He had a 'very good record there' and was 'vouched for' by the Australian Director of Naval Intelligence. Asserting that these recommendations were 'far better than anything M.I.5 can produce', and that 'the state of affairs in the Far East does not leave room for any red tape', Section G.2 wanted to take on Kendall without further ado.

But a fastidious secretary in Personnel (as G.2 explained to her head of section) 'was a little doubtful' because this was 'contrary to your orders'. Personnel had their way and the following day a 'trace enquiry' on Kendall was telephoned to MI5, who replied a day later that there was 'nothing recorded against'. Even though the correct procedure was apparently followed, it was not much of a vetting process. Kendall had completed the standard application form (in use since 1938) on which the first entry was 'Recommended by', with space provided for the names and addresses of three referees. But Kendall filled in none of these. By mid-January 1942 his recruitment was complete: on 30 December he had signed the Official Secrets Act; on 8 January he had 'seen the doctor', and the following day he completed the 'secrecy form' relating to pay ('Disclosure to any person of emoluments received, will lead to instant dismissal').[49] The security risks which accompanied the sometimes rather casual wartime checks were inevitably magnified when able recruits were taken on trust, a factor which enabled the Cambridge-educated Soviet spy Kim Philby to slip into the Service, initially to work in the Iberian branch of the counter-intelligence Section V in September 1941.

Naturally the Service was always on the lookout for suitable candidates and from time to time individuals with unusual specialist skills were recommended. In November 1942 an MI5 officer passed on to SIS a letter from Detective Superintendent Westland of the Aberdeen city police concerning a thirty-seven-year-old man called John Ramsay. Ramsay had been born in Scotland of Lithuanian parents named Ramensky, but had changed his surname at the start of the war. As Westland described him, Ramsay was a 'clean living' kind of man: he did not swear, smoke or drink and was 'an excellent specimen of physical fitness'. But, more to the point, he was 'the most neat and tidy safe breaker in Britain to-day . . . His safes are all opened by means of explosives and, from a professional point of view, to see them after he has finished the job is a treat in itself, because the work is so neatly done.' Although Ramsay had twice been sentenced to five-year prison terms, the policeman went on to give him a remarkable character reference: 'In spite of his convictions, I look on him as a real gentleman and a person who would not do a mean action nor commit a mean crime . . . Personally, I think he would make an excellent Commando.'

SIS looked into the possibility of employing Ramsay, but regretted that 'owing to his knowing no other languages than Lithuanian and English, it does not appear possible for us to use him'. But they passed him on to the Commandos, who were glad to have him, and he eventually served in 34 Troop 30 Commando (the Special Engineering Unit, Military Section) with whom his safe-blowing skills were put to good use.[50]

By the end of 1942 SIS had endured a very testing sequence of trials by both battle and bureaucracy. The Service got its share of blame for the series of British setbacks, especially during 1940, which to a greater or lesser extent were suffered by all the armed forces. Above all, it was sharply criticised for not adequately meeting urgent and understandable demands for timely operational intelligence. The perceived need for action of some – any – sort, moreover, inspired the proponents of special operations and fuelled the growth of SOE, which became a sort of cuckoo in the clandestine agency nest. While Menzies was well aware of the importance of intelligence-gathering, and strove hard himself to defend it, he had fought in the trenches during the First World War and was also well aware that *of itself* intelligence is valueless. He made this clear in a Service circular of 10 November 1942 highlighting 'the real reasons for the existence of S.I.S.'. In wartime, he wrote, 'all Intelligence about the enemy, whether collected by secret means, or by open field Intelligence, should be based on the old dictum that "Intelligence is the mainspring of Action"'. It followed, therefore, 'that S.I.S.'s prime function is to obtain information by secret means which may admit of or promote action . . . Information on which no action can be taken may be of interest, it may be useful for records or for the future, but it is of secondary importance.' Remarking that 'a definition of what constitutes "action" should not be necessary', he nevertheless provided one: 'It must in the ultimate resort spell a movement of operations which result in the death of one or more of enemy nationals, or the defeat of some of his projects.' He concluded this manifesto with a reminder of the last war, about which there was some belief that it ended 'because the enemy was defeated by means of the spoken, written word, or some other ancillary war activity'. This was not the case: 'Germany was defeated because the German Armies were beaten,' and it was clear that SIS would have failed in its primary function if it did not materially contribute to the defeat of German arms in this war in which they were currently engaged.

11

The European theatre

The work of SIS in Northern and Western Europe during the first half of the war falls naturally into two parts. First, there was the period of the so-called Phoney War from September 1939 until April–May 1940 when, after the conquest of Poland (where the spoils were divided between Germany and the Soviet Union), there was a kind of armed stand-off between the Allies – Britain (along with the empire) and France – and Germany. Over these six months or so SIS sought to develop and extend its coverage of German intentions and capabilities from a ring of stations in neighbouring countries, all of which were themselves anxious to remain neutral and were therefore especially sensitive about foreign intelligence agencies operating on their soil. The second period began after the German onslaught in the spring of 1940 which resulted in the occupation of Denmark, Norway, the Low Countries and France. This disrupted (and in some cases completely extinguished) SIS operations, which were further hampered by Italy's entry into the war alongside Germany in June 1940. The Service now faced the formidable problem of re-establishing itself in German-occupied territory. At the same time there were efforts to mobilise resources in the remaining neutral countries – Sweden, Switzerland and Iberia – both to target Germany itself and to attack the Germans' own foreign intelligence operations. Finland, which was neutral at the start, also offered apparently promising opportunities, but having fought (and lost) the Winter War against the Soviet Union in 1939–40, it moved closer and closer to Germany, becoming a full ally by the end of 1941.

Early wartime days

The first of a number of SIS withdrawals in the face of German advances during the war occurred from Poland in September 1939. On 1 September the Germans invaded. Two days later Britain and France declared war. German forces advanced so rapidly that on 5 September British diplomats, a military mission which had just arrived and the SIS station were all evacuated from Warsaw to Łuków, a small town fifty miles to the south-east. Here Sophie, the twenty-year-old wife of the SIS station chief, Major John Shelley (he was fifty-one), was killed in a German air raid. They had been married only since 21 February. Heading south towards the Romanian frontier, Shelley, using his secure SIS wireless, signalled London that 'as matters here now look like becoming SAUVE QUI PEUT and this place will become extremely dangerous', he had told the three female staff 'to prepare to leave but they begged to remain'. Not everyone was as cool under fire as Shelley's 'three stout-hearted and courageous girls'. While the female staff could stay, Shelley asked permission to send home two male colleagues 'who are quite useless in crisis [to] prevent panic and anxious to leave'. In fact they all escaped, with Shelley and his female secretaries reporting to Broadway on 28 September.[1]

In October 1939 the Polish intelligence service established its headquarters in Paris, but in the early summer of 1940 moved to London following the fall of France. In Paris a close liaison was established through the SIS station chief, Wilfred 'Bill' or 'Biffy' Dunderdale (nicknamed 'Wilski' by the Poles), who as head of the A.4 section at Broadway continued to be the chief SIS link with Polish intelligence after he too had to decamp from Paris to London. In Britain SIS offered financial, technical and logistical support, while the Poles (who had a very productive and extensive European-wide network of agents) agreed to pass on all the intelligence they acquired apart from any concerning internal Polish matters, an arrangement which, though not without its strains, worked thereafter to the great benefit of the Allied war effort.

For the SIS station in Helsinki across the Baltic Sea, the war effectively began on 21 August 1939 when more or less out of the blue the Soviet–German non-aggression pact was announced. This left the Finns to the mercy of their old enemies, the Russians, who invaded at the end of November. The Finns also felt badly let down by the Germans, which made it easier for Harry Carr, the long-serving SIS head of station, to work against both Germany and the Soviet Union. Carr's formidable range of Finnish contacts included senior officers in Finnish Military Intelligence such as Colonel Reino Hallamaa, head of the Radio-Intercept and Cryptographic Branch. In January 1940 Menzies asked Carr to find out if the Finnish authorities had 'procured any Soviet cryptographic material which could be communicated to us'. Carr immediately replied in the affirmative and it was arranged that Colonel John Tiltman of GC&CS should travel out to Finland, where he was presented by Hallamaa with a Red Army code-book taken off a dead Russian officer and which 'bore the marks of a bullet'. GC&CS noted afterwards that it had been 'of real assistance' to their cryptographers.

During 1940 Finland became something of a refuge for intelligence people of various sorts. After the German invasion of Denmark on 10 April, Sidney Smith, just a fortnight after taking over as the SIS representative in Copenhagen, moved to Helsinki. Head Office had wanted him to be based in Stockholm, where he could keep in touch with his agents, but this was vetoed by both the minister, Victor Mallet, and the Stockholm SIS head of station on the grounds that it would cause 'confusion'. With cover as a diplomatic courier, therefore, Smith travelled weekly to Sweden to meet agents. One of his contacts, a former Russian diplomat long resident in Denmark, tried to continue reporting through the United States legation in Copenhagen, but the Americans refused to pass the information on. Meanwhile, when it became apparent that the Russians were about to occupy the Baltic states, London decided to close down the Tallinn station and relocate some of the staff to Helsinki, from where they continued to run some Baltic agents. The fall of France brought an unexpected bonus for Carr in the shape of George Alexeev, head of the French secret service in Finland, who offered his whole agent network if SIS would provide the funding, an offer which London gratefully accepted. In September 1940 another Estonian contact, agent 'Outcast', who had been an important source on Soviet matters, turned up in Helsinki. Outcast, a Russian émigré formerly living in Berlin, had escaped from Tallinn with German help, but at the price of agreeing to work for the Abwehr Russian section. In Helsinki he told SIS that he would in future be visiting Finland regularly, and offered to work for the Service against the Germans. He appears to have been a valuable source, providing political, military and economic reports from within the Reich. In November 1940 he reported from his Abwehr control that 'German command [was] preparing (June) campaign against U.S.S.R.

which would begin Spring 1941 possibly earlier.' In his signal to Head Office Carr added that such a startling indiscretion by an Abwehr officer to his agent seemed 'incredible', warning that 'possibly [the] statement [had been] made for propaganda purposes'. London evidently agreed, since no further hard evidence remains in the archives of what would otherwise have been a unique intelligence coup.

After the German invasion of Russia in June 1941, SIS's position in Finland became increasingly precarious. During June and July Carr managed to get all his staff out to Sweden, and made arrangements for maintaining contacts after he too had to leave. While some of the agents were able to travel to Sweden themselves and others could use secret couriers, Carr also set up a link through the United States legation (which remained in Helsinki until the summer of 1944). After Britain broke off diplomatic relations with Finland in August 1941, the USA became the 'protecting power' (looking after British interests) and a British representative remained in the United States mission. Carr arranged for him to receive material from Alexeev (the Frenchman, who continued to work in Finland until the autumn of 1944). There was also intelligence from a Baltic network, run by a senior Estonian officer also working for the Swedes, Germans and Japanese. He left packages for Alexeev to pick up at a 'dead letter box' in a Helsinki public lavatory. Contact with Outcast, however, was lost when his handler (another Russian émigré) was arrested in August 1941. But Carr had wisely set up a drill for fall-back contact in Stockholm which Outcast duly implemented, though not until May 1942.

Until shortly before the war Oslo had been a sub-station of Stockholm, but over the summer of 1939 an independent station under Lieutenant Commander J. B. Newill was established. In September Frank Foley, the longstanding SIS man in Berlin, was posted to Oslo with general responsibilities for Scandinavia as a whole, evidently on the assumption that he would be able to meet former contacts permitted to travel outside Germany, and also be well situated to recruit neutral residents who could visit the Reich. In the event not much was achieved beyond Foley putting GC&CS in touch with Norwegian cryptographers who had succeeded in breaking some German diplomatic codes and were working on German and Russian naval and military cyphers.

Following the German invasion, the Norwegian military high command withdrew from Oslo north towards Lillehammer. Foley and his staff went with them and provided secure wireless communications through which the Norwegian Commander-in-Chief, General Ruge, appealed desperately for help from the British and French governments. On 14 April Foley added his own commentary. Norway, he said, 'has lost her arsenals and supplies in towns captured by Germans. They are fighting almost with bare fists . . . Unless help comes at once there will be a first class disaster from which allies will, I submit, find it difficult to recover.' General Ruge 'fears he will not be able hold out much longer. Please take his word most earnestly. You cannot conceive pitiable condition material this army but men fine types.' Foley's secretary, Margaret Reid, afterwards compiled a vivid account of the retreat under attack from German bombers, eventually reaching Molde on the west coast where they embarked for Scotland on 30 April. During one air raid the SIS wireless operator, H. C. Edwards, collapsed. 'He was unconscious for over an hour,' recalled Reid, 'and part of the time delirious and calling out for his wife and Commander Newill.' 'In all probability', she thought, it was 'due to overstrain and too little sleep'. He died a few days later.[2]

On his return to London Foley was put in overall charge of operations in Scandinavia (with Newill as section head), the Low Countries and those involving de Gaulle's Free French movement. Inevitably there was a period of confusion while the arrangements needed to underpin a successful co-ordinated clandestine effort evolved. Not only was there friction between SIS and SOE, but there were internal differences between the Norwegian armed services themselves, and establishing satisfactory liaison with the Norwegian government-in-exile took some time. Meanwhile on 10 June wireless contact was established with agents in Haugesund (on the coast south of Bergen), but the group was broken up by arrests in August 1940. With SIS clearly under pressure to re-establish a presence in Norway, two large groups of agents were infiltrated in September by a motorised fishing boat from the Shetland Islands: 'Skylark A' (destined for Oslo) had twelve agents, and 'Skylark B' (Trondheim) twenty-one. By April 1941, with the Norwegians and SOE separately sending in their own people, Newill complained that without any central control there were 'many examples of line crossing' which 'increases the hazard to our agents to such an extent as to make their work almost impossible'.

Although Claude Dansey's appointment in May 1941 as an adjudicator between SIS and SOE eased the inter-agency problems, progress was slow. In July 1941, other than some intermittent communications from Skylark B, all the Norwegian section could report was the early stages of four additional operations, three of which aimed to provide ship-watching reports from along the coast. During 1941 a series of operations identified by Greek code-names were initiated. Most of these emanated from suggestions by Norwegian escapees that they should return to Norway equipped with a wireless set, or that they had contacts (particularly in shipping circles) who could already operate a set and who would willingly act as observers. One operation was 'Epsilon', run by Newill's successor, Eric Welsh. In particular this investigated German interest in heavy water, an important component in the development of an atomic bomb, and produced by the Norsk Hydro hydroelectric plant at Rjukan in south-central Norway. In October 1941, Leif Tronstad, a professor of chemistry in Trondheim and a member of the Skylark B network, escaped to England where he was interviewed by R. V. Jones, an Air Ministry official seconded to SIS's scientific section (which he headed), and Professor Frederick Lindemann, Churchill's scientific adviser.[3] Based on Tronstad's information Welsh (a scientist himself) proposed the destruction of the plant by bombing or sabotage. 'The removal of this source of supply', he wrote, 'would completely cripple any designs the Germans may have with regard to this type of weapon and on the other hand, the Allies are not in a position to use this potential weapon themselves for at least eighteen months, as they are only now considering building a suitable plant in America.' Following the disastrous failure of a Combined Operations raid, the machinery was temporarily disabled and heavy-water stocks destroyed in a well-executed SOE sabotage attack in February 1943. This demonstrated, at least in this instance, that SIS intelligence and SOE operations could successfully and productively be integrated.

The most sustained demand for Norwegian intelligence came from the Admiralty, who wanted rapid information about German naval movements along the coast. Trondheim became particularly important after the main German battle fleet was based there in January 1942. In April the newly appointed Deputy Director/Navy, John Cordeaux, complained that 'we are very scantily served at present in Norway, being represented only in Bodo, Trondheim, Bergen and Oslo', but efforts to recruit and infiltrate more agents brought a marked improvement over the following

year. The need to provide coverage for the Admiralty at Kirkenes on the
Russian frontier in the far north-west of Norway (where there was a
U-boat base) led to a disastrous co-operative venture with the Russians.
Two SIS agents equipped with radios were flown by Catalina flying boat
to an airbase at Lake Latkha in Russia in August 1942. The Russians had
agreed to receive the agents and drop them by parachute near Kirkenes.
Far from despatching them within days, as promised, the Russians held
the agents incommunicado for two months and then dropped them,
with only their summer equipment, in Finland instead of Norway. They
were quickly apprehended and handed over to the Germans who brought
them to Oslo, where they were interrogated under torture and shot. 'I
am', minuted Cordeaux in October 1943, 'most distressed to read this
dreadful story and of course now bitterly regret that we attempted co-
operation with the Russians.'

The German conquest of Norway not only brought the hitherto rather
poorly resourced SIS station in Sweden into the front line, but it also
naturally heightened the Swedes' vigilance concerning any foreign clandestine activities which might threaten their neutrality.[4] Besides, as
with other European neutrals in the early years of the war, while there
were undoubtedly individuals with pro-British leanings, there were also
many pro-Germans in Sweden. The station chief in 1939, Lieutenant
Commander John Martin, had no more than ten regular agents and sub-
agents on his books, with four more on probation. Early in 1940 a group
of Section D agents, primarily gathering shipping intelligence for the
Ministry of Economic Warfare, were arrested, and all were sentenced to
prison terms of hard labour ranging from eight to fifteen months.[5]

Worse was to come. In April 1940 an SIS Section D team was uncovered
by the Swedes. They were operating under business cover and aiming to
sabotage northern Swedish port installations handling iron-ore exports to
Germany, an operation specifically urged by Churchill. The leader of the
group, A. D. Rickman (who had attracted the attention of the Swedish
Security Service by his contacts with German émigré journalists), was
arrested and a mass of compromising material found in his flat, including fifty-three kilos of gelignite, detonators and electric timing devices.
The minister, Victor Mallet, complained to London that 'our sleuths
seem to be thoroughly bad at their job: so far they have achieved little
in Sweden beyond putting me and themselves in an awkward position'.

Martin was not at all happy either. 'Frankly I feel very bitter after all the hard work and time I have given up to help them', he cabled London, 'that they should, by their own negligence or inefficiency or both, have compromised me like this.' The Rickman debacle, moreover, demoralised Martin's most important single Swedish source, who had been reporting on the information revealed to the Swedes by Rickman and his associates. 'Effect of this case on source deplorable,' wrote Martin. 'He stated frankly that previously he felt he was working with people who knew their job but now feels large portion of 22-land [UK] S.I.S. composed of inexperienced amateurs.'[6]

Section D's incompetence in Sweden was one of the factors undermining Laurence Grand's position back home and contributing to the creation of SOE as an independent agency. Martin never lost his antipathy to special operations, and the situation in Sweden illustrates SIS–SOE relations at their worst. In March 1941, for example, after the arrest of three SOE Norwegian agents, Martin complained to Menzies that he considered 'activities of S.O. organization having serious results and impairing our relations with Swedes . . . [It] embarrasses me and increases my difficulties. They cross my lines and tap my resources with resulting serious confusion.' Menzies, in turn, asked Frank Nelson at SOE to 'consider issuing instructions for your people to lie low and to act with the utmost discretion for the time being'.

The fall of Denmark and Norway in 1940, and the expulsion of the British from Finland in 1941, meant that by the beginning of 1942 Sweden had become a hive of SIS activity. Additional staff were sent in, and sub-stations opened in Malmö and Gothenburg. From the capital, albeit under very close Swedish surveillance, Martin's Stockholm station worked Swedish and Danish cases, and assisted with Norwegian operations, while Harry Carr's Helsinki station-in-exile worked Finnish and Baltic cases. The most important of the Norwegian operations involved contact from November 1941 with scientists who had access to valuable intelligence on German progress towards an atomic bomb.

Despite this activity, London wanted more from Stockholm, and in February 1942 Menzies told Martin that he was 'seriously alarmed at lack of [military, naval and air] information from first hand sources in North Germany, German Baltic ports and Denmark', and that he hoped that under Carr's supervision 'a service to North Germany and Denmark' might be worked up, both directly and through the Baltic states. Martin continued to have problems, not all of his own making. In April 1942 the head agent of the Czechoslovak intelligence service (run by the Czechoslovaks from the UK), along with three members of his network, was arrested. The Czechoslovaks reported, using their own code, through the SIS Stockholm station. Among the documents captured were their coding materials and, having read all their back telegrams, the Swedes took particular exception to one message referring to the possibility of sending typhus-infected lice into Germany, as they naturally felt their position would be badly compromised if the Germans got to hear of it. Martin, of course, suspected the hand of SOE behind it, and so, indeed, it turned out, SOE being in touch with at least two of those arrested. The press coverage in Sweden was considerable and Mallet was once more embarrassed.

In December 1942 Martin was replaced as Passport Control Officer by Cyril Cheshire (a fluent Russian-speaking timber merchant in civilian life), who, in the undoubtedly more favourable circumstances of 1943–5, markedly increased the productivity of the Stockholm station. Martin had certainly been under very heavy pressure in 1939–42, and he bore the brunt of the move from a peacetime to a war footing, along with the burden of coping with the fallout from the early excesses of Section D and SOE. Under the circumstances he seems to have kept his head remarkably well, and he also retained the confidence of the minister, which was no mean achievement.

Switzerland

In September 1939 SIS had a station in Geneva, headed by a Passport Control Officer, with an assistant and a wireless operator. Following the outbreak of war, however, Claude Dansey and the greater part of his Z Organisation relocated from London to Switzerland, which was believed to be a better base for penetrating Germany. Dansey and at least four colleagues initially set up rather insecurely in a Zurich hotel, where Dansey had to warn his staff, 'Don't call me colonel.' Eventually the team was given cover as the visa section of the Zurich consulate, with Dansey as consul. After Menzies became Chief in November, Dansey was posted back to London and his deputy unsteadily (he had a drink problem) minded the station until February 1940, when he was replaced by Count Frederick 'Fanny' Vanden Heuvel, who remained in charge for the rest of the war. Heuvel was a cosmopolitan figure of Italian origin who had been brought up in England and had a successful business career. An acquaintance of Freddie Browning's, he had worked for Cumming in France and Switzerland from 1916 to 1918.

An SIS agent arrested in Switzerland in October 1939, while under interrogation, had already blown Dansey's cover as Z. So concerned was Dansey to secure this agent's release that in late November 1939 (before Menzies's official appointment as Chief) he personally visited the President of the Board of Trade and got Gladwyn Jebb to see Sir Horace Wilson at the Treasury in order to sanction some sort of trade deal with the Swiss – a suggestion was an increase in the import quota of watches from £30,000 to £50,000. Dansey had good reason to be nervous, as the arrested agent alleged that he had received all his instructions from him (Dansey). 'Why this gratuitous lie', fumed Dansey, 'when I had only just been put in touch with him I cannot understand.' Dansey's own Swiss sources now said that it was too dangerous for them to meet him in public as he was effectively 'brûlé' (blown). After discussions with a Swiss intermediary a deal was struck and the agent released and returned to England.

The possibilities for establishing robust networks of agents targeting Germany and Italy, which had originally been the main purpose of the Z Organisation, markedly deteriorated after the war had begun. Already highly sensitive about their neutrality, the Swiss made life difficult for all the foreign intelligence services operating in their country: French, German and Italian, as well as British. Early in 1940, they successfully penetrated the SIS Zurich station with a Swiss national who had been living in London and had applied for permission to return home, upon which the Z Organisation promptly recruited him without any apparent preparation to work in Switzerland. But he revealed himself to the Swiss authorities, who used him to keep tabs on SIS, a role he played for some time until his case-officer was alerted to his duplicity by an anonymous informant. It is scarcely possible that this man was recruited without Dansey being consulted, but the manner in which he was engaged is of a piece with the hasty quest for personnel in the difficult early wartime days.

Matters were not improved by the refusal of Dansey to permit his officers to do any counter-espionage work or of Valentine Vivian to deploy anyone from Section V in Switzerland. One officer, posted to Switzerland towards the end of the war, afterwards asserted that this was principally due to the personal antagonism between the two men, 'who were at no time on speaking terms throughout the war, a deplorable state of affairs'. Another difficulty with the Swiss operation concerned communications. There was an SIS wireless set at Geneva, but it could be used only for receiving messages as the Swiss authorities did not permit foreign missions in the country to send enciphered messages except through the Swiss Post Office. Before the fall of France messages went in a diplomatic bag through Paris, and after May 1940 it was possible for British members of the mission who had diplomatic status and were over the age of forty-five to travel through Vichy France to Spain and Portugal and thence by plane to London. This ceased after the Germans occupied Vichy in November 1942, but it was thereafter found possible to bribe South American diplomats to carry the bags out. 'Two journeys and retire for life' was the saying. For additional security, letters for the diplomatic bags were sewn into their envelopes. Cypher telegrams could still be sent, but SIS had to use one-time pads for this, which, as Switzerland became more isolated, came to be in very short supply, as getting material into the country was as difficult as getting it out. These communications difficulties meant that often only messages of the highest importance could be sent by cable, and that much intelligence collected in Switzerland reached London only after a considerable delay. Because of the lack of continuous secure communications, moreover, London was unable to send out any signals intelligence material, which was another handicap for the Swiss station.

Among the best wartime agents in Switzerland, Halina Szymańska, remembered by one SIS officer as 'a very attractive and formidable personality', began working in late 1940. Szymańska's husband had been Polish military attaché in Berlin, where the couple had become acquainted with the Abwehr chief Admiral Canaris.[7] After the defeat of Poland, Canaris had arranged for Szymańska to escape to Switzerland, where he put her in touch with the Abwehr representative in Zurich, Hans-Bernd Gisevius. Although nominally working as a secretary in the Polish legation in Berne, Szymańska became a Polish intelligence agent (though paid from British funds) and began to cultivate Gisevius for information about German policy and internal conditions. As well as passing information to the Poles, with their agreement she also reported directly to SIS using the code-name 'Z.5/1'. In January 1941, for example, she reported details of German aircraft stocks, Gisevius's belief that there would now be 'no invasion Great Britain but aerial bombardment on increasing scale also submarine activity', and 'no action Balkans before March'. Three months later Gisevius told Szymańska he was 'convinced hostilities between Russia and Germany will start early in May'. Much of this intelligence was very sound. The German invasion of Yugoslavia and Greece was launched on 6 April, and Operation 'Barbarossa', the invasion of the USSR, had originally been planned for May, but was postponed until 22 June 1941.

The most intriguing aspect of the Szymańska–Gisevius relationship, however, is the role of Canaris, or 'Theodor' as SIS called him. There has been much speculation about the precise nature of this sensational Swiss link between the intelligence services of Britain and Germany and whether, for example, Canaris and Menzies were in personal contact. The SIS archives reveal that Gisevius (though never an SIS agent) was a regular source of intelligence. Between August 1940 and December 1942 Geneva sent London twenty-five reports with information provided by him. Almost all of this was channelled through Szymańska. Although Vanden Heuvel told London that Gisevius was 'first and foremost acting as intermediary for Theodor', this is not unambiguously supported by the evidence, and only nine of the reports specifically quote Canaris. Indeed, Vanden Heuvel's assertion may have been calculated to boost his station's intelligence product as much as anything else. One report, however, was based on a dinner Szymańska had with Canaris in Berne on 19 October 1941. This is the only recorded face-to-face meeting between Canaris and anyone reporting directly to SIS. Canaris had just returned from a tour of the Russian front and reported the difficulties the German forces were experiencing there on account of severe winter weather. Hitler, he said, had miscalculated and had 'counted on support from dissatisfied elements in Russia itself, which had completely failed to materialise'.

Both Canaris and Gisevius were involved with opposition groups in Germany, but the extent to which their contacts with foreign intelligence agencies in Switzerland – Polish, British and American (from the spring of 1943 Gisevius also passed on information to Allen Dulles, representative in Berne of the United States Office of Strategic Services) – constituted treason is debatable. While Canaris and Gisevius may certainly have been keeping both their own and their country's options open, cultivating Polish and British contacts was legitimate Abwehr business which could produce valuable intelligence and even provide them with a channel for spreading disinformation. On 28 March 1941, for example, Szymańska reported a definitive statement from Gisevius, 'German troops in Libya *not* [emphasis added] for offence purposes'. Two days later, in fact, German and Italian forces launched their drive into Cyrenaica.

Venlo and work in the Low Countries

One consequence of the Z Organisation's move to Switzerland was that Dansey's man in the Netherlands, Sigismund Payne Best, was transferred to work under Richard Stevens, the SIS station chief at The Hague. Best brought with him what appeared to be extremely promising contacts with an anti-Nazi network inside the German army. Early in October 1939 Stevens told London that Best was 'reasonably confident' that he could arrange for 'two highly placed 12-landers' ('12' being the code for Germany), Generals von Rundstedt and Dorsheim, to visit Holland 'in the near future'. They were, he reported, members of an organisation which sought to 'overthrow the present regime and establish a military dictatorship'. What the Germans wanted, however, was 'some sort of assurance' that, if they succeeded, the British government would 'be prepared to treat with them'. Stevens consulted Sir Nevile Bland, the British minister at The Hague, who gave his support, but because of his diplomatic status was not prepared to take part himself without instructions from London. Further enquiries by Stevens revealed that, as well as Rundstedt, a General Wiedersheim and an Oberst (Colonel) Teichmann were involved in the opposition group.

Within a fortnight direct contact had been established. On 17 October Teichmann, 'speaking discreetly by telephone', reported that Wiedersheim had attended an army commanders' meeting with the Nazi leader Heinrich Himmler at which the generals had 'refused to undertake any major action of any kind against France or England' and had 'insisted that everything be done to obtain peace'. Teichmann further said that conditions were 'such that only small impetus required to set ball rolling and to get rid of Nazis'. Here was intelligence apparently coming from the very highest German military circles, and with it the seductive possibility of bringing down the Nazi regime. SIS was playing for high stakes indeed, and the potential prize was so glittering that critical faculties both in the Netherlands and in London were dangerously blunted. Years afterwards an SIS contemporary at The Hague remembered 'the almost overbearing confidence of Stevens, who seemed to be completely in the pocket of Best', and a diplomat at the British mission recalled that Stevens, 'who was a man of immense ambition, saw in this a possibility literally of winning the war off his own bat, and this completely clouded his operational judgement'.

But if Stevens and Best were dazzled, so too, apparently, were the Chief in London and even his political masters. While Sinclair was in his last illness (he died on 4 November), and perhaps not fully able to engage with developments, Rex Howard, his chief of staff, and Menzies, his deputy, were kept fully informed, as was the Foreign Secretary, Lord Halifax, and the Prime Minister, Neville Chamberlain, who gave his personal approval for SIS to continue discussions with the Germans. Although some officials and politicians were not very optimistic about the possibilities of success, on 1 November the War Cabinet authorised the continuation of negotiations.[8] Halifax also circumspectly briefed the French ambassador in London about the covert contacts said 'to emanate from German military elements . . . anxious to get rid of the Nazi régime'. In the Netherlands, although it was still a neutral country and keenly anxious not to offend Germany, the head of Dutch Military Intelligence, General J. W. van Oorschot, supported SIS and provided an intelligence officer, Lieutenant Dirk Klop, to accompany the SIS men when meeting the German representatives.

There was surely an element of wish fulfilment about the whole affair. It may have seemed too good to be true, and so it was. From the start, alas, it was a brilliantly conceived and executed double-agent operation run by the Nazi Sicherheitsdienst (SD: security service). Although General Wiedersheim actually existed, he never turned up to any of the five meetings Stevens and Payne Best had with supposed emissaries. But the Germans tantalisingly increased the pressure in early November. After a meeting with a 'Hauptmann Schaemmel' (actually the SD officer Walter

Schellenberg, who was running the operation), Stevens told London on 7 November that a 'coup d'état will be definitely attempted' whatever the British government's attitude might be. The same evening he telephoned London to say that 'to-morrow, the big man himself is going to meet us'. But the next day (phoning at midnight), although they had had another 'satisfactory meeting', due to a German military conference which Wiedersheim apparently could not avoid 'big man did not come, but sent most cordial message, and probably coming tomorrow'. Following this meeting Stevens proposed flying to London to report in person and hoped to brief a senior Foreign Office official to carry on the negotiations.

The scene of the Venlo incident as depicted in the Amsterdam newspaper De Telegraaf, 30 December 1939.

So it was that on 9 November 1939 – a grey, overcast day – Stevens, Best and Klop (himself masquerading as the British 'Captain Copper'), along with Best's driver Jan Lemmens, headed for Venlo on the Dutch–German frontier. The rendezvous was at the Café Backus, situated beyond the Dutch border post and about 150 yards short of the German one. In a script prepared for a radio broadcast after the war, Stevens described a peaceful scene on the day: 'No one was in sight except a German customs officer who was strolling towards the Dutch customs house and a little girl who was playing ball with a big dog in the middle of the road.'

'Schaemmel', standing on the café veranda, waved a greeting. The man in charge of the German snatch squad, captured and interrogated by MI5 late in the war, told his side of the story: 'As soon as Schellenberg recognized the approaching car of the two British agents he gave the arranged signal by taking off his hat.' Firing machine guns in the air, the squad rushed forward and captured Stevens, Best and Lemmens. Klop opened fire, and was himself fatally wounded.

Beyond the wider fact that Stevens and Best had been completely taken in by the Germans, their tradecraft that day was deplorable. Stevens was carrying some coding material, and Best had a list of agents' names and addresses with him. They travelled to Venlo in Best's own distinctive American Lincoln Zephyr car. Perhaps because there had been two previous meetings at the same venue, no one thought to reconnoitre the area ahead of time on 9 November, and there was no contingency plan in case things went badly wrong. Stevens's and Best's own attempts at security, keeping the dealings with 'Schaemmel' and the others completely to themselves at The Hague station, meant that there was no opportunity for any of Stevens's colleagues to assess the German emissaries or the operation as a whole. Stevens's head agent, moreover, had himself taken on an assistant, Folkert van Koutrik (code-named 'Wallbach'), in the summer of 1939, who was shortly thereafter turned by the German Abwehr, and proved to be a very valuable source indeed, so much so that by the autumn of 1939 the Germans had a pretty clear picture of the whole SIS operation in Holland, a fact which clearly informed their subsequent interrogation of Stevens and Best.

The Venlo disaster came at a bad time for the Service. The changeover at the top and the early wartime pressure to produce results, combined with enthusiastic initiative on the ground (not always a bad thing), meant that the operation was pressed forward with perhaps more despatch than should have been the case. The fact that Best was Dansey's man, moreover, cannot have helped such ambitions as Dansey may have had for Sinclair's job. Stevens and Best, however, were not acting independently and, albeit based on their own judgment of the case, proceeded only after seeking approval from London. The participation of the Dutch, who maybe had more to lose than the British if the operation went wrong, was also significant, and can only have encouraged Stevens and Best to press on with the contacts.

But the damage from the affair was very great. The Service's reputation inevitably suffered, and the Germans made tremendous propaganda capital out of it. For the rest of the war the painful Venlo experience coloured British opinions generally (and Menzies's specifically) about responding to apparent German opposition elements. The capture of Stevens and Best, who spent the rest of the war in a series of prisons and concentration camps, gave the Gestapo a glorious opportunity of interrogating 'members of the British Intelligence Services in positions of authority' and obtaining a picture of the organisation's activity. How much actual information they got from the two SIS officers, and how much from their double agent van Koutrik, remains uncertain. By mid-December 1939, however, the Germans were able to construct detailed and largely accurate charts of both Stevens's and Best's agent networks and in the autumn of 1940 their Informationschaft GB provided some fairly accurate information about SIS head office and the Z Organisation, quoting both Stevens and Best. Postwar interrogation of German intelligence officers suggested that, while van Koutrik had provided names and addresses of Stevens's Hague station agents, 'they knew nothing of the Best organisation prior to the Venlo incident'. Whatever the truth of the matter, it is clear from the German interrogation reports on Stevens and Best that both men provided plenty of information about SIS, if only because they believed the Germans already knew a lot.[9]

The Dutch government were deeply embarrassed by Venlo, and Anglo-Dutch relations suffered accordingly. A complete breakdown in diplomatic relations was saved only by Sir Nevile Bland's considerable emollient skills, but General van Oorschot had to resign and the Foreign Office instructed SIS forthwith to cease all activities in the country. Rodney Dennys, head of the counter-espionage section, which operated separately from the Stevens–Best networks and had not been compromised, protested strongly and after Menzies had weighed in on his behalf was allowed to continue working, provided he moved his headquarters to Brussels. But when the Germans invaded in May 1940, Dennys, who evidently had not completely relocated to Belgium, spent a day and a half at The Hague burning files and card indexes. During the invasion Major Monty Chidson, the fluent Dutch-speaker who had briefly headed The Hague station in 1937, in one of D Section's few real successes managed to seize the bulk of Amsterdam's industrial diamond stocks (essential for machine tools) and, with the help of two Dutchmen, to bring them safely to England.

SIS's relations remained frosty with the Dutch government-in-exile after the Germans occupied the Netherlands. From the summer of 1940, nevertheless, the Service managed to slip in a few agents. A Dutch naval officer, Lodo van Hamel, for example, was dropped in by air on the night of 28–29 August. Some went in by sea, including Pieter Tazelaar, put ashore at 4.35 a.m. on 23 November at Scheveningen near the seafront casino in full evening dress and smelling of alcohol, wearing a specially designed rubber oversuit to keep him dry while landing. Rather than leaving him 'somewhere on the dunes', the aim was for him immediately to be able 'to mingle with the crowd on the front'. Having landed on the beach, his colleague Erik Hazelhoff sprinkled a few drops of Hennessy XO brandy on him, to strengthen his 'party-goer's image'.[10] But without reliable contacts inside the Netherlands these agents were all sent in blind, which made the effort especially hazardous. Van Hamel, for example, was soon captured and executed by the Germans. Of fifteen agents sent in over the eighteen months from June 1940, all but four lost their lives, a fate which intensified Dutch ill-feeling towards SIS. The Special Operations Executive, meanwhile, began working actively with the Dutch, producing a considerable amount of intelligence. When John Cordeaux became responsible for operations in the Low Countries in the spring of 1942, he found that SIS was 'in the humiliating position of obtaining no information ourselves, but being graciously allowed to pass on . . . intelligence obtained by S.O.E.'. Cordeaux, however, managed to establish a fresh SIS liaison with the Dutch government-in-exile, and after the nightmare of Operation 'North Pole', when during 1942–3 SOE's Dutch operations were disastrously penetrated by German intelligence, he was able (in conjunction with SOE) to build up productive networks over the last two years of the war.[11]

The SIS operation in Belgium, which had been under heavy pressure in the immediate prewar period, expanded rapidly after the outbreak of the war. Under what was known as the '13124 Plan', Edward Calthrop, the head of station and Passport Control Officer in Brussels, began to recruit agents initially in the east of the country to give warning of any concentration of German troops across the frontier. Should Belgium be invaded it was hoped that the network could continue as a stay-behind organisation. The head agent was the sixty-year-old Walthère Dewé, who had run the celebrated Dame Blanche organisation during the First World War. His agents in 1940 seem to have been well selected and at least two of them survived to operate after Belgium was occupied. They were given radio transmitters and some rudimentary Morse code training, and were instructed to send their signals blind. Confirmation of receipt was to be provided through coded messages in talks and poetry readings broadcast by Radio des Beaux-Arts, an SIS Section VIII venture operating from England but 'purporting to be a small broadcasting station financed by philanthropic old Belgian ladies desiring to bring something of beauty to an ugly war clouded world'. Sustaining this fiction proved difficult after the occupation as the technicians in Britain had to make sure that their transmissions did not overrun the German-directed electric power cuts imposed across Belgium. This perhaps over-elaborate system was not a great success, but Gambier-Parry extracted two useful lessons from the experience. 'Ab initio training of an agent who had no knowledge whatever of signalling' was not 'a practical proposition', and personnel would have to be recruited for wireless communications in the field with some existing signalling experience. The second lesson was that stay-behind schemes were inherently problematic. Gambier-Parry noted that the operation planned in Belgium 'under pre-invasion conditions suffered the handicap that these conditions became revolutionised after occupation by the enemy', and that the 'subsequent infiltration' of agents was a much more successful procedure. Inevitably this was fraught with danger. The first agent, Henri Leenaerts, was flown in on 18 August 1940, but the Lysander which carried him was unable to land and was lost on the return flight, killing the pilot and agent.

In fact, the most productive source of intelligence from inside occupied Belgium came from a partial revival of La Dame Blanche under Dewé, who ran a network successively called 'Cleveland' and later 'Service Clarence' until he was captured and shot by the Germans in 1944. Their intelligence covered a broad range of subjects, including information on aircraft hangars; troop and train movements; the state of Belgian industry; reports on the movement of munitions and munitions depots in Belgium (as well as some in neighbouring Germany); drawings of fortifications around Zeebrugge; and reports on the effects of local RAF attacks on German defences in the Low Countries.[12] In May 1941 it was reported that the

Cleveland organisation was 'the only one now working in Belgium', but by the end of the year three further networks had been established with courier lines working into Spain. These doubled as escape lines for British service personnel, which, although important and valuable, markedly increased the problems of security. As with other Allied countries, SIS operated in Belgium in co-operation with the government-in-exile in London, though here, too, there were difficulties arising from internal rivalries and the fact that the Belgian King and part of the Cabinet remained in Belgium. While the Belgian Sûreté de l'État developed a close liaison with SIS, the military Deuxième Bureau was more interested in sabotage and resistance, if not also (as some claimed) plotting to re-establish the King with a crypto-Fascist regime. During 1942 additional trained wireless operators were infiltrated and the supply of intelligence improved. In April the Air Ministry noted that reports from Belgium during February and March 'had added very considerably to the picture of the German night fighter organisations', while in June (echoing the achievements of La Dame Blanche a quarter of a century before) the War Office commented on the 'accurate, comprehensive railway information' being regularly provided by SIS sources which 'very frequently provides important confirmation of troop movements reported by other agents'.[13]

France

The main SIS concern in France was Biffy Dunderdale's 45000 network and his very close relationship with the French Deuxième Bureau, and subsequently with the Cinquième Bureau, formed at the outbreak of war to oversee clandestine intelligence work. Dunderdale was SIS's chief link with the Bureau head, Colonel Louis Rivet, and with Colonel Gustave Bertrand, who ran the French cryptanalytical branch. Although he had recruited agents to gather German military intelligence, Dunderdale was unable to keep them going in the chaotic weeks following the outbreak of hostilities. There were, he wrote, 'insurmountable difficulties in travelling across frontiers and even in France itself', due to the 'very severe control and complete disorganisation of civilian traffic'. Over the winter he came to depend almost entirely on information from Rivet's organisation. Following the rapid German advance into France after 10 May

1940 Dunderdale and his staff had to withdraw from Paris. On 10 June he found himself near Orleans, quartered next to the largest ammunition dump in France, and cheerfully reported to Menzies the observation of the French colonel in command that if the dump went up it would result in an 'instantaneous and painless death'. But the French were beaten and Menzies called the SIS team home.

Partly due to French sensitivities, stay-behind preparations in France were continually frustrated until May 1940, by which time it was too late to achieve anything meaningful. At the last minute the head of Dunderdale's Special Communication Unit managed to organise a wireless link with Bertrand, which in the immediate aftermath of the capitulation was the only direct SIS contact with France. A further difficulty lay in the fact that the majority of SIS's French contacts were with men who continued to serve under the Vichy regime which, after the surrender to the Germans in June 1940, survived as a quasi-independent government responsible for a large part of southern and south-eastern France. The Vichyists were vehemently opposed to the Free French General de Gaulle, while in their turn the Free Frenchmen (who inevitably constituted a highly promising source of potential agents) heartily despised Vichy and all its works. Faced with this conundrum, and under immense pressure from the government and service ministries to get intelligence out of France, Menzies deputed Dunderdale to head Section A.4 and continue to foster contacts with Bertrand and his Vichy colleagues, while Commander Kenneth Cohen, who had been in Paris as part of Dansey's Z Organisation, was made head of Section A.5 and deployed to work with the Free French. Although in the anxious summer days of 1940 this division of responsibility may have seemed to Menzies to be the only option, the potential for competition, disagreement and friction was very great, and was heightened by the fact that, while Cohen was responsible to Dansey (the Assistant Chief), Dunderdale reported directly to Menzies himself.

By late June 1940 the War Office was urging SIS to get agents into France as soon as possible. Clandestine pick-up operations and insertions started as early as 18 June, when Major Norman Hope of Section D led an abortive mission to rescue General de Gaulle's wife. On 23 June, three men were landed on the French coast to ascertain the morale of the people. But, as Major Hubert Hatton-Hall, head of SIS's Army Section, argued, wherever the target area was, the 'important thing is to enlist agents who belong to those areas & who know their way about & to provide them with WT communications'. None of this could be magicked out of thin air, but in late July Commander Frank Slocum's new Operations Section landed Dunderdale's first A.4 agent, a young cavalry cadet called Hubert Moreau, the son of a French admiral, near Douarnenez in western Brittany. Moreau stayed for four days, and, operating out of Mylor Creek in Falmouth Harbour, Cornwall, he went on to make two more trips in August and September.[14] Above and beyond whatever intelligence was acquired, the expeditions demonstrated that, although difficult, it was possible to infiltrate agents by sea, and contacts made in these early days contributed to the marine reporting system which developed along the French coast.

LONDON.

25th December, 1940.

Dear

The following is the agent's report which I have received as a Christmas message. I am told that it is not altogether original and that a somewhat similar version was in circulation in Rome a year or two ago. All the same, it is an amusing effort.

"Communique. Fête de Noel supprimée par ordre autorité Allemande. Plus possible de la célébrer. La Sainte Vierge et l'Enfant Jesus sont evacuées. Saint Joseph est mobilisé. Les Trois Rois sont en Angleterre. Les bergers sont arrêtés. Etoile est occultes. Etable requisitionné. Le Boeuf est à Rome. L'Ane est a Berlin."

Yours ever,

Air Commodore A. R. Boyle, C.M.G., O.B.E., M.C.

Evidently hoping to raise spirits at Christmas 1940, this letter from Menzies to Archie Boyle of Air Intelligence, asserts that the festival had been abolished 'by German authority'.

Clandestine landing by sea was not the only option and on 20 August 1940 the Royal Air Force formed No. 419 Flight at the North Weald fighter station to assist in the delivery and extraction of SIS (and SOE) agents in enemy territory. New aviation techniques had to be learned by the unit employing the limited available aircraft (obsolete Whitley bombers and army-support Lysanders). The first attempted operation pre-dated the formation of the flight by several days. In a report prepared in April 1942 Claude Dansey summarised it: 'In August, 1940, our first effort was made of landing an agent by Lysander. We were inexperienced, we were groping in the dark, and the first essay was a failure. What happened has never been known with exactitude as the plane did not return and we never heard of the agent or his wireless set.' It was a bad start but things soon improved; for the period October 1940 to August 1941, ninety operations were planned, of which forty-eight were cancelled before take-off. Of the remaining forty-two, four were unsuccessfully attempted, with the remaining thirty-eight involving the delivery of fifty-seven agents and the return of eighteen with the loss of three aircraft. It was not just a case of transporting people and delivering supplies; the operations were able to bring important documents back to Britain from the field.

Through the summer and autumn of 1940, the intelligence return was nevertheless disappointing. In November all three service liaison officers in SIS complained about the meagre product. The head of the Air Section, Group Captain F. W. Winterbotham, declared that 'with the exception of some reports from deserters and Free Frenchmen who have managed to get across to England, reports from agents on the German Air Force in France and Belgium have been practically nil'. Dansey responded by saying that to give a list of agents put back into occupied France would convey 'little or nothing' in itself, though it 'would show a record of disappointments'. The main problem was one of communications; satisfactory radio links had not yet been established and other means of communication, for example through Switzerland, meant that information when received was 'completely stale'.

Matters had improved by early 1941, when Dunderdale's organisation had agents and postboxes in occupied and unoccupied France. One important network (code-named 'Fitzroy' and later 'Jade') was set up by Claude Lamirault, who had been active in prewar extreme right-wing and anti-Communist circles. John Cordeaux wrote that he was 'as tough as any Chicago gangster' and 'rather an "ugly customer"' (so much so that SIS 'had certain misgivings about him'), but his 'burning hatred of the Germans' evidently outweighed his pro-Fascist political leanings. For the first two years of the war, moreover, the Russo-German non-aggression pact could provide anti-Communists with an additional justification for resisting the invader. Already versed in clandestine activity, Lamirault recruited agents 'from the most varied walks of life', including government officials, leading businessmen, factory workers, railway officials and prostitutes. Initially these agents provided information on economic and railway subjects.

Another network, code-named 'Johnny', provided good intelligence about the naval base at Brest, from March to June 1941 reporting on the positions, condition after bombing and state of seaworthiness of the German battle cruisers *Scharnhorst* and *Gneisenau*, while 'Felix' was the first to report the arrival of the heavy cruiser *Prinz Eugen* in June 1941. Human intelligence of this type was especially valuable, as it was only from the early summer of 1941 that the code-breakers at Bletchley Park were able to crack the German naval and dockyard Enigma cyphers. But the A.4 networks suffered a series of setbacks in 1942. In February Felix was disbanded after the capture of its wireless operator, and in April the Germans raided the Fitzroy headquarters at Sartrouville, capturing another radio operator. Lamirault was back in England at the time and insisted on being dropped blind into France, where he salvaged the remains of his group and managed to evacuate six important agents out through Spain and Gibraltar.

After the fall of France Dunderdale re-established contact with Rivet and Bertrand, who, although continuing to work for the Vichy regime, offered to supply SIS with information. Dunderdale, travelling as 'John Green', flew to Lisbon where on 5 September 1940 he met Rivet's representative, 'Victor', in the church of St Geronimo. Victor expressed his willingness to work on a reciprocal basis and also help the British with potential sabotage work in Spain and Libya. Dunderdale gave him a wireless transmitter and codes and reported to Head Office that for him reciprocity meant sending the French 'harmless stuff' while 'exploiting every opportunity of obtaining information'. Dansey, responsible for developing work with the Free French, meanwhile warned Menzies that liaison with anti-Gaullists could cause friction and political complications (as in fact it did), but SIS's contacts with the established French intelligence community had been so close and productive that, as Menzies put it in the spring of 1941, 'although my policy was queried, I insisted on renewing W/T contact with the French Deuxieme Bureau', after the fall of France.[15] It was a good decision, since through his unique position Bertrand (or 'Bertie' as he was referred to in telegrams) was able to provide advance warning of Abwehr and Gestapo intentions against SIS agents, as well as information on Italian and German troop and ship movements to North Africa, German dispositions in the Balkans and losses on the Russian front.

The false passport used by 'Biffy' Dunderdale (travelling as 'John Green') when meeting a representative of the Vichy French intelligence service in Lisbon in September 1940.

Back in England Kenneth Cohen at the head of A.5 had the difficult task of liaising with Colonel André Dewavrin – whose nom de guerre was 'Colonel Passy' – the head of the Free French Forces' Intelligence.

Agents infiltrated into France through Spain included Gilbert Renault, an ardent Gaullist, who by mid-1941 had started networks along the French Atlantic coast and established a courier line to Spain. One agent, employed by the Germans in Brest, sent him complete plans of the harbour defences and reported movements of German naval craft. Renault's organisation, which became known as the Confrérie de Notre-Dame, eventually covered most of France. Another extensive network was run by 'Navarre', a right-wing hero of the Great War and leading member of the veterans' organisation Les Anciens Combattants. Using war veterans' clubs and various charity enterprises as cover, by mid-1941 his organisation ('Kul') had spread into much of the unoccupied zone and, to a lesser extent, Brittany, parts of northern France and Paris, as well as having agents in French North Africa. 'Most of these agents', noted Cohen, were 'what might be termed "enthusiastic volunteers" of the officer type, rather than trained spies', and they were consequently sometimes ill prepared for the efficiency of the German security forces in France. Navarre himself was arrested in July 1941, but, thanks to the efforts of Marie-Madeleine Meric (later Fourcade), Kul continued to function. With Fourcade taking the code-name 'Hérisson' (Hedgehog), and later under the new name 'Alliance', it established its headquarters in Marseilles.[16]

By the end of 1941 A.5 had established particularly good coverage of the French Atlantic ports, where German U-boats and commerce raiders were based. But the growing size and consequent vulnerability of the networks resulted in a number of them, including the Confrérie de Notre-Dame, being penetrated by the Germans. Into 1942 there was a growing list of arrests, especially of wireless operators, but the Confrérie and Alliance nevertheless managed to provide a large volume of information from most parts of France. This was passed to the United Kingdom by wireless, by couriers through Spain, by sea operations to the Brittany coast and by aircraft pick-ups (of which by mid-1941 there was about one every month). Probably the most important intelligence was the very detailed coverage by a Confrérie cell of the German radar station and its defences at Saint-Bruneval, north of Le Havre on the French Channel coast. Along with air reconnaissance, this helped enable the successful British raid in February 1942 in which precious examples of the German equipment were captured.[17]

During 1942 Fourcade's Alliance organisation was threatened by the activities of 'Bla', a thirty-nine-year-old former farm manager in Normandy who had lived in France for about twenty years before the war. Escaping from the German advance, he had made his way to England in June 1940 and been recruited as an agent by SIS. He parachuted into southern France near Pau in August 1941, intending to operate a wireless set for Alliance and establish a network in Normandy. He began to report directly to London in February 1942, but inconsistencies in his identity checks, among other things, had begun to lead London to suspect that he might have been compromised. In May SIS received reliable information that Bla had been arrested by the Germans, who were using him for a deception operation. Hoping that he might still be loyal, Menzies decided in turn to play him as a double agent through the XX (or 'Twenty') Committee, an interdepartmental body set up in January 1941 which ran the tremendously successful British wartime Double-Cross System. He also wanted to give Bla the chance 'to escape from the enemy's clutches' and return to Great Britain. A rendezvous was arranged in July, when Bla did not appear, but one of the leading Alliance agents narrowly evaded arrest by Abwehr officers lying in wait for him. The following month, with mounting concern, London instructed Bla to hide his set and get to Spain or Switzerland where he should report to the British authorities. By this stage the alarm bells were also ringing at SOE, who knew Bla as 'Blanchet'. One of their agents had spotted him in Lyons, and Major Maurice Buckmaster, the head of SOE's F (Independent French) Section, told SIS that he was signalling to France to warn them that Blanchet was a 'most dangerous individual' and they 'should have no dealings with him whatsoever . . . If possible suggest to him that he makes for Spain,' he continued. 'If he persists in worrying you you are fully authorised to dispose of him as neatly as possible.' In September 1942 there were various sightings of Bla in Pau and Toulouse, and a chance encounter in Marseilles with another British agent, 'Heron', led to his capture in early October by Alliance agents masquerading as policemen.

Bla was taken to an Alliance safe house where he was interrogated by Marie-Madeleine Fourcade (among others) and confessed to 'having given to the Boches all details known to him about us'. They first tried to kill him 'without him knowing it', by putting lethal drugs in his food, but this failed and merely alerted the unfortunate man to 'the attempt we were making'. When he was killed he faced his fate with what Fourcade reported as 'extraordinary moral courage' and 'astounded us by his calm attitude in facing punishment'. 'The way he died', she wrote, 'did something to mitigate his past record.' Although in her memoirs Fourcade relates that an 'execution order' was received from London, nothing so explicit survives in the relevant files, and her contemporaneous report asserted that over the weekend when Bla was in Alliance hands no contact was established with London. A subsequent minute, nevertheless, by the Free French Section in Broadway recorded that as the leading members of Alliance were 'known personally to [Bla] the danger was such that eventually we instructed them to do away with him should the opportunity occur'. Bla's fate was naturally suppressed. When his widow made enquiries about him towards the end of 1944 she was simply told that the authorities had had no information of his whereabouts 'since 1942'. As one SIS officer minuted, 'if any sleeping dogs should be let lie I think this is one'.

A.4 and A.5 represented passionately opposed French political opinions. The files contain accusations and counter-accusations, with the Free French accusing Dunderdale of purloining Frenchmen before they had a chance to declare themselves for de Gaulle, and Dunderdale complaining about the unwillingness of the Free French to co-operate. After Dewavrin had complained to Dansey about Dunderdale's hostility to de Gaulle, in February 1941 Menzies tried to calm things down by giving Dunderdale the primary task of collecting intelligence from the ports in German-occupied France, authorising him to contact de Gaulle's staff direct for any personnel required 'so long as there is no possible overlapping', while adding that A.4 agents 'need not of necessity join De Gaulle, but if they can be persuaded to do so, the less bother will occur'. The maintenance of two parallel SIS French sections, while administratively inefficient, was a pragmatic solution to the intelligence opportunities which emerged after the fall of France. But it certainly ran risks. As the Beirut station warned in May 1942, 'any suspicion that [the] British were in contact with Bertrand would sow deepest seed of distrust in heart of even our best friends among Free French'. Dunderdale also provided SIS liaison with Polish intelligence organisations in France, drawing on contacts he had made before the war through Bertrand. This also irritated the Free French, who complained that the Poles were not only allowed to operate much more independently than they were, but were also permitted directly to recruit French agents of their own. Towards the end of 1941 the Polish F2 network in France had 210 French and only forty Poles. But it was very productive. The Marine Section, based in Bordeaux under 'Doctor', noted German submarine movements out of Bordeaux, Brest and Le Havre. Doctor also ran a cell called 'Italie', which reported German troop movements on Italian trains. It was the collation of information about troop transports and a tank division going south with a report about desert-war training in a Prussian camp that first suggested to London that the Germans might invade North Africa.[18]

The threat of invasion and conditions in Germany

For about a year from the fall of France SIS was under sustained pressure to provide intelligence on the likelihood of a German invasion of Britain. What the Service was able to glean can be followed in the reports for the Foreign Office and the service ministries, which from May 1940 were also supplied to Desmond Morton for the Prime Minister. The available human intelligence fell into two main categories: detailed eyewitness observations of German operational preparations, and higher-level information, mostly from Berlin, about German strategic intentions. In July 1940 agents reported the arrival of paratroop battalions in Norway and Belgium, including a *Landungskorps* (special air landing force) which had been transferred from Austria. In September Menzies sent Morton (for Churchill) a very detailed series of reports from an A.4 agent who had just made his second visit to northern France. The agent had cycled along the north coast of Brittany and returned with maps showing German garrisons, gun-emplacements, airfields and troop concentrations, photographs of German activities at Douarnenez and Lorient, and reports of German soldiers practising amphibious landings. On into the autumn, agents' reports confirmed the probability of an invasion. On 30 September fully equipped German troops were observed to have embarked on seven cargo ships at Bayonne, only to disembark two days later. On 20 October the German War Ministry ordered that three *Einsatztruppe* (special contingents) were to be despatched, one to Oslo and two to The Hague, each contingent being accompanied by two English-speaking interpreters. The Navy Section weekly summary for 21–28 October noted ships of four and five thousand tons lying in Hamburg harbour waiting to take on troops, and on 4 November a French agent watched a German invasion exercise at Étaples, using rubber boats with ten to twenty soldiers in each.

The best of the higher-level reports about possible invasion came from Menzies's 'very well placed and reliable German source'. This was 'A.54', Paul Thümmel, who had offered his services to the Czechoslovaks in 1936. They continued to run him, first from the Netherlands and later from London after Colonel František Moravec and the core of the Czechoslovak Intelligence Service had been spirited out of Prague by SIS in March 1939. Thümmel was a well-placed Abwehr officer who was able to provide first-class intelligence (which came via Switzerland) about German capabilities and intentions.[19] Between April and December 1940, designated '12022/A' by SIS, he supplied at least fourteen reports specifically concerning the invasion question, and the way in which they were processed demonstrates how SIS broadly handled intelligence at this time. The subject matter was classified as political, which meant that the primary circulation of the material was to the relevant section of the Foreign Office, in this case the Central Department. Other copies (of which, apparently, no more than thirteen were made) were sent to the Permanent Under-Secretary (who was only personally sent reports judged to be of special importance, and internal evidence suggests were for him to show to the Foreign Secretary, Lord Halifax), the PUS's private secretary (who was sent copies of all reports), Major Morton (for the Prime Minister) and the service departments. The only copies of the reports which have survived are those sent to Morton and which he (as required) returned to SIS.

Thümmel's first mention of an assault on Britain was in 'an unavoidably delayed report' of 2 May, circulated on 19 May 1940. 'Intense preparations for air attacks on England', he warned, 'are proceeding,' but the invasion itself had 'been postponed, because all available troops are being used in Norway'. In July he reported that the invasion had been further postponed pending clarification of Soviet intentions in the Balkans. On 13 August SIS circulated a report which had been received 'within the last few days' from their 'very well placed German source'. It asserted that the attack on Britain was 'not to be expected within the next fourteen days'. An expeditionary force was being assembled in Paris, Brussels and The Hague, but the troops would not be ready for at least three weeks.

LIEUTENANT-COLONEL VIVIAN.

    Mr. Jebb asked me a few days ago if we could ascertain
the name of "Lord Haw-Haw". I said I would try to find out
his identity, and was told last night by a private
acquaintance that it is William Joyce of the British Fascist
Party. On asking how this was known, I was informed that
his first wife recognised his voice and also his child, who
suddenly turned pale on listening-in and said that it was
Daddy talking.

    Can you ask M.I.5. if it is possible that it is William
Joyce, or alternatively, is it a well known fact? At one
time it was thought that Baillie-Stuart was on the air.

Note:

    Since dictating the above, I hear it is a well known
fact that Joyce is "His Lordship". *also that*
M.I.5 share this view #.

                                        20th December, 1939.

*Menzies's response to an enquiry about the identity of the German propaganda
broadcaster, 'Lord Haw Haw'.*

This intelligence was clearly of interest at the highest level. 'P.M. saw Lord
Halifax's copy,' noted Morton. On 19 September Thümmel reported that
the 'fact that the attack on Britain had not yet taken place' was 'due
chiefly to weather conditions and secondly to the British air raids'. This

report was circulated on 21 September, just two days after being made, a remarkably quick process repeated in the next report, five days later, which also put the delay down to bad weather. By October Thümmel was reporting that the attack would not now be until 'early 1941', and on 28 December, having been present at a speech given by Field Marshal Keitel (Chief of the Oberkommando der Wehrmacht – the German Armed Forces High Command), he said that Hitler had decided on a spring invasion of Britain, perhaps at the end of March 1941. Keitel also forecast an attack on Greece in support of the Italians, but 'said he would let the Italians stew till the spring as the main German purpose was to syphon off British troops from North Africa'.

Thümmel was not the only person reporting about Germany in 1940. Regular reports on morale and other matters were assembled from a number of sources. A report in September contained information from two 'North Europeans' (most probably Swedes), who had visited Berlin, and an 'eminent Swiss physician', who had visited Munich and Vienna. A 'German manufacturer who arrived in Budapest from Hamburg' had said that the shipbuilding yards of Blohm and Voss had been completely destroyed by air raids. The following month a report entitled 'Germany: miscellaneous indications' drew on information from 'a Swede of standing, who has many friends in Berlin', 'a traveller of Austrian nationality, of a Swiss firm', 'the correspondent in Finland of an important German newspaper' who had just spent a month in Germany and 'a well placed neutral in Berlin'. These people were not 'agents', as the report explained; all their information had been acquired 'by trustworthy indirect means, i.e. none of these individuals is a conscious source of ours'. The SIS team in Switzerland were always on the lookout for information. Late in 1940 the Geneva station was advised that an employee of the United States embassy in Berlin would shortly be visiting Switzerland. 'She should only be asked to give information about conditions in Germany,' came the instruction, 'and <u>not</u> asked to work for us.' Hard military information was the most difficult intelligence to acquire. On 27 December 1940 Malcolm Woollcombe noted: 'It is piteous to find ourselves in this state of ignorance' about events and production inside Germany. Nevertheless, one agent did get through at this dark hour, a Yugoslav ex-naval officer, 'Rauf', who had been recruited in Trieste. Rauf visited Berlin in late 1940 and (according to his postwar medal citation, now the only record of his work) reported on the Junkers aircraft factory, and also 'gave important information on a newly-established aerodrome in the vicinity'.

Iberia

Once the Germans had occupied western France down to the Pyrenees and the Spanish frontier, it was widely feared that Spain would be their next victim. The right-wing government of General Franco, moreover, provided an accommodating environment for pro-German groups and SIS found itself having to devote considerable efforts to counter-espionage work. There was also the problem of dealing with Sir Samuel Hoare, ambassador in Madrid from June 1940 to December 1944, whose prickly combination of knowledge and authority (as both a former Foreign Secretary and a former intelligence officer) with a tendency to windy overreaction made him a difficult colleague. This was demonstrated in September 1940 after Hoare was told by his own 'secret sources' of an alleged 'confession' to the Spanish Security Police by three men posing as Belgians that they were British agents working for the Passport Control Officer (and SIS representative). Although the men were 'plants', apparently engineered by Falangist (Spanish Fascist) and German elements, Hoare, fearing that the incident could escalate into a major anti-British demonstration, panicked and ordered the Passport Control Officer to leave the country. He also wanted the newly arrived SIS head of station, Leonard Hamilton Stokes, to go; SIS to cease all work (especially along the frontier with France where Hamilton Stokes had been setting up an early-warning network against a possible German invasion) and to burn its archives; and the Passport Control Office to be run on a skeleton basis, dealing only with legitimate passport matters. Hamilton Stokes complained to Menzies that his 'position vis-à-vis YP [the ambassador] has become extremely difficult and embarrassing and reputation of S.I.S. has suffered'. Menzies responded with cool good sense. 'A mere statement unsupported by reliable evidence that certain persons are working for the Passport Control Officer', he signalled, 'should neither perturb the Embassy nor the Spanish authorities who happen to be friendly or neutral. This is just a bluff by the Germans to get our organisation shut down and YP has fallen for it.' Hamilton Stokes, he said, should 'tactfully' point out to Hoare that the men had 'never been employed by us' and that as the Passport Control Officer's name was well known, he was 'naturally a scapegoat'.

In the end the Passport Control Officer went home and Hamilton Stokes grumpily stayed on in Spain. Not only were relations with Hoare difficult, but he also had to work with the naval attaché, Captain Alan Hillgarth, an adventure novelist and personal friend of Churchill, who played a central role in collecting intelligence about enemy submarines in Spanish waters (Hoare described him as 'a veritable sleuth'),[20] and was permitted to communicate directly with Menzies in London. Over the winter of 1940–1 Hamilton Stokes endeavoured to build up his networks, exploring possibilities with, for example, opposition elements in the Confederación Nacional del Trabajo (National Labour Confederation). The potential for the public embarrassment (or worse) of the British in Spain if contacts such as these became known was another factor in Hoare's nervousness about SIS activities. This was exacerbated by Hamilton Stokes's liaising with the British military authorities to set up escape lines for Allied servicemen out of France. Already in August 1940 Frank Foley had raised the possibility of working with the Basques who had 'a complete S.I.S. organisation started during the Spanish Civil War' with excellent secret contacts and routes across the French frontier. But, as Foley delicately put it, arrangements with any such groups raised 'certain difficulties caused by considerations of higher policy', especially as the Basques, it seemed, in return for co-operation would demand British support for their political claims.

In the spring of 1941 SIS representation in Spain was boosted by the addition of a Section V officer, Kenneth Benton, to work under Hamilton Stokes. But, reflecting the animosity between Dansey and Valentine Vivian in London, Benton was separately instructed by the former to concentrate on developing communications across the Franco-Spanish frontier and stay-behind networks in Spain, and by the latter to devote himself to counter-espionage duties. After some irritable exchanges, Hamilton Stokes was confirmed as in overall charge of SIS activities in Spain, while Benton focused on the developing work in the territory south of Madrid, as well as counter-espionage across the whole country. Meanwhile Hillgarth (who doubled up as the SOE representative in Spain) had set up his own counter-espionage system, code-named

'Secolo', targeting German attempts to sabotage British ships in Spanish ports. Some positive work was at last being done. By the early summer of 1941 Hamilton Stokes had become cautiously optimistic and reported that over many months of patient and difficult work he had gradually re-established Samuel Hoare's confidence in SIS.

But it was not to last. Two high-profile incidents disturbed the harmony, the first of which was the Claire case. Early in 1941, 'Paul Lewis Claire', a French naval officer who had transferred to the Royal Navy after the fall of France, was taken on by Commander Slocum's O Section in SIS to help run clandestine sea operations in French waters. By July Claire was in Spain where he was arrested at the frontier apparently trying to get to Vichy France. Subsequently, as Hoare cabled to London on 23 July, Claire had gone to the Vichy French naval attaché in Madrid, to whom he had 'divulged many secrets of British S.S. in Spain and elsewhere'. Since 'French Embassy are now trying by every possible means to get him to Vichy', Hoare was 'accordingly faced with the dilemma (1) capturing or killing him and running the risk of irrevocably compromising the Mission. (2) Letting him get to France with the information that will destroy our present intelligence organisation in Spain and do even greater harm elsewhere.' Hoare wanted immediate instructions as Claire was expected to visit the embassy the following day to get his British passport. At SIS headquarters Frank Slocum advised that Hillgarth had been 'asked to take what steps he can to intercept Claire'. He also suggested that SOE might be approached 'to see if there is any possible step which could be taken in Spain or France to liquidate Claire' and wondered 'whether we could kidnap Claire's wife or any member of his family in an effort to bring Claire to heel'. Convinced he was a traitor (and Hillgarth afterwards said Claire had admitted his treachery), and aware that he possessed damaging information, including the identities of at least one agent network in northern France, Menzies said that if Claire could be intercepted, 'belief that he may learn something more to divulge may make it possible to get him to Gibraltar by road with assurance car will wait and bring him back to Madrid. Action Gibraltar', he added, 'will be arranged.'

What then happened can be followed in a series of telegrams mostly from Hamilton Stokes 'for C.S.S. only'. At 1.00 a.m. on 25 July he reported that 'in conjunction with Y.N. [Hillgarth] I have lured Claire to Embassy and rendered him unconscious. He leaves tonight under Morphia for Gibraltar by car.' There was good news at 6.13 p.m.: the kidnap had been 'satisfactorily accomplished'. Menzies responded by drafting a signal for Gibraltar instructing that Claire was 'to be arrested on arrival, charged with treason and kept under close arrest until opportunity of sending him home. On no repeat no account whatsoever is he to be allowed to escape.' But this signal was cancelled when, early the following morning, '51000' (the SIS representative in Morocco, currently in Gibraltar) informed Hamilton Stokes that 'consignment arrived in his ?town completely destroyed ?owing to over attention in transit. 51,000 states salvage being quietly disposed of tonight . . . Damage regretted but I submit it is for best.' In a despatch a few days later 51000 explained that during the drive south the unfortunate Claire had recovered from the drug and had begun 'shrieking for help and calling [*sic*] so much attention'. His captors had 'hit him on head with a revolver' with the result that he had died. 'It could not have been a worse affair,' wrote Hoare to Anthony Eden. 'As to ignorance of conditions the airy suggestion that we should intercept him in his journey to France shows how totally ignorant S.I.S. are of work in a semi hostile country stiff with German Gestapo. As it is with great personal risk to ourselves and still greater to the existence of the mission we have got rid of him – he is dead.' Though SIS was certainly at fault – Menzies frankly admitted that Claire should not have been sent to Spain – this criticism was less than fair. Hoare had himself raised the admittedly risky possibility of kidnapping Claire, and he later told Cadogan that 'had it not been for Hamilton Stokes' very efficient service, the man would now be in Vichy giving away every kind of secret to the Germans'. Rather ignoring the fact that Hamilton Stokes was himself an SIS officer, Hoare asserted that 'once again we have had here to save S.I.S. from a catastrophe'.[21]

There was some embarrassing political fallout. German and Vichy French diplomats in Madrid complained to the Spanish Foreign Ministry, and on 12 August Radio France broadcast a report of the affair, asserting that as the car passed through 'a small village in Andalusia' the prisoner 'tried to attract people's attention by shouting . . . [but] the Englishmen declared "Don't get upset, it's only a member of the Embassy gone mad and we are taking him to a Sanatorium"'. Two days later the London *Daily Telegraph*, under the headline 'Nazis invent a kidnapping', reported 'one of the highest flights of fancy from the Nazis' propaganda depart-ment', which alleged 'a gangster-like kidnapping of a Frenchman by British secret service agents in Spain'. In fact the German story was pretty accurate, but one Foreign Office official thought that 'the D.T. has done quite well and no doubt other papers would take the same line', a senti-ment with which Menzies agreed.[22] The official story (as communicated by Commander Ian Fleming of Naval Intelligence to the British Red Cross in July 1942) represented Claire as 'missing believed drowned', en route to Britain on the SS *Empire Hurst*, sunk by enemy aircraft on 11 August 1941. After the war, in order to protect SIS, it was decided to pay Claire's widow a pension, 'however repugnant it may be to reward the de-pendants of a traitor'. As Valentine Vivian minuted about the matter, 'It may be that "murder will out" in any case, but we stand to lose so much in this case if it does, that we ought not voluntarily to take the slightest scintilla of risk.'

The second affair which threatened to disturb SIS's position in Spain was that of Lieutenant Colonel Dudley Wrangel Clarke, who had been run-ning a strategic deception section at GHQ Middle East in Cairo since the late autumn of 1940. Using cover as a war correspondent for *The Times*, and aiming with the help of SIS to make contacts to assist his deception work, Clarke travelled to Lisbon and Madrid where, some time after call-ing on Hamilton Stokes, on 17 October 1941 (as the British embassy reported to London the following day) he 'was arrested in a main street dressed, down to a brassière, as a woman'. He initially told the Spanish police that he 'was a novelist and wanted to study the reactions of men to women in the streets'. Later he asserted that in fact 'he was taking the feminine garments to a lady in Gibraltar and thought that he would try them on for a prank. This', added the embassy, 'hardly squares with the fact that the garments and shoes fitted him.'[23] A telephoned press report from Madrid to Berlin which SIS intercepted said that 'Wrangal Craker, the Madrid correspondent of the London "Times"', had been arrested. Reflecting the 'unusual circumstances of these times' and the 'working methods of British agents', he had been discovered 'dressed as a woman'. 'Craker' had 'unusually big feet with a remarkable . . .' and here the inter-cept tantalisingly broke off with an 'indecipherable passage'. In response to anxious cables from Menzies, concerned about a possible leakage of in-formation, Hamilton Stokes reported that while the police were inclined to the theory that Clarke was a 'homosexualist', the German Gestapo had intervened and alleged he was a spy. On 21 October, however, Clarke was released from prison and the embassy got him away to Gibraltar the same evening.

On arrival in Gibraltar Clarke insouciantly claimed that the 'incident in Madrid was carefully calculated' and 'nothing (repeat nothing) whatever compromised'. He asserted, indeed, that the affair had usefully confirmed that his cover still held with both the Spaniards and the Germans. Clarke's eccentricity evidently reinforced his aptitude for secret work and the episode does not seem to have affected his own position, since he returned to Cairo and went on to have a brilliant career in deception. Hamilton Stokes, meanwhile, worried that his situation might have been jeopardised, while Hoare inevitably blamed the unwelcome publicity on SIS, though the Service could scarcely have predicted Clarke's foray into undercover work, if that is what it was.

Hoare's ambivalence about SIS, on the one hand anxious that covert activities be limited as much as possible so as not to upset relations with the host country, and on the other supportive in some areas (especially counter-espionage) and quick to exploit the capabilities of officers on the ground, reflected a common ambassadorial attitude towards intelligence matters. Late in 1941 there was a row involving Menzies, Hoare, the Foreign Office and Hamilton Stokes over Menzies's (and apparently Hoare's) desire to boost the Passport Control staff in Spain to monitor suspect individuals travelling from Europe across the Atlantic. But when Hamilton Stokes injudiciously revealed London's exasperation with Hoare over his refusal to contemplate embassy cover for extra SIS staff, the ambassador bluntly declared that 'after the episodes of [the PCO in September 1940], Claire and Clarke I have ceased to have any faith in SIS London'. In January 1942 Hoare, asserting that 'various S.I.S. agents' had 'apparently become dupes of the Germans in the war of nerves' and were merely peddling 'sensations', suggested to Alexander Cadogan that he should look through recent SIS reports 'and thus check their usefulness'. The Foreign Office view, however, was that intelligence reports from Spain had 'been particularly good lately, and not in the least alarmist'. Peter Loxley (Cadogan's private secretary) thought that Hoare was simply 'running a hunt against the S.I.S. these days' and that his 'present strictures' were 'quite unjustified'. Cadogan firmly told the ambassador that over the past month SIS reports had in general been 'balanced and accurate'.[24]

Later that year SIS had a striking success when (through agent networks and signals intelligence) it helped finally to neutralise Germany's infrared surveillance system (code-named 'Bodden') aimed at detecting Allied shipping passing through the Straits of Gibraltar. Intelligence about Bodden obtained by SIS and the Admiralty was used by Hoare from May 1942 onwards to embarrass Franco into ordering the abandonment of the whole undertaking, which was being carried on by the Axis in Spain and Spanish Morocco. By December 1942 Menzies could happily tell Peter Loxley at the Foreign Office that he had learned from 'most secret sources' (signals intelligence) that Hoare's protest of 20 October had 'had a very healthy effect in Spain', leading to the dismantling of Bodden.[25]

The intelligence challenge in Portugal was similar to that in Spain, though at the beginning the work was bedevilled by staffing problems. As in Spain, SIS objectives included monitoring German fifth-column activities, establishing a stay-behind network in case of a German invasion and penetrating occupied France, though an additional priority was Italy. Yet when, an ex-banker and MI5 officer, was sent out in June 1940 to assist the existing one-man SIS operation, he spent his first three months complaining (albeit with some justification) about the poor level of security in Lisbon, so much so that Menzies eventually lost patience with him. 'The war is at [a] stage', he wrote in September, 'at which risks must be taken and the question of being compromised [must] take a back seat.' This seems to have had some effect and in November he reported that he had established a line of agents in northern Portugal whereby people, letters or parcels could be smuggled over the Spanish frontier in either direction. In February 1941 a Section V officer, Ralph Jarvis, was sent out to take over as Passport Control Officer and build up the counter-espionage side. Jarvis and his newly appointed assistant, whose health was poor, did not get on, and the assistant was replaced by Philip Johns in June 1941.

Between 1940 and 1942, while the SIS team in Portugal failed to obtain any significant intelligence from Italy, it did manage to build up a reasonable coverage of shipping movements in and out of the country. Lisbon was also a main base for the transatlantic Ship Observers Scheme, run by William Stephenson in New York during 1941, whereby 'observers' were planted among the crews of neutral ships with the job of reporting on any suspicious matters. Through a combination of signals intelligence and Section V information, by 1942 Jarvis was well on his way to achieving almost complete coverage of enemy intelligence operations in Portugal, including the German Waterfront Organisation set up to obtain shipping information from Allied seamen in Lisbon. A dossier of its illegal activities was prepared which the ambassador submitted to President Salazar, with the result that the organisation was suppressed. Despite these local successes, London was not satisfied with the overall quality of the Lisbon station's work. 'Cut out ruthlessly redundant Economic and C.E. [counter-espionage] stuff, and concentrate on essential, viz. Armed Forces and Italy,' Menzies instructed Johns in April 1942. The following month Claude Dansey told him that the most important requirement was the development of an organisation 'for watching over North-West ports in 23-land [Spain]'. The British ambassador, moreover, thought that Johns was too closely involved with anti-Salazar groups, and (according to Dansey) had described some of his political reports as 'rubbish', so it was decided to move him, and he was replaced in December 1942.[26]

Some of SIS's Iberian work was linked to that of MI9, a Directorate of Military Intelligence section formed in December 1939 to provide an organisation to facilitate the escape of British personnel from prisoner-of-war camps and to develop techniques to assist servicemen to evade capture if stranded behind enemy lines. The military disasters of the spring and summer of 1940 resulted in the capture of thousands of British troops, while others sought sanctuary by crossing the frontier into neutral Switzerland or Spain. Members of Allied aircrew shot down over enemy territory added to their number. Embryonic escape lines soon began to establish themselves in the enemy-occupied Netherlands, Belgium and northern France and similar, if less dangerous, activities began in the Vichy-controlled southern zone. The work was among the earliest forms of resistance to occupation and relied heavily on the zeal of the population and a few intrepid British servicemen, such as Seaforth Highlander subaltern Ian Garrow, who declined to escape across the Pyrenees in order to set up a sound and effective network in France.

Inevitably word of these activities reached SIS. An authoritative work on the subject states that Menzies met with the head of MI9 on 6 August 1940 and 'offered to set up an escape line to run from Marseilles into Spain'.[27] Unfortunately no record of the meeting has survived in Menzies's (somewhat sparsely maintained) appointments diary, but there is no question that SIS took a keen and early interest in the lines that had begun to stretch from the Low Countries through the occupied and unoccupied zones of France and across the frontier into neutral Spain, and along which intelligence as well as people could travel. Claude Dansey managed the SIS side. He maintained his customary caustic view of operations and frequently gave the impression that his engagement was as much to deny any other government department the opportunity to meddle on the Continent as it was to rescue British personnel. He employed a small group of army officers on MI9's books, such as J. M. (Jimmy) Langley and Airey Neave (later to become a Conservative MP and be murdered by Irish terrorists), who possessed first-hand experience of escape and handled the organisation's affairs in London with skill and sensitivity. Other SIS/MI9 officers, such as Donald Darling and Michael Creswell, were employed in Spain, Portugal and Gibraltar to oversee the end of the lines.

MI9 attracted a remarkable collection of characters. The range extended from the outstanding bravery of men and women such as the Belgians Albert-Marie Guérisse ('Pat O'Leary') and Andrée de Jongh, to the despicable behaviour of the British traitor Harold Cole, whose treachery led to the deaths of some fifty escape-line helpers. The bulk of the work was done by men, women and sometimes children, who offered safe houses and acted as couriers for the extremely dangerous business of moving Allied servicemen through enemy territory and across closely guarded borders. The German security forces tended to treat the organisation as seriously as any of SIS's intelligence-gathering networks, and the penalties for anyone arrested were as grave as those for being caught carrying out espionage.

12

From Budapest to Baghdad

The 'nightmare scenario' for British strategic policy-makers in the 1930s posed by the potential simultaneous challenge of three great powers – Germany, Italy and Japan – affected and perplexed SIS just as much as any of the armed services, and although Sir Hugh Sinclair had striven to sharpen up the Service with this threat in mind, there was neither the political will in Whitehall nor the money available for him to do very much at all. Inevitably – and rightly – the main focus was on Germany, but this meant that intelligence operations in the Mediterranean, the Middle East (where in any case it was hoped that Britain's ally France could help out) and further afield in Asia were comparatively neglected, at least until the situation was brutally transformed by the German conquests in Northern and Western Europe, the entry of Italy into the war in June 1940 and that of Japan in December 1941.

South-east Europe

The rapidly escalating demands placed on SIS during 1939 and 1940 stretched the Service's resources almost to breaking point and it is clear that in seeking to maintain (if not also extend) its coverage in south-east Europe the Service was pushed to find qualified officers for the region. The stations in Austria and Czechoslovakia had been closed down (and the SIS representatives' cover blown) following the Nazi advance into both countries in 1938 and 1939. In February 1938 Wilfrid Hindle, a former journalist with no intelligence experience, had been sent out on probation to reinforce the Prague station. Three months later Harold Gibson, his boss in Prague, despite having noted that Hindle was handicapped by a lack of German-language skills, recommended him 'for permanent employment', while advising that he would need 'further instruction before being given an independent post'. Nevertheless, having been forced out of Prague, in April 1939 Hindle was appointed Passport Control Officer and head of station in Budapest, where the former incumbent had been sacked for incompetence. In September 1939 he was joined by another officer with a slightly chequered intelligence career, who had briefly been employed by SIS as Assistant PCO in Riga in 1929–30. He had evidently not made a success of this and the Service offered him no further work. In 1939, however, he reappeared and, judged suitable 'for subordinate employment in this organisation', had been re-employed to help out with Passport Control in Berlin. Assisting Hindle in the Budapest office were six secretarial staff and a wireless operator. The station had twenty-one agents on a retainer (others were 'paid by results'), of whom in the autumn of 1939 two were funded by the Ministry of Economic Warfare.

There were smaller stations in Bucharest, Belgrade and Sofia. The representative in Bucharest was Harold Gibson's brother Archie, who had journalist cover as a correspondent for *The Times*. In the late summer of 1939 he had one secretary, a wireless operator and fourteen main agents, most of whom were still only on trial. In Belgrade, a former colonial policemen, was head of station. He had been hired in November 1936 to assist in Berlin, and transferred to Yugoslavia by September 1939. Late that year, to help build up intelligence on German and Italian troop movements, a sub-station was opened in Zagreb which (among other things) was a convenient location to debrief agents from inside Italy. Much the largest operation in south-east Europe was in Athens, where the Passport Control Officer and head of station had over a dozen staff and seventy salaried agents (whose retainers ranged from £1 to £200 per month, with the majority receiving between £10 and £20). Assessing the Athens operation early in 1940, Captain Cuthbert Bowlby, a sailor who had joined the Service in 1938 and had become head of the Middle East Section, noted that the station 'must be considered from rather a different angle than others' since 'in dealing with Greeks it is no exaggeration to say that to be a S[ecret] S[ervice] agent is quite a normal profession, a situation which must make it difficult to get an agent to do more than a certain amount for a certain sum of money. It follows, therefore, that if you want big results you must pay well.'[1]

From the start of the war until the summer of 1940 the main intelligence requirements from the region were political and economic, the former to underpin the broad British policy of securing a neutral Balkan bloc of countries which together might resist Axis advances, the latter to reinforce the economic blockade which the more optimistic British strategists hoped would help cripple the German war effort.[2] Exchanges between Bucharest and London about a potential new agent reveal the sort of thing that was required early in the war. In September 1939 Archie Gibson reported that a local commercial traveller in medical goods was an excellent prospect as he could legitimately visit Germany. But London did not want just any old information. 'General observations on countryside, or local gossip from doctors and chemists useless', they signalled. 'Information German activities must be directly or indirectly from <u>inside</u> German organisations and must be confined to specific items, with in each case expressly specified sub-sources.' There was also a note of requirements from the Ministry of Economic Warfare, who wanted information on 'details and quantities of commodities passing to and from Germany, distinguishing between rail and Danube traffic'. London did not rate the political reporting from Romania very highly. Gibson's own recruits were described as 'mostly local journalists', who were 'fairly prolific', but 'their output on the whole is worthless. They are occasionally right, as often fantastically wrong, their subsources are vague and nebulous, and we are never in a position to say what, if any, weight can be attached to anything they report.' In February 1940, when Gibson reported a potentially promising contact with Hermann von Ritgen, the German press counsellor in Bucharest, David Footman in London warned (with Venlo undoubtedly in mind) that 'personal contact in wartime between one of our representatives (even one without official cover) and a senior member of the staff of a German legation is a very delicate matter. It may well result in an exceptional coup or in a first-class flop.' Later information suggested that Ritgen, a 'Nazi agent and propagandist', was himself probably aiming to penetrate SIS, and Gibson was briskly told to 'discontinue contact'.

In 1939–40 Laurence Grand's Section D worked on schemes to deny Romanian oil and other strategic supplies to the Germans, both by direct action in the Ploeşti oilfield north of Bucharest (which supplied 20 per cent of Germany's prewar needs) and also by blocking the Danube at the Iron Gates, where the river cut through the Carpathian Mountains and for three miles flowed through a narrow gorge along the Romanian–Yugoslav frontier. Grand's chief local expert, Julius Hanau (rather obviously code-named 'Caesar'), the Belgrade representative of the British engineering firm Vickers, devised a scheme to blow up the cliffs at the gorge, and, when this was thwarted by the vigilance of the local police, proposed in May 1940 to sink barges carrying cement and scrap iron, crewed by Section D men, which would block the river for an estimated three months. Hanau was active elsewhere, and in February 1940 George Rendel, the British minister in Sofia, complained that he had been in Bulgaria endeavouring to get one member (at least) of the local British community 'to take on a job connected with placing bombs in German ships and possibly tearing up railway lines'. With the conventional diplomat's suspicion of clandestine work, Rendel wrote that it filled him 'with misgiving to feel that irresponsible agents of this kind may be wandering about here without my knowledge doing things which may completely undermine the political position which we are so laboriously struggling to build up'. During the First World War Rendel had served in Athens and his 'recollections of the deplorable activities of such people as Compton Mackenzie in Greece during the last war only tend to increase my uneasiness'.[3]

Despite Grand's own optimistic claims for the achievements of Section D (which he made during the Hankey inquiry), neither it nor its successor SOE actually did very much to disrupt German strategic supply lines in 1939–40. But, despite the worsening political climate following the fall of France, when it hardly seemed as if Britain could avoid defeat, SIS managed to build up some intelligence assets in south-east Europe, a number of which even survived German domination of the whole region after the middle of 1941. One paradoxical consequence for SIS of German success was the encouragement of close relationships with the intelligence services of defeated allies, such as Czechoslovakia, Poland and France. In Hungary, thanks in part to Harold Gibson's close liaison with the Czechoslovak intelligence chief František Moravec, SIS inherited some intelligence assets. In June 1940 the Bucharest station was given permission to engage a contact formerly working for French intelligence. This man, who proved to be an excellent stay-behind agent, worked continuously until his arrest in February 1944 and was backed up in 1943–4 with Polish radio operators. He ran a very productive network (code-named 'Nannygoat'), which by 1943 included French,

Greek, Swiss and Romanian nationals, Catholic priests, businessmen, oil company workers, a police inspector and a source in the Romanian General Staff. One contemporary recorded that he 'started his wartime work with the disadvantage of having the appearance of a typical stage spy'. He had 'a slight stoop and a generally sinister appearance' and 'could have played the part of a spy in any theatre without further make-up'. But 'he had all the attributes of a successful head agent in real life. He was brave, resourceful and possessed of an extremely strong security sense.' Arguing for the award of a military decoration, Menzies told the Foreign Office that he was 'regarded by the War Office as one of our best and most reliable sources'. Another colleague noted the 'high importance of a British decoration to a foreigner, which he will be able to show at the end of the war, or perhaps before that if he is forced to leave enemy territory'.[4]

In Belgrade, efforts in 1940 to exploit Yugoslav sources for information about Austria and Czechoslovakia produced negligible results, but in the spring of 1941 both SIS and SOE (the two organisations here working closely together) mobilised their political and military contacts in the country behind the coup of 27 March 1941 which deposed the pro-Axis Regent, Prince Paul, in favour of a pro-Allied regime. As elsewhere, too, SIS's secure radio communications were used to transmit appeals for help from beleaguered local forces. At the beginning of March, for example, Archie Gibson sent a plea from General Stojanović, the Assistant War Minister and an 'old acquaintance', for British arms, without which 'they had no possibility of offering effective resistance to any German attack'. The coup was a tremendous British propaganda success, though unfortunately short-lived as it also precipitated the German invasion of both Yugoslavia and Greece. But SIS was able to give a little warning to Belgrade. At 10.20 a.m. on 5 April 1941, drawing on signals intelligence (though disguising it as a human source), Menzies sent a message to Gibson: 'Inform Yugoslav General Staff that from very reliable agent we learn that German attack will begin early tomorrow morning the 6th.' The invasion, in fact, began at 5.15 a.m.[5]

SIS activities in Greece in the early months of the war showed the same mixture of political, military, economic and special operations work as elsewhere in the Balkans. In February 1940 the Athens head of station complained that he had so many demands for economic information that it was jeopardising, 'from our point of view', more important armed forces work. Among the latter were increasing calls for information about Italy, which, having invaded Albania the previous spring, was threatening further advances in the region. He worked on a scheme to establish agents in the Dodecanese Islands (who would report back through Turkey), and in April 1940 London signalled Athens, Belgrade and Malta urging them to send 'additional tip and run agents' to Italian Adriatic ports, to watch for 'the assembly of transports or troops for an expeditionary force'. The Athens station, meanwhile, also built up productive relations with the Greek security police, who began to supply SIS with increasing amounts of information about German activities in the country. After the Italians came into the war in June 1940, and rightly anticipating that they might attack Greece (as happened at the end of October), evacuation and stay-behind plans were prepared. In London, Bowlby noted the possibility of locating a station in neutral Turkey 'opposite the Dodecanese', and also that agents in Corfu, Patras, Crete, Salonika and Samos had been provided with wireless sets.

In order to boost the naval work in Greece an additional officer was sent to Athens in May 1940, and, although there was a personality clash with the head of station (so much so that Menzies complained the situation was 'most unsatisfactory, and retards our primary objective, which is to make every effort to win the war'), by September the British naval attaché in Athens reported that the new man (who had good sources in Greek naval circles) was getting 'much valuable information' and was 'of great assistance to me'. Following the Greeks' spirited and successful response to the Italian invasion of October 1940, there were well-founded concerns that Germany might come to the Italians' aid. In a review of 'German offensive plans' prepared for the Foreign Office at the end of December 1940 Malcolm Woollcombe reported 'on very good authority' (possibly A.54, the Czechoslovak agent Paul Thümmel) that the Germans were contemplating an attack on Greece at the beginning of March 1941 'via Bulgaria', and that 'German troops would also pass through Yugoslavia, with or without that country's permission'. Information 'from a most secret and very reliable source' (signals intelligence) confirmed the concentration of German military and air units in Romania to secure the oilfields; in addition, judging by their disposition, 'it appears probable that the operation aims southward across the Bulgarian frontier'. This proved to be a pretty accurate prediction, although opinion was divided in London as to whether the Germans were also planning to invade Turkey. The attack, when it came on 5 April 1941, was directed against Yugoslavia and Greece.[6] Twelve days later Yugoslavia capitulated and Greece had fallen by the first week of May.

SIS in Turkey

SIS had a modest presence in Turkey at the start of the war. Based in Istanbul, the SIS representative, Arthur Whittall, had an assistant, a secretary, two messengers and twenty-four agents on the books. Over the next two years the situation was transformed as Istanbul became one of the great espionage entrepôts of the war. Although neutral, the Turks were well disposed towards the Allies and, especially fearing Italian ambitions in the region, concluded a treaty with Britain and France in late September 1939, promising mutual assistance in the event of aggression by another European power against any of the signatories. This brought practical benefits for SIS: first, enhanced co-operation (initiated by the Turks) on secret service matters, though it was not until 1942 that this produced significant returns; and, second, Turkish acquiescence in the establishment of an SIS sub-station at Smyrna (İzmir) on the Aegean coast of mainland Turkey, to which the Athens station could relocate if forced to withdraw from Greece.[7] After the German occupation of Greece, in fact, the Smyrna station, along with Cairo, became the main bases for the repenetration of the Greek islands and mainland. Headed by Lieutenant Commander Noel Rees, an Old Harrovian whose family had longstanding business interests in the region, and with a ready supply of patriotic Greeks willing to serve as agents, Smyrna was ideally placed for clandestine sea operations, though missions were also launched from harbours further south, such as Bodrum, more conveniently placed for targeting Rhodes, headquarters of the enemy's Dodecanese Command, and Leros, where the Italians had an important naval base. In this part of the world classical names for operations and agents were clearly irresistible. When Harold Gibson and Cuthbert Bowlby went on a tour of inspection in June 1942, they noted the 'Dido plan' for a coast-watching service around Marmaris and an organisation at Mytilene (Mitilini), run by agent 'Agamemnon', who made a fortnightly motor-boat run to a sub-agent on the island of Khios.

In January 1941 Menzies posted the very experienced Harold Gibson to take charge of operations in the region. Within six months, as SIS representatives withdrew from the Balkans in the face of Axis advance and relocated in Istanbul, Gibson found himself responsible not only for Turkey, but also for 'stations-in-exile' from Sofia, Bucharest, Budapest, Belgrade and Athens. He had furthermore to liaise with the Turkish authorities, as well as local Polish, Czechoslovak and Yugoslav intelligence organisations, and maintain good relations with a British embassy unsettled (as was so often the case) by the growing number of SIS, SOE and other analogous personnel, working none too clandestinely in a country whose continued neutrality in these early years of the war was essential to the British. Much of SOE's Balkan work was run from Turkey and Gibson, too, was worried about the dangers of SOE activities being exposed, as the otherwise accommodating Turks could not be expected to discriminate between different British secret services. Yet he was not against SOE per se, and could only recommend (as he did in November 1941) that increased security measures be adopted by all concerned.

Early in 1942 Menzies told Gibson that he was seriously concerned about the lack of armed forces information from the Balkans and was sending Frank Foley (whom he used during the war as a kind of roving troubleshooter) to review the position. Foley's report of 28 March 1942 usefully provides a snapshot of SIS's work in Turkey approximately halfway through the war. Overall, he thought that the situation with Romania was good, and for Turkey reasonably satisfactory. Intelligence from Bulgaria was mainly provided by the Turks. He was optimistic about Greece, notably a promising scheme for penetrating the Dodecanese Islands, but intelligence from both Yugoslavia and Hungary was poor, though in the case of the latter some lines were opening up through Romania. Foley reported that Gibson had established extremely cordial relations with the British ambassador, Sir Hughe Knatchbull-Hugessen, who himself spoke of Foley 'in the warmest terms'. Hugessen's attitude towards SIS, nevertheless, was one of 'pained tolerance'. This clearly irked Foley, who told Menzies: 'I consider your service here is contributing at least as much to war effort as Y.P.'s [the ambassador].' He also suggested (though this was not likely to cut much ice among some diplomats) that the Foreign Office 'be pressed to instruct their Y.P.s to provide your representatives with proper status, accommodation etc. as an integral part of their staff'. The 'provision of facilities for our success here', he added, 'should be regarded as important index of strength' of the alliance with Turkey. 'Reverse attitude is serious handicap to your organization's work.'

Foley concluded his report with praise for Gibson, who was 'practically indispensable' in Istanbul and who, 'in most discouraging circumstances', had 'worked with great ability and energy'. On the whole he thought Gibson was well served by his staff, and, although improvements were undoubtedly desirable, it was now 'very difficult to find right men'. Reflecting on the problems of current recruitment, and perhaps, too, acknowledging Service personnel weaknesses exposed by the challenge of war, Foley observed that 'an intelligent layman who had come much into contact with SIS' had remarked that 'we are too ready to be satisfied with "good second-raters"'. In Turkey, Foley thought that only Gibson, his brother Archie's assistant from Bucharest and one other officer could be exempted from this criticism. 'Satisfied with "good second-raters"' was strong stuff indeed, and Foley's worries illustrate not only an important degree of critical Service self-reflection, but also the sometimes painful progress of the organisation towards full professionalism. Coming, moreover, as it did from a longstanding Service colleague, it was clearly something which Menzies had to take seriously. Evidently Foley had been concerned about the issue for some time, as he urged the Chief to give consideration to the long-term suggestion he had discussed with him shortly before his departure to create a 'directorate for dealing with personnel and technical matters on a plane commensurate with [the] importance of SIS'.

Gibson, another Service veteran, could write with similar frankness to Menzies, as he did in September 1942 when he reported that Hugessen was trying to bring SIS under strict embassy control. While the ambassador refused to concede that any Service officers could have diplomatic status, he was otherwise prepared to support them on the understanding that SIS was allowed to operate in Turkey only with his consent, and as his 'guests', an attitude which clearly irked Gibson. 'I consider we are here to do a job of work,' he signalled London, 'not as members of a house party.' He 'deplored the tendency, which seemed pretty general among the British Diplomatic Service, to treat members of the "C" Organisation as poor and rather disreputable relations'. He observed that 'the war we were fighting was not a kid glove affair and we should take a leaf out of our enemy's book and cease drawing the line between pure diplomacy and the rougher stuff without which the fight could not continue'. Another of Hugessen's irritating criticisms was that some members of SIS were not of the right social standing, and he had cited the case of one member who had been given diplomatic status in 1939 and who was subsequently discovered to have been a 'cabaret keeper' ('shades of Curzon!!' commented Gibson). Hugessen further described SIS as a 'cancer it was desirable to remove from the diplomatic body'. One SIS colleague found this attitude 'nauseating', and felt it disclosed 'a venomous die-hard' Diplomatic Service attitude towards SIS under the 'veneer of professional suavity'. For the Istanbul head of station the main issue was 'the status and utility of our Service . . . vis-à-vis the Diplomatic service'. Gibson thought Hugessen's antediluvian attitudes implied that he was more concerned to defend the privileges of diplomats 'than in helping us to pursue a ruthless war', and he pressed Menzies to assert the Service's legitimate role 'on the highest level', otherwise 'the chiefs of our diplomatic service are not likely to change their pusillanimous and peace-time mentality'.[8]

Another facet of wartime SIS, demonstrating how everyone mucked in, is illustrated by a 'most secret and confidential – not for publication' medal citation of 1943 for a woman who had been 'engaged on the clerical side of intelligence work in a Balkan country on the outbreak of war'. This secretary began to take on 'direct intelligence work . . . In an atmosphere of accumulated strain as the Nazis strengthened their hold on the country', she 'performed most of the tasks of an intelligence officer, including the delicate work of contacting agents, which bore no slight risk in that Balkan war atmosphere'. When the Germans moved in, she 'came to a nearby neutral country' where she 'continued to do similar work', the whole period covering 'several years of unbroken foreign service interspersed with long spells of strain and overwork'.

The Middle East stations

In 1939 few people foresaw how important the Middle East and North Africa would become as a theatre of enemy activity and military operations. On 22 August that year, however, anticipating the possibility that in the event of war communications might be interrupted, Sinclair instructed his four stations in the region – Jerusalem, Cairo, Aden and Baghdad – that Major John Teague, the Jerusalem station chief, was to be the senior SIS representative in the Middle East. Teague, who had been in post since 1936, ran the largest operation, with seven officers and a similar number of support staff. In Cairo, Desmond Adair, a fluent Arab-speaking cavalryman, was head of station. In the 1920s and 1930s he had spent ten years in the Egyptian army and Sudan Defence Force, before being taken on by SIS in July 1936. He then spent a couple of months being trained in Jerusalem under Teague, before being posted as assistant to the Cairo station chief, whom he succeeded in July 1938. By the beginning of the war, Adair had an assistant of his own, five support staff and over forty agents on the books. He was also responsible for the Aden station at the mouth of the Red Sea, where another fluent Arab-speaker, who had worked for the police and Air Intelligence in Iraq, had been appointed joint SIS and MI5 representative in August 1936. The smallest of the Middle Eastern stations was at Baghdad, established only in March 1939, though there had previously been a station there in the early 1930s. Here the sole SIS representative had fourteen agents, three of whom (reflecting the strategic importance of Iraqi and Iranian oil) were dedicated to Ministry of Economic Warfare work.

In December 1939, John Shelley, who had been head of station in Jerusalem before serving in Warsaw, was sent out to strengthen the SIS presence in the region, and to concentrate especially on getting better information on the Italians. Based in Cairo, over the next two months he visited Palestine, Syria, Iraq and Iran to review the overall situation for Menzies. He reported (on 8 March 1940) that the Jerusalem station was 'most efficient', with an 'adequate staff'. He had interviewed the Palestine civil and military authorities, who told him that the 'burning question' was Jewish illegal immigration which they said was 'encouraged by 12-land [Germany]', and that German agents 'were being included amongst the illegal immigrants'. What they wanted was help from SIS to stop the flow. In contrast to this perceived Jewish threat (and reflecting the different ways in which the Service could be pulled), Shelley was approached in Jerusalem by a former contact from the Jewish Agency, the main Jewish organisation in Palestine, which worked ceaselessly to protect Jewish interests and facilitate Jewish immigration, offering the Agency's help for

intelligence work. Shelley was happy to accept the offer, passing it on to
Teague to exploit. The Palestine Director of Immigration had told him,
moreover, the 'interesting item of information' that Jews were returning
from Palestine to Italy as 'conditions for Jews in Italy had improved', and
Shelley may have seen an opportunity here to boost his coverage of Italy.

Part of Shelley's mission was to build up links with Allied intelligence
agencies, including the French, based in French-administered Syria, the
Poles, who were currently running their organisation from headquarters
in Paris, and the Czechoslovaks. In Syria he 'established a most cordial
liaison' with the local Deuxième Bureau representative who told him that
there were active German agents in the area. The Frenchman added that
he had so far not got any information from the Poles, but that he understood they were 'très bien installées' in Iran. When he reached Baghdad,
Shelley found the 'efficient and hardworking' SIS representative there so
overworked and understaffed that it was 'impossible for him to travel and
recruit new agents'. Here he recommended the appointment of 'a good
male secretary (possibly of the retired N.C.O. type)', which Menzies subsequently approved.

Travelling on to Tehran (it took six days because of snow on the road),
Shelley began planning for a full SIS station in Iran, which could, among
other things, improve coverage of the Soviet Union. This was something
the existing Baghdad-run SIS agents in Iran (mostly British businessmen) were reluctant to do. 'Men of this kind,' remarked Shelley, 'while
prepared to take reasonable risks, will not risk their businesses, which
are their means of livelihood, by doing anything which might get them
into trouble with the [Iranian] Government, and they consequently will
not undertake the active role of running agents across the frontier into
95-land [the USSR].' With the Indian Intelligence Bureau already working on Russia from a base in Meshed, Shelley recommended that SIS
should operate from Tehran and Tabriz in the north of the country. He
also spoke to local French and Polish intelligence officers, discovering
that the latter were not only already getting agents across the frontier
into the Soviet Union but also developing networks within Afghanistan.
Although unable to meet any Czechoslovaks, he reported that in Iran
they appeared 'to offer a very fruitful recruiting ground for agents'.[9]

Menzies's original idea had been that while Shelley would be attached
to army headquarters in the Middle East, he should co-ordinate the

supply of intelligence to the air force as well. But this arrangement came up against inter-service rivalries and the RAF objected to him being integrated with the army. Menzies then decided to appoint a more senior officer, Sir David Petrie, to be General Manager for the Middle East stations, with direct access to the regional commanders of all three armed services. The sixty-year-old Petrie was a very experienced intelligence hand. Born in Aberdeen in Scotland, he became a career policeman in India before the First World War, ran intelligence agents in East Asia, headed the Indian Intelligence Bureau for seven years between the wars, and in 1937–9 both assisted in the reorganisation of the Palestine police and reported for SIS on intelligence requirements relating to British East Africa. From May 1940 Petrie and Shelley (who served as his staff officer until moving on to SOE in September) became the Inter-Services Liaison Department (ISLD), with Petrie being put in overall charge of SIS across the region, including Egypt, Palestine, Iraq, Iran, Turkey, Ethiopia and East Africa. His organisation was responsible for obtaining and distributing locally all kinds of information from Greece, the Balkans, Italy and enemy-occupied North Africa. Agents themselves were run by individual stations (including those from Greece and Yugoslavia which after the German conquest of the Balkans operated primarily from Egypt), though they were kept physically separate from ISLD and each other.

Targeting Italy

In March 1940, Frederick Winterbotham complained that the intelligence position regarding Italy was 'lamentable'. 'I cannot believe', he wrote, 'that Italian Air Force Officers in Budapest, Italian engineers and merchants in Belgrade and Sofia are all unapproachable. This is the side from which we need to penetrate since the French use their own opportunities to the utmost.' By early May the situation had not improved. Cuthbert Bowlby conceded that it 'has become abundantly clear in the last week or so that the Armed Forces are not satisfied with the amount of information they are getting on Italy'. While the Belgrade, Athens and Malta stations had been 'endeavouring under pressure from headquarters to remedy this deficiency in Italy and Sicily', and Cairo had 'sent several rather expensive agents' into the Italian possession of Libya, this had all been 'without so far achieving much result'. Bowlby suggested trying to acquire information 'from further afield, i.e. North and South America, where enormous Italian colonies exist'. Dansey agreed and said that in his capacity as Z he had 'put up proposals about a year ago' that 'in anticipation of war, recruiting centres should be established in New York, Buenos Aires or Brazil'. Although 'it will be expensive', it was still 'worth doing'. Beyond an unsuccessful attempt to enlist Italians in Canada, no co-ordinated large-scale effort to recruit Italian agents in the Americas was ever launched. But Dansey continued to promote the idea. In October 1942 he asked that the station in Rio de Janeiro should look for possible agents in the 'large Italian colonies in South America'. New York, he lamented, 'never seems able to find the right people'.

The demand for intelligence intensified further after Italy came into the war in June 1940. In August London told Swiss, Balkan, Eastern Mediterranean and Iberian stations that the Service 'urgently' required Italian economic and industrial intelligence. Nothing much seems to have resulted from this, although it was reported that some information was being obtained from French sources. Two months later a signal from Malta (where the MI5 Defence Security Officer was also head of the SIS station) suggested inserting agents into the Italian colony of Libya from French-ruled Tunisia. In the spring of 1940 an SIS officer, Major A. J. Morris, had been sent to Tunis to set up a sub-station in liaison with the French authorities, but they arrested him after the British shelled the Vichy French fleet at Oran on 3 July. Morris was taken to Casablanca where he was allowed to escape by an anti-Vichy policeman and he eventually got back to Malta in September. He thought that owing to 'extreme anti-Italian sentiment throughout Tunisia and his [own] personal friendship with several officers it would be possible for him to obtain ?reliable information on local situation and on possibility restarting organisation for 32-land [Italy]'.

But the penetration of Italy proved to be extremely difficult. When Rex Howard asked in January 1941 what progress the Athens station had made in getting agents into southern Italy, a laconic unidentified official wrote across his minute 'None'. Anxious for information on the 'probable reinforcement of Albania and especially Libya by Italian forces', the War Office enquired about SIS's port-watching organisation in Italy. This had been run by the Vienna station before the war, but had broken up following the expulsion of the Service from Austria. Despite efforts from both Athens and Malta, SIS had not subsequently 'succeeded in establishing any permanent watchers'. But even when the Vienna organisation had been working (and apart from the great difficulty of establishing reliable wireless communications) the information provided had been 'far from complete', especially since 'troops naturally embark at night from guarded quays and sources cannot keep a 24 hour watch. No doubt', added one jaundiced officer, the Admiralty 'would like us to have established a network of agents at all ports, all equipped with W/T, and able to see in the dark, and have free access to all docks'.

Attempts to penetrate Libya had been no more successful. Bowlby noted Cairo's failure to do so, though this was not 'for the want of trying'. Early in 1940 six agents had been despatched 'at considerable expense and risk, but they were never able to achieve very much owing to Italian vigilance and difficulties in getting them there and back and communications'. An agent, working from French-controlled Tunisia, had produced 'a large and expensive Libyan Arab organisation', but it had not had 'time to get going properly before the French collapse'. Events on the ground from late 1940, however, changed the situation dramatically when an offensive launched on 9 December from Egypt into Libya met with spectacular success. By early February 1941 British and Commonwealth forces had advanced some 400 miles, the Australians had taken Benghazi and up to 100,000 Italian prisoners had been captured. One idea raised in SIS was to comb the prisoner-of-war camps for potential agents. Bowlby was not optimistic. 'Italians make very bad agents,' he wrote, 'and although many of them dislike the Fascist regime yet they love their country and dislike danger. I am afraid that any attempt of this kind will merely be treated as a beneficial repatriation scheme.'

The Italian reverses in Libya prompted Hitler in February 1941 to send the Afrika Korps to help. By the end of April, Axis forces under General Erwin Rommel had driven the British back to the Egyptian frontier. The simultaneous collapse of the Balkans further undermined SIS's opportunities to penetrate Italy. By June, with the Admiralty urgently wanting to keep track of 'possible reinforcement of Libya from Italian ports', and complaining that SIS had provided only four reports from Italy and Sicily over the previous six weeks, Bowlby reported that it was hoped shortly to penetrate Sicily from Malta, and 'N. Italy' from Switzerland. Dansey, however, warned that it might take four months to improve the situation which in any case depended, 'to a very great extent, on how long Spain and Switzerland remain unoccupied by the Germans'. Although neither country was invaded, and despite the fact that both the Lisbon and Madrid stations were told to concentrate on Italian work, the dismal performance continued through 1941. Dansey hoped that the Geneva station could step up its reporting but noted in November that the agent working the traffic out of Switzerland through the Simplon railway tunnel had been arrested and this had 'made them very careful, for which one cannot blame them'. Almost despairingly, the Army Section at Broadway conceded, 'the truth is that since we lost 44000 station [Vienna], we have never been able to organise a proper service against Italy. I find it difficult to see how we are going to do so now but will go on talking to all and sundry about it.'

Over the next year various stratagems were considered. One officer believed that 'far more could be accomplished by bringing "high-ups" out of 32-land [Italy] rather than putting agents in'. The Lisbon station identified a prominent musician who had been engaged to perform at an International Musical Congress in Venice in September 1942. The Naval Section wanted him 'to ascertain what battleships are in Venice during his visit or have been in Venice during July and August', but no record survives of any response. It was proposed to form a film company in Portugal which could seek production facilities in Italy, gathering intelligence along the way. The Cairo station suggested looking for 'active anti-fascists' among Italians being repatriated from East Africa, but Dansey glumly observed that this had already been tried on a previous convoy where the 'Fascist special police' had been 'very well represented on board' and had warned against any Italians speaking to potential British agents. They had taken 'very active steps' to 'see that this warning was carried out' and he feared that 'the worst may have happened to the one useful contact that was made'. Reflecting on the position in December 1942, an officer in the SIS Army Section noted that despite exerting 'all the pressure I could' on the production side 'to produce information on Italy', there had been 'little result'. Up to the present, he wrote, 'the difficulties have been very great', but he had hopes for an improvement on two grounds. First was 'the continued failure of Italian arms with the consequent further lowering of morale. This should not only make the task of an agent in Italy far easier, but should make available many more candidates for the penetration of Italy.' Second was 'the increasing German hold over Italy', which 'might well secure for us the active co-operation of considerable elements among the Italians themselves'. Presciently (as it turned out), he thought that 'the combination of these two circumstances might give us our opportunity'.

Operations in North Africa

Sir David Petrie stayed in Cairo only until December 1940 when he was called back to London to conduct an investigation into SIS's troubled sister-service, MI5. Teague was temporarily brought in from Jerusalem to replace him, but when Petrie was appointed head of MI5 in April 1941, Cuthbert Bowlby was sent out from London to serve as regional supremo, with responsibility for the Balkans as well as the Middle East. Both at Broadway and in Cairo Bowlby had to cope with the dramatic ebb and flow of the Desert War in North Africa. In early 1941 he had favoured establishing an advanced base in Libya (first in Bardia just across the Egyptian frontier, then in Tobruk further west) from which parties could be sent out into the desert behind enemy lines, but this proved unfeasible when the Afrika Korps pushed the British back into Egypt during April. After his move to Cairo, Bowlby also had to fight SIS's corner institutionally and establish good working relations with the Middle East military headquarters. This was not only necessary from an intelligence perspective, but also essential if SIS was to obtain the resources required for reorganisation and expansion. That Bowlby managed to improve relations with the local authorities owed much to his ability to get on well with colleagues, but he was severely overworked and his health suffered in consequence. Towards the end of 1941 he had a spell in hospital, but assured London that he was not 'breaking up'. 'Far from it,' he declared, 'it is only result of unbroken period of toil since I arrived.'

There was, too, the matter of relations with SOE, who were also competing for scarce resources. Both SIS and SOE needed air support, and the scarcity of aircraft was a constant concern. Although it was agreed at the beginning of 1942 to have a dedicated RAF unit in the Middle East for all SIS and SOE operations, even by 1943 there were fewer than five long-range aircraft available for both agencies, with the result that the despatch of SIS agents, as well as much SOE equipment, was frequently delayed. Bowlby and the Middle East head of SOE, Terence Maxwell, petitioned London to champion their needs, and when, on one of his visits to the Middle East, SOE handed Churchill a paper on the subject they got a few more long-range sorties at SIS's expense and some further temporary friction between the two agencies ensued. These problems were eased in mid-1943 by the creation of 334 Wing (Special Duties) under Wing Commander R. C. Hockey, operating out of airfields in North Africa and later Italy. Early in 1942 Bowlby also complained to London that SOE was trying to take over responsibility for the local MI9 organisation. He reported that SIS had built up a strong relationship with MI9 and worked closely with them. The principal interests of SOE, he said, were more to get large numbers of people into enemy countries than out of them, and to mix escape work with offensive duties would be disastrous to the former. Besides, he thought that SOE was 'more anxious to take over our transport and communications facilities than our responsibilities'. This apparent SOE empire-building was blocked. Bowlby later described Maxwell as having a 'form of megalomania', and a further proposal from him that all clandestine organisations in the Middle East should be co-ordinated under one individual (assumed to be Maxwell himself) was also stillborn after Henry Hopkinson in the Foreign Office declared it 'unthinkable'.

Actual intelligence work continued alongside bureaucratic infighting. From Malta Major Morris ran some groups in Tunisia, mainly 'patriotic and stout-hearted Frenchmen . . . working without the knowledge of the [Vichy] French authorities'. In January 1941 three French soldiers who had escaped to Malta in a small boat brought news of Morris's previous contacts in Tunisia and the existence of a clandestine organisation which was ready to operate but needed wireless sets. The leader of the French party, André Mounier, a thirty-eight-year-old lawyer who had been working in Tunis at the start of the war, returned with radio equipment before the end of January and developed a network which reported continuously for the next five months, transmitting 232 messages to Malta between 9 January and 28 June.[10] On 25 February they provided the first report of German troops disembarking at Tripoli and just under a month later made 'a most valuable identification' of German tanks. As SIS reported afterwards, this was their first appearance 'on African soil and was to delay our conquest of Tripoli by nearly two years'. Early in March a coast-watcher was installed at Kelibia on the east side of the Cap Bon penin-sula to monitor the movements of Italian convoys, and on 5 April Malta reported that an Italian ship 'had been torpedoed as a result of an agent's information'. In order to provide cover in Tunis a small company, the Société d'Étude et des Pêcheries, was floated, and a scheme established whereby money could be transmitted through a local resident.

At the end of June 1941, the Mounier network, having become involved with SOE activities, was compromised following an unsuccessful SOE attempt to sabotage a French tanker at La Goulette. Although Mounier and two associates were safely extracted, another dozen colleagues were arrested and the property of the Société d'Étude et des Pêcheries seized. Reflecting afterwards, the setback was blamed on 'entanglement' with SOE and a general lack of security, including 'too much independent action by young enthusiastic agents in Tunis'. Over the next few months agents were reinserted from Malta by submarine, motor boat and air. SIS managed to acquire in England two ex-Norwegian German-made Heinkel He-115 seaplanes for Service operations. Morris recalled that they had 'very great difficulties' with the local RAF commander 'over the maintenance and camouflage of these aircraft', and that 'the greatest danger was from the trigger-happy R.A.F. fighter pilots during our prac-tices'. They were used operationally, but on 22 September one of the Heinkels, carrying Mounier himself, 'a born leader and . . . one of our most valuable men', was lost en route to Tunisia. Meeting agents at the other end was also very difficult. One foreign diplomat in Tunis who was helping SIS observed that the use of cars was extremely strictly control-led, and there was 'absolutely no possibility of having a car waiting for a man anywhere outside the centre of Tunis. Anywhere else it would be such an object of curiosity that the addition of a brass band would not render it any more remarkable.'

The same month, however, 'Dick Jones', who was to lead the most successful of the wartime Tunisian groups, was recruited in Cairo and brought to Malta by Morris. Under his 'conditions of service', Jones was to be paid seventy-five Egyptian pounds per month (about £2,500 in modern values), of which E£60 was to be paid directly to his wife. 'In the event of your mission being successful and that you return in person', he was to be paid E£1,000 (equivalent to £34,000), and 'in the event of your death owing to enemy action whether due to being shot as an agent or whether due to any other enemy action', his wife was to receive E£3,000. If he were reported missing, or definitely taken prisoner by the enemy, his wife's allowance of E£60 was to be continued for six months, and if he had 'not returned by that time a gratuity of E£1,000 . . . will be paid to your wife'. While the money must surely have been a factor, Jones also appears to have been impelled by idealistic motives, which he described in a letter to his wife, apparently written before he was infiltrated into Tunisia. His case-officer in Malta thought this was of such interest that he forwarded a copy to London. 'The letter,' he wrote, 'although somewhat flamboyant, tends to show why he [Jones] is doing the work on which he is now employed.' 'All my previous undertakings of this nature have been fun,' wrote Jones, 'undertaken from a love of adventure . . . This affair is quite different: it is a question of a very definite aim and ideal.' Jones's 'chief objective' was to 'avenge myself on the Fascist regime'. Secondly, he said he wanted 'to defend Liberty which I value more than life and I am convinced that after a Nazi-Fascist victory Liberty will no longer exist. Thus the only thing I can do, and I have already done it, is to put myself at the disposition of the English who are defending the Liberty of the world.'

Described as an 'outstanding personality', Jones was an Egyptian Jew who had served in the Italian colonial army and 'could pass for an Italian'. With 'the help of Jewish colonists', and equipped with both Tunisian and Fascist Italian identity cards, he was to penetrate Libya through Tunisia. But the operation started very badly. In late November, having safely landed Jones and another agent off a submarine, the British Commando who had rowed them in was forced to swim ashore after his boat capsized. As they attempted to get him some dry clothes, the alarm was raised and French police arrested all three, along with weapons, two suitcases, one containing a wireless set, and the other '200,000 lire, 300,000 francs, £5,000 sterling, some gold louis, two bags with about eleven diamonds and a bag of turquoises', as well as 'a brown wooden box containing chemicals for the production of invisible ink'. The two agents were tried, convicted and sentenced to twenty years' hard labour. Six days after the Anglo-American landings in North Africa (Operation Torch) on 8 November 1942, which prompted the Germans to occupy Tunisia, the

SIS men and a large number of pro-Gaullist prisoners were released by the French authorities, enabling Jones to organise an intelligence network which was to be especially productive over the following four months.

Working from Egypt, Cuthbert Bowlby was involved with the Africa Bureau project, by which the SIS Middle East station (ISLD) and those at Cairo, Casablanca and Dakar co-operated in penetration operations, many of which were implemented by the Long Range Desert Group (LRDG), which had been formed in the summer of 1940 for reconnaissance, intelligence-gathering and special operations deep behind enemy lines. Throughout 1942 the LRDG delivered ISLD agents into enemy territory to carry out SIS tasks in North Africa.[11] Late in April 1942 it was reported that a group led by '52901', a Jewish academic in his sixties, was about to leave Siwa near the Libyan frontier and be taken by the LRDG to El Abiar, where 52901 'had introductions to friendly sheikhs'. From here, close to Benghazi, the group was to report on enemy troop deployments. Two other groups, planned to go during May, were targeted on Tripoli. One was led by an Italian Communist who had lived in Libya for ten years; the other mostly comprised Free Frenchmen who were to be airlifted into Tunisia and reach Tripoli from the west. Demonstrating that the Africa Bureau remit was not confined only to the north of the continent, plans were being worked on for a fourth group, also Free French-led, to penetrate Madagascar. This plan was overtaken by the British invasion of the island early in May, and the North African operations were disrupted by Rommel's two counter-offensives, though 52901 and his group managed some reporting in May–June 1942. Rommel's first offensive, in January 1942, pushed the British past Benghazi. The second began on 26 May and was not halted until the beginning of July when the Afrika Korps reached El Alamein, just fifty miles from Alexandria. Fearing that Cairo might fall, along with the bulk of Middle East Command, SIS moved all but a skeleton staff to Jerusalem where it remained until the end of the year.

As it existed in 1942 the structure of the regional SIS headquarters in the Middle East – ISLD – echoed that of SIS headquarters in London. GC&CS and the Radio Security Service had a regional office which came under Bowlby's command. The various SIS stations collected intelligence which ISLD distributed, mostly through the inter-service Middle East Intelligence Centre. Counter-intelligence was the responsibility of Security Intelligence Middle East (SIME) which had an analogous role within Middle East Command to that of MI5 at home, primarily responsible for protecting British secrets from the enemy. An SIS representative was attached to SIME and, on the whole, excellent relations were maintained between the two organisations, producing highly satisfactory results in the field of counter-intelligence in general and of double agents and deception in particular. SIS and SIME combined with Dudley Clarke's A Force (responsible for theatre deception operations) in a Special Section formed on 30 March 1942, principally to co-ordinate double-agent operations. Having much the same function as the XX Committee in London, in order to go one better it was locally known as the XXX Committee. The main source of counter-intelligence information, as elsewhere in the war, was GC&CS, whose material (code-named 'ISOS' – 'Intelligence Service Oliver Strachey', after a senior member of the Bletchley Park staff) was received and distributed by the local SIS signals organisation under Major Rodney Dennys, appointed Section V representative in Cairo in November 1941. In contrast to the high-level skirmishings which sometimes broke out in London between Valentine Vivian of SIS and Sir David Petrie of MI5, Dennys recalled that relations between SIS, SIME and A Force were 'close and cordial, because the officers concerned liked and respected each other. Outside regular office meetings, we usually met for a drink or a meal at least once a week, where ideas could be floated or kinks ironed out.' The '"severe formalism" of inter-departmental relations in London', he wrote, 'found no echo in Cairo'.[12]

Up to the summer of 1942 the record of SIS in the Eastern Mediterranean and North Africa was decidedly patchy, as it was for British and Commonwealth forces generally. But the elements for success were gradually falling into place. Those SIS representatives who survived in post, having had to cope with almost continuous retreat in the opening war years, became battle-hardened and, with hard-won experience, were gradually able to take stock and begin to establish productive agent networks in enemy-occupied territory. The extraordinary breakthroughs in signals intelligence, moreover, transformed the intelligence situation in a whole range of areas, especially that of counter-intelligence and deception. Furthermore, the entry into the war of the Soviet Union in June, and of the USA in December 1941, massively boosted the Allied cause.

All this contributed to the successful battle of El Alamein in October 1942 which finally turned the tide in the theatre, and laid the basis for the expulsion of Axis forces from North Africa by the early summer of 1943.

Syria, Iraq and Iran

The liaisons with French intelligence colleagues in the Middle East which John Shelley made when he toured the region in early 1940 promised much. Some records from June 1940 indicate the sort of operation which was contemplated. On 4 June Shelley reported from Cairo that the senior French intelligence officer Gustave Bertrand had told him that the chauffeur of the Italian ambassador to Iran, who regularly carried Italian and German mail between Tehran and Baghdad, was in French pay 'and will deliver mails at agreed place if a mock bandit ?attack made on car. He adds that Italian soldiers accompanying car would have to be over powered. Asks whether we can arrange.' Shelley added a warning from Petrie that in any such operation 'there must be no risk of bungling which would compromise British Government'. Shelley doubted 'if we yet have adequate organisation', and added his own opinion that 'drugging Italian soldier and changing bag much simpler operation with far fewer complications. Better still if we could open, photograph and re-seal [bag] and thus be able to repeat operation.' In London Bowlby rejected 'any attempt at banditry', as it would be bound to invite retaliation and would inevitably be blamed on the British government. Shelley's suggestion, he wrote, 'holds out the best chance of any really valuable result', though it would be a very difficult operation to execute and could probably be carried out only once. Valentine Vivian agreed with Bowlby ('sound common sense') and thought something of the sort was 'worth doing', but 'only if it can be done [?regularly] and in such a way that it does not become known' (which was surely rather an unnecessary point to make). He suggested that Bertrand should be asked to obtain 'through chauffeur an exact and detailed account of journey, so that we can judge whether any opportunity of secret opening & scrutiny presents itself'. Only then could permission for the operation be considered.

But joint Anglo-French ventures were (for the moment) swept away by the fall of France, after which British activities in Syria and the Lebanon were severely restricted by the Vichy authorities. In March 1941 Teague reported from Jerusalem that the United States consul-general in Beirut was 'well disposed' towards the British and had granted him diplomatic-bag facilities for communications into Syria. The following month (as the British were retreating from Greece) there were fears that the Germans might occupy Syria, and London asked Teague if he were in a position to give early warning of such an eventuality. Teague explained that he had a portable wireless set in Beirut and one en route to Aleppo. In addition, an (unidentified) American diplomat in Beirut was 'always ready to help' and could give some warning. Teague thought that he could 'do something' with local smugglers. There was also an embryonic anti-Vichy organisation which might be able to assist. 'So', he reported, 'from one source or another we should have very early intimation of German landing there.'

In the end there was no German invasion, but Teague's Syrian sources were able to provide Middle East Command with the complete Vichy French order of battle before the British Commonwealth and Free French operation which wrested Syria from Vichy control in June 1941. Teague thought that the subsequent formal British presence in Syria was a 'temporary and God-sent opportunity to consolidate the organisation against the probable time when we shall no longer be there'. Illustrating the difference between SIS's long-term approach to intelligence-gathering and the more immediate concerns of, say, its armed service colleagues, he shrewdly (though expansively) observed that the 'primary task of the present' was the establishment of 'effective organisation for all possible contingencies in the future'.

On the political side, Teague told Menzies in July 1941 that relations with the Free French were extremely strained. He considered that for the British, 'it is like trying to live amicably with a jealous, touchy and domineering wife'. At every corner the Free French saw sinister British plots. De Gaulle had appointed General Georges Catroux as Commander-in-Chief of the Free French Forces in the Levant, and, although he was 'more reasonable' than de Gaulle, even he presumed that the British were out to annex Syria to the British empire. When Catroux became de Gaulle's representative in Syria, an SIS agent (source 'Volcano') in the former's headquarters passed over copies of Catroux's and de Gaulle's correspondence which provided a picture not only of de Gaulle's attitude towards the British in the Middle East, but also of his intentions regarding French North Africa. Volcano, who continued to operate until the summer of 1943, was a highly prized asset, some of whose product was fed directly both to the Foreign Office and to Churchill through Desmond Morton.[13]

The Allied invasion of Syria had partly been triggered by a pro-Axis seizure of power in Iraq, led by Rashid Ali early in April 1941. Baghdad station sources had been predicting a coup for the end of March. During the crisis one SIS agent gathered valuable information from Iraqi army officers of troop dispositions, on the prearranged line for retreat decided on by the Iraqi army and on the attitude of Middle Euphrates tribes to the revolt, but the Baghdad representative reported that the intelligence 'unfortunately arrived too late to be used owing to the removal of our transmitting sets'. British forces quashed the rising, but *The Times* enquired if the Foreign Office had been taken by surprise and 'What was our Intelligence Service doing?'[14] Within SIS it appeared that the Eastern Department in the Foreign Office had failed to pass on all of its reports, so much so that a set of extracts from the weekly political summaries was assembled showing that the Baghdad station had been warning of the specific possibility of a coup from the beginning of the year.

During 1941 the issue of using Anglo-Iranian (formerly Anglo-Persian) Oil Company (AIOC) employees for intelligence work surfaced after the head of the Baghdad station, set up a local network without going through the proper channels established by SIS with the AIOC head office in London. In March 1941 Bowlby observed that the station was using several individuals who had 'not had the official sanction of their Company to carry out our work, although the Manager out there knows of their activities which he allows but does not like'. The local manager's attitude was 'understandable in view of the extremely delicate relations existing between the Company and the Iranian Government'. Vivian was not at all happy that Baghdad had 'consciously side-stepped' the existing 'perfectly good & close liaison' (by which the Service had agreed not to use company employees except through the head office) and he felt that the Service could not expect AIOC 'to be very much impressed by our good faith'. Nor were they, and after a meeting in London at which an AIOC representative 'made it quite clear that the repercussions resulting from the Iranians having any cause for complaint against the Company would be disastrous, not only to the Company but also to the conduct of the war', the Service had to agree to terminate 'the employment of any employees of the Company'. In May Vivian and Malcolm Woollcombe, however, had a meeting with AIOC, who reassured them that they were still 'quite prepared to volunteer to 82000 any information of real inside importance, which may happen to come to their knowledge'.

The SIS station at Tehran for which Shelley had laid the foundations at the beginning of 1940 began operating in April. The first full-time representative, whose instructions were to concentrate on the Caucasus and South Russia, stayed barely a year, by which time little progress had been made in penetrating the Soviet Union. In April 1940 London asked Tehran to look into the possibilities of using as agents smugglers working across the Soviet–Iranian frontier. Evidently nothing resulted, for in January 1941 the Army Section at Head Office noted that the Soviet Central Asian Military District was 'a veritable "black spot" to us as 83000 [Tehran] has so far failed to obtain a single item of military information from this area'. It was hoped, however, that matters might improve as an additional officer had been sent out at the end of 1940 specifically to concentrate on Soviet military information. Before Germany invaded the Soviet Union on 22 June 1941 and it came into the war on the Allied side, very real fears that Russia might fight on the Axis side sharpened the need for intelligence about both its intentions and its capabilities. While noting that there had been a recent 'very satisfactory improvement in our U.S.S.R. O. of B. [order of battle] etc. information', in February 1941 the Director of Military Intelligence urged SIS 'to establish without delay further trans-frontier contacts particularly in Moscow, the Caucasus, Central Asia and Eastern Siberia'. 'I think DMI is right,' noted Hubert Hatton-Hall. 'We may well be fighting USSR in another year.'

The head of station in Tehran was replaced 'temporarily' by Wilfrid Hindle (the former head of station in Budapest), who stayed until the end of 1942. After the German invasion of Russia SIS operations against the Soviet Union were suspended, but there was much enemy activity in Iran and, in order to forestall a feared pro-Axis take over, British and Soviet troops occupied the country in August 1941. Hindle became so keenly concerned with security questions that it seems to have undermined his intelligence duties. In September 1942 he produced a string of allegations which ruffled feathers high in the Foreign Office. He complained about one consul who was 'extremely friendly' with a Nazi-sympathising

German-born woman, a British subject by marriage, who reportedly had been employed by Spanish intelligence in North Africa. When a cabaret which the woman opened, backed financially by the consul, was put out of bounds to British troops, the consul strongly protested to the British minister. Hindle also reported that an officer attached to Sir John Dashwood (who had come from the Foreign Office to review the security of the mission in Tehran) had 'spent much time in the company of a suspect cabaret girl'. He claimed, too, that there had been various security leaks from the mission and that an unnamed member of the British legation, in reply to a comment from some non-official on the number of secretaries on the staff, had announced: 'Of course they are not all really secretaries. For example, there is Hindle, who is really in M.I.6.' Hindle was moved on from Tehran, but the affair illustrates how a legitimate concern for security could become unreasonably magnified and corrosively affect the perspective and work of an SIS officer.

13

West and East

During the Second World War SIS dramatically expanded its operations in both North and South America, and, as Japan appeared to pose an increasing threat to British interests in Asia, there was a modest expansion of activities in the Far East. Before 1939 there were three SIS stations in the Americas: '48000' in New York, where the Passport Control Officer (with the curious telegraphic address 'Subsided New York') had responsibility for 'U.S.A. and Dependencies'; '72000', based in Panama, responsible for 'Mexico, Central America & all South American countries lying North of, but not including, Brazil and Peru'; and '75000' at Montevideo covering the rest of South America. Although the New York office was to become the most important single overseas SIS station of the Second World War, in the early autumn of 1939 it was something of a quiet backwater. The whole station comprised only nine people: the Passport Control Officer, Captain Sir James Paget, who had been in New York since August 1937, an assistant PCO, four Examiners (whose duties were mostly concerned with actual Passport Control work) and three secretaries. At this time the station appears to have had no agents at all on the books, which reflected Sinclair's order in June 1938 to cease operations against United States targets.

William Stephenson and the creation of BSC

All this was to change over the next six years. For the first eighteen months or so of the war, before the Lend-Lease agreement of March 1941 when the USA formally committed itself to supporting the British war effort, Britain was faced with a situation where a great proportion of its war production, supply, shipping and foreign investment was situated in a country which had no obligation to protect it, and within which there were substantial minority communities sympathetic to the Axis powers. Although the specific acquisition and security of supplies was in the hands of a British Purchasing Commission, SIS had to provide much of the necessary information, and also step up counter-espionage and subversion work. But this required close liaison with the FBI, which was eventually established through the person of William Stephenson.[1]

Stephenson had first come to SIS's notice in the summer of 1939 when he offered to put his British Industrial Secret Service (later Industrial Secret Intelligence) at the disposal of the British government.[2] In 1939–40 he provided information about Scandinavian matters, especially Swedish iron-ore supplies to Germany, which Section D were keen to disrupt, and he evidently impressed SIS sufficiently for Menzies to use him in April 1940 as a go-between with J. Edgar Hoover of the FBI. Stephenson was ideal for the job as he could reach Hoover through a mutual acquaintance, the boxer Gene Tunney, whom he had met as a fellow member of an inter-service boxing team in Amiens in 1918. The first Paget learned about this mission was a cable from Menzies informing him that Stephenson 'is doing nothing against America and is known to us. Should an enquiry reach you from Hoover you can say he is all right.' Stephenson visited Hoover on 16 April and (as the American record dryly put it) 'discussed arrangements for co-operation between the British Intelligence Service and the Federal Bureau of Investigation'.[3] That evening Stephenson excitedly reported to London: 'long Washington conference completely successful . . . Will co-operate fully with all resources . . . Have undertaken all communications strictly unofficial personal and secret between him and C.S.S.' Code-names were given to the two men: 'Our chief is S. M. Scott' – Menzies – while Hoover was to be 'H. E. Jones': 'Jones sends Scott assurances of goodwill and of desire to assist far beyond confines of officialdom.'

While London reminded both Paget and Stephenson 'that any liaison resulting from this must be entirely unofficial', Hoover took very good care to clear the arrangement with President Roosevelt's secretary, General Edwin M. Watson, and ensure that the White House had no objection to the proposed relationship (still apparently kept secret from the State Department) between the FBI and SIS. Stephenson stayed in

America for over a month and had a number of meetings with Hoover who, he told Menzies, had invited him to 'procure official position to remain Washington as your personal contact'. Menzies liked the suggestion and appointed him Passport Control Officer at New York in place of Paget (who was ordered home and rejoined the navy), explaining to Gladwyn Jebb that Stephenson had good contacts with an official who saw Roosevelt daily, and he thought that this would prove of 'great value'.[4]

As Paget received his orders to leave, the controversial former SIS New York representative, Sir William Wiseman, turned up in London offering his services. The previous autumn Broadway had rejected a suggestion that he might organise propaganda in the USA. By this stage Wiseman's notable success as an 'agent of influence' during the First World War had been rather eclipsed by the reputation for self-promotion which he had acquired among Admiralty circles (and put about by the former naval attaché Sir Guy Gaunt whose *amour propre* Wiseman had offended in 1915–17). 'Beyond indulging in an inordinate amount of intrigue,' Sinclair had written in October 1939, 'it is not known that he achieved any signal success.' Wiseman was, he continued, 'extremely shrewd, and although mistrusted by most people, nevertheless manages to worm his way into the confidence of prominent persons'. So it happened in June 1940 when Wiseman persuaded the Foreign Secretary, Lord Halifax, to suggest that he be found some substantive role in America. But Menzies would have none of it. 'Both my predecessors made it clear that in their view Wiseman should never be employed again by this Organisation,' he wrote, adding enigmatically: 'They had their reasons.'[5]

Stephenson arrived in New York to take over as Passport Control Officer on Friday 21 June 1940. The following day France signed an armistice with the Germans, leaving Britain and the empire to stand alone. The official history of what became (from January 1941) British Security Co-ordination, which Stephenson had caused to be compiled in 1945, states that, before he left London, he 'had no settled or restrictive terms of reference', but that Menzies 'had handed him a list of certain essential supplies' which Britain needed. Menzies also laid down three primary concerns: 'to investigate enemy activities, to institute adequate security measures against the threat of sabotage to British property and to organize American public opinion in favour of aid to Britain'. With his headquarters on the thirty-fifth and thirty-sixth floors of the International Building in the Rockefeller Center, 630 Fifth Avenue, Stephenson built up a very extensive organisation, recruiting many staff from his native Canada, although Menzies sent the intelligence veteran C. H. ('Dick') Ellis to be his second-in-command. The New York organisation expanded well beyond pure intelligence matters, and eventually combined the North American functions not just of SIS, but of MI5, SOE and the Security Executive (which existed to co-ordinate counter-espionage and counter-subversion work): intelligence, security, special operations and also propaganda. Agents were recruited to target enemy or enemy-controlled businesses, and penetrate Axis (and neutral) diplomatic missions; representatives were posted to key points, such as Washington, New Orleans, Los Angeles, San Francisco and Seattle; American journalists, newspapers and news agencies were targeted with pro-British material; an ostensibly independent radio station (WURL), 'with an unsullied reputation for impartiality', was virtually taken over; and close liaison was established with the Royal Canadian Mounted Police. Stephenson also ran special operations throughout the western hemisphere and from July 1942 to April 1943 was put in charge of all SIS's South American stations.

'Wild Bill' Donovan and liaison with the USA

United States intervention on the Allied side was, of course, the ultimate British aim and in 1940–1 Stephenson played a central role in building the closest possible Anglo-American relations. Making contacts and lobbying at the highest levels of the American administration was a key objective, though one which inevitably overlapped with the conventional diplomatic activities of the British embassy in Washington. Both Stephenson and the British ambassador, Lord Lothian, for example, worked to cultivate Frank Knox, the recently appointed United States Secretary of the Navy, who was known to be strongly pro-British and anti-Axis. Stephenson's entrée to Knox was through an existing acquaintance, Colonel 'Wild Bill' Donovan, who was to become the leading figure in American secret intelligence and operations during the war. Donovan came from a poor Irish-American background, but had been a classmate of Roosevelt at

Columbia Law School. He earned the nickname 'Wild Bill' when fighting against Pancho Villa with General Pershing's expedition to Mexico in 1916 and went on to command the New York Irish 'Fighting Sixty-Ninth' regiment on the Western Front, returning home as America's most decorated soldier. In the later 1930s he was used by Roosevelt for fact-finding missions to Ethiopia and Spain and came to oppose the USA's prevailing isolationist foreign policy. He was to be an extremely important ally. As Stephenson told Menzies in December 1940: 'A Catholic, Irish American descent, Republican holding confidence of Democrats, with an exceptional war record, places him in an unique position to advance our aims here.' Though he was pro-British, this was 'from a practical American stand-point and really simple fundamental that only Britain is between Hitler and America'.

On 10 July 1940 Lord Lothian reported that Knox was sending Donovan to England to investigate 'Fifth Column methods'. Lothian recommended that Donovan, as an 'influential adviser', be 'given every facility', even to the extent of meeting the Prime Minister. On 15 July Stephenson wired Menzies to tell him of the proposed trip, adding that Donovan was personally representing Roosevelt, Hoover and Knox. The visit was a tremendous success, not least because of Menzies's efforts. He told Stephenson that Donovan had 'been put in contact with all leading Government officials and Ministers'. Meetings with both Churchill and the King had been arranged, and he visited factories and military bases, returning to the USA convinced of Britain's resolve to hold out, an opinion diametrically opposed to the reports of imminent and inevitable defeat being sent to Washington by the Boston Irish-American ambassador in London, Joseph P. Kennedy.[6] Kennedy remained an impediment to closer Anglo-American relations. On 26 November 1940 Stephenson reported that the ambassador was in California telling movie magnates 'that they will eventually have to look to Hitler for their market' and had 'addressed service officers with such alarming effect that Knox has informed President "If that son of a bitch comes anywhere near my people again there will be trouble for him. As undoing Donovan's good work."'

Following Wild Bill's visit, Menzies told Stephenson that Donovan had been convinced of the necessity for the 'closest co-operation' between the FBI and SIS, and was also prepared to advocate that Army and Naval

Intelligence should similarly co-operate with the British. For his part, Stephenson was delighted to report that Donovan had 'strongly urged our case regarding destroyers and other matters' to the United States government, and it seems clear that Donovan's strongly expressed views (as well as Lothian's and Stephenson's lobbying) played a significant part in paving the way for the September 1940 agreement by which the USA agreed to provide the United Kingdom and Canada with fifty badly needed destroyers in exchange for rights to bases in British possessions. Stephenson reckoned that Menzies indeed had played a crucial role in cultivating Donovan. 'Give yourself fifty pats on [the] back sometime,' he cabled on 4 September. 'Without Colonel, it could not possibly have happened at this time.'[7]

Another developing liaison which personally involved Menzies concerned signals intelligence. In October 1940 Stephenson told Menzies that the American Military and Naval Intelligence departments now favoured a 'full exchange' of all known information on enemy and other codes and cyphers. Having discussed the matter with the armed service Directors of Intelligence in London, Menzies agreed that 'a pretty free interchange of cryptographic information' would benefit both the United Kingdom and the United States, and proposed that an American expert be invited to Britain to discuss the matter. If the expert 'made a favourable impression', work on Italian and German cyphers could be considered. There was, however, a limit to what might be covered, as Menzies explained to the Director of Military Intelligence. He had discussed the matter with Sir Alexander Cadogan, who agreed that 'we cannot possibly divulge our innermost secrets at this stage'. Menzies's main interest, in fact, was in sharing expertise in attacking Japanese codes, but he worried that restricting any discussion to Japan would 'almost certainly give a measure of offence, as clearly indicating that we have something to hide'. That was perhaps the least of the government's worries, as one official, bearing in mind that GC&CS had been attacking American diplomatic signals traffic for years, minuted: 'What will they think if they find we have been reading their own stuff?' On Menzies's advice, however, Churchill agreed not to limit the discussions to Japan.[8]

The Americans, who brought with them a reconstruction of the Japanese diplomatic cypher machine code-named 'Purple', visited Bletchley Park over several weeks early in 1941. The discussions went very well, and, at

```
New York

    26. 11. 40.
    1917


    27.11.40.            M.Y.T.
                         P.B.S.
       1055              27.11.40.
                         1200



Following is for C.S.S. only.
A.     KENNEDY is doing a great deal of harm here to our cause.
B.     He is now busily affecting MOVIE magnates on west coast.   He
       tells them that they will eventually have to look to Hitler for
       their market.
C.     He has addressed service offiers with such alarming effect
       that KNOX has informed President " If that son of a BITCH
       comes anywhere hear my people again there will be trouble
       for him.   As undoing DONOVAN's good work."
```

A caustic signal from William Stephenson in New York about the anti-British
Irish-American Joseph Kennedy (father of President John F. Kennedy).

the behest of the Chiefs of Staff, Menzies secured Churchill's permission to reveal 'the progress which we have made in probing German Armed Forces cryptography', though for the moment the discussions were to be 'confined to the mechanized devices which we utilise and not to showing the results'. Although this decision 'was thought inadvisable in some quarters', Menzies firmly defended it as 'a wise one', as it led to GC&CS acquiring important new Japanese material.[9] This American cryptographic mission to Britain marked a very significant step in the developing Anglo-American intelligence relationship, and the episode illustrates the extraordinary extent to which the British were prepared to reveal (albeit with some understandable reservations) among the most sensitive of all their intelligence secrets to an as yet still neutral United States. The visit, too, was a part (if a very secret part) of that process by which the United States administration, and eventually public opinion, moved away from isolationism and gradually swung towards support for Britain.

With Menzies's encouragement, Stephenson took on responsibilities throughout the western hemisphere which involved both liaising with the Americans and developing intelligence work on his own behalf. Noting that the Admiralty needed information about enemy activities in Mexico, in September 1940 Menzies suggested to Stephenson that if American sources could not provide the information required he should build up a separate SIS organisation there (which he did). Stephenson also worked with the FBI, which from June 1940 to 1946 ran its own Special Intelligence Service throughout Central and South America.[10] In November 1940 one of Stephenson's men in Mexico City passed information to the FBI for the American authorities that four German ships intended to run the British blockade in the Gulf of Mexico, with the result that the ships were stopped by the United States Navy. The FBI was also concerned about the possibility of Axis sabotage throughout the Americas, and when Hoover learned in October 1940 that the Italians were withdrawing $3,850,000 (equivalent to $59 million today) from United States bank accounts for transmission by diplomatic courier to Rio de Janeiro, it was assumed that the money might be used to fund this. The State Department, now well aware of the SIS–FBI liaison, favoured some sort of 'joint effort' between Stephenson and Hoover to intercept the funds. Menzies suggested that Stephenson put 'most imperative pressure' on a Pan American airline executive to 'purloin Bags' en route, and he also endeavoured to ensure that the British authorities in Trinidad and elsewhere in the Caribbean would try to intercept the bags if they came through British territory. Menzies recognised, however, 'probability is route via Central America', and although he could alert local British representatives to the passage of couriers through the region, 'obviously unable to instigate action these countries'. In fact, although two-thirds of the money got through to Brazil, Stephenson was able to help as one Italian courier travelled via Mexico City with $1,400,000. Stephenson's local representative tipped off the Mexican police, the courier's bag was opened, ostensibly (as diplomatic bags were supposed to be sacrosanct) by 'a new and inexperienced clerk', and the money discovered, confiscated and placed in a blocked account.

During the autumn of 1940 liaison with the Americans increased across the board, though this coincided with an American Presidential election during which Roosevelt had to defend himself against accusations of being too pro-British and recklessly abandoning American neutrality. Stephenson and Menzies meanwhile played a central role in oiling the wheels of the expanding Anglo-American relationship. In November (after Roosevelt had been returned for a third term as President) Stephenson advised Menzies that Donovan, 'presently the *strongest* friend whom we have here', was at Roosevelt's request planning another trip across the Atlantic, visiting the Mediterranean as well as Britain, before returning to the USA, 'to repeat his good work of last occasion and also to combat forces of appeasement here which are gaining ground again'. As with Donovan's previous visit, Menzies oversaw all the arrangements. Writing to Desmond Morton in December, he noted the high importance of Donovan's friendship for the United Kingdom and argued that, 'commended by Mr. Churchill for what he has already done for us and directed as to his future course of action in the mutual interests, much can be achieved here more quickly than by any other means'. This was a clear attempt to secure a Prime Ministerial audience, though Morton could promise nothing definite. 'The Prime Minister', he replied, 'knows well the value of Donovan to us, though rightly or wrongly he considers Donovan to be over optimistic.' Morton offered to give Donovan lunch and 'remind the Prime Minister' of his 'propinquity'. Menzies also lobbied Cadogan, passing on Stephenson's opinion that Donovan had 'more influence with the President than Colonel House had with Mr. [Woodrow] Wilson'. This seems to have had the desired effect and Churchill turned up trumps. Not only did he have Donovan to lunch in 10 Downing Street, but he also instructed that, during an extended tour of the Mediterranean, Middle East and Balkans, 'every facility' should be

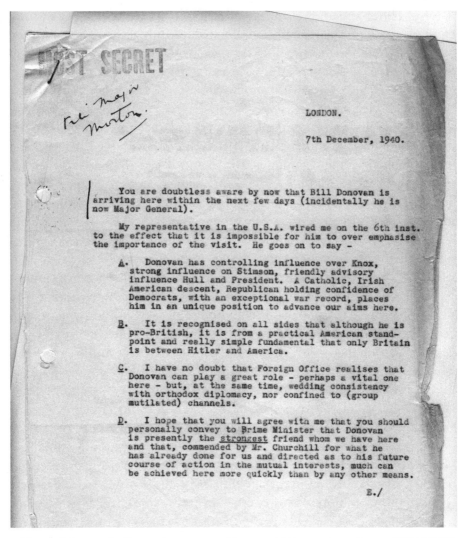

MOST SECRET

LONDON.

7th December, 1940.

You are doubtless aware by now that Bill Donovan is arriving here within the next few days (incidentally he is now Major General).

My representative in the U.S.A. wired me on the 6th inst. to the effect that it is impossible for him to over emphasise the importance of the visit. He goes on to say -

A. Donovan has controlling influence over Knox, strong influence on Stimson, friendly advisory influence Hull and President. A Catholic, Irish American descent, Republican holding confidence of Democrats, with an exceptional war record, places him in an unique position to advance our aims here.

B. It is recognised on all sides that although he is pro-British, it is from a practical American standpoint and really simple fundamental that only Britain is between Hitler and America.

C. I have no doubt that Foreign Office realises that Donovan can play a great role - perhaps a vital one here - but, at the same time, wedding consistency with orthodox diplomacy, nor confined to (group mutilated) channels.

D. I hope that you will agree with me that you should personally convey to Prime Minister that Donovan is presently the strongest friend whom we have here and that, commended by Mr. Churchill for what he has already done for us and directed as to his future course of action in the mutual interests, much can be achieved here more quickly than by any other means.

E./

Menzies's letter of 7 December 1940 to Desmond Morton, introducing 'Wild Bill' Donovan to the Prime Minister.

afforded to Colonel Donovan, 'who has great influence with the President' and who had been 'taken fully into our confidence'.[11]

Although Stephenson's North American position as Director of British Security Co-ordination was formally 'registered and welcomed' by the United States government at the end of January 1941, some members of the administration, notably the anglophobe Assistant Secretary of State,

Adolph Berle, remained suspicious about the activities of BSC and the closeness of the Anglo-American relationship. In March Berle noted that Stephenson, although ostensibly involved with the protection of British supplies, was developing 'a full size secret police and intelligence service', with a string of 'regularly employed secret agents and a much larger number of informers, etc.'. Berle was not necessarily opposed to protecting British ships and munitions, but believed that this should be done only with official authorisation and in conjunction with the FBI.[12] During 1941 Stephenson's burgeoning activities also began to concern Menzies, who worried that with his multifarious responsibilities to SOE, MI5, the Security Executive and the Ministry of Economic Warfare he might be losing sight of his primary duty to SIS. Stephenson had been asked to identify potential agents in North America for deployment into occupied Europe. 'Hope that in this question you will remember that the old Firm has constant and imperative needs,' wired Menzies. Stephenson could exploit United States neutrality by recruiting agents locally who 'after training by Ellis as to Service requirements' could be sent to Lisbon or Switzerland. Stephenson might utilise Spanish ships to put agents into France through Bilbao or Santander. Giving an indication of current SIS priorities, Menzies said that he really 'wanted high class agent in Vichy for political information as to Government's plans and true position of [Admiral Jean] Darlan', the supposed strong man of the Vichy administration.

During the early summer of 1941 Admiral Godfrey, the Director of Naval Intelligence, accompanied by his personal assistant Commander Ian Fleming, travelled to the USA to review and improve Anglo-American intelligence relations. He went out with SIS's support and, liaising closely with Stephenson, appears to have been in part responsible for persuading Donovan to accept (and getting Roosevelt to agree to) appointment to the position of Intelligence Co-ordinator. As Stephenson envisaged it, Donovan was the ideal person to head an American equivalent of BSC, and he reported to Menzies on the eve of Godfrey's visit in May 1941 that he had 'been attempting [to] manoeuvre Bill into accepting job of co-ordinating all 48 land [USA] intelligence'. Once Godfrey arrived, Stephenson organised a private meeting with Knox, Henry Stimson (the Secretary of War) and Robert Jackson (the Attorney-General), hoping that this would 'induce immediate decision, which would otherwise be long delayed through usual "official channels"'. For his part, Godfrey (who stayed with Donovan in his New York apartment) was 'profoundly impressed' by the work being done by Donovan and believed that his 'energy and drive' would 'probably be decisive in obtaining results desired by [British] Chiefs of Staff, namely full co-operation in realms of Intelligence'. Godfrey suggested to the chairman of the Joint Intelligence Committee, Victor Cavendish-Bentinck, in London that Churchill might be asked to send Donovan a 'personal message of exhortation', though Cavendish-Bentinck wisely vetoed the idea. 'Risk of leakage, although small, must be taken into account,' he warned, 'and if message ever became known it would expose Colonel Donovan to the imputation of being a British agent instead of the splendid free-lance that he is.'

In his memoirs Godfrey recalled that he had a very difficult time trying to penetrate the Washington bureaucracy, and had not realised how bad relations were between the United States army and navy. He consulted Stephenson who in turn sought advice from, of all people, Sir William Wiseman, who engineered Godfrey an invitation to the White House.[13] On 12 June Godfrey wired Menzies and the Admiralty, stating that the previous evening he had dined with 'Flywheel' (the codename for Roosevelt) and afterwards had had an hour's interview alone during which he was 'cross-examined closely about co-ordination of intelligence and Allied question'. Godfrey was careful not to mention Donovan by name, but there was clearly only one man for the job and Stephenson signalled on 19 June that Roosevelt had appointed Donovan to be co-ordinator of all forms of intelligence (including special operations). 'You can imagine', he wrote, 'how relieved I am after three months of battle and jockeying for position at Washington that "our man" is in a position of such importance to our efforts.' Donovan's position as Co-ordinator of Information (COI) was the precursor to his appointment to head the new Office of Strategic Services (OSS) in June 1942. With both the COI organisation as it evolved and the OSS, Donovan presided over a combined intelligence and special operations organisation which more closely resembled Stephenson's BSC than Menzies's SIS. Claude Dansey, neatly bracketing the two 'Bills' together with his underlying antipathy to special operations, complained in April 1942 that 'there was not much in Donovan for S.I.S.'. He was 'completely sold on publicity and this he can find in S.O.E. operations. Further, that 48000 [Stephenson] is urging him on down these noisy paths.'

The rapid growth of OSS into a large and formidable agency, which owed much to the help and advice provided by Stephenson and his people, and its impact on SIS, reflected the positive, as well as the ambivalent and difficult, sides of the Anglo-American 'special relationship' during the Second World War and after. Within the undoubtedly close, productive and mutually trustful intimacy of the partnership, there were inevitable zones of competition and conflict, underscored by the fierce enthusiasm and apparently unlimited resources which the Americans poured into the Allied war effort after the Pearl Harbor attack of December 1941. And while the Anglo-American wartime alliance was as close as any alliance had ever been (and perhaps would ever be), neither party was ever completely going to abandon its own national sovereignty. Beyond the very extensive common endeavour to defeat the Axis powers, each country retained its own essential interests, not least in that most private and jealously protected state function of intelligence. 'My duty', wrote William Phillips, the OSS head of station in London, was to serve Donovan's goal of a global American intelligence service, 'by developing independent American sources of information' and 'resisting all efforts of the British Secret Information [sic] to gobble us up'.[14] Indeed, it was testimony to the perceived power and efficiency of SIS that American intelligence officers should see the situation in such potentially adversarial terms.

The nature of the apparent challenge posed by OSS as a comprehensive (or substantially so) covert agency, running propaganda and special operations along with pure intelligence, went to the heart of what intelligence work might be and what an intelligence agency might legitimately or appropriately do. From the mid-1930s, under the pressure of anticipated and actual war SIS had intermittently taken on a whole range of covert activities, not all of which were exclusively concerned with the gathering of foreign intelligence from foreign sources. Under similar pressures, and massively reinforced by William Stephenson's restless business gifts and entrepreneurial flair, BSC developed with astounding speed into an impressively wide-ranging organisation, and one which provoked favourable comment from visiting officers. 'How much I admire the wonderful set-up you have achieved in New York,' wrote Admiral Godfrey. 'As the prototype of what such an organisation should be, I consider it beyond praise.' F. T. 'Tommy' Davies, a senior SOE man, who had begun in Laurence Grand's Section D, was 'much impressed' by the 'very harmonious relationship' between BSC's three sections of SIS, Security and SOE and claimed that an 'immense advantage' was gained 'by a quick and complete inter-change of intelligence'.[15] When Richard Gambier-Parry visited BSC in late 1941, he came away very struck by Stephenson's 'immense application, photographic memory and driving force', and spoke highly of the overall efficiency of the operation, as well as the excellent relations both within its headquarters and between it and the numerous agencies with which it liaised.

But once the USA came into the war much of BSC's security and intelligence work could legitimately be taken over by the FBI and other United States agencies. Indeed, an irony of the USA becoming an ally at all was that the State Department and United States service departments' consequent determination to be the controlling influence in the western hemisphere, and to stop all foreign and clandestine activities in the USA, whether by friend or foe, actually threatened BSC's existence. As Stephenson reported to Menzies in January 1942, the so-called McKellar Bill then before Congress would require the registration of all 'foreign agents' and the detailed disclosure of particulars concerning agents' appointment, remuneration, business and activity. This, wrote Stephenson, 'might render work of this office in U.S.A. impossible as it is obviously inadmissible that all our records and other material should be made public'. Menzies was less worried, however. He thought the bill did 'not in fact appear to curtail the activities of S.I.S., since you obtain moneys from the Embassy which need not pass through any bank. Your agents are all secret men unknown to any person outside the organisation and it should be impossible for the Americans to check up on their activities.' In any case, 'your S.I.S. activities are not now very great, since all Fighting Force information obtained from American sources should be forwarded through the British Missions in Washington', which had been formed 'now that America is in the war'. Nevertheless, after some vigorous lobbying by Stephenson and others, the bill was amended so that agents of the Allied 'United Nations' would be exempt from registration and need only report in private to their own embassy.

By mid-1942 BSC had passed its zenith (although Stephenson stayed on until the organisation was wound up in 1945). In October 1942 Menzies responded to a request from Stephenson for additional staff with the unwelcome news that he was considering whether 'your already large

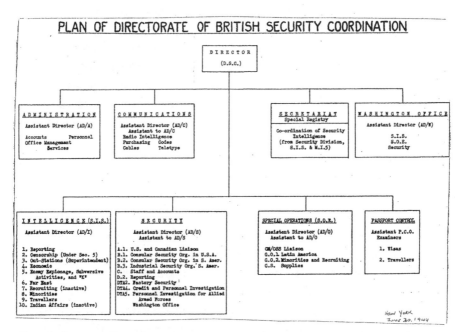

British Security Co-ordination organisation chart, June 1944, showing the wide range of activities within William Stephenson's North American empire.

staff should not be reduced rather than increased'. By the New Year, after Air Commodore Payne (Deputy Director/Air) had been out to inspect the SIS stations in the Americas and had discussed the situation with Ellis, Menzies was taking a harder line. 'I am disturbed by the size of the S.I.S. staff in your New York and Washington offices,' he wired on 2 January 1943. He thought there was not 'now any justification for increasing the staff at S.I.S. stations in Central and South America' and bluntly instructed Stephenson 'to effect a 25% reduction in the executive staffs, and a 25% reduction in the clerical personnel' of the New York and Washington offices by 31 March. Stephenson protested (with some reason) that 'figure of 25 percent seems arbitrary and haphazard without basis on which it is computed', and, noting that he had a total of twelve SIS executive personnel (there were about the same number of clerical staff), a 25 per cent cut would mean a reduction of three officers. He proposed, nevertheless, reductions in staff dealing with South American work, but complained about Payne's evidently adverse report

('pettifogging charges based on malicious gossip which seemingly moti-
vated misrepresentation of our activities'), and warned that 'should
B.S.C.'s position here become sufficiently weak then real danger' would
be the gradual 'subordination of our established position in this ?entire
hemisphere to Jones [Hoover]'. This final point appears to have struck
home in London, as, although there was a gradual reduction of the SIS
presence in the USA, Menzies did not press the need for drastic cuts.

BSC's intelligence work

Beyond the BSC Official History of 1945, clearly designed to show the
organisation in the best possible light and based on records which were
subsequently destroyed, no comprehensive record exists of its work.
Although a sizeable proportion of the many thousands of telegrams between New York and London have been retained, very few of the more
substantive letters and reports that went by diplomatic bag appear to have
survived. One 'annual report' (it is not clear how many of these there were
in all), however, exists. Completed in June 1944 and covering a period
from March 1943, it provides a useful picture of BSC's intelligence work
during the second half of the war. Within the intelligence branch three
sections (each with two officers) actively processed various kinds of information. The Reporting Section handled 'European theatre reports obtained from 48-land [USA] sources', prepared the Western Hemisphere
Weekly Intelligence Bulletin, compiled 'data pertaining to 48-land politics' and had 'liaison duties'. By mid-1944 the first of these had effectively
been superseded by the work of the OSS London office, through which
an increasing volume of reports were being channelled. Valentine Vivian
thought that the Western Hemisphere Bulletin, while 'well prepared' and
'interesting', was 'not an S.I.S. function' and 'not worth what it costs'. A
similar observation might be made about the political reporting, which
was more properly embassy work, and in any case was 'not usually sent
to Headquarters in the form of reports' but was merely 'available as background material etc'.

The 'Superintendent's section', though 'for all practical purposes [a] part
of the B.S.C. organisation', handled material from the Latin American
stations and in fact reported directly to London, while circulating some

relevant reports locally and to Canada. The Economic Section supplied information about the USA and Latin America for the Ministry of Economic Warfare in London. Among the material provided was intelligence about the activities of the United States Alien Property Custodian, which had control of enemy companies, such as the German chemical concern IG Farben. Aware that the Custodian had 'embarked upon an ambitious scheme' for increasing exports to Latin America, and 'mindful of the fact that some of these [enemy] companies had been restored to German control after the last war', the Economic Section 4 'decided to keep a covert eye on the Custodian's activities'. It was ascertained that he was negotiating supply arrangements with companies in Mexico, Brazil and Colombia, 'a development which was pregnant with undesirable implications'. Little, if any, of this had been reported by the Custodian to the British ambassador, 'but H.M.G. was kept informed by Section 4'.

The largest SIS section, with five officers, dealt with 'XB': counter-intelligence and 'enemy activities and subversive activity'. The report asserted that among the 'tangible results' of XB work was the 'arrest, and/or prosecution and conviction' by the US authorities of 'seven key enemy agents' and some twenty associates. The section naturally liaised closely with the FBI, and from October 1943 had been jointly investigating Communist activities, especially in South America. One longstanding interest of SIS in North America was 'Indian activities', and 'an up to date card index' of Indian nationalist and other suspects had been compiled, drawing principally on official United States sources. During 'recent months', however, there had been 'a noticeable reluctance on the part of U.S. official and other circles to collaborate with information relating to British Indian nationals'. This was felt to be due 'to the latent American dislike of the popular conception of British imperialist suppression of Indian nationalist aspirations', rather than 'any officially inspired policy'. This work, in any case, had been the responsibility of an individual officer who had returned to England, and the study of Indian activities was scheduled to cease at the end of June 1944.

William Stephenson's 1945 Official History asserts that among BSC's most significant achievements was the penetration of the Italian, French and Spanish embassy staffs in Washington, while, thanks to the amorous activities of agent 'Cynthia', both the French and Italian naval cyphers were obtained. The history also maintains that Cynthia was responsible for short-circuiting an Italian attempt to scuttle merchant ships interned in US ports. The SIS files contain nothing about any role Cynthia may have had against the Italians but there is some material to corroborate her part concerning the Vichy French. A report from Lisbon in October 1940 noted that Cynthia (Mrs Elizabeth Pack, an American married to a British diplomat, who had worked for SIS in Poland before the war) was 'on a visit from Washington'. Lisbon raised the possibility of her again being useful to the Service, noting that she was 'great friends' with a strongly anglophile American naval intelligence officer. 'He is aged about 40, unmarried; and she is undoubtedly rather attractive.' The officer and some of his colleagues 'were apparently anxious to be of use to England' and had offered to give her information for the British authorities. London passed on the contact to Stephenson who was given permission in March 1941 to employ her at a salary of $250 per month 'for a three months' probationary period to cover diplomatic and inside foreign circles in 48-land capital'.

According to the BSC History, Cynthia began an affair with the Vichy press attaché, Charles Brousse, in the early summer of 1941 and subsequently provided copious amounts of information from the Washington embassy for SIS, so much so that Menzies complained about the volume of material, asking 48000 to be more selective and concentrate on United States–French relations and telegrams from the French naval attaché. In June 1942 he particularly requested information about a new cypher the ambassador and naval attaché were using. As narrated by the BSC History, Cynthia and Brousse masqueraded as lovers in order to spend nights in the embassy and organise it so that a locksmith could get access to the safe. New York reported that on the first attempt it took too long to open the safe, which was ascribed to Cynthia's 'nervousness', and there was no time to make photostats of the code-books. The History relates that there was a second, successful attempt (and it includes two photographs of the Vichy cyphers), but there is no independent confirmation of this in the archives.[16]

SIS in Latin America

The BSC Report for 1943–4 estimated that the annual total expenditure on all SIS's Latin and South American stations came to something just short of £200,000 (£6,600,000 today). Demonstrating the huge expansion in activity across the hemisphere, this was well over ten times the budget allocated in 1939–40 for the whole region. In the spring of 1938 a local British resident, Captain Reginald 'Rex' Miller, had been appointed to Montevideo with cover as Civilian Assistant to the Naval Attachés in South America. He would, wrote Gladwyn Jebb from the Foreign Office, 'perform certain special duties in connection with Intelligence matters. It is not desired to give any more publicity to this appointment than can be avoided.' Miller was a Spanish-speaking businessman, and, although he had no previous experience of intelligence work, he did very well in South America where he remained until 1946.

Beyond the gathering of political and economic intelligence, the wartime work of SIS's South American stations was of three main types. First was naval intelligence, involving, as London instructed Panama in September 1939, 'penetration of Mexico to watch German activities especially supplies to raiders and submarines', or as Miller put it in a report on Uruguay in February 1940, 'investigating the activities of the German Legation and their possible relationship to maritime alarms, excursions, movements, etc.'. The second included monitoring and attempting to penetrate the sizeable local Axis communities, identifying enemy intelligence agents and assessing threats to Allied political and economic interests. Third was a range of other covert activities, sometimes special operations alongside SOE personnel who were run out of Stephenson's BSC office in New York. Of these, naval intelligence, at least in the first half of the war, absorbed the greatest amount of time and money. Some matters were excluded from the Service's purview, presumably not having been raised by customer departments. In 1943, for example, London queried a proposal to engage a Peruvian agent involved in the drug business on the grounds that 'we are not (repeat not) particularly interested in the manufacture and export of cocaine'.

Miller's SIS work naturally intensified after the outbreak of war. On 25 September the Foreign Office were informed that he had deployed agents to gather intelligence for the Ministry of Economic Warfare. By October he was complaining that some of his agents were overworked, and at the beginning of December he asked for a full-time assistant to run SIS work in Brazil. In December the naval attaché in Buenos Aires worried about Miller's health breaking down under the strain of overwork. This was especially important as the majority of the attaché's information 'on enemy movements' came from sources under Miller's control. 'That part of his organisation that deals with enemy activities within his countries', claimed the attaché, 'provides material of the greatest use, the ultimate effect of which it may be hard to exaggerate.' The Admiralty view seems to have been decisive and Miller got his assistant. At the beginning of 1940 Miller, with two secretaries in his office, secured permission to spend up to £160 a month on a network of a head agent and eight under-agents to target Nazi organisations in Uruguay. Five months on he raised the problem of underfunding in Chile, where he was faced with an 'exceedingly efficient and co-ordinated German penetration'. Here his SIS organisation of 'some eight to ten members', costing £150 a month, could not 'do more than cramp the enemy's style'. In November 1940 Menzies approved a proposal from Miller for an officer to run operations in Chile, Peru and Bolivia, and in February 1941 Major Henry Higman (who had briefly been Passport Control Officer in Madrid and had been working in Head Office) was appointed as '76000' to head an independent station at Santiago.

Admiralty concerns about the region were underpinned by the Battle of the River Plate, when British warships forced the German pocket-battleship *Admiral Graf Spee* to take refuge in Uruguayan territorial waters, where it was scuttled on 17 December 1939. Although this was a rare early success in the war, the mere presence of the German ship in the South Atlantic sharpened fears that other enemy warships, including submarines and disguised armed merchant-raiders, sheltering and even reprovisioning in remote parts of the South American coast, could operate in the area, threatening vital British sea-communications. With the Mediterranean effectively closed to British merchant traffic, vessels sailing to the Middle East and India, as well as the Far East and Australasia, had to go round the Cape. By the end of 1940, indeed, German raiders, operating chiefly in the Atlantic and Indian Oceans, had caused the loss of fifty-four merchant ships totalling 367,000 tons.[17]

In May 1940 Miller reported that a ship-watching service had been established on the Argentine coast of Patagonia, but with a long coastline, a very scattered population and only eleven sub-agents the task was one of 'considerable difficulty'. Miller had to depend mainly on 'a few isolated Englishmen working farms on or near the coast' and it was 'not a practical matter to draft strange agents into these areas of few inhabitants. Hundreds would be required to assure any certainty of results.' He raised 'the possibility of equipping ocean going fishing craft for this purpose'. The following month a sub-agent reviewed the position in Chile, with similar challenges of a long coastline and scattered population. In the province of Aysen, eight hundred miles south of Santiago, moreover, there was 'a large proportion of German settlers' and the previous summer 'a party of Germans supposed to be a scientific expedition' had 'explored the province' and, 'no doubt, mapped the country very thoroughly'. This work, noted the report ominously, was *not* 'on behalf of the Chilean Government'. As the establishment of a shore organisation was 'a physical impossibility', Miller suggested the alternatives of keeping watch by sea or air.

In London this was interpreted as a firm proposal for coast-watching from the air. Reflecting that the cost 'of such a service would be very considerable', SIS asked the Admiralty's opinion 'as to its desirability and value'. Meanwhile Miller proposed an ad hoc arrangement by placing an agent on a local oil company plane engaged in survey work. This was enthusiastically welcomed by the Admiralty in August 1940, 'as there is a raider somewhere in these parts now and it might be hiding in some uninhabited inlet in Patagonia'. But the arrangement was only a stopgap and in December the Admiralty issued an explicit instruction to SIS to make searches by aircraft 'of the coast lines of East South America, including Southern Brazil, Argentine and the Terra del Fuego – both Argentine and Chilean'. This was easier said than done. Herbert Taylor, head of the American section in Broadway, sounded out an oil company executive who estimated that, apart from any local political problems which the scheme might encounter, it would cost £10,000 to set up and run in the first year. In January 1941 Taylor noted that 'the problem is obviously bristling with difficulties', but since the Admiralty were 'most anxious for something to be done', he thought 'we must explore every possibility before saying we are unable to help'.

Miller in Montevideo came up with a solution which involved buying a plane for the local manager of an English-owned sheep farm in the southern Argentine. For the rest of the Patagonian coast he believed that commercial pilots flying in the area 'could be persuaded to act as observers for monthly retaining fee' and to cover the Chilean coast funding could be provided for a local British ranch owner 'nominally [to] purchase an amphibian aeroplane for his own use'. Miller estimated that, 'excluding cost of aircraft', it would only cost £2,500 per annum. Having secured Foreign Office and Admiralty approval, the purchase of a plane was agreed in March 1941. The business, however, dragged on for some time. It was argued that getting a plane from the USA would be 'far quicker' than using British channels. 'If the Air Ministry is brought into it,' minuted one official, 'and then M.A.P. [Ministry of Aircraft Production], it would seem that we will just about be getting approval for the purchase by the time the war is due to end.' After a plane had been ordered (from the USA), but not delivered, some local British supporters offered to buy one themselves 'as part of their war contribution', which Miller gladly accepted. Meanwhile hangars and landing-strips had to be constructed at farms down the coast, and insurance (a nice touch) arranged for both plane and pilots. On 13 December 1941 the first survey was run. 'Source', reported Miller, 'was not able to fly over all the coast line but was able to see the greater part. There was nothing to report.' He speculated that the existence of a British plane flying over the coast at irregular intervals 'may act as a deterrent to enemy activities'. In London Taylor said the report was 'of considerable interest and we are very glad that this reconnaissance has now got under way'. In fact, no raiders or submarines were spotted by subsequent flights either. A similar coast-watching operation in Chile, involving both a plane and an eighty-ton schooner, also failed to spot any enemy activity, though a Chilean police source in November 1941 provided 'reliable information to the effect that a submarine of unknown nationality had been reported east of Castro', which suggested that the exercise might not have been at all futile.

The moment of maximum threat had passed, as, indeed, had the moment of maximum need in 1940–1 when, without the precious 'Ultra' signals intelligence obtained from German Enigma cyphers which later informed naval operations, the Admiralty were desperate for information from whatever source. Money was clearly no object. Early in 1941 Miller raised the possibility of buying information from a disaffected German embassy employee about the location of raiders, including the pocket-battleship *Admiral Scheer*. Despite 'not attaching very much weight to the report', Admiral Harwood, commander of the Royal Navy's South American Division, thought this possible source of information should be followed up, 'in view of the present raider position'. Miller reported that, having laid down certain conditions about the information – that it would have to be tested for genuineness and that 'informant must state name of raider, armament, speed and approximate whereabouts' over a period of fifteen days – a price of '105,000 Argentine pesos (approximately £6,250)' had been quoted. Even though he also warned that 'this might be a plant with object of:– 1. Leading our ships into a trap, or 2. Diverting them', on 3 March London accepted the staggering cost (equivalent to something over £200,000 in current values) and Miller was instructed to go ahead.

Four days later there was information, though the source had not been able to fulfil all of Miller's conditions. He stated that an 11,000-ton raider called *Handelsschiff* or *Hilfskreuzer* (literally, 'merchant vessel' and 'auxilary cruiser'), flying the British flag, was scheduled to take on spares between 15 and 16 March at a specified position near Annobón island in the Gulf of Guinea off the African coast. 'Failure of source to answer every question we asked', suggested Miller, 'seems to me to support his genuineness.' Naturally the source was now keen to be paid. After waiting for two weeks without hearing anything, he put to Miller his suspicion that the raider had been caught by the Royal Navy, who were 'keeping it dark and trying to swindle him'. He was, nevertheless, 'still willing to play provided he is satisfied he is not being "done"'. London told Miller (for his personal information only) that 'owing to raider activities attempt at interception had at last moment to be abandoned', but he could tell his source that 'owing to last minute mechanical breakdown his story could not be proved or disproved', and that 'at your discretion' he could 'pay source up to five hundred (repeat five hundred) pounds as token of good faith'. By committing what was still a very substantial sum of money (equivalent to over £18,000) just to keep him sweet, it is clear that Broadway not only regarded Miller's German embassy source as highly promising, but was also extremely keen to acquire this particular kind of naval intelligence. The episode illustrates the lengths to which the Service was prepared to go when presented with the possibility of recruiting one of those very rare individual agents apparently in a position to provide highly specific information which could be used directly by the armed forces for operational purposes. But, for whatever reason (the archives do not reveal whether the £500 was paid or not), the source dried up and SIS had to fall back on more generalised, and inevitably much more chancy, coast-watching networks to keep a lookout for German raiders.

After Pearl Harbor there was an intensification of intelligence interest in the Argentine and Chile. It was thought they would 'offer better opportunities' than other South American countries since they were the only ones that maintained diplomatic relations with Axis Powers. In February 1942 the Air Ministry supplied a questionnaire on the Japanese aircraft industry; the War Office wanted any travellers coming from Japan to be quizzed about troop sightings ('Did you observe at ports or there [*sic*] vicinity troops in tropical kit, also tanks?'); SIS's Economic Section wanted general information about Japanese industry and the supply of strategic commodities, as well as any 'expedients adopted by enemy concerns to elude our and American economic control'; while the counter-espionage Section V wanted 'detailed information' regarding 'Japanese, German and Italian espionage organisations, and on their use of neutral diplomatic communications, particularly Spanish bags'. Undoubtedly reflecting SIS's own activities, Section V insisted that 'the influence of axis organisations on local police forces must be constantly watched' and also raised the possibility of 'the use of bribery in high places'.

In March 1942, arguing that 'Argentine is assuming increased importance, not so much for fear of axis internal coups but because she is almost only remaining country where enemy agents can operate with comparative freedom', Miller asked for an additional £885 a month to investigate Japanese activities there. When questions were raised in London about the cost, Taylor defended Miller by noting that 'Japanese activities' could 'include all sorts of things', such as 'establishing naval bases for raiders', and that, in any case, '75000 is an experienced representative and I think time has shown that we may trust him to spend money wisely.' A year later Miller re-emphasised the importance of work in the Argentine, 'the one remaining free territory for enemy activities in this hemisphere'. The enemy, moreover, were 'well entrenched, spend lavishly, and have many years start on us'. He also warned about conceding influence in the region to the Americans, and was 'more convinced than ever that so far as this country [the United Kingdom] is concerned, grouping of the whole of this Continent, regardless of race or prejudice, as a 48-land [USA] sphere of influence in which we are only secondarily interested' was 'to build up a policy on a false thesis. We have had', he continued, 'and we still have influence in this country' which 'we cannot transfer to our 48-land Allies even if we could'.

Another of Miller's tasks was making clandestine acquisitions for the British Purchasing Commission in New York. Among the highest-priority Ministry of Supply requirements were metric machine-tool parts, essential, for example, for the manufacture of Bofors anti-aircraft guns. These could be obtained only from 'machine and tool makers' in Switzerland, who needed German transit permits before the goods could be exported. SIS in Montevideo, therefore, was endeavouring to secure them 'through Argentine "cloak" firms'. Miller also obtained other items, such as watches and diamonds, more straightforwardly from smugglers. When in April 1942 he asked for additional staff to help make these acquisitions, London queried whether SIS should be doing this at all. Conceding that the work was 'of great importance to the war effort', Valentine Vivian argued that it still 'didn't alter the fact that it is well outside our charter'. 'Is it sound', he asked, 'from the S.I.S. viewpoint that 75000 shd be doing this fraudulent trading and smuggling? It might easily draw attention to his more legitimate work and might well lay him open to a request to leave the country.' On the other hand, he recognised that Miller might be 'the only man on the spot with the "noûs" and drive to do it'. So it appeared to be, and it was decided simply to charge the cost of additional office staff to the Ministry of Economic Warfare.

SIS's relations with British diplomats in South America were generally quite good. Early in 1942, reflecting on his three and a half years running the main regional station, Reginald Miller noted that, despite his feeling that ambassadors were 'inclined to be jealous of their privileges', he had never 'had any difficulty' with them, partly, he thought, 'because I have adopted a co-operative attitude'. Whenever he was in Buenos Aires the ambassador did 'not hesitate to discuss with me and often asks my views on any matter of interest'. In Montevideo, moreover, he found that the new ambassador 'looks upon me almost as his unofficial counsellor', a state of affairs which had 'definite advantages for our organisation'. This could have disadvantages, as in Lima, where the SIS representative complained to Miller in May 1940 that the embassy staff had 'a tendency to look upon him as a local private detective'. But Miller recognised the importance of keeping professional diplomats sweet and in May 1945 reported that Evelyn Shuckburgh, who had been chargé d'affaires in

Buenos Aires for over a year, would shortly be in London en route to a new posting in Prague. He was 'still a young man' (in his mid-thirties), but 'an extremely able one, and will I think go a long way in his profession'. As he was 'most friendlily disposed towards our Organization and even has no little respect for its efficiency', Miller thought it would be 'a happy idea for him to have the pleasure of a talk with somebody at H.Q.'. This suggestion may not have been entirely disinterested as when 'P.12' did see him in July Shuckburgh 'expressed great appreciation for the work of 75000'. But Miller's prediction was sound, as Shuckburgh (later Sir Evelyn) continued on a distinguished Foreign Office career, serving as the Foreign Secretary's principal private secretary in the early 1950s and later as ambassador to Italy.

British diplomats in the region were not averse to doing a bit of espionage on their own account, as Henry Higman discovered when he arrived in Chile in July 1941. So far as the entire British mission in Santiago was concerned, 'secret intelligence', he reported, was regarded as 'just everybody's business'. The existing head agent (theoretically being run by Miller in Montevideo) was not very good, with the result that the naval attaché had effectively become the SIS representative, and had developed a network of agents of his own. Higman rightly felt that combining covert work of this sort with conventional attaché duties was extremely risky, but was faced with the 'very real' difficulty that his colleague was 'now so mixed up with and enthusiastic about "C" [secret service work] that he may feel sore if he feels that he is not being kept fully conversant with future developments'. The first secretary, furthermore, was operating an extensive intelligence-gathering operation which Higman was 'supposed [to] take over as a going concern'. This included 'running, and contacting quite openly – or at least with the most rudimentary precautions for security – a number of very doubtful foreign agents', and, worst of all, an elaborate telephone-tapping operation actually located in the British embassy itself. Higman was told that tapping the phone of a German-owned bank had produced 'most valuable' economic intelligence, but he was extremely concerned about the extent to which the position and security of the embassy had already been compromised.

Higman set to work sorting out the SIS operation in Chile, laying off some of the unsatisfactory agents he had inherited, who included a 'French morphine addict' claiming close contact with the German intelligence service, an anti-Hitler former German army officer and a 'Chillian [*sic*] Irishman'. He wanted to get the telephone-tapping operation out of the embassy building, but when he found that the cables could not be moved without arousing suspicion, a special room was constructed in the basement. By December 1941 the calls of the German embassy propaganda office and two banks were regularly being monitored. When the Santiago station was closed down at the end of 1943 and Higman brought home, he reported that telephone and postal interception had been among the best sources of intelligence. Up to eight phone lines could be monitored by two operators working simultaneously, and for postal work Higman said that he could 'obtain, examine, photostat and return to circulation mail addressed to any Post Box'.

Relations with the diplomats could be upset by the most unexpected things. In March 1942 the British consul-general in New York despatched thirteen crates of SIS wireless equipment to Chile. Although he had been instructed to label them as 'office furniture', the shipping documents (addressed to the British ambassador) read: 'Secret English confidential material, nett weight not revealed, declarable value not revealed'. This 'act of stupidity', wrote Menzies, 'may annoy the Ambassador and prejudice him against my representative in Santiago although it was no fault of his'. Sometimes, too, things just went wrong, as when in September Higman's deputy in Peru reported a 'quarrel ending in blows between his head agent 414 and a dismissed sub-agent 416'. The head agent, it seemed, had been swindling the sub-agents, 'retaining ?part of their pay'. In revenge the sub-agent had 'initiated proceedings against 414 citing British ?Consulate as supposed employer of 414'. A local lawyer had been in touch with the consulate who were 'sending representative to disclaim such fantastic story'. This set the alarm bells ringing in London where Taylor worried about the potentially damaging fall-out of the affair, especially back in Britain. Reflecting that it 'may have serious repercussions with YP Lima [the British minister]', he suggested that Higman go immediately to Peru to handle the matter, 'the object being that YP Lima should not repeat not send telegrams to ZP [the Foreign Office] on this subject if it can be avoided'. Happily, Higman was able to report 'situation seems less serious than supposed'; the minister was 'most understanding and helpful and has not repeat not telegraphed ZP'.

In 1942 it was decided to post a representative to Cuba for

counter-espionage work. The method used to establish secure commercial cover illustrates how readily the Service was able to work with private companies, especially in wartime. The officer concerned had previously worked in Havana for a British firm. Felix Cowgill of Section V decided that the managing director of the company should be 'given some of the reasons why his re-employment would be in the national interest' and be asked 'to have the idea that he again needs a representative in Cuba in view of the expanding possibilities there. After due consideration he might decide that [the officer] is the very man for the job.' If this were done, argued Cowgill, it would reduce talk in the company office 'to a minimum'.[18] In another case, where a British firm were going to withdraw their representative (who was a very productive SIS source) from the Argentine because of a wartime drop in business, the Service persuaded them to keep him on by agreeing to meet half the costs of his salary.

Across South America SIS successfully identified and countered Axis agents. In March 1940 Miller reported one agent foiling the attempted sabotage of a British vessel in Montevideo. A sub-agent 'hit the saboteur over the head with a sandbag, stole his suitcase and is forwarding one of the bombs home to the D.N.I. now'. In May he 'obtained shorthand notes of recent inner Nazi party meetings in Buenos Ayres which indicates considerable fifth column progress in Argentine', and in October he reported efforts to penetrate the German embassy in Buenos Aires, 'hoping to make contact with' an embassy telephonist 'through the German mistress of a well known Englishman' in the city. None of these individuals would necessarily have been aware of SIS's interest, and, indeed, if they were, it might have made it more difficult to exploit them for intelligence purposes. From within the sizeable local Ukrainian community 'reliable and sound information' had also been obtained about German efforts to persuade them 'to become Nazi-minded'. Using press and shipping-office sources, Miller was 'receiving copies of the majority of the neutral shipping passenger lists, and through [agent] 75141 and his contacts we are able to obtain very accurate details of outgoing passengers and both in-coming and outgoing cargoes of a suspicious nature'. Miller emphasised that collating this material was quite a challenge. 'The sorting of masses of trivial information,' he wrote, 'the card-indexing of hundreds of names, a daily report of two or three pages to me, the typing out of passenger lists, the translation of data received in Spanish and, in fact, the hundred and one details inherent in any form of widespread organisation, all take up considerable time.'

No.	Name and Address	Nationality	"Class A" Birthplace and Date	Occupation
41	DILLINGSHAUSEN, Nicolaus Eduard von Rio de Janeiro.	Esthonian	Katentach, 1904	Engineer

Nicolaus Eduard von Dellinghausen

Arrived in Brazil from Germany before the war as representative of Stahl-Union. In 1941, by arrangement with Stahl-Union, he became Managing Director of Cia Ferro e Carvão. DILLINGSHAUSEN allowed Schlegel's transmitter to be transferred to his fazenda in Minas, for which participation in Axis espionage activities he was tried on 19.11.1942 and sentenced to 8 years imprisonment.

| 42 | DIAS, José Ferreira, (Alias "José da Burra") Rio de Janeiro. | Portuguese | Santo Tirso, Portugal, 1888 | Dock Checker. |

Employee of Hermann Stoltz in charge of stevedores. Made regular trips around Guanabara Bay in the Company's launch "Hansa" listing Allied ships which were photographed by Walter Augustin, who accompanied him. Tried on 6.10.1943 and sentenced to 20 years imprisonment. Retrial 29.10.1943, when sentence was reduced to 7 years. A further trial of the Hermann Stoltz group is due to take place shortly.

'Purple primers', collating SIS's information about suspected enemy agents, were prepared for many neutral countries. This extract is from the Brazil volume.

One result of this kind of work – repeated in station after station – was the so-called 'purple primers' (after the colour of their binding), country-by-country lists of enemy personnel, of which a number have survived in the archives. In a Uruguay example of October 1943 individuals were classified under five headings: A – 'Known and suspect espionage agents'; B – 'Known and suspect agents, informants and sub-agents'; C – 'Axis or pro-Axis persons using prominent positions as cover for subversive activities'; D – 'Persons acting on behalf of enemy interests'; and E – 'suspect fifth columnists'. In the first two categories were 'all our registered XB cases' (counter-espionage targets), while the other classifications 'deal with persons who we believe either give assistance to them or who themselves are in line for a higher classification'. Of 174 people in the Uruguay primer, fifteen were in category A and thirty-eight in category B. By contrast, a December 1943 primer for Brazil included 238 category A people, though unlike the Uruguay volume it listed a large number who had been tried and convicted of espionage in the local courts. They did things differently in Peru where the primer was divided up into subject categories, such as 'Commercial espionage', 'Gestapo', 'Peruvian Axis collaborators', 'Sabotage' and so on. Reflecting the success of both Allied and indigenous efforts to curtail Axis activities in the country, the Lima station reported that, of eighty-seven subjects identified in 1941, forty-three had been 'deported or repatriated'.

Other work in South America shaded into special operations territory, and here lines were sometimes crossed with operations run out of 48000 in New York. In March 1941 the SIS representative in Rio de Janeiro (where a separate station had been established in April 1940) complained to London that an officer, 'Agent 75265', had been sent to him from New York to 'be employed by me and at the same time undertake work for 48,000 of nature of which I am ignorant'. Agent 75265, in fact, was involved in a proposed SOE operation to sabotage the Italian airline LATI (Linee Aeree Transcontinentali Italiane) which operated between Italy and Brazil. The service was regarded as a major loophole in the British blockade of Nazi-occupied Europe, carrying 'German and Italian diplomatic bags, couriers, agents, diamonds, platinum, mica, Bayer chemicals, propaganda films, books and all sorts of men and materials back and forth over the route'. In part because one of the Brazilian President Vargas's sons-in-law was chief technical director of the airline, the Brazilians refused to restrict LATI in any way. The Rio head of station argued that sabotage would only temporarily interfere with the service, and might, moreover, give the Germans in Brazil, who were 'in a position [to] do more damage to our interests here than we are to theirs', an excuse to indulge in reciprocal sabotage. After SOE agreed to drop this project, BSC in New York came up with another scheme to forge a letter from the airline's president in Italy to an Italian executive in Brazil. At BSC (using a genuine letter acquired by SIS in Brazil) much work was put into getting paper and other details absolutely right. By November 1941 a letter had been produced insulting the Brazilian President (the 'little fat man') and aligning LATI behind Brazilian opposition groups. After the letter was leaked to the Brazilians through the American embassy in Rio (the Americans being completely fooled into thinking it genuine) the desired result was obtained.[19] LATI was closed down in Brazil and all its assets seized.

In early 1942 when Brazil broke off relations with the Axis powers, SIS in Rio reported the American embassy's opinion that the 'LATI letter' had 'been one of the main factors in persuading President Vargas to turn against the enemy'. SIS, which never came clean to the Americans about its role in the affair, took some quiet satisfaction in bamboozling their diplomats in Brazil as (according to the Rio head of station) the US ambassador, Jefferson Caffery, and some of his staff were strongly anglophobic Irish-Americans who indulged in constant anti-British activities, even after the USA had entered the war. Despite this local Anglo-American tension, the position throughout the region, even before Pearl Harbor, was one of close co-operation. In November 1940 London had laid down 'as a general principle' that 'all information of interest to Americans should be shown to them'. At the end of January 1942 the SIS representative in Rio again complained about SOE agents being sent to Brazil who 'know too much about us; nor have they shown sufficient discretion. I consider that here at least S.I.S. is far more important than S.O. which must depend on S.I.S.' By March SOE was pushing to extend its activities generally in South America, but the US State Department objected, and with South American governments beginning to line up on the Allied side, by late 1942 the Axis threat in the region was ebbing away. On 30 October Stephenson in New York wired Menzies that in view of improving coverage of SIS in South America 'am proposing to close down SOE there'. Menzies telegraphed back: 'Am convinced eminently sound proposal.'

SIS in the Far East 1939–41

Although Britain's strategic priorities during the first two years of the war were naturally concentrated first on the threat to the United Kingdom itself and subsequently on its interests in the Middle East, Mediterranean and North Africa, the possibility of a direct Japanese challenge in the Far East remained a worry. But there were few enough resources to deploy in the region. At the start of the European war SIS had five main stations across the Far East. In Shanghai the veteran Harry Steptoe produced mostly political and economic information on China. Frank Hill at Peking (Beijing) was working mainly on military information from North China. At Hong Kong the responsibilities of a one-man station run by Alex Summers extended from northern French Indo-China in the west across southern China to Formosa (Taiwan) island in the east.[20] A separate station was run by Lieutenant Commander Charles Drage, who had been based in Hong Kong since 1933 and had primary responsibility for Japanese military intelligence. By 1939 there was a rapidly growing demand for this, but one which SIS was ill equipped to meet. In the summer of 1940 Drage relocated to Singapore, whither the regional inter-service intelligence organisation, the Far East Combined Bureau, had moved the previous year. The Singapore station itself was headed by Major J. H. Green, an army officer with twenty years' intelligence experience in Burma who had been appointed Assistant Defence Security Officer in 1938, and who was responsible for Burma, Malaya, Siam (Thailand) and French Indo-China. Stretched enough in Europe to respond to the challenges of Germany and Italy, SIS, like every other part of the British defence and security community, had little to spare for the Far East, where the probability of full-scale war with Japan was widely (and somewhat complacently) discounted.

In 1940 two additional stations were established. One was at Chungking (Chongqing) where, with cover as the press attaché at the British embassy, Walter Gordon Harmon's primary (and difficult) role was liaison with Chiang Kai-shek's Nationalist Chinese intelligence service. Harmon was an Englishman who had been born and bred in China, and had been employed in the Salt Gabelle, the body which administered the Chinese salt tax. The other station was at Manila, where Gerald Wilkinson, a British businessman based in the Philippines whose father had worked with Menzies during the First World War, was appointed SIS representative with responsibility (as Menzies told the Foreign Office) 'mainly to find out certain information which the Ministry of Economic Warfare require'. Wilkinson, in fact, had been working under Hong Kong since 1936, briefed not only to cover the Philippines' defences but also to work on the penetration of Japan. In October 1939 he had reported a contact who might be able to secure 'a Japanese or Japanese-speaking Philippine ready to go to Japan and stay at some naval station with [the] object of gathering naval information', but nothing appears to have resulted from this. In the meantime Wilkinson developed a close relationship with the American military authorities in the Philippines, which was later to prove very beneficial for Anglo-American liaison.

Apart from concentrating on Japan and Japanese targets in China, the SIS stations in the Far East were also asked for information about the USSR. Reflecting concerns arising from the Nazi–Soviet Pact, late in December 1939 Broadway announced that 'the penetration of Vladivostock is now of high importance not only for Russian information but as a possible German base'. It instructed the Far Eastern stations to 'telegraph what prospects you see of getting suitable sources for obtaining the above information in the near future'. Only two of the stations appear to have responded positively. Singapore signalled that a 'local Russian' had volunteered to work for them, and asked the Shanghai station if visas for Vladivostok were obtainable and what steamship sailings there were to the Russian port. After Shanghai replied to both questions in the negative the potential agent rejected the mission as not being 'a practicable proposition'. The response from Hong Kong was initially more hopeful as the SIS representative there was currently 'negotiating for purchase of up to date plans of Vladivostock'. Although the source (a White Russian) was 'an utter blackguard', he had 'always delivered the goods hitherto'. A 'report on Vladivostock Harbours' was indeed delivered in September 1940, but a later note (which described the Russian as both a 'chronic alcoholic' and 'totally unreliable') said that it 'proved of little value'.

One of the problems for SIS in the region was that the very longevity of its representatives, coupled with the general gossipy lack of security that pervaded official and expatriate circles in the Far East and a near-fatal tendency to underestimate the enemy, meant that the identities of SIS representatives were widely known and their efforts to step up operations in 1939–40 readily compromised. One officer at Broadway, who had served in the Tokyo embassy in 1940, ruefully reflected afterwards that the Japanese police had been able to give him 'a fairly detailed outline of our S.I.S. work in China'. The activities of Steptoe and Hill, he added, were 'known to most European residents in the Far East, for so-called Embassy cover does not mean a great deal unless a man does some definite Embassy job in addition to S.I.S. work'. By 1939 the Service's Japanese and Formosan port-watching organisation had moved to Singapore, but here it ran into security difficulties when members of the local Jewish community denounced Drage's South African-born assistant to the police as a Nazi agent. In January 1940 Drage moved back to Hong Kong, but seems not to have been able to maintain the flow of reports, many of which had been marked in London as 'of considerable value'. Additional efforts to penetrate Japan were uniformly unsuccessful. Drage attempted to work up a network based in the Japanese community on the United States Pacific coast, but it produced no more than a few preliminary reports. Further evidence of how vigilant and suspicious the Japanese security services were of British residents was the arrest in January 1940 of one Vincent Peters, and his subsequent eight-year prison sentence 'for military and economic espionage'.[21]

In July 1940 the Chief of the Intelligence Staff on the Far East Combined Bureau, Captain Wylie, delivered an extremely critical review of SIS's work in the region. Not only was the information the Service provided poor, but the SIS representatives themselves barely co-operated with each other. Wylie suggested that a regional director be appointed to sort out these problems.[22] Menzies accepted the criticism and asked Godfrey Denham to review the position. Denham, a very experienced former head of station at Shanghai and Inspector-General of the Straits Settlements Police who had gone into business after retiring from the public service, visited Singapore in February 1941, agreed with Wylie that a regional controller was required to sort out the situation and, pressed by Menzies, took on the job himself. By August he was established within the Far East Combined Bureau (FECB) in Singapore with the station number '69000' and had been directed by London to 'control all the representatives in the Far East', receive 'the Bureau's criticisms on their work' and 'obtain questionnaires' for SIS.

While Denham was able to improve SIS's general relations with the FECB, he was unable to do much about the dearth of Japanese military information. In October 1941 an FECB review of 'sources of intelligence' reported very unfavourably about the Service. There was the inevitable tension between the armed services' urgent operational needs and the more reflective political intelligence which was SIS's stock-in-trade. There was also a problem about the integration of SIS work with the intelligence effort as a whole, a difficulty exacerbated by the absence of any SIS representative on the FECB itself. The original idea had been for Denham to be a member of the Bureau, but this 'had not been fully

implemented'. The FECB view, however, was that naval and air officers 'with up-to-date technical qualifications' could usefully replace SIS
personnel and, this being the case, it would actually neither be necessary
nor desirable for SIS to be represented. The absence of SIS on the FECB
may in turn have facilitated the sweeping criticisms of the Service in the
review. SIS was seen as far too independent: 'A great number of telegrams
sent home to London direct from S.I.S. without previous reference to the
F.E.C.B. seem far from the truth and wasteful of public money.' It would
be better if the 'majority of S.I.S. reports' were submitted to the FECB
for comment prior to despatch to London.

The review went on to make specific criticisms of SIS coverage of the region. The 'Northern Area – including Manchukuo' (Manchuria) was 'the
least satisfactory of all. There is no doubt that the present Peking representative is incapable of carrying on the service, still less of developing it.
In view of the importance of this station in event of a Russo-Japanese war,
the appointment of a first-class man to Peking is of urgent importance.'
The situation in Japan and Japanese territories was a little more satisfactory. They were 'being penetrated on a very small scale from Manila', a slow
process but one which 'shows promise'. It was suggested that more information 'could probably be obtained from Nanking'; south China and
Thailand were 'improving'; French Indo-China was 'reasonably good' but
too dependent on French sources. Further afield, it was noted that 'no air
intelligence' was received from SIS 'regarding the U.S.S.R. East of Lake
Baikal'. Finally, the report reflected circumspectly on the provision of
signals intelligence, but here again there was nothing positive to report
about SIS, which had 'at no time produced anything of value'.

PART FIVE

WINNING THE WAR

14

The tide turns

SIS grew spectacularly during the war. This is reflected in a summary of SIS's wartime accounts drawn up by Paymaster Sykes in June 1945. Sykes broke down the total sums into three main sub-divisions: 'S.S.' (secret service), GC&CS (signals intelligence) and 'Section 8' (Gambier-Parry's technical branch). In 1940–1 the total expenditure was just over a million pounds, with 'S.S.' spending £889,000 (as opposed to £117,000 in the mid-1930s), GC&CS £79,000 and Section VIII £111,000. Three years later secret service spending had increased more than threefold to £2,828,000 and Section VIII's fivefold to £569,000, but GC&CS's had risen over sixteenfold, to £1,302,000. Numbers of personnel had increased commensurately. In April 1939 there had been forty-two officers in SIS (of whom fifteen were special operations – Section D, later hived off into SOE) and fifty-five secretaries. At the beginning of 1944 SIS had 837 people working at headquarters: 307 officers and 530 secretaries, as well as an unknown number of other support staff, including janitors, cooks and cleaners. Section VIII and the Radio Security Service had 190 officers and 4,783 other ranks (which included wireless operators abroad), while GC&CS had a total of 7,847. As for SIS personnel abroad (excluding the Mediterranean Command, for which figures were not available), there were 253 officers and 322 secretaries.[1] These figures do not include numbers of agents, which are effectively incalculable. In 1946, for example, Menzies, evidently including anyone who served even in the most minor capacity, claimed that during the war 'we had 25,000 French agents working with S.I.S. and the D.G.E.R.' (the French secret service).[2]

Headquarters reorganisation

The growing size and responsibility of SIS continued to put pressure on its administrative structures. Following the 1942 reforms, when the service Deputy Directors had been brought in and the production side tidied up, further changes were made in the spring of 1943. Partly to improve liaison with the War Office, and partly to ease his administrative load, Menzies had his old friend General Sir James Marshall-Cornwall transferred from SOE to SIS and appointed Assistant CSS on 29 March. The intention was that he should understudy Claude Dansey (who had been redesignated Vice CSS in October 1942), and act for him in his absence. Marshall-Cornwall, who had served in the Intelligence Corps during the First World War and had been military attaché in Berlin from 1928 to 1932, remained as ACSS for the rest of the war but his time at SIS does not, on the whole, seem to have been particularly happy. It was apparently intended that he should relieve the sixty-seven-year-old Dansey of some of his burdens, assuming responsibility for his territorial concerns across Europe. He took over the supervision of Mediterranean stations, but Dansey held on to his French operations. In the careful words of Robert Cecil (who succeeded Patrick Reilly as Menzies's personal assistant at the end of September 1943), writing long afterwards: although 'showing signs of wear', '"Uncle Claude" remained sufficiently himself to resist intrusion into the secrets of the networks he was developing in France in anticipation of D-Day'.[3] Marshall-Cornwall, too, had a tendency to bypass existing arrangements, which upset the occasionally somewhat Byzantine SIS chains of command. Both John Bruce Lockhart in Bari and Harold Gibson in Istanbul grumbled about his 'interference'. The former told Cuthbert Bowlby that Marshall-Cornwall's 'complete ignorance and misrepresentation of the facts' had caused 'indignation and resentment' and he objected strongly to Marshall-Cornwall's 'practice of addressing or repeating insulting and entirely ignorant letters to my officers without consulting you or me first'.

At the same time as Marshall-Cornwall's appointment, Valentine Vivian's designation was changed from DCSS to Deputy Director/SP. Although in practice his duties did not change, and he remained in charge of security and counter-intelligence, the new title, sharing that of Deputy Director with the three service appointees, could widely be interpreted as an effective demotion. Combined with Marshall-Cornwall's appointment as Assistant Chief, and Dansey's confirmation as Vice Chief, this change undermined any claims Vivian might have continued to nurse for the position as Menzies's number two. A more unambiguously positive appointment in March 1943 was that of Commander Kenneth Cohen to the new position of Chief Staff Officer, Training, which was designed to make training more comprehensive and systematic than hitherto. The administrative side at Head Office was further reinforced in September when Menzies, responding to concerns which colleagues such as Frank Foley had felt, created a new post of Deputy Director Administration who was to be responsible for 'recruitment and administration of all personnel, officers and secretaries; works, buildings and transport; welfare; finance . . . and the general running of the machine except in regard to Section VIII' which was to 'remain autonomous in the above respects'. To fill the post, which he held for the rest of the war, Menzies brought in Air Commodore Harald Peake, an able businessman (albeit also an Old Etonian) who had been serving as Director of Air Force Welfare. As with the case of Vivian, this appointment marked another change from the old order, as Peake supplanted Rex Howard, who had been chief of staff since before the war. Howard's own post was 'put into abeyance', and he was reduced to being chief staff officer to Air Commodore Peake.[4]

Over the turn of the year 1943–4 the experiment of combining armed service representation with geographical responsibilities was abandoned. Of the three service Deputy Directors, only Bill Cordeaux was adjudged to have been a complete success. Menzies separated the two functions, creating a series of 'controllerates' covering wide geographical areas, and with primary responsibility for production. Cordeaux was made Controller Northern Areas (CNA), Cohen Controller Western Europe (CWE) and Marshall-Cornwall (whom Menzies consistently supported) Controller Mediterranean (CMed). A Controller Far East (CFE) position was later created to which Dick Ellis was appointed. Payne and Beddington continued as Deputy Director/Air and /Army respectively, while Commander Christopher Arnold-Forster became Deputy Director/Navy, which he combined with being one of Menzies's personal assistants.

The administrative changes in SIS are also reflected in the increasing formalisation of arrangements at Broadway. The small Head Office community which had existed before the war had been run by Sinclair as if it were a family business. Individual officers had ready access to the Chief and no one worried very much about the niceties of hierarchy or the proper channels. Menzies continued this style of management, but it became increasingly difficult to carry on as the Service grew and the pressure of work expanded exponentially. Robert Cecil recalled that, without any prescribed arrangements for individuals to communicate with the Chief, 'queues formed outside his room at the end of the corridor, imperfectly controlled by lights, which showed whether or not he was occupied'.[5] This complete free-for-all was unsustainable, and although Menzies remained remarkably accessible, by October 1943 an appointments system was in place and staff had been circulated with a list of the times (9.45–10.45 a.m. and 2.45–3.45 p.m.) when the Chief was *not* available to see people.

Like all other wartime government offices, Broadway was overcrowded and scruffy. A secretary who joined in September 1943 thought that, whenever it was that the office had been built (actually in 1924), she did 'not think it had ever been refurbished, or redecorated'. The floors were 'covered in worn lino, quite dangerous in places, walls were a mucky grey/white/cream, and the rooms were lit with bare light bulbs: only senior personnel were allowed to have desk lamps'. The offices were so dark that at the back of the building, which looked into a courtyard, there were what she remembered as 'long panels of silver painted wood' placed outside the windows and slanted in order to reflect light in. She herself worked with three other people in a 'large gloomy room in the front of the building, grottily furnished'. When she first started, her hours were 9.30 to 6.30 six days a week, 'but we could choose which day of the week we wanted off', and she was allowed one week's holiday for every three months worked. A great many of the staff were 'serving officers who wore uniform (except on a Saturday, when they all wore tweeds)'.

This secretary worked in the Finance Section under Paymaster Sykes, 'a fearsome gentleman in naval uniform, very deaf', and some of her early duties concerned staff salaries, another area where the pressures of war forced rationalisation and change. Before the war the practice in both SIS and MI5 had been for salaries to be paid free of income tax. In his second report on the Secret Service (which focused primarily on MI5) Lord Hankey raised the matter and suggested that, while it was probably unwise to alter the basis of existing salaries, the situation might be regularised for future appointments, with salaries subject to tax. In August 1940 Sir Horace Wilson, Permanent Secretary at the Treasury, told Menzies that there was really 'no option' but to adopt this proposal. Menzies was appalled, describing it as a 'drastic change'. Members of SIS, he told Wilson, were 'just as anxious as anybody else to make their proper contribution to the war expenditure', but SIS salaries were so comparatively low that in order to make up for the deduction of income tax 'a very considerable additional payment would be necessary'. It was still the case, moreover, that there was no pension provision for SIS officers. Security was also a consideration. Menzies was concerned that if tax deductions were made from Service salaries, and even if the information was restricted to only a few tax officials, the potential leakage of information about SIS personnel would be 'deplorable and fraught with the utmost danger'. But the huge expansion of wartime staff, with many individuals being seconded from the armed services, made it difficult to sustain the traditional, idiosyncratic system. The Treasury had their way and from April 1942 all new appointees paid tax. But everyone, even the Chief, was still paid in cash, and the paybooks were all written in pencil, 'ready to be rubbed out if anyone tried to prove there was an SIS'.

Training and communications

Commander Cohen's appointment as Chief Staff Officer, Training, in the spring of 1943 marked another move towards professionalisation. The war years saw the beginnings of a more coherent and co-ordinated, if rather modest, training regime. Up to this time, with the exception of codes and signals, training had been decentralised and varied considerably from section to section. The sort of thing that might be done is illustrated by the bespoke training programme Rex Howard devised in summer 1941 for the novelist Graham Greene, due to go to Freetown, Sierra Leone, in November. Greene was detailed to visit Sections I–IV (Political, Air, Naval and Army respectively), V (Counter-espionage) and VI (Economic), who would be asked to describe their work to him, and also their requirements from the West Africa area. Section V would instruct him in the 'general question of C.E., enemy methods, hints on security and telephones'. Greene would be instructed in codes and wire-less procedure. Howard noted that, 'if possible', Greene should see an agent being trained and also be instructed in secret inks. He would need to read 'Instructions to Representatives' and 'Notes for S.I.S. officers', along with the instructions given to the current representative at Lagos. Howard himself would meet Greene for discussion 'regarding S.I.S. Organisation at home and abroad. Relations with other Government Departments. Objectives, methods and the question of personal cover. Symbols for Departments and Sections. Post-boxes, cut-outs, agent dou-bles, [and] provocateurs.' Greene would then see Frank Foley for instruc-tion regarding the training of agents, and other officers for 'discussion on censorship', telephonic communications and security. Finally, Greene would be introduced to the Deputy Chief, Valentine Vivian. Beyond this specific SIS training, in order for the rather unmilitary Greene to main-tain cover as an army officer, he was also sent to a general course for Intelligence Corps officers at Oriel College, Oxford, for the sole purpose 'of being given the most elementary instruction in soldiering, so that he could wear battledress without embarrassment'.

However comprehensive and detailed individual programmes like this might be, it was clearly an inefficient way of providing training for a rap-idly expanding Service. Among the signs of the new approach to train-ing and tradecraft was a memorandum prepared by the Army Section in February 1942 on 'S.I.S. Stations abroad: their operations and special tasks'. Compiled at Rex Howard's request, this embodied general prin-ciples, 'based on personal experience'. That the training arrangements were becoming much more systematic is illustrated by a 'P.9 [Norwegian Section] Agents' Training Sheet' from 1943 which set out a list of twenty-one separate possible training requirements, including 'Security' (at the top), through various types of communications, 'Principles S.I.S.', 'Arrest information', 'Pistol', 'Unarmed combat', to 'First Aid', 'Photography' and 'Parachute'. Against each of these were boxes for completion under four headings: 'Whose responsibility', 'Training commenced', 'Training completed' and 'Remarks'.[6]

Commander Cohen's new Training Section began in a modest way. The first officers' course, run in the summer of 1943, had only three stu-dents, but there was a steady expansion. Ten officers attended the second course in September, and by this stage the section were helping overseas stations with training instructions and manuals. Individual officers could now be directed to specific programmes, as was Graham Greene's fellow writer Malcolm Muggeridge, in August 1943. 'P.11', the head of the Africa Section, suggested that, 'time permitting', Muggeridge, home from Lourenço Marques and expected to return there (though in the end he did not), 'should do a short refresher course with our Training Section to bring his ideas up-to-date. The "Tradecraft" lectures in particular should prove helpful.' The Training Section was keen to expand its activities and when in April 1944 it responded to a request from Major Frederick Jempson of the Belgian Section to train an individual agent 'in the best means of conveying documents through occupied territory', especially 'the best methods of sealing and packing films so that we could tell on arrival whether or not they had been tampered with en route', it reflected on including the instruction on general training courses. In November 1944 Menzies told Sir Alexander Cadogan at the Foreign Office that the new training arrangements would help Service *esprit de corps*. In order to overcome problems of compartmentalisation arising from 'an enforced separation of some of the Sections, solely due to housing difficulties', he had 'introduced a training system which gives numerous officers of the S.I.S. a wide insight into its various functions'. He was also currently 'experimenting with a similar course for selected members of the female staff'.[7]

Communications were at the heart of SIS wartime operations. Gathering intelligence was difficult enough, but the whole exercise was vitiated if the information acquired could not be got back to London, or wherever it was of use. Section VIII's outstanding achievement in developing and refining radio transmitters and receivers made an indispensable contribution, but at the sharp end it was up to individual men and women to operate the equipment in often very hazardous circumstances. A letter to Head Office in March 1943 from 'Magpie', a British radio operator working in the Lyons area in France, described conditions on the ground:

> For the moment I have to change places after each transmission, with only one set this means that it has to be carried from place to place in order to maintain daily contacts. Owing to the absence of other means of transport this has to be done mostly on foot. Last Sunday I had to walk 9 miles carrying MED [his radio set] and the aerial, you can guess what a sport that is. Incidentally, the handle

of the case is not strong enough, mine broke twice. I can tell you it is not very easy to carry without a handle.

Magpie proposed that, to avoid the risky moving of a radio set from place to place, more sets should be provided, which could be left 'in different parts of or outside the town'. Balancing Magpie's complaints (which considering the life-and-death circumstances in which he worked seem rather mild) was appreciation for the support he got from London. 'I must thank Home Station', he wrote, 'for their work during the last months, contacts always having been made very rapidly. You may be sure that all of us here do our utmost to make these contacts a success.' Commenting on the letter, Kenneth Cohen noted that Magpie's network had been more or less on the run during the previous two months and suggested that his difficulties bore out the case 'for more W/T sets in each group'. London was able to respond, and after Magpie had been in the field for six months there were thirty radio sets working in his network, for which he recruited and trained the operators locally.

Apart from the vagaries of weather, air pressure, power supply, local security arrangements and so on, reliable wireless communication also depended on the most scrupulous attention to detail in the preparation of signals, as is illustrated by one case in January 1944. Section VIII broadcast a signal for a Free French agent code-named 'Bonita Granville' informing him to be ready for a message at 1300 the next day. A signal of this sort was generally sent blind to a number of agents without acknowledgement by them, and London had no means of knowing for certain that the message had been received until actual contact was made at the time specified. Agents, however, also made regular contact at prearranged times and, as it happened, this agent's next scheduled contact was at 1200 the following day, when, after passing other traffic, the signal about contact at 1300 as requested by P.1 (the section which ran Free French networks) was repeated, and acknowledged by the agent. But at 1300 the agent did not respond to London's call. At 1400, however, the Free French communications training section based at Ealing in west London (who regularly monitored the traffic with France) telephoned Section VIII to say that Bonita Granville was calling London. Contact was made and a further message was sent asking him 'to listen to us at 2000 the same night'. The agent replied asking: 'check and repeat your encoding'. London did so, but the agent twice more asked them to 'check and repeat'. 'After this it is said that the agent in exasperation made the signal "Merde, merde, merde!!" and closed his station.'

What had gone wrong? Gambier-Parry himself investigated the case, personally coding and recoding the messages, which 'came out correctly as sent by the operator'. Only when he compared the coding substitution table used in France with the master copy in London did he discover that, 'owing to the misplacement of one figure in one line of typing out the copy', a coding error had resulted in the first message asking Bonita to call at 1400 (which he had done), and the second asking him to call at '3000', which he naturally could make no sense of. A mistake of this sort could have had extremely serious consequences. Gambier-Parry's investigation of the matter revealed the care rightly lavished on the system. The master substitution tables – each of which had ten vertical and horizontal columns, and a hundred different versions of which were used – were typed in the office at Whaddon Hall and a carbon copy on flimsy paper given to the agent. But the tables were 'retyped on tough paper for the station where they receive a considerable amount of handling from day to day'. Gambier-Parry reported that the mistake had occurred in the re-typing, 'despite the fact that the invariable practice is to have the retyped copy checked by two people independent of the person who has typed it'. He had identified the original typist (who made the copy six months previously) and 'admonished him for his mistake', though he argued to Menzies that it was 'a human error of which the chances of recurrence are extremely remote'.

Secret writing was a tried and tested method of communication, but it, too, could be problematic. In late 1942 Cyril Cheshire, head of the Stockholm station, had a job persuading a Danish agent, '161', who was 'naturally of a timid nature', to take back to Denmark some new tablets for making 'invisible' ink. The tablets were supplied in a Swedish box 'which had previously contained stomach pills. I assured 161 that in case of need he could prove that these pills were for his own personal use and could demonstrate this by taking one.' But, he continued, 'I have no idea whether this will have any ill effect on this valuable agent, but I am hoping for the best.' Back in Broadway a colleague noted, 'not toxic to any great degree', and Cheshire was reassured that the 'developer, although slightly toxic, would not harm him in smallish doses'. While 'the whole

SECTION V. — Continued.

5/308 SHOES Q.A.
5/310   ,,   Q.

       5/308 exposed.   5/310 exposed.

      SIGNET RINGS   These rings are of varying shapes and mechanism.   They are primarily intended for the carrying of suicide tablets, but can also be used for small jewels, micro-photographs or messages written on very small pieces of fine paper.

5/314   SIGNET RINGS This type has a screw-on top which must be unscrewed by a turn to the right to reveal the concealed cavity.

5/315   SIGNET RINGS The top of this ring is pivoted in one corner, allowing it to be opened by a sliding movement. The concealed cavity is below this sliding lid.

5/316   SIGNET RINGS The top of this ring has a single pivot in one corner allowing it to be opened by a sliding movement. A miniature compass is concealed in the cavity thus revealed.

5/317   SIGNET RINGS The top of this ring has an inlaid stone or jewel. This has to be prised out to reveal the concealed cavity beneath.

Some of the many ingenious types of concealing devices prepared for the use of SIS and its agents.

packet might put him under for a bit', it was 'unlikely to bring about his demise'.

The conveyance of reports by agents or couriers out of occupied Europe was considered by Bill Cordeaux in a review of SIS operations after the war. Most documents were 'photographically reduced in size' and various concealing devices were used. Reflecting that 'ingenious concealing devices are a favourite subject with writers of spy stories', Cordeaux remarked that 'in practice there is not a great deal to say on the subject. Once a person is suspected of carrying secret papers, it is almost certain that a rigorous search will discover them.' Concealing devices, therefore, were 'normally only designed to evade a routine examination', for which 'a quite simple device is adequate'. Among this type, 'the well tried ones of hollow hairbrushes, nail brushes and tooth brushes, the backs of pocket mirrors, fountain pens, pencils, the soles of shoes, cakes of soap, tooth paste and shaving cream were all used'. The most popular were creamy substances, such as toothpaste and shaving cream. Reports, reduced to 'about a square centimetre', would be wrapped in a condom and buried in the centre of the pot of cream concerned. In February 1944 John Bruce Lockhart in Italy reported using animals 'with false shoes, tails, horns etc' to get matter through controlled areas. 'A shorn sheep, for example,' he wrote, 'if well fitted with a woollen skin sewn onto light gauze can conceal under it on the flat of its back a number of largish documents.' He also claimed to know of a case where a false horse penis had improbably been employed. 'Contrary to popular belief,' asserted Cordeaux, 'suitable parts of the human body, such as the inside of the mouth, hollow teeth, the aenus [sic] and the vagina were not often used.' In one instance, however, a sleeping-car attendant on the Trieste–Lausanne train brought reports from a network in north Italy to Switzerland 'wrapped in greaseproof cloth' and concealed in his anus. The fastidious Cordeaux remarked that the transference of 'reports from the agents to our representatives, and their subsequent transcription into readable form are just another example of the varied and not uniformly pleasant nature of the duties of an S.I.S. representative'.

Counter-intelligence

Beyond the signals intelligence and technical branches of the Service, the department which grew most dramatically during the war was the counter-intelligence or security Section V. Before the outbreak of the war it had comprised three officers: Valentine Vivian, who had run the section since its creation in 1925, an assistant, and Colonel Felix Cowgill, who began work in March 1939, apparently 'on the understanding that he might in due course expect to succeed Vivian, aged 52, as the anti-Communist expert'.[8] Cowgill, the son of a missionary, came from the Indian Police where he had served as personal assistant to Sir David Petrie when he had been Director of the Delhi Intelligence Bureau. It had become apparent in the 1930s that the Germans were targeting SIS networks abroad and before the war two Section V officers were posted overseas: one to Brussels and Rodney Dennys, who had been sent to The Hague in 1937. Dennys later claimed that 'after Cowgill's arrival he, rather than Vivian, became the driving force' of the section and 'it was almost entirely due to his initiative, drive and abilities that Section V not only grew rapidly in size and efficiency, but also was the one H.O. section that really had a finger on the pulse of its sub-organisations in the various Theatres of war'.

Allowing for some special pleading on the part of a former Section V officer about the excellence of his branch, its expansion was certainly impressive. By 1945 it had 163 officers, three times the size of any other single Head Office branch, apart from Gambier-Parry's mammoth Section VIII. In addition, Section IX, which was created in May 1943 to take on the study of Communism and Soviet espionage (which the focus on Germany had caused to be largely neglected), numbered thirty-two officers by Victory in Europe Day, making a grand total of 195 SIS counter-intelligence officers at the end of the war. The growth of Section V was stimulated not only by its counter-intelligence work, but also by the fact that from the end of 1940 Menzies entrusted Cowgill with the security of GC&CS signals intelligence material which was beginning to come on stream and which came to be known as ISOS. Having its own officers in stations abroad with their own cypher communications, this section became something of a service within the Service, arousing some resentment of its position and the resources it absorbed. The high seriousness, moreover, with which Cowgill took his responsibilities over the precious ISOS (and related) material, which was vital both for counter-intelligence and later deception operations, and the extremely tight restrictions which he imposed on its distribution, caused some friction, both within the Service and in its relations with other bodies, MI5 above all.

The expansion of Section V was initially assisted by its sister service. In June 1941, for example, MI5 approved an SIS request to release staff for the section, though not without some internal dissent. 'Its work is so essential to our Service', minuted one MI5 officer, 'that . . . we are fully justified in making this sacrifice.'[9] There was, however, a strong and growing feeling in MI5 that SIS had no business trespassing in what was essentially MI5's primary concern. On 17 April 1942, Sir David Petrie, now head of MI5, while assuring Menzies that he wrote 'with the single purpose of doing better a most important job', made a bid to take over Section V altogether. He sent Menzies a paper arguing for the amalgamation of Section V with B Division of MI5, which was responsible for investigating all threats to security. His case was founded on 'the basic desirability, or indeed, necessity, of handling a single subject as a whole instead of in two parts. The German espionage organisation', he declared, 'does not recognise our artificial divisions of a home and a foreign field, but operates without regard to geographical or other boundaries.' There was currently 'an immense duplication of effort . . . most particularly apparent with respect to ISOS'. Nor, he argued, 'can there be any real doubt as to which of the two organisations, S.S. [Security Service] and S.I.S., should belong the united whole'. It would be MI5, 'who are the executive body responsible for arresting and prosecuting enemy agents directly'. Petrie further proposed that MI5 should in future have direct liaison with GC&CS (hitherto arranged through Section V) and full access to all ISOS counter-intelligence material. MI5, furthermore, would direct the intelligence-related work of the Radio Security Service (which had been handed over to SIS on Petrie's recommendation only a year before) and would retain the direction and planning of all double-agent cases under the control of the XX Committee.[10]

Unsurprisingly, this proposal did not go down at all well in SIS. Vivian prepared a draft reply (which does not survive in the archive) which he did not expect Menzies 'to approve as it stands, since I have "dipped my pen in vitriol"'. Menzies's reply of 11 May, while not vitriolic, was a detailed, frank and robust rejection of Petrie's case. He started with an exaggerated definition of the purport of Petrie's proposal: 'that Section V. of S.I.S. should be absorbed into M.I.5, [and] that you yourself as the latter's Director General should assume exclusive control of the Section V. functions'. Petrie, furthermore, and here Menzies quoted from the MI5 paper, would have 'the right to communicate information and to issue directives as to what was required for the proper discharge of security functions everywhere'. He cast severe doubt on MI5's competence to carry out delicate counter-intelligence operations in foreign territories of which they had no experience. Neither he nor the Foreign Office would agree to the transfer of Section V since the intelligence it circulated was of far wider than simply security significance. It was 'unsound', moreover, that Menzies, 'as the Director of the G. C. & C. S., and being acutely aware of the vital importance to the national interest of preserving the secrecy of its material as a whole, should relinquish responsibility for the treatment of any portion of its output', or 'any measure of control over XX agents abroad', where SIS understood operational risks and conditions better than MI5. Past proposals for the amalgamation of SIS and MI5 (for example in 1927 and 1931), he argued, had had 'the virtue of logic, which the present one has not'. Besides, he concluded, the dangers of separation had been exaggerated and 'good liaison and good will should prove the solvent'.

Petrie did not take this lying down. His reply on 5 June, which had a slightly sarcastic tone, corrected the inaccuracy of Menzies's definition of his proposals: he had not suggested that he should assume 'exclusive' control of Section V functions, but was merely advocating the 'unified direction of counter-espionage as a subject'. He introduced some shrewd new arguments. Until a year before, he wrote, Section V had consisted 'of only a handful of officers, and was in very deep water'. As a consequence it had drawn 'considerably' on MI5 staff: 'Are we to accept it then that they alone are capable of handling the products of C.E. intelligence by some esoteric method outside our comprehension and competence?' He observed that both SIS and SOE had 'for months past been suffering serious losses of agents on the continent' because of German penetration, and asserted that SIS was 'not producing enough C.E. material because of "operational" claims', and was 'falling down over "operational" [activity] because of your neglect of C.E., so that the vicious circle is complete'. He acknowledged that amalgamation of SIS and MI5 had been rejected in the past and said that 'speaking for myself' he did not favour complete amalgamation, on the (faintly odd and certainly debatable) grounds that he did 'not believe that as a race we show to any advantage in handling big organisations'. He assured Menzies that MI5 had 'no wish to usurp your authority over the G. C. & C. S.', though he 'should have thought that since ISOS intercept material is of such great significance to my Department . . . you could have expected us to have quite as catholic an appreciation of the need of safeguarding it as anyone else'. Petrie concluded by telling Menzies that he intended to take the matter up with Lord Swinton, to whom he reported as head of the Security Executive.

Petrie's appeal to higher authority had what was presumably the desired effect in bringing Menzies round to a more accommodating position. 'The letters you and I have exchanged . . .', he wrote on 28 June, 'have certainly cleared the air, and if I may say so allowed us to blow off a little steam.' Menzies had taken the wise course of having an 'informal talk' with Petrie, and, having given 'very careful thought' to the matter, now conceded 'that the general basis of your original proposals is logical'. Although he gracefully accepted the need for 'a single unified body responsible for studying the activities of the enemy secret services and for co-ordinating and directing action to counter them', he still could not accept that 'this unified Contre-Espionage body should be divorced from my organisation and incorporated into M.I.5'. What he proposed instead was a *joint* section. Considerable discussion ensued into the autumn of 1942 over the details of how this might be arranged, including sharp differences of opinion about where this new body should be located, Menzies wanting it to be at the Section V base in St Albans, Petrie insisting that it should be in central London. But no joint section was ever created and by October the two services had formally agreed merely to hold regular bi-weekly liaison meetings, and even this appears to have petered out after a few months.

Yet both Petrie and Menzies had agreed on the principle of close co-operation, and Menzies's change of attitude seems to have been important in bringing to pass what he had predicted in his first letter to Petrie, that 'good liaison and good will should prove the solvent'. At a practical level, moreover, Section V and B Division officers actually appear to have been able to co-operate on a more or less satisfactory basis all along, despite occasional bouts of agency rivalry. Robert Cecil, for example, cited 'first hand evidence [albeit from unspecified sources] that MI5 had full access to all relevant ISOS from the very beginning and that at the working level co-operation was good, as indeed the fruitful outcome testifies'. Relations between SIS and MI5 certainly improved markedly from late 1942, especially after Section V did move from St Albans to Ryder Street

MOST SECRET

LONDON

15th March, 1943.

This places me in an uncomfortable position. You know as well as I do the valuable work which Philby is doing for me. At the same time, I realise the importance of first-class representation in Spain in the days ahead. I also have some qualms of conscience about interfering with the career of so able a man as Philby is.

After full consideration of all the circumstances and after consulting those immediately responsible for Philby's work, I have come to the conclusion that the Allied cause will best be served by leaving Philby where he is.

I hope that when he communicates this decision to Deakin, Roberts will make an opportunity of emphasizing that the essential nature of Philby's contribution to the war effort compels his present employers regretfully to refuse to let him go, and that they hope that this refusal will not prejudice Philby's own personal interests.

I have not liked, without your permission, to tell Philby what has happened. May I have your permission to do so?

P.K. Loxley, Esq.

Stewart Menzies to Peter Loxley of the Foreign Office refusing a request to transfer Kim Philby, later exposed as a Soviet agent, out of SIS. This letter demonstrates how trusted and valued Philby was by his unsuspecting Chief.

in St James's in July 1943, which greatly facilitated personal contacts between the two agencies.[11]

By 1943 Section V was organised into six main territorial sections – Kim Philby heading the especially important Iberian one – each responsible for counter-intelligence in specific areas across the world. There were also four specialist sections: one processing and analysing GC&CS material; another devoted to double-agent operations; a third which liaised on censorship with the various agencies concerned; and the last dealing with vetting (an important wartime innovation) and arranging facilities for agents to enter and leave the United Kingdom. The GC&CS section used ISOS to help assemble the details of enemy intelligence organisations and individuals which were collated in the purple primers. Dossiers of German intelligence personnel were prepared for the use of the armies in the field. As regards double agents, broadly speaking those run in the United Kingdom and from British military bases abroad were an MI5 responsibility, while those operating in foreign countries came under SIS. In practice, it was a combined SIS–MI5 joint effort within the machinery of the XX Committee in London, the XXX Committee in Cairo, and the XXXX Committee, based first in Algiers and later Caserta in Italy. Each of these committees had broadly the same tasks, among which was the provision of 'foodstuff' or 'chickenfeed' – information – for the double agents concerned to pass on to the enemy, and the degree to which this information might be false, true or 'true-ish' was a matter of very careful judgment. The committees also had to co-ordinate double-agent activity in their areas, implement deception schemes and, by studying the questionnaires given by the enemy to double agents (among other things), prepare appreciations of enemy plans and intentions.

North Africa

Reflecting on the performance of SIS during 1942, F. H. Hinsley noted the Service's marked improvement across the board, but especially so in the Middle East and Mediterranean. By the end of the year, he wrote, 'the SIS was at last accepted as "a serious intelligence agency"' in this theatre.[12] Cuthbert Bowlby and John Teague were always invited by General Sir Harold Alexander (C-in-C Middle East) to his very exclusive morning meetings and they were granted ready access to the Cabinet-level Minister of State in the Middle East, the Australian R. G. Casey. SIS's position was certainly boosted by the increasing volume of signals intelligence which it was able to supply, but this was reinforced by valuable human intelligence, especially from Tunisia, which became the last bastion of the Axis forces in North Africa, as Anglo-American forces advanced from the west following the Operation Torch landings in November 1942, and British Commonwealth forces approached from the east through Libya.

From November 1942 the Dick Jones network in Tunisia supplied a mass of intelligence. Jones, who had begun to organise among fellow prisoners in the Tunis Civil Prison, was able to start almost immediately following his release on 14 November. Using an existing SIS radio which had been kept hidden in Tunis, he made contact with Tony Morris, SIS head of station in Malta. On 20 November Morris reported to London that Jones had 'organized group of about 20 (repeat 20) de Gaullists who left prison with him'. His 'gang' consisted of 'determined men' who had arms and sabotage material 'and can assure results on receipt of prompt reply. Many others', he added, 'ready to join.' Within three hours London had replied: 'Under no circumstances' was Jones to 'participate in sabotage . . . Please impress upon 78 [Jones] that he must confine himself to his duty of producing information which is of vital importance at the present juncture.' But they also asked if the 'gang' might be taken under SOE's wing, so long as Jones himself was not involved or compromised in any way. When Morris reported that there was no SOE organisation in Tunis, London softened its position. 'Notwithstanding vital importance of maintaining intelligence work', it directed, sabotage 'by persons disassociated from our own activities' would 'certainly be welcome'. In this instance, moreover, it was prepared to leave the initiative to Jones and his colleagues in Tunisia: 'While active operations are in progress, we appreciate here that in last resort men on the spot must be best judge of how to assist in defeating enemy.'

Reviewing the work of the Jones group, one agent summarised their activity as providing 'general information' on the strength, organisation, armament and location of enemy troops and supply dumps; sea and air traffic, including 'tonnage and nature of cargoes landed'; and the 'results of bombing, damage and effect on the morale of the native population in particular'. The detail provided can be illustrated by a report sent through the newly established SIS station at Algiers in late November 1942: 'Petrol dumps as follows: on quay opposite maritime station clock tower Bizerta, also in wood at road Ernk to Fishery and Sidi Ahmed Road at end Sebra Bay, also at road junction two (rpt. two) kilometres southwest Bizerta–Mateur–Ferryville railways junction'. Jones himself is credited with having first reported by wireless the arrival of the monster fifty-six-ton German Tiger tanks later the same month, and his was the most productive of five groups operating in Tunisia (involving in all some fifty men and women). Their peak period was the first and second weeks of January 1943, when their reporting 'embraced practically every branch of enemy activity, including enemy intentions and French political tendencies. Military, air and shipping intelligence supplied was voluminous – indeed, for reasons of security,' reported Morris afterwards, 'it was necessary to curb the almost continuous flow of messages.' At one stage, in fact, the Malta station was decoding up to thirty reports a day. The productivity of these Tunis agents helped to raise SIS's reputation with the military. 'After a very cold initial reception,' one officer told Kenneth Cohen in February 1944, 'the information from our Tunis groups became so operationally valuable that First Army were literally hanging on our daily signals to them.'

The extent and enthusiasm of the Jones network led to security lapses, which were exploited by Inspector Marty, a Gestapo collaborator in the French police. A series of arrests in January 1943 led the police to Jean Coggia, a twenty-five-year-old former medical student who had been part of André Mounier's network and subsequently worked alongside Jones. Arrested in Bizerta, Coggia was taken to Tunis for interrogation. Here, 'while awaiting the arrival of the notorious Marty', though still handcuffed, he managed to escape and rejoin Jones. The following month, as they endeavoured to cross over to Allied-occupied territory, Jones and Coggia, both disguised as Arabs, were caught by enemy soldiers after an exchange of fire which left Coggia with a bad wound in his shoulder. The prisoners were brought to Tunis on 23 February 'and Coggia was hurried to Marty's office, first-aid for his wound being refused'. An Italian officer, who was described as being attached to the SS, recounted to a Gaullist policeman what happened then: 'although exhausted and suffering from loss of blood, Coggia maintained a complete sangfroid, and during a long night of interrogation and torture, resolutely refused to reveal anything.

Indeed, he so taunted Marty and his fellow inspectors, that the black-guardly Marty finally lost all control and finished him off by shooting him in the neck with a revolver.' The Italian said that a German SS officer present 'was unable to stomach the scene and finally left, declaring that these were "Russian methods"!'. Jones, who managed to persuade his captors that he was in fact a British officer, was taken to Germany where, with the help of a sympathetic Abwehr major, he eventually gained formal prisoner-of-war status. After spending some time in a prison cell next to the celebrated anti-Nazi Pastor Dietrich Bonhoeffer, he ended up at the famous Colditz Castle.[13]

The group survived and reorganised after the loss of Jones and Coggia. Despite further arrests in March 1943, they continued to supply Malta with vital military information until 'Allen', an Englishman who had taken over the leadership, was himself caught on 15 April. He had been denounced by an Italian who lived in the flat below, and when the police came to arrest him, Allen jumped out of a second-floor window, but broke his leg and was quickly stopped. As reported afterwards, 'at the time of his arrest, his real identity was unknown, and he might have got away with his story of being a Spanish petty thief, had it not been for a slight carelessness in his disguise'. He had dyed his hair black, but the dye had not been renewed, 'with the result that the roots disclosed the natural red shade, while the ends remained jet black'. Following the Axis surrender in Tunisia in May 1943, Morris summed up the performance of the Dick Jones team as displaying 'high grade "morale"' but 'low grade security'. The 'whole "esprit"' of the group was 'based on great daring and disregard of danger, and these admirable and lovable traits brought them many recruits. On the other hand, this same daring (often amounting to rashness), together with a taste for good fellowship and good living, were largely responsible for their final undoing . . . In the type of work in which they were engaged, over-confidence is as great a pitfall as faint-heartedness.' Morris drew 'two outstanding lessons' from the experience: '(a) what can be achieved under brilliant leadership, and (b) the inevitable results of over-confidence and lack of security precautions'.

Elsewhere, the price of discovery was equally grim. After Axis troops had occupied Corsica in November 1942, a number of SIS agents were infiltrated on to the island from North Africa. In April 1943, while waiting to rendezvous with a submarine, two agents from group 'Auburn' were arrested by Italian troops. One of the men, a British-born Belgian merchant navy officer called Guy Verstraete (cover-name 'Vernuge'), who had unfortunately been carrying plans of the island defences as well as some English-language intelligence reports, was very badly treated by his Italian captors. 'In spite of three months of the severest interrogation and the foulest tortures,' reported a French colleague, 'he never gave anything away.' For a fortnight he was forced to use his chamber-pot as a container for food. His right leg was broken at the ankle, fingernails and toenails were torn out and cigarettes stubbed on his chest. He was sentenced to death by firing-squad in July. A report received in London the following October said that he placed his right hand on his heart and told the soldiers to 'aim well'. Then, raising his left hand and declaring 'Vive la Grande Bretagne,' 'he died a brave man ["il est mort en brave"]'.[14]

The Torch invasion of French North Africa precipitated not only the despatch of German troops to Tunisia, but also their entry into unoccupied France. This fatally undermined the Vichy regime and its hold (such as it was) over French overseas territories. Over the next few months there was an awkward period of uncertainty over who would assume the leadership of what had now become known as the Fighting French. Churchill had thrown his support behind Charles de Gaulle in 1940, but the United States, which had recognised the Vichy government and whose first major commitment to the war in the west was in North Africa, regarded him with suspicion. After Admiral Jean Darlan, the Vichy-appointed Commander-in-Chief of French armed forces, called a ceasefire on 11 November 1942, the United States commander, Dwight D. Eisenhower, had him confirmed as the political head of French North Africa, a move which disgusted the Gaullists. In the wings, moreover, was General Henri Giraud, who, having been taken prisoner at the fall of France, had escaped from Germany to Vichy in the spring of 1942 and appeared (especially among Americans) to represent an acceptably anti-Axis French leader.

Algeria was the first part of metropolitan France (as it was regarded by the French) to be liberated from Axis control, and after the ceasefire the political and military focus shifted to Algiers where Eisenhower established his headquarters. Giraud, having been smuggled with SIS help out of southern France on a British submarine, arrived on 9 November. By 12 November SIS had established a presence there under the code-name 'Orange', and Menzies in London pressed the unit for news: 'in particular

we wish to know nature of Giraud's relations with Eisenhower, his attitude towards Darlan and the latter's general orientation'. Two days later
Algiers signalled that the Americans were backing Darlan as they hoped
that through him Vichy supporters could be brought round to the Allied
cause. Meanwhile Giraud was 'somewhat unwillingly' to be kept in the
background. His staff were reported as being 'fully aware grave danger [to
Giraud's ambitions] if Darlan can continue to convince 48-landers [the
Americans] his value'. On 17 November, having managed to get out of
France, the Deuxième Bureau chief, Louis Rivet, and his air intelligence
specialist, Georges Ronin, arrived. Menzies asked Orange to assure Rivet
'that his arrival is really heartening news'. Evidently anxious to keep the
French liaison exclusive to SIS, Valentine Vivian told Algiers that he was
sending out Winterbotham, head of the Air Section at Broadway, to meet
Ronin. 'Try and persuade him and Rivet', he continued, 'to keep clear of
S.O.E. and other newly formed intelligence services' (perhaps a reference
to OSS, which had also set up a station in Algiers). 'We trust they will stick
to old friends who are, as always, ready to help them in every direction.'
So anxious was Menzies to keep the French out of SOE's clutches that in
January 1943 he asked for Rivet to be given an oral, personal message informing him that since 'our previous association' (before the fall of France)
'sabotage' had been 'divorced from me'. A senior officer of SOE was to visit
North Africa shortly 'and I would like you to know that they have nothing
repeat nothing to do with S.R. [intelligence]. I forbid the use of my agents
or organisation for this purpose as disaster would inevitably follow.'

Ronin, who asserted that the Deuxième Bureau still had 'considerable
possibilities' in France and the Low Countries, suggested that they might
establish a liaison station in London and, following Winterbotham's visit
to Algiers, Ronin and Paul Paillole came to London for ten days over
Christmas 1942. Here they met most of the SIS high command. Paillole
recalled Dansey as being 'rather strange' ('un curieux personnage'), but
added that Menzies, who spoke with an air of authority, treated Dansey
with respect. The two Frenchmen also met de Gaulle's intelligence chief,
André Dewavrin, amicably enough it seems, and had some preliminary
discussion about co-ordinating activities.[15] Menzies's 'ultimate hope' was
'to get one combined bureau amalgamated with [the] fighting French'.
He recognised, however, that 'this will not be easily attained', and indeed co-operation between the various French organisations remained

highly conjectural for some time. In the meantime SIS had to work with Dewavrin's BCRA (Bureau Central de Renseignements et d'Action) and Rivet's set-up largely as separate entities. The assassination of Admiral Darlan by a maverick anti-Nazi French royalist on Christmas Eve 1942 simplified the political situation and during 1943 de Gaulle gradually gained the upper hand. Giraud faded from the picture, and by the winter of 1943 Rivet's organisation had been merged into the Free French BCRA.

Italy

All through 1942 coverage of Italy proved a very hard nut to crack. An Italian Jew recruited in Tunisia by André Mounier was given wireless training in Malta and landed on the west coast of Sicily by submarine. When he began transmitting, 'we discovered by the check question method [by which the operator could use a prearranged answer to show he was under duress] that he had come under enemy control'. Rather than break off contact, Dudley Clarke used him as part of his brilliantly successful deception operation before Operation Torch, sending the agent 'questions and warnings' which implied that Sicily was to be the target rather than North Africa. A second operation involved the landing by submarine of two Italian ex-prisoners-of-war on the coast near Livorno in Tuscany. They had claimed to have anti-Fascist friends and that they would be able to pose as soldiers on leave, for which they were provided with false documents. But, as their case-officer recalled, 'they were a very happy go lucky pair and we never heard of them again', rather confirming Cuthbert Bowlby's prediction in January 1941 that recruiting agents from among captured Italian servicemen might 'merely be treated as a beneficial repatriation scheme'.[16]

By the spring of 1943, when it was clear that the defeat of Axis forces in North Africa was only a matter of time (the capitulation came on 13 May), pressure to get agents into Italy stepped up sharply. On 18 April London instructed Algiers that 'considering the grave importance of southern Italy, you must take that as your first target'. But Algiers replied ten days later that the prospects were not very promising. 'All our experience so far', they signalled, 'emphasises difficulty in finding

suitable Italians willing to enter Italy or islands.' They had consulted the
Deuxième Bureau 'who admit their prospects almost zero'. Sicily and the
southern mainland would now be under intensive security, which would
make it especially hazardous for operations. 'Trained Italian agents have
always been and are likely to continue to be so scarce that their quick loss
in hot areas would appear uneconomic.' The Auburn network in Corsica,
which had been asked to attempt the penetration of Sardinia, was 'now
virtually wiped out'. But there was one hopeful note. Algiers viewed recruiting prospects in Tunis 'with relative optimism', as after its capture
'truly patriotic Italians may take more stock in our victory. A few such
should be worth many traitors or cranks.'

Early in May Menzies sent out his newly appointed Assistant Chief, Sir
James Marshall-Cornwall, to review the situation on the spot. Perhaps
the most important recommendation which Marshall-Cornwall made
was the posting of an extremely able young officer, John Bruce Lockhart,
to help out in Tunis. A St Andrews-educated schoolmaster in peacetime,
a nephew of Robert Bruce Lockhart who had served in Russia during the
Revolution and a keen player of real (court) tennis, John Bruce Lockhart
had been recruited to SIS only in January 1942. Before becoming involved with counter-intelligence and double-agent operations in the
Middle East, he had spent some time in Cairo working on German order
of battle and (as he recalled years later) 'six glorious weeks' with 'a Buick,
a bag of gold and a heart full of hope' in the Caucasus organising stay-
behind teams in case the Germans penetrated through the mountains.

In June 1943, reflecting the shifting geography of the war, Menzies
moved Bowlby and the regional SIS headquarters from Cairo to Algiers,
where he was instructed to 'ensure all liaison with British and Allied
Staffs'. This, as is so often the case, was easier said than done. The French,
having established their seat of government in Algiers, resented having to
refer operational requirements back to London. The Americans were inclined to act entirely off their own bat, and in early July Bowlby worried
that, without proper liaison with SIS, OSS would 'undoubtedly turn to
S.O.E.' for assistance in running their own agents. He reported that the
intelligence authorities at the Allied headquarters in Algiers were 'most
anxious' for closer co-operation between OSS, SOE and 'other interested
parties', such as Dudley Clarke's A Force deception team, counter-intelligence and SIS. 'My experience of working with the Americans in

Mideast', added Bowlby, 'is that one must at any rate give the appearance of co-operating with them completely . . . To hold back in any manner is a game at which they are likely to be more adept than we, and I feel we should lose by it.' While this observation has an air of cynical calculation, Bowlby also stressed the overall importance of co-operation. 'I should like to be certain', he signalled, 'it is clearly understood in H.O. [Head Office] that all operational and intelligence activities in North Africa are carried out on a complete fifty–fifty basis. It is most unfortunate that an organisation such as ours should, by unwillingness to co-operate, fail to fall in with this general spirit so carefully fostered by the Commanders in Chief in North Africa.' In July, Menzies, having spoken in London to Colonel Donovan of OSS, emphasised the 'necessity for harmonious collaboration with Americans and of pooling our resources, training and transport', and instructed Bowlby to set up a co-ordinating committee (with French representation) to deal with the problem.

The maintenance of good Allied co-operation was undoubtedly intended to reinforce SIS's enhanced reputation, which was itself underpinned by the high quality of operational intelligence the Service had been able to supply from Tunisia. Although an SIS group (with the cover name of 'No. 1 Intelligence Unit') was attached to Alexander's 15th Army Group, events moved too quickly following the invasion of Sicily on 9–10 July 1943 for it to replicate SIS's performance in North Africa, even had it been able to draw on any existing networks of agents. Enemy resistance ceased in Sicily on 17 August, and already by the end of July John Teague in Cairo was proposing that SIS should aim to be 'ahead of operations. We should', he said, 'look over Italy to Austria.' As soon as a station was established on the Italian mainland, it should make the penetration of Austria and south Germany 'one of its primary duties'.

On 23 August Menzies raised the role of SIS with Alexander. The 'original intention' was that it 'might be useful for providing tactical information by sending Agents through the line', but this had not happened and Menzies's opinion now was 'that proper S.I.S. function is the provision of Intelligence on a long term basis provided by agents working on the enemy's lines of communications'. Alexander agreed. 'Up to present in Sicily', he cabled on 29 August, 'S.I.S. unit has not been able to provide any reports of tactical importance and in my opinion it is not likely that they will be able to do so in future except in the case of prolonged static

conditions.' He recommended, therefore, that SIS units be 'retained under centralised control for work of strategical interest'.

After Allied forces had landed on the Italian mainland at Reggio
and Salerno, and Marshal Badoglio's government (which had ousted
Mussolini in July) capitulated on 8 September 1943, hopes were high
that the Germans might withdraw, at least to the north of the country.
But the German commander, Field Marshal Kesselring, resolved to resist,
and the Italian campaign became a costly slogging match as the Allied
armies inched their way up the peninsula from late 1943 and through
the following year. During this campaign SIS, in addition to developing
its own organisation in Italy, ran a second set-up in conjunction with
the Italian secret service, SIM (Servizio Informazione Militare), now
working for the Allied cause. One early, and perhaps disturbing, result of
this was the news from SIM officers in October that their cryptographic
section had previously broken the 'diplomatic cyphers' of United States
military attachés, the 'Russian confidential cypher', and those of Turkey,
Yugoslavia, Greece, Portugal, Egypt, Brazil and Belgium. The results had
been 'passed to Germans and Hungarians' who could 'now presumably
decypher all above cyphers'.

In October 1943 Bruce Lockhart was posted to take charge of No. 1
Intelligence Unit, by this time based at Bari on the southern Adriatic
coast of Italy. He found the unit in bad shape. Agent recruitment, training and security were all very lax, and he reported (in a letter which
Bowlby described as 'helpful and honest . . . a rare combination in this
racket!') that it was 'common gossip among the rougher element in the
town that I.S.L.D. is the easiest way of making soft money (what A.C.F.
[the African Coastal Flotilla which provided sea operations support] refer
to as "our repatriation scheme")'. Bruce Lockhart rapidly began to sort
out the unit and build it up into a very efficient operation, assisted by 'five
or six SIS pre-war secretaries . . . who were absolutely first-class'. He was
notably good at managing the personnel under his command, and keenly
aware that sustained hard work had to be balanced with moments of rec-
reation, as illustrated by one response to a request for equipment. 'Hope
to have a rugger ball for you shortly,' signalled London, 'and some tennis
balls. Please remember these are not easily come by. We do our best.'[17]

Under Bruce Lockhart's command Bari became the base for SIS operations, first into German-occupied northern Italy, and then also into the

Balkans and Central Europe. From late 1943 various schemes were mooted for the penetration of 'southern Germany', effectively, in fact, Austria, which had been integrated into the Reich since 1938. One involved the recruitment of Austrian and Italian prisoners-of-war in North Africa and their repatriation by means of an existing escape route through Spanish Morocco, Spain and France. Another suggested recruiting agents among partisans in northern Croatia and smuggling them into Lower Styria. Two-man agent/wireless-operator teams would be dropped in blind to establish 'advanced bases' (one was proposed to be in 'the Brenner Pass area'; another on the Slovene–Austrian border) to which agents would report. Nothing came of this ambitious scheme, and in February 1944 Bruce Lockhart, while conceding that his section ('44200') dedicated to penetrating Germany was under-performing, noted the real difficulties with which it was faced. There was a shortage of air support; blind-dropping agents was 'useless'; some of the proposed agents were unsuitable. One, indeed, could 'not possibly pass as Italian due to Prussian accent'. Bruce Lockhart thought that better results might be obtained by infiltrating foreign labourers and specialists. One of his colleagues complained about the poor quality of the Austrians he had been given. 'The supply of even half-way suitable types is strictly limited,' he observed, and, even if he sent some off, he doubted if he would 'ever hear from them again'. 'Leaving aside all wishful thinking', and drawing a striking parallel, he argued that SIS was 'in much the same position, even at this stage of the war, as the 12-land [German] service when they are looking for 22-landers [Britons] to work for them in 22-land'. SIS of course got 'plenty of rats that leave the sinking ship, and we shall get more, but precious few are prepared to go back to gnaw another hole in her bottom'. Not much was achieved until the spring of 1944 when two largely self-contained sections were set up. The first, for the penetration of northern Italy, was under Major Brian Ashford-Russell and the second, for Yugoslavia and Central Europe, under Major James Millar.

The Balkans

During the second half of the war SIS in several places dealt directly (and productively) with Communists. Across the Balkans both SIS and SOE found themselves working against Axis forces with Communist resistance and partisan groups. But the Western Allies were also supporting and mobilising centrist and right-wing elements in occupied Europe, and as victory began to seem increasingly likely, tensions also began to emerge between domestic political groups, looking to winning not only the war but also the peace that would follow. Furthermore, as Soviet armies began to roll back the Germans and move towards Eastern Europe, concerns were raised, both in London and by the men on the spot, as to the political consequences of this advance, in both the short and the long term.

Greece was a case in point, where resistance coalesced into two main groups: the rightist National Democratic Hellenic League, EDES, broadly aligned with the Greek government-in-exile, and the Communist-backed National Liberation Front, EAM, with its military wing, ELAS, the National Popular Liberation Army. British engagement with these groupings, at least in 1942–3, depended less on any perceived political leanings than on their efficiency in fighting the enemy. Responding in August 1942 to Greek complaints about the 'British Secret Services' (which included both SIS and SOE) consorting with elements 'hostile to the King and the Government', for example, SIS recognised that it was 'only natural' that SOE's 'operations are connected with subversive elements'. If 'they are using Communists, which we have every reason to believe is correct, they have chosen these men because they are more active against the Axis than the other elements in the country'. At this stage SIS's main Greek operation was based in Smyrna, where Lieutenant Commander Rees was running boats into Greece, supporting escape lines, but not producing much intelligence from the Greek mainland. All through 1942 there were concerns about the lack of information. Menzies (as always) was being pressed for military intelligence by the service departments, while the Foreign Office wanted better reporting on the admittedly complicated and confused political situation. In Cairo an office was established with the main function of penetrating Greece, not only from North Africa but also through Smyrna. Matters improved in 1943 when (among others) a network of agents run by Rees – called 'S' sources – began to report. 'S.41' was recruited in September 1942 and sent military and naval information from Salonika, much of it based on train-watching. Another agent, 'S.30', who had previously worked for the Italians against the Turks, was regarded as 'a most valuable source' who in

1943 alone, up to his arrest in July, had supplied thirty-nine reports on the Dodecanese, including air, army and naval information which had received 'very favourable criticism' from the service ministries.

In 1943 some SIS officers were dropped into Epirus in north-western Greece, primarily to report on German order of battle in Greece. One of these was Nigel Clive, who had been recruited by the Service in December 1941 and had served as assistant to the Baghdad representative, before engineering a move to Cairo in a successful effort to get a more active job. Equipped with a money belt containing a hundred gold sovereigns and under the pseudonym 'Jim Russell', he parachuted into Greece in December 1943 along with a wireless operator and a regular Greek army officer to help with liaison. Clive's duties were not particularly covert. Formally attached to SOE's Allied Military Mission at EDES headquarters, he served in British battledress and lived openly among the partisans in the Greek mountains. As Clive claimed afterwards, one unusual circumstance of his posting was that his SIS predecessor, an alleged Greek-American called Costa Lawrence, had been shot dead by an SOE officer, an Irishman named Spike Moran. Although Clive was well aware of the intermittent tensions between SIS and SOE, this seemed to take things too far, and it emerged that Moran had believed Lawrence was a traitor and thought that he was about to be betrayed to the Germans. Moran himself and his SOE colleagues were actually very helpful to Clive, who was able to collect a great deal of information about the German forces, finding Greek interpreters working for the enemy to be especially willing to assist. Clive remained in Epirus until the German withdrawal from Greece in the autumn of 1944, and from April 1944 he began also to report on the political competition between the rival Greek resistance groups, in effect predicting the civil war which erupted at the end of the year.[18]

Turkey, meanwhile, remained a lively centre of intelligence activities during the second half of the war. The enemy scored a notable success with the famous spy 'Cicero', Elyesa Bazna, Albanian valet to the British ambassador in Ankara, Sir Hughe Knatchbull-Hugessen, whose sloppy attitude to security enabled Bazna in 1943 systematically to photograph highly classified documents and sell them to the Germans. SIS were involved in the investigation after the leakage of secret information from the Ankara embassy was revealed both by signals intelligence and by an

OSS agent in the German Foreign Ministry, but the full story did not emerge until after the war.[19] At the same time as the Cicero crisis, SIS struck an outstanding blow against the Abwehr by recruiting and organising the defection of Dr Erich Vermehren and his wife Elisabeth. Vermehren, an anti-Nazi Roman Catholic who had won a Rhodes Scholarship to Oxford just before the war (but had been prevented from taking it up on account of his refusal to join the Nazi youth organisation at school), had been assistant to Paul Leverkühn, the senior Abwehr officer in Turkey, since October 1942. His wife was a cousin of Franz von Papen, the German ambassador in Ankara, and had family connections with Adam von Trott zu Solz, a leader of the July 1944 plot to assassinate Hitler.

The Vermehrens' case officer was Nicholas Elliott, who had been Section V representative in Istanbul since the spring of 1942. An assessment after the war recorded that Elliott handled the Vermehrens with 'consummate skill and sympathy, but with just the necessary touch of firmness'. Vermehren had got in touch with the British assistant military attaché in Istanbul, who passed him on to Elliott. The first contact was made on 18 January 1944 and on 21 January Elliott told Felix Cowgill in London that he had recruited Vermehren, whom he described as a 'highly strung, cultivated, self-confident, extremely clever, logical-minded, slightly precious young German of good family'. Vermehren, he said, was willing to work for SIS as he was 'intensely anti-Nazi on religious grounds', and also because his wife and her family had been persecuted by the Nazis. Vermehren had produced 'a quantity of detailed information' about the Abwehr organisation in Turkey, which had 'fully convinced' the SIS station of his bona fides. Over a four-day period in late January, Vermehren managed to bring out important Abwehr files for SIS to photograph, including an organogram of the complete Abwehr set-up in Istanbul, and he was able to give SIS details of current Abwehr operations in Turkey and the Middle East.

On 25 January Elliott was tipped off by a contact in the Turkish secret police that they knew Vermehren had been in touch with the British. Reasoning that it would not be long, therefore, before the Germans got wind of this, with Turkish assistance he arranged for the Vermehrens and two other anti-Nazi Abwehr officers to be smuggled out to Cairo through the SIS station at Smyrna. Because of Vermehren's supreme access, his defection completely compromised and demoralised Axis espionage throughout the region. Leverkühn, who was reported to be in 'a hell of a flap' over Vermehren's flight, was recalled in disgrace to Berlin. Apart from its impact on German operations in the Near and Middle East, the Vermehren defection had a very significant impact on the struggle for intelligence supremacy in Germany between the Abwehr and Himmler's Sicherheitsdienst, which ended with the latter absorbing the former. It was also one of the factors leading to Canaris's downfall. As Michael Howard has concluded, the entire German intelligence service 'was thrown into a state of confusion just at the moment, in the early summer of 1944, when its efficient functioning was vital to the survival of the Third Reich'.[20]

In Bucharest the productive head agent, Nannygoat, continued to provide a variety of intelligence. In the summer of 1942 he was asked to confirm the identification of five Italian divisions deployed in Romania. The following year he supplied a 'news reel film purporting to show fortifications on French coast' and reported that a sub-agent claimed to 'know German engineers willing [to] desert bringing new bomber range 3,000 kilometres'. 'Shall I make further enquiries,' he asked in July 1943. 'This is probably the Heinkel 177,' replied London: 'ZA [Air Ministry] very interested. Please go ahead.'[21] Nannygoat's contact seems not to have delivered the wavering German engineers, but the exchanges between Head Office and Istanbul demonstrate the range of information which any one agent might provide.

Nannygoat's network also illustrates the polyglot nature of wartime intelligence-gathering. He himself had originally been a French agent, and his own organisation included several different nationalities. This, of course, could bring risks. In November 1943 he acquired some Polish wireless operators, three of whom were arrested the following February 'due to discovery in Warsaw of Polish organisation working to Bucharest'. By the spring of 1944 Nannygoat (no left-winger he) was wiring 'for instructions as to what course to pursue in the event of Russians arriving in Bucharest before British'. 'In principle,' replied London, 'we would like as many agents as possible to remain undisclosed to Russians but feel that those who are likely to be arrested should be protected by us.' In June 1944, however, 'after denouncement by two Frenchmen', Nannygoat was put under house arrest by the Romanian authorities, who suspected him of working for the British. But in the confused Romanian politics of the moment, with the Germans in retreat and the Russians on their doorstep, 'working for the British' could be an advantage. As reported afterwards, Nannygoat secured an interview with Colonel Traian Borcescu, head of Romanian counter-intelligence. He admitted that he 'was head of a British Intelligence Service in 14-land [Romania] and warned him that if he and his collaborators were not released Borcescu and his colleagues would have to suffer for it'. This 'produced an electric effect'. Nannygoat and some of his agents were released and put on a plane for Istanbul on condition that he would if possible try to secure British help for Romania.

15

From Switzerland to Normandy

SIS's enhanced performance in the Mediterranean and North Africa, which had become apparent by the end of 1942, was reflected elsewhere, as increasing numbers of networks were established, techniques were refined, liaison with Allies was improved and, despite the continuing (and in some cases intensifying) oppression of enemy occupation forces, growing numbers of individuals were bravely prepared to offer assistance in all sorts of ways to intelligence, escape and resistance organisations across Europe.

Switzerland

For most of the Second World War the main SIS representative in Switzerland was Frederick 'Fanny' Vanden Heuvel, based in Geneva. He and his staff established contacts with Swiss intelligence, mainly in order to get their co-operation in escape and evasion. The Swiss assisted by putting escapees quietly over the frontiers into France at appropriate spots and times. In the spring of 1943 Dansey produced a report on SIS activities in Switzerland which showed that the Service had agents operating in or into France, Germany, Italy, Yugoslavia, Belgium and the Netherlands, and contacts providing periodic reports from Turkey and Norway. The main effort was on Germany and France. In Germany there appear to have been agents in eight main industrial and communication centres, including four in Berlin. In Switzerland itself, the train-reporting service continued, while economic reporting, primarily for the local Ministry of Economic Warfare representative, had become a major commitment.

The files indicate good military intelligence on Italy too. A report of May 1943 from Geneva, marked up by Menzies as 'v. important', recorded that 'Z.101' had identified twenty-four special trains loaded with torpedoes and sea mines and that 120 German naval personnel had passed Brenner destined for Venice. Between 9 and 12 May, Z.101 noted approximately 25,000 German troops in trains to north Italy, en route to Verona, Piacenza and Bologna. Following the collapse of Italy, thousands of British prisoners-of-war were liberated, and many crossed into Switzerland where they were interned. Many of them, however, especially air crew, were badly needed in the United Kingdom. SIS, in conjunction with SOE, organised the clandestine escape through France of a number of these, it is said at the rate of some six every three weeks. On 26 October 1943 Menzies sent a personal message to Vanden Heuvel offering his 'thanks and congratulations' for the work of SIS staff in Switzerland. 'After four years isolation and heavy work,' he wrote, 'I realise that all must feel the strain but the results should be a consolation and satisfaction to you.'

By this time SIS in Switzerland was receiving a detailed picture of internal German conditions and the effects of heavy Allied bombing. A source in Berlin reported that '90 per cent population still spend every night in cellars.' The people were generally 'apathetic' and there was 'no evidence [of] riots or demonstrations but could not visit working class quarters. Little hate against the British despite intensive propaganda, but people hope reprisals will be sufficiently effective to stop air raids.' There was great faith in the possibilities of an unspecified secret weapon, which was 'relied upon to work miracles but if it fails or proves non existent reaction will be serious and probably revolutionary'. The Air Ministry in London lauded these reports, affirming that they were 'of considerable value and largely accurate', since they added details to the more general evidence from signals intelligence 'and provided an assessment that the RAF was unable to obtain from aerial reconnaissance when the weather was bad'. Another source visited Berlin from August to November 1943 and reported that there were no signs of internal demoralisation and that public services were functioning satisfactorily. Among workers and soldiers, he noted, Hitler was still considered a 'demigod'. Heavy bombing, while materially devastating, seemed to have had the effect of stiffening resistance and determination for revenge.

Reflecting the continuing value of the close Anglo-Polish intelligence relationship, a precious supply of information from high German military circles came to SIS from an impressive Polish intelligence network code-named 'Darek', run by Major Szczęsny Choynacki, with cover as the Polish deputy consul in Berne. After the Germans (who knew the net-work as 'Jerzy') began in the early summer of 1943 to read Choynacki's radio traffic and break up his organisation, they concluded that at least one of his agents had well-informed access to Hitler's headquarters. This was probably 'JX/Knopf', one of the ninety-three Darek sub-sources re-corded by SIS. Evidence survives that Knopf reported between February 1942 and April 1943. He mainly supplied intelligence on the Russian campaign, but also considered a few other matters, such as the possibil-ity of an Italo-German offensive aimed at the seizure of Suez, and troop dispositions in Tripolitania. A surviving Knopf report, dated 12 February 1943, and described as 'from "contacts in the O.K.W." [German high command]', discussed the 'state of mind' at the headquarters following the defeat of the German Sixth Army at Stalingrad. 'Despite their prodi-gious efforts, their heavy casualties, illness and, in some sectors, the loss of the greater part of their equipment', German army morale was 'far from broken; indeed it is very good. For this reason all rumours of an imminent break-down of the German military front in the East are quite untrue.' MI14 (the German order-of-battle branch of British Military Intelligence) regarded Knopf as having 'very good contacts', and when 'reporting from his usual sources, he is more often sound than not'. The information, however, could not 'be accepted without some confirma-tion, but when it is clear and factual and is in line with our own views [a necessarily double-edged judgment this] or with information from other sources, a high degree of confidence can be placed in it'.[1]

One of the most interesting relationships was that between Vanden Heuvel and Allen Dulles, the OSS representative in Switzerland, who ar-rived in early November 1942 (and who later served as Director of the CIA from 1953 to 1961). Although they would ultimately share intelli-gence, from the beginning controversy surrounded Dulles. In January 1943 Broadway warned Vanden Heuvel about him, suggesting that he was likely to 'lend himself easily to any striking proposal which looks like notoriety'. Although the SIS head of station and Dulles had mutual friends in the United States and were personally on friendly terms, Vanden Heuvel himself concluded that Dulles was 'out for himself and clashes of interest are bound to come'. Competition for agents seemed

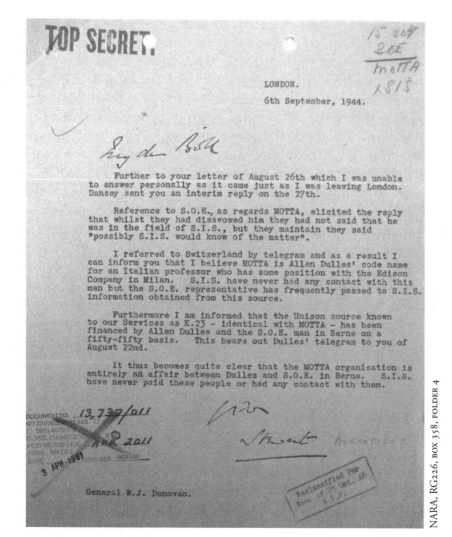

TOP SECRET.

15 304
20E
MOTTA
X SIS

LONDON.

6th September, 1944.

My dear Bill

Further to your letter of August 26th which I was unable to answer personally as it came just as I was leaving London. Dansey sent you an interim reply on the 27th.

Reference to S.O.E., as regards MOTTA, elicited the reply that whilst they had disavowed him they had not said that he was in the field of S.I.S., but they maintain they said "possibly S.I.S. would know of the matter".

I referred to Switzerland by telegram and as a result I can inform you that I believe MOTTA is Allen Dulles' code name for an Italian professor who has some position with the Edison Company in Milan. S.I.S. have never had any contact with this man but the S.O.E. representative has frequently passed to S.I.S. information obtained from this source.

Furthermore I am informed that the Unison source known to our Services as K.23 – identical with MOTTA – has been financed by Allen Dulles and the S.O.E. man in Berne on a fifty-fifty basis. This bears out Dulles' telegram to you of August 22nd.

It thus becomes quite clear that the MOTTA organisation is entirely an affair between Dulles and S.O.E. in Berne. S.I.S. have never paid these people or had any contact with them.

DOCUMENT NO. 13,737/011

Stewart menzies

General W.J. Donovan.

The closeness of the wartime Anglo-American intelligence relationship is confirmed by the friendly tone of this letter from 'Stewart' (Menzies) to 'My dear Bill' (Donovan).

especially acute. In typically acerbic fashion Dansey observed that the dollar was an 'unfailing magnet' and that Americans 'everywhere swallow easily and are not critical'. He therefore thought it essential for SIS to work as closely as possible with Dulles (and the French, Poles and Swiss), otherwise the 'only people who will profit by this madness will be the Germans and agents who get paid by three and even more masters'.

The potential for disaster was demonstrated by Dulles's first contact with the Abwehr representative, Hans Bernd Gisevius, in January 1943, which he reported back to Washington on a cypher which the British ascertained (through their Polish agent Halina Szymańska) had been broken by the Germans. In the middle of April Dulles told Vanden Heuvel that he had seen Gisevius, who had just returned from Berlin and had told him that forty large flying boats had recently been built in Rotterdam to be used for the heavy bombing of London manned by suicide squads. Despite having been alerted to the problem with the cypher, Dulles had reported this to Washington in two telegrams. Dansey thought that Dulles had been 'stuffed' by a deliberate piece of German disinformation. Clearly agitated, he told Vanden Heuvel: 'could you report to the fool [Dulles] who knows his code was compromised if he has used that code to report meetings with anyone, Germans probably identified persons concerned and use them for stuffing. He swallows easily.'

Vanden Heuvel, nevertheless, was keen to exploit Dulles's contact with Gisevius, who in July 1943 (responding to questions supplied by SIS) told Dulles about rocket projectile tests at 'Peenemuende or Swinemuende', for which his source was an Abwehr colleague. Gisevius expressed great concern lest Dulles's communications were unsafe, since discovery would certainly lead to identification of the original source, and he suggested to Dulles that he should pass the information 'through British channels for extra safety' (which he did). The information stated that damage caused by air raids at Friedrichshafen included works producing the steering mechanism for rockets, which could lead to up to three months' delay in them being put into operation. The main production of rocket bombs was taking place at Frankenthal. The source believed that no other important factories were there other than some sugar refineries and for this reason the source urged that the information must be used with the greatest discretion. The course also stated that Hitler was taking a close personal interest in the production of the projectile.

In September 1943 Szymańska reported that Gisevius, who was 'highly nervous', had (for the first time) told her about the 'V' (for 'Vengeance') weapons being developed. He said he was giving all the details he could

'as [a] Good German', because he firmly believed the new weapon was serious and would certainly lengthen the war even if it could not affect the
eventual result. Although London remained desperate to glean more information on V-weapons, particularly over rocket sites, scales of production and the date for which firing was planned, Gisevius proved unable
to help further. According to Szymańska, by February 1944 Gisevius had
become persona non grata among his German colleagues and friends.
Dansey told Vanden Heuvel that he feared Gisevius's usefulness was 'now
quite impaired. 189 [Dulles] has compromised him beyond redemption.'
Dansey was further alarmed since Dulles was 'flooding' Washington
with Gisevius information, representing it as being from 'an important
source'. When Szymańska saw Gisevius again in February 1944 his position (and that of Canaris) had worsened considerably, particularly after
the defection of the Vermehrens in Turkey the previous month. A year
later Gisevius told Szymańska that he had been deeply involved in the
July 1944 plot to assassinate Hitler and that after its failure he had managed to evade arrest by lying low in Berlin for three months.[2]

Scandinavia

Cyril Cheshire, head of the Stockholm station from December 1942
until the middle of 1945, expanded and developed the work started by
his predecessor, John Martin. Reviewing the station's output in October
1944, Bill Cordeaux at Head Office noted that Cheshire had worked up
the number of reports from fewer than four hundred a month 'to an average of about 700 per month, the majority of the increase being Armed
Forces information'. Much of this resulted from the exploitation of
Dutch, Danish, Norwegian and Baltic contacts, among businessmen and
others who were able to travel between Sweden and German-occupied
Europe. One especially valuable Danish agent, a businessman recruited
in December 1942 and code-named 'Elgar', was a frequent visitor to
Stockholm where his company had an office. Other business connections
took him to Germany, Finland and Romania, and he acquired information from fellow countrymen working for German heavy industrial
companies manufacturing war matériel. During 1943 he recruited some
twenty sub-sources, including a diplomat in Hamburg; technical workers

in Peenemünde on Usedom island in the Baltic, where the Germans had a weapons-testing site; an employee in the Berlin office of Donau Flugzeugbau, which manufactured Messerschmitt aircraft in Hungary; and a man in the Danish lighthouse service, able to debrief lighthouse-keepers for shipping information.

Conveying material to Cheshire in Sweden required some ingenuity. In the autumn of 1943, for example, Elgar brought three hundred reports on film concealed in glass bottles hidden in one of three barrels of acid imported for business purposes. In November Cordeaux noted that he was 'among the first' to report on the V-1 (described at the time as a 'rocket gun') and that he had supplied a photograph of a rocket which had landed on the Danish island of Bornholm in the south-western Baltic Sea. He had 'provided valuable night fighter information, Finnish chemical warfare equipment and valuable reports from his sub-agents and his own journeys in Germany, Finland and Roumania'. One of his sources had provided 'ground photographs of air raid damage in Hamburg'. But it was too good to last. Elgar was arrested by the Germans in January 1944 and his network disintegrated. Although roughly treated in captivity, he was transferred to a sealed camp in Sweden in April 1945, and was suspected by some of having been an enemy agent. The evidence from surviving accounts of German interrogations of him does not support this in any convincing way, and SIS afterwards decided that he had provided information to his captors simply 'in order to save his skin'. While he gave the Germans accurate descriptions of SIS staff in Stockholm and of Danish contacts in Sweden and the United Kingdom, he also gave invented information with sufficient plausibility at least to worry the Germans, if not to convince them, claiming, for example, that SIS had 'succeeded in establishing important groups in Berlin, Hamburg, Bonn, Königsberg and Vienna' and that English-trained sabotage teams had been deployed in the Danish islands of Zealand, Funen and Falster.

Like all the other neutral capitals in Continental Europe, Stockholm was full of dubious characters offering information to whomever would pay. One such was agent '36439', a Russian émigré who had been a Z Organisation source before the war. In late 1943 this agent claimed to have a penetration source in the Japanese legation, agent 'Eve', recruited in June 1943, who provided copies of Japanese despatches and re-enciphering codes; and an economist in Berlin, who, apart from reporting in his own right, retailed gossipy information from an old contact who was a housekeeper in the household of Reichsmarschall Hermann Göring, the head of the German Air Force.

From April 1943 a trained Section V representative, Peter Falk, was posted to Stockholm under Passport Control cover to run a separate Sweden station devoted to attacking the German intelligence service, not only in Sweden but across Scandinavia and elsewhere. Falk's chief target was Dr Karl-Heinz Krämer, the German assistant air attaché in Stockholm since November 1942. Krämer was a flamboyant character who, as one of SIS's contacts in the Swedish police complained, 'always travels in a fast sports car and was therefore very difficult to follow'. He was, in fact, an officer of the Abwehr's Air Intelligence Section (Luft I) and had been posted to Sweden to develop intelligence operations against Britain and the USA. SIS's interest comprised the need not just to identify and (if possible) neutralise him as an Abwehr officer, but also to assist MI5 in closing down any potential intelligence operation in Britain itself. Late in 1943 signals originating with Krämer and containing intelligence from and about the United Kingdom were acquired by OSS in Switzerland. Further messages purporting to come from Abwehr agents in Britain (including one code-named 'Josephine'), which contained a mixture of plausible speculation and some apparently factual statements, subsequently appeared among British signals intelligence. While MI5 eventually concluded that the alleged Krämer network was fictitious, suspicions remained that he was getting information from Swedish diplomatic sources in Britain. SIS in Stockholm meanwhile mounted a successful operation against him.[3]

In early December 1943 luck took a turn with a walk-in. A 'strongly anti-Nazi' Austrian woman, separated from her Swedish husband, came to the British legation and asked to speak to 'someone who spoke German'. Fielded by an SIS officer, she 'did not disclose the nature of her business until she had been safely conducted . . . out of the reach of S.O.E., YN [the naval attaché], etc.'. The woman then declared that her best friend, also Austrian, worked as a maid for Krämer and had chanced upon some important-looking documents which she had copied. These appeared to be drafts of telegrams about air intelligence from Britain and included a 'request to Josefine [sic] for information'. This first contact duly led to a meeting with the friend and to the recruitment of both women. Throughout 1944 the maid supplied more message texts and other papers from Krämer's desk, waste-paper basket and coat pockets. Moreover, after coolly borrowing and copying the key to his desk drawer which he always kept locked (by taking its impression in a dish of butter), she was able to abstract and copy by hand no fewer than eight current and old passports, which showed his travel movements since 1938. These included a short visit to England in the month before the outbreak of war, which naturally sounded alarm bells in London.

After the end of the war, when SIS were able to interrogate Krämer himself, and assemble reports from both German and Swedish sources, it appeared that the energetic and creative Krämer had been misleading both the British and his own Abwehr superiors. His reports from 'very reliable sources' were mostly reworked second-hand material acquired from intelligence-peddlers in Sweden and elsewhere, though amid this was information derived from genuine Swedish service attaché reports originating in London. Although MI5 had effectively rumbled Krämer before the end of 1943, there were residual worries about him up to the early summer of 1944, especially in the tense few weeks before Operation 'Overlord' (the invasion of France by Allied forces), when it was feared that even the slightest security lapse could jeopardise the invasion. Learning in May 1944 that Krämer had been 'laying aside considerable savings every month', and was suspected of pocketing 'quite large sums from the expenses allowed for paying agents', Peter Falk thought that the German might be susceptible to being 'bought' by SIS, especially since he had briefly been involved in running a concentration camp and believed that he was on the Allies' list of war criminals. But Broadway vetoed the proposal. 'We cannot do business with war criminals to save their necks,' wrote a Section V officer. 'There is surely nothing very important that this peculiarly unpleasant rat could give us if he was allowed to leave the sinking ship,' added Cuthbert Bowlby on 11 June, 'and the "leakage" is now so much less dangerous than before "Overlord" started.'

During the second half of the war, the Helsinki station-in-exile under Harry Carr continued to operate from Stockholm. In December 1942 Menzies congratulated Carr for 'considerable progress in work of your station during last six months'. This was 'particularly commendable bearing in mind handicap of working from outside your own country'. Carr's product had been boosted by the re-emergence in May 1942 of his pre-war agent Outcast, who was now working for the Abwehr. Outcast was briefed to report specifically on the results of RAF raids on Berlin and other German cities. His early reports, sent by secret writing to a cover address in Sweden, were not very useful but his stock in London rose dramatically after some detailed and accurate reporting on the results of the Battle of Berlin, the RAF's heavy bombing campaign launched against the German capital from November 1943, and on which he was debriefed by Carr himself in Stockholm. Carr provided a large-scale plan of Berlin while Outcast 'produced little scraps of paper concealed all over his person with what seemed to be unintelligible scribbles on them in pencil'. The resulting report reached the Air Ministry before they got any clear photographic intelligence and 'some weeks later', recalled Carr, 'we were delighted to see our typewritten report, almost word for word, in the Air Ministry's periodic Intelligence Summary, which had been sent to the Air Attache in Stockholm'.

Following his May 1942 visit to Stockholm, Outcast whetted the appetite of his Abwehr employers with the prospect of securing information on the United Kingdom, and possibly even establishing a source there through his good Swedish connections. This scheme eventually developed into a fully fledged double-agent operation. With the help of T. A. 'Tar' Robertson of MI5, Outcast passed a mixture of genuine and fictitious information ('foodstuff') to the Abwehr, which enhanced his value to them and justified his regular visits to Stockholm. This, in turn, meant that he could be debriefed in person, and it thus improved his reporting. By the end of 1942 he had begun to include information on the power struggle between the Abwehr and the Sicherheitsdienst, a subject of great interest to him as well as to London, since he belonged to a circle of Abwehr officers regarded as close to Admiral Canaris. In early 1943 he was evaluated in Head Office as 'the best source for information on the German interior produced so far in the war'.

Outcast was known to Swedish Military Intelligence as an Abwehr agent and he supplied them with information on the German–Russian aspects of the war. In turn, he reported to Carr the Swedes' views on the progress of the war, which were of considerable interest to London, especially when the tide began to turn against the Germans. Late in 1942 Outcast established contact with the Japanese military attaché in Stockholm, General Makoto Onodera, who recruited him as an agent. By 1944 Outcast was providing Onodera with American deception material supplied through

SIS. Outcast's reports continued to be very well received in London throughout 1943. One in particular, on conditions in Poland and Polish attitudes towards the Russians and the Germans, aroused great interest in the Foreign Office and was shown by Menzies to Churchill. When in late 1943 Outcast, ill with tuberculosis, wanted to move with his family from Berlin to Stockholm, SIS was supportive, and he managed it early in 1944. But the Swedes refused to let him stay and he was evacuated to Britain, where he died the following year. In a postwar SIS evaluation he was described as 'one of the most successful spies against Germany that the 1939–45 war produced'.

Other agents reported from inside Germany, as is illustrated by a telegram from Carr dated 1 October 1943 with a report from a source travelling 'from Belgium to Stockholm who was in train standing in Hanover Hauptbahnhof during raid September 22nd/September 23rd'. The station remained intact 'but railway lines about 150 metres outside station (in direction of Berlin) were smashed and five full trains standing on lines were destroyed or badly damaged by bombs and fire'. The district north of the station 'suffered greatly from bombs and flooding resulting from burst water main pipes. Inhabitants seen escaping from this district wading knee deep in water.' In early 1944 a report from a Finnish source raised a difficult dilemma for Harry Carr where professional duty cut across personal feelings. The agent told him that the Germans had taken a party of Finnish officers on a tour which had included launching sites for V-1 flying bombs in north-west France and had 'boasted to them how London would be obliterated by the pilotless machines'. At the time Carr's mother and sister were living together in a top-floor flat in Norwood, south London, which he realised was right in the line of flight of V-1 bombs heading for central London. Apart from looking after his sister (who was working as an ambulance driver), Carr reckoned his mother 'had no special reason for remaining in the London area', but he could not 'disclose the secret agent's report to them'. In the end he wrote her a letter 'saying that I considered she had stuck to London long enough, and suggested that she should go away for a bit', and stay with relatives in Bournemouth on the south coast. His mother ignored the advice and remained where she was. As Carr had feared, in June 1944 one of the very first 'doodlebugs' aimed at London landed near her flat, blew in the dining-room window and caused quite a lot of damage. Fortunately, however, his mother was in another room at the time and his sister was out.

While in April 1942 Bill Cordeaux had complained that there were only four SIS 'stations' (here meaning networks) in Norway, in June the following year Broadway sent Stockholm a list of twenty-three Norwegian stations whose members and agents might appear in Sweden seeking assistance. They extended from Kirkenes in the far north, through Tromsö (two stations), Trondheim (three), Bergen (two), to Stavanger, Kristiansund in the north-west and Oslo (four). There was no shortage of patriotic volunteers for these stations and the Norwegian section at Head Office (P.9) established a training school in London at 14 Brompton Square. While the 'primary objective' of the Norwegian shore stations was 'the obtaining of sighting reports of major units of the main German battle fleet' (especially the battleship *Tirpitz*), their activities varied significantly according to the personalities of their members and the range of their contacts. Intelligence on German naval movements was collected from direct visual observation as well as from agents recruited locally. This was all backed up with extensive logistical support. Motorised fishing vessels, motor torpedo boats, submarines and aircraft were all used to infiltrate agents. Once ashore each station needed support, for example, in charging accumulators to power their radio sets, as well as couriers to deliver intelligence and warning of German counter-measures, such as arrests, searches and roadblocks. Visual reports on the *Tirpitz*'s movements, along with Ultra decrypts and photographic air intelligence, locating the ship and its defences in Altafjord, northern Norway, contributed to the planning of a daring midget-submarine attack which in September 1943 disabled the warship for three months.[4] For a year from late 1943, the 'Aquarius' station in Stavanger had a useful agent in the police headquarters whose command of German led to his being employed in liaison duties with the German military. Thus he was able not only to supply detailed information about the local German forces but also to influence the course of security investigations.

One of SIS's most successful Norwegian agents was Oluf Reed Olsen, whose report of his second operation, a six-month spell from May 1944 based near the seaport of Kristiansand on the south coast of Norway, gives a flavour of the challenges presented by working in enemy-occupied territory. Olsen and his wireless operator were dropped in by parachute, and the operation (code-named 'Makir') began very well. 'I had an excellent landing', he wrote, 'in the middle of a blueberry bush approx. 10 metres from one of the corners of the light triangle' (set up to mark the landing zone). 'The reception were on the spot and ready with a cup of warm tea.' A few days later, Olsen, who was carrying his wireless set, found himself alone in a railway compartment with a German SS officer, who 'became extremely interested in the bag containing the radio set and kept on staring at it'. Olsen managed to move to the next carriage, but mildly observed in his report that 'it would be a great help if the radio sets could be packed into an ordinary leather bag with a good lock on it'. A camp was set up on a forested hillside near the fjord entrance to Kristiansand from where shipping movements could be monitored. A contact in the harbour police recruited two German sailors who had been planning to desert and who had sought his assistance in escaping to England. They 'were keen to join and fight for the side which they thought right', but the Norwegians persuaded them that they could best serve by staying on and collecting military information. 'This they agreed to do, and all seemed so easy that we were almost wary of a Gestapo trap.' Olsen told them 'that if anything went wrong, they would be given a safe passage to Sweden' but, 'on the other hand, if they double-crossed us, their death warrant could be considered signed'.

Apart from reporting shipping movements and providing daily weather reports, the Makir station had also to report on U-boat activity along the adjacent coast, as well as German order of battle in the area. Olsen, who was careful about security, described the routine as follows:

> The main contacts in the town collected reports from their respective sources and placed them in the post-box: twice a week the post-box in town was emptied by the man who was responsible for sending food to the camp, and the reports which had thus been collected were sent with the food courier twice a week. There were always two on this job as it was necessary for one man to go ahead empty-handed in case of bumping into a control. In this way four men were constantly employed on this part of the work. Every fourteenth day the timing was put forward one day to avoid regular traffic. The couriers met each other at pre-arranged places in the forest and at each meeting the place was changed again for the next time.

The men's tents were 'well camouflaged from the air and ground, which proved itself when the owner of the property, together with 2 berry-pickers, passed not more than four yards from the main tent without discovering the camp'. Silence was the rule; boots were forbidden; 'and gym-shoes were worn whether it was wet or dry'. They also 'had considerable trouble' from one colleague 'being prone to snoring, but the person concerned soon became used to being woken up 10 times a night'. At its peak, too, the station transmitted up to ten messages a day, and had to relocate more than once in order to evade German direction-finding units.[5]

The Low Countries

The Netherlands and Belgium together posed particular problems for British intelligence operations. Both were densely populated small countries, which made it extremely hard to find suitably remote locations for air dropping zones. Furthermore, as they both lay under the Allied bomber route to the German industrial heartland of the Ruhr, anti-aircraft defences were especially concentrated and made it exceptionally difficult for aircraft to grope around at low level trying to distinguish the faint lights of a reception committee. While both were geographically well placed for sea operations from Britain, the enemy in consequence specially built up maritime defences and security measures so that this method soon became prohibitive. The military importance of the two countries to the Axis also meant that a high priority was given to them by the German security services, and although the Sicherheitsdienst and the Abwehr were often at each other's throats, their efforts constituted a very serious threat to SIS, which was compounded by the disasters suffered by SOE in both Belgium and the Netherlands.

By the autumn of 1942 German successes in Belgium had resulted in a situation when, as an official SOE history put it, the agency's 'organisation in the field was no more than a mirage created by the Gestapo'.[6] In March 1942, following a wave of arrests, Claude Dansey began to worry about the SIS organisation in Belgium. He told Frederick Jempson (head of the Belgian Section in Broadway) that 'unless some drastic steps are taken with or without the consent of [Fernand] Lepage [the London-based head of the Belgian Sûreté de l'État] you will soon be without any agents left in Belgium'. Dansey (wisely in the light of SOE's experience) wanted to double-check whether any of SIS's wireless operators had been compromised. Only then might they 'devise some steps to save what is left'. But the news was not all bad. In April 1942 R. V. Jones in the Scientific Section noted that Jempson had produced two valuable reports, one of 17 February giving the position of the first known German Radio Direction Finding (RDF) station for controlling night fighters; and one of 28 March locating the first identified 'decimetre' directional wireless communications station in Belgium. Jones added that, 'as all our attacks on the Ruhr' had to pass through Jempson's territory, 'these constitute an important section of the main German air defence system and the more we know about them, the less our casualties'. Early the following year another agent, assisted by a compatriot employed in forced labour by the Germans building a new radar station at Lantin, near Liège, bribed his way into the building where over several nights he made detailed sketches and notes of all he saw. Supporting SIS's case for a gallantry award after the war, the Air Ministry assessed his achievement as 'making among the most outstanding air intelligence received during the war from clandestine sources'. This had enabled counter-measures to be developed which the ministry said saved 'the lives of hundreds of Allied airmen and many of our night bombers'.[7]

The most successful Belgian network was Service Clarence, which was effectively administered by Hector Demarque after the First World War espionage veteran Walthère Dewé ('Cleveland') had been forced to keep a low profile. Dewé was later shot by the Germans while fleeing from arrest in January 1944. Clarence provided regular technical intelligence, including reports about the removal of uranium salts to Germany, and one agent working in a German headquarters near Breskens just across the Dutch frontier reported on German minefields and the disposition of enemy forces along the Belgian coast. A contact in a Belgian oil company provided not only information on military and other road traffic but also petrol and cars for the network to use. Information on enemy communications and movements, especially on the Belgian railway system, continued to be a priority target and, as in the First World War, Belgian agents produced most impressive results. Service Clarence, for example, continued to provide reports on the RAF bombing of German cities, including Hamburg, Düsseldorf and Cologne; intelligence on batteries at Zeebrugge and Ostend and on the defences at Knocke; and photographs of German anti-aircraft gunners, aerodromes and gun emplacements. The network also produced reports on V-weapons, including Peenemünde (4 January 1944), while from an entrepreneur working for the Germans and travelling in northern France an agent gleaned sightings of seventy-metre-long platforms (9 January 1944). Thereafter there were regular reports from Service Clarence on V-rockets.[8] The 'Luc' network acquired information from the head office of Belgian State Railways and was able to give advance notice about the transport of German troops and equipment through Belgium and northern France. Luc agents also tapped into the State Railways' private telephone system, as well as the teleprinter service between the State Railways and 'the German Railway Transport Office which controlled the running of all military trains'.

The Belgian networks faced considerable problems in getting information out of the country. Towards the end of 1942 SIS began to send new ground-to-air 'Ascension' radio sets to the Clarence network. Developed by Gambier-Parry's Section VIII boffins, this new device allowed agents to speak directly to an aircraft flying near by. Since it dispensed with the need for Morse code, it was easier for inexperienced operators to use, and because they did not require lengthy call-sign procedures, transmissions were more difficult to locate by direction-finding.[9] The Ascension sets were used with some success in Belgium and elsewhere, but the system was not very useful for long messages which still had to be smuggled out by courier across long and precarious land routes. One officer in Broadway complained in January 1943 that, although they were receiving a large number of reports from Belgian sources, the information contained in them 'has been so old that they have become valueless'. During the last week of December 1942, the Military Section had sent eighty reports to the War Office, the contents of which revealed an average time lag of three and three-quarter months. An officer asked if anything could be done to speed up delivery, but Hubert Hatton-Hall, head of the section, commented: 'I imagine that we are very lucky to get this stuff at all & that there is little chance now of speeding up.' In May 1943 Jempson told Dansey that all his courier lines with Belgium had broken down following arrests at collecting and forwarding centres in Paris, Lyons and Toulouse. Jempson therefore asked Demarque if he could open a

Sir Stewart Menzies, Chief of SIS from November 1939 to June 1952.

Margaret Reid (Frank Foley's secretary), whose personal diary vividly described the nightmarish retreat from Oslo in 1940.

A Gestapo photograph of Richard Stevens (head of station at The Hague), taken after his capture at Venlo with Sigismund Payne Best on 9 November 1939.

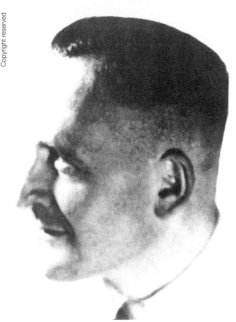

Liaison benefits: The former Czechoslovak president, Edvard Beneš (third from left), and František Moravec (third from right), head of Czechoslovak Military Intelligence, exiled in London (*top*). Next to Beneš (in uniform) is SIS's Harold Gibson, who engineered the dramatic rescue of Moravec, his staff and secret files from Prague in March 1939. 'A.54' Paul Thümmel (*left*), the high-grade Czechoslovak agent in the Abwehr whose reports were shared with SIS.

LORIENT   7.9.40

Entry to Port. Showing on horizon cargo boat prepared for invasion

Naval Base, On left old Cruiser "Conde" in centre Naval Barracks

Naval Base. Closer view, Naval Barracks on right, 5 fast Minesweepers
                                          moored alongside.

Naval Base. Close up view of 5 fast minesweepers

Early intelligence product from Nazi-occupied France: agent photographs taken in Brittany on 7 September 1940, showing the entry to the port and the naval base at Lorient.

A hurriedly-taken shot of German troops manoeuvring a gun onto a fishing boat at Douarnenez, 6 September 1940.

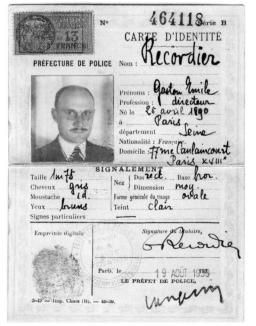

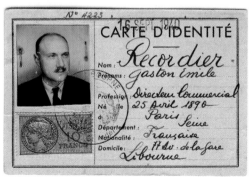

False identity documents prepared for Gilbert Renault, the outstanding leader of the Confrérie de Notre-Dame organisation in France.

SIS in North Africa: Desmond Adair, head of station at Cairo. A photograph taken in late 1941.

© C. Cohen

Wood / Detour

Photographed in Cairo in the spring of 1942 (from the left) Cuthbert Bowlby (chief SIS representative in the Middle East), Elizabeth Dennys, her husband Rodney (head of the Middle East counter-intelligence section) and Kenneth Cohen (SIS liaison with the Free French) (*left*); 'Dick Jones' (*right*), SIS's most successful agent in Tunisia, sketched here by J. F. Watton while both were prisoners at Colditz.

The acerbic Claude Dansey, Assistant Chief of SIS during the Second World War.

Sir Samuel Hoare, successively SIS officer, Cabinet Minister and Ambassador to Spain.

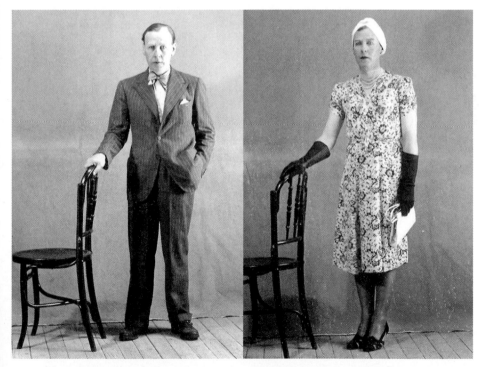

Spanish police photographs of the unfortunate Dudley Clarke, arrested in Madrid dressed as a woman in October 1941.

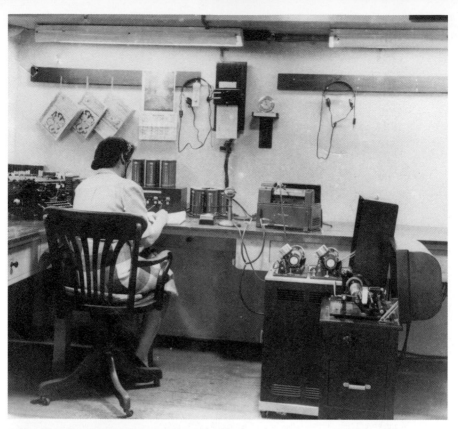

SIS's productive phone-tapping operation in the basement of the Santiago embassy.

Anglo-American Intelligence heroes: 'Wild Bill' Donovan presenting William Stephenson with the United States Presidential Medal of Merit, November 1946.

Sir Hughe Knatchbull-Hugessen (Britan's ambassador to Turkey) and Winston Churchill at Adana airfield, January 1943.

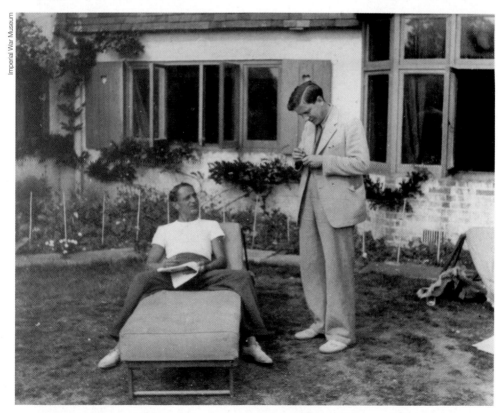

SIS's worst traitor, Kim Philby (*standing*), with Paul Dehn when both were instructors at SOE's Beaulieu training establishment, 1941.

Norwegian operations: the shipwatchers' environment (*top*); keeping in touch with London; wireless communication was pivotal in ensuring intelligence reached SIS headquarters rapidly, but radio operators had to evade the watchful enemy security forces; agents had to keep vigil in exposed coastal positions throughout the year, including the harshest of winter conditions (*middle*). Ready for action (*bottom*): Oluf Reed Olsen (*right*) and a colleague still wearing their 'striptease' parachute jump suits the morning after their landing in Norway, 7 May 1944. Although evidently a posed photograph, a revealing air of devil-may-care resolve suggests why Olsen was one of SIS's finest Norwegian agents.

GENEVA   VCSS/II/III/)
1.7.43   IV/P.3   )
1428   VCSS   )

1.7.43   3.7.43
1715   1725 DST   *VCSS have cop J*
              PEC

Following for V.C.S.S.

Your telegram 774.

A.   Do not think that you can count too much on plan as it is
rough pencil sketch not to scale, probably drawn from memory
by P of W. Have photographed in two negatives two inches by
one inch.

B.   Plan shows railway from ZINNOWITZ running to north east tip
of island. At railway terminus there is submarine and aerial
experimental station. Factory making rocket projectile, part
above and part below ground, located to south. Comparing
sketch with atlas one concludes projectile factory is on
extremity west of PEENEMUNDE Bay, ?almost opposite land
promontory at FREEST.

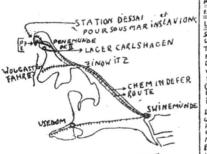

ATELIER DE FABRICATION
ET D'EXPERIMENTATION DE
L'OBUS A FUSÉE.

SE TROUVE A P?... EN PARTIE
SUR TERRE, EN PARTI SOUS-
TERRAIN
FUSÉE EN VOL. LONGUEUR
DE 10 METRES. ELLE EST
VISIBLE PENDANT LE
VOL. ASPECT EN CIGARE
GARDE SA DROITE PEN-
DANT LES PREMIERS 50KM
PUIS ATTITUDE DE BALLES
DOUM-DOUM C'EST LÀ LE
GRAND PROBLEME OU ELLE
POSERAIT A L'HEURE ACTU-
ELLE. - AU DEPART ELLE EST
MONTÉE SUR UN DISPOSTIF LE
FORME CUBIQUE. DES BOUTE-
ILLES CONTENANT DU GAZ S'Y
TROUVENT. - AU DEPART SUR-
GIT UNE FLAMME - LA FUSÉE
TOURNE SUR SON AXE SELON
UN MOUVEMENT ENTIRILLE ET

PLAN GENERAL DE L'ILE
D'USEDOM

S'ENVOLE. - DISTANCE PARCOURUE SUREMENT 150 KM. PROBABLEMENT
250KM. - L'USINE SUPERIEUSEMENT GARDÉE. 1 POSTE TOUS LE 10 M.
LE S.R. ALLEMAND CHERCHE DES AGENTS EVENTUELS

TRANSMIS PAR JEAN L'AVEUGLE

ACCUSEZ RECEPTION: BBC EMISSION POUR LE
GRAND-DUCHÉ.
    "FIR DE BLANNE JANG 1-2-3-4 ARTHUR DE
JANG ASS DO"

FAMILLE MARTIN

An early fragment of intelligence about the German V-weapon development site at Peenemünde in East Prussia, this sketch map was passed to SIS in Switzerland in June 1943 and is seen here with the Geneva station telegram of 1 July alerting London to its existence.

Illustrating the variety of experience of SIS officers during the Second World War, John Bruce Lockhart (*top left*), who served in uniform as head of station at Bari, 1943–5, sending agents into occupied territory; 'Fanny' Vanden Heuvel (*top right*), a Papal Count who with civilian cover as an assistant press attaché was head of the Geneva station, 1940–5; Nigel Clive (*bottom*), pictured here (*right*) with Greek army Lieutenant Mario Maniakis. Clive's paramilitary role from December 1943 saw him attached to an SOE Military Mission behind enemy lines in north-west Greece.

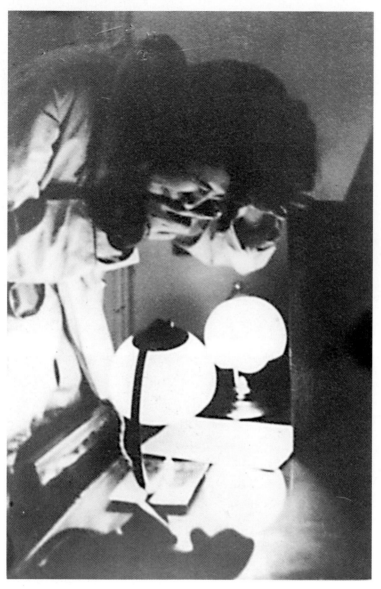

An extremely rare image of an agent at work: the double-agent 'Ecclesiastic' photographing British documents, Lisbon 1944. This photograph was taken by her German target presumably to hold as insurance over her. It only survives because she promptly passed it on to her British case officer.

SIS's Belgian operations: Hector Demarque (*top*), a colleague of Walthère Dewé in the Belgian telephone company RTT, who took over leadership of Service Clarence in 1940; and (*bottom*) 'Colonel Page' (Frederick Jempson, *first left*), head of SIS's Belgian section, in an Army Mess room, Brussels, November 1944.

A photograph taken by
Kenneth Cohen in August
1944 and captioned by
him: 'De Gaulle's officers
returning to France by MTB
after landings'. Airey Neave
of MI9 is second left.

Philip Keun, a leader of the 'Jade'
network who was arrested in
Occupied France in June 1944
and murdered at Buchenwald
concentration camp three months
later.

Kenneth Cohen (*left*) and Guy Westmacott receiving the Légion d'Honneur at Les Invalides,
Paris, September 1945.

Edward James, senior SIS officer in Burma 1947.

John 'Sinbad' Sinclair, postwar Vice Chief of SIS (and Chief 1952–6), seen here as Director of Military Intelligence visiting 15th Army Group in Italy on 16 March 1945. On the left is the American General Mark Clark.

northern route through Sweden. Eventually he found someone and sent an Ascension message to London that one of his agents would call on the British military attaché in Stockholm: 'He will give the name Buelemans and will say: "Aucun chemin de fleurs ne conduit a la gloire."'[10] The contact appears to have been made but in the end little intelligence came through Sweden.

SIS's problematic relations with the Dutch began to improve in 1942 after Bill Cordeaux took charge of operations to the Low Countries and Captain D. O. 'Charles' Seymour took over as head of the Dutch section. One of the section's problems concerned the employment of Dutch nationals, whom the government-in-exile wanted to keep for themselves in specifically Dutch formations. To get round this difficulty, Seymour proposed in September 1942 to look for men with British passports, but who were, 'to all intents and purposes, purely Dutch', and he asked the service liaison sections in Broadway to 'do all in your power to trace every likely individual'. The first trained agent of SIS's new Dutch set-up left for the Netherlands in March 1943. Because it was (rightly) thought that the existing British clandestine networks in the country were compromised, 'Hendrick' parachuted in blind, 'with no organisation to receive him and even without strong hope that his identity cards and other documents were correctly forged'. Cordeaux described him as a strong Calvinist, who was 'utterly fearless and regarded his task as a mission from God'. He encountered great difficulties from the start, when his Ascension radio-telephony set failed to work. He managed, nevertheless, to build up a network involving some three hundred members, which by the end of 1943 'was providing a steady and useful, if not very prolific series of reports'. Hendrick's attempts to return to England vividly illustrate that it was as difficult to get agents out of occupied Europe as it was to get them in. One scheme involved seizing an air-sea rescue motor boat in Scheveningen harbour, but the engine refused to start and Hendrick escaped only after a lengthy shooting-match. On a second occasion he got as far as the Pyrenees, when a snowstorm forced his party back from the Spanish frontier. Hendrick was arrested shortly afterwards and spent the winter of 1944–5 in prison subjected to intermittent bouts of violent interrogation before he was liberated by advancing Allied forces in the spring of 1945.

France

In August 1943 Menzies learned that the French Committee of National Liberation in Algiers, which had formalised the joint leadership of Giraud and de Gaulle over all anti-Axis French forces, was deliberating on the future of French clandestine services. He alerted the British Minister of State in Algiers, Harold Macmillan, to the importance of SIS's relationship with the Fighting French. 'Since 1940,' signalled Menzies, 'have maintained close collaboration with de Gaulle's special Bureau here known as B.C.R.A. [Bureau Central de Renseignements et d'Action].' 'Organization', he continued, 'built up in France with much difficulty in collaboration my service and B.C.R.A. has now reached stage where most important results being obtained.' He quoted a letter he had just received from the Director of Military Intelligence 'saying that the intelligence supplied by this joint French–British service has been of greatest value to General Staff particularly during last month', adding that the War Office 'would view with great misgiving any action which might interfere with our relations with B.C.R.A. and perhaps decrease the flow of military information'.

Menzies, evidently worried that SIS's liaison with the Gaullists in London (and its monopoly of the information produced by the link) might be jeopardised by some new arrangement based in North Africa, naturally emphasised the productivity of joint espionage operations in France, while not unduly troubling Macmillan with any of the accompanying problems. There was a universal expansion of clandestine activity in France during 1943, but that of SOE and resistance organisations, who concentrated on special operations more than intelligence, often cut across SIS's information-gathering networks. There were also continuing and overlapping tensions between different groups, including Gaullists, anti-Gaullists, conservatives, Communists, former Vichyists and those with ostensibly no politics at all. Internal French political competition, moreover, was sharpened as victory over the Axis became more likely and also as the Gaullists began to get the upper hand in the battle for acceptance as the legitimate French government-in-waiting.

One of the most important Free French networks in the early part of the war, the Confrérie de Notre-Dame, remained important in northwest and northern France, but by the summer of 1943 London reckoned that the network was in some trouble. Fearing that he knew too much and was a security risk in France, Dewavrin had brought the inspirational leader Gilbert Renault out, but in his absence rivalries among the hierarchy undermined the organisation. In March 1943, moreover, 'Espadon', a former port employee in Bordeaux, who had been providing shipping intelligence and helping to courier information about coast defences in Brittany, was arrested after helping two British fighter pilots to escape.[11]

There was better news of the 'Davis' group, based around Nice, which had originally been associated with the Confrérie, but had become an independent outfit by mid-1943 when a journalist with the cover name 'Chavagnac' took charge. A handful of his original telegrams still remain on file, giving a flavour of the material coming from the network, and also illustrating the difficulty of disentangling intelligence from special operations. In late July 1943 Chavagnac offered to blow up railway locomotives which the Italians were trying to remove from Nice. On 28 July he noted the arrival in Nice of Field Marshal von Rundstedt, commander of the German Army Group West, and two days later gave precise details of his journey back to Paris by special train, information which could have been used to inform an attack on the general. But the timings were very tight. Chavagnac's 30 July telegram noting that Rundstedt's train 'will leave Sete on the first of August at 1525 hrs. and will arrive in Paris (Gare de Lyon) on the second of August at 0925 hrs.' took over a day to be processed and was passed to the Air Ministry only at 7.45 p.m. on 1 August. On 2 August Chavagnac reported that three German divisions were moving out of the Montpellier–Port Vendres region, and were thought to be going towards Italy. On 14 August he signalled that twenty-seven German trains with about eleven thousand troops and nine Italian trains with five thousand troops had passed through Cannes towards Italy between 6 and 9 August.

The Davis network was highly regarded in Broadway. A March 1944 minute noted that over the previous six months it had been the most productive 'of any of our organisations'. In June it was added that Davis had 'frequently received bouquets from the Air Ministry and War Office, who also often express astonishment at the volume of Davis' output'. The Admiralty considered Davis to be in the 'top drawer' and the Ministry of Economic Warfare also commented favourably on the value and number of economic reports produced by the organisation. London believed that

FOURCADE, *NOAH'S ARK*, PLATE 7

Marie-Madeleine Fourcade was described by SIS's Kenneth Cohen as the 'copybook "beautiful spy"'. Top left shows how British forgers could change her appearance for false identity papers.

this success was due to Chavagnac's 'administrative ability and common sense', combined with 'a complete disregard for his own safety'. Early in 1944, however, 'two minor members of the organisation divulged their knowledge of it to the Germans'. After failed attempts 'firstly to evacuate them by a pickup operation and secondly to execute them', and fearing that the network had been seriously compromised, Chavagnac was brought out and the organisation split into thirteen independent groups, which all continued to supply 'valuable intelligence'.

An annotated breakdown of Marie-Madeleine Fourcade's Alliance organisation drawn up in August 1942 demonstrates the reach of one of the largest and most important SIS French networks. One hundred and forty-five individuals are listed, organised into ten different groups. The largest of these, led by 'Panthère', had thirty agents, among whom were an electrical engineer and wireless operator who 'has some serious sources in the Beauvais region'; an 'industrialist, Paris and Nord'; a Paris-based female friend of Panthère, 'a very cultured woman and enterprising' with 'contacts in medical circles'; a businessman able to travel between the two zones of France and to Germany; a police commissaire 'in charge of the surveillance of the coast in Brittany'; an engineer who divided his time between Lille and Grenoble; and a port employee in Brest who 'possesses information on movements of all German boats which he can pass on to us'. At its peak in the spring of 1943 Alliance was reckoned to have over two thousand agents, couriers and contacts right across France. Organised into three main geographical regions, each of which was divided into a number of sectors, it was run along military lines and concentrated broadly on military intelligence, including information on U-boat bases in western France and, from 1943, V-weapons.

A snapshot of life for an Alliance agent on the ground is provided by 'Pierre Verrier' ('Seagull'), a civil airline pilot before the war, who, among other things, helped make arrangements for landing operations. Debriefed on his return to England in April 1943, he reported that he had had 'very little trouble' with the French police, and that 'the most patriotic and the easiest ones to get on with were those belonging to the pre-war regime'. He claimed that the Gestapo, who 'combined excessive politeness and the utmost brutality in the accomplishment of their duties', were 'overwhelmed with work'. Sometimes they were 'remarkably stupid', as when they had come to arrest two brothers. At the house they 'asked one of the men if his brother was at home'. He replied that he would go and see, and both men managed to escape while the Germans waited patiently for him to return. 'Whilst they were in the house,' moreover, 'a young local boy came in, went upstairs to the attic, dismantled and packed the W/T set and walked out without being molested.' More ominously, however, Verrier added that 'in every small town and village' the Gestapo had 'at least 2 or 3 denouncers'. Verrier, too, had good advice for other agents. 'When in lonely country districts where he was a stranger, looking for suitable landing-grounds,' he said that 'he made a habit of visiting 2 or 3 farms to enquire for food.' This could provide him with an alibi. Should the police ask him why he was in the district, 'he could answer that he was looking for food', and 'indicate farms where he had called and where, should the police check up on his story, they would find it to be true'. Another observation was that when a stranger went to live in any locality for a length of time, it was 'not safe for him to be there without receiving correspondence'. If, 'in the normal way', he did not receive letters, 'he should write letters to himself. A person who does not receive any correspondence', asserted Verrier, 'is apt to be looked upon as a person in hiding.'

Despite Verrier's somewhat dismissive remarks about the Gestapo, the Alliance organisation was very badly hit by enemy penetration and arrests during 1943. Its sheer size and centralisation, along with some lax security, proved fatal for many of its members. The German occupation of south-east France in late 1942, moreover, deprived Allied sympathisers of what had been a comparatively safe haven. Early in 1943 it was clear that the Germans had become aware of a clandestine organisation whose members took the names of animals as pseudonyms. In January and February a series of arrests disrupted the network in Toulouse, Marseilles, Nice and Lyons, where the Gestapo chief, Klaus Barbie, directed the torture of two young female Alliance members, 'Hummingbird' and 'Mouse'. German pressure forced the network to move its headquarters from Lyons to Paris, but in the summer there was a further series of blows. In June, 'Elephant', one of the principal figures who had remained at Lyons, and the network's chief supplier of forged documents, was arrested. The following month the head of the south-west region in Limoges narrowly evaded capture by the Gestapo, but some of his staff were captured. Further arrests followed in Toulon, the Alpes Maritimes and even Paris. With the whole organisation under extreme pressure, its leader, Marie-Madeleine Fourcade, was brought out to London.

Only after the war did it become apparent that the disasters of 1943 were in part due to at least one traitor in the Alliance ranks. Elephant's capture seems to have been down to an Alsatian, Jean-Paul Lien ('Lanky'), who had penetrated the organisation for the Germans. Lien also engineered the arrest of Fourcade's effective second-in-command, Léon Faye ('Eagle') on his return from a brief visit to London in September. Faye, whose party included 'Magpie', a British radio operator who had been sent to work with Alliance in October 1942, was picked up with incriminating documents, three million francs, arms and other equipment which they had brought over from England. Others awaiting Faye's arrival in Paris managed to get away when the Gestapo began to search the block of flats where they were gathered. More arrests followed, and by the late autumn of 1943 most of the Alliance groups in north-west France and the Rhône valley had ceased to function. Many of the network's members were shot by the Germans. Faye was executed at a camp in eastern Germany early in 1945. Magpie was more fortunate. In a rare wartime example of a spy-swap, the British, negotiating through the Swiss protecting power, managed to exchange him for a German officer and he arrived back in the United Kingdom in February 1945.[12]

The Davis and Alliance organisations came under Kenneth Cohen's P.1 section at Broadway, which handled most of SIS's French work. Numerous other intelligence networks developed under Cohen's aegis, with and without Free French co-operation. One was 'Sosie', a large and extensive organisation working mainly in the north-east of the country, and the smaller networks included 'Triboullet' and 'Jove'. Their primary means of communication was by radio, but some used courier lines through Spain, while others were provided with air and sea pick-ups. The growth of intelligence activities in France during 1943 produced a growing backlog of intelligence reports because of inadequate communications out of the country. The problem was eased by the development of an independent organisation to handle the material. This was set up by a French diplomat in Madrid (using the code-name 'Alibi'), who had already run a successful line across the Franco-Spanish border, and who managed to establish wireless communications with networks in France.

All through the war Biffy Dunderdale, P.5 at Head Office, continued to work with separate French networks. In June 1943 he reported that, apart from Polish intelligence, he still got information from his old Deuxième Bureau contacts (with a special line to Bertrand), and also from the Jade organisation. The Polish service had some thirty networks in occupied and neutral Europe, and three hundred agents were employed primarily on SIS work. Dunderdale's section organised their travelling and transport facilities, while a centre at Stanmore, just north of London, produced agent equipment including radio sets. Some of the Polish networks were very productive. One based in the south of France run by 'Lubicz' (Zdzisław Piątkiewicz) had 159 agents, helpers and couriers, who in August and September 1943 provided 481 reports, of which P.5 circulated 346. Dunderdale's other organisations were rather smaller. He recorded the Deuxième Bureau as having nine stations and Jade four in mid-1943.[13]

In the autumn of 1942 Claude Lamirault had begun to rebuild the Jade organisation. One group on the Swiss frontier was organised to smuggle urgently needed precision instruments out of Switzerland and

across France in fruit boxes, though this was not a great success. There
were also sub-groups in Marseilles, Bordeaux, Lyons and Paris (it was
in the capital that Lamirault established his headquarters). Each group
had independent communications with London, and relied on the centre
only for funds and instructions. The Jade Bordeaux group, which actually came to be centred on Paris, was led by Philip Keun ('Admiral' or
'Deux'), a Dutchman raised in England and France who had worked for
the French Marine Deuxième Bureau and whom Bill Cordeaux described
as 'an international adventurer with more than his fair share of charm
and cunning'. Along with Roman Czerniawski, who had been part of
the Polish F2 network, Keun set up his headquarters in a convent which,
happily, the Gestapo regarded as above suspicion. Czerniawski had been
arrested in 1941 and recruited as an agent by the Germans, but got back
to London in October the following year where he pledged to continue
to work for Polish and British intelligence and was thereafter run as double agent 'Brutus' by the XX Committee.[14]

One of Lamirault's most impressive achievements, which helped enormously in his work, was the acquisition of an official identity card and
badge used by the Vichy police. Both card and badge were sent to London
by courier, faithfully copied by SIS's false document section and returned
to France. The false badges allowed Lamirault and a few chosen members
of the Jade group to pass through police cordons, but in the end it was
the fake identity card that caused his downfall. He was arrested in Paris
on 15 December 1943, trying to force his way into a hotel as a police
inspector, but suspicions were raised, and in resisting arrest he shot a real
policeman. The following day he was handed over to the Gestapo, who
transferred him to Fresnes prison. Attempts were made to rescue him but
they failed. He was deported to Dachau, but survived the war only to be
killed in a road accident back in France in May 1945. Philip Keun was
also arrested, in June 1944, and murdered at Buchenwald the following
September.

Intelligence product

In November 1942, Menzies asked that Dunderdale should provide him
with a fortnightly progress report, drawing his attention only 'to items of

outstanding interest'. 'Where there is no such item', he instructed that he 'would prefer the paragraph to be as short as possible'. Although it is difficult to ascertain exactly who was providing what for Dunderdale's P.5 section, the surviving reports give a flavour of the intelligence his agents were sending back. In October he reported telegrams from 'Bertie' (Gustave Bertrand) giving the names of the heads of French armed forces intelligence and the Vichy French Intelligence Service itself. The next month he stated that his 'Vichy France Section' was providing 'outstanding' information on French North Africa, including photographs of beaches on the Moroccan Atlantic coast from Agadir to Mazagan; the boom and net defences at the port of Oran; 'description, equipment and cargo movements' at Nemours in Algeria; from occupied France 'a scheme and report of coastal defences' around Bayonne, and a report about construction work on a submarine shelter in Bordeaux; and from the then still unoccupied zone a report detailing the difficulties of recruitment for the Vichy army. A telegram from his Polish source 'Rygor' (Major Mieczysław Słowikowski) on 8 November stated that from 6 November all shipping movements in the port of Algiers had been suspended. Clearly the authorities there had got a sniff of the impending Torch offensive. Ships at sea had received orders to return to the nearest port, while the French submarines *Caiman* and *Marsouin* were being held at readiness in Algiers.[15]

During November 1942 P.5 agents reported on coastal defences at Toulon and Marseilles; the names of commanders of all ships of the French naval forces larger than minesweepers taken from a secret document held by the French Ministry of Marine; details of a German staff headquarters in the Château de Kerlivio near Brandérion in Brittany, with a sketch showing strongpoints which should be destroyed in the event of operations; changes in the armament of the destroyers *Gerfaut* and *Guépard* and the cruisers *Algérie* and *Dupleix* at Toulon, with plans; reports on the arrival of the Italian Piave and Legnano divisions in France (with the Italian headquarters at Cannes and staff headquarters at Nice), along with the general Italian order of battle; German troop movements on the French Mediterranean coast and air order of battle across France. From Germany itself, Dunderdale's agents reported on the output of the Schichau shipyards at Elbing in East Prussia, and details of ships under construction or repair in Kiel, Stettin and Lübeck. There were also reports of extensive preparations being made in Germany for gas warfare, including one that 'Infantry Battalion 151' had carried out exercises with poison gas at Białystok in Poland; positions of U-boats and their bases in Danzig, with yard serial numbers of submarines under construction; and an OKW appraisal of Soviet and German intentions and the Eastern Front situation dated 30 November 1942.

In 1943, there were reports on Italian naval units on the south coast of France ('a prompt reply to a query', according to Dunderdale); the position of ships and air-raid damage in Genoa; more reports on German preparations for gas warfare; and submarine construction at Gdynia, Königsberg and Katowice. In France there were reports on the coastal defences in the Marseilles region and the political situation in both France and North Africa following the Allied landings of Operation Torch. In February 1944 reports arrived on German troop movements to the Eastern Front and a survey of the situation in Italian-occupied Corsica, giving the strength of the occupation forces (20,000–25,000) and identifying units and their locations, with notes on coastal defences, accompanied by two maps and twelve photographs. In March there were reports on the state of the French fleet at Toulon after scuttling; Gestapo arrests in the French Foreign Ministry; a copy of a questionnaire submitted to German SS agents in France; and the drinking-water supply in Tunisia. From Germany came reports on the shipyards at Pillau and Königsberg in East Prussia; the position of the German naval headquarters at Copenhagen; and military convoys for the Eastern Front.

During the spring reports came in on coastal defences along the Mediterranean west of Nice; the defences of Fréjus–Saint-Raphaël aerodrome and beach; and radio-location stations south of Morlaix in Brittany. Names of the German naval staff at Toulon were provided, together with Axis units and the principal radio installations at the Toulon naval base as well as details of torpedoes used in German motor torpedo boats. A Jade agent provided details of damage at the U-boat base in Bordeaux during a daylight raid on 17 May. From the early summer onwards there were increasing numbers of reports on coastal defences, not only along the Mediterranean, but also along the English Channel, the Atlantic in Brittany and south to the Spanish frontier. In July and August reports were received on German troop movements in France; aircraft production; 'danger areas' in Brittany; German-occupied aerodromes;

the manufacture of propellers; the movement of troops to Italy and the Italian-occupied zone in south-eastern France; and German air order of battle in Poland. At the end of June there was a report on the state of work at shipyards in Bordeaux, Nantes, Saint-Nazaire, Saint-Malo, Le Havre, Rouen and Dunkirk. There was also intelligence about telecommunications – buried cables at Lorient, details of lines between Rouen and Cherbourg and a repeater station at Le Mans.

From the autumn of 1943 reports about German rocket weapons came with increasing frequency from Dunderdale's P.5 networks. The Germans had, in fact, been developing two V-weapons: the V-1, a pilotless jet-propelled plane launched from a ramp; and the V-2, which was a longer-range rocket. Both carried about a ton of explosive. SIS played a major role in providing intelligence about these programmes. In 1940 the Service had passed on vague reports of German experiments with long-range weapons, but it was not until late 1942 onwards that more specific information began to be received. Elgar, the Danish engineer who was able to travel in Germany, provided three reports about a new rocket weapon between December 1942 and March 1943. Another source reported in January and February 1943 that a factory had been built at Peenemünde to manufacture a rocket, and a third source in February reported that a rocket with a ten-ton warhead and a range of a hundred kilometres had been developed there. During March Broadway acquired a much more detailed report from 'a most reliable and expert source which has provided most valuable information over a long period'. The report, which described a series of rocket trials, drew on information provided by forced labourers from Luxembourg who had been drafted to work at Peenemünde. Further information came through Switzerland. As recalled by one SIS officer, the SIS station in Berne received from a Luxembourger 'a very dirty ragged sketch plan of some big contrivance being constructed by the Germans at an island call[ed] Peenemuende sometime in 1943. This filthy sketch plan seemed to make little sense and it referred to a launching of a "pilotless aeroplane" which had a range of 250 kilometres.' The head of station, Fanny Vanden Heuvel, was away at the time and his assistants decided 'to telegraph the most we could make out of this piece of paper. When Fanny returned he chided us for being such fools as to believe such nonsense, and said we would undoubtedly get a rocket from Dansey for wasting cypher groups!' But Broadway's reaction was quite the opposite: Berne was congratulated for 'most valuable information' and told 'that anything further on this subject should always be telegraphed "Most Immediate"'. Corroborative information about the installations at Peenemünde from Polish sources and RAF photographic intelligence enabled an extremely detailed plan of the facility to be prepared and used for an Allied air raid on 17–18 August 1943 which so badly damaged the site that the weapons programme was put back by at least two months and the Germans had to disperse both the experimental facility and the manufacturing side to other locations across the Reich.[16]

SIS agents also helped to pinpoint V-1 and V-2 launching sites in France. The most outstanding contribution was made by Michel Hollard and his 'Agir' network. Hollard, sales representative for a company that made gas generators for motor cars (a job which allowed him to travel all over France), offered his services to the British assistant military attaché in Berne in January 1942. He was at first rejected, but the report he left, on the French motor and aero industries, was graded so highly that, when he turned up again in May, SIS recruited him at once. Hollard built up a network, including many railway workers, and began by reporting on economic matters and German order of battle in France. In August 1943, however, one of his agents drew his attention to a site near Rouen where the Germans were imposing unusually precise specifications on the French building contractors. Masquerading as a labourer, Hollard investigated for himself and found mysterious 'miniature runways' being constructed which were all carefully aligned on bearings pointing towards London. The Berne station was not particularly impressed by the information, but when it was sent on to London it was realised that they were launching-ramps for the V-1 flying bomb. Hollard was instructed forthwith to concentrate exclusively on locating other such sites, which he and his colleagues did with extraordinary success.

By October 1943 Agir had located over a hundred V-1 sites, and Hollard, who had 'an arrangement' with the Chef de Gare at Rouen, was able to measure and take a series of photographs of a railway truck-load of V-1s. In addition, he stole an architect's blueprint of a V-1 site which allowed London to construct an exact scale model which, complemented with photo-reconnaissance, enabled the RAF to carry out effective bombing of the sites (which Agir in turn reported on). One of Hollard's sub-agents, 'Z.187', was an eighteen-year-old Frenchman who came to the British mission in Berne hoping to go on to England to join the Free French forces. When told that this was not possible he offered to work as an agent. SIS arranged for him to be taken on by Swiss Military Intelligence (which facilitated crossing and recrossing the frontier) and simultaneously join the Agir organisation. He helped identify V-1 sites and pinpointed the first V-2 launching site at Watten, near Calais. He also regularly supplied conventional military intelligence, among which was a German General Staff map showing the deployment of an infantry division in the Pas de Calais region – alleged to have been specially prepared for an inspection tour by Hitler – in 'complete detail down to platoon formations, with all the defence works drawn in, including underwater anti-tank and anti-personnel obstacles along the shore'. Z.187 was caught in June 1944 and never heard of again, presumed shot by the Gestapo. Hollard was more fortunate. Having crossed the Swiss frontier ninety-eight times before being betrayed and arrested in February 1944, he survived the war.[17]

SIS and D-Day

Operation Overlord, the successful invasion of France on 6 June 1944, in which some 150,000 troops were landed at a cost of little over 5,000 casualties, was a stunning achievement in terms of Allied and inter-service co-operation, careful planning, logistics, timing and, not least, the courage of the individual soldiers, sailors and airmen involved. It was also a tremendous intelligence success. Indeed, no previous military operation in history had been so well supported and sustained by the intelligence available for the assault and its range and quality were a testament to the combined efforts of many agencies: signals intelligence from Bletchley Park; aerial reconnaissance from the RAF; deception operations run by the XX Committee; and detailed surveys of the beaches themselves obtained by COPPs (Combined Operations Pilotage Parties), sometimes lying offshore for days in midget submarines measuring tidal currents and beach gradients and taking sand samples.[18] But there were limitations to what could be done. Signals intelligence, for example, which was so valuable where the enemy used wireless, could provide only fitful coverage about the deployment of static German forces, as in northern France, who relied principally on land-lines for their communications. Much of the information about this came from the kind of material that was SIS's stock-in-trade: old-fashioned human intelligence – humint – gathered by a host of individual agents and helpers over the preceding two years and more.

Information on German deployment, coastal defences and communications in northern France, such as that provided by Dunderdale's P.5 networks, was carefully assembled by section MI14 in the Directorate of Military Intelligence (for German order-of-battle information), and the Combined Intelligence Section (CIS) of General Headquarters, Home Forces, which had been given responsibility for collating all intelligence along a thirty-mile-deep coastal strip from Den Helder in the Netherlands to the mouth of the River Loire in France. From June 1942 to May 1944 CIS produced a series of weekly reports, code-named 'Martian', which systematically laid out the intelligence under seven headings: strategic survey; enemy forces; topography and maps; transport and industry; police and civilians; air; and naval. The reports were illustrated with aerial photographs, reproductions of documents and plans of coastal defences supplied by agents.[19] From March 1944, MI14 began to issue more detailed 'weekly notes' or 'weekly summaries', classified 'TOP SECRET(U)', which provided a greater emphasis on German troop dispositions, general order of battle and the nature of fortifications on the northern French coast.[20]

In order to sustain the supply of tactical intelligence for the invasion forces during and immediately after Overlord, and aiming also to provide an alternative network in the tactical areas around the Normandy bridgehead should existing clandestine organisations fail as a result of enemy counter-measures, in late 1943 the 'Sussex scheme' was developed. This was a joint scheme between SIS, the American OSS and the Free French BCRA. Fifty intelligence targets were identified, half in the planned operational area of the British 21st Army Group and half in that of the United States forces. Each was to be covered by a French two-person team. But there were delays in assembling the agents and wireless operators, as not only had the BCRA in London to refer all matters to Algiers for a decision, but it had been decreed that General de Gaulle and his staff were not to be given details of Overlord until the actual day the invasion was launched. There were also problems with the personnel themselves. Just before Christmas 1943 Kenneth Cohen (Chief Staff Officer, Training, and chair of the inter-Allied Sussex Committee of Three running the scheme), complained to Tony Morris in Algiers that the men the Free French were supplying were of 'low medical category or indifferent morale' and that 'at present rate we shall fail to implement our operational undertakings to the Chiefs of Staff, and responsibility for this will lie with the French'. For his part, Morris thought that 'the whole B.C.R.A. attitude of mind seems to be much more directed towards internal politics and the Mouvements de Résistance than towards the collecting of military information'.

So concerned were Cohen's committee about the risk of contacts with potentially compromised existing agent networks in France (and in keeping with the intense security maintained for all aspects of Overlord) that they considered the risky possibility of dropping the teams in blind. In the end, however, they decided to send in a preliminary 'Pathfinder' mission to prepare the way, when the twenty-five-year-old 'Jeanette Gauthier' was parachuted in on 6 February 1944. Based in Paris, she travelled west to Alençon, and south to Lyons, Bordeaux and Châteauroux, locating suitable dropping zones and arranging reception committees. Between February and April 1944 she personally met the first nine Sussex teams that parachuted into France and led them to safe houses in the Paris region.

Considerable effort was put into agent training, which was modelled on SOE experience and run by British and American officers based at Prae Wood in St Albans, close to the Sussex administrative headquarters at Glenalmond, a commodious Victorian house where Section V had been located earlier in the war. The training programme included a week-long exercise where pairs of potential agents were scattered across England, given locations of safe houses and instructed to send information (for example about military convoys) back by radio. A report of the fourth of these exercises, based in the East Midlands in early May 1944, gives a flavour of what was involved. With an emphasis on 'tradecraft and its practice', the students performed well and no one was 'arrested in "flagrante delicto"'. The local police were in on the exercise and the trainees 'all had to be brought in on an obviously framed up charge in order to undergo the experience of interrogation'. The police reported afterwards that the teams had stood up well to questioning (one individual was 'interrogated for some 8 hours' by the Nottingham Police) and they were commended for the hiding of 'maps, documents and compromising papers', as 'searching of their rooms in their "safe" houses in no case produced any result'. On the radio side, '105 messages were sent, of which only 2 were indecipherable and of the remainder 70% were without fault'. The students were carefully debriefed afterwards. One female radio operator had put her partner in danger by telling the police that she had met him in Nottingham, while unbeknown to her he had claimed to have no 'friends or acquaintances' in the city. This was a salutary lesson and the training officer observed that the woman now seemed 'to have grasped the importance of detail and of co-ordinating cover stories'. Only one participant refused to play the game, and had made 'little or no attempt to learn his cover story or to apply it under interrogation'. His attitude was 'that the matter was quite childish and he was merely there on an exercise which in fact was well known to the police concerned'. This did not go down at all well and he was 'severely talked to about his general manner during the exercise'. He admitted 'that he played the fool', and his partner thought he had offended 'from a feeling of "je m'en foutism"', but 'that he would in fact take the matter very seriously if it were the real thing'.

At the time of D-Day, although only fifteen Sussex teams had been dropped into France, ninety-five students had completed their training, and by mid-June twenty teams were in the field, reporting both by wireless and using the new ground-to-air Ascension device. Between 5 and 8 June, one team, 'Ossex/6', sent in reports which, along with German order-of-battle details, first identified the Panzer Lehr Division, about which one Supreme Headquarters Allied Expeditionary Force (SHAEF) officer remarked: 'If the Sussex scheme produced no other intelligence, it would have been worth while for these reports alone.' Following the invasion, other teams supplied immediately useful information, such as 'Brissex/20', who on 7 July reported on German barge traffic along the Seine, as a result of which 'the R.A.F. took immediate action', sinking twelve barges 'during the following 24 hrs. from the details given in his message'. By the end of August 1944 over thirty of the forty-five Sussex teams despatched had made radio contact with base, and up to 800 messages had been sent.[21]

During the run-up to Overlord the possibility of a co-ordinated assassination operation was discussed. Targeted killings had been contemplated at intervals since the beginning of the war and this was in part what SOE potentially existed to do. In May 1942 SOE-trained Czechoslovaks had assassinated Reinhard Heydrich, the German Protector of Bohemia and Moravia. Another SOE operation, 'Ratweek', in 1943–4, aimed to kill as many collaborators and members of the German security forces as possible across Europe, though in France it was successful only in Lyons where one agent 'disposed of' eleven individuals.[22] In April 1944 SHAEF, suggesting that likely victims might include Rommel, Rundstedt and possibly also Vichy collaborators, asked the Foreign Office to raise the matter with SIS (and curiously not with SOE). Menzies wanted clearer guidance as to what precisely was required, but, assuming 'that they must be thinking of the removal between now and D. Day of personalities whose liquidation might actually assist the Overlord operation', he said that 'the compiling of lists would seem to be a fairly simple matter'. Nevertheless he was worried that any such action 'might automatically lead to reprisals against hostages or United Nations personnel in enemy hands', and wished to know 'exactly what effects it is hoped to attain by the action proposed'. SHAEF came back with the proposal that, rather than German military commanders, the sorts of people they had in mind were 'para-military and civilian German personnel in key positions in France whose removal at the critical moment might really be a blow to the German war effort'. These might include 'Abwehr and S.D. [Sicherheitsdienst] characters, important political figures, transport chiefs, heads of supply and other economic organisations etc'. They did not want any French names, as they were 'strongly in favour of leaving it to French resisters to select their own victims'.[23]

On 11 May Menzies told Peter Loxley that while SIS had prepared a list of possible targets (which he was not as yet forwarding to him), the Service did not believe that their removal would 'have much, or indeed any effect on the efficient functioning of so widespread and highly organised a machine' as the Germans had in France. He also recommended that Loxley consult Bill Cavendish-Bentinck, the chairman of the Joint Intelligence Sub-Committee, on the matter. Cavendish-Bentinck agreed with Menzies 'in disliking this scheme, not out of squeamishness, as there are several people in this world whom I could kill with my own hands with a feeling of pleasure and without that action in any way spoiling my appetite', but because it was 'the type of bright idea which in the end

produces a good deal of trouble and does little good'. Above all there was
the risk of bloody reprisals. Nevertheless, if the French liked 'to assassinate Germans or collaborators', he added, 'we should not deter them', but
'we should steer clear of this business' and 'should not ourselves designate
persons to be liquidated, either German or still less French'. He noted the
likelihood 'that for every successful assassination' there would be 'two or
three failures' and observed that 'if assassination were easy many states-
men and high officers would have come to a violent end'. Looking to the
future, Cavendish-Bentinck worried that if German civilian officials were
murdered in France, it would 'probably start a wave of murderings' which
might continue after the British had occupied enemy territory, 'with the
result that members of our Control and other Commissions will become
poor risks for the insurance companies'. Cadogan shared these negative
opinions and SHAEF were informed accordingly.[24]

SIS's part in Overlord drew on its experience in North Africa and the
Middle East and reflected the successful organisation which had been developed there in 1942–3. Thus, as well as the Sussex teams, echoing SIS's
No. 1 Intelligence Unit which had been attached to Alexander's 15th
Army Group in Italy, No. 2 Intelligence (Unit) Section (or, more succinctly, but no more revealingly, No. 2 I(U) Section) was attached to the
headquarters of General Montgomery's British 21st Army Group, and
provided the link to SHAEF on intelligence matters, both with London
and in the field. On 8 June Menzies appointed Colonel Guy Westmacott
to take over the section, with an officer who had hitherto been running
the Sussex programme as his deputy. In a move that signalled the start
of the Service's anticipated peacetime deployment in formerly occupied
Europe, the deputy was given the symbol '27000', which belonged to
the head of the Paris station. He was charged with obtaining 'information deep behind enemy lines', both 'by the recruiting and infiltration of
special agents and by establishing direct contact with S.I.S. organisations
previously controlled from the U.K.'. At Broadway, No. 2 Intelligence
Unit came under Commander Cohen, who now as Controller Western
Europe (CWE) was responsible for SIS operations 'in France, Belgium,
the direct penetration of Germany and Czechoslovakia; also the clandestine activities of M.I.9. in those areas'.

Three other types of SIS section served with Allied formations in the
field. There were a number of Special Counter-Intelligence Units, attached

to major headquarters, which distributed sensitive signals intelligence material from Bletchley Park and were responsible for the security of that material. There were Special Liaison Units which handled Bletchley Park air intelligence and passed it on to theatre air headquarters. Finally, there were the paramilitary Special Communications Units which had been set up by Gambier-Parry to handle all SIS's field communications.[25] No. 2 Intelligence Unit's role in the provision of tactical battlefield intelligence fell away after the Allies had broken out of the Normandy bridgehead in mid-August and begun rapidly to move eastwards, soon overrunning most of the Sussex teams in the process. Thereafter, it acted as a link for the passing of information from London to 21st Army Group. Following the Allied landings in southern France on 15 August, and the liberation of Paris a week later, by the end of September all but a few parts of eastern France had effectively been liberated. On 23 October the Allies recognised General de Gaulle's administration as the provisional government of France and for SIS the task now became a combination of closing down wartime French networks, settling remaining obligations to agents (including those who had worked for SIS in preference to de Gaulle), sorting out its future deployment in the country and establishing the basis of postwar liaison with the French intelligence authorities.

16

Victory in Europe

D-Day did not by any means mark the end of the war, and SIS could not rest on such intelligence laurels as it had earned by the invasion's success. Although victory over Germany was increasingly regarded as inevitable, sustained stiff enemy resistance on the Eastern and Western Fronts left the Allied forces (including SIS) with much yet to do. But the process by which legitimate governments would be re-established in formerly occupied countries, and anticipations about the political balance of postwar Europe, began to preoccupy planners in the East and the West. SIS had a part to play in these developments, and especially so with the growing appreciation of the Soviet Union's intentions to drop even the pretence of Allied co-operation and pursue self-interested (and understandable) ambitions to ensure its security by dominating Eastern and Central Europe.

Belgium and the Netherlands

In the run-up to D-Day, Service Clarence had continued to supply excellent intelligence for SIS, such as a map of the Pas de Calais defences; details of German defence installations at Belgian ports; the numbers of troops and trains passing through Belgium to France and the Netherlands; information on German air force activity across a range of airfields in the region; and news about the gradual arrival in Belgium of the SS Adolf Hitler Division. The network also provided notes from Germany on the jet engine of the Messerschmitt Me-262 fighter and continued to procure information on V-weapons.[1] In mid-May 1944, Frederick Jempson, head of the Belgian Section in Broadway, reported that Service Clarence had suggested reorganising their communications

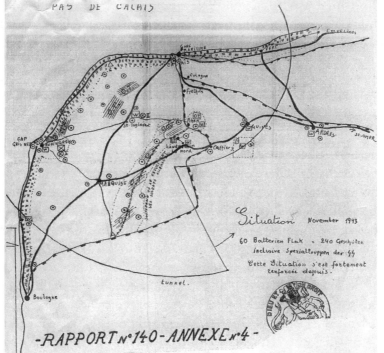

*A sketch map of German defences at the Pas de Calais made by a
Service Clarence agent in November 1943.*

in anticipation of the expected invasion. In order to speed up the flow of
intelligence they proposed dividing the network into nine sections, each
with a wireless or Ascension operator. The sole Ascension operator currently in Belgium, code-named 'Player', had been in the field since early
1943, but had fallen ill and been ordered to take 'a complete rest for 3
months'. Another operator, whom he had trained, had been arrested in
March 1944. While London was keen to help, skilled operators could
not be conjured out of thin air. Commander Cohen approved a scheme
whereby a wireless and two Ascension operators, 'specially chosen and . . .
amongst the best Agents now available', would be sent out 'during the
next moon period if possible'. Codes and sets for three locally recruited
'professional radio operators' would also be dropped, and 'other wireless operators will follow'. The first three agents, all 'Ascension-trained',
parachuted in on 4 July, but it took a further month before another six

operators (three Ascension and three wireless) were dropped in on 4 and
5 August. One of these agents was specifically instructed to concentrate
on 'German rail transport arrangements'. Reflecting the careful security
which now applied to the infiltration of agents, and to prevent the agents
from carrying any compromising material with them, such as a British
box of matches or bar of chocolate, a note on the file recorded that they
were searched twice, by Jempson in London and 'before leaving aerodrome by the Escorting Officer'.

Brussels was liberated on 3 September 1944, and soon afterwards the
SIS unit attached to 21st Army Group headquarters reached the city. On
18 October London told the head of the unit that to meet the army's
needs he should speed up the delivery of information, concentrating on
'operational intelligence, not only from opposite his front, but from well
on the flanks'. Before continuing its advance into the Netherlands, officers
were hived off to form the nucleus of an SIS station, initially to liaise with
the Belgian Sûreté, which was also in the process of re-establishing itself
in Brussels. Accompanied by the Sûreté chief, Fernand Lepage, Jempson
himself landed at Arromanches in Normandy on 11 September and arrived in Brussels two days later, basing himself at the Hôtel Métropole.
Here his priorities were V-2 weapons (reports were still coming in of V-2
tests at Venlo in eastern Holland) and the penetration of Germany. On
15 September Jempson reported that he was sending a Service Clarence
man into the Reich to prepare a reception committee for six agents to be
dropped in by parachute during the next moon.

By 1944 SIS's Dutch Section, P.8, was running five networks in the
Netherlands reporting through some thirty wireless sets, and they were
part of a standing committee with their Dutch opposite numbers BI
(the Bureau Inlichtingen), SOE and its Dutch equivalent BBO (Bureau
Bijzondere Opdrachten). Paralleling this London organisation was the
NBS, the Nederlandsche Binnenlandse Strijkrachten (Dutch Forces
of the Interior), which was created to co-ordinate Dutch resistance. In
September it set up a headquarters in Brussels, including SIS and SOE
representatives. After the first Allied troops crossed the Dutch frontier on
11 September, it was widely assumed that the Netherlands would soon
be liberated, and resistance groups stepped up their activities. A national railway strike was called to assist the Allied advance. But the costly
failure of the ambitious operation to seize a bridgehead over the Rhine

at Arnhem was followed by a period of military stalemate which lasted through the winter. Behind the enemy lines, German security units, reinforced by withdrawals from France and Belgium, punished the Dutch for their premature action. Food supplies collapsed and the civilian population suffered appalling privations, with an estimated fifteen thousand people dying of hunger. While SIS wireless links carried news of the suffering to the outside world, money and letters of authorisation from the Dutch government to spend large sums on relief measures were dropped in with Dutch and SIS agents.

Meanwhile No. 2 Intelligence Unit, which had moved to Eindhoven, continued to supply tactical military information and serve as the link for the transmission of intelligence from both London and agents across enemy lines. In early 1945 some thirteen SIS wireless sets were reporting from German-occupied territory. But, based now in the Netherlands itself, the SIS team were also able to exploit an unexpectedly rewarding new source by tapping into a Dutch electricity company's private telephone network which had lines connecting company offices and the private homes of employees across the country. Using one of these private telephones in Allied-occupied territory, communication was established with points in the enemy-occupied zone, from which agents were able to provide a mass of tactical information with such speed that in a number of instances air strikes could be called up against the particular target reported. But casualties were especially heavy during the final campaign for the Netherlands. Of eighty-nine agents sent out from England, or infiltrated through enemy lines, thirty-nine were arrested and twenty-eight were shot or died in German captivity.

The Germans' counter-attack in the Ardennes, the Battle of the Bulge (their last major offensive of the war), launched on 16 December 1944, shook easy assumptions that the war was effectively over. For a moment it seemed as if the new Brussels station would have to be put on a renewed war footing. London instructed it to alert existing Belgian networks 'with a view to creating strong stay-behind organisations'. Within hours Brussels had replied: 'agents in situ, crystals issued and all sets working to Section VIII, who are requested to begin listening forthwith. Further teams being sent to Liège area.' But the German offensive quickly ran out of steam and the stay-behind teams were not required. Marking the improved situation, at the start of February 1945 London cancelled the wireless plans and operator codes of no fewer than fourteen Belgian net-works. Apart from attempts to penetrate Germany, the Brussels station thereafter turned to the demobilisation of wartime agents, liaison with the Sûreté and the question of an SIS peacetime set-up in the country.

Targeting Germany

When the Berlin station closed at the outbreak of the war, its residual functions had been transferred to London. Contact was lost with most of its agents, though a few of the better ones were reactivated after the war. A few German agents were already being run from London or from third countries and continued to be run, but with increased difficulty, dur-ing the war. By the spring of 1943 operations against Germany carried out from the United Kingdom had become the responsibility of the P.6 Section, acting partly as a station-in-waiting in London. This was led by Major Reginald Simon Gallienne, a Channel Islander who had studied French and German at Oxford and had then taught in Breslau (Wrocław), Germany, in the late 1930s and had joined SIS from the Intelligence Corps in July 1942 on appointment as P.6. Assisting him in the section were an old Germany hand and interwar veteran of the Service, and an-other officer, who had been born and educated in Hamburg, had worked as a chartered accountant and merchant banker specialising in Germany, and had joined SIS in late 1942.

During the autumn of 1944 the Service began to lay the basis for a re-constituted German section. In November the old Berlin station symbol, '12000', was revived for the officer who had been P.6 since late June 1944. While he stayed in London, Lieutenant Colonel G. M. 'Paul' Paulson, with the 'German' designation '12600', was posted from the SIS station in Paris to command No. 2 Intelligence Unit and make active prepara-tions for penetrating Germany. P.6 officers looked for potential agents among German prisoners-of-war in the United Kingdom, targeting Communists, Social Democrats and others with less obvious reasons for opposing Nazism. But it was slow work and the returns were meagre, as a report in November 1944 made clear. Only four teams had been des-patched. 'Ewen', a member of the Sudeten Social Democratic Party, had been 'launched to Sudetenland from Adriatic' in May 1944: 'Nothing heard since'. 'Chip' and 'Rance', a Briton and a German ex-prisoner: 'Operation launched 10/11 April 44. Contact made with W/T op. but nothing heard since mid-September 44.' 'Chip' was the thirty-five-year-old Philip Frank Chamier, whose father was British and mother German. Having been brought up in Germany, he spoke the language like a native. The Service employed him in 1938–9, when he made several trips to Germany, photographing airfields and gathering 'useful' military information. After working as an interrogator of German prisoners-of-war in Egypt, in February 1942 he offered 'to go to Germany' for SIS, as he wanted 'to do something worthwhile before war is over'. 'I am all for his going,' minuted one officer at Broadway; 'mustn't let slip a chance of getting a man into Germany if he has any potentialities, and can be trusted.' But it was over two years before Chamier and his German-born radio operator, Friedrich Reschke, were dropped into the Reich. Postwar interrogation of German security officials revealed that shortly after they landed Reschke had betrayed Chamier, who was 'very brutally treated' by the Gestapo in a vain effort to get him to work for them as a double agent. There was no certainty about his ultimate fate, though one report asserted that, held in a Berlin prison, he had been killed during an Allied air raid in 1945.[2]

The third team comprised 'Hamish' and 'Geoffrey', two Germans: 'Operation launched from Adriatic 5/6 Sept. 44, but dropped in wrong area and agents were captured by Yugoslav partisans. We await their release.' The fourth team (two Germans again), were also dropped in the wrong place, and dramatically so, 'in Slovakia instead of near Vienna'. One had been picked up by Slovak partisans; of the other there was 'no news'. Even had the agents survived to report back to London, it is not clear that they could have produced much useful intelligence, beyond humdrum 'de visu' (observation) reports of such things as enemy troop movements, the kind of thing which (as demonstrated by Service Clarence in Belgium) only really became useful if supplied in large quantities from a multiplicity of sources. On the other hand, had the Germans been able to dig in and hold their western defence lines, and if the Reich had taken longer to collapse than it actually did, then even low-level tactical information would have been of value to the advancing Allied forces.

In mid-December 1944 a well-placed and experienced German intelligence officer from the Reichssicherheitshauptamt (RSHA: state security organisation) contacted the newly reopened British embassy in Paris and explained that he had been sent by his superior on a special mission to make contact with the British government, mentioning Churchill and Lord (formerly Sir Robert) Vansittart in particular. When asked to explain, he outlined a vague plan for the many Germans who were against Hitler and the continuance of the war to co-operate with the British in avoiding the destruction of Germany and the dismantling of its industrial base by the Russians, Americans and French. This, he added, could lead only to Germany's absorption into the Russian sphere of influence, which would surely be unacceptable to the British. He claimed that, although he did not represent an organised resistance movement, his immediate superior had a very wide range of longstanding contacts in the Wehrmacht, heavy industry and the professions. During an initial debriefing, he produced some useful tactical intelligence about German military dispositions and immediate plans, including sabotage in the Dutch–German border region. He identified some German agents in the Netherlands and France; explained that the Germans had had advance knowledge of the Arnhem landings from captured Dutch agents; fingered a Dutch traitor in Queen Wilhelmina's staff; mentioned a number of operations for infiltrating agents to Ireland by sea; and described plans for a resistance movement within Germany. His mission was believed in Broadway to be 'apparently part of German plans to disrupt Allied relationships'.

The Foreign Office and Anthony Eden (the Foreign Secretary) shared this view and SIS was authorised to debrief him further only on the understanding that the Soviet and United States governments were informed of his arrival, and it was emphasised to them that no attention was being paid to any political suggestions he might make. Frank Foley then questioned him (now given the code-name 'Dictionary') in Paris and concluded that he was 'a character of the highest importance and that provided he is interrogated fully at an early date, his evidence will prove invaluable as it will add enormously to our knowledge of the inner political, military and SD [Sicherheitsdienst] circles in Germany'. On Foley's recommendation Dictionary was brought to the United Kingdom for further interrogation, and over the next six months became SIS's most productive human source of the war on German counter-intelligence matters, producing a mass of detailed organisational and historical information (for example, about Venlo), as well as details of personalities, ranging from leading political figures to individual intelligence officers, much of which could naturally be cross-checked by reference to signals intelligence material.

Over the turn of the year 1944–5 Paulson's unit continued to work steadily on penetrating Germany. Arrangements were made with the help of CSDIC – the Combined Services Detailed Interrogation Centre – to process prisoners-of-war captured by 21st Army Group in Belgium and identify potential recruits for reinfiltration. Lists of possible contacts in twenty-three German cities and towns were prepared. In London, Kenneth Cohen drew up a detailed standard format for monthly progress reports on the number of missions despatched by the unit and their success or failure, the number of recruitments made and reports sent, and so on. A great deal of attention was paid to such operational details as transport, false documentation, civilian clothes and comforts (among other things, P.6 was asked for '3 jars of operational rum and 6 small flasks'). A few more agents were parachuted into Germany with wireless sets in late 1944 and early 1945, but produced little or no intelligence, though after the end of hostilities some of the survivors were retasked as agents in Germany. SOE was simultaneously trying to mount similar drops for a deception operation, 'Periwig', designed to persuade the Germans that there was an active domestic resistance movement supported by the British. This caused something of a clash of priorities between the two agencies, which SIS won, and various restrictions were put on the SOE effort. But there was also co-operation. SIS allowed two of its agents recruited in North Africa, one French and one Alsatian, to be used for an SOE plan (Operation 'Longshanks') aimed at persuading the Germans that Field Marshal von Rundstedt was plotting to overthrow Hitler and was in secret communication with the Allies.

One of the earliest P.6 agents parachuted into Germany was an anti-Nazi Yugoslav who had been recruited by SIS in Uruguay, where he was working in the construction industry. He was brought to the United Kingdom in 1944, trained for undercover work and provided with a false identity as 'Josef Bauer', a 'cement worker' employed in Germany by the Berlin firm of Siemens-Bauunion. On the night of 2/3 October 1944 he and 'Brian', his German-Jewish radio operator, were dropped into southeast Germany, near Heilbronn, from where they had to make their way to Magdeburg, east of Berlin, where Bauer was to be based. His objectives were to report on 'military and air identifications', 'production figures of industrial concerns', 'air-raid damage', 'morale of the population' and 'tendency of the Nazi movement to go underground'. By 11 October the two men had reached Berlin and made contact with an agent of the SIS Stockholm station who smuggled out a secret-writing letter from the agent asking for additional German identity documents and describing Berlin as 'unbeschreiblich kaput' (indescribably finished). But he was arrested by the Gestapo on 28 October, having been denounced by an informer, and Brian was shot the following day at his lodgings. Postwar interrogation of one of the German security officials involved revealed that Bauer had 'taken two poison pills' which failed to work and under questioning had revealed his radio operator's location. There is no conclusive proof of his ultimate fate, though another postwar report presumed that he had subsequently been executed. In late 1944 Broadway estimated the average life of an agent in Germany at three weeks.

As 21st Army Group moved into Germany, No. 2 Intelligence Unit continued to mount short-range operations ahead of its advance. In February, for example, Operation 'Fugitive' was designed to assist 'in the mounting of a feint attack across the [River] Roer', near the Dutch–German frontier just north of Maastricht. Two Dutch agents were put across the enemy lines to spread false information among local villagers about Allied troop concentrations. This they did, and also returned with information about German troop dispositions. The army subsequently expressed themselves as 'highly satisfied with the result'. Paulson noted, however, that, while 'our fundamental job is to help the Army in any way we can', 'this sort of operation does NOT really come into our brief'. SIS was also asked to consider what could be done in the Kiel and Schleswig-Holstein region in view of the possibility that the Army Group might have to fight its way into Denmark. Although an officer with Danish experience was sent out, in April 1945 Kenneth Cohen in London reflected the SIS view that 'generally speaking we had hoped to be released from such operations and from short-term infiltrations which from recent experience are quickly overrun and have little opportunity in the present disorganised state of German formations of providing military intelligence of value'. He was 'most anxious' that Paulson's unit and P.6 'should now begin to concentrate on longer term schemes'.

Reviewing the work of No. 2 Intelligence Unit three weeks before the

German capitulation Paulson confirmed that he had discontinued most 'short-term tactical missions' and now considered that for the immediate future SIS's role in Germany was 'to prepare the ground for future clandestine work by investigating the possibilities of placing long-term agents behind our own lines and in "British" [meaning British-occupied] Germany generally'. He would continue 'the investigation of likely recruits and the search for personal and other documents for which we have already been asked by H.O.', and also 'prepare lists of, and if possible with great care to make contacts with, individuals who may be of use in the future'. Meanwhile plans were made for the post-hostilities SIS organisation in Germany. The headquarters unit was to be called the War Office Liaison Group, with an establishment of thirty, under 12000, and Paulson ('12600') as second-in-command. Headed by Gallienne, No. 2 Intelligence Unit would continue to serve as the link between SIS and the local army headquarters, but it was to be renamed No. 5 CCU (Civil Control Unit).

Scandinavia

Although Finland was allied to Germany from the summer of 1941 until late 1944, during this period some of Harry Carr's old contacts in the Finnish intelligence community kept in touch with him while his station was in exile in Stockholm, as did various Finnish agents reporting on both Finnish and German matters, including Axis shipping movements. Towards the end of 1943 Colonel Reino Hallamaa (head of Finnish signals intelligence) met Carr and told him of plans to evacuate key members of his staff and all his records from Helsinki to Sweden to prevent them falling into the hands of the Soviets should Finland be forced out of the war. Hallamaa proposed that SIS should take over the lot and move them to the United Kingdom, where they could continue to work on the Soviet target. Before returning to Helsinki he gave Carr a German Enigma machine for secret communication with him in Finland (presumably in blissful ignorance of Bletchley Park's successes in breaking Enigma cyphers). Carr immediately raised the proposal with London, where it was considered by Menzies himself, who turned it down flat, on the grounds that he did not want a group of Finns (at

Supreme Headquarters
ALLIED EXPEDITIONARY FORCE
Office of the Supreme Commander

12 July 1945

Dear General Menzies:

I had hoped to be able to pay a visit to Bletchley Park
in order to thank you, Sir Edward Travis, and the members
of the staff personally for the magnificent services which
have been rendered to the Allied cause.

I am very well aware of the immense amount of work and
effort which has been involved in the production of the
material with which you have supplied us. I fully realize
also the numerous setbacks and difficulties with which you
have had to contend and how you have always, by your supreme
efforts, overcome them.

The intelligence which has emanated from you before and
during this campaign has been of priceless value to me.
It has simplified my task as a commander enormously. It
has saved thousands of British and American lives and, in
no small way, contributed to the speed with which the enemy
was routed and eventually forced to surrender.

I should be very grateful, therefore, if you would express
to each and everyone of those engaged in this work from me
personally my heartfelt admiration and sincere thanks for
their very decisive contribution to the Allied war effort.

*Sincerely
Dwight D. Eisenhower*

Major General Sir Stewart G. Menzies
   KCMG, CB, DSO, MC
The War Office
Whitehall
London, SW1

*Thanks from General Eisenhower to Menzies for the
Bletchley Park intelligence which saved 'thousands of
British and American lives'.*

this time officially enemy nationals) working on cryptographic matters in the United Kingdom. Under the code-name 'Stella Polaris', Hallamaa proceeded with the evacuation to Sweden all the same, and offered his records to the French, who gratefully accepted them. Biffy Dunderdale, in turn, learned of this from his French contacts and was able to arrange for SIS to get copies of the material. Thus the Service in the end obtained the material without having to make any embarrassing commitments. After the end of the war, the Swedes found Hallamaa (who had remained in Sweden) a bit of a hot potato, and, at the request of the French, Carr helped to have him smuggled out through Denmark and Germany to France where he went to ground under an assumed name.

On 12 September 1944, in Moscow, Finland signed an armistice with the Allies, following which, as a defeated enemy, it came under the oversight of an Allied Control Commission, led by Colonel General Andrei Zhdanov, the senior Soviet political officer on the Leningrad Front. This was the first of a series of similar postwar Allied military administrations in defeated enemy countries, within which (or alongside which) SIS would seek to operate. In Finland (as elsewhere) the leading position of the Soviets presented particular challenges for the Service, especially since the Foreign Office line at this stage was to avoid making any trouble with the Soviets, who were still, in name at least, allies. Top-secret Foreign Office instructions to the British members of the commission underlined this point. British officers were to establish 'frank and friendly relations' with their Soviet colleagues and refrain from contacts with Finns which were 'likely to give offence to the Soviet authorities', but they were also to note that while 'our ultimate policy is to ensure a Free and independent Finland . . . it must always be remembered that Finland is a conquered country and will have to work her passage home'.[3] The Helsinki station's exile ended in March 1945 when Rex Bosley was posted to reopen it, operating initially under the control of Harry Carr in Stockholm. Bosley was a gifted intelligence officer (nicknamed 'the Ferret'), whom Carr had recruited in Helsinki just before the war and who had been a most effective assistant thereafter. After Carr had been called home in May 1945, following a long postwar leave becoming Controller Northern Area with responsibility for all of Scandinavia in September, Bosley took full charge of the Helsinki station, based initially in the office of the British Political Representative, but in 1947 as Assistant Information Officer in the legation.

Relations with the Soviets affected the management of a liaison contact run by Carr's Helsinki station-in-exile. This was '43931', the former Estonian Director of Military Intelligence, Colonel Richard Maasing, a fierce anti-Communist who had been helped by the Germans to escape from Estonia in 1940, had done some work for the Abwehr and had then come to Sweden, where he offered his services, reporting on German military matters, both to SIS and to the Japanese military attaché in Stockholm, General Makoto Onodera. Maasing was regarded as a valuable contact, though after the German defeat at Stalingrad in early 1943 he began mainly to produce reports (which he supplied not only to the British and Japanese, but to the Swedes as well) on the Red Army as it swept westwards. An old intelligence hand, he had consistently refused to reveal his sub-sources to SIS. In 1942 he fiercely resisted a demand from London that he 'come clean in the whole matter of his organisation'. Observing that obtaining information on German intentions was 'most difficult, dangerous and thankless work', he claimed that he and his men were working for a cause and would continue to do so whether SIS needed the results or not. In late 1944 Onodera's cables to Tokyo (which Bletchley Park were reading) showed that Maasing was more forthcoming about his sources to Onodera than to SIS, prompting renewed concerns about his reliability. Besides, the Foreign Office had banned direct work against the Soviets, and as their importance to the Allied cause grew, London became increasingly nervous about the risk of them finding out that SIS was associating with such an anti-Soviet character. Head Office therefore instructed that Maasing be given an ultimatum to reveal his sub-sources or the relationship be terminated. He again refused and was paid off. Carr later discovered that one of the officers in Head Office who had strongly advocated the ultimatum was Kim Philby, who would presumably have passed on to his Soviet masters whatever Maasing revealed about his sources (whom Carr believed included Communist Party members still in the Soviet Union).

In the later stages of the war the various SIS groups in Sweden handled an increasing amount of counter-espionage work. Peter Falk, the Section V representative posted to Stockholm in April 1943, had quickly established liaison with Norwegian and Polish opposite numbers, as well as the Swedish security police. He also took over from the SOE station two agents with access to the German legation. One of these was a German woman refugee who worked for the German legation's Press Section. Although her access to material of real intelligence interest was limited, her presence within the legation enabled her to report on German personalities and their coming and going, thus providing valuable background and targeting information. She received daily news briefings from Berlin and visited Germany and Finland for Falk. She was never paid, but was given British nationality in 1945 and resettled in the United Kingdom. In April 1944 another specialist Section V officer was posted to Stockholm to concentrate on liaison work with the Danes. Towards the very end of the war, counter-espionage work began to loom larger, as SIS sought to encourage the Scandinavian countries, when hostilities ceased, to round up those of their nationals who had worked as agents for the Germans, or were pro-Nazi. The information which emerged from the Krämer case added to Falk's knowledge of suspects in Sweden and set the basis for increased counter-espionage exchanges with the Swedes, who became more inclined to co-operate as the Allied victory became more certain.[4]

The Bari station

In August 1944 Cuthbert Bowlby, who had been designated H/Med since October 1943, began to consider long-term strategy in the Mediterranean theatre and press London for guidance about this. Reflecting the changed focus of military operations, he proposed concentrating the regional SIS effort in Italy and Istanbul, and running down the Middle East headquarters in Cairo. Arguing that Austria should be the main base for SIS activities throughout south-east Europe after the war, he raised the possibility of working into the Soviet sphere from there, as well as from Italy and Bulgaria. Although he stressed that such operations would not be 'palatable' to the Soviets, he thought that they 'could be undertaken without their knowledge, provided that it is skilfully and methodically thought out'. London considered such planning to be premature. Although he had raised the matter generally with Bowlby the previous September, Menzies now preferred 'to await the experience which we may gain from our first contacts with the 95-landers [Soviets] in our joint missions in the 91-land [Balkan] countries'. Reflecting the unusual consequences of fighting a war alongside a past and potentially future enemy, Marshall-Cornwall realistically thought it unlikely that 'any of our present personnel' in the Mediterranean could be used in renewed operations against the Soviet Union. But, as he observed to John Bruce Lockhart (who had also raised the matter of forward planning), SIS needed to 'draw a clear distinction between post-armistice plans and peace plans'. For the moment all that Bruce Lockhart (and Bowlby) need consider was the former. Planning for the longer term was not their business, but would be conducted in London.

Bruce Lockhart's No. 1 Intelligence Unit was one of the SIS successes of the war. From later 1943, following the Italian capitulation, it had a sub-section liaising with the Italian Military Intelligence service, SIM, which had particularly good right-wing and Italian army sources. Another sub-section, which was kept completely separate, developed contacts among Italian opposition groups, including the Communists. Bruce Lockhart brought over from North Africa a leading party activist – with the appropriate cover-name 'Rosso' – to 'establish the Communist Party in Southern Italy', gave him wireless sets and got him to organise his comrades in the north 'to transmit military intelligence to us'. Bruce Lockhart, moreover, personally fetched Rosso's wife and child 'from a hovel in Tunis' and brought them to Italy, for which, he recalled some years later, 'I suffered an orgy of osculation not only by the wife but by [Rosso] – a very unpleasant memory.' The networks in northern Italy, which proved to be an extremely fruitful source of valuable information, were run by Brian Ashford-Russell, an ex-Commando who had been badly wounded and taken prisoner in North Africa. Having lost the use of his left hand, and being left-handed, he had managed to get himself repatriated under the Geneva Convention as unfit for further military service. He made a tremendous success of his task. Reporting on him in mid-1944, Bowlby described his performance as 'astounding'. 'As far as I can remember,' he wrote to Menzies, 'during my 6 years in your organisation, nothing very much has ever been produced from Italy, which makes the results achieved all the more meritorious. Somehow he has made Italians enthusiastic about this kind of work which is no mean achievement.' Bruce Lockhart reported in August that he ran his section 'like clockwork', was 'very loyal', and 'once given instructions, no matter how much he disagrees with them, he carries the instructions out to the letter'. Here Bruce Lockhart dryly added that he had 'found this a somewhat rarer virtue in [SIS] than in the Army'. Ashford-Russell, however, was not perfect. Bowlby described him as 'a man of extreme (there is no other word) personal ambition which prompts him to aspire to quicker promotion than is the normal practice in this organisation'. But he was also 'extremely able'. Bowlby and Bruce Lockhart, therefore, had 'ignored the former, except to tell 32300 [Ashford-Russell] not to be a B.F. [bloody fool], and concentrate on the latter, our main objective being to obtain information which might assist in defeating the Axis'. In this, he concluded, 'our efforts have been fully rewarded'. Menzies shared Bowlby's concern about Ashford-Russell's personal ambitions. 'Past experience', he wrote, had demonstrated that 'conceit' was 'a dangerous trait for those engaged in our particular trade' and (perhaps with Venlo in mind) he could 'call to mind several disasters from this characteristic, which generally means that the individual despises his opponents, with dire consequences'.

But London continued to worry about 'liaison' with 'Communists, Socialists and Patriots'. Bruce Lockhart explained that the reason why SIS had to 'remain on friendly terms' with the Communists in the liberated area was 'partly in order to obtain recruits', but 'far more to obtain access to their organisations North of the [enemy] line', adding that it was 'fair to say that 80% of the information coming from North Italy is obtained from Communist, Socialist and Patriotic organisations' and it was 'doubtful whether without their help we could even have got our network started'. Lest the station should be suspected of having gone off the rails politically, in July 1944 he reassured Bowlby he was satisfied that 'in our relations with the Communists and Socialists', SIS had not 'gone beyond what was strictly necessary for obtaining military information'.

Ashford-Russell ran most of these networks, and through him SIS provided the Italian Communists with communications equipment and codes for them to report back on enemy order-of-battle information, but the Service also routinely monitored all Communist signals traffic. By this means, and through a British officer openly based in the Party headquarters in Naples (though not formally acknowledged as being SIS), the Service gathered much political intelligence as well. Shortly before the fall of Rome in June 1944 Palmiro Togliatti, General Secretary of the Communist Committee for Liberated Italy and future leader of the post-war Italian Communist Party, arrived from Moscow. Although he ejected the SIS representative, he promised that Communists would continue to supply information, but from now on this was limited to military matters. In the spring of 1945, when it was clear that the Germans were beaten, and much of northern Italy was in Communist hands, Togliatti terminated the wartime marriage of convenience with SIS. While the volume of intelligence from Communists fell off in early 1945, other left-wing groups continued to supply a considerable quantity of information through Ashford-Russell's head agent in Milan, who was a political activist. From May to September 1944, in a series of reports marked by this agent's 'wide experience . . . of men and their problems', he covered the partisan organisation and operations, the dispositions and morale of the Germans, Italian Fascist forces, propaganda, politics, economics, the Church and the press. In October, having briefly come out to Rome for consultations, he and a colleague were infiltrated back behind enemy lines in the unhappily named operation 'Wop/Risky' (a title both offensively inappropriate and insecure, since the point of a code-name is ideally to bear no relation whatsoever to the operation in question). They were flown from Bari to Lyons in France, and proceeded to Chamonix where they climbed to 12,000 feet and on foot crossed a corner of Switzerland into Italy. Since it was 'undoubtedly the hardest' mountain crossing, the Germans did not 'consider it worth watching'. This agent continued to report for the first four months of 1945, until the end of the war in Italy.

Another of Ashford-Russell's agents (not, in this case, a Communist), 'Dragonfly', had been recruited in South America and operated in Rome for four months during early 1944. He 'used to lunch regularly' with Herbert Kappler, the SS chief in the city, 'and report back to us on the meetings'. He sent large numbers of messages by wireless, and, despite being warned of the dangers of enemy direction finding, refused to cut down the volume of signals, arguing that 'risks had sometimes to be taken and he would not abandon his post at this critical moment (shortly before the fall of Rome)'. In the end he was caught red-handed (though 'while the door was being forced open he had time to burn all his papers'), and was shot at Dachau several months later.

Reflecting afterwards on the success of his Bari operations into northern Italy, Bruce Lockhart recalled that by the end of the war they had had 'about 30 or 40 wireless sets coming up daily giving German order of battle and troop movements'. This had made them 'somewhat swollen headed' and 'we thought we knew all the answers', but 'we didn't realise how easy it was being made for us', as army headquarters could audit SIS product against very good prisoner-of-war interrogation intelligence, 'first-rate aerial photography and first-rate Sigint'. This 'admirable collateral' meant that 'as soon as an agent or group started to send something unlikely or improbable all lights flashed at G.H.Q. and straight away the information was shown up as being phoney'.

Bruce Lockhart's other section was headed by Major James Millar, who was posted to Bari in January 1944. Millar, a Scot educated at St John's College, Cambridge, had joined the Service in March 1939 and had served briefly in Berlin and Zagreb, before being posted to Bari to work on Yugoslavia and Central Europe. This included 'Germany south of River Main, Czechoslovakia, Hungary and Austria', though the penetration of Germany was carefully described only as 'an ultimate objective'. Within six months, Bowlby, by now himself installed at Naples, reported that Millar (along with Ashford-Russell) had 'produced excellent results' and 'merited several bouquets from our local customers'. Yugoslavia was another of those places where SIS had to work with Communists. The domestic resistance movement was dominated by two mutually opposed groups: the Partisans, led by Josep Broz, 'Tito', the prewar leader of the Yugoslav Communist Party; and the virulently anti-Communist Četniks, under the royalist General Draža Mihailović. Although at the start the two groups had to some extent co-operated, and Mihailović had been backed by the Allies, signals intelligence and reports from SOE missions in Yugoslavia gradually revealed that the Četniks were increasingly collaborating with Axis forces against the shared Communist foe. Churchill became convinced that the leftist Partisans were much more likely to draw German troops away from the west and in February 1944, therefore, the government resolved to withdraw backing for Mihailović and support only Tito.[5]

In SIS, which seriously began to target Yugoslavia only after the Italian surrender, differences remained about whom to support among the resistance. For some, old anti-Bolshevik habits died hard. In April 1944, following a visit to Bari, Bowlby worried that Millar and his staff were 'far too Tito-conscious'. He complained that 'pictures of Tito cover the walls' of Millar's office and he asked London to send out large photographs of King George VI and Queen Elizabeth, 'to be hung in some prominent place' in the office. This, he felt, 'should have the desired effect of intimating to 35,600 [Millar] that there are limits to local partisanship'. Bruce Lockhart appreciated Bowlby's point about Tito, whom he considered was certainly a 'tool of the Russians'. He argued, nevertheless, that Millar was right 'in putting all his money on Tito' as this was 'undoubtedly his best chance of obtaining good military information'. So it was, and most of the intelligence which SIS acquired about Yugoslavia came from overt SIS and SOE liaison with the Partisans. As Bruce Lockhart noted in May 1945, although it was 'not an SIS problem in the precise sense of the word', the Yugoslav intelligence which Millar produced was nevertheless 'consistently on a very high level' and 'at one period YM [the army] and YA [the air force] were almost entirely dependent on the intelligence produced by 35600 [Millar] for their planning'.

Worries about left-wing politics affected individual SIS officers as well, including one of the men in Millar's section, Kenneth Syers, who had been recruited into the Service in late 1942. Educated at King's College, Cambridge, he had been a journalist before the war, then a British Council lecturer in Yugoslavia from 1939 to 1941, and spoke fluent Serbo-Croat. In August 1943 he was dropped into Yugoslavia as an officer-agent, was brought out in November 1943 and served in Bari before spending another spell in Yugoslavia from May to September 1944, after which he was posted home to Section I (Foreign Office liaison) in Head Office. He had first come to the notice of David Footman (head of Section I) in the latter part of 1943 'when he sent us a series of reports on the political aspects of the Partisan movement', the quality of which was, in Footman's experience of political reporting, 'quite unique'. 'They were endorsed by [Fitzroy] Maclean,' the British representative with Tito, and made 'a considerable impression on the Foreign Office including the strong pro-Mihailovist element then there'. His reports, in both quantity and quality, had been 'of greater value than perhaps those of any other officer in our Mediterranean station'. But, on his posting to London, Syers's political opinions came under close scrutiny. While Footman admitted that they were 'undoubtedly Left', he was prepared to believe Syers 'when he says he is not a member of the Communist Party' and the very fact that he had had 'trouble with the Partisan authorities seems to show that this is correct'.

Valentine Vivian was not happy about Syers, who was, he said, among a number of SIS officers who were 'so far Left as to be scarcely distinguishable from Communists'. Although, having looked at Syers's file, he found no evidence to support his contention, in November 1944 he nevertheless asked Roger Hollis of MI5 to look into Syers's background. Towards the end of the year, Syers announced his intention to marry an SIS secretary, who had worked most recently at Bari. When Rex Howard checked up on her, he discovered that she was a niece by marriage of Maxim Litvinov, the prewar Soviet Foreign Minister, a fact which, curiously, did not appear on her file. Vivian then raised the matter with Kim Philby, who also wrote to Hollis. Hollis replied in January 1945 that MI5 had no record of her and 'nothing of great relevance' on Syers. Two months later, however, Hollis reported that they had evidence that connected Syers to 'a certain Communist in the Army Education Corps named Hobsbawm, who was before the war an undergraduate at Cambridge' (and who subsequently became a very distinguished historian). When Vivian passed Hollis's letter on to Philby, saying 'I don't much like the look of this,' Philby rallied to Syers's defence, though in terms which seem remarkable, given the benefit of hindsight and his own role as a Soviet agent in SIS:

> Syers seems to be remarkably unfortunate in his choice of friends! I have had several conversations with him recently and he has consistently reiterated his intention of taking up journalism at the earliest possible opportunity. It would seem, therefore, his connections with Communists are less sinister than might be supposed, since it is hardly conceivable that the C.P.G.B. [Communist Party of Great Britain], or any Soviet organisation, would dream of letting him leave S.I.S. once he had got his foot well inside it. Moreover, he makes little attempt to conceal his interest in Marxism and Marxists – an attitude which is hardly consistent with sinister designs.

In July Philby still professed that he was at a loss to know what to advise about Syers and suggested pressing Hollis for more information. This time Hollis was more forthright, noting further contacts between Syers and Eric Hobsbawm and at least one other 'leading Party member'. He advised that Syers and other similar left-leaning officers in SIS should be allowed to 'return to journalism or whatever work they wish to follow as soon as this can be done'. So it was to be. Syers, the suspected Communist sympathiser, left to work for the Liberal-leaning *News Chronicle*, while Philby, the unsuspected Soviet spy, stayed on.

Dealing with the Soviets and penetrating the Balkans

SIS's relations with the Soviet Union during the Second World War were extremely problematic. The USSR and its global ambitions, having been a major target for SIS since the revolutionary years, remained so for the period from the Nazi–Soviet Pact of August 1939 until Hitler's invasion of the Soviet Union in June 1941. But, all of a sudden, the USSR became an ally, and a British mission was sent to Moscow to underpin good inter-Allied relations, facilitate support for the Soviet war effort and, it was hoped, encourage the exchange of (among other things) information which might be of mutual benefit. Right at the start, too, it was also seen as an intelligence opportunity. In July 1941 Admiral Godfrey, the Director of Naval Intelligence, wrote to Menzies about the possibility of embedding intelligence officers in Moscow who could work on acquiring information about the Soviet navy. It was, he declared, a 'golden opportunity to obtain that intelligence regarding the U.S.S.R. which we have lacked for so long'. But there were worries in Broadway that any such operation 'would only result in compromise'. Menzies argued that 'the Anglo-Russian alliance against Germany' had 'not altered my policy of endeavouring to obtain U.S.S.R. Armed Force information', but Godfrey would appreciate 'that I have to tread very warily as regards any further steps I may take'. The British ambassador and mission in Moscow, he continued, were 'most anxious that nothing should be done which may in any way impede their efforts towards a successful collaboration with the U.S.S.R. authorities, the result of which may have much influence in winning the war'. Despite the somewhat elliptical language (and demonstrating that Menzies was clearly alive to the political ramifications of the proposal), this was a definite SIS refusal to meet a direct request from a customer department.

Intelligence, however, was central to the new Anglo-Soviet relationship. Having rallied to the Soviet side in the summer of 1941, there was actually very little practical assistance that London could offer, and when an Allied supply mission, including United States representatives, arrived in Moscow in the autumn it became abundantly obvious that the bulk of any available war supplies would come from the USA. In the meantime, as Bradley F. Smith has observed, 'out of a combination of necessity and desperation', the British Military Mission in Moscow under General

Noel Mason-Macfarlane 'always came back to intelligence exchange as the best available method of aiding the Russians and demonstrating Britain's military prowess and importance'.[6] But the best British intelligence was based on Ultra material, and there was never any suggestion that the USSR could be let into the secret in the way the USA had been earlier in the year. Menzies was instructed to 'work out a scheme' for transmitting 'highly secret information' to Macfarlane, who, in turn, was told 'to pass on nothing to the Russians likely to compromise our sources of information'. Apart from the marking 'from most reliable sources', Ultra material, which was transmitted to Moscow over a dedicated, secure SIS wireless link, was paraphrased and massaged to obscure its origin. When Churchill pressed Menzies in July 1941 to send Ultra-based material to Moscow, Menzies observed that the immediacy of the information (which was of course one of its greatest strengths) could jeopardise the source if it were sent without some delay. 'It would be impossible', he wrote, 'for any agent to have secured such information' and transmitted it so quickly. He therefore arranged for the gist to be buried among other War Office material, and the Soviets to be tipped off that SIS had a 'well-placed source in Berlin'.[7]

Even so, Menzies worried about the security of Ultra and the volume of material being provided. In September 1941, on a copy of an Air Intelligence signal to Moscow containing from 'most reliable sources' (evidently German air force Enigma decrypts) information about Luftwaffe dispositions on the Eastern Front, he minuted: 'I am very <u>concerned</u> about these comm[unication]s & I think [we] sh[oul]d refuse to let this type of info[rmatio]n go forward.' Intelligence security did not just apply to the Soviets. In August 1941 London sent Macfarlane a complaint from the Turks that their military attaché in Moscow 'was getting very little information from our M.A.'. Since it was 'very important to maintain good relations with the Turks', London requested that Macfarlane pass on 'what information you feel possible'. Menzies thought that this might be 'dangerous' and asked Commander Denniston at Bletchley Park about Turkish cypher security. Denniston reported that 90 per cent of the Turks' diplomatic signals and 'all' military attaché messages between Moscow and Ankara were 'practically fully legible . . . Hence it may be assumed that any information passed to the Turkish Ambassador or M.A. may be read by the enemy.'

In September 1941 SOE signed an agreement with the Soviet intelligence agency, the NKVD, to co-operate in subversive activities in all countries outside their respective spheres of influence. An SOE mission was established in Moscow under Colonel George Hill, an old Russian hand and longstanding anti-Bolshevik who had worked for SIS during the post-revolutionary period and rejoined the Service in Section D at the start of the war, subsequently transferring into SOE. In the face of the German push towards Moscow during the winter of 1941, all foreign missions were evacuated to Kuibyshev, a provincial city on the River Volga. Here Hill cheered up his colleagues by inventing ingenious vodka cocktails.[8] While the NKVD were aware of Hill's role, there was also an unavowed SIS representative in the party who began to develop contacts in the parallel Polish and Czechoslovak military missions for intelligence. The most productive of these was Colonel Leon Bortnowski, code-named 'Perch', who was the Polish intelligence service representative in the USSR from August 1941 until September 1942. Although Bortnowski was avowed to the NKVD he offered to pass on information to SIS from his own Polish network and released Polish prisoners-of-war. A shopping list was prepared in London, with the Air Section asking for information about Russian aircraft production and the transfer east of aircraft factories. The Naval Section wanted Bortnowski to ask the Russians 'what warships, especially battleships, aircraft carriers and cruisers are building in Japan' and if the Germans had 'any gas, other than those known in last war'; the Economic Section were primarily interested in oil production and the 'condition of the railway system'; and the Political Section requested information about morale, 'with special reference to whether there is any serious or organised opposition to the Soviet regime'. Bortnowski was able to supply some economic material, but there were complaints at Broadway about its quantity and that he was unable to respond to supplementary enquiries. For one officer this merely illustrated 'how unsatisfactory' it was 'to rely on Foreign representatives to get us our information', as the source was both 'in a delicate position' and 'not under our control'. 'We, as an organisation,' he continued, 'should and must rely primarily on our own intelligence collecting weapons rather than those of our Allies, friends or neutrals.'

In December 1941, however, Bortnowski did supply what were described as 'authentic Russian documents', Soviet General Staff intelligence reports concerning Turkey, Afghanistan and India, which showed that the USSR was 'very well informed about British activities in India and elsewhere', and for which London sent a special message of thanks.[9] In May 1942 the possibility was raised of using Polish agents to 'find out something' about the 'policy and present activities' of the Comintern. David Footman in Broadway appreciated that 'our representative has, of course, to watch his own step very carefully in Soviet Russia, but the Poles might not have the same diffidence about making these enquiries'. Valentine Vivian saw merit in the proposal. 'We should, I think, be wrong', he wrote, 'not to keep abreast of Comintern (a) Policy & (b) activities. The directives we have seen to the C.P.G.B., and the tactics now being employed, show that Communism may at the end or <u>towards</u> the end of the war be a force to reckon with.' But, he added, 'policy with regard to anything Russian' is 'delicate'. Frederick Winterbotham, now in the counter-espionage Section V, thought the whole proposal was 'very undesirable'. 'Our man in Kuibishev' might pick up 'scraps', he argued, but this 'would in no way compensate for the risk of the Soviet authorities discovering, or suspecting, what he was up to'. Faced with this opposition, Vivian dropped the notion.

In December 1942 it was proposed to send an avowed SIS officer to the Soviet Union to act as Hill's assistant and work on the 'exchange of information' with the Soviets, though Broadway recognised that this would be a 'difficult task'. All the Allies found the Soviets hard to deal with in this respect. Colonel Stanisław Gano, the Polish intelligence chief, said that while he had 'supplied the Russians with a fair amount', he had 'received nothing in return except questionnaires of a very childish nature', and Hatton-Hall, head of the Army Section at Broadway, regretfully observed that it was 'hopeless to expect the Russians to reciprocate. We must be prepared to get nothing back.' Lieutenant Cecil Barclay, a twenty-eight-year-old sailor who had been hired by SIS in 1938 to assist in Section X (the telephone-tapping department), and had subsequently stayed on at Head Office, was posted to Moscow in June 1943. Over the next two years he acted as the conduit for signals intelligence material, and, as had been expected, most of the traffic was one-way. In November 1944, however, he was given some captured German code-books, of which one ('Schlüsselanleitung zum Rufzeichenschlüssel' – 'key instruction to call-sign key') provoked great excitement at Bletchley Park. It would, declared the Director, Commander Edward Travis (Denniston's successor), 'mean that one of the biggest difficulties of the moment will be solved. In other words, Barclay has got a catch.'

On 13 October 1943, Vivian told Peter Loxley that 'about six months ago' he had obtained Menzies's approval to establish a small unit (Section IX) to concentrate on the 'illegal' or underground aspects of the Communist movement in foreign countries, and to handle cases of Communist or Soviet penetration and espionage. An MI5 officer, J. C. Curry, had been seconded to the section and SIS now wanted to adopt 'a cautious, forward policy' of tackling this target, including the exchange of information with allies. Recognising 'the extreme delicacy of the matter', Vivian assured Loxley that 'few have been made aware of the nature' of this work. Sir Orme Sargent (Deputy Under-Secretary at the Foreign Office) was immediately enthusiastic: 'I quite agree to the proposal . . . in fact, I am surprised that this branch of our intelligence services should have been allowed to fall into desuetude.' Sargent was keen to know how far Communist organisations operating in the Balkans had taken root among the population, 'and how far they are being supported by Moscow'. Loxley therefore quickly told Vivian that the Foreign Office had no objection to SIS developing Section IX's work, 'provided that discretion is observed, and provided that you do not do anything in the U.S.S.R. itself (despite Soviet espionage in this country)'.[10]

As Soviet forces moved towards Berlin in April 1945, Barclay suggested that the 'time had come' to start on counter-espionage within Germany, and asked Broadway if there were 'any special addresses in Berlin which interest you and what do you want from them'? He could also pass to the Soviets lists of names of the more important German intelligence officers 'suspected of remaining in Berlin', or (and here he reflected prevailing concerns that the Nazis would seek to preserve some clandestine organisation after their defeat) staying 'elsewhere in east to work underground'. London replied with a list of eighteen intelligence service addresses in the Berlin area, along with nineteen 'Mil. Amt' names, including that of the organisation's head, Walter Schellenberg. (The Militärisches Amt had been created in June 1944 when Himmler's SD had swallowed up the Army Intelligence Abwehr.) There were also nine officers' names specifically from Amt VI (the overseas branch of the SD), including 'Obersturmbannführer Eichmann'. While London had 'no definite evidence of a stay-behind network being set up in territory occupied by the Russians', they added seven names of officers 'known to have been employed in intelligence work against Russia'. Barclay's raising of the issue and Broadway's ready supply of names and addresses were a product of that brief period at the end of the war when it was believed that Anglo-Soviet intelligence co-operation (such as it was) would continue, if only in the pursuit of Nazism.

That this might not be the case should already have been apparent from experience in the Balkans and Eastern Europe, where the insertion of SIS teams following the liberation of countries by Soviet forces proved to be extremely problematic. As early as the spring of 1944 Harold Gibson had secured Menzies's cautious approval to take soundings in Turkey, 'with a view to obtaining our representation in all Russian occupied Balkan territories'. Gibson then prepared a paper for Likhterov, the Soviet military attaché, suggesting that SIS could 'offer certain facilities and contacts' in areas occupied or likely to be occupied by the Soviets, which could be 'exploited to mutual advantage'. Although Likhterov had been encouraging (if non-committal), in August London directed that liaison with the Soviets would be handled by Barclay in Moscow. In the meantime Gibson continued planning for SIS representation in Romania and Bulgaria. On 23 August the twenty-two-year-old King Michael of Romania, who had seized power from Marshal Ion Antonescu, surrendered to the Soviets and the following day declared war on Germany, thus committing his army against the Axis forces still in the country. The following day Gibson sent the first of several increasingly pressing requests to London for permission to proceed to Romania. 'In my opinion,' he wrote, 'it is important to stake our claim quickly and no time should be lost in moving forward as soon as possible.' From Naples, Cuthbert Bowlby urged that a party be sent at once. On 27 August Gibson asserted that the Soviets were 'badly in need' of operational intelligence from Romania, which his contacts could help supply. This 'should surely help justify' his presence or that of another SIS officer. But London was discouraging. The following day Menzies signalled that the Foreign Office had promised not to despatch personnel into the zone of Soviet military operations without Moscow's explicit agreement and Gibson was instructed to stay put. There was better news about Bulgaria, which announced its withdrawal from the war on 26 August 1944. Two days later Menzies announced that the Foreign

Office had lifted its objection to the despatch of an SIS party and instructed Gibson to make preparations, but not to take action just yet.

In London, meanwhile, the Foreign Secretary, Anthony Eden, approved a proposal that SIS should be allowed to operate in all liberated territories, but with 'one stipulation', that 'no party should be sent into Roumania in advance of the official mission' in order 'to avoid possible complications with the Russians'.[11] Gibson continued to lament the 'loss of a great opportunity', especially since the Americans in the shape of OSS were planning to send in a party. He was further exercised by the hold-up in permission to enter Bulgaria. 'Regarded from this end,' he signalled in September, 'the delay in moving S.I.S. parties into the Balkans has been catastrophic,' and the Service had 'lost a unique opportunity of getting there first . . . and being on the spot to pick up and direct important contacts'. SIS had instead 'been forestalled by our go-ahead American colleagues who could act unrestrictedly and were not afraid to do so. Result is they have strong and energetic teams in Bulgaria and Roumania already functioning to good purpose.' Menzies would not budge about Romania, though he was prepared to let Gibson go to Bulgaria. In the case of the former, while he appreciated Gibson's 'disappointment', the Foreign Office line was clear, and he 'must abide by the higher policy laid down'. As to the latter, the wisdom of London's caution was soon demonstrated. In mid-September Gibson and a small SIS staff moved to Sofia by road from Istanbul. But on 25 September they (and the OSS mission in Bulgaria) were peremptorily expelled by the Soviet authorities.

Echoing Gibson's feelings, Cuthbert Bowlby wrote a 'slightly despondent' letter to Menzies regretting the British failure to exploit the situation in Bulgaria and Romania. SIS, he said, had 'naturally come in for a good deal of criticism', which he had staved off by citing the Foreign Office ban. Nevertheless, surprise had been expressed that a secret organisation such as SIS should be prevented from operating anywhere it wished at any time regardless of official restrictions: 'What, they say, is the use of being a secret organisation if you are tied by the same rules which govern open activities?' Here Bowlby was voicing a common attitude about SIS (and similar agencies), but one which dangerously confused operational matters with policy considerations. With the former, secret operations might well not be bound 'by the same rules' which governed 'open activities'. But the latter was entirely different. Menzies, who claimed to

Bowlby that he was 'just as disappointed' by the turn of events, carefully observed: 'You must realise . . . that at no time, and especially not in war time, can our functions be carried out with a total disregard of Government policy.' In this particular case, moreover, there could have been 'very little prospect of any penetration' remaining unknown to the Soviets. The Foreign Office feared that the entry of intelligence personnel into an area which could properly be described as within 'the zone of military operations of our allies' might have been resented 'as bitterly as we should resent the unannounced arrival of 95-land [Russian] personnel in, let us say, 13-land [Belgium]'. In the event, moreover, the Foreign Office's apprehensions had been justified by events, and the suggestion that the Soviets had welcomed the Americans and were surprised by the British failure to appear on the scene was 'now shown to be wholly at variance' with the official view taken in Moscow.

Iberia

SIS in both Spain and Portugal played a central role in the hugely effective double-agent operations which played such a major part in the successful deception of the enemy, over for example the Torch landings in North Africa in November 1942, the invasion of Sicily in July 1943 and Operation Overlord in June 1944. While the running of double agents was in practice a joint SIS–MI5 responsibility (through the XX Committee), MI5 took primary charge of those operating in the United Kingdom, and SIS of those in foreign countries. During 1944, for example, some 113 double agents were operating under Section V's control. One of the most successful of all wartime double agents, the Spaniard Juan Pujol, code-named 'Garbo', was first handled by an SIS Section V officer, Ralph Jarvis, in Portugal after a tip-off from an American diplomat. Pujol had been taken on to spy in Britain by the Germans in Madrid, but he had only got as far as Lisbon, from where he supplied a series of fictitious reports, which he told Jarvis he collated from British guidebooks, maps and newspapers. SIS brought Pujol to England in April 1942, following which he was run by MI5, and became the Germans' apparently most successful agent, with a network of twenty-seven sub-agents across the country. Up to March 1943, when he acquired a wireless, all his reports

were conveyed by secret writing in letters notionally carried by an airline employee working on the London–Lisbon run, but actually organised entirely by SIS, as was the transmission of his German case-officer's
replies.[12]

A particularly good example of a double-cross operation run almost
entirely by SIS was that of agent 'Ecclesiastic', a glamorous twenty-two-
year-old Central European woman living in Lisbon. Having worked for
a while for the Polish intelligence service targeting Italian diplomats, by
June 1944 (when she was taken on by SIS) she was the mistress of an
Abwehr officer, Franz Koschnik. Perhaps reflecting the stage of the war,
along with a 'certain amount of patriotism' and 'financial reasons', among
the motives ascribed to her by the Lisbon station was: 'wants to keep her
head above water by working for allies'. Having concluded that there were
'obvious possibilities in this lady', SIS intended at first simply to achieve
'penetration of Abwehr', but within a week the possibility was raised of
her passing 'foodstuff' – deception information – to the Germans, since
another double agent, 'Artist', had reported that Koschnik was 'short of
material'. Koschnik, for his part, wanted Ecclesiastic to cultivate British
and Dutch aircrew flying between Portugal and Britain to obtain reports
about the damage caused by V-1 flying bombs.

In August SIS arranged for her to get a secretarial job at an office staffed
by British RAF personnel (in civilian clothes) which had been set up
to provide technical assistance to the Portuguese government under the
Azores Agreement of October 1943. Although there were in fact no 'technical air secrets' in the office, it was assumed that the Germans could
'easily be led to believe that such material' was to be found there. One of
Ecclesiastic's case-officers was the flirtatious 'Klop' Ustinov (father of the
actor Peter Ustinov), an MI5 man posted to SIS's Section V in Lisbon.
His speculative eye for a pretty woman and keen appreciation of female
charm is evident in the report of his first meeting with her. He dryly
observed that while Ecclesiastic considered the cultivation of her lover as
'part of her official duties', these duties were 'not too onerous'. Koschnik,
he deduced, was 'very fond of the girl, and it needs a woman much less
womanly than Ecclesiastic to resent such homage to both her physical
charm and no doubt also to her mental quality'. Ecclesiastic, he added,
was 'very intelligent indeed' and she clearly enjoyed 'the game of mobiliz-
ing her ample female resources against normal male instincts'. This, he

asserted, explained why her 'appreciation of the rôle we are assigning to her is at present more romantic than practical and why her cohabitation with Koschnick [sic] has – from our point of view – not yielded greater results so far. I made it clear to her that to live with the Abwehr is not quite helpful enough and that more concrete results must be achieved before her activities for us can be termed a success.'[13]

Although Ustinov had initially concluded that Ecclesiastic would serve better as a 'transmitting' than a 'receiving station', she in fact proved to be a real success in both directions right through to the end of the war. Up to the early spring of 1945 (when Koschnik's appetite for information fell off markedly), Ecclesiastic provided him with a stream of material prepared by Flight Lieutenant Charles Cholmondeley of MI5, including details about a new aeroplane and other developments (some on crumpled-up pieces of paper apparently fished from waste-paper baskets); convincingly scribbled notes of overheard phone conversations; and letters containing aero-technical gossip (on authentic Air Ministry notepaper) to Air Commodore Fullard (head of the RAF mission), one of which Koschnik had Ecclesiastic herself photograph before she returned it to the office.[14] Perhaps for insurance, to show Ecclesiastic that he had evidence which could be used against her, he himself photographed her doing this, giving her a copy. She, however, passed it on to SIS and this rare image of a spy at work survives in the archives. In January 1945 a letter to Fullard from the genuine Air Commodore J. M. 'Jack' Easton at the Air Ministry was planted as part of the Ministry of Home Security's 'V.2 deception plan'. In it Easton complained (among other things) about far-fetched enemy claims of damage to central London. 'The best of the bunch is the total destruction of Piccadilly Circus and Leicester Square which the enemy propaganda put out some time ago. I can assure you', he wrote, 'that the Cafe Royal is still in business, and I will treat you to lunch there when you are next home.' But even deception had its limits, as the covering note to SIS in Lisbon made clear: 'Easton would like to add that the invitation to lunch does not repeat not hold good and is merely inserted to add verisimilitude to the letter.'

From September 1944 to the end of February 1945 Ustinov met Ecclesiastic twenty-six times, passing her 'foodstuff' and receiving a steady supply of information about Koschnik and his Abwehr colleagues. At the beginning of December, Lisbon reported that she was 'now very valuable from the penetration point of view'. London agreed 'heartily' and raised the possibility of Ecclesiastic targeting another Abwehr officer, Rudolf Baumann, whom they suspected might be organising German sabotage activities in France. She rose to the challenge. On 9 January 1945 Ustinov reported that she was 'continuing to work on him . . . in the direction of softening his belief in victory', but 'even two prolonged kissing bouts at his flat, one of which lasted 35 minutes, have not had the desired effect'. Although Baumann does not seem to have succumbed to Ecclesiastic's charms, Koschnik remained infatuated. By mid-April, with Germany on the verge of final defeat, while he had lost all interest in Ecclesiastic's 'foodstuff', 'his interest in source as a woman remains as great as ever'. As Fullard's office was closing down at the end of April, Ecclesiastic's position was about to alter. But the Lisbon station congratulated themselves on a successful operation. 'A year's activity', they reported, had 'passed without major upheavals and setbacks. Source, not unlike the nymph Arethusa, emerges clear and unpolluted (from the intelligence point of view) for new tasks in other spheres.' The first of these, they thought, might be to 'follow and report on the twilight of the TLW [Technische/ Luftwaffe] god in Lisbon'.[15]

17

Asia and the end of the war

SIS was not as successful in the Far East as it was in the West. This partly stemmed from the fact that between the wars it had been even more starved of resources there than elsewhere. But the intelligence challenge was also much greater. Though this was never completely so, indigenous peoples in enemy-occupied territory across Asia were in general less likely to help the Allied cause than was the case in Europe. Differences of race and ethnicity meant that there were in any case fewer potential officers or agents who could melt into the background. The sometimes uneasy Allied relationship with both the Nationalist Chinese and the Americans posed further problems from time to time, and the apparent successes of SOE in the Far East tended to eclipse the less dramatic work of SIS. But the Service did have achievements out East, especially in Burma from 1944 onwards, ship-watching along the south Chinese coast and in anti-Japanese work elsewhere in the region, though much of the latter information came from liaison sources.

The Japanese onslaught

As in Europe, SIS's experience in the Far East in the early war years was one of retreat, and following the Japanese onslaught which began on 7 December 1941 with the surprise attack on Pearl Harbor, Hong Kong fell on Christmas Day and Singapore on 15 February 1942. SIS and other British personnel in Peking and Shanghai were interned by the Japanese. Frank Hill, Harry Steptoe and other staff were eventually repatriated in the autumn of 1942. Alex Summers, who got his last radio signal out of Hong Kong on 26 December 1941, was imprisoned with many others of the British community in the Stanley Camp for the rest of the war. His security was evidently better than that of some SIS colleagues. While he managed to maintain his cover as simply a local businessman, he reported afterwards that during his captivity the Japanese 'made several inquiries as to the whereabouts of 28002 [Charles Drage]'. Godfrey Denham and his colleagues left Singapore in early January 1942. 'There was a wholesale burning of some of our records,' he reported from India at the end of March, 'but 28,002 successfully managed to get away practically all of his most important records which I may mention here have proved of great value since our advent in India.'

Understandably enough, the catastrophic defeats of 1941–2 were followed by a period of recrimination and backbiting in which SIS got its share of the blame. While the Service's intelligence from Japan itself had clearly been pretty poor, there is some evidence of accurate reporting on forward Japanese dispositions in the latter half of 1941. Responding in March 1942 to criticisms levelled by the Australian General Gordon Bennett of poor British intelligence,[1] SIS asserted that twenty-one reports on Japan's 'preparations for Southward Move' had been issued to the War Office and the Far East Combined Bureau between 30 November and 7 December 1941. These described a steady build-up of Japanese army and air force units in Indo-China, and included a report in early November that Japanese reinforcements 'for ultimate despatch to Indo-China' were arriving at Hainan Island (south-west China), and another in mid-November that the 'Japanese [were] preparing to attack both Thailand and Burma'. On 5 December a source had reported thirty transports at Camranh Bay in southern Vietnam (one of the Japanese assembly points). 'Strength of troops ashore estimated 48,000,' continued the report, 'with 250 aircraft.'

In August 1943, reviewing his work at Singapore, J. H. Green maintained that his liaison efforts had been particularly successful. Emphasising the personal factor, he reported that his liaison with Dutch and French colonial intelligence organisations in the Netherlands East Indies and French Indo-China was 'founded entirely upon friendship and mutual trust'. When he began in 1938, official contacts with the British services had been prohibited by the Dutch (in keeping with their policy of neutrality), but he 'commenced liaison with my friend Lovink' (the local Dutch intelligence chief), who organised a false passport for Green to visit Batavia (Jakarta). The Governor-General of the colony was in on the relationship and (rather like General van Oorschot in The Hague) turned a blind eye to the contacts 'provided that neither the Dutch nor the British Service Chiefs should know of it'. But the connection produced useful material. Lovink's signals intelligence branch provided analysis of Japanese broadcast weather forecasts 'as to time and place of invasion', as well as two captured German cyphers and 'two Chinese ciphers required by our cryptologists', which were handed over to the signals intelligence section in Singapore. Green claimed that in 1941 his French liaison in Indo-China, code-named 'Sectude', had kept in clandestine contact using an unauthorised radio. From him 'we received ample warning of the attack upon Siam [Thailand] and Malaya. A two months' notice, a one month's notice, a week's notice and two days' notice. The last warning gave the correct date and the actual places selected for the landings and the strength and movement of the enemy invasion fleet.' Following the declaration of war, we received 'full and last minute details of their [Japanese] Air and Military reinforcements to Indo-China and Siam and the location and construction of operational bases'. Green was 'extremely proud of these successes. The full warning of the invasion', he claimed, 'was possibly the S.I.S.'s most spectacular success in the Far East over a period of years.' But, however good this intelligence may have been (and in the circumstances it was understandable if Green hyped it up a bit), it could not be of much use without sufficient military forces in the region and their appropriate deployment. 'Had we been in a position to adequately oppose the Japs or to advance against them,' he wrote, 'our organisation and the information given would have been invaluable and perhaps adequately appreciated.'

There were, in any case, problems with processing the material. Although Green's reporting was apparently very well received by the War Office in London during the days immediately after the Japanese invasion, it does not appear to have contributed much, if anything, to the actual defence of Malaya. In May 1942 he asserted that much of his intelligence had been disregarded. 'Evidently', he wrote, 'the pile of information which conclusively proved that a Japanese attack upon Siam and Malaya was to occur in the first week of December 1941 was set aside as "I" staff were told by a visitor from Siam that owing to Monsoon any attack would be impossible before March.' Another 'important contributory factor', he claimed, was the 'lack of any scientific system of collation. Owing to frequent changes of officers information which had been filed was soon forgotten.' He added, moreover, that 'information which supported pre-conceived ideas or previous deductions was over-valued and information which did not support such deductions was devalued, "lost" or even sup-pressed.' Denham had a similarly low opinion of the Far East Combined Bureau. 'It is quite apparent', he told Menzies in March 1942, 'that much of our information never percolated through to the right persons in the right form.' Although these SIS views were doubtless influenced by the benefit of hindsight, Green certainly identified a perennial intelligence-assessment problem in the existence of preconceived ideas, which could properly be addressed only by the establishment of effective inter-agency and inter-service machinery for collating, processing, testing and evaluat-ing the whole range of raw intelligence material available.

Green's agent Sectude continued transmitting until January 1942 when Japanese surveillance obliged him to sign off, but he did so with a cheery message: 'Of course nothing changed between us. Listen in. Goodbye. Good luck.' The agent had told Green to monitor the English-language broadcasts of Radio Saigon for particular phrases. 'You are listening to Saigon', for example, was to mean 'shipping concentration in Saigon river', and 'Good night to you all' at the end of a broadcast meant 'rein-forcements sent to Malaya'. In February Calcutta reported that 'informa-tion from 65100 [Sectude] by Saigon broadcasts' was 'being received in Burma'. Some direct contact was maintained with Sectude, who request-ed a replacement wireless set in August 1942 'to operate from Hanoï'. In January 1943 one of Green's agents swam across the Red River at Hoikow (Haiku), where the railway crossed the border between China and French Indo-China, only to be told that Japanese surveillance made wireless op-eration difficult and so intelligence collected by Sectude was brought out by courier across the Chinese border to Kunming.

Advance warning of the Japanese attack was also passed to the Americans through Gerald Wilkinson in Manila. Two telegrams sent by Wilkinson to the SIS sub-station in Honolulu have survived in the archives (though only as paraphrases). On 26 November, citing 'Secret source (usually re-liable)', he reported that the Japanese would attack the Kra isthmus (in southern Thailand) from the sea on 1 December 'without any ultima-tum or declaration of break with a view to getting between Bangkok and Singapore. Attacking forces will proceed direct from Hainan and Formosa. Main landing point is to be in Songkhla area . . . American military and Naval Intelligence Manila informed.' The second signal was sent on 2 December and comprised the text of a wire which Menzies had sent to Wilkinson. 'Most immediate,' it read. 'We have received considerable intelligence confirming . . . accelerated Japanese preparation of airfields and railways [and] arrival since November 10th of additional one hundred thousand troops . . . and considerable quantities fighters, medium bombers tanks and guns (75 mm).' The conclusion at Head Office was 'that Japan envisages early hostilities with Britain and United States. Japan does not ?intend attack Russia at present but will act in South. You may inform chiefs of American Military and Naval Intelligence Honolulu.'² These reports were only two of many indicating heightened Japanese activity, and whether or not the intelligence made any practical difference to the defence of Malaya, the 26 November prediction was remarkably accurate. The main Japanese landing on 8 December was indeed at Songkhla in southern Thailand. SIS, however, does not appear to have had any knowledge of the perhaps tactically more important landing further south at Kota Bharu, just inside Malaya.³

Gerald Wilkinson went on to play an important role as the main British liaison with the American General Douglas MacArthur, reporting through Menzies eventually to Churchill himself. In the dark days before the fall of the Philippines Wilkinson used his SIS secure radio link to transmit MacArthur's urgent appeals for reinforcements as well as family messages from members of MacArthur's personal staff which he passed on to the New York station for delivery. He accompanied MacArthur to Australia when he established his headquarters there in March 1942, and provided Menzies with a steady stream of reports on the position as viewed by MacArthur and his staff. When in September 1942 the Director of Military Intelligence pressed for 'information from the SW Pacific area', Menzies noted that 'apart from my endeavours to penetrate Japanese occupied territory by an organisation based on Australia, I consider that my representative attached to General MacArthur is as well placed as anyone to obtain American information on the subject'.⁴ Wilkinson admired MacArthur as a commander but was less impressed with his character. While he was 'shrewd, selfish, proud, remote, highly-strung and vastly vain', and had 'imagination, self-confidence, physical courage and charm', he had 'no humour about himself, no regard for truth' and was 'unaware of these defects'. He mistook 'his emotions and ambitions for principles'.[5] MacArthur later sent Wilkinson as his personal representative to report to both General Wavell (the British Commander-in-Chief in India) and the American Joint Chiefs of Staff in Washington. Wilkinson's career also illustrates some of the personal costs of service during the Second World War, as his wife and two daughters were interned by the Japanese in the Philippines. After the war Wilkinson was publicly accused by MacArthur's acerbic intelligence chief, General Charles Willoughby, of leaving his family 'to fend for themselves', but he vigorously rebutted the accusation and secured a full retraction.[6]

Regrouping in India

During January 1942, Drage, Green, their staff and some agents withdrew from Singapore to Calcutta where Denham took general charge of SIS operations in the region. With the move to Calcutta, SIS's intelligence priorities shifted from the Pacific rim to the more immediate Japanese military challenge threatening north-east India through Burma and Australia from the East Indies. But Denham was concerned about the infrastructure of the SIS organisation in the Far East and gloomy about the overall situation in India. With the fall of Singapore clearly in mind, he wrote to London in March: 'everything seems to me to be chaotic, and there is very little preparedness for dealing with a state of war; nor in fact is there to my mind among the civilian population any realisation of what may happen'. Denham's morale cannot have been improved by the in-fighting within the Service in Calcutta, where Green accused Drage of indulging in intrigue and regarded Denham as unprofessional and too apt to sacrifice SIS's core interests for the sake of temporary political advantage with the military establishment. On the other hand, unlike Green, who was an intelligence case-officer, Denham was a bureaucrat and an adept political operator attempting to create an environment within which SIS might have some chance of surviving in India. He had, in fact, strong views about the military's fundamental misconceptions concerning the role and functions of SIS and the way in which it recruited, controlled and protected its agents. He told Menzies in March 1942 that the Director of Military Intelligence in India 'harbours a somewhat childish resentment against our organization because it is not under Military control'. He thought that none of the Military Intelligence people in India had 'any real field experience', and it was 'very easy' for them 'to shout for information when sitting at the seat of custom, [and] if information is not forthcoming then someone, to their mind, must necessarily be to blame' (and that 'someone' was usually SIS). Warming to his theme, and echoing widely held SIS opinions about Military Intelligence officers, Denham declared that they were 'usually grossly ignorant regarding the difficulty in obtaining the information, and what steps have to be taken in building up an organization of our nature'. Denham was 'sorry to have to make these observations', but he wanted Menzies 'to know what sort of people we have to deal with and that their criticisms are usually not of any real value'. This grumble about Military Intelligence evidently struck a chord with Menzies who, marking the relevant passages in his distinctive green pencil, commented, 'the old, old story', and, in the margin, 'too true'.

Menzies recalled Denham in May 1942 (though he did not leave until October), and replaced him with Colonel Leo Steveni, an Indian Army officer with family business connections in pre-revolutionary Russia. He had served with Military Intelligence in Russia at the end of the First World War and had been British military attaché in Meshed, north-east Iran, in the early 1930s. He had been taken on by SIS in 1939 and early in 1940 was posted to Section IVB, 'to make a speciality of military information from the Far East'. Under continued pressure from the military authorities to produce intelligence and faced with a rapidly expanding and proactive SOE presence, whose can-do approach was welcomed by the hard-pressed soldiers and airmen in India, Steveni was put in an exceptionally difficult position. In order to protect SIS's continued existence and autonomy in the region, in the short term he had paradoxically to dance to the military's tune and respond to their demands for immediate operational information. As an Indian Army man himself, Steveni perhaps more readily appreciated their needs, but his approach upset the old intelligence hands in SIS. Green was particularly frustrated by the army's ignorance of local conditions. He had worked in Burma for years, had 'trained the original Burma Intelligence Corps' and had brought local experts on to his staff, including former Burma Police intelligence officers.

Green believed that the best approach was through the 'back-door', via Kunming in south-western China, from where he could re-establish contact with his existing, reliable agents, targeting them on the Japanese rear areas and then towards the battle zone. The army view was that they needed agents put directly across the front line. Steveni accepted this and, 'under pressure from the D.M.I. – through 69000 [Steveni]', Green was compelled 'to attempt what the Army and the other "I" organisations had attempted and completely failed to do – to send in agents over the land frontier and through the fighting line. I know this frontier', he continued, 'and its problems probably better than any man and, had I been backed, we should by now [he was writing in August 1943] have been reaping ample results, instead of floundering to disaster in attempting the almost impossible.'

One network for which Green had held high hopes was run by Major Louis Cauvin, who, before the Japanese invasion, had been an immigration official at Padang Besar on the Malaya–Thailand border. Between October 1940 and September 1941, Cauvin had recruited a group of Sino-Thai agents to operate in Thailand. After he had to withdraw southwards in the face of the Japanese advance, Cauvin began work on a stay-behind organisation, recruiting mainly from among Malayan Communist Party members who, being familiar with clandestine work, were well suited to be agents. Towards the end of January 1942 Green signalled from Singapore that he had arranged for Cauvin 'and one Chinese operator' to 'stay behind Japanese lines' and 'to operate communist intelligence service which now covers the whole peninsula'. The party grew to include three Royal Signals personnel, led by John Cross, who, equipped with a suitcase radio and a signal plan for contact with a control station in Singapore, Java or Burma, were to provide the base communications for Cauvin's 'all-asiatic intelligence unit'. After a meeting on 27 January in Singapore with the secretary-general of the Malayan Communist Party, Cauvin's party (known as ISLD Station A) entered the jungle near Kota Tinggi in Johore, some twenty-odd miles from Singapore. Cauvin's intention was to try to recontact some of his agents in Thailand. Green thought it 'a brave but foolhardy enterprise as he had to travel 300 miles through Japanese-occupied Malaya, where there were no Europeans left, before he even reached the Siamese border'. 'He has not been heard of since,' added Green. In fact, ISLD Station A spent the next three years in Malaya under the protection of Communist guerrillas, until the survivors of the party were exfiltrated by submarine in May 1945. But their radio communications proved unreliable and, despite meticulous signals watches, they were unable to establish regular contact with any SIS signals units. Java and Burma were too swiftly overrun by the Japanese, and the frequencies Cross had been allotted were judged in 1945 to have been quite wrong for the distances that actually had to be attempted.[7]

While unable to transmit intelligence, the group were able to receive it, and they assembled English-language propaganda which was distributed clandestinely by the Malayan Communist Party in the 'Emancipation News' and the 'Victory Herald'. Like all jungle dwellers, ISLD Station A had to live off the land, moving camp some thirty times to evade the Japanese occupying troops and subsisting on scanty rations. Cross noted that at one point in April 1944 daily meals consisted of wood potato flour and two small fish per man. The health of the whole party suffered, and Cauvin's condition declined rapidly up to his suicide in July 1944. At the end, there was not a lot to show for the party's efforts, which in any case were more special operations than intelligence. All Cross could find to say in his postwar report was that they had kept themselves 'intact as a unit', used their 'technical resources to spread the news of Allied fighting progress' and given the anti-Japanese forces as much advice as they had been 'willing to take in their resistance activities'. Thus they had 'at least been something of a nuisance to the Japs'.

In November 1942 Steveni reported to London that ISLD had thirteen current and projected operations in hand, though only one had been completed successfully, a preliminary reconnaissance of the Akyab area on the Bay of Bengal near the India–Burma frontier over ten days in late October by two agents put in and picked up by sea. GHQ India were recorded as having been 'very pleased' with the information. Of the other operations, one had failed because of inadequate support (damage to a radio set badly packed by the RAF and their failure to drop a spare), while another had been delayed by the naval officer-in-charge at Chittagong failing to follow instructions. A third operation had had to be postponed 'owing to inadvertent arrest of our agents by Police on way to their destination'. This was the result of poor co-ordination. Green claimed that although he had made arrangements 'with the Corps Intelligence and Bengal Intelligence', his agents had been 'arrested and beaten by the British officer of the Security Police'. On a second attempt to cross through the battle lines, the two men were 'attached to a party who were taking a Burman fifth columnist to be publicly executed in a border village'. But the escort allowed the prisoner 'to escape into enemy territory'. There was, remarked Green, 'little wonder that the agents, upon whom we had spent so much time and money', and who assumed that they could now be identified, 'refused to carry on with the work'.

Green had contacts across the political spectrum. Apart from his links with the Malayan Communists, through the Special Branch in Singapore he had established a relationship with George Yeh, local representative of the Nationalist Chinese Kuomintang's intelligence service. Green admired the professionalism of the Chinese, noting particularly that their 'bumping off organisation was efficient'. Yeh supplied him with twenty potential agents who were taken to India and 'carefully trained for specific work in parts of Malaya, Siam and Indo-China'. To Green's intense irritation, however, Steveni insisted on deploying them on an ill-planned operation to collect information along the Malayan coast. In the absence of any well-established (let alone productive) networks of agents across Japanese-occupied territory, potentially the most valuable approach for SIS was to forge a close liaison with the Chinese. But this was difficult to achieve in a region where not only was there a range of Allied agencies, British and American, all trying to do the same thing, but also there were at least five rival Nationalist Chinese intelligence organisations. SIS's local contact with one Chinese intelligence service in Singapore was small beer compared to the much more valuable liaison which SOE had with the Nationalists in China itself. Based in the Nationalist capital Chungking (Chongqing), the SOE representative Findlay Andrew's main Chinese contact was General Wang Ping-shen, a close colleague of the Nationalist leader Chiang Kai-shek. SOE partly financed the Resources Investigation Institute (RII), a sub-section of Wang's propaganda and intelligence organisation, the Institute for International Studies. London complained to Delhi in March 1943 that they had 'no knowledge of S.O.E. activities in China other than Findlay Andrew's connection with Wong [*sic*] who runs R.I.I.'. But they knew that while the RII ran some special operations, it also collected 'much intelligence which we get from S.O.E.', and about which government departments commented 'very favourably'. At present the information was 'political and economic with some military identifications concerning Japan and Japanese occupied China', but SOE planned to expand the organisation 'to include other types of information'.[8]

A possible additional source of information was Mao Zedong's Chinese Communists. Although the Communists and Nationalists had formed an uneasy common front against the Japanese in 1937, internecine hostilities had resumed from early 1941 and any British contacts with the Communists had to proceed with considerable discretion. In mid-July 1942 Gordon Harmon in Chungking reported that he had been visited by the private secretary of General Zhou Enlai, the 'political head of the Chinese Communist Party', who gave 'evidence of a really genuine desire to co-operate against the Japanese'. The Communist emissary handed over a report which, although ascribed to human sources, was clearly derived from signals intelligence. It described a major reorganisation of Japanese intelligence in China and was an intercept of a message from the Japanese embassy accredited to the puppet regime in Nanking to the Japanese consulate-general in Hankow (Hankou). Harmon wisely noted that he had to be 'extremely careful in contacts with this organisation'. In London, Section V thought the source 'seems very promising'. Alastair Denniston of GC&CS confirmed that part of the message had been received in Bletchley Park but not the rest, and while the Admiralty had 'no means of checking the truth' of the report, they thought it 'very likely' and were 'prepared to believe it'. Although Chungking reported in August a further contact promising 'a considerable amount of information' and a personal message from Zhou Enlai that he 'wished to collaborate closely in Anti-Japanese effort', the source appears to have dried up shortly thereafter. An attempt the following year to extend coverage in China and possibly develop contacts with the Communists was neatly thwarted by the Nationalists. SIS proposed to send Frank Hill, the former head of station at Peking to open a new post in Sian (Xi'an), 350 miles north-west of Chungking and a centre of Communist activity. Taking a necessarily circuitous route because of the war situation, Hill was allowed by the Nationalists to travel only as far as Chengtu (Chengdu), actually further from Sian than Chungking. London reckoned that Hill had queered his pitch with the Kuomintang by having already made indiscreet contacts with Communists in Chungking, and so they wanted him safely out of harm's way. In the event Hill's health deteriorated and he was withdrawn in October 1943.

Although SIS was ostensibly working alongside allies, China proved to be an extremely hostile intelligence environment. Gordon Harmon was confirmed in October 1942 'as representative of S.I.S. working in free China, vis-à-vis the British ambassador and Central Government authorities in Chungking'. But he did not himself run any agents and came under increasing criticism in London. In December 1943 P.14 on the China desk in Broadway thought Harmon had been unwarrantedly puffed up into 'the position of THE Chinese expert – a kind of Pope of China whose infallibility must not be questioned'. Yet 'he has never supplied any S.I.S. intelligence, only hand-outs from the Chinese Officials – in fact, any rubbish that they wished to palm off on us'. Claude Dansey, he asserted, had 'picturesquely described this as "drainpipe stuff"'. An analysis of all 119 reports of Far Eastern material circulated from January to October 1943 revealed that the biggest suppliers of information were first, SOE (thirty-four reports), and, second, United States diplomatic sources (twenty-one), which, while useful as 'background material', was 'not, in the main, S.I.S. information, but . . . information acquired by members of the American diplomatic and consular services in the ordinary course of their functions, and quite open and above board, as it were'. The next largest was nine reports provided by '43931', the Estonian Colonel Maasing, whose information came from the Japanese military attaché in Stockholm, General Onodera. Harmon himself had only directly produced seven reports, of which 'two at least' were dismissed merely as 'expressions of opinion – competent views, but not true S.I.S. information'. Despite pressure to remove Harmon, Menzies preferred to 'wait awhile'. Harmon had the backing of Steveni in Delhi (to whom Menzies had delegated the regional direction of the Service) and stayed on in Chungking for another year. With Hill having broken down in the autumn of 1943, Menzies, perhaps as the least worst option, decided to stick with Harmon, who was recognised as 'a difficult and touchy person to handle but one whose standing with the Chinese is such that his potentialities are enormous'.

The problems of co-ordination within India and, above all, of providing intelligence for the armed services generally, led to the growth in Delhi of an Inter-Services Liaison Department, rather along the lines of the ISLD in Cairo, and roughly mirroring the functions of SIS headquarters in London, though it was more weighted to circulation and liaison than the production of intelligence. Its structure was military and, no doubt, so too was its ethos. Green was not impressed and thought that in Delhi money was being 'squandered upon extravagant buildings and overpaid staffs. Bigger, better and more ostentatious appears to be the slogan.' Under Steveni the two stations in Calcutta retained their separate identities. Early in 1943 both Green and Drage were replaced, the former by Colonel Reginald Heath, who took over responsibility for the collection of intelligence on Burma, Malaya, Thailand and French Indo-China, the latter by an officer who was given charge of 'Japanese occupied areas of China and the Japanese Empire'. Heath, who had been mobilised in Malaya as a local volunteer naval reservist before being recruited to be Green's assistant by SIS in late 1940, had worked for the Anglo-Swiss Nestlé milk products company before the war, spoke Malay and had a 'good knowledge of business shipping' in the region. The other officer, who came from a famous family of wine merchants and had briefly worked in the Azores for the War Office special operations section MIR (later subsumed within SOE), had been working as Drage's assistant since June 1941.

SIS in Mountbatten's Command

Changes in the overall Allied command in the theatre affected SIS further. In August 1943 Admiral Lord Louis Mountbatten, King George VI's glamorous, charismatic and politically astute cousin, was appointed Supreme Allied Commander, South-East Asia. Mountbatten brought a distinct sense of dynamism and urgency to the command and under him a significant degree of cohesion was at last brought to the role of intelligence and clandestine operations in the region. During the autumn of 1943, as he was assembling his new headquarters at Kandy in Ceylon (Sri Lanka), Menzies took the opportunity to replace Steveni, who had not been a great success in what was admittedly a tough assignment. In August 1943 Brigadier Beddington, the Deputy Director/Army, whose geographical responsibilities included Asia, sounded out Gerald Wilkinson for the job, but he was not attracted by 'an area where our organization is so ineffective, the obstacles so difficult and the future requirements so great'.[9] The following month, however, Beddington found a candidate in classic SIS

fashion. At his club he met a cavalryman, Brigadier Philip Bowden-Smith
– 'Bogey' – 'whom I had known for years' and who was 'looking very de-
pressed and worried. He told me [wrote Beddington in his memoirs] that
he had just been told that he was considered too old [he was fifty-two] to
take his Tank Brigade on Active Service, and that he was soon going to
be out of a job.' Beddington raised the possibility of his becoming 'our
head man in India' and brought Bogey to see Menzies, 'and it was agreed
that if he came satisfactorily through two months strenuous training (for
it was work he had never done before) he would be appointed'. He also
had to be vetted by MI5 (demonstrating that the recruitment process
at this stage did not entirely depend on the old-boy network). Having
passed his training, he arrived in India in February 1944, where, according to Beddington, he 'proved a great success'.[10] A personnel report in
1945 (another innovation marking the steady professionalisation of the
Service) was positive, albeit a little more measured. It gave him a 'satisfactory' grading as 'Head of S.I.S. in F.E. [Far East]'. Overall, he had 'done
his utmost under very difficult circumstances and did not spare himself in
any way. Covering a gigantic area, he travelled by air continuously under
conditions of sometimes great hardship and has gained the genuine affection and respect of all his officers.'

Another improvement was Mountbatten's appointment of a 'bluff
and hearty' sailor, Captain G. A. Garnons-Williams, to head the P,
or Priorities, Division, with the task of co-ordinating all clandestine
activities within the Command, including SIS, SOE, OSS and 'political
warfare'. With experience in Combined Operations (he had been involved,
under Mountbatten, in setting up the Commandos in 1940), Garnons-
Williams was well qualified for the job. Although he had no specific
intelligence background, he became an SIS officer and on 22 November
1943 drew up a 'doctrine' for Bowden-Smith which revealed considerable understanding of SIS's own perception of its role. The doctrine
emphasised the extent to which Bowden-Smith (unlike Steveni) needed
to keep SIS at a distance from the military command structure. 'We are
an independent organisation . . . only concerned with obtaining illicit
information which we collect from sources with whom the services are
not in touch. We are', he wrote, 'only collectors and distributors, not
collators.' SIS's work did 'not over-lap with that of other Intelligence organisations, and as far as possible we must avoid becoming involved with

Service "I" organisations.' Furthermore, 'it must be remembered that we work for many Government Departments' and therefore could not 'always guarantee to tackle any particular task at short notice, for our existing agents may be otherwise employed or unsuitable'. Evidently reflecting on the existing situation in India, Garnons-Williams thought it 'of the utmost importance that all quarrels, jealousies and backbitings with other services cease forthwith'. Other services had also been informed of this and he had 'been given powers by the Supreme Commander, S. E. Asia [Mountbatten], of dismissal against any Officer who so offends'. Finally he stressed the continued autonomy of SIS in the region. 'Although clandestine services in S.E. Asia are co-ordinated it does not mean that the services concerned part with their individuality in any way. Integration ceases at the co-ordinating committee, of which I am Chairman, and the policy for services must be that of intelligent self-interest.' Perhaps with the Americans in mind (as much as other British agencies), Garnons-Williams added that whatever degree of co-operation was achievable, 'this does not mean exposing the secrets of our service to another'.

Before leaving for India, on 23 December 1943 Garnons-Williams went to see Menzies, who outlined to him the instructions he was giving to Bowden-Smith. They provided for 'centralised direction and decentralised execution' of SIS operations in the theatre. Bowden-Smith was given a directive which made plain the need for him to serve the interests of the Supreme Allied Commander, though it conferred the right to refer to London if the demands made appeared 'inimical to S.I.S. interests or policy'. Yet it was clear who would be in effective control. All policy and intelligence requirements were to come through Garnons-Williams. Moreover, while Bowden-Smith was to be 'in complete charge of the administration' of his stations and staff, should he 'wish to dismiss any officer' he had to 'obtain the concurrence' of Garnons-Williams. And if Garnons-Williams wished to dismiss an officer, Bowden-Smith had to 'carry out his wishes' unless they were 'entirely contrary' to his views, in which case the matter should be referred to Menzies. Reflecting the extent to which Menzies himself remained directly involved in the management of the Service, he instructed Bowden-Smith to 'keep me frequently informed through P.14 [the Far Eastern Section in Broadway] of the progress of the organisation entrusted to you'; nevertheless, 'on matters of first importance you will correspond with me direct'.

Garnons-Williams afterwards maintained that he had taken on 'a supposedly impossible task in October 1943'. When he reached India in January 1944 he found that 'ISLD [SIS] and Force 136 [SOE] stank in every ones' nostrils' and he faced a 'constant struggle to overcome the ill feeling between the Fighting and Clandestine Services and the internecine suspicions between the Clandestine Services themselves'. By the end of the war, however, he claimed that 'the battle in Burma as far as Rangoon redounded to the credit of the Clandestine Services which were used and controlled as a whole'. Writing to the Controller Far East in Broadway on 25 August 1945, he said that 'those senior high Intelligence officers who had experience of the Libyan and N. African campaigns' had 'stated that the Clandestine Intelligence in Burma was far in excess of that supplied to Alexander and Montgomery. I had Slim [commander of the Allied Fourteenth Army] in my War Room yesterday,' he continued, 'with Keith Park [the air force commander] and Mountbatten, and they were more than complimentary.' Whether Garnons-Williams's self-reported success was quite as outstanding as he claimed, his P Division certainly made a difference and markedly improved the co-ordination of SIS, SOE and OSS during the last eighteen months of the war.

There was also a surge in operations from the spring of 1944.[11] In Operation 'Bittern I' an agent and wireless operator reported from the northern Shan States between May and September 1944, attracting praise from Mountbatten's United States deputy, General 'Vinegar Joe' Stillwell, for their coverage of Japanese troop and supply movements. In February 1944 (Operation 'Blow') four agents were parachuted in to cover the Japanese airfields in the Katha district, 150 miles north of Mandalay. They spent nine months behind enemy lines and produced seventy-four reports (twenty-one graded 'A' and fifty-three 'B'), earning an MC for the Burmese officer who led the team. Operation 'Bulge' involved a five-agent team under a British officer who had been a planter in Burma before the war. They were dropped into the Maymo/Mandalay area, where the officer was well known, on 29 November 1944 to report on Japanese troop and supply movements. The leader of the group broke his ankle on landing, but carried on with a sixty-pound load nevertheless. The team came under pressure from the Japanese, who had become aware of the ex-planter's identity, but they continued to operate until their wireless batteries failed in March 1945.

Some operations were not successful. 'Bracket', the landing of two Burmese agents ('65538' and '65539') on Ramree island, off the west coast of Burma, in December 1943 came to grief when the agents concerned, on their way back and not far from the Indian border, spent a convivial evening with a party of Japanese soldiers, during which one of the agents boasted of his (prewar) visits to India. No comment was made at the time but the next morning a Japanese officer asked to see the two men. When their belongings were searched 65538 was found to have hidden some current Indian rupees in a handkerchief tied around his thigh. 'Without further ado the Japanese officer smashed a large stick which he was carrying, down on to 65538's head which knocked him unconscious.' The officer then kicked the unfortunate man again in the head and had him shot dead. Had the officer paused for reflection and interrogated 65538, the other agent might also have perished, but he managed to escape and make his way back to Calcutta.

The administrative problems raised by having to mount and maintain operations by land, air and sea over such great distances could be solved only by an armed-services approach to logistics. To a considerable extent, logistics, climate and terrain determined the shape of operations, which became more military in concept and numbers. It may have been an inability to adjust to a quickened operational tempo and a vastly increased scale of activity that prevented Green and Drage from being as successful in India as they had been before. The traditional single agent gave way to operations involving groups of agents, usually with some military experience (particularly in Burma), operating from a jungle base and, in this respect, not unlike SOE. Training, too, required military and naval skills, the latter provided at Camp Z in Ceylon, for example, for Operation 'Mullet', which aimed to land agents for an observation post on an island off the west coast of Malaya in February 1944. But the venture was a catalogue of disasters. Setting off from the British naval base at Trincomalee by submarine, the eight-strong party had originally planned to seize a junk off the Malay coast to take them to their destination, but no suitable junk was found and the first attempt was abandoned. A second attempt was cancelled twenty minutes before zero hour when the submarine concerned was ordered away on patrol. The landing eventually took place on 23 February, in four folboats (collapsible canvas boats) with stores for six days. 'Our landing was compromised from the start as we ran into fishing craft 50 yards from our landing place.' It was decided to abort the mission, but the submarine 'observed no signal from us and [dived] at 0527 hrs. and we were left paddling about in enemy waters in broad daylight'. That evening, 'after 2½ hrs. rowing, with one Folboat nearly full of water [and] all torches unserviceable', they at last made contact with the submarine, were taken back to Ceylon and the operation cancelled. During the operational post-mortem the inadequate condition of the folboats caused much heart-searching, since they had been rigorously inspected before leaving SIS stores in Calcutta (a thousand miles from Trincomalee) and again before loading aboard the submarine. After investigation, it was established that during the delays between the various attempts to launch the operation, the boats had been used by officers of the submarine depot ship for harbour parties with personnel from the Women's Royal Naval Service, a contingency which had not, evidently, been taken into account in the operation's planning.

Despite Garnons-Williams's best efforts, the inevitable tensions and problems of co-ordination between SIS and SOE surfaced from time to time. This was exacerbated by the fact that SOE's stock-in-trade of special operations and support for indigenous resistance groups was more readily appreciated by the military men in South-East Asia Command than SIS's purer intelligence work. As a result SOE had become the predominant British clandestine agency in the region, in terms of both operations and intelligence. Officers at Fourteenth Army headquarters, moreover, had also come to admire OSS's more integrated operations and intelligence structure, so much so that in January 1945 Slim's chief of staff, General George Walsh, proposed amalgamating SIS and SOE and subordinating them to the OSS, which he regarded as an altogether more effective covert organisation. This was a non-starter, but Garnons-Williams still had to work out some acceptable arrangement.

As in Europe, there was the underlying issue of what sort of intelligence was required. In the spring of 1945 Garnons-Williams wrote to Bowden-Smith and his opposite number, Colin Mackenzie, who headed SOE's India mission, seeking to establish priorities between long-range intelligence on political, economic and social targets and more immediate operational intelligence. Fighting SIS's corner (which as an SIS officer himself was quite understandable), and with the end of the war in mind, he observed that SOE's involvement in intelligence-gathering should not be taken as a precedent. He thought it 'important that we preserve a long range view in which the British Secret Intelligence Service shall (a) carry out its proper function and (b) have an eye to the future'. The 'greatest danger in the past', he asserted, had been 'interference' with SIS 'by the Military and other Organisations', and, with Mountbatten's support, he was currently endeavouring 'to undo the harm which has been done in the last two or three years'. While Bowden-Smith and Mackenzie both responded by stressing the valuable intelligence contribution of their agencies, it was clear that SOE was by far the more productive, and Garnons-Williams laid down that current operational intelligence work should be handed over to SOE (or OSS), so that SIS could concentrate on the future. In comparison to the large SOE organisation, he stressed that, 'by long-range standards', the 'small Service of S.I.S.' was 'infinitely the most important'. Garnons-Williams also argued that 'no single member of I.S.L.D. in this Theatre will be of the slightest use after the war because he is completely and absolutely "blown" already and the organisation will have to be built anew'. A further factor was signals intelligence which 'fortunately', he said, was 'unknown to all except 5 officers!' in South-East Asia Command. But nothing should be done to jeopardise the agency – SIS – which controlled it. 'I would myself', added Garnons-Williams, 'rather see the whole of agents work, except for political, social and economical intelligence, handed out to Force 136, Z Force or OSS and leave ISLD to its true role.'[12]

Working relations between SIS and SOE on the ground (as was the case in other theatres) appear to have been markedly better than the more institutionalised relations at higher levels, especially in London. Just as Garnons-Williams was endeavouring to iron out inter-agency co-ordination, local SIS–SOE relations were damaged by a visit in May 1945 from London of Colonel George Taylor of SOE's Director of Far East Group and Commander J. P. Gibbs, recently appointed SIS Controller Far East. So unhelpful was their attitude that Mountbatten himself was moved on 23 May to write a joint letter of complaint to Menzies and the head of SOE, Colin Gubbins. 'Much as I liked both Taylor and Gibbs, and enjoyed their visit from a personal point of view,' he wrote, 'I am sorry to have to tell you both that your two representatives . . . have not helped me in the prosecution of the war.' Indeed, until their visits, Mountbatten claimed, SOE and SIS had been 'collaborating in a far more friendly

and get-together spirit'. He fully backed Garnons-Williams's proposals
for giving operational intelligence the first priority. 'No one', he wrote
emolliently (though with a sting in the tail), 'could be more insistent on
the absolute necessity of true S.I.S. operations, but I am afraid I cannot
allow them to interfere with my over-riding urgent military Intelligence
and clandestine needs, in view of the rapid campaigns I am now planning.' In a private postscript to Menzies alone, Mountbatten added that
he 'entirely' sympathised 'with the need for setting up your organisation
with a view to the postwar Intelligence' and did not 'seek to interfere with
any steps' Menzies might take in this matter. Indeed, Mountbatten was
'prepared to do anything' he could to help.

Broadway had to accept a scheme giving priority to SOE for the collection of immediate operational intelligence (though in the event, with
the unexpected capitulation of Japan on 14 August 1945 following the
atomic bomb attacks on Hiroshima and Nagasaki, the wartime structure
soon lapsed). Gibbs, however, in an otherwise amiable letter of 1 August
to Garnons-Williams (whose only son had married Gibbs's only daughter in July the previous year), effectively accused him of letting down
the SIS side. 'You have no real knowledge of our firm,' he wrote, 'and it
is not possible that you should have, partly because there is [sic] never
any opportunity for giving you any training, and partly because you are,
of course, Dickie's [Mountbatten's] man, and he is not only completely
S.O.E.-minded, but also, being a German, only has a military point of
view.' 'For heaven's sake,' he added, 'remember that the military point
of view is the last thing that interests our firm.' Garnons-Williams was
quite unrepentant. Replying on 25 August, he conceded that 'the firm'
was 'not interested in war', but argued the 'inescapable fact' that 'in this
theatre it was fully committed to military activities when I took over,
admittedly without proper resources, and so had to be used in a military
manner'. He claimed that he had 'succeeded from the overall point of
view, with the honest help of Bogey [Bowden-Smith] in detail and administration, in making it [SIS] function in this part of the world after
beginning on an extremely bad wicket'. As for the 'peace time setup', that
was 'your affair', and for the immediate future Garnons-Williams had secured Mountbatten's approval 'to exclude Bogey from coordination, only
coming to me for transport. I have told Bogey not to put his operations
into me at all. In fact,' he concluded, 'his Service is being put back into

the obscurity from which it should never have been taken three years ago; that, I know, will make you feel happier.'

China

During 1944 a total of 566 operational reports were received from all SIS posts in China, most of which were passed on only to the local military authorities.[13] Some 150 reports, however, were sent to London, of which 116 were graded 'A' or 'B'. In January 1945 SIS reported to the United States General Albert C. Wedemeyer, recently appointed chief of staff to Chiang Kai-shek, that the Service had forty-one staff in China, all men, including communications and support staff, distributed among ten stations, the largest of which were Kunming (nine), Nanping (nine) and Chungking (five). The Kunming station and its south-west China sub-posts operated into north-east Burma, French Indo-China and Thailand in support of British and United States/Chinese military operations in Burma, and had done so since at least 1942. Chungking, by contrast, was a liaison station within the British embassy, in touch with Chinese intelligence organisations and other government bodies, such as the Maritime Customs and the Salt Gabelle, from which SIS sought to recruit personnel. Of the forty-odd SIS representatives, twenty were agent-running case-officers (this information was *not* supplied to Wedemeyer) who between them, over the course of the war, controlled upwards of four hundred agents and contacts of all nationalities. SIS told Wedemeyer that the Service in China was 'a non-operational organisation whose sole object it was to produce information for the benefit of Naval and Air Task Forces in the China Theatre', and underpinned this benign view by showing the general a telegram from the United States Army Air Force confirming the accuracy of an SIS report about air-raid damage to Japanese shipping at Amoy in south-east China.

The station in Nanping, upstream of Foochow (Fuzhou) in Fukien (Fujian) province, and another smaller station originally at Wenchow (Wenzhou), south-east of Shanghai, had a coast-watching function among others, and were probably the source of the intelligence on shipping in Amoy. Other stations ran agents who visited Japanese-occupied territory and in their turn recruited resident agents. Why did these people become agents? The head of the Kweilin (Guilin) station, a former policeman who with Chinese Communist help had escaped from Japanese internment in Hong Kong in 1942, offered some thoughts in December 1943. 'What constitutes a promising agent', he wrote, 'is about as explainable as "horse-sense"', but there were a few who would 'work under a feeling of patriotism or loyalty to the British cause'. But the majority were 'out for pecuniary gain, and of these only a rare few will be satisfactory in a strict business sense'. He hazarded that 'perhaps the best field for the general raw material of agents' was 'to be found in the young lower middle class of country bred Chinese adult', who showed 'a fairly shrewd sense of proportion in regard to expenditure' and had 'an inherent knack of adapting themselves to the changing circumstances of war. Their minds are receptive to ideas,' he concluded, 'although initially they are chronically unobservant.'

The intelligence provided by SIS on local Japanese activity in China can never have been more than useful, rather than essential. Shipping was another matter, as Allied attacks on shipping affected Japanese forces across South-East Asia as far afield as Singapore, Malaya and the Dutch East Indies, all targets for Allied reoccupation. By mid-1944 coast-watching – the observation, identification and reporting of enemy shipping – had become a major requirement for some SIS stations in China, and Calcutta was seeking suitably qualified personnel to support it. Not only did officers need to have appropriate language qualifications, 'they must, if possible, have had sea-going experience and be able to instruct on naval matters'. SIS told General Wedemeyer in January 1945 that the output from all the Service's Chinese stations amounted to some seventy intelligence reports a month. While 'a large proportion of these reports' were 'of background or static information', he calculated that during the forty-one days between 1 December 1944 and 10 January 1945, '21 operational sightings of enemy shipping off the China coast were passed to American air and naval liaison officers for operational action'. Information also came from the ports in south China. In May 1944 a sub-source working as a coolie in the Hong Kong naval dockyard reported on the completion of a vessel in the shipyard, as well as giving some details about dockyard staff. Reflecting the difficulties in getting information out, this report was not circulated until November 1944. Coast-watching was not confined to the shore. SIS acquired a junk in Foochow and equipped it with a wireless set. It made its first voyage in December 1944 crewed by members of the Nanping station. A month's costs for the junk, including repairs and the crew's pay, came to 71,500 Chinese dollars, about £120 at the going black-market rate (and approximately £4,000 at current values).

The end of the war found SIS's China stations generally well informed about Japanese activity in China, including the operations of Japanese political warfare units under the generic term 'kikan'. As late as June 1945 the Wenchow station was still reporting on the 'Ume' (plum) Kikan, the Japanese organisation controlling puppet military bodies in Chekiang (Zhejiang) province. SIS reported on suspected Japanese agents in Hong Kong, such as an unidentified woman who made weekly journeys on a military train to Canton, 'sometimes accompanied by other women, usually young', whom the source believed were 'being trained for espionage purposes by the Japanese in Canton'. They also reported on the location and personnel of Japanese intelligence organisations in Peking and Canton. But while the SIS stations in China had done much to meet their wartime task, they were not similarly well informed on Communism, the forte of the prewar SIS China stations. In January 1945 General Wedemeyer had told representatives of British and United States clandestine organisations operating in China that they were not to interest themselves in 'matters which pertain to the internal affairs of China, i.e. they were not to have anything to do with the Communist question, etc.'. The Japanese as a common enemy had formed the only basis upon which the presence and activity of Allied secret services in China were tolerated in wartime. Peace was to be another matter.

18

Postwar planning

As the war drew to a close SIS, like everyone else, began to think about the postwar situation. In this respect the Foreign Office were quicker off the mark than most, commissioning a review of postwar intelligence needs and organisation in 1943–4 which was strikingly to lay the basis for the future development of SIS.

The Bland Report

During 1943 a number of people began to think about the future of the intelligence machine. In March, Duff Cooper (then head of the Security Executive) suggested to Churchill that a committee be set up to consider the matter, and proposed that there should be a unified Secret Service combining MI5, SIS and SOE into three branches: Information, Security and Operations. Churchill was not so keen. 'Every Department which has waxed during the war', he wrote, 'is now considering how it can quarter its officials on the public indefinitely when peace returns. The less we encourage these illusions the better.' Churchill was against a committee being set up, but suggested that monthly meetings between the heads of the three organisations (which Desmond Morton could attend on his behalf) might enable 'causes of friction' to be 'smoothed away and common action promoted'.[1]

Like previous suggestions for the formal co-ordination of secret agencies (for example the 1940–1 Secret Service Committee, or the Joint Planning Staff proposals of May 1942, which had proposed 'unified control' of SIS and SOE),[2] this proposal came to nothing. A Secret Service Committee meeting was held on 9 April 1943 at which 'it was pointed out that on matters of common concern liaison between the [secret] Services was already extremely close'. There were monthly meetings, for example, between SOE and the Foreign Office, at which Menzies was present, and 'S.I.S. and the Security Service had their own extremely close liaison'. It was bluntly agreed that Churchill should be told 'that monthly meetings of the Secret Services were not considered necessary' and that meetings could be arranged 'as occasion required'. Co-ordination, thus, continued on an ad hoc basis, but the problem of intelligence organisation generally remained in the air. When Geoffrey Vickers at the Ministry of Economic Warfare suggested in May 1943 that after the war a special department should be set up to collate economic intelligence, Denis Capel-Dunn, secretary of the Joint Intelligence Sub-Committee, counselled caution. 'Among the many lessons I have learned during the past 2½ years,' he wrote, 'one has been how unsatisfactory it is for small, or indeed large, independent organisations to grow up with indeterminate responsibility, e.g. S.O.E., the Security Executive, with all its ramifications.' The 'future of economic intelligence', he continued, 'cannot possibly be considered apart from the future of the intelligence organisation as a whole'.[3]

At about the same time that Vickers's idea was being discussed, Peter Loxley was also contemplating the matter. The thirty-eight-year-old Loxley was an extremely well-regarded official, 'quite the most promising of the younger men at the Foreign Office', who was killed in an air crash flying to the Yalta conference in February 1945.[4] Like previous private secretaries to the Permanent Under-Secretary, he provided one of the main links between the Foreign Office and SIS, so much so that the Service was occasionally described in official minutes as 'Mr. Loxley's friends'. On 2 April 1943 Loxley wrote to Menzies that postwar planning was 'in the air' and it struck him 'that the time has come when you ought to be doing some serious future planning for S.I.S.'. He thought that a number of matters needed particular attention, including recruitment, which appeared to him to be haphazard, and conditions of employment, which under existing conditions offered neither security of tenure nor pensions. He also felt that the Chief should have a designated deputy. At the moment Menzies was carrying far too great a personal burden, and on the rare occasions when he was absent, there was 'no one man in charge of S.I.S. as a whole'; instead, 'four deputy directors, plus Vivian and probably one or two others, each continue to run his own sectional affairs but without anyone of them really overseeing the whole organisation'. Loxley finally raised the question of the relations to be established in the post-war world between British diplomatic missions and SIS representatives abroad.

Perhaps prompted by Loxley, during April 1943 the SIS Board of Deputy Directors were urged to begin thinking about forward and post-war planning. At the end of the month, the chief of staff, Commander Howard, circulated a paper on the 'Re-establishment of S.I.S. posts in Europe', which raised questions both of the scale of the planned postwar organisation and of the cover under which representatives would oper-ate. Another quite urgent problem was that of recruitment. The Deputy Director/Army had reported 'that we have now reached the limit of can-didates from the War Office'. The other services, moreover, 'have been practically barren for some time'. It was suggested that more use might be made of women, 'at any rate under present war conditions'. This raised an important question. The number of women employed by SIS increased enormously over the war, though almost invariably they were used only in subordinate clerical and office support roles. Even when they were employed, entrenched male attitudes caused problems. Reporting 'dif-ficulties' among the secretaries in his station at Bari in southern Italy, John Bruce Lockhart observed that 'most of the male officers are fairly pudding-like and are either misogynists or else consider that a woman's place is the bed and the kitchen, certainly not the mess'.

Inside the Foreign Office, Loxley argued that it was a particularly op-portune moment to consider the future of intelligence organisation gen-erally. Reflecting the fact that the Office was less pressed by work at this stage of the war than was anticipated would be the case after it had ended, and because he and his colleagues had 'a very real interest in the matter', Loxley argued that 'there is every advantage in our trying to clear our own minds on the subject while there is still time to do so at leisure'. He 'diffidently' put forward the case for a 'single Government intelligence body devoted to the study of military intelligence in the widest sense of the term'. This would be like the Joint Intelligence Sub-Committee (JIC), but 'more unified'. He was not sure which government department should take responsibility for this organisation, but thought perhaps it would be the Ministry of Defence, although he observed that the Foreign Office had a major interest in 'what may loosely be called civilian, as op-posed to service, intelligence'.[5]

This matter essentially concerned the organisation of intelligence-assessment, but, as Loxley observed at the end of August 1943, 'intertwined' with the role of the JIC after the war was 'the future organisation of intelligence relating to foreign countries'.[6] SIS was central to this discussion and early in October Cadogan appointed a three-man committee under Sir Nevile Bland to report on 'the future organisation of the S.I.S.'. Bland was at the time ambassador to the Netherlands government-in-exile. Having first been posted to The Hague in September 1938, he had had the disagreeable task of fielding the diplomatic fall-out from the Venlo incident in 1939, an experience which could have prejudiced him against SIS. But he was already well acquainted with intelligence matters, as in the 1920s he had been private secretary to five successive permanent under-secretaries, and had been secretary to the Secret Service Committee in the 1920s. The other two members of the committee were Loxley, Bland's successor in that crucial private secretary position, and Victor 'Bill' Cavendish-Bentinck, who had been chairman of the Joint Intelligence Sub-Committee since the beginning of the war. The surviving documentation confirms that Loxley was the key member of the group. He acted as secretary and prepared the text of the report, which among other things addressed all the issues he had raised in his original letter to Menzies. Bland told Cadogan that the 'principal credit' for the report was due to Loxley, who was no doubt also responsible for the lightly ironical tone which suffuses parts of the text. From the very start the committee worked 'in conjunction with "C"', and Loxley circulated drafts not only to his fellow committee-members, but also to Menzies at SIS.[7]

The Bland Report – 'Future Organisation of the S.I.S.' – which was completed in October 1944, is a crucial document in the history of the Service. Despite the vicissitudes which SIS had suffered thus far during the war, its continued autonomous existence was powerfully embedded in the report. Its findings formed the basis for the organisation of the Service as it emerged after 1945. And if, as seems to have been Loxley's intention, the report was designed as a pre-emptive strike, seeking to es-tablish the Foreign Office vision of SIS's future role and relationship with the rest of government, then it was outstandingly successful. Menzies, too, could hardly have hoped for a more favourable result. Summarising the 'cardinal points' of the report for Cadogan, Bland stressed first that

FUTURE ORGANISATION OF THE S.I.S.

Report of a Committee set up by Sir A. Cadogan on the 8th October, 1943.

I.—GENERAL.

WE have conducted our enquiry on the basis that it is essential to have a highly efficient British Secret Service in peace-time.

In the course of our enquiry we have covered a larger field than we originally intended and we have made various recommendations, especially designed to ensure that both the Foreign Office and the Staffs of the Armed Services will continue to receive all possible assistance from the S.I.S.

In the present chapter we wish to confine ourselves to making certain recommendations of a general nature: our more detailed recommendations will emerge in the following chapters. Our general recommendations are :—

(1) The range of countries and subjects to which its customers wish the S.I.S. to devote attention after the war is an extensive one. Nor do we believe that it should be otherwise. Experience gained during the war has shown only too clearly how much this country lost from the financial starvation of the S.I.S. during the lean years between the two wars and how much money we have had to expend during the war in order to obtain intelligence that could have been obtained so much more easily and cheaply before the war began.

The opening section of the 'Bland Report', which laid the basis for the postwar Service.

SIS and GC&CS 'must always remain under the direction' of the Foreign Secretary. Second was the conclusion that 'no secret organisation should again be allowed to operate abroad', except under the direction of SIS. Thus was SOE's future decided (at least by the Foreign Office). Bland further proposed that SIS 'must start to build up a really secret organisation behind its existing, much too widely known, façade', and the report also included a remarkably forthright and positive manifesto for the future role of the Service, embodying an assumption that in the postwar world human intelligence would be of enhanced importance:

> S.I.S., however costly, is far the cheapest form of insurance in peace time against defeat in war, but to be effective it must be efficient. It can only be efficient if staffed with the best men we can get. We can only hope to get the best men if we can offer them first class pay and prospects. We must never again try to run the S.I.S. on the starvation level of the lean years between 1920 and 1938. It is necessary to emphasise the importance of an efficient S.I.S. now more than ever, inasmuch as it seems unlikely, in the light of developments in cyphering, that we can count indefinitely on obtaining the bulk of our most valuable and secret information through the G.C. & C.S.[8]

The report itself is a substantial thirty-eight-page document, in which all aspects of the Service were considered. Recruitment, as Bland had indicated in his letter to Cadogan, was fundamental to its success, but it was also 'the most difficult of all the problems that at any time face C. If . . . the S.I.S. does not succeed in attracting the right men, first-class results cannot possibly be forthcoming.' Good pay was essential, and the prewar practice of seeking recruits 'among men with private means or enjoying a pension from some other service, merely to enable the S.I.S. to economise in salaries', was firmly dismissed. The committee recommended that 'men between the ages of 30 and 45 who of their own volition would prefer a change of employment', as well as 'a fair proportion of young men when they leave the University', should be targeted. With a nod towards the modern world they also pointed out 'that the S.I.S. has been backward in employing women'.[9]

Bland stated that the 'main task' of the SIS was 'to obtain by covert means intelligence which it is impossible or undesirable for His Majesty's Government to seek by overt means'. It followed that, with the exception of some counter-espionage work conducted 'for the better protection of its own agents', SIS did 'not collect intelligence for itself but for its clients'. Consequently, if waste was to be avoided, it was 'at all times important that S.I.S. should know what its clients want'. Requirements should be clearly indicated, and an appendix to the report included Foreign Office and service ministry priorities for SIS in the postwar period. But the committee also thought – and here perhaps is evidence for Menzies's own discreet role in the formulation of their report – that it was 'almost equally important that consumers should not try to foist on to the S.I.S. work which it is not really the latter's function to perform at all'.[10] Consumers were 'apt to do this in three main ways': by asking SIS for information which, 'at any rate in the first instance', could be obtained overtly; 'by putting enquiries to the S.I.S. on quite trivial matters' (though what constituted, or who decided, what was 'trivial' remained undefined); and by expecting the Service 'to perform digestive work', summarising and collating reports, which was properly the task of the consumers.

The Bland committee wanted to sort out the relationship between the Service and its consumers. Central to this was the role of the Foreign Office and Bland recommended that the wartime innovation of seconding a member of the Foreign Office as personal assistant to C should be continued after the war. This official would handle all liaison matters between the two departments, and a second Foreign Office representative would be attached to Major Woollcombe's Political Section to deal with the transmission of SIS intelligence to the Foreign Office. The committee similarly thought that the policy of appointing senior service representatives to SIS should be continued (though not as deputy directors, but as senior naval/military/air representatives). Bland argued that 'the ideal arrangement would be attained' if these officers were 'of high reputation' and if it were understood that their career prospects would be enhanced by secondment to SIS.

Turning to the matter of SIS representation abroad, the committee pondered the various arguments for the Service operating under diplomatic or independent business cover. It had been suggested to the committee that, with or without the knowledge of the company concerned, SIS could recruit employees of British firms operating in foreign countries, or 'suitable Chairmen of British Companies' could be asked 'to provide cover in their offices abroad for regular S.I.S. personnel'. In the former instance the committee worried about possible conflicts of interest, and in the latter it thought that 'such obliging Chairmen are likely to be few'. While the committee were considering this matter, Claude Dansey wrote to Peter Loxley that he had been hearing 'on all sides that everyone is recommending the use of "Big Business" for S.I.S. in the future'. Dansey was scathing about the possibilities and sent Loxley a memorandum about his difficulties with 'Big Business' before the war. 'The plain truth', he asserted, 'is that the men in Big Business can never see beyond their own financial interests' and would not directly help SIS. From the war itself, he asked, could anyone 'quote an instance' of any firm which had 'ever delivered [a] drawing of machine tools – something which was very hard to come by – I doubt it'. He concluded: 'The best service business can render to S.I.S. is to give cover to agents whose loyalty is primarily to S.I.S. and not to the business concerned,' and he was 'happy to say that there are here and there business firms which will give such cover without any questions, merely asking that every reasonable precaution shall be taken to prevent them being compromised'.[11]

Bland concluded that the best prospects would come from 'the creation of small businesses which would in fact be solely run in the interests of the S.I.S.'; the recruitment of established British businessmen who ran their own private concerns and would 'have no-one to fear in the shape of a board of directors in London'; and 'the obtaining of cover from semi-national and often non-profit making British institutions with offices in foreign countries'. These could include British railway companies or the British Overseas Airways Corporation. Another possibility was the British Council, though it was somewhat grumpily noted that the Council had 'never been ready in the past to lend the smallest assistance to the S.I.S.'.

As for official cover, which hitherto had in some cases been highly problematic, the committee had 'no hesitation in recommending that, in the absence of very strong reasons to the contrary', the Foreign Office should accommodate SIS personnel, though not necessarily with diplomatic or consular rank. 'The advantages of obscurity', they noted, 'may often outweigh those of official standing.' No single title, moreover, should be reserved for SIS representatives, and 'it would seem desirable to ring the changes and to use as well, according to circumstances, such titles as

Assistant Naval, Military or Air Attaché or Assistant Commercial Secretary. We note', continued the report dryly, 'that consumer Departments are always eager to receive high-grade secret intelligence, but that they are apt to show much less enthusiasm when they are asked to lend S.I.S. representatives the cover of their name.' Whatever cover was adopted, Bland was sure that the SIS representative should live up to it: 'If he has business cover, he must genuinely do business. If he is the Assistant Commercial Secretary or is a member of a Consulate, he must perform a sufficient amount of commercial or consular work, not only to deceive the natives of the country but also to sustain his apparent rôle among his colleagues at the Mission.' The committee also reiterated the practice that SIS representatives attached to British missions 'should not work against the country in which they are stationed without the prior knowledge and consent of the Foreign Office'. In the past, they noted, this 'used to be a firm rule', but during the war there had 'been a considerable relaxation of standards and in neutral countries the rule is probably now as much honoured in the breach as in the observance'.

One area where this rule could be modified was counter-espionage, which the committee thought in foreign countries 'need seldom be in any way compromising'. SIS representatives in this field would 'be openly known to the police and the deuxième bureau of the country concerned, and will in many cases be actively collaborating with them'. These representatives, moreover, could safely retain the title of Passport Control Officer which almost all SIS personnel abroad had used before the war. 'This fact', remarked the report, 'became so widely known that little extra harm would have been done by affixing a brass plate "British Secret Service" to the door of their office.' There was even some advantage to using the PCO designation since 'if all C.'s counter-espionage representatives bear this title and none of his other representatives do, it should furthermore act as a red herring to draw away to the former, who do nothing compromising, the attention of foreign police authorities which should really be devoted to the latter. Indeed, it is arguable that the more that C.'s counter-espionage representatives are really thought to be gatherers of secret intelligence, the better.' Commenting generally on the particular importance of counter-espionage in wartime, the committee noted that it was 'a branch of activity which demands, when at its height, heavy expenditure on staff, card indices and other records' and 'it would be a great mistake if the main branch of the S.I.S. were to be handicapped after this war through the expenditure on counter-espionage work not being ruthlessly pruned when it is no longer of major importance'. There was, moreover, a potentially difficult political dimension with counter-espionage work, and in an early draft of the report Bland firmly recommended that SIS 'should not direct its energy to investigating the activities of political organisations', such as 'Communists, Anarchists, &c . . . unless specially directed to do so, and then only for such time as may be considered absolutely necessary'.[12] The committee also recognised that there was much 'duplication and overlapping' in this area between SIS and MI5, and it was 'grossly wasteful to have two separate bodies covering so much of the same ground'. They therefore recommended that 'at an early date' there should be a separate inquiry into the division of responsibilities between the two agencies.

Counter-espionage was an area which the committee thought was 'always likely to be a fruitful field for collaboration' between SIS and secret services in other countries. During the war there had been very close contact between SIS and 'the secret services of our Allies', with the result that those services were 'now all very familiar with the personnel and to some extent the methods of the British S.I.S. This may not matter to-day,' reflected Bland; 'but we do not consider that it is a state of affairs which should be allowed to prevail for a day longer than is necessary once the war is over.' The committee did not support ceasing all collaboration with Allied secret services as after the war it could 'yield good fruits'. They felt, moreover, that 'token open collaboration with the secret services of other countries may serve to conceal the fact that our real energies have been diverted to other channels'. Collaboration (or 'liaison' as it came to be known) 'should only occupy a small part of S.I.S.'s energies', which should primarily be directed towards developing an entirely self-sufficient 'postwar organisation whose methods and personnel and other secrets should be entirely unknown to any foreign secret service'. Reflecting, among other things, continuing assumptions about Britain's future status as an autonomous Great Power, the committee affirmed that 'it is upon itself, and upon no one else, that the S.I.S. should in the main rely'.

Bland also addressed the tricky topic of special operations. Noting that SOE's 'present activities' were not within their terms of reference, the committee somewhat disingenuously reported that they 'therefore thought it wiser not to ask any members of the Organisation to appear before us'. But having consulted quite a few other people, including departmental heads in the Foreign Office, as well as 'certain Service representatives', they observed that it was 'impossible to conduct any enquiry into the S.I.S. without coming across numerous examples of the harmful impact upon it of the present existence of a second, independent secret organisation functioning in the same fields'. The report therefore decided it to be 'inconceivable that there should exist in peace-time any secret organisation operating in foreign countries that is not responsible to the Foreign Secretary'; that SOE should be wound up as an independent organisation; and that such special operations functions as it was thought appropriate to retain should be managed by SIS.

This had been the Foreign Office view for some time. In December 1942 Cadogan had written to Charles Hambro at SOE, explaining that the Foreign Secretary had 'firmly concluded' that after the war there would not be room for two secret services, and that no clandestine organisation would be allowed to operate on the Continent except under Foreign Office control. At the time it is evident that SOE themselves did not necessarily accept this as a final decision, and they certainly envisaged a long-term postwar presence in former enemy-occupied countries (a role which they proposed to the Chiefs of Staff Committee in May 1945).[13] But a different view was taken elsewhere. In April 1944 Bill Cavendish-Bentinck wrote that he could not 'believe that anybody in their senses and outside S.O.E. seriously contemplates that organisation continuing after the war separate from the S.I.S. and not firmly under F.O. control'. In June, when Rex Leeper, British ambassador to the Greek government, raised with Peter Loxley the question of SOE having any potential postwar role in the Balkans (to which Leeper was vehemently opposed), Loxley told him about the Bland committee and added that it was considering 'a variety of matters of mutual interest to the Foreign Office and my friends [SIS] in the postwar world'. 'Between ourselves,' he told Leeper, 'we shall almost certainly recommend that, if and when any organisation for covert action is required, it should be made part of my friends' organisation and should on no account be a separate body.' Implying that this effectively was a Foreign Office stitch-up, Loxley asked Leeper to 'keep all the foregoing to yourself, especially the part about the Bland Committee, as S.O.E. are not in on this at all'.[14]

Bland did not by any means dismiss the entire idea of special operations, merely noting the unlikelihood of there being much call for them after the war. In notably cautious and conditional terms the committee thought, however, that it would be a 'mistake to abandon the principle that in almost any foreign country occasions may arise when it may be useful for His Majesty's Government to resort to bribery, &c., for the furtherance of their foreign policy (this in contrast to the strict S.I.S. practice of only paying money for the collection of intelligence)'. The committee thought that SIS should establish a small department to preserve and develop expertise in this field (including 'deception') and prepare specifically for 'secret action in time of war'. The Foreign Office view was that the Middle East was the only region where such action was likely to be necessary in the foreseeable future. Various British agencies had for years paid 'subsidies' to regional leaders, but the committee also thought that an independent organisation might be necessary to run 'news agencies, broadcasting stations, &c., which, while appearing to be Arab controlled, are in fact vehicles for the dissemination of the British point of view'. Bland considered a further variety of special operations, including 'the employment of private individuals to work on political parties, specialised groups, &c., in foreign countries with whom they might have some influence'. It was suggested that there might be elements – such as 'opposition parties, minority groups, press, labour, business or ecclesiastical organisations' – with which 'Englishmen of standing in different walks of life' might be able to form closer and better contacts than could British diplomats. While this kind of activity – 'the exercise of persuasion and influence by private persons' – might not necessarily be particularly compromising to the British government, the committee delicately noted that it might not 'seem desirable that there should be too obvious a connection between the Foreign Office and private individuals'. Although not expressing 'a view on the merits of the proposal', the committee thought that it would 'in practice prove desirable to entrust the task to C.'.

Consideration of special operations naturally brought the committee to the technical aspects of secret work. It was accepted that the large wireless communications section which had grown up during the war would be very substantially reduced. Menzies told the committee that he thought it 'most unlikely that in peace-time' it would be necessary to provide agents with their own wireless sets. Assuming that the Foreign Office would develop its own wireless communications, it was thought that SIS could use it, and, moreover, that the costs of developing and maintaining secure communications could be transferred from the Secret Vote to the Foreign Office budget. As well as specialised wireless equipment, Bland noted that in wartime, 'and to some extent in peace time', secret organisations also required 'secret inks and similar processes, microfilms, forged documents, seals, &c.', and 'sabotage and counter-sabotage equipment, including certain types of arms'. Obviously research in these matters 'should not be abandoned when the war is over', both to maintain British expertise and to keep up with 'scientific developments in other countries'. Bland's view was that this work, though itself highly secret, did not need to be borne on the Secret Vote, and that a new research department should be established for this purpose, which would have an analogous position to that of the GC&CS. The Chief of SIS would be its Director-General, and, since its work would be of most interest to the armed services, they, or the Ministry of Defence, could meet its costs.

Bland's recommendations regarding the financing of future research reflected the committee's general opinion that all possible expenditure should be accounted for openly: 'We reach this conclusion partly on principle and partly because we see practical objections to the Secret Vote being larger than necessity dictates.' The committee argued that the larger the Secret Vote, 'the greater the risk of parliamentary comment and criticism at home'. On the other hand, too much economy could be very risky and the committee expressed 'the strongest hope that it will be remembered how starved of funds the S.I.S. was from soon after the end of the last war until the Secret Vote began markedly to increase once more in 1936, and what increasingly great dividends the S.I.S. has paid since it has had ample funds at its disposal'. Thus they also wanted 'to sound an earnest note of warning against again allowing the Secret Vote to be reduced too far'. The committee assumed that the wartime figure for the Secret Vote would be published. This had risen from £179,000 in 1936 to £15 million in 1943 (of which SIS's share had been £117,000 and £4,170,000), and they worried about the impact this might have on public opinion. 'We are concerned', they wrote, that 'there may be an idea among the British public that something like a Gestapo has been operating in our midst during the past few years, and lest a reaction against the employment of secret means to obtain information about the views and activities of British subjects may lead to an ill-informed revulsion against the S.I.S.' They suggested that this possibility could be countered by the Prime Minister, or a senior military figure such as Field Marshal Montgomery, making public statements which confirmed the high importance of the intelligence provided by the secret service.

The last subject covered by Bland was the Government Code and Cypher School. The committee noted that GC&CS had 'performed its task brilliantly' during the war, though this success had been largely unexpected. Reflecting views expressed even at the time of the Hankey inquiry in 1940, they remarked that during the last war it was 'generally thought' that 'never again could cryptography pay such a dividend as it was paying then. One is almost forced to make the same observation again to-day, for it seems unthinkable that we shall ever be able to read more traffic than we can read now. But it is highly rash to prophesy,' and they agreed 'that no time, labour or money should be spared to permit the G.C. & C.S. to read everything that is readable'. Nevertheless, 'the probability that cryptography is a wasting asset strongly reinforces the need for a first-rate S.I.S.'. As for the relationship between SIS and GC&CS, the committee decided that they 'should emphatically not recommend removing the G.C. & C.S. from the supreme control of C. since we are strong believers in the unified direction of all secret intelligence work directed against foreign countries'. But the committee, evidently aware of the danger of depending too readily on signals intelligence, were opposed to any complete integration of SIS with GC&CS 'since it could only result in the long run in making the personnel of the S.I.S. feel they could rely on the fruits of cryptography, instead of having to bestir themselves to obtain intelligence through agents'.

Peter Loxley sent a draft copy of the report to Menzies, who said that he was 'in general agreement with the main recommendations'. It was clear (and no doubt comforting to Menzies) that the committee counted 'on the organisation of an S.I.S. of far greater efficiency in the Peace era than it was possible to create before the War'. Finance was obviously fundamental, and, allowing for as much spending as possible being provided on Open Votes, Menzies hazarded that 'an effective Foreign S.I.S. should be maintained for under 1 million per annum'. He disagreed with the proposal to appoint 'senior service advisers', who, he reckoned, would lack 'sufficient practical experience of S.I.S. work to enable them to accept extensive executive responsibility'. Liaison with the service ministries was much better secured by the Service Circulating officers – 'in constant liaison with the individual sections of the Service Department concerned' – assisted by able junior active service officers, seconded to SIS for two or, preferably, three years. Menzies noted the long-term nature of counter-espionage and asserted that funds should be provided for it. He agreed that 'the C.E. budget must be reduced very materially below its wartime level', but warned against doing this too drastically. With an apt allusion, he observed that 'a counter-espionage service cannot be built up between a Munich and a declaration of war'.

Menzies agreed that there should be a separate inquiry into MI5. The present position was 'not satisfactory' and steps should be taken to eliminate 'the present duplication of records and of research even though complete amalgamation of effort may prove to be neither practicable nor desirable'. Menzies, indeed, was fiercely anxious to maintain SIS's monopoly of foreign intelligence-gathering and he strongly deprecated as 'highly detrimental' any proposal 'which permitted M.I.5 to run a foreign Intelligence Service in any country parallel to, or in competition with, S.I.S.'. As for SIS's relationship with GC&CS, Menzies said he was not yet in a position to offer firm advice, as this would have to await the conclusion of 'a far reaching investigation' which he had ordered about the future of signals intelligence work.[15]

One part of the report which particularly exercised Menzies was the specific injunction that SIS's counter-espionage section 'should not direct its energy to investigating the activities of political organisations, *e.g.* Communists, Anarchists, &c.'. This, he argued, ran 'directly counter' to what he had 'thought to be the Foreign Office wishes in this matter'. He noted that the 'Foreign Office desiderata in regard to Europe' (provided in an appendix to the report) included as the first priority to watch for any revived 'attempts by Germany to spread her influence in other countries', and second 'to observe Russian activities . . . and the activities of national parties or groups in different countries who look to Moscow for leadership or support'. Menzies added that in October 1943 SIS had been 'expressly encouraged to build up an organisation' to deal with 'this type of work' (hence the creation of Section IX). 'In general,' Loxley himself had written, 'we can count on the N.K.V.D. and other Soviet organisations pursuing covert aims and activities in contradiction to the overt policy of the Soviet Government, but with the latter's blessing.' These activities, he added with a nice touch of ironic understatement, 'are not likely to be for our benefit'. It was 'only common prudence to learn as much as is possible about these aims and activities', and it should be possible to do so without running any 'undue risk – provided that you do this through foreign Communist parties outside the U.S.S.R.'. With an observation which was sadly much truer than even he might have suspected, Loxley concluded: 'The Russians would surely think that we were fools not to do so when it is absolutely certain that they have a wide network of agents here.'[16]

Menzies felt that a blanket prohibition on dealing with 'these semi-political matters' would impose on him an 'impossible' and 'unwarrantable handicap'. 'In its more detailed aspects,' he argued, 'the study of Communism abroad is irremediably linked with counter-espionage Intelligence.' He had, moreover, appointed a senior officer to co-ordinate all aspects of this work and proposed 'to establish a separate section charged to deal with this particular subject'. Menzies wanted the restriction deleted from the report. He convinced Nevile Bland, who thought he had made an 'irrefutable case'.[17] Loxley was less impressed, and thought that Menzies's comments were 'the pure milk of the doctrine of Colonel Vivian' (not inaccurately casting the veteran head of Section V as an inveterate anti-Communist). Forwarding Menzies's paper to Cadogan, Loxley observed that while the Foreign Office certainly wanted SIS to watch 'Russian activities', which might, for example, include studying 'the Communist Party in e.g. Greece', he thought it wrong 'that S.I.S. should go witch-hunting and study Communists for their own sake. The Communist Party', he continued, 'is a legal party in this country and it would be a great mistake if the S.I.S. ever came to be regarded as an instrument of the Right Wing.' Loxley was 'frankly scared of the "Indian policeman" outlook in connexion with counter-espionage'. Loxley also thought Menzies was wrong to resist the appointment of senior service officers to SIS. 'The Service Departments', he wrote, 'will always make trouble if they aren't allowed a nominee of their own at Broadway.'[18]

After further consultations with the Bland committee members and Cadogan, Menzies formally proposed some revisions for the report before a final version was circulated. Regarding SIS relations with the service ministries, it was conceded that 'Senior Service Representative' would replace 'Senior Service Adviser', but the only substantial amendment concerned potential counter-espionage activities. Evidently responding to Loxley's worries about the potential political leanings of the Service, Menzies asked that the non-political nature of SIS activities should be firmly embedded in the text. Following a statement that SIS 'may from time to time be required to investigate the activities of foreign political groups or parties, e.g. Nazis, Communists, Anarchists, etc', he requested Loxley to include the following significant admonition, which covered Service activities generally as well as his own specific responsibilities as Chief:

> We think it important that those concerned in the S.I.S. should always bear in mind that they are not called upon to investigate such organisations because of their political ideology; and that they should therefore only engage in such investigations when there is prima facie evidence that the organisation in question may be used as instruments of espionage, or otherwise when specifically requested to do . . . We consider it to be of great importance that the S.I.S. should avoid incurring any suspicion that it is the instrument of any particular political creed in this country, and we believe therefore that C would always be well advised to seek guidance from the Foreign Office as to what political parties in foreign countries need special watching, and for how long.[19]

Loxley accepted this, and Menzies's statement, almost exactly as drafted, was included in the final version of the report.[20] There was, of course, an advantage to having such a resounding and perhaps emblematic declaration of political disinterest placed on the record. And by following the correct constitutional line that the Foreign Office directed the work of the Service, it could usefully release SIS from having repeatedly to rehearse the impartiality argument every time a party political organisation was targeted for investigation.

The final version of the Bland Report was printed, and circulated to a very limited number of people, in December 1944. The service ministries were not slow in responding. Indeed, the Chiefs of Staff had evidently already got wind of the proposal to wind up SOE and maintain only a small special operations section within SIS after the war. Towards the end of November, clearly hoping that this was not a fait accompli, they expressed reservations about it to the Prime Minister. Edward Beddington (the Army Deputy Director) and Lionel Payne (Air), whose opinions had been canvassed by Peter Loxley during the writing of the report, both broadly concurred in its conclusions and strongly supported the importance of having senior service representation at the existing Deputy Director level in SIS. The service Directors of Intelligence were less unanimously accommodating about the report, however. While the Director of Military Intelligence (DMI), John 'Sinbad' Sinclair, thought that 'the question of senior Service representation to the SIS' was 'of utmost importance', filling the post was a difficult exercise. The army, he maintained, would be most unlikely 'to appoint a first-class officer . . . to an appointment which is so completely out of the normal run of Army work. Still less are they likely to do so if the appointment is in no way executive.' One possibility was that the post be abolished and the responsibilities taken on by the DMI or his deputy. The Director of Naval Intelligence (DNI), Edmund Rushbrooke, was more blunt. The appointment of naval representatives had 'been tried and failed dismally'. Officers selected 'either had nothing to do, having no executive authority, or else were absorbed into the S.I.S. organisation and ceased to be Service representatives'. Rushbrooke argued that the service Directors of Intelligence could quite well 'protect S.I.S. from unreasonable requests', and he suggested that 'C' himself could appoint three senior SIS officers, who had been members of the fighting services, to administer the work of their respective arms.[21]

There was disagreement among the services about the future of SOE. While for the navy Rushbrooke strongly concurred 'that S.I.S. should absorb S.O.E. after the war and that a separate S.O.E. should never be revived', Sinclair, reflecting the army's more particular interest in SOE's expertise, wanted the matter put before another committee 'to consider the control of all secret organisations'. Sinclair's views generally about the future organisation of SIS are of particular interest, as in September 1945 he transferred into the Service as Vice Chief and succeeded Menzies as Chief in 1952. Again clearly at this stage reflecting the War Office view, Sinclair asserted that it was 'completely unacceptable that cover for SIS representatives should be provided by appointment as Assistant Military Attache', and he suggested that the Ministry of Defence (rather than the Foreign Office) should assume overall responsibility for the Service. Sinclair was agnostic about the future relationship between SIS and the Code and Cypher School. He conceded that 'it <u>may</u> be desirable that both organizations should be under the same Chief', and allowed that this was 'essential while the present "C" continues in office'. Sinclair also commented on the question of recruitment (which was to be a major concern of his after he joined SIS). 'The Committee', he wrote, had 'not mentioned that the war expansion of SIS took place at a very late date. In consequence many desirable recruits were already employed by the Forces, SOE, MEW, etc.' He therefore recommended that 'one senior member of SIS' should be specially responsible for this matter, and 'maintain and revise annually lists of suitable recruits'.[22]

One aspect on which the service Directors agreed was the future importance of scientific and technical intelligence. Edmund Rushbrooke observed that weapons of war were becoming more complex, 'e.g. Radar, Rockets, Jet propulsion, Atomic energy, etc'. SIS officers in the field, therefore, would have to be well briefed about the latest developments. Rushbrooke proposed that 'a small number of specially selected, skilled scientists and technicians should join S.I.S. in order to act as technical advisers'. These individuals, moreover, 'should be of sufficient scientific status to enable them to gain an entree when necessary to foreign academic and university scientific circles'. It was in 'such a milieu', he argued, 'that early information of interesting developments may be obtained'.[23]

While the Bland Report was being considered, the Joint Intelligence Sub-Committee commissioned Cavendish-Bentinck and Denis Capel-Dunn, the JIC secretary, to prepare a study on 'The Intelligence Machine'. Like Bland, Cavendish-Bentinck and Capel-Dunn stressed the need for the 'strongest possible Secret Service in peace', but they also argued that only one agency should be responsible for counter-espionage, and that, since scientific and technical intelligence was likely to be of the highest priority, SIS should concentrate on this specific target. This clearly reflected the armed service departments' intelligence priorities, as did their proposal that the whole intelligence machine should be co-ordinated by the JIC, under the general direction of the Chiefs of Staff. They further suggested that there should be a Central Intelligence Bureau, headed by the Chief of SIS, which would gather and collate material from all existing intelligence sources.[24] Menzies, however, objected to this. He felt that the JIC should remain a non-executive and co-ordinating body, over-seeing the whole machinery of intelligence. 'It was', he claimed, 'quite impracticable for a consultative committee of this kind to wield any ex-ecutive authority over organisations that had executive functions.' As the head of an intelligence-gathering agency, he also thought it wrong that he should head the proposed Central Intelligence Bureau, a consumer organisation. In fact, something of the Bureau concept was established when, without involving SIS or Menzies, in August 1945 the Chiefs of Staff set up a Joint Intelligence Bureau to take over (primarily from the Ministry of Economic Warfare) the collection and study of information on transportation, defences, airfields and various economic subjects.

Although Cavendish-Bentinck was associated with both the Bland Report and the JIC study, the two papers broadly embodied different conceptions of how SIS, in both organisation and function, might fit into the wider government framework. The JIC paper reflected the op-erational, technical and scientific priorities of the armed services, which, moreover, dominated intelligence requirements in wartime. By contrast, the Bland conclusions embodied the longer-term, more political needs of the Foreign Office, which tended to be more apparent in peacetime. At the command level throughout the war (as had been the case in 1914–18), SIS was under continual pressure to integrate its organisa-tion and activities into the military machine. For the most part, arguing both security considerations and a sustained obligation to gather politi-cal as well as military intelligence, the Service resisted these attempts to erode its autonomy, although in some places (notably South-East Asia Command) it was unable fully so to do. What the Cavendish-Bentinck and Capel-Dunn paper represented was an attempt at the highest level, once victory was in sight, to ensure that the peacetime organisation of 'the intelligence machine' largely matched the wartime needs of the serv-ice departments and their particular perceptions of what intelligence was about. Why this attempt failed was in part down to superior Whitehall footwork by the Foreign Office as opposed to the service ministries; but it also reflected the anticipated peacetime intelligence requirements. It may also indicate a more profound British uneasiness with military and potentially militarised organisations which the Bland committee hint-ed at in the concern their report expressed about public suspicions that 'something like a Gestapo' might have been operating in Britain. For

British decision-makers, and perhaps also for the British people, part of the price of winning the war was the ostentatious rejection of those very military values and strengths which had largely made victory possible. In institutional terms, SIS, even though it embodied many military qualities and to a very great extent served the needs of the armed forces, was much more likely to survive and flourish in the postwar world as an explicitly *civilian* organisation under the accommodating supervision of the Foreign Office.

PART SIX
FROM HOT WAR TO COLD WAR

19

Adjusting to peace

Although the conclusions of the Bland committee in December 1944 laid out the broad principles upon which SIS was to develop in the post-war years, the assumption underlying the report that there would be a breathing space after victory had been secured during which the machinery of British intelligence (and, indeed, perhaps the country as a whole) could regroup and reorganise proved over-optimistic. The realities of the postwar world, in which renewed challenges for Britain and SIS, especially those posed by the Soviet Union, combined with national exhaustion and virtual bankruptcy, soon swept away any sense of euphoria. The unexpected change in government following the July 1945 general election, when the Conservative Party and Winston Churchill were decisively defeated by Labour under Clement Attlee, meant that SIS had a new set of political masters. Although Labour had been an integral part of the wartime coalition administration, and Attlee (among other Labour ministers) had been inducted into the existence and role of SIS, the reforming zeal which Attlee's Cabinet brought to the whole range of government focused attention and resources on domestic matters and national reconstruction. But it also underpinned a readiness to review the postwar intelligence organisation and SIS's place within it.

Whitehall warfare

In the summer of 1945, following one of Bland's recommendations, Sir Findlater Stewart, who had been head of the Security Executive and a member of the XX Committee, had already begun an inquiry into the Security Service, MI5. The perennial question of whether MI5 and SIS should be merged into a single organisation was considered briefly but rejected, and Stewart produced a draft directive for MI5's peacetime operations which confirmed that it existed solely 'for the purposes of the Defence of the Realm' and that its responsibilities were confined to British territory. 'M.I.5', wrote Stewart, 'should continue to be responsible for obtaining "counter intelligence" in the Empire by the means used in the past. But', he continued, 'the acquisition of intelligence, including counter-intelligence, by secret means elsewhere, must remain a matter for S.I.S.' Attlee (after consulting Menzies) approved the directive in April 1946, though only after his Foreign Secretary, Ernest Bevin, had insisted that the Foreign Office's intelligence role was formally recognised by adding a sentence to the effect that 'on matters affecting the Foreign Office or the responsibilities of S.I.S., no action should be taken, except after consultation with the Foreign Secretary'.[1]

By the end of the war SIS's relations with the Foreign Office operated on a number of levels. At the top, important policy matters were handled through regular personal contact between Menzies and the Permanent Under-Secretary, Sir Alexander Cadogan, who was succeeded by Sir Orme 'Moley' Sargent in February 1946. At a lower level the Permanent Under-Secretary's private secretaries (notably Peter Loxley before his untimely death in February 1945, his successor Tom Bromley, and Aubrey Halford from the beginning of 1946 until the spring of 1949) played an important role in day-to-day contacts. From 1943 the Services Liaison Department in the Foreign Office, which came directly under the Permanent Under-Secretary, dealt with military planning and co-ordinating bodies, such as the Joint Intelligence Sub-Committee and the Joint Planning Staff.[2] Cavendish-Bentinck headed this department and was also chairman of the JIC until July 1945 when he was succeeded by Harold Caccia. Caccia, in turn, was followed in the autumn of 1946 by William Hayter, who served until the end of 1949, by which time the Services Liaison Department had been replaced by the Permanent Under-Secretary's Department, which took over the work of both the Services Liaison Department and that of the private secretary to the Permanent Under-Secretary so far as it involved SIS and the other intelligence agencies. From early 1942 there had been a further link between the Foreign Office and the Service through the appointment of a Foreign Office representative in SIS Head Office with the designation of 'personal assistant to the Chief'. Patrick Reilly and Robert Cecil had successively held the post until the latter was posted to the Washington embassy in April 1945. SIS officers occupied the position until October 1946, when there was a reorganisation of the Chief's personal staff and Terence Garvey (who had been a private secretary to the Permanent Under-Secretary) was appointed to the new position of Foreign Office Assistant to CSS, which thereafter became the main link between SIS and the Foreign Office.

Early in 1946 Harold Caccia prepared a paper on the work of SIS which provides a useful snapshot of the Service in the immediate postwar period. Menzies, he asserted, was 'doing all in his power to ensure that intelligence of the kind that only he can get will be provided'. Caccia, at least, was convinced, and his covering minute reflected the Foreign Office view, that by the beginning of 1946 the Soviet Union had already become the principal threat. 'The main target is, of course, Russia,' he wrote, 'and in view of the difficulty of piercing the iron ring of Russian controlled territory "C's" field is wider and task harder than ever before.' He argued that three things were necessary from the consumer of intelligence: 'patience, support and interest'. Patience was required 'because it may take years to get an agent into the position of trust from which alone he can supply the information required'. Support was necessary 'because the Secret Service will not be able to do the job without the necessary funds' and interest 'because the test is value to the consumer and it is as old as it is true that you get the Secret Service that you deserve'.

In his paper on SIS, Caccia raised a series of important issues for the postwar Service. These included the allocation of resources, both in terms of the overall Secret Vote and as between signals intelligence (in the broadest sense) and human intelligence; and tasking, with the linked issues of the SIS–MI5 division of responsibilities and the question of special operations. He began by listing different 'clandestine methods' by which the Service (including the Government Code and Cypher School) was currently organised to obtain intelligence. These included intercepted telegrams; intercepted telephone calls (marked as 'very secret, & not known outside F.O.'); and 'Agents' reports'. He noted that the advantage of intercepted communications was 'that we get from them the actual correspondence of foreign governments or their representatives', while reports from agents were 'mainly intended to cover quite a different field, namely those questions about which it is difficult, if not impossible, for regular representatives to get information by ordinary means'. He illustrated this by citing 'the activities of communist parties' as 'an example of the sort of question asked'. Caccia then turned to the organisation of intelligence, noting that Menzies had 'since the end of the war reviewed his whole organisation to try to ensure that he will be able to provide what is wanted in peacetime over a long period'. There were 'two main problems': '1. how to divide expenditure between . . . "intercepted" intelligence and . . . agents' reports, and 2. how to recast his organisation for getting the kind of agents' reports which will be required in peacetime'.

Caccia recognised that the machinery for signals intelligence was 'by its nature costly and uncertain', but observed that all departments had 'been anxious that this branch should be maintained if not at a wartime rate at least at a high scale for the sake of the "hard news" that it gives'. He reported that Menzies was 'reorganising and rehousing his "factories"'; was in negotiation with the United States and the Dominions 'for exchange'; and that he had got Treasury sanction for much of the 'listening expenditure' to be borne on the open Post Office Vote. In terms of human intelligence, Caccia noted that SIS had now to refocus its principal efforts on political rather than the military intelligence which had been the priority during the war. Major reorganisation was required, moreover, since during the war SIS had 'worked so closely with other Secret Services that many of its staff have become "blown"'. There was also the problem of accommodating SOE's residual functions of 'training and research in this country and the collection abroad of those kinds of intelligence that are useful for S[pecial] O[perations] in war; suitable landing grounds, demolition targets, etc.'.[3]

In a further note on the work of the Services Liaison Department prepared in February 1946 for the new Permanent Under-Secretary, Sir Orme Sargent, Caccia confirmed that Menzies was engaged in a 'root and branch reorganisation' of 'every single one of his various activities' which, he thought, would 'certainly not be completed before the end of the year'.[4] Menzies, in fact, had begun planning for the postwar Service early in the spring of 1945, evidently as a response to the Bland Report, with the 'C.S.S. committee on S.I.S. organisation'. He himself took the chair, though the day-to-day work was handled by his deputy chairman, Maurice Jeffes, who had been Director of Passport Control since 1938. The other full members of the committee were Dick Ellis, Bill Cordeaux and Kim Philby. Thus Menzies included a balance of long experience

(Jeffes, Ellis and Cordeaux) and comparatively new blood (Philby), though in the latter case also presumably ensuring the distribution of the committee's proceedings to the Soviet intelligence service.

When they reported on 13 November 1945, the committee stated that their overall aim had been 'to plan for a practical peace-time S.I.S. organisation, which will be capable of rapid expansion in time of crisis'. They explicitly built on the Bland conclusions and both formalised and streamlined the structure of the Service as it had developed over the second half of the war. The committee proposed that SIS be divided into four main branches: Requirements, Production, Finance and Administration, and Technical Services. At the highest level of command it recommended that the Chief should be supported by an officer 'to perform the duties of a true deputy . . . responsible to C.S.S. for the work of all four Branches'. Embedded in this proposal was an implied but definite criticism of the haphazard wartime practice of appointing every now and then a VCSS, DCSS and/or ACSS responsible for only partial areas of work. Each of the four branches would be headed by a director, and those directors could collectively act as an executive committee 'when this may be deemed necessary'.

The Requirements Branch was to be 'responsible for indicating and defining intelligence targets, for assessing production and for guiding and assisting the Production Branch and Stations in the fulfilment of intelligence requirements'. It was also to 'maintain close liaison with G.C. & C.S., in order to ensure that the greatest mutual advantage shall be obtained from intelligence received'. Reflecting Bland's emphasis on the need to improve SIS's requirements dialogue with its consumers, the CSS committee proposed dividing the branch into seven sections, each responsible for a different intelligence area: political, counter-intelligence, scientific, economic, naval, military and air, along with a co-ordination section, which might estimate 'the degree of success achieved by S.I.S. in meeting requirements' as well as producing general background and information papers. The committee also suggested staffing levels for each section, with counter-intelligence (headed by Philby) being the largest with ten officers. This reflected the inherited importance of its predecessor, Section V, and the prevailing assumption that Nazi organisations would continue to pose a major threat after the war. It was also to provide advice for overseas stations about 'penetrating, countering and disrupting' foreign secret services and 'subversive political movements'. Scientific intelligence was thought especially important and had been 'assigned almost the highest priority in the S.I.S. brief'. 'Even though the results may be few and far between,' concluded the committee, 'they are likely to be of overriding importance,' and it was felt that 'the discovery of the majority of the world's scientific secrets' was 'more likely to occur as a result of information from S.I.S. sources than any other'. Thus the Scientific Section was allocated a specific research and collation function which it was hoped would be an improvement on the wartime experience, as 'the somewhat lamentable story of ad hoc committees created to deal with "Crossbow" [German V-weapons] strongly underlined the advantages of centralising the intelligence within a trained unit'.

In parallel to the tasking function of Requirements was the intelligence-gathering function of the Production Branch, responsible for 'obtaining all forms of secret intelligence' and also undertaking 'such Counter-Intelligence activities in the field as fall within the sphere of S.I.S.'. There is a hint here of the overlapping functions of MI5 and SIS which periodically troubled inter-agency relations, but it also embodies a significant use of the term 'counter-intelligence', which became the preferred SIS terminology and denotes active attack on the intelligence services of other countries, rather than the more defensive 'counter-espionage'. Implicit in the usage is the SIS belief that 'counter-intelligence' is to a great extent directed towards the protection of its own operations and security as well as towards the more generalised security of the state. The committee envisaged that the Director of Production would also 'superintend and co-ordinate all double-agent and deception activities'. It proposed creating five Regional Controllers, responsible for the operations of 'all S.I.S. Stations and organisations', as follows: Western Europe (CWE), covering the Low Countries, Iberia, Germany, Austria, Switzerland and Italy, as well as West, Central and Southern Africa; Northern Area (CNA), responsible for Scandinavia, Poland, Czechoslovakia and the USSR; Eastern Mediterranean (CEM), covering Hungary, the Balkans, Turkey, the Middle East as far as Iran, and North-East Africa; Far East and Americas (CFE&A), 'responsible for all countries east of India, and also for the Western Hemisphere'. The fifth, Controller Production Research (CPR), was proposed to be 'responsible for all agents controlled direct from Head Office', as well as 'talent-spotting' for the other Regional

Controllers. This arrangement operated from late 1945, though in May 1947 the Western Europe Controllerate was divided into an Eastern and a Western Area.

On the production side one organisational anomaly remained which even the tidy-minded root-and-branch reformers on the CSS Committee were unable to remove: the Special Liaison Controllerate (SLC), which constituted the rump of Biffy Dunderdale's wartime empire and embodied his carefully nurtured liaison arrangements begun with the prewar French and later adding the wartime Polish intelligence service. In what was effectively an independent station based near London, Dunderdale ran an operation 'with a highly specialised staff of Russian-speakers, mostly of Russian origin' engaged in collecting, processing and distributing Russian-language material, some of which was provided by the Poles. Sensitive to Dunderdale's status in the Service, if a bit hazy about what he actually did, the committee also 'understood that there still existed certain personal links of long standing between S.L.C. and elements of the former French IIième Bureau' and 'agreed that such links, whatever they were, should remain undisturbed'. All the committee could suggest was that Dunderdale's outfit might in general eventually come under the new Directorate of Production.

The other two branches proposed by the CSS committee were to provide administrative and technical support for the 'core business' of the Service. Among the responsibilities of the Director of Finance and Administration was to be training, and the committee made the revolutionary (for SIS) suggestion that 'a Training Section should form part of the post-war organisation'. Specific recommendations were made for 'Officers' Initial Training' for all new entrants to the Service, 'Advanced Technical Training' – an annual course for 'Officers at Head Office and Stations abroad', and 'Secretaries' Training'. The underlying aim was to bring SIS into line with current training practices in the armed forces and business. 'It is the policy of the Services,' they noted, 'and indeed of most large commercial firms, for all members of such services or firms destined for responsible positions in them first to obtain a good general knowledge of all departments and branches of the work. It is believed', they continued, 'that this principle should also apply in our case.' The 'advanced technical training' was primarily intended for SIS officers, but could also be adapted for agents and even carried out at the stations abroad where they were to be run. Among the subjects it could include were secret inks, letter codes, micro-photography, radio communications, tradecraft and the 'latest developments in concealing devices, document copying and special gadgets'.

Another area for improvement under Finance and Administration was the Registry, which for sensible security reasons had been evacuated to St Albans at the beginning of the war. When most of the rest of Head Office returned to central London less than a year later, the Registry stayed put. Inevitably it had expanded enormously during the war – its prewar staff of six increasing over tenfold – but the inconveniences and delays in moving documents between St Albans and London meant that some Head Office branches began to develop their own independent filing systems. The vitally important 'central personality reference index' also suffered, and by the end of the war had become so unreliable as a vehicle for tracing potential contacts and agents, that (as a subsequent SIS report observed) the Service became 'dependent to an unhealthy degree on the relatively comprehensive index maintained by MI5'. The Central Registry was brought back to Broadway, and an effort was made to reconstitute the Service's archives and personality records. Some improvements were made, but the branch remained understaffed throughout the 1940s. This was also true of security matters. In November 1945 Menzies appointed Valentine Vivian, the wartime overlord of Sections V and IX, to be his Security Policy Adviser under the designation 'A.S.P.'. Establishing the security of the Service on a proper basis was an important development, though at the start Vivian was given no machinery to carry out his responsibilities. Matters improved, however, after he was made Inspector of Security in February 1947, with a staff officer to assist him.

Absorbing SOE

The fourth main branch proposed by the CSS Committee was Technical Services, which was to ensure that SIS had 'at its disposal every type of technical apparatus or process required for the acquisition and communication of intelligence', and it was the only part of the committee's work which took much account of the mooted absorption of SOE into SIS. An ad hoc sub-committee on technical requirements, with representatives from SOE and the War Office, was set up under Air Commodore Jack Easton, who had served in Air Intelligence during the war and been brought into SIS in August 1945, becoming Assistant Chief in November. Faced with SIS proposals concerned almost exclusively with communications, and SOE ones focused on the development of devices and equipment, Easton's sub-committee had to try to combine and rationalise the two sets of requirements and propose realistic and economical arrangements for the future. This they did rather successfully, with the establishment of workshops on two separate sites, one concentrating on communications and the other on weapons and analogous technical devices. In due course (as suggested in the Bland Report) much of the cost of these establishments was met from the Open Vote of the Foreign Office and the Ministry of Supply respectively. Further Secret Vote funds were saved by the emergence from Gambier-Parry's Section VIII in 1946 of a new Diplomatic Wireless Service under Foreign Office direction, which took charge of all the government's secure communications requirements.

By the time the CSS Committee reported in November 1945, SOE's fate had been well sealed. There was an effort to establish a continued independent role after its parent department, the Ministry of Economic Warfare, had been abolished in May 1945. Cavendish-Bentinck uncharitably thought that Colin Gubbins (who had succeeded Charles Hambro in September 1943) 'saw himself as continuing indefinitely as head of S.O.E. equal to C and under a Director-General of the Secret Services'. But the Foreign Office remained determined to take it over as part of SIS. Cadogan told Bevin it was 'essential' that Menzies thenceforth should be head of both organisations; Bevin agreed and put the matter to Attlee, who on 23 August 1945 confirmed that there should be 'a single head – that head being C'. In November, on the advice of an ad hoc committee chaired by Cavendish-Bentinck (which included Menzies and Gubbins as well as representatives of the service ministries), the Chiefs of Staff Committee defined a limited planning and training role for a much reduced SOE. It was to maintain a cadre organisation which would have 'adequate clandestine contacts', 'up to date information regarding potential objectives' and 'covert communications capable of functioning at short notice on the outbreak of war'. Suggestions from within SOE that it might play an active role in occupied Germany and Austria against any Nazi revival, or a possible Soviet threat, got short shrift from Sir

Orme Sargent in the Foreign Office. 'All this seems to me excessively dangerous,' he minuted on 28 November, at a time when there were still widespread (if, as it turned out, wildly unrealistic) hopes that the wartime alliance with the Soviet Union might continue in some form. 'It is one thing to arrange for S.O.E. to maintain an organisation in this country in peace-time capable of quick and effective expansion in time of war, but it is quite another matter for it to embark on activities against Russia, or indeed any other friendly country, in present circumstances.' It would be 'time enough' to do something of the sort when the government 'decided to prepare for war against Russia – if, indeed, when that time comes, there is found to be any place for the tricks and contraptions used by S.O.E. in the last war with such dubious results'. He described SOE's activities in Germany against unregenerate Nazis as those 'of a secret police', and a 'dangerous and invidious task' for which SOE was neither equipped nor originally created to perform.[5]

The absorption of SOE by SIS marked a stage in the progressive assertion of Foreign Office control over all clandestine activities overseas, a policy with which Menzies apparently fully agreed, as demonstrated by the draft of an important 'directive to be issued to the Chief of the S.I.S.' which he submitted to Harold Caccia in January 1946. Indeed, the fact that Menzies could write his own terms of reference demonstrated both his sensitivity to the requirements of his political masters and the high degree of mutual confidence which had been established between them.

> In time of peace [Menzies's draft stated] it is essential for political reasons and also on grounds of economy that the S.O.E. organisation should be reduced to a small staff at home and that no operations or preparatory work should be carried out abroad unless and until authorised by the Foreign Office. The only exception to this ruling is in the case of certain activities in the Middle East and India which have been specifically authorised . . . Special operations with secret Intelligence are to form a unified Secret Service controlled and administered by you.

Caccia agreed on 2 February 1946 that this draft not only correctly reflected 'the decisions of the Chiefs of Staff' but also met 'Foreign Office requirements satisfactorily', and a circular telegram to British diplomatic

representatives across the world in March 1946 laid down that henceforward there would be 'a single Secret Service and C's local representative'
would be 'solely responsible in your country'. The Secret Service would
'not undertake any activity other than obtaining intelligence without specific prior approval from the Foreign Office. In particular clandestine
recruitment for resistance movements has been banned.'[6]

Winding up SOE took several years. The scale of the exercise is illustrated by the fact that special operations accounted for £500,000 of SIS's
1946–7 estimated Secret Vote allocation of £1,750,000, more than the
entire MI5 share (£325,000).[7] Beyond special operations, moreover, SOE
made a significant contribution to the postwar SIS in terms of technical capabilities and training expertise. On the technical research and development side, two establishments were set up, one building on SOE's
special strengths in such matters as sabotage, explosives, fuses, weapons
and various chemical tasks, while the other, drawing on the experience of
Gambier-Parry's Section VIII, focused on communications and electronic
development. But SOE's greatest legacy lay in training, which during the
war had developed on a much more extensive and thorough basis than
that of SIS. Much of the SOE Training and Development Directorate
was taken into SIS, and by the late 1940s was providing courses not only
for officers, but also for secretaries and agents, who could be instructed
in such matters as 'black' frontier-crossing operations, by land, sea or air
(including by balloon). In his first progress report to the Chiefs of Staff
on special operations, covering the first six months of 1946, Menzies
expressed the hope that 'almost all the staff of the joint Secret Service'
would have 'received training during the next two years. Officers', he
noted, would 'receive instruction in both S.O. and S.I. subjects' so that
they would 'be able to undertake both types of work'. Progress, in fact,
was not quite as rapid as Menzies had predicted. By mid-1947 fewer
than forty officers had been on special operations courses, though all SIS
recruits who attended the newly introduced 'General Course' (a hundred
in 1946) were given 'a short period of general instruction on the nature
and requirements of S.O. work'.

SIS's absorption of SOE was not universally approved. Field Marshal
Lord Montgomery, who served as Chief of the Imperial General Staff
(CIGS) from 1946 to 1948, regretted the loss of SOE's independent ex-
pertise and attempted to reopen the whole question of special operations

and secret intelligence organisation. In November 1946, during a discussion about the importance of Greece (where British forces were supporting the anti-Communist side in the civil war) and Turkey, he told the Chiefs of Staff Committee 'that special operations in Turkey might prove to be of considerable value', and he got the committee to agree to 'a review of the control and responsibility for the S.O.E. organisation'. The following March he launched an outright attempt to shift responsibility for the whole secret service (including operations *and* intelligence) from the Foreign Office to the Ministry of Defence. He argued that 'the system of control adopted in peace should conform as closely as possible to that required for war'; that the use of special operations as a means of furthering British policy 'should not be lost sight of'; and that 'at present all the emphasis' was on secret intelligence, and it was 'not possible' while the Foreign Office was 'in control in peace to employ fully those "unacknowledgeable" activities which may be required in furtherance of British interests'. The Ministry of Defence, furthermore, was already responsible for some inter-service organisations, and if it took over SIS, 'the Foreign Office would be relieved of the embarrassing responsibility for approving "unacknowledgeable" activities'.[8] Neither SIS nor the Foreign Office was much swayed by this generous offer, and although Montgomery got the Chiefs of Staff Committee to agree with him, his attempt to prise SIS away from the Foreign Office soon came to a shuddering halt. 'Monty' was not a success as CIGS. Whatever his skills on the battlefield, the doctrinaire, brusque and hectoring style he brought to the corridors of power in London was no match for the perhaps more subtle and feline skills of veteran Whitehall warriors like Menzies.

But it was not just a matter of Menzies outmanoeuvring Montgomery in some deft bureaucratic quadrille, since it is clear that neither the Foreign Office nor, in fact, the Ministry of Defence was in favour of altering the responsibility for SIS. As the Minister of Defence, A. V. Alexander, told the Chiefs of Staff in June 1947, the transfer of SIS to his ministry was 'not practical politics. Even if the Foreign Secretary were well disposed towards the idea, which he is not,' he added, 'I do not favour the transfer of the Secret Service to the Minister of Defence.'[9]

Managing the Service

Reconstructing the bureaucratic structure of SIS during and immediately after the Second World War is gravely hampered by the absence of some central administrative records. It is clear, for example, that after the appointment of the three armed service Deputy Directors in the spring of 1942, a Board of Deputy Directors (which it seems may have acted broadly as an executive committee) was formed with Claude Dansey, as Assistant Chief, in the chair. There is evidence that this body had meetings at which some notes of the proceedings were kept, but no full minutes of any specific meeting, let alone a complete set of its minutes (if indeed one ever existed), has been found in the archives. Under the reformed structure introduced following the recommendations of the Chief's reorganisation committee, from November 1945 there was a 'Weekly Meeting of Directors', and the Director of Production held regular meetings of his Regional Controllers, in which a wide range of matters was discussed, including administration, finance, recruitment, personnel, training and requirements. In the absence of any records of Directors' meetings (which do not, apparently, survive for the 1940s), these minutes comprise the main central SIS records for the postwar period.[10] The Regional Controller meetings were superseded in January 1947 by the 'VCSS's production conference', which covered much the same range of business as its predecessor.[11]

During 1946 the structure recommended by the Chief's reorganisation committee in November 1945 was broadly adopted for the postwar Service. In the spring of 1946 (reflecting changing priorities), a Director War Planning was appointed. The Requirements Directorate – handling tasking and relations with customer departments – came into being under Claude Dansey, and the existing Circulating sections became known as 'R.' sections.[12] In 1948 a liaison section, R.8, was created to handle relations with the SIS Production side, as well as the Government Code and Cypher School. Reflecting the increased importance of the Soviet target, the counter-intelligence section, R.5 (which had taken over the wartime Sections V and IX), was divided in two: R.5/Int. for counter-intelligence generally; and R.5/Com. to concentrate on Communism. When John 'Sinbad' Sinclair, the Vice Chief, took over direct responsibility for Production in January 1947, he created three Chief Controllers:

Europe (CCE), which encompassed the existing Northern and Western European areas; MidEast (CCM), which covered the Mediterranean, Balkans and Middle East; and Pacific (CCP), to cover the Far East and the Americas, though Dick Ellis, who held this position from May 1947, continued to style himself Controller Far East. Kenneth Cohen, who had been Controller Western Europe since early 1944, became Chief Controller Europe and John Teague became Chief Controller MidEast. With broadly equivalent status was Dunderdale as Special Liaison Controller and the new Controller Production Research, who set up a front company to provide commercial cover for his activities.

The Head Office postwar reorganisation did not, however, satisfactorily resolve the inherent conflict between the Requirements division, organised on a worldwide basis, and Production, based on specific geographical regions. The two extremes, as Sinclair observed in March 1949, were 'control by stations' and 'control by targets'. If the former were strictly applied, a controller and his production staff might 'ignore possibilities of finding agents on his door-step in England and of lines being run, or that could be run, by other Controllers into his area'. But if the latter were applied, it 'would lead either to unco-ordinated orders to Stations or to friction in Head Office' (or, of course, both). Examples of targets being attacked from geographically remote stations occurred during the war, when much of the small amount of intelligence SIS was able to collect about Japan came from sources in diplomatic missions across the world. The tension between 'station' and 'target' in part explained the apparently anomalous existence of the Controller Production Research section running agents from the United Kingdom, and the survival of Dunderdale's SLC networks. In October 1948 the Controller Production Research told the VCSS's production conference that although some of his British agents overseas, many of whom operated under business cover, were prepared to work under the local SIS representative, other firms and individuals were 'not prepared to play except on the basis that all contact would be in the U.K.'. In these cases all he could do was to 'keep the Controller concerned informed'. The same applied to any Controller proposing 'a scheme for running a line into another Controller's area', and Sinclair laid down that in such cases Controllers (including CPR) and Dunderdale should inform each other of any projects for each other's areas. In matters of disagreement, Sinclair himself would make the final decision.

The modernisation of SIS practices and procedures brought with it an increasing bureaucratisation of work. From the Second World War onwards the Service could no longer be run in the more informal way that Admiral Sinclair and his colleagues had been able to enjoy. Size alone – the postwar Service was ten times the size of the prewar – meant that paperwork and proper office procedure were essential for efficient operation. The formal acquisition of Foreign Office approval for operations, the drawing up of detailed station directives, regular and systematic training, close attention to and the organisation of regular feedback from customer departments all became routine in the late 1940s. Briefing the Middle East stations in May 1946, London stated that it was important for the benefit of those who came later that 'lessons learned' in the running of agents and operations should be reported back to Head Office from time to time. Such lessons were 'of the greatest value' to the training staff. Reflecting the difficult economic circumstances of the time, London additionally pointed out that 'whereas during war funds for legitimate S.I.S. targets were not limited by financial considerations, the strictest scrutiny will, from now onwards, be required'. Future budgets, they instructed, would 'necessitate a much more detailed and close estimate', owing to the more limited resources at the Service's disposal. In order to get some systematic sense of how well SIS was serving its customer departments, moreover, intelligence reports were sent out accompanied by a Comment Sheet (or 'crit sheet', as it was commonly known), asking the customer to grade the report from 'A' to 'D'. Detailed statistics were kept at Head Office of the number of 'A' and other crits scored by stations. But, as is so often the case with performance-indicator schemes, there is the risk that measures of performance themselves become targets. So it was with the crit scheme. It was found that stations sometimes pursued 'A' crits on easy targets to the detriment of devoting effort to more difficult and more important requirements, a tendency reinforced by customer departments with voracious appetites for low-grade intelligence doling out 'A' crits in order to encourage the flow of reports. Thus a system introduced for the best of intentions did not always produce the desired result.

Budget considerations (as ever) underpinned all Service activities during the later 1940s. Menzies believed his initial peacetime allocation was adequate for SIS's needs, but, as austerity began to bite in Britain, allocations were cut across the board and all spending was closely scrutinised.

The old system where the Chief himself, or Pay Sykes, personally scrutinised and authorised the spending of even relatively minor sums of money, did not survive the war, and with the appointment in January 1946 of
a senior Air Ministry official (and former Lancashire county cricketer) to
be the new Director for Finance and Administration (as recommended
by the Chief's reorganisation committee), civil service procedures and
accounting systems were gradually introduced. This took time, but in
November 1949 Sinbad Sinclair reported to his production conference
that Finance and Administration would in future provide Regional
Controllers with a monthly statement of expenditure in their area 'only
one month in arrears'. Station accounts would be provided three months
in arrears, and Controllers were sternly instructed that they 'must not
go beyond their Budget allocations without the matter being referred to
V.C.S.S. through D.F. & A.' But old habits (if that is what they were)
died hard. The same month Ellis (Controller Far East) reported a proposal 'made by the Far East for raising funds through the sale of opium
confiscated by the Customs Authorities'. Ellis said that the matter had
two aspects: the 'moral issue of dealing in opium' and 'the legal financial
aspect'. In this case he had advised 'Far East' against the operation on
the reasonable argument that 'time would have to be devoted to it at the
expense of Production work', and on the mildly more surprising grounds
(though it is just possible that this was a joke) that 'we might get involved
with rogues and undesirable characters'. His colleagues were not against
the matter in principle and agreed 'that there might be occasions in which
raising funds by irregular means would be justified', but they would have
to be approved on a case-by-case basis. SIS's new postwar situation, thus,
meant that not only was there generally less money available but that
any schemes proposed would be much more closely scrutinised by the
Foreign Office than hitherto.

Relations with MI5

Between 1946 and 1950 much time and effort of both Menzies and his
MI5 opposite number was taken up with sorting out the relative responsibilities of the two services. While MI5's primary concern was for security intelligence within the United Kingdom – usually defined as 'up to

the three-mile limit' – and in British territories overseas, SIS's was for gathering intelligence outside British territory. In practice the dividing line between the two agencies was rarely very clear-cut, and arguments about their respective areas of responsibilities were endemic in the relations between them. During the war, distinctions had become particularly blurred, both accidentally and deliberately, through the activities of such bodies as the Security Executive, British Security Co-ordination in New York, Security Intelligence Middle East (SIME) and Security Intelligence Far East (SIFE). MI5 increased its representation overseas especially in the Middle East, where British forces were widely deployed. By 1944 SIME, GHQ Middle East's counter-espionage and security organisation, had links extending to India, Algiers and Italy. After 1945, as Britain pulled in its horns across the world and with pressure for decolonisation being applied at home and abroad (especially from the United States), the question of what was domestic and what was foreign intelligence became increasingly difficult to answer.

Disagreements between SIS and MI5 were especially problematic in the Middle East, where SIME operated in a number of foreign countries. In January 1947, Sir Percy Sillitoe, whom Attlee had appointed Director-General of MI5 the previous spring, wrote to the Foreign Office arguing that the SIME system should continue. William Hayter thought that Sillitoe's objective was 'the establishment of a permanent M.I.5 organisation in the Middle East, involving the suppression of C's organisation there'. Hayter argued that, since SIS had 'greater and more lasting responsibilities in that area', MI5 'should only operate in Palestine [still a British mandate], and that C should be responsible for everywhere else' with 'a representative in Jerusalem to maintain liaison with M.I.5 there'. Menzies thought that Sillitoe had even greater ambitions. 'The logical conclusion of this argument', he wrote, 'is that there should be a single world-wide secret service under his control.' This contention, asserted Menzies, had 'already been rejected by Findlater Stewart. Furthermore,' he added a touch acerbically, 'I cannot but feel that the energies of the Security Service would better be devoted to the problems confronting it in this country, where I suspect that a great deal of work could usefully be done in combating Communist penetration.'[13] The dispute rumbled on for nearly two years. Late in 1948 Sillitoe took his case to Sir Edward Bridges (Permanent Secretary to the Treasury). 'We are faced with a situation', he wrote, 'in which S.I.S. is given an ill-defined security responsibility which overlaps with mine.' The resulting failure of colla-tion, and 'uncontrolled and unsystematic duplication', was producing 'a weakness in our national security' and, 'incidentally, a wastage of man-power'. But another official, Eion Donaldson, was not convinced. 'Root of the trouble', he minuted, 'is the tradition of hostility between M.I.5 and S.I.S. which results in mutual reluctance to exchange information and in a general atmosphere of non-cooperation.' Sillitoe should be told that he 'cannot be given complete and undisputed authority for the study from every standpoint of all subversive activities wherever they may oc-cur', as this 'would interfere with the appreciation of political intelligence from the Foreign Office angle which is, and must remain, the function of S.I.S.'.[14]

But Menzies and Sillitoe managed to patch things up between them-selves. Towards Christmas 1948, after a lunch together at Menzies's club, White's, Sillitoe went to Bridges to tell him that 'the atmosphere between S.I.S. and M.I.5 had completely changed'. Menzies had proposed a joint working party 'from the point of view that there were gaps between them which ought to be filled, and also [Menzies was a keen huntsman] that they ought on occasion to be able to chase the fox over the boundary into the other hunt's territory'. 'I hope', noted Donaldson, 'the Christmas spirit will inspire the huntsmen!'[15] Apparently it did. Meeting during the first half of 1949, the working party agreed that neither service was 'charged with the task of collecting straight intelligence in British (includ-ing Commonwealth) territory' and that this constituted 'a serious gap'. By 4 July a joint 'memorandum of agreement' had been agreed. It assumed that the two services would ultimately share headquarters in London, and that collation work on Communism and hostile intelligence services would then be integrated as far as possible, together with any other areas of overlap where economies might be achieved, including the two reg-istries. While the employment of secret agents in foreign countries was reserved exclusively to SIS, MI5 might 'in certain circumstances' apply to the Foreign Office for sanction to maintain a liaison officer in a foreign country. But such liaison would normally be through SIS channels. MI5 agreed 'to seek straight Intelligence on behalf of and in collaboration with S.I.S. in British territories, within the limits of its own constitutional sanctions and its collecting resources', and special liaison arrangements were made for the services jointly to run cases. On SIS's side this was primarily handled by the Controller Production Research section.

After the agreement had been settled, Sir William Strang, who had succeeded Sargent as Permanent Under-Secretary at the Foreign Office in February 1949, wrote to Menzies enquiring about its practical results. Reflecting the overall government emphasis on economy, he felt sure that Menzies would 'bear in mind the necessity, in these hard times, of confining representation abroad to what is necessary to the exclusion of what is only desirable'. In September 1949, Sillitoe proposed that SIME should close down in Greece, the Lebanon, Amman, Turkey and Iran, leaving the field to SIS, but that it should continue to work in Iraq where he had been 'specially requested by the Foreign Office to negotiate with the oil companies in the hope of exercising some measure of supervision over their security'. He also proposed to hand over SIME's secret agents in Egypt. Menzies agreed with these arrangements, apart from Greece, where he said it was not possible for SIS to take over SIME's work altogether while British troops remained there (as they were to do until January 1950).[16] In practice (and rather like the situation between SIS and SOE during the war), relations on the ground between SIS and MI5 were quite good. In April 1947, for example, Menzies had assured Hayter of the 'very satisfactory collaboration' between SIS and the Security Service 'during and since the war'. Information was 'exchanged on an entirely satisfactory and friendly basis'. SIME and SIS representatives, he asserted, had 'for the past year regularly collaborated in the writing of papers for the J.I.C. Middle East, basing themselves on the information available to each organisation'.[17]

In the matter of 'British' or 'foreign' territory, and SIS's role therein, British India was a special case. By the beginning of 1947 it was clear that the territory would become independent (as it did on 15 August, when it was partitioned into India and Pakistan), and SIS began to consider what intelligence arrangements would be necessary in the future. On New Year's Day 1947 a meeting of representatives of MI5, SIS and the India Office's intelligence organisation, Indian Political Intelligence (IPI), met to consider the issue. On security matters it was hoped that proper liaison could be established between MI5 and whatever Indian security organisation was established. As for SIS, it was recognised that even if the independent government of India was 'willing to liaise in a friendly manner, it was improbable that they would, either on account of inefficiency or lack of interest, be able to furnish all the information required by H.M.G.'. Thus it was proposed that SIS should set up a covert organisation in post-independence India, which, as Menzies explained to Hayter in January 1947, would take over some of the work currently done by IPI, including intelligence about India itself and also about its neighbouring countries, which were all 'without exception either contiguous to the Soviet Union, or are the object of actual or potential Soviet penetration'. Aubrey Halford in the Foreign Office agreed, believing that 'it would be wise to assume the worst, that is, that the Indian Government will be either unwilling to co-operate with our intelligence organisations, or at the best, wholly unreliable even if they agree to do so. Even if', he added, 'India acquires Dominion status, she can never be in quite the same category as Canada or Australia.'[18]

In the spring of 1947 Sir David Monteath, the Permanent Under-Secretary at the India Office, produced a brief on future intelligence liaison with India which proposed the incorporation of IPI into MI5, where it would continue to operate in co-operation with SIS, which itself would carry out covert operations in India. Sending this brief to the high commissioner in Delhi, Sir Terence Shone, Monteath noted that 'in theory Secret service cannot operate in British Commonwealth territory, but we feel that for this purpose we should be wise to treat India as a foreign country'. Since this ran counter to the 1946 MI5 Directive, the Prime Minister's approval had to be obtained, which was done in March 1947. Menzies chose a former Indian policeman, to head his new covert station in India, which was established in August. Although he went with cover as an 'economic adviser', Shone felt that he was too well known as a security official and protested about the appointment, but Menzies insisted and Shone withdrew his objection, though he warned the Foreign Office that if things went amiss, 'you will remember my reluctance'.[19]

Things did go wrong. In March 1948 Dick Ellis reported to a production conference that the officer's D.I.B. [Delhi Intelligence Bureau] background had been resurrected and was considered sufficiently dangerous politically to lead him to suggest his immediate recall'. For the meantime he was bringing him home on leave, 'with a distinct possibility of his not returning', and he felt that this probably meant 'the abandonment of a permanent representative's post and a fresh approach on C.P.R. lines', that is to say with some sort of 'natural', rather than diplomatic, cover. When a new high commissioner, General Sir Archibald Nye, was appointed to India later in the year, he took the view that an SIS station was not necessary at all in Delhi and that British intelligence requirements could be met through the existing MI5 Security Liaison Officer. Again the matter went to the Prime Minister, who now decided that SIS should withdraw completely from India at the end of 1948. This decision established a precedent which became known as the 'Attlee doctrine'. Attlee's instructions about India came to be regarded by the Commonwealth Relations Office (which in July 1947 had been formed in place of the Dominions Office) as establishing a general principle, understandably supported by MI5, that SIS could not undertake any intelligence-gathering activity in any Commonwealth country without the full knowledge and approval of that government. In terms of the old white Dominions – such as Canada and Australia, which were beginning to set up their own foreign intelligence organisations – the 1948 decision was not unreasonable, but in terms of newly independent ex-colonies in Asia (and later in Africa) the 'doctrine' threatened to hamper SIS's operations, especially against the perceived worldwide threat of Communism.

Recruitment and conditions of service

Significant improvements in recruitment and conditions of service were introduced in the mid-1940s, closely following the Bland Report recommendations, and they brought the arcane world of intelligence firmly into the ambit of the modern civil service. This was also marked by the appointment of the new Director of Finance and Administration, and although he was primarily a financial specialist, his regime marked the emergence of SIS as a civilian career service, rather different from the armed services attitudes and standards which had hitherto prevailed. Again following Bland (and in this instance rather in advance of other government departments), Regional Controllers were asked in May 1946 'to consider where, both at home and abroad, women could be employed as officers'.[20] The Director of Production told them 'that several women officers were now available for posting and added that it was accepted policy that they should be employed in those appointments for which their qualifications and experience suited them'. Later that year he ruled that women 'should be recruited on the same level as male officers, i.e. they should be able to be sent abroad to foreign stations'. While 'there was no reason why a woman officer should not eventually become a representative . . . this would be the exception rather than the rule', but he observed that currently a 'minor Station' had been under a woman officer since May 1946. But there was also the problem of obtaining Foreign Office agreement to any such appointment. In April 1949 they refused SIS's application for cover for a woman officer in a Middle Eastern station. At home in the postwar years, too, there was a persistent shortage of trained secretaries, which the Service tried in part to address by running a hostel in Belgravia 'where junior girls who could not find accommodation in London could live very cheaply'.

In 1948 a Recruiting Office was established for the first time (in clear recognition of the need to compete with other organisations and services for the best talent), and the following year the Civil Service Selection Board was brought in to help find suitable candidates. In January 1948 instructions were issued defining the three main types of officers the recruiters were to look for. In the first place were 'General Intelligence Officers' who should be 'men of character, integrity and intellect, combined with imagination and subtlety'. This was a clear echo of the Bland Report recommendation that SIS 'train up more of a team of all-rounders than at present exists' and reflected the CSS Committee's view that 'the S.I.S. officer of the future, engaged on producing intelligence, should be able to fulfil the requirements of any of the Intelligence sections'.[21] Second, there were 'Unofficial Assistants' who would work under natural cover, who should be 'more hard-boiled, in whom integrity and intellect, whilst important, are less essential'; and, third, there were those to be recruited 'on short-term engagements for special and interim purposes'.

The recruitment process continued in practice to involve a mixture of the informal and formal, as recalled by one officer who joined SIS in 1947. Having served in the Guards during the war, ending up with the rank of major, he had spent eighteen months in business before he started to investigate the possibilities of a career in the Foreign Service. Told by a friend 'that a special department of the Foreign Office was looking for new entrants', he expressed interest and was approached by an individual who took him to lunch twice at his club, Boodle's in St James's Street, and quizzed him generally about his life and background. Evidently having passed muster, the candidate was then questioned in some depth at the War Office by a 'Miss Connolly', and further interviewed by a five-member board chaired by the head of the Economic Requirements Section: 'Many questions were put to me, but no information was given of the department for which I was being interviewed.' A week later he was told he had been accepted and he was instructed to report to the SIS headquarters at Broadway.

Cover while assessing potential employees was a perennial difficulty. After a 'Secretaries Combined General & Overseas Course' in February 1947, one of the students complained that 'at her first interview' she had been 'offered an immediate overseas post to an unnamed place at an unnamed salary' and had been 'told only that the work would be interesting'. She said that 'naturally her parents would not agree to so vague an offer' and any cover story that she now gave them was insufficient. They could not 'understand why she was not given a detailed offer, such as would be given by an ordinary business firm, at her first interview'. Vivian, now the head of Service security, neatly summarised the problem as concerning 'our dealings with men and women, who may never become members of S.I.S. but to whom sufficient information must be given (a) to enable them to know whether they want to join us, [and] (b) to enable us to know whether we want them to join us'. No satisfactory solution was found to the problem, though once the Civil Service Selection Board was brought into the recruiting process, Vivian hoped that some formal acknowledgement would be possible that candidates were being considered by the Services Liaison Department (or some such appellation) of the Foreign Office. Above all, he felt that the Service 'should jettison the various amateurish and inconsistent little tricks which we have been compelled to adopt in the past by the purblind reluctance of the Foreign Office to admit any connection with us except behind closed doors and which are far more calculated to betray us and embarrass the Foreign Office than a clear statement of truth'.

Nevertheless, while the Service remained officially unacknowledged, the recruiters had to continue to dissemble as plausibly as they could. Different candidates were told different things, none of which was very convincing, for example that it was a department 'in close touch with the other fighting services', or that it was 'a civil department which works

abroad . . . under the general administration of the Foreign Office',
but which had come into being 'as a result of the Ministry of Defence'.
One successful candidate reported the problem of reconciling the
selection procedure (which he naturally reported to his immediate family) with his eventual cover. The first letter he received had been from
the 'Government Communications Bureau' (which cover name an SIS
conference in February 1946 viewed as 'blown and unsuitable under
new peace time conditions'). The presence of armed forces officers on his
interview board made it difficult to reconcile with the work being
connected with the Foreign Office. 'Only at the last stage (after signing
on)', he wrote, 'is the candidate told the full truth,' and what 'lie (cover)'
he should tell for external consumption. 'In the meantime a suspicious
(and dangerously accurate) idea gets about.' When his actual cover was
eventually 'trotted out', the effect was embarrassing: 'Why all the elaborate selection procedure for a [mere] Passport Examiner (my cover)?' It
was, he added, 'difficult to fool an intelligent questioner'.

Conditions of service were also modernised. In came a grading structure, comparatively generous rates of pay ('below the scale of average
industrial remunerations and slightly above those of the Foreign Office' –
though equal rates of pay for men and women had to wait for some years
yet), and an internal provident fund. In 1946 supplementary payments
were introduced for language proficiency. Out went tax-free salaries
determined by the Chief in the light of an individual's private income and
armed forces pension (if any), and not to be discussed with anyone else.
The Bland Report had also recommended the establishment of a proper
pensions scheme linked to salary and length of service, but this was more
problematic. Since 1943 SIS employees who reached sixty could receive
a pension, but this was paid on an ad hoc basis out of the Secret Vote.
In 1946 the Treasury considered, briefly, introducing a superannuation
fund on the civil service model (on the grounds that 'we are, in effect,
committing the Exchequer to a future pension liability of which
Parliament has not been given any intimation'). The difficulties of managing such a scheme while maintaining secrecy were thought too great,
however, and Sir Edward Bridges ruled in October 1946 that 'we should
go on as at present and take the risks there may be in finding these
pensions as they arise from the current S.S. vote'.[22]

Bringing SIS into line with other parts of government and armed services was the introduction in 1946 of annual reports for officers, including such matters as 'general conduct' ('Of temperate habit: Yes or No?'); professional and intellectual ability; language qualifications; and 'Whether recommended for promotion'. The Service also began to think about the welfare of its members. Subsidised luncheon facilities were provided in the basement of Broadway Buildings. Though inexpensive, these 'were somewhat frugal, and less than pleasantly housed'. This was clearly not enough for some, as in September 1946 it was reported that Menzies had noticed that 'a small number of officers . . . seemed to be extending their luncheon hours beyond the allotted 1½ hours' (which was already felt to be generous). Officers were reminded that 'this period should never be exceeded for other than Service reasons'. Reflecting a continuing distinction between 'officers' and 'other ranks', from 1948 senior members of the Service could use 'the slightly more salubrious, waitress-served (and more expensive) facilities of the Broadway Club', which operated as a kind of senior common room within the headquarters building where colleagues could discuss Service business with comparative freedom. For younger officers a mark of favour was to be invited in the first instance to be an 'evening member' of the club, allowing them to meet their seniors informally over drinks. But even in Broadway security had to be observed and Sinclair reminded officers in November 1947 'that there should be no secret talk in front of messengers, etc., in lifts and corridors and at the time of the emptying of waste-paper baskets, etc.'.

On a number of scores postwar reforms were held up pending the anticipated move into a new headquarters building. Broadway, where the headquarters had been situated since 1926, was grossly overcrowded, and sections of the Service were spread across a range of buildings in both central London and the home counties. There were also security concerns that, especially among liaison services, 'Broadway' had come to be used as a synonym for SIS. In May 1944, for example, after it was reported that both OSS and SOE officers in Cairo had been 'referring to S.I.S. as "Broadway"', instructions were issued that officers should 'refer to this organisation as "C", never as Broadway, S.I.S. or any other symbol'. In October 1945 the Director of Production said he was 'somewhat alarmed by the extent to which the term "Broadway" was used in telephone conversations from the Field to Head Office', a practice he described as 'thoroughly insecure'.

The CSS Committee, noting that the present premises were 'most un-satisfactory', looked into the question of a new headquarters building which might have to accommodate both SIS and the Government Code and Cypher School. It rejected a suggestion that SIS 'should be placed in the country', for example at Eastcote in north London, where GC&CS had moved from Bletchley Park in 1946, as being 'quite impracticable'. Having ascertained from the Ministry of Works that any new building in Whitehall would take at least five years before it was available, the committee told Menzies that 'immediate and most active steps are re-quired on the highest level'. Menzies, who, like many others, felt a strong sentimental attachment to the old place, was not so keen on moving out of Broadway. In 1949, however, the Ministry of Works found a site in Marsham Street, Westminster, for a purpose-built headquarters to be shared by SIS and MI5, with the latter being the avowed occupant. Work actually started on the project, but was suspended following a freeze on government building, and separate arrangements were subsequently made for the two agencies. SIS did not get a new headquarters building until it moved into Century House in Lambeth in 1964.

Technical developments

SIS's scientific research and development organisation after the war was concentrated in two main branches. The SOE development team joined SIS in a new Directorate of Training and Development, and SOE's Station XII at Stevenage, with its wealth of wartime experience, became responsible principally for clandestine equipment of all sorts and special operations matters, such as sabotage, explosives, fuses, drugs and other chemical tasks. SIS's wartime technical establishments were amalgamated into the Government Communications Centre, which dealt with radio communications and electronic development. Since this branch also managed the Foreign Office's secure communications, it was adminis-tered jointly by SIS and the Foreign Office. Because both establishments took on a support role for agencies other than just SIS, arrangements were made (as envisaged in the Bland Report) for their funding to come from the Open Vote. Paralleling research and development was the administra-tion of stores and equipment, including transport. An experienced army quartermaster colonel with the designation Q was brought in to manage this side of things. Q Branch also took over a photographic-reproduction and training team, which was housed in Broadway alongside a printing and roneo (reprographics) section which had existed since before the war.

Beginning in September 1947 the Training and Development Directorate produced a series of 'Development News Letters' to inform colleagues about their work. 'The task of the Development side of D.T.D.', declared the first newsletter, 'is to evolve items of equipment for specialised work. We need [for example] a special type of silent weapon; we do not therefore have to do research work on either guns or silencers. That we leave to the research establishments, but we take their guns and their silencers and adapt them to meet our special needs.' The range of work undertaken (and also therefore the kinds of activities that SIS operations might include) was indicated by the 'five main lines' currently under investigation. First was 'a device which will increase the security of operators on burglarious enterprises'. Infra-red equipment having been found to be too heavy, a torch which cast a 'deep red light' was being worked on. Second was 'a knock-out ampoule or tablet which will behave in a reasonably predictable manner', bearing in mind 'the variability of human beings'. Third was 'a method of opening combination safes', an 'intriguing' subject about which the experts were 'not without hope'. They were experimenting with electronic devices 'and not the sandpapering of finger tips which, we are convinced, was never an effective method of "finding the gap"'. Fourth was 'a gun silencer which does not become less silent with use'. The department had already developed such a gadget and it needed only 'to be adapted to a specific weapon when the requirement arises'.

The final problem was the 'destruction of paper', not at all an easy task, but one which the painful experience of the war suggested was worth addressing, bearing in mind the problems stations had experienced destroying documents ahead of the German blitzkrieg in 1940. In addition to the instances where a courier might need to destroy paper quickly, as well as the 'daily destruction of waste' in a building where fires might not be permitted, the research team focused on 'the destruction of all those files you have kept till the last moment' – inevitably those would include the most secret and most valuable papers – 'and the last moment comes a little sooner than you expected. There is no time now to shovel the stuff in the fire because a determined man could hit you with one hand and pull the stuff out of the stove with the other.' Various techniques were being tested, including accelerated burning and the chemical destruction of paper. Acid, for example, would destroy paper but at normal temperature this might take several days. A mechanism therefore had to be devised to raise the temperature both to char the paper (as 'charred paper is easily soluble in sulphuric acid') and to speed up the process as a whole. But no foolproof system had been developed yet. While the aim was to ensure 'the rapid destruction of a filing cabinet full of files' and 'we hope the paper will disappear in the short time it takes a man to run up a flight of stairs', the 'way things are going it will have to be a short, fat, man with gout and broken wind'.

Postwar development work also reflected the special operations possibilities which were being discussed for the Service, as well as the challenge of infiltrating agents into hostile territory. In January 1948 the problem of throwing tracking dogs off the scent was being addressed, and tests conducted with different substances, including osmic acid which had 'the power to destroy the sense of smell for about a fortnight and if its effect is to thoroughly bewilder the dog for even one day we shall have achieved something'. The following year a detailed report was produced on air-supply operations, clearly drawing on wartime experience, and some 'notes on dogs' indicated how far research had gone on this topic. Aniseed had been suggested for putting off tracker dogs. 'Everyone whom we thought knowledgeable on this subject' had declared that 'a dog could not resist aniseed', but 'when we tried it we found dogs "couldn't care less" about aniseed or any other nice thing' if they had 'been trained to indicate man scent'. Someone had proposed that 'bear fat or cheetah fat' would awaken 'atavistic memories' in a dog 'and he will run from these substances. We doubt it, and not without reason. During the last war a piece of bear fat was obtained and offered to a dog. It was eaten faster than a week's meat ration.' Another approach was to mask human scent and experiments were being planned with deodorants, though this was thought to be no more than 'chancy', since to neutralise human scent a heavy concentration of the substance would be required which did 'not seem practicable under operational conditions'.

A 'Development Progress Report' for December 1949 further illustrates the range of work being done at the time and the extent to which SIS liaised with other government departments on technical matters. An investigation into the use of helicopters had been started with the RAF's Transport Command Development Unit and a prototype compass for use in folding canvas boats had been 'tried satisfactorily by Admiralty departments'. The War Dog School in Germany was working on the problem of evading tracking dogs, and a request for a 'full investigation' on 'the use of hypnotism and/or drugs during briefing and interrogation' had been placed with the RAF Medical Services Directorate, who were also being asked to study 'the uses of plastic lenses as a method of simulating severe cataract of the eyes so as to avoid conscription for forced labour'. A remote 'train count device' was being given preliminary testing by the back-room specialists before SIS subjected it to field trials. Andrew King, the Controller Eastern Area (created in May 1947 to cover Germany, Austria and Switzerland), had 'submitted a requirement for drugged cigarettes' and it had been established that 'cocaine was the only likely drug . . . which would produce the effect desired'. But it had 'been impossible to obtain a sufficient quantity of cocaine in this country' to manufacture enough cigarettes. An investigation on the 'use of biological and chemical warfare agents by saboteurs' had been referred to the Microbiological Research Centre at Porton Down, who had replied that biological warfare agents were 'not sufficiently specific in their action to make possible their use by saboteurs'.

Meanwhile, the problem of destroying paper had been 'satisfactorily solved'. The original aim of destroying a filing cabinet full of files proved to be so difficult that the technicians 'asked for a review of the absolute minimum of documents that could be held, and finally got an agreement that code books and three top secret files would suffice'. This had a total weight of nine pounds of paper 'when the hard covers of the code books were removed'. With this new target, progress was rapid and, 'under laboratory conditions', by interleaving the documents 'with oxygen carrying material', they succeeded in destroying the lot in less than two minutes. The next stage was 'to mock up a safe to see if the paper could still be destroyed under rigid security conditions'. About forty spectators assembled for an outdoor trial which went spectacularly well, as one account testified: 'For perhaps fifteen seconds after initiation there was no appreciable change other than a small trickle of smoke from the vent holes at the base of the safe. Then, as combustion got under way, the volume of smoke increased, soon to be replaced by long, roaring tongues of flame.' Some spectators said afterwards that they felt the safe was 'on the point of explosion' and they noted that 'so great was the force of gas issuing from the jets that the safe was lifted some inches off the ground'. The writer was unable to confirm this 'as by that time he had retired to a place of safety behind the building'. A usable safe producing a less violent combustion process was developed, in which 'hardly any flame emerged from the vent holes, although large quantities of smoke made the immediate area uninhabitable'. But the research and development section were able to celebrate a job well done and the production of a satisfactory incendiary safe in which nine pounds of paper could be 'completely destroyed in just under 2 minutes'.

20

Deployment and operations in Europe

Even before the Second World War had ended SIS began to wind down its massive wartime structure, both in Europe and across the world. During 1945 this process went on in parallel with postwar operational planning and the deployment of resources to meet the anticipated challenges of peacetime. Initially, much effort was put into meeting the possibility of a continuing, if residual, Nazi threat, but before very long this was decisively supplanted by a renewed Soviet threat, which was to preoccupy the Service for many years to come. By June 1946 the Joint Intelligence Sub-Committee had concluded that the Soviet Union should be 'the first charge on our intelligence resources' in terms of its war-making capacity and warlike intentions. And, although Attlee and Bevin had initially wanted to cut SIS down, by late 1947 the Foreign Office Russia Committee's representations and Bevin's own experience of the Soviets' behaviour had finally convinced the Foreign Secretary that there was no longer cause for optimism that friendly relations could be maintained in the face of their anti-Western and expansionist campaigns.[1]

Finishing wartime business

Dismantling SIS's worldwide wartime network took some time. Paying off agents was not just a monetary matter. Delicate decisions, for example, had to be made involving recommendations for awards and decorations. There were security considerations, too. Former agents had to be trusted, or paid (or a combination of the two), not to publish their memoirs or tell tales in the pub, especially in parts of the world, such as Eastern Europe, where there was a significant continuing intelligence effort. Widows and orphans also had to be taken care of. Winding up the Jove

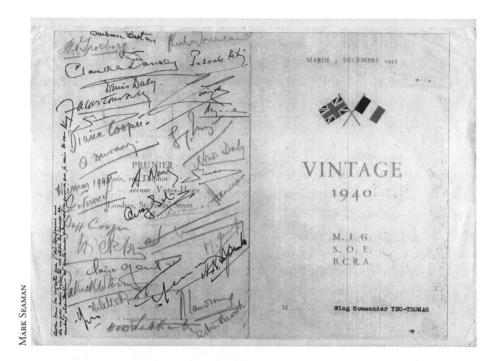

*The resistance hero 'Tommy' Yeo-Thomas's menu from a dinner for British and
French colleagues celebrated at Prunier's restaurant in Paris, 4 December 1945.
Among the signatories are Stewart Menzies and Claude Dansey.*

network, which had operated around Lyons in France, provides a typical
example. A total of just over a million francs (about £5,000, or £161,000
in current value) was paid to the network's forty agents, with the majority
receiving between ten and twenty thousand francs each, the equivalent of
three months' stipend. In January 1945 the Paris station had sought approval to pay 60,000 francs (£300) each to the families of nine Jove agents
shot by the Germans. Approving this, London instructed that 'apart from
normal individual receipts, you should obtain from Jove [a] written statement stating this sum is in full settlement of all British financial liabili-
ties', adding that 'you may of course add British appreciation of the work
he and his friends have done, which will be further expressed in due
course as your recommendations for awards are put through'.

In March 1945 the Controller Western Europe raised the matter of
awards for three Frenchwomen who had worked with the Sussex teams:

'Jeanette Gauthier', and two Resistance helpers: Andrée Goubillon and Marguerite Kiel. Gauthier, who was described as 'unquestionably the heroine of the Sussex plan', had been 'absolutely selfless' and 'beyond all praise'. The other two had run 'continued and very real risks of death over a prolonged period, showing constant, unselfish devotion to the national cause'. Kiel owned a Paris café and Goubillon was married to the owner of another one. Over a period of seven months Goubillon had sheltered over twenty Sussex agents, and hid their wireless equipment in the cellar of her café in the Rue Tournefort near the Panthéon.[2] But the possible grade of award being considered – officer (OBE) or member (MBE) of the Order of the British Empire – depended on the perceived social status of the proposed recipient. Jeanette Gauthier, who unusually was a commissioned officer in the French army, was thought eligible for the OBE. The other two, however, although they were perfectly respectable women, were (apparently) 'not what may be termed "Ladies"', and so were put down for MBEs. This pedantic concern with precise social hierarchies was thought sufficiently ludicrous by Kenneth Cohen in March 1945 that he composed some doggerel verse on the subject:

How do you feel
About Marguerite Kiel?
Can Andrée Goubillon
Dance the cotillion?
At what social summit
Stands Mlle. Jeannette?

Their assets, their accents, their undies laid bare,
Then, only then can we apportion the share:
B.E.M.s may be spared for intelligence chores
But O.B.E.s are reserved for the silkiest drawers.[3]

Another illustration of what was happening at the time comes in a signal to the Paris station in the summer of 1946. An officer who had worked during the war in south-eastern Europe, now himself retired, had been re-engaged on a one-off basis to tie up some loose ends. 'For your information only,' instructed Head Office, 'he has been authorised to contact one French ex-Balkan head agent with object firstly of liquidating outstanding claims on us and secondly of arranging compensation for widows of three dead French ex-Balkan sub-agents.' London was sending out a package containing 'a certain quantity of gold which you should deliver via any cut-out you may select' to the retired officer at a private Paris address, 'preferably late at night or before nine a.m.'. Evidently fearing that he might fall into old habits, London added that, other than the planned payment of ex-agent debts, the emissary had 'been strictly instructed on no account to contact your office and to indulge in no repeat no intelligence activity while in Paris'.

Rather than just paying agents off, in June 1945 London suggested to Reginald Miller in South America that 'where an agent has given us service and is in possession of certain information it may save considerable difficulty later if he can be fixed up in some job rather than being let loose on the world with potentialities for blackmail'. But this was easier said than done, and Miller reflected bitterly on the attitude of local British-owned companies where he had tried to find a job for an ex-agent. 'You would be shocked', he cabled London, 'if you knew how unwilling all British firms so far approached are to do anything of this nature where their businesses are concerned. That we have fought a bloody and costly war for several years so that they may continue to possess these businesses, cuts very little ice.' London, however, was 'not in any way surprised' at this attitude and, indeed, thought that it would 'become more so, hence our anxiety to try to get any arrangements made while there are still some memories of the war'.

A more sombre legacy concerned Bla, the agent who had been killed by members of the Alliance network in southern France in October 1942, leaving a wife and children. In late 1945 his widow approached the SIS head of station in Paris (27000), saying that she had 'heard a rumour that her husband had been executed as a double agent and she wanted either to know the worst, or to put the rumour down'. He discussed the matter with Marie-Madeleine Fourcade, who had led the network. She thought 'that although we may have to tell Mme [Bla] the truth to prevent her getting involved in proceedings to put these rumours down, (which she threatens to do) we should not make the facts known officially for the sake of the children'. He added that the death could be made to look like suicide, as 'the body was in fact found in the sea, and the newspapers of the time put it down as suicide'. On instructions from London, 27000 told Madame Bla 'that we had irrefutable evidence that her husband, after his arrest by the Germans, accepted to work for them'. He had been 'contacted again by us (I purposely did not indicate whether the "us" was 99532 [Alliance] organisation or S.I.S.) in Marseille, and admitted his guilt and committed suicide'. He added that any attempt to clear Bla's name 'must end in disaster'. If Madame Bla 'kept quiet, nobody but ourselves would know the truth and her name and that of her children would be saved'. Sympathetically (if somewhat disingenuously, as he was also clearly concerned about protecting SIS's reputation), 27000 added that 'the main thing was to prevent her children and his family in [the] U.K. from learning of his downfall'.

Priorities and practices

In intelligence matters, as in other spheres, British (and Allied) attitudes towards Germany at the end of the war were very much coloured by memories and lessons learned from the First World War and the peace settlement which had followed. In part, the principle of unconditional surrender and the absolute need for Germany's defeat to be demonstrably total to both the world at large and the German people themselves stemmed from a sense that the German, or Prussian, militarism which had allegedly been a major cause of the earlier conflict had been insufficiently crushed. Now any trace of that dangerous infection had to be thoroughly extirpated, and a high priority for SIS was its role in dismantling the mighty German war machine and ensuring that 'never again' would be a fact, rather than just the pious hope it had evidently been between the wars. In 1944 the Bland Report had predicted that 'close on the heels of victory' SIS would have 'to assist in the rooting out of members of the enemy intelligence services and the forcible disbandment of those services themselves'. One of the Service's 'prime tasks' would be to ensure that the Abwehr and Sicherheitsdienst were 'effectively broken up and that remnants of the Nazi party do not succeed in maintaining an organisation underground, whether in Germany itself or in some foreign country'. Additionally, 'by the examination of captured documents and the interrogation of arrested persons, the S.I.S. should be able to acquire a fund of valuable material about the general methods of the enemy secret services'.[4]

This last objective involved the Service with German former intelligence officers whose thorough debriefing could throw much valuable light on the intelligence successes (and failures) of the war. British interrogators, for example, carefully investigated the German side of the Venlo debacle. With the growing Soviet threat in mind, German counter-intelligence expertise on Communist networks and techniques was much in demand (by United States as well as British agencies), leading the Service to deal with some pretty unattractive former (and not so former) Nazis. One such was Sturmbannführer (Major) Horst Kopkow, a leading German expert on Soviet intelligence, who had been head of Gestapo Amt IV 2A, dealing with war sabotage. Kopkow's particular wartime target (which he had attacked with some success) had been the Soviet 'Rote Kapelle' network, but it was also reported in 1945 that he had an 'encyclopaedic' knowledge of the German intelligence service. After he had been arrested by British forces in May 1945, Kopkow co-operated fully with his captors and was interrogated over the next few months, producing a voluminous series of reports, rated as only second in value to the information provided by the Nazi intelligence chief Walter Schellenberg. During 1947 Kopkow was held for some time by the Allied War Crimes Group on suspicion of having mishandled prisoners and of having executed United States airmen. He was also interrogated in connection with the execution of British prisoners at Gross Rosen in Silesia. In March 1948 the War Crimes Group shelved the case for lack of evidence and 'provisionally released him for special employment under an "I" agency here [SIS] who, however, have specially requested that the case against him should not be dropped'.[5] In order to facilitate Kopkow's future use, SIS faked his death. A cover story was invented that he had died while interned in the United Kingdom, a death certificate was issued to that effect and a false identity was created for him as 'Peter Cordes'. He lived under this name for a while, but later appended his real name to the alias and settled openly in West Germany.

At the beginning, along with the final subjugation of Germany, followed by Allied military administration in separate British, American, French and Soviet Occupation Zones, 'denazification' and eventual postwar reconstruction, there was also a wide public assumption – an optimistic emotional hope as much as any rationally derived belief – held with varying intensity, that the wartime alliance with the Soviet Union would survive in some shape or form. In SIS, with its historic professional suspicion of Communism, there was less confidence in Moscow's bona fides, but the Service was not unaffected by the prevailing mood. Allowing Harold Gibson, a prewar Passport Control Officer and from his time in Istanbul undoubtedly blown to the Soviets as an SIS officer, to go into Bulgaria in September 1944, for example, makes sense only in the context of assumptions about a continuing alliance of some sort. But the hard-nosed Soviet refusal in Bulgaria to accommodate British and American intelligence officers, even as part of an Allied Military Mission, provided a rapid corrective to any expectations of postwar co-operation. For some time after the war had ended, however, the Foreign Office, not perhaps from starry-eyed expectations about friendly relations with Moscow but for sound diplomatic reasons, continued to enforce the formal prohibition on direct SIS work against the Soviet target first imposed during the war. But this did not at all mean that SIS ceased to target Communist and Soviet expansionism in general – far from it. As it became clear that there was no realistic prospect of any Nazi revival, and especially as the Soviet Union tightened its grip on Eastern Europe, much of the Service's work became focused on Communism and Communist-related affairs.

The re-emergence of a kind of renewed 'Great Game' between Britain (as part of the Western Alliance) and Russia, with a priority on the gathering of long-term political intelligence, took SIS back to familiar territory and for many in the Service it was a welcome move away from the incessant wartime demands for immediate, short-term operational information. By the late 1940s, however, the situation had changed markedly. The Iron Curtain now divided the Moscow-dominated bloc of countries in Eastern Europe from the West. During 1948 the Communist seizure of power in Czechoslovakia in February and the Berlin Blockade from June demonstrated a hardening of Soviet control in the East, and the Communist conquest of China the following year confirmed the global extent of the challenge. For SIS the position in respect of intelligence-collection in these territories to a certain extent reflected that in Europe following the German victories of 1940. Such intelligence sources as there had been were mostly swept away, the overt collection of information was gravely impaired, and the demands on SIS escalated to include the most trivial details of everyday life in these obsessively well-protected countries. The very success of British intelligence during the war, moreover, with the matchless signals intelligence and the development of productive agent networks in occupied Europe, left some customer departments, notably the armed forces, with quite unrealistic expectations of what SIS could be expected to provide in these new circumstances. On the other hand, accumulated wartime experience, together with the absorption of SOE into the Service, fuelled a greater willingness than hitherto in SIS to undertake special operations and, certainly, to use wartime expertise for the infiltration of agents into Communist-bloc countries, where (as during the war) it was assumed there would be viable resistance networks to provide support for them.

That there was also a Communist threat nearer to home was confirmed after the defection in September 1945 of Igor Gouzenko, a cypher clerk at the Soviet embassy in Ottawa. This became known as the 'Corby' case, the name apparently chosen from the Corby's Canadian whisky favoured by the officers working on the case. According to the SIS archives, the first notification London had about Corby was on 9 September, two days after Gouzenko and his family had been taken into protective custody by the Royal Canadian Mounted Police. The message, transmitted over secure SIS channels through Sir William (Bill) Stephenson's British Security Co-ordination office in New York (as was all the cable traffic on the subject), was from Norman Robertson, Permanent Under-Secretary to the Canadian Department of External Affairs, to his British counterpart, Alexander Cadogan. A 'statement made yesterday . . . by clerical officer of Soviet Embassy in Ottawa', read the cable, indicated that 'Soviet agents' were operating in Canada. This was 'supported by convincing documentary [evidence of] political and scientific espionage'. The investigation was 'proceeding in consultation with Stephenson and F.B.I.'. Further details followed in a flurry of telegrams on 10 September, including the fact that Soviet espionage in Canada was being run by Nikolai Zabotin, the military attaché in Ottawa, who was running a GRU (Soviet Military Intelligence) bureau with a staff of sixteen. A British atomic scientist working in Canada, Dr Alan Nunn May, was named as having passed both information and samples of Uranium-235 to the Soviets, and while the Soviet embassy were showing 'signs of alarm at disappearance of official', Ottawa had 'no way of knowing to what degree they suspect that information about their activities has come to our knowledge'.[6]

While the Soviets may have suspected the worst from the start, they soon got confirmation from their man in SIS, Kim Philby. A signal on 17 September from Moscow to Philby's Soviet intelligence controller in London, Boris Krötenschield, confirmed that information from 'Stanley' (Philby's Soviet cover name) about 'the events in Canada . . . does correspond to the facts'. At the London end, although Menzies was closely involved, the Corby traffic was primarily handled by Philby as head of the counter-intelligence Section IX, and he was also the principal point of contact for MI5, who naturally had a direct interest in the case. On 12 September Philby produced a draft précis of the case so far (probably for Menzies, who had to give Attlee a personal briefing about the matter on 13 September), which is notable for its cautious and soothing tone, including predictions of developments which he had already engineered himself. 'It would appear', he wrote, that the defector's 'information is genuine though not necessarily accurate in all details'. There were 'signs that his disappearance has caused some alarm in the Soviet Embassy', and it was also 'possible, therefore, that other members of the network will have been warned, and in particular that the contact between May and the Soviet agent in the U.K. will fail to materialise'. In a covering note, Philby suggested 'we send out to Canada someone who really knows what he is talking about in the matter of Soviet espionage . . . I doubt whether any of our officers on the spot are competent to tackle the problem.' He suggested Jane Archer or Roger Hollis from MI5. His preference, significantly, was for Hollis rather than Archer, whom he considered the abler and more knowledgeable, and therefore more of a threat.[7]

Philby also attempted to restrict the circulation of Corby material. In his note to Menzies he proposed that communications should henceforth be left to the intelligence organisations, rather than the politicians. The information from Canada, he wrote, confirmed 'an assumption which any responsible person must have made long ago, viz. that the Soviet Union is using every means, fair and foul, to discover the extent of our progress in atomic research'. What remained, therefore, was merely a 'technical job of investigating the extent, ramifications, nature, technique etc of Soviet organisation involved, and of endeavouring to assess the value of the information which it may have received'. Bevin and Cadogan, however, were convinced of the high political importance of the affair. It coincided with a bad-tempered Council of Foreign Ministers in London at which it was feared the Soviet delegation might demand access to atomic secrets, and they insisted that all Corby telegrams should continue to be passed to them. So, although all traffic went through Philby, he does not seem to have restricted what was shown to the Foreign Office and Downing Street. But he was more successful with MI5. When consulted by Menzies, Bill Stephenson welcomed the idea of sending out an MI5 expert to assist in the interrogation: 'yes, please send immediately', he cabled, and Hollis, who flew out on 16 September, became the linchpin of Gouzenko's interrogation. Cables passed between Hollis and MI5 through Stephenson and Philby, an arrangement which MI5 found unsatisfactory and slow. Philby, despite giving constant reassurances that he would let both sides see all communications as soon as they were received, seems to have been adept at weeding out, amending or just delaying key messages, without ever quite going too far, making it hard for MI5 to insist on alternative channels.[8]

Nunn May, meanwhile, remained at liberty. A telegram to him from Moscow with instructions to make contact in London on 7 October had been intercepted and Menzies thought that 'May should be allowed to travel in hopes of giving us an opportunity of identifying his London contact and possibly others.' This was agreed by MI5 (whose responsibility it was) and the scientist returned to Britain to take up a post at King's College London. In Canada Gouzenko named a series of Soviet agents and told his interrogators that the Soviet Union was 'preparing already for war against Western democracies' and that a 'large proportion [of] diplomatic representatives of Russian satellite states' were 'Moscow agents'. Faced with the Corby revelations of Soviet covert aggression, both Cadogan and Bevin favoured a public response, with the arrest of suspected Soviet agents and formal trial, a course of action which it was recognised might involve the public humiliation of the Soviet Union.[9] But there were wider political considerations and neither the Americans nor the Canadians were willing to act. President Truman, hoping to sustain some of the apparent Allied amity displayed at the Potsdam conference in July 1945, and faced with domestic pressure to keep atomic secrets firmly under United States control, was reluctant to upset things by washing dirty Soviet espionage linen in public, even after the FBI had uncovered evidence of an extensive Soviet intelligence network operating in the USA itself. This caused frustration on the British side, especially after Nunn May on 7 October failed to meet his Soviet contact (who had, of course, been warned off in part through Philby's machinations).

All through the autumn Washington maintained an effective veto on action, President Truman refusing to discuss the case with Attlee when he visited Washington in November. On 21 November Menzies told Stephenson that the delay was 'most disappointing', and, while he understood that the FBI did not want to compromise their investigations into the Soviet network, he thought such compromise was unlikely since the Soviets had already been tipped off. 'Meanwhile', he wrote, 'Corby scents are growing rapidly colder since it is already well over two months since first alarm was given.' The Russians, moreover, were 'being given ample time to prepare their case in advance and also possibly to organise counter action'. Menzies's frustrations were understandable, and were amplified perhaps by the fact that by this stage he had effectively become simply a spectator of the Corby affair. Apart from the high politics involved, MI5 were in any case the lead agency for security and counter-espionage matters.

After the affair eventually became public early in 1946 – the Canadians set up a Royal Commission to inquire into the matter, while in England Nunn May was arrested and confessed – Harold Caccia of the Foreign Office, and chairman of the Joint Intelligence Sub-Committee, asked Menzies what, following the revelations of Soviet espionage in Canada, was 'the possibility of repercussions should Russia endeavour to produce a case against S.I.S., with a view to distracting attention'. Menzies told him that there was 'no danger whatsoever at present of any charges being made against S.I.S. for activities within the U.S.S.R.', or Soviet satellite countries, for the simple reason that 'no widespread British organisation has yet been set up'. He had, 'of course, individual agents who might conceivably be arrested', but he regarded those risks 'as somewhat remote in view of the precautions [unspecified] which have been taken'. He added that he would 'be failing' in his duty if he 'did not encourage the rapid building up of organisations within the satellite countries and where opportunities presented themselves for using these to obtain information from within Russia'. But he added an 'old French saying – "On peut pas faire le S.R. [Service de renseignements] avec le curé"'. He hoped, moreover, 'that within a year I shall have a far wider network than exists at present' and assured Caccia that 'particular caution' would be 'exercised during the next few months'.[10]

Both in private and in public, the Corby case certainly focused minds on the active Soviet challenge to the Western world. But it also highlighted the real difficulties politicians and officials in Europe and America faced in responding to this evident threat. A vigorous public reaction carried risks of poisoning diplomatic relationships and making 'peaceful coexistence' between East and West (if that was the overall aim) even more difficult than it was already. In fact, what Corby did was to confirm for many the role which *covert* agencies might play in under-pinning British and Western interests in the developing Cold War. But the problem, as ever, remained one of not getting found out, and the Foreign Office, in particular, were anxious to keep SIS operations under close scrutiny. Replying to Menzies on 12 March 1946, Caccia noted that while Sir Orme Sargent was glad to know that satellite projects were being examined, he was 'most anxious that you should not start anything new in these areas without our knowing', and asked Menzies for 'some explicit reassurance' on this matter, 'owing to the political risks involved'.[11]

Special operations was another possible approach. Following the absorption of SOE, not only did the postwar Service have an enhanced operational expertise, but the Chiefs of Staff Committee in February 1946 had explicitly given SIS 'the task of collating, examining and assessing information bearing on future clandestine operations, and the selection of potential objectives for attack by clandestine methods'. In March, just as the Foreign Office was sending a circular telegram in-forming its representatives that 'the Secret Service will not undertake any activity other than obtaining intelligence without specific prior approval', Menzies was forming a planning staff in SIS to prepare outline plans for special operations in foreign countries. Although Foreign Office approval was required for any such operations, during the later 1940s the Service came under intermittent pressure from the armed services to develop this side of things, as illustrated by Field Marshal Montgomery's brief cam-paign in 1946 for the Chiefs of Staff to take over SIS. Another enthusiast was Air Chief Marshal Sir John Slessor, who promoted the notion of an SOE-type campaign of subversion, sabotage and propaganda against the USSR. At lunch with Menzies in January 1948, he raised the possibility of 'psychological warfare and S.O.E. operations', but was dismayed at the modest level of commitment which Menzies envisaged. While Slessor thought 'something of the order of at least £10 million a year' was 'the minimum sort of scale to which our secret operations to win the cold war should be considered', he was 'alarmed to find that "C" was thinking in terms of £½ million', which seemed to Slessor to be 'derisorily inadequate'.[12] While Menzies's 'inadequate' conception of special operations spending may indicate a certain lack of enthusiasm for the whole idea, the Service did develop guidance on the subject. By early 1949 an 'S.O. Handbook' had been produced with detailed instructions, for example, on 'Clandestine Air Operations', primarily intended for use in the event of another war and clearly drawing on the experience of 1939–45. 'General Instructions on S.O. Planning' laid down broad guidelines, noting that all operations had to have Foreign Office sanction, and emphasising (among other things) that 'the use of Emigré groups' was 'at present banned', although 'contact with selected individuals' was 'likely to be authorised in peace'.

If émigré groups were off-limits, then occasions when Soviet-bloc nationals came to the West might provide opportunities for exploiting. At a production conference in August 1947 Harry Carr 'proposed an effort be made to contact and recruit satellite athletes attending next year's Olympic Games in England'. Sinbad Sinclair was attracted by the idea and asked Controllers to explore ways 'whereby stations might obtain the names of local entrants'. The Controller Production Research was given the job of trying 'to unearth a suitable British intermediary in Olympic Games circles'. But, before approaching the British athletic authorities, it was decided 'to sound M.I.5 on the scheme'. And there the matter stopped. MI5 were reported as 'not hopeful' and the scheme was abandoned.

The difficulty of cover for SIS representatives, which the Bland committee had pondered in 1944, continued to exercise the Service after 1945. One response (and a means to enhance security for SIS representatives overseas) was the development of what came to be known as 'the doctrine of the UA', or 'Unofficial Assistant' as a security cut-out. The main principle of this 'was that a representative should never contact agents direct, but transmit his requirements to them and receive his reports from them through the medium of a carefully selected and trusted third person, generally a local (and if possible British) resident or business man'. When the matter was discussed at a production conference in November

1946, P.7, responsible for part of Northern Europe, said that in his area they had largely failed to find any suitable people for the task. 'Most of the more important businessmen, who might have been suitable,' he reported, 'were either too busy to give the necessary time to the work,' or, if prepared to work, 'demanded unconditional assurances, which we could not give, that if their businesses were to suffer through their connection with us, we should be responsible for any financial losses they might incur'. John Teague thought the problem was not insurmountable, and that a representative could select 'a small number of unofficial assistants who would develop and run, at his direction, "cells" of agents'. The 'ideal Unofficial Assistant', moreover, would be 'a carefully selected, unobtrusive person, with an extensive knowledge of the country in which he was operating'. While it was felt that such ideal candidates might be hard to find, the conference confirmed that 'it was undesirable that representatives should handle agents direct. Whenever possible, unofficial assistants and/or cutouts of a more passive character should be interspersed.'

Another problem for the postwar service was a basic one of acquiring and keeping agents. At a conference in October 1947 the Director of Production raised the matter of 'incentives to agents, whether financial or of another nature'. He observed 'that whilst during war time many agents worked for the organisation for patriotic motives, now in peacetime this motive had, to a large extent, disappeared, although the dangers incurred by agents, particularly in "iron curtain" countries, had not decreased'. He said it was 'arguable' that the 'zeal of agents' might be increased by offering them more money, 'e.g. persuading an agent to go for three months to difficult and hostile territory on the promise of payment of say £1000 down' (equivalent to about £28,000 in modern prices), but he felt that 'incentives of a non-financial nature' might be more attractive. These might include such things as naturalisation as British citizens, or the arranging of education in England of an agent's children, or 'trade benefits', by which a British company might take on an agent as its representative in the country concerned.

At subsequent conferences further suggestions were made, including payment in 'gold, diamonds or dollars', rather than the local currency, and whether life assurance policies could be provided for which the Service would pay the premiums. In this case, although there were 'considerable technical difficulties', Finance Branch thought that there was 'a possibility of making [the] necessary arrangements'. Clearly if agents were simply prepared to work for money, that would be the easiest solution. But it was not always so. In October 1946 Harry Carr, the Controller Northern Area, reported on an actual case which had cropped up on his patch involving a Finnish subject resident in Sweden who was a potential agent. The Finn had 'made it clear that he was prepared to work for the British but on the sole condition that if, at any time, by reason of his activities, threats were made to him that he would be deported to Finland and handed over either to the Finns or Russians', SIS would 'promise either to give him a visa for entry into the U.K. or to ensure that sufficient assistance was given to him to enable him to escape repatriation to Finland'. This man 'had made it clear moreover that money as a reward for his services would not be considered as an inducement'. But Sinclair believed that the Service was unable to make any hard and fast guarantees of this sort. 'We could not go much further', he said, 'than to inform agents that subject to us being satisfied of their good faith and zeal on our behalf, we would take every possible step to prevent them falling into the hands of the Russians,' but 'each case would have to be examined on its own merits'.

Germany

SIS's postwar existence in Germany began in June 1945 with a top-secret paper by the intelligence chief in Field Marshal Montgomery's British 21st Army Group, Brigadier 'Bill' Williams, on 'Clandestine intelligence within the British zone'. Williams laid down that SIS's No. 2 Intelligence (Unit), now renamed No. 5 Civil Control Unit, and the various Special Counter-Intelligence Units, combined as No. 7 Civil Control Unit, were both authorised to run agents in the British Zone of Occupation in Germany. No. 5 CCU was 'responsible for obtaining long term political, economic and military intelligence by clandestine means'. Happily for SIS, and marking the change from war to peacetime functions, Williams instructed that the unit would 'not receive demands for specific intelligence'. No. 7 CCU's task was 'the running of penetration agents' for counter-intelligence purposes. P.6, the German section in Broadway, decided to use some of their existing agents, mainly recruited from among

German prisoners-of-war, 'to lay the foundations of our post-war organisation in Germany'. Only those 'who have either already proved their worth in the field or whose loyalty, in view of their background and present status, is unquestionable' would be selected.

This proved to be over-optimistic. The quality of the agents, their origins, background and motivation varied considerably. Only a handful worked on beyond the end of 1946. One of the most productive, 'Tudor', lasted in Berlin until 1949 and did, indeed, produce valuable political intelligence for much of his active life but became an 'administrative headache'. A very promising agent, 'Upton', a prewar Jewish refugee and Pioneer Corps volunteer, well educated and well connected, produced valuably for a few months but then opted to return to the United Kingdom for demobilisation. Another P.6 agent, 'Merrick', who had been dropped in by parachute near Hamburg in December 1944 and was overrun in April 1945, remained out of touch until 1946, when he contacted the Berlin station and was then run from Berlin into the Soviet Zone. In 1947 he bodily carried a Soviet 85mm armour-piercing shell over to West Berlin, and topped this in 1948 with a Soviet aircraft propeller. He was trained as a stay-behind agent, but was later sacked for 'incurable inefficiency'. A relic branch of SOE, ME 42, which had moved into Germany with the 21st Army Group, was also busy in 1945 infiltrating recruited German prisoners-of-war (known to SOE as 'Bonzos') into prisoner-of-war camps in order to try to identify unregenerate Nazis who might be planning to form a resistance movement. This unit, which SOE had intended to be the spearhead of future SOE operations in Germany, was entirely taken over by SIS at the end of 1945.[13]

Over the winter of 1945–6, the SIS representation in Germany was transformed into an element of the Intelligence Division (Int. Div.) of the Control Commission for Germany (British Element), of which it ostensibly formed the Technical Section, located in Bad Salzuflen, north-east of Bielefeld. No initial directive has survived for the new station, but, considering the overwhelming preoccupation of the Control Commission with ensuring that there could be no resurgence of German militarism or Nazism while the establishment of democratic government got under way, it is likely that SIS's primary initial intelligence role was to penetrate and report on the German economic and political scene, with particular reference to the persistence of Nazism and the role of the

German Communist Party. In mid-June 1946 the chief of the United States Strategic Services Unit (successor to the OSS), Crosby Lewis, reported that 'while there was complete agreement that the principal target for intelligence operations for both British Services and the Americans was the Soviet Union', the British were 'placing a higher priority on activities inside Germany' than the Americans, and appeared 'to be concerned with building up within the British Zone and elsewhere in Germany a long range under cover series of contacts and agents which will serve their interests after the Allied occupation of Germany is over'.[14] Any possible future threat from the Communist East was at first perhaps a secondary concern. On the counter-intelligence side, however, retrospective reporting on the German intelligence service soon gave way to the need to cover Russian intelligence activities in the British Zone.

In November 1946 Simon Gallienne was appointed head of station at Bad Salzuflen and senior SIS officer in Germany. Ostensibly he was head of No. 1 Planning and Evaluation Unit within the Intelligence Division, into which the two Civil Control Units were subsumed. This was one of a series of anodyne cover names which SIS adopted for its German units. Also at Bad Salzuflen was No. 4 Economic Assessment Unit; at Hamburg No. 5 Regional Rehabilitation Section; and at Düsseldorf the Rhineland Statistics Recording Unit. A perhaps apocryphal story relates that when an SIS secretary was asked by a male acquaintance what they did in No. 1 Planning and Evaluation Unit, she replied that 'in the morning we plan and in the afternoon we evaluate what we planned in the morning'. By November 1947 Gallienne had thirty-eight officers and fifty-three administrative staff under his command. He was 'responsible to C' for all secret intelligence and special operations activities based in Germany. His main intelligence targets were 'the Russians' and 'international communist parties and the degree of Russian influence over them'. Along with these were targets which were mostly common to all SIS stations: 'the scientific development by any country of new weapons or methods of war' and 'the intention and capability of any foreign country to wage war, together with its economic potential and relations with the economies of other countries'. As for special operations, Gallienne was instructed to plan for action to be taken in the event of a Soviet invasion of the West, probably including scorched-earth policies, sabotage and stay-behind organisations.

SIS's sources of intelligence in postwar Germany included defectors, of whom quite a few crossed over during the late 1940s. Indeed, defectors came to be seen as an easier and more satisfactory source of intelligence on Soviet matters than agents laboriously infiltrated into, or recruited from, the Soviet Zone, Poland or even the USSR itself. In Berlin in October 1947 Lieutenant Colonel Grigori Aleksandrovich Tokaev (code-named 'Excise'), a distinguished aeronautical engineer, was the first high-level Soviet defector in Germany. Both SIS and MI5 were able to interrogate Tokaev (who produced a great deal of intelligence of varying quality), but were only peripherally involved in handling the defection. SIS, however, was soon active in trying to use Tokaev to encourage the defections of other Soviet officers known to him as having dissident tendencies and a new post was created at Bad Salzuflen to co-ordinate policy and the efforts of outstations to provoke defectors.

The encouragement of other defectors did not always go to plan and Tokaev became involved in an embarrassing episode in the spring of 1948. A Russian officer acquaintance of his, Colonel J. D. Tasoev (code-named 'Capulet'), who was working in the American Zone, had been earmarked for possible recruitment by SIS. In April it was learned that Tasoev was being posted back behind the Iron Curtain, and, using the Chief of the Imperial General Staff's plane, Tokaev, with an SIS minder, flew to Germany to meet him. There Tasoev announced that he, too, wanted to defect, and, without consulting anyone, Tokaev's SIS escort brought him back to England. This upset everyone: the Russians protested about his having been 'abducted'; the Foreign Office complained when they found out, as did the JIC, who were supposed to handle all defections; and MI5 grumbled because they had not been consulted at all. To make matters worse, Tasoev, as Sargent told Bevin on 12 May, 'overcome by a fit of remorse and in a mood of Slavic penitence', now wished 'to give himself up to the Soviet authorities to pay the price of his treason'. He had attempted to escape and had had to be placed under restraint in a police station. He was eventually returned to the Soviet Union, but SIS had to take the blame for the very unwelcome publicity, with lively press speculation and questions asked in parliament. Bevin was very annoyed and asked specifically 'that he should never again be put in such a false position'. Menzies tried to defend the Service's role in the affair, though William Hayter in the Foreign Office thought he 'would have done better to have admitted frankly that he made a bad muddle of all this'.[15]

Using SIS lines to help exfiltrate individuals from Communist Eastern Europe – in a kind of revival of SIS's wartime association with the escape organisation MI9 – raised questions of what the Service was actually for. In the autumn of 1947, not least to test the possibility of safe routes for agents out of Poland, SIS agreed to make a plan to get the former Polish Prime Minister, Stanisław Mikołajczyk, whose life was threatened by Communist groups, out of the country. The scheme came to nothing and Mikołajczyk escaped with the help of British and American diplomats. But when the Foreign Office asked for assistance with the escape of a locally employed member of the Warsaw embassy staff, Mrs Buyno, doubts were expressed as to whether SIS should be involved at all. Buyno was apparently aware of British clandestine activities in Poland and, if arrested (as was feared was about to happen), could throw suspicion on the whole mission. Terence Garvey, the Foreign Office liaison officer with SIS, noted that the Service had helped with Mikołajczyk because of his importance, and had accepted the risk that had the 'operation been undertaken and failed your friends [SIS] would have thereby lost one of their best sources of information on Poland'. Regarding Buyno, it was 'just conceivable that C's people in Germany' might be able to help, 'but the German station, like the rest of C's organisation, exists mainly to obtain intelligence. We cannot expect them at short notice to risk destroying their intelligence networks in Eastern Europe for the purpose of pulling minor Foreign Office chestnuts out of the fire.' Sir William Hayter agreed: 'C's organisation exists to provide intelligence. Its use for other purposes can only be justified in very exceptional cases of major importance.'[16] In the end, SIS, keen to test out an existing commercial escape line, did agree to help and Mrs Buyno and her son were safely conveyed to the United Kingdom by the end of the year.

SIS had some success against the German Communist Party (KPD), though not at the highest levels. A counter-intelligence review for 1947 asserted that 'we can safely say that we know all we want to know about the organisation and methods and plans of the KPD up to Kreisleitung [district leadership] level', but the policy-making levels were yet to be penetrated. One promising agent who began to produce in late 1947 was 'Cook', a former SOE woman agent who worked her way into left-wing circles in Hamburg and reported on them to both SIS and (under SIS control) the KPD, which was her target for long-term penetration.

Regarded by SIS as a talented spy, though not a very good reporter, she died before fulfilling her potential. In the desperate circumstances of postwar Germany, SIS ensured her loyalty with food, 'as under a regime of 1500 calories a day a tin of bully beef speaks with a loud voice. [She] knows on which side her 500 grammes of bread are buttered.' But it was not just food or cigarettes or money (though all were important) that bought the loyalty of individual Germans. In the aftermath of the war a significant number were willing to become SIS agents for patriotic German motives, allying themselves with a country which had defeated Nazism. Once a new, democratic German state was established some of them fell away. There were also more personal reasons. One important agent's wife was in a concentration camp at the end of the war. SIS found her, close to death, and reunited the pair, which the agent thereafter re-garded as an unrepayable debt.

Towards the end of the 1940s SIS in Germany had over one hundred officers and two hundred secretaries, forming the largest overseas repre-sentation in any one territory. In February 1948 John Bruce Lockhart succeeded Gallienne as head of station and was simultaneously appointed Director of the newly formed Analysis Division of Int. Div., responsible for its agent-running operations. He thus took charge of all British cov-ert human intelligence work in Germany, reporting directly to Menzies. This move significantly improved the co-ordination and quality control of the operations carried out by 120 case-officers. It also, in due course, offered the opportunity of recruiting the ablest Int. Div. personnel into SIS. Later, Bruce Lockhart reckoned that Germany was the 'nursery of SIS', and the place where, more than anywhere else, the Service first be-gan to learn how to adjust to the transition from war through occupation to an uneasy peace and then to the Cold War. Among the new realities which had to be faced was the total dependence of both political and military customers on human intelligence, initially on Germany and then on the Soviet Union and its allies, in contrast to the rich wartime sup-ply of signals intelligence, air reconnaissance and prisoner-of-war inter-rogation reports. Another was the initial disagreement between the main London customers, the Foreign Office and the Chiefs of Staff, about the Soviet Union: was it still an ally or was it the next enemy? Then, once the answer to this question had become clearer, there was the increasing realisation by SIS of the immense difficulty of penetrating a highly alert and paranoid Communist state at anything more than the most pedestrian level. This, above all, was to lead SIS into some disastrous operations (especially those involving émigré groups) which were to cast a shadow over its experience of the next decade.

Central Europe and the Balkans

For SIS Austria presented a similar challenge to Germany: a defeated enemy country divided up into Allied Occupation Zones, where the initial task of watching for any possible Nazi revival swiftly changed into one of monitoring and, if possible, penetrating the Soviet Communist target. Initially, as in Germany, SIS worked within a military Control Commission, but as the military structures were run down the problem of long-term cover emerged. The head of station in Vienna, George Young, a wartime recruit with degrees in modern languages from St Andrews and economics from Yale, worried in August 1946 that his staff of over twenty officers and secretaries would be too large for satisfactory embassy cover. Besides, most of the present representatives were already blown to many people in the British military administration, to most of his American opposite numbers and (this was, after all, Harry Lime's Vienna) to 'a great number of more or less shady individuals who have connexions of one kind or another with wartime intelligence bodies and who have after demobilisation or repatriation taken up their peace-time activity here'. Musing on the problem of cover in general, Young observed that 'the moment one starts to collect intelligence one is blown to somebody and it is only a matter of time before a Security Service catches up on one. The problem', he thought, 'always appears to me not how to keep from being blown but how to keep persona grata with the local authorities and ensure that in our shadier operations we are several jumps ahead of [a] hostile Security Service. Maintaining cover is a battle of wits not a defensive action.'

In February 1947 Menzies got the Foreign Office to make a special case for Vienna to accommodate a larger SIS presence than usual. 'In view of the probable sterility of the stations in countries further east,' argued Menzies, 'we should do all we could to help them in countries where they can operate with comparative ease and safety.' SIS proposed to station five officers, six women secretaries and '2 British handymen or drivers' at Vienna. Hayter agreed and told the British mission in Vienna that since conditions in Austria were 'more favourable' for SIS's work 'than else-where in Eastern Europe and we should like to do what we can to provide them with a base from which they can work eastward in comparative safety', he hoped that the existing Austrian Statistics Unit could be ab-sorbed into the diplomatic mission. This was agreed, but in 1947–8 SIS activities in Austria were disrupted by fears of Soviet penetration. Officers from London (including the Controller Eastern Area, who was responsi-ble for Germany, Austria and Switzerland) came out to investigate secu-rity and concluded that the main problem was lax attitudes among the Field Security Section, responsible for the safety of the British occupation forces, but who liaised closely with the SIS Civil Control Unit and ran a number of agents themselves.

Late in 1947 the Vienna station became aware of an Austrian former SS officer who as a black marketeer regularly travelled in and out of the Soviet Occupation Zone. Over a period of several months he had also helped three Russian soldiers to defect: a lieutenant and two non-commissioned officers. After interrogating him, SIS decided that he was working purely from right-wing political motives. He was 'still a fairly convinced Nazi' who thought that 'Germany would lead the world again' and that anti-Communist activities would 'qualify him for an exalted position within the Greater German Reich'. It was 'thought unlikely', however, that he was 'tied up with any organised underground Neo-Nazi movement', nor was there 'reason to believe' that he was 'in touch with any other Intelligence organisations'. This being the case, and giving him the cover name 'Subaltern', it was decided to recruit the Austrian, who 'agreed to work for us but refused to take any direct payment'. He was instructed to look out for potential defectors and also report on the military situation in the Soviet Zone. SIS was especially interested in a 'high-level defector' who might stay behind for some time to 'acquire documents or specific information'. While Subaltern, whose contacts were mainly 'ladies of easy virtues who are in touch with Russians', identified a number of low-level possible defectors, it was quickly realised that finding any high-level candidates would be 'a slow and wearying undertaking dependent upon circumstances which are very often against us (i.e. frequent postings, non-fraternization orders etc.)'. In the meantime, therefore, he was told to concentrate on collecting information about Soviet troops and military matters 'until such time as we think that a high-level defector would need his undivided attention'. During early 1948 Subaltern produced a few military reports for the Vienna station. 'We still hope however', they reported to London in May, 'that his female contacts will one day produce the desired defector.'

A report reviewing work in Austria in the very late 1940s suggests that the Subaltern operation produced no significant result during those years. Indeed the officer who took over as head of station in April 1949 admitted that they had 'not made satisfactory progress' in penetrating Communism in Austria. Although he did 'not wish to make excuses', he asserted that they were 'constantly handicapped by the fact that the Austrians simply do not enjoy intelligence activity'. This was partly due 'to the Austrian temperament, which is not naturally adventurous', and partly due to their desire to emulate Switzerland 'and adopt an attitude of sunny neutrality towards the contending great powers'. He reviewed the possibilities for an Unofficial Assistant 'moving in the right circles' to begin penetrating Communist organisations and reported that two had already 'posed as Fellow Travellers' but 'without the faintest possibility of reaching' active Communist sources. Another possibility was finding a willing member of the Austrian socialist party, the SPD. Although the party was 'the enemy of communism' it 'inevitably' had 'a certain fluidity with that organisation'. Then there was the possibility of 'planting a man ourselves'. One idea was to find 'a young student who needs a little financial help to continue his University studies and who would be willing, in return, to join the communists and work for us'. But this would be 'a very long term project'. The 'only way of working oneself quickly into the inner circles of the communists' would be to join them 'as a traitor from some other organisation', but he recognised that it was 'virtually impossible' to find a leading member of, say, the SPD who was 'willing to ruin his political career and be an object of extreme contumely among his friends, simply in order to get intelligence for us'. Whatever tactics were adopted for the work on Austrian Communism, he observed that there was competition with the Americans for likely agents, and they were 'paying enormous sums as retainers'.

The difficult and unrewarding effort which SIS had to mount in Eastern Europe is well illustrated by the experience of postwar Bulgaria where

Tony Brooks, an exceptionally brave and able officer who had served with SOE in France during the war, was sent to Sofia as head of station in May 1947. His posting began badly with an unpleasant journey out, during which he, accompanied by two female secretaries, spent five days in the train between Paris and Sofia, including long spells in Balkan railway sidings. Their luggage, too, was stolen at Domodossola in northern Italy. In Sofia Brooks had diplomatic cover and the British minister, John Sterndale Bennett, insisted that he spent most of his time on Chancery work, leaving little enough opportunity for him to develop the SIS duties he had been sent out to perform. Sterndale Bennett, in fact, was so nervous about the possibility of his mission being compromised by SIS activity that he strictly limited what Brooks could do even covertly. While claiming to appreciate his difficulties, in July Head Office urged Brooks to ascertain if there were any British residents in Bulgaria who could be taken on as Unofficial Assistants. 'In the circumstances,' cabled London, 'we would consider even an indifferent Briton far better than any Bulgarian, however able and well-placed.' If there were no suitable Britons, perhaps he could investigate French or Swiss possibilities, who would not be 'suitable for building up any very long-term projects' but 'might be valuable in tiding over your present difficulties'.

A review of Sofia's production from June to October 1947 showed that Brooks had only nine main sources in Bulgaria, three of whom were British. There were two lawyers, an engineer and a Bulgarian Jew, 'not heard of recently'. Another source had 'faded into oblivion'. Over five months Brooks had supplied some fifty reports, of which London considered thirty-nine were good enough to circulate. But only four reports had been graded 'A' for quality, and two of these had come from the British Military Mission in the country. This was thin enough, and Brooks was becoming increasingly frustrated, but in October Sterndale Bennett ordered him to cease SIS activity altogether, claiming that during a recent visit to London Menzies had agreed to this. Although Brooks presumed that this 'was a misunderstanding', he had to comply all the same. In January 1948 he reported that he had studied all possible Unofficial Assistants or cut-outs among friendly nationals with the dispiriting result that only three individuals seemed remotely suitable: a Bulgarian (who could, however, be an agent provocateur) and two Americans who 'were the most terrible social gossips which, to my mind, is the greater danger'.

Matters did not improve during 1948. In May Brooks returned to London to discuss the position in Sofia. Aubrey Halford from the Foreign Office confirmed Bevin's wish that 'every effort was to be made to penetrate the Iron Curtain', and that 'pressure would now be brought to bear' on Sterndale Bennett to lift his ban on SIS activity. Although this had the desired effect, Brooks reported in July that in practice 'all normal processes for collecting intelligence are barred'. The Bulgarians had begun to put great pressure on both the United States and British missions. A junior member of the American legation had been caught red-handed giving money to a Bulgarian for information, and a clerk of Bulgarian origin at the British legation evaded a similar fate after a car chase through the streets of Sofia and was later expelled by the Bulgarians, accused of spying. Brooks reported that there were no Britons available to be Unofficial Assistants and he had also drawn a blank regarding 'friendly foreigners'. He painted a 'dismal picture' of the increasingly stringent surveillance imposed by the Bulgarian authorities. At the present time he thought the activities of his station could 'never hope to get beyond the following: the reporting of overt information; reporting of rumour and gossip, and items from personal observation'. Falling back on his wartime SOE experience, he could also prepare special operations plans, 'selecting landing grounds and dropping zones', and scouting locations for caches of wireless sets and other stores. Finally, he also thought he might be able to assist other stations 'by posting letters inside iron curtain and delivering supplies to agents by means of dead letter boxes'.

Even this was optimistic. Paul Mason, who succeeded Sterndale Bennett as British minister in February 1949, was equally uncooperative, so much so that Brooks thought he wanted simply to close the station down altogether. SIS got caught in a tussle between the Bulgarian and British authorities to reduce the size of their missions in each other's country. Brooks hazarded that Mason believed that if he was compelled to reduce his staff 'he might as well get rid [of] our representative and not one of his own'. Brooks, in fact, stayed put in Sofia until the end of 1949, keeping the position warm for his successor. But the Bulgarians continued to put pressure on the mission generally, threatening to close down their wireless sets in August, intermittently harassing the staff and accusing the British, American and Yugoslav missions of being 'nests of espionage'. Things got so bad that in November 1949 Brooks sought (and got) specific instructions from London in case he had to close down the station altogether. These specified the destruction of papers and the return of SIS cyphers 'by confidential bag forthwith'. The gold reserve was to 'be handed over to the Caretaker officer and a receipt obtained'; local currency was to be left with the mission (again having secured a receipt); and all other notes were to be returned to Head Office. Cameras and photographic equipment were also to go back to London, while secret-ink materials were to 'be destroyed on the spot'.

Bearing in mind the manifest difficulties facing SIS representatives based in Iron Curtain countries, particular efforts were made to penetrate the Soviet bloc from neighbouring states. Yugoslavia was a special case. Marshal Tito, the Communist wartime resistance leader, had to defeat internal opposition from right-wing groups before establishing a stable government in 1948. After he broke away from the Soviet Union that summer, for a time the survival of his regime was in doubt. In July it was reported to SIS that Tito himself had approached the Swiss authorities about the possibility of seeking asylum there. The political situation in Yugoslavia stabilised and Tito survived to preside for another thirty years over an ultimately unsustainable ethnic federation, but SIS made little progress in the country during the 1940s. In 1947, using an agent under business cover, the Service acquired extremely detailed information about Yugoslav civil and military petroleum installations and reserves, but subsequent efforts to continue the flow of information by recruiting an employee of a Western oil company as an Unofficial Assistant came to nothing.

Greece, where from 1946 until victory in October 1949 the royalist government (backed by Britain and the USA) fought off a Communist guerrilla challenge, had a significant SIS presence in the postwar years. In May 1946 Broadway decided that there should be a main station at Athens (under Nigel Clive, who had had a distinguished SIS war record), with sub-stations at Salonika and Florina, both well placed in the north of the country for operations into the neighbouring Communist states. The local representatives were to concentrate on the penetration of Greece (particularly Communists), Albania, Yugoslavia and southern Bulgaria. Reflecting the close control which London kept over money matters, all expenditure on agents had to stay within already approved budget estimates, although the head of station was authorised 'in the case of urgent necessity' to spend up to £150 (equivalent to slightly over £4,000 today) 'without previous reference to Head Office'.

The experience of SIS in Greece in the late 1940s illustrates the extent to which even the most carefully made plans were hostage to unexpected and unpredictable events. During the summer of 1948 an Unofficial Assistant (known as '025') working in an Athens airline office was instructed to monitor Eastern bloc airline crews passing through the city with a view to recruitment as agents. In September he reported contact with a Czechoslovak pilot whom he had met previously while working in Paris shortly after the war, and London told him to investigate the possibilities. The following month 025 engineered a social meeting during which he established that the pilot (who was married with an infant child) would 'undertake any work on our behalf if we can assist him to evacuate his family from Prague to one of the western democracies'. Agent 025 arranged another meeting on the Czech's next trip but just before Christmas 1948 the plane the pilot was flying crashed in poor weather en route to Athens.

Another aborted operation in 1948–9 also involved a pilot, in this case a Serb who had flown for the RAF during the war. A committed anti-Communist, he had gone to Greece in 1945 and in September 1948 was working as a labourer north of the Greek capital. The head of station in Athens spotted him as a possible agent, and after both London and the SIS station in Belgrade reported 'no trace' against his name, he approached him and ascertained that he was 'willing to go as resident agent to obtain information from areas north and east of Belgrade', as well as in the Niš area further south. Subject to 'thorough training', Athens thought he would make 'a potentially useful head-agent' for Yugoslavia. The man was taken on, and London and Athens began to think about whether he should be infiltrated by sea, or overland from either Greece or Trieste. He underwent an intensive training course (including radio communications) through the winter and spring of 1948–9. All was going well when the agent 'developed very sudden and serious tuberculosis' and was hospitalised in August 1949; the operation was cancelled. A third operation, code-named 'Contemplate', which involved close liaison with the Greek air force and the acquisition of photographic intelligence across the frontier with Albania, Yugoslavia and Bulgaria by using a specially equipped Spitfire aircraft, had temporarily to be abandoned when a Greek minister vetoed the project.

But there were successes, too. Reviewing work in the spring of 1949, albeit not long before the rebel surrender, Athens reported extensive coverage of the Communist movement through a network code-named 'Damocles', which included intelligence provided by some very highly placed agents. There was also a Macedonian hashish smuggler who toured southern Yugoslavia collecting military and economic intelligence (mostly troop dispositions and railway information) which London assessed as 'of a fair quality'. He went across the frontier about once every three weeks and was paid £10 for each report he delivered to a local head agent who in turn was paid £10 a month as a retainer. London thought that 'for the risks being run and for the results achieved, expenditure is remarkably low', and, since the Macedonian was the only contact regularly reporting from the area, gave their approval for Athens to continue paying the two men. In the north-east of Greece, the Athens station had also managed to assemble 'an undoubtedly brave and determined team' of anti-Communists who crossed into Bulgaria in March and April 1949 and reported back on troop deployments and Bulgarian support for Greek Communist rebels. By the close of the year, however, with the end of the Greek civil war, SIS acknowledged 'that our customers do not seem to be particularly interested in south Bulgaria any longer'. Thus the 'efforts and risks' of penetrating the region might be 'hardly worth while' in the future.

France and Spain

In October 1944, when Menzies told Cadogan that the battle for France was 'over' and that he wanted the Foreign Office to lift the ban on the penetration of France which had been imposed before the outbreak of war, he initiated an illuminating discussion about the appropriateness (or otherwise) of spying against friendly states and allies. Richard Speaight in the Foreign Office wanted to continue 'indefinitely' the ban on SIS working in France except in co-operation with the French authorities. He pointed out that it was government policy to cultivate the closest possible relations with France and 'we regard Anglo-French solidarity as one of the chief bulwarks of our future security'. If SIS started to penetrate France, he minuted, it was 'likely to be caught out sooner or later & such a revelation wd. strike at the root of the spirit of intimate collaboration with the

French Govt. which we are so anxious to build up'. The 'best means of obtaining intelligence from France' was 'through the Embassy & its extensive ancillary services . . . If', he continued, 'our overt representatives there do their job properly, they shd. be able to supply us with initially all the stuff that "C" could hope to obtain through covert channels.'

This was the classic sceptical diplomat's dismissal of the role of secret intelligence. Cavendish-Bentinck could not have disagreed more. 'We have suffered during this war from bans on carrying out S.I.S. work in certain countries,' he began. This included Italy in the early 1930s. As for France, 'during the two years prior to the outbreak of war, we were lamentably badly informed'. ('Yes, indeed,' minuted Cadogan by this statement.) 'We should have known . . . that the French Army was not going to be our bulwark,' continued Cavendish-Bentinck. He argued that 'in a couple of years time, if not sooner', the French might become 'extremely nationalistic and xenophobe, with the result that those who are really in the know will not be chattering to foreigners as freely as has been done in the past'. Since he believed that 'first class sources in foreign countries cannot be created at short notice', but required 'careful and <u>prolonged</u> cultivation', Cavendish-Bentinck thought that Menzies should 'think out very carefully a plan of S.I.S. operations in France' and submit it to the JIC, who could 'then consider whether the ban on secret service operations in France can be raised'.[17]

Peter Loxley thought similarly and reminded colleagues that as part of the Bland Report the Foreign Office had given Menzies a list of post-war tasks, including, for France, 'in general any French groups whose sympathies incline them towards Germany'; 'hidden Russian activities' in France; and 'any French groups or parties of totalitarian tendencies'. 'We cannot have it both ways,' he added; 'if we want "C" to provide us with first class information from France, we must allow him to operate more or less freely there. If, on the other hand, Mr. Speaight's view is approved, then we must in fairness cancel our existing directive to "C".' Although he wanted to modify the prewar ban on operations in France, Loxley nevertheless conceded 'that in the interests of our relations with the French authorities we must walk carefully' and that Cadogan should see SIS's general plans before they were put into operation. Cadogan agreed and wrote to Menzies along these lines.

A few days later Loxley discussed the matter with the British ambassador

in Paris, Duff Cooper, who assumed that SIS would have a representative working in France with the Deuxième Bureau. Should, however, SIS
wish to conduct any secret operations in France without the knowledge
of the French authorities, Duff Cooper thought that he had better not
know anything about it, to which Cadogan minuted in the margin 'Yes'.
In February 1945, nevertheless, when Menzies sent A. J. 'Freddie' Ayer,
the Oxford philosopher who had been working for SOE in New York
and France, to Paris, Duff Cooper was informed about it. Ayer's job,
for which he had embassy cover, was not to run operations but, in a
'purely preparatory and exploratory role', to establish contacts who could
be exploited by SIS in the future. Reflecting on the arrangement after
Ayer had returned to London in October 1945, Duff Cooper wrote to
Cadogan to say he was not sure if he wanted to 'repeat the experiment'.
He was 'averse to having as a member of my staff, working in the embassy,
someone of whose activities I know nothing and over whose movements
I have no control'. Rehearsing all-too-familiar ambassadorial attitudes of
a sort which had strained relations in the past, he also wanted to 'draw a
very rigid line' between 'the activities of the diplomatic service and those
of the secret service'. 'A diplomatist', he wrote, 'has as much right to consider himself insulted if he is called a spy as a soldier has if he is called a
murderer,' and while he 'knew, of course, that the secret service existed',
he 'believed it would be quite impossible for a member of it to adopt the
cover of a secretary or attaché in an embassy'. Embassies were kept under
very careful scrutiny; foreign servants were employed and the covert activities of a member of staff could hardly be concealed for ever. 'No secrets
are kept indefinitely,' he asserted: 'Everything is known in the end.'[18]

By the time John Bruce Lockhart was posted to be head of the Paris
station in January 1946 it is clear that the ban on SIS reporting on France
had been relaxed. Writing to London in August, he discussed domestic
French politics, including details of French Communist Party finances
and reflections on Communist penetration in the French army and air
force (an understandable interest, bearing in mind that Communist
and leftist parties consistently won over a quarter of the vote in postwar
French general elections). Much of this was based on a combination of
documents supplied from the French intelligence services and what Bruce
Lockhart called 'gossip'. Bruce Lockhart's successor, who took over in
October 1947, continued to concentrate particularly on the Communist

target. A year later the Controller Western Area (CWA) in London noted that the Paris station had two main responsibilities: '(a) Liaison with the French intelligence services, and (b) Procurement of intelligence by secret means on behalf of SIS'. But there was in practice a conflict between the two functions since the task of at least some French intelligence departments with whom the head of station was asked to liaise was precisely to prevent secret intelligence activities by foreign services. In order to reduce the risk of compromising SIS operations, Paris was instructed to limit the amount of work undertaken which 'could be construed by any of the local authorities as being anti-French'. With a brief analysis of the Paris station's 'present penetration activity', the CWA concluded 'that apart from attacking the enemies of France on French soil no accusation could be levelled against the station that it is, in any way, pursuing activities inimical to the French state'. Even in neighbouring countries – Belgium, Spain and Italy – there was no current anti-French penetration work.

Duff Cooper's successor as ambassador, Oliver Harvey, nevertheless, took a similarly dim view of secret intelligence work in France and in September 1948 protested to the Foreign Office about a reported instance of SIS operating in the country. Hayter wrote to Menzies asking for a 'brief account of your present activities in France' to use when soothing Harvey – whose views, Hayter said, were not shared by the Foreign Office's Western Department, nor indeed by Bevin. Kenneth Cohen, as Chief Controller Europe, having consulted Menzies, drafted the response for Hayter. It confirmed that relations with the French were 'of a cordial and fruitful nature'. Indeed, the main current difficulty was 'largely in keeping pace with French demands for co-operation'. There was no doubt that it was 'in the general interest that these relations should continue'. It was noted, nevertheless, that SIS staff also maintained 'certain contacts of a "direct nature". I have', continued the draft, 'never made it a secret from the French that I am not prepared to rely entirely on their own estimates of Communist activities in France and that I make a practice of pursuing direct enquiries into these matters.' A further activity concerned 'the uncovering of illegal immigration and arms-running organisations in connection with the Palestine dispute'. SIS's efforts here, it was claimed, 'have had considerable success', but due to divergent French and British policies towards Palestine, they had 'sometimes been a cause of friction'.

Postwar requirements, and agent-handling, can be illustrated by the instructions given to a British businessman based in Spain (the brother of an existing SIS officer), agent 'ΟΙΟΙΟ', who began work at the end of 1945. Reflecting his position and expertise, the primary requirements were economic, including background material relating to 'civil aviation between Spain and Portugal and U.S.A.', 'What, if any, strings are being pulled by Spain or foreign big business . . . in connection with trade negotiations with France and Switzerland?', and 'particulars of any outside and backstairs influences, domestic or foreign, at work in high quarters in connection with the British/Spanish trade relationships'. Political intelligence was less of a priority, but the agent was asked to keep an eye out for material about the Monarchist movement, the Spanish Communist Party, and 'information on any German attempts to hide key-men, plans, loot, etc. in Spain'. The agent's first report contained quite a lot of information evidently gathered from open sources, and prompted a mild rebuke from his SIS handler, which provides us with a useful indication of what the Service regarded as core business. 'It should be remembered', wrote the case-officer, 'that it is the function of H.M. Embassies and Consulates to provide the F.O. with overt information, general surveys of the situation, etc. We do not, therefore, require such material from our sources. What we do require is factual, specific and well authenticated items of information which are not accessible to Embassies and Consulates through overt channels.' He added that 'the most valuable type of secret political material is documentary', and every effort should be made to acquire it. The Service was 'always interested in reports based on off the record remarks made by individuals who are known to be in a position to speak with inside knowledge and authority on the subject under discussion and who do not know that their remarks will get back to this country'. Such information was particularly valuable since direct liaison with Franco's intelligence authorities was ruled out by the Foreign Office. It was, commented Aubrey Halford in June 1948, 'useless to pretend that C's representatives can have a personal liaison with the Franco secret police without bringing the Embassy into it', and the Spanish would be bound to 'want something in return' for any help they gave. Writing to Menzies, Hayter acknowledged that it would be 'gratifying' to receive intelligence on Communist methods and activities, but that the Foreign Office felt 'the price the Spaniards are asking is too high, namely that we should in effect condone the regime'.[19]

Late in 1948 an opportunity was taken of giving a questionnaire to a well-placed Briton who had worked alongside the Service during the war and was travelling on vacation to Spain. Aware that he had good political connections, the Political Requirements Section in Broadway asked if he were 'able to talk confidentially with important political persons or with responsible persons close to Franco' and whether he could collect information on 'any movements towards the restoration of the monarchy on the part of left wing democrats, monarchists and Franco respectively'; on the attitude of the Roman Catholic Church towards Franco and domestic political issues; and on 'evidence of any secret discussions between the U.S.S.R. and Franco's regime'. In keeping with the growing emphasis on economic intelligence, he was also asked to report on authoritative Spanish attitudes towards the 'chaotic economic conditions' in Spain and 'Hispano-Argentine commercial relations'.

The example of one potential agent who worked in France and Spain further illustrates both postwar intelligence priorities and also how a fly-fishing technique of tempting and reeling in people could be applied in practice. The target in this case was a former wartime contact, now resident in France. In February 1948 the head of the Madrid station reported that the man, who was 'extremely well informed as usual', had visited Spain where he had had 'several long talks' with an SIS colleague. Thinking that he might make a good source for French political information, an initial approach was made 'on the basis of [a] mutual interest' in international Communism. The target said he was 'willing to meet a representative once a week' to provide information on this topic. Madrid recommended proceeding on the basis that 'for the time being' the main subject should be restricted to Communist matters, 'that the contact should be regular and great interest maintained', and, 'if properly handled, it will not be long before subject lets himself wander into the field of normal political matters as well'. Aware that the right psychological attitude was required, Madrid added that 'subject should not be allowed to gain the impression that he is being fitted into an existing machine. This impression might make him shy off.' The Paris station took up the baton and through the spring of 1948 began a series of meetings with the target 'on a purely social basis'. Paris reported that the individual had now got a job with an international humanitarian organisation, which would involve him travelling frequently in the 'Russian satellites' in Eastern Europe, and added their impression that he would 'be prepared to carry out an observation mission for us' during his visits to Eastern Europe, and 'would accept payment', though they said that 'neither point was, of course, discussed directly'. The target would be based in France, moreover, and was apparently prepared to 'pass us information about such subjects as Communist penetration of French administration, [and] Communist blackmail against non-Communist French politicians'. The only evident snag was a worry that he might 'also be in touch with French Intelligence' and might already 'have been recruited by them to carry out similar missions'.

SIS had considered using international humanitarian organisation cover before. In April 1946 there was a discussion about the possibility of getting an agent working in one such agency. Despite the fact that it was assumed that the agency in question was already 'completely pen-etrated' by the Communists, it was felt that in certain countries where such organisations operate, 'e.g. the Balkans and other Russian domi-nated countries, it might well be the only way in which an S.I.S. officer could get into contact with the people of the country owing to the almost complete isolation in which the Embassy staffs lived'. Head Office was keen to proceed with the operation. 'This looks even more promising than we anticipated,' minuted one officer, particularly as the organisation was 'reported to be Communist penetrated'. Even if he were working for French intelligence, 'I do not consider it constitutes a reason for turning him down.' In France, meanwhile, a representative in Paris had 'estab-lished very friendly relations with subject', who was aware he was dealing with British intelligence and now appeared 'to be upset' that contact was being maintained only on 'purely social lines' and that no 'shop matters' were being discussed. London therefore cabled that 'relations' could now be put 'on business footing'. The potential agent should be asked to re-port on the degree of Communist penetration, but London considered it 'advisable [to] leave French political questions in abeyance until we know subject better'. Paris then proceeded formally to recruit the agent, who was obviously raring to go. 'Source appeared to jump to the conclusion', reported Paris, 'that we were interested in establishing, through him, a "reseau" [network] through Europe.' One drawback of such a scheme, said the agent, was that the Americans, who provided most of the money for the organisation, 'and were manoeuvring themselves into most of the key positions, were, he strongly suspected, working on similar lines'. On the other hand, a point in the scheme's favour was that this particular humanitarian organisation was thought to be 'the only one that stood a chance of continuing to function throughout Europe for a period of several months after the outbreak of hostilities'. Thus 'it was worth while trying to exploit it as a means of establishing a secret network'.

The potential agent also offered information on Communists. He had, he said, an acquaintance in the French Interior Ministry with a source in the French Communist Party, who was being blackmailed by the police into handing over copies of 'secret reports and minutes'. The acquaintance, he added, occasionally told him 'the gist of these reports'. Having been hooked, the quarry now, ironically, started to force the pace and, fearing that things were beginning to move too quickly, SIS began to back-pedal. In mid-1948 the Paris station recommended that the agent should be told there was no intention 'of pursuing at the present stage his scheme of working up a "network"', nor did SIS want to develop the French Communist Party source, whom the Paris station had 'strong reasons' to suppose was 'bogus' and copies of whose reports were, in any case, already being received through service attaché channels. Nevertheless, as the source appeared to be 'sincere in his desire to help us, it would be unwise to discourage him', and they suggested that he should in the meantime be 'supplied with innocuous questions' about Communist penetration of the international organisation. London felt that the outlook was now 'rather disappointing on the whole, particularly if this high grade potential source can only be fed with innocuous questions'. There were, however, renewed concerns that the source was already working for French intelligence, and there the matter appears to have rested, as there is no indication in the records that he ever developed further as an agent.[20]

Scandinavia

Work in postwar Scandinavia was inevitably dominated by the Soviet Union and a widespread sense that the region was part of the front line in the Cold War. This was especially so in Finland, where fears of a Soviet-supported coup, backed by Communist members of the government, periodically agitated Finnish politics in the 1940s. Rex Bosley, head of the Helsinki station from March 1945, had to tiptoe very gingerly indeed through the complexities of Finnish postwar life. He cultivated a wide range of Finnish contacts – 'several hundred' according to Bosley at the end of 1949 – many inherited from Harry Carr's long service in the country as well as from other prewar relationships. There was certainly no shortage of potential agents; the problem was more one of selecting, targeting and running them, without the Soviets (who kept a very close eye on British contacts with Finns) becoming aware. Some approaches from within Finnish armed service circles seeking British support for right-wing political intervention had to be treated with great caution. Bosley also tended to gravitate towards conservative political contacts, though he ranged as widely as he could. In January 1948 he told Carr (who had become Controller Northern Area in Broadway) that 'very few matters of any importance in this country escape our knowledge'. Furthermore, 'from time to time we do manage to glean certain items of interest from the Soviet Union despite the ban on any efforts in this direction'. On the other hand, the station had not succeeded in penetrating either the Finnish Communist Party or the Soviet strategic enclave at Porkkala, on the coast south-west of Helsinki and, even by mid-1949, barring lucky breaks, they regarded the acquisition of political, naval or military intelligence from *inside* the Soviet Union as beyond them.

In Sweden the postwar SIS station was directed to concentrate first on the Soviet Union, followed by Germany. The third target was Poland and subsidiary targets were Finland, Denmark and Norway. 'On no account', instructed London, 'are you to conduct any espionage against Sweden.' During 1946 directions were added about preparing for a possible third world war. 'Although it is assumed that the United Kingdom will be free of a major war during the next ten years,' Broadway (no doubt with the experience of the Second World War in mind) pointed out that 'international crises may develop with great suddenness. Hence, it is advisable and necessary to make certain arrangements in advance, to be put into effect in an emergency, in order to preclude the complete collapse of our secret organisations and communications.' Wireless sets designed to survive burial underground, 'for eventual transportation to Finland and the Baltic States', would be supplied and were intended to be used by 'stay-behind agents in enemy occupied territory'. With engaging frankness the directive continued: 'scepticism as to the potential success of such a scheme certainly exists in the light of previous experience; however, such plans should be pursued and agents for operating these W/T sets should be found with a view to being trained at a later stage'.

Throughout the late 1940s, the Soviet Union remained the main target for SIS in Sweden, as it was elsewhere. A new directive in November 1947 added the Swedish Communist Party to the list of targets, including the extent of Soviet control over it. The embargo against spying on Sweden was repeated, but in terms that suggested it was now derived from a more general SIS doctrine: 'In principle you should not work against the country in which you are stationed, but you should report any information on it which comes your way.' The instruction on liaison with the Swedes undoubtedly reflected that for any similar non-Communist states. The head of station in Stockholm was to 'maintain and develop your close and friendly relations with the Swedish Intelligence and Security Services with the object of exploiting their intelligence work and of obtaining as much information through these channels as possible . . . while at the same time continuing to build up your own network independent of the Swedes'. Similarly, the archives of the Swedish postwar intelligence T-Office show that a high level of surveillance on British representatives was maintained, even as liaison contacts were being developed.[21] The quite precise directives issued to Stockholm, as to other stations, marked a new development in Service practice and the introduction of a management regime wherein Head Office issued clear intelligence objectives, closely related to general intelligence requirements and stated government policies. As a November 1947 directive made clear, there was a new emphasis, too, on the need to send officers, secretaries and (where appropriate) Unofficial Assistants and agents back to the United Kingdom for training 'in accordance with the training programme now being drawn up'. While these instructions reflected the growing professionalism of the Service and a necessary explicit integration of its work with official British foreign policy aims, they also inevitably marked increasing bureaucratisation, as 'targets' and 'programmes' threatened perhaps to erode the buccaneering individuality of the tiny prewar Service.

Instructions issued to Leslie Mitchell, who became head of the Copenhagen station in July 1945, further reflected modern bureaucratic practice by asking him to prepare a three-year plan for the station showing both short- and long-term objectives. In a review of the station's tasks in July 1948, Mitchell cautiously noted that 'as far as our major target, the Soviet Union, is concerned, it would be more than optimistic to rate our chances at successful and resident penetration at all high'. Mitchell commented on various methods available for penetration of the USSR: commercial travellers – 'a failure for secret intelligence'; members of Trade Delegations – 'of limited interest'; Baltic refugees and deserters – 'not productive and low-grade'. He maintained that the station's 'most successful line' concerned merchant shipping, and claimed that 'no Danish ship sails to Soviet ports without this station's knowledge'. Yet for all Mitchell's professionalism and clear organisational skills there was still some quite severe criticism in London about the station's lack of political, military, counter-espionage and scientific product, further demonstrating the difficulties for even the best-run stations to acquire precious intelligence about the Soviet target.

Reflecting the extremely close relationship between SIS and the Norwegians during the war, SIS's postwar situation in Norway differed slightly from the other Scandinavian countries. The primary focus for the SIS representative, posted to Oslo in June 1945 and head of station from March the following year, was to build on the wartime legacy. In April 1946 the station was enjoined to exploit liaison with the Norwegian intelligence service 'to the utmost advantage'. Although (as was now the case elsewhere) he was told he 'should not work against the country in which you are stationed', this evidently did not rule out keeping a watch on Communist and hostile intelligence activities in Norway, let alone running agents from Norway against other targets. In July 1946 London specifically encouraged Oslo to recruit agents in Norwegian 'Cultural, Labour and Party Organisations' which had relations with the USSR, with a view to their being able to visit the Soviet Union in due course and gather intelligence there. 'Such penetration', they thought, 'offers one of the best chances of getting behind the formidable barriers of Russia.'[22]

Reporting on FOII (the Norwegian intelligence service) in January 1947, the head of station said that its policy, born of the nation's experience, was 'Norway for the Norwegians', and the activities of any potentially hostile power would be the target of its intelligence operations. Since the United Kingdom did not pose a threat to Norwegian sovereignty or security, active co-operation with SIS was natural and extended even to discussions about the joint running of agents. Although in the head of station's opinion this 'far exceeds official governmental policy', he felt that members of the Norwegian government knew of and approved the liaison. By contrast, Colonel Wilhelm Evang, the acting head of FOII, told SIS of his irritation when the Americans were discovered in late 1947 trying to bribe a Norwegian policeman and one of them was expelled. By January 1948 Evang had become increasingly ill-disposed towards the Soviets, who were regularly caught out spying against Norway.

In March 1947 SIS agreed to pay the Norwegians £1,000 a year to help finance the establishment in north Norway of an intercept operation against the USSR, the results of which were found to be 'most valuable'. Other proposed joint operations included the penetration of the Murmansk region across the Norway–Soviet frontier and the placing of an agent in Spitzbergen to report on Soviet activities in the area. But there were also instructions to pursue other targets independently of the Norwegians. These included placing or recruiting agents in Norwegian merchant ships and in Norwegian firms trading with the Soviet bloc, and in the Norwegian airline service to Poland, as well as targeting the Norwegian Communist Party. The Oslo station was charged with penetrating Soviet and satellite missions in Norway and with recording, collating and periodically reporting information which came to light about local counter-espionage cases. Early in 1949 Norwegian officers travelled to London for detailed discussions about war planning (which also involved United States participation), stay-behind schemes and SIS provision of training and technical support.[23]

21

A worldwide Service

SIS's postwar deployment after 1945 was increasingly concentrated in countries where the threat of Communism was seen as most immediate, and also in those places where it was thought that threat might effectively be challenged. In practice this meant that resources were focused on countries bordering the Soviet bloc in both Europe and the Middle East, and, after 1949, in Asian countries on the fringes of Communist China. But the Service retained a worldwide reach, even though budgetary considerations compelled it to reduce its representation to the bare minimum where the perceived threat was not so great. This was undoubtedly the case in Latin America. At the end of the war there were ten, usually one-man, stations. Within a few years only those at Buenos Aires, Mexico City and Rio de Janeiro survived. SIS had even less involvement with Africa, where in the late 1940s, apart from the British Dominion of South Africa, there were only two independent countries, Liberia and Ethiopia. Security in the British territories was the responsibility of MI5 and, apart from a small station in Addis Ababa, which was geared more to the Middle East than to Africa, it was reckoned that any intelligence concerning the colonies of other European countries could be acquired in the appropriate European capitals. Across the Middle East, beyond sizeable stations in Istanbul, Cairo and Jerusalem, SIS was pretty thinly spread, and tackling Communism in Iraq and Iran largely depended on liaison services. Palestine, which for SIS constituted a major commitment, was highly unusual in the postwar world in that Communism was hardly an issue. Here 'end of empire', the quest of Jewish people for a secure 'national home' and the terrible legacy of the Holocaust combined to fuel a troubling, combustible and violent situation for which in the end neither Britain nor its security and intelligence agencies, including SIS, could do much to help.

Palestine

Although SIS had an important station in Jerusalem, the gathering of intelligence about Palestine (which counted as part of the British empire) was shared with the Criminal Investigation Department of the Palestine Police, Military Intelligence and MI5. SIS, indeed, had no direct role in the sharp and violent campaign waged between British forces and Jewish insurgents from 1946 until the unilateral British withdrawal in May 1948, and which included (among others) the assassination in September 1946 of a former SIS officer, Desmond Doran, who had transferred to Security Intelligence Middle East (SIME) in October 1942. In December 1946 Broadway estimated that SIS's sources were rather better on the Arab than the Jewish side, and that Jerusalem was the only political intelligence station in the Middle East 'to have penetrated effectively the Communist organisations of its own area'.

The threat posed by militant Zionist groups, such as the Irgun Zvai Leumi and the Stern Gang, threatening enough in Palestine (where, for example, in July 1946 the Stern Gang blew up the King David Hotel in Jerusalem with the loss of ninety-one lives), extended to Continental Europe and the United Kingdom itself. In 1946–7 Irgun units launched sabotage operations against British military installations in Germany, planted a substantial bomb (which did not explode) at the Colonial Office in London, threatened to assassinate Bevin and Attlee, sent letter-bombs to Cabinet ministers and blew up the British embassy in Rome (where the SIS office was badly damaged). SIS helped track Zionist units, and reported (wrongly) to MI5 that the Irgun leader Menachem Begin had altered his appearance by plastic surgery.[1] Of particular concern was the question of Jewish illegal immigration to Palestine, which had troubled the British administration since the 1930s. The quotas which the British had established in order to prevent the Jewish population in the country from growing uncontrollably (which would inevitably exacerbate communal tensions) proved increasingly difficult to enforce. This was especially so in the context of the Holocaust when the legalities of the situation seemed both cruel and pettifogging in the face of the evidently desperate desire to reach Palestine of people who had survived savage persecution and the death camps. On the other hand, British responsibilities to the non-Jewish population of Palestine, the government's hope that some sort of communal balance might be maintained, and the need to maintain good relations with the leaders of oil-rich Arab states led the British authorities to maintain strict limits on the numbers of Jews who were permitted to settle in the territory.[2]

But how could this be enforced? Towards the end of 1946 the government sought advice from SIS and a paper was prepared containing 'proposals for action to deter ships' masters and crews from engaging in illegal Jewish immigration and traffic'. It did not pull its punches: 'Action of the nature contemplated is, in fact, a form of intimidation, and intimidation is only likely to be effective if some members of the group of people to be intimidated actually suffer unpleasant consequences.' The 'falsity of stories based only on "notional" unpleasant incidents', it argued, would 'soon be discovered' and it was 'essential that "whispers" and rumours should have some factual backing'. This could be arranged through overt British government warnings, or by covert action, which covered a range of possibilities, such as spreading rumours of terrorist action against ships, or actual sabotage against vessels, 'to prevent a ship from sailing' or disable it after leaving port. Among a range of options was 'the discovery of some sabotage device, which had "failed" to function, after the sailing of a ship'; 'tampering with a ship's fresh water supplies or the crew's food'; and 'fire on board ship in port'. In a covering letter, Menzies reflected on the idea of blaming the action on some specially created, and apparently powerful, Arab organisation, though this might be objected to on the grounds that it could 'tend to increase tension between Jew and Arab in Palestine and it might encourage Jews to take reprisals against Arabs'. Alternatively, rumours could be spread 'in vacuo', and 'something of a mystery' made of the organisation behind them, though he thought this was 'not likely to be as convincing as the proposal to link the whispers with an Arab terrorist organisation'. Whatever was decided, he felt that the strictest secrecy should be maintained 'as any leakage might have a grave effect on Anglo-American relations, apart from ruining all chances of success'.[3]

Opinion in the Foreign Office was generally against the more drastic proposals, taking the view that the risk of discovery was too great. Peter Garran of the Eastern Department thought that 'these are the kind of actions which can be justified in wartime but not I am afraid in time of peace and they would be likely to involve us in serious difficulties with the countries in which they were carried out'. Nevertheless, following a meeting on 14 February 1947 between SIS and representatives from the armed services, the Colonial Office and the Foreign Office, Hayter told Menzies that he should go ahead provided there was 'no risk of casualties being incurred'. SIS should not kill people or disable ships after sailing and arson attacks 'must be arranged, if at all, [only] when the ship is empty'; tampering with food or water was also prohibited. In effect this was taken to mean that there should be no direct attacks on ships actually carrying refugees.[4] Thus was the perhaps aptly named Operation 'Embarrass' born.

For some time both SIS and MI5 (who had a responsibility for security in Palestine) had been keeping watch on illegal Jewish traffic, which was code-named 'Trespass'. Information was gathered on refugee camps in France and Italy from which parties of prospective migrants journeyed to Mediterranean ports where ships would (they hoped) convey them to Palestine. British agents identified particular camps in Milan, Bari and the heel of Italy used by the Trespass organisation as 'transit camps for illegal immigrants. Prior to an illegal embarkation, there would be a large decrease in the number of refugees at the Rome camps and they would all turn up at one of these camps demanding, and being given, asylum for a few days pending their departure in an illegal immigration vessel.' British officers at the camps were alerted to the process and worked to disrupt the traffic. In France one agent located an unofficial refugee camp and provided details (including photographs) of 'suspect ships' in harbours along the Mediterranean coast near Marseilles.

Informed by the Trespass intelligence, in early 1947 an Embarrass team was set up in Broadway with instructions 'to slow down the flow of illegal immigrants into Palestine'. The brief made clear that, 'although suspicion would be accepted, the primary consideration was to be that no proof could ever be established between positive action against this traffic and H.M.G.'. Knowledge of the operation within SIS was very carefully monitored (indoctrinated personnel were described as 'Embarrassed'), and a special communications network, 'Ocean', was set up dedicated exclusively to Embarrass traffic. Outside the Service a few individuals in MI5 and the Foreign Office (including Orme Sargent) had outline knowledge of the scheme, although in May 1947, after consulting the Foreign Office, Menzies instructed his representatives in Athens, Cairo and Rome to 'approach their heads of Mission personally and tell them the story'. With a budget of £30,000 (£875,000 in current terms), although in the end only £13,000 was actually spent, the operation had three aspects: direct action against potential refugee ships; a propaganda campaign; and a deception scheme to disrupt immigration from Black Sea ports inaccessible for direct action.

A team of former SOE personnel was deployed in France and another in Italy, though actual attacks were mounted only in Italy. British limpet bombs and timers were supplied. Since huge numbers of such weapons 'had been supplied to resistance movements in Europe during the war and had not been accounted for', this was not thought to constitute any security risk. But very careful thought was given to the agents' cover. In the first place the British individuals involved needed a good reason for their presence abroad, and this included business, visiting friends, holidaymaking generally and taking a Mediterranean yachting trip. If things went wrong and these stories were broken, 'they were under no circumstances to admit their connection with H.M.G.'. Instead, they were to claim that they had been recruited 'by an anti-Communist organisation formed by a group of International Industrialists, mainly in the oil and aircraft industries', said to be directed from New York, which aimed to stop illegal Jewish immigration into Palestine on the grounds 'that the Russians were infiltrating Communist Jews into Palestine through the Jewish Escape Groups, thus endangering the various interests of the Group in the Middle East'. To do this the international organisation had recruited agents 'of the ex-Commando type', who were trained in 'an old manor house' near Oxford in England. Agents were warned that this cover 'was their final line of defence and, even in the event of a prison sentence, no help could be expected from H.M.G.'.

During the summer of 1947 and early the following year attacks were made on five ships in Italian ports. A priority for the sabotage team was to ensure that any target ship was unloaded and that there were no personnel on board. One ship was reported as 'a total loss' and two others were damaged. Limpet mines planted on the other two were apparently both discovered. In one case a mine was knocked off, later recovered by divers and 'its English origin established', but the local harbour master thought this was 'not surprising as the Arabs would of course be using British stores'.

As part of the propaganda side of the operation, and in order to divert suspicion from the British, a notional organisation called the Defenders of Arab Palestine claimed responsibility for work against Jewish immigration into Palestine. Letters prepared in Broadway on 'typewriters of appropriate nationality' and posted in Paris were sent to the British Prime Minister and Foreign Secretary (among other prominent personalities) and major newspapers, implicating Soviet Russia in the immigration. It was, claimed the letters, 'Russia's intention to force the establishment in Palestine of a Jewish state which looks to them rather than the West for inspiration and support . . . Faced with the alternatives of a war between Arab and Jew in Palestine or the seizure of that country by the Jews', the Defenders declared that they would 'carry the fight into those lands where these troubles have their roots'. There was no intention to harm 'innocent Jews' or 'cause further trouble in Palestine'. 'We shall', they warned, 'attack only those who are directly involved in Jewish Illegal Immigration and those who assist them.'

Contrasting with this attempt to implicate Russia in the movement of Jews, the deception scheme aimed to suggest that the *British* were using the traffic to get agents out of Eastern Europe. Thus it was hoped that the Soviet authorities would act to impede it. A faked British government document was prepared suggesting that not only was the 'British Secret Service' exploiting Jewish emigration channels in Bulgaria and Romania to exfiltrate agents to the Middle East, but that 'Jewish migrants from behind the "iron curtain" were a valuable source of information on Russian activities in that area'. In February 1948 the document was planted by an officer from Broadway in the Casanova night club in Vienna, which was 'known to be frequented by the MGB [Soviet intelligence service] and believed to be under Russian control'. In the hope that the local postal censors would report it to the Soviet authorities, various letters were also posted in Bucharest hinting at this British scheme, but by the time Embarrass was stood down at the beginning of April 1948 (anticipating Britain's weary withdrawal from Palestine on 14 May) there was no indication that the deception scheme had had any effect whatever.

Reflecting on the matter afterwards, one SIS officer reckoned that perhaps the biggest missed opportunity had been a planned operation to disable the *President Warfield* in the small French Mediterranean port of Sète during the early summer of 1947. The ship had been shadowed by an SIS-controlled yacht carrying sabotage-trained agents, who planned to disable the ship by placing a limpet mine 'on the hull with a three or four day time delay'. While this was to enable 'the yacht to be in Italian waters before the explosion occurred', it also inevitably meant that the agents could hardly guarantee that there would be no casualties. In any case, after the French government assured the British in May 1947 that they would themselves take steps to stop the immigrant traffic, the Foreign Office placed a strict embargo on Embarrass operations in France and the yacht was instructed to 'proceed to other targets in Italy'. The *President Warfield*, however, sailed from France in July with a cargo of 4,500 refugees and became internationally famous as *Exodus 1947*. On its arrival off Palestine the ship was seized by British security forces (during which operation three people were killed) and the immigrants forcibly returned to Europe, in the full glare of extremely critical press publicity, especially in France and the USA. 'The cost', mused one of the SIS officers involved, 'both direct and indirect to H.M.G. must have been enormous.' The affair presented Zionists with 'a first rate propaganda weapon and even among our friends sympathy was shown towards the illegal immigrants'. All of this, the officer argued, 'could have been spared if the F.O. had permitted the S.S. [SIS] to take the appropriate action against the President Warfield when they suggested doing so'. Hazarding that the actual cost would have been an improbable £100, and that any British involvement would have been 'impossible to trace', he suggested that it would 'be difficult to find a more glaring example' of the value of special operations in peacetime or of the inability of the Foreign Office 'to appreciate the use to which they can put the operational weapon which they have at their disposal in the S.S.'.[5]

Despite the case of the *President Warfield*, and uncertainty over the deception side, Operation Embarrass was judged on the whole to have been a success, especially in demonstrating the capabilities of special operations in peacetime, which presented different, and in some ways greater, challenges than in wartime when, for example, 'the greatest risk occurred during the operation itself and, once the operator was clear of the area, the operation could be considered a success'. But in peace the risk of compromising the British government 'was the greatest danger and the association of an Englishman with the event afterwards [an irrelevant factor in wartime] would have been disastrous'. In September 1947 SIS claimed that the deterrent effect of the ship attacks had caused a complete cessation of sailings from Italy. The following spring they noted that a number of potential emigrant vessels had left Italian waters and that the Jewish organisers of the illegal immigration had lost confidence in the chief provider of ships 'as they consider him to be too compromised to be of any further use'. In terms of the actual special operations, the final Embarrass report concluded that 'careful planning and attention to detail' had enabled the smuggling of large sums of money as well as explosives across frontiers and proved that the Service could carry out sabotage while maintaining 'complete cover' for the agents concerned, thus 'enabling them to have freedom from suspicion for future action in the countries concerned'. Above all, the operation had been 'carried out in peace in the interests of H.M.G. without any suspicion of H.M.G. being aroused'. As for the propaganda side, and reflecting on the relative press coverage of different episodes, SIS wryly concluded that a lesson from the operation was that 'from a purely publicity aspect, a failure involving the discovery of the limpet was of greater success than an actual sinking'.

On 8 May 1948, six days before the proclamation of the new independent state of Israel, Nigel Clive, who had been head of the Athens station, took over in Jerusalem. A month later he reported his initial impressions of Palestine. 'I think we are wrong', he wrote, 'if we persist in thinking of it as a country and wronger [sic] still if we think of Jerusalem as a capital – even a future capital.' The situation in the region, he thought, was 'roughly' back to what had obtained just after the First World War 'when there was a major dispute over the ownership of this area and where there is now again likely to be some land-grabbing'. There were, too, opportunities for SIS. The early days of the Israeli state, he argued, 'are those in which they are likely to be most vulnerable. The longer we leave them to settle down the less chance there will be of our finding chinks in their iron curtain.' Thus he hoped that the situation could be exploited to SIS's advantage. But the violence and chaos of the First Arab–Israeli War which accompanied the birth of the new state put the lives of British personnel in Jerusalem at risk and in July obliged SIS temporarily to relocate the station to Amman, when Clive was replaced as head of station.

But Broadway remained keen to keep some representation in 'the Jewish areas of Palestine'. Since it was 'considered impossible under present circumstances for a male officer to work there effectively' (but why is not clear), in August the Service (with Foreign Office approval) proposed to attach 'a woman intelligence officer' to the British consulate in Haifa, ostensibly as one of the consul-general's secretaries. But the consul concerned, Cyril Marriott, would have none of it. Already worried by the unsettled situation and the arrest on espionage charges of five British employees of the Jerusalem Electric Corporation (one of whom was sentenced to seven years' imprisonment, but released in November after his conviction was quashed),[6] Marriott said that the arrival of 'an English woman' would undermine his current advice that the country was unsafe 'for wives and children'. If she did come, however, she should 'realise that she would be the only English woman here and therefore conspicuous and that she would be under constant watch by Jewish intelligence'. Moreover, if Marriott had to provide accommodation for her, a 'bathroom and lavatory' would have to be installed in his office premises 'where existing arrangements in living quarters are for men only'. Appointing women to work in the region proved a continuing problem with the Foreign Office. In the spring of 1949 Broadway proposed posting a woman to take charge of a sub-station in the new British legation at Tel Aviv, but the Foreign Office refused to agree. When the Service proposed sending a female secretary to Amman in August 1949 the ambassador, Sir Alec Kirkbride, who was 'extremely sensitive about the question of [female] secretaries', urged that if they 'must send a woman she should be a person of a certain age and if possible of forbidding appearance, well able to take care of herself'.

In the late 1940s Israel remained 'a high priority target' about which SIS reckoned in November 1948 the British government was 'likely to maintain a lively interest for some time to come'. In September a production conference in Broadway had been told that 'coverage of Israel was negligible' and in December the head of station was instructed to remain at Amman with a nucleus around which a new station in Jerusalem (which SIS envisaged would be the base for its effort against Israel) could be built. By October the following year Britain's relations with Israel had sufficiently normalised for SIS's Middle East Controllerate (the new name for the Eastern Mediterranean Controllerate) to propose that an officer in Tel Aviv would serve purely for liaison – which would 'undoubtedly be difficult and tricky' – with the Israeli authorities, hoping to use 'their assistance in recruiting and running agents into the USSR or the Balkans'.

Meanwhile, the 'penetration of Israel itself' could be co-ordinated from Jerusalem. The Controller in London, John Teague, cautiously agreed that an overt liaison officer could 'in due course' be posted to Israel, though he also raised in this specific instance a general problem with any serious liaison. He felt that while the Service stood to gain 'a good deal of useful information' about the USSR and the Eastern bloc generally, 'we could be sure that the Israelis would extract the maximum returns and, unless our representative was very cunning, get to know too much about our own organisation and exploit it'. Writing in November 1949, Teague had doubts about the proposal to target Israel from Jerusalem, which had been partitioned between the new state and the rump of Palestine, amalgamated into Jordan following the Arab–Israeli war of 1948–9. There was, he noted, 'a large and strongly-held military barrier' running through the city, 'which it is a major operation to surmount', and it made running operations there quite unfeasible. Once, however, Jerusalem was 'no longer divided by this physical barrier, we should immediately establish an officer . . . there with the idea of making it our principal office for work into Israel'. Even the veteran Teague, with a quarter of a century's experience of the region, cannot have anticipated how long it might take before the city would be united.

The Far East

In August 1945 SIS was left with a sprawling deployment in India and China, generally geared to supporting the military needs of Mountbatten's strategy for the war against Japan. Indeed, for all that it regarded itself as independent, it had in effect become an intelligence-gathering tool in the hands of G. A. Garnons-Williams's P Division at the headquarters of South-East Asia Command. SIS's stations had been positioned more to support the military campaign in Burma and the recovery of Malaya than to gather the longer-term intelligence required to support a re-established British presence in the region. With the prospect of Indian independence (which came in August 1947), SIS moved its regional headquarters, the Inter-Services Liaison Department, from Delhi to Singapore, where Donald Prater became Far East Controller, with a staff of eight officers and seventeen secretaries. In September 1947 Dick Ellis, the Chief Controller

Pacific in London, reviewed the state of SIS in the Far East before embarking on a tour of the area. In China there were stations at Hong Kong, Tientsin (Tianjin), Shanghai, Nanking and Urumchi (in the north-west); outside China there were stations at Tokyo, Batavia (Jakarta) and Hanoi, and plans for stations in Bangkok, Rangoon, Kabul and Seoul. Ellis was generally disappointed with the lack of intelligence being produced in the region but attributed it to difficulties with accommodation and the degree to which officers were obliged to become involved in their cover duties, an unwelcome feature of the postwar operating environment.

In China, SIS had few assets of its own, and was for the most part dependent on the nationalist Chinese Kuomintang for intelligence. In late 1946 a senior Kuomintang intelligence officer educated in Japan and a former SOE contact proposed to the Nanking station an elaborate scheme to establish a bogus press agency in Shanghai which would collect information on Soviet activity, using White Russians (and some Japanese) previously employed by the Japanese against the same target. While there was some initial enthusiasm for the idea (which involved paying a salary to the contact), the situation very soon became confused partly because of what Nanking called the 'unrealistic rate of exchange and China's chaotic economy'. London, moreover, had no faith in the contact, whom they described as 'an adventurer out to feather his own nest, a bluffer and not too good even at that game', and the scheme was dropped. Ironically, while the information on Soviet activity that the agent provided was unreliable, his analysis in early 1947 of where the Kuomintang stood in relation to the Communists was entirely sound, though it went unremarked in London, perhaps because by then it was unremarkable. The Kuomintang, he asserted, 'today find themselves in a parlous condition'. They were 'losing both territory and influence'. There was 'no doubting' that 'at the conclusion of the war the Kuomintang were militarily far superior to the communists', but they had 'succeeded in dissipating much of this advantage' and it was 'open to question' if they were 'now any stronger than their foes'.

It was, nevertheless, to be nine months before SIS started seriously to make plans in the face of Communist conquests in China. In March 1948 London cabled Singapore to instruct the Tientsin station to 'make immediate plans for stay-behind organisations with necessary communications in areas likely to be over-run by Communists particularly Peking

Tientsin area and South Manchuria'. But there were problems getting anyone to take part in a stay-behind scheme. The head of the Tientsin station assumed that local British firms would remain after the takeover, but found them reluctant to co-operate, displaying a 'regrettable attitude' with 'a mixture of complacency, optimism and fatalism'. There was a more fundamental problem (reflecting the new postwar conditions) in that 'virtually no Chinese – one may perhaps say literally none – could be trusted to work honestly for us for as much as twenty-four hours once our backs were turned unless we had some powerful hold over them'. This was 'an indisputable fact' and the reason for it was obvious. 'It is quite irrelevant', declared the Tientsin representative realistically, 'to say that a considerable number of reliable Chinese were available during the war against Japan. The Japanese were foreign enemies. The communists are neither foreign nor, in the eyes of the vast majority of Chinese, enemies.' It was, in any case, far too late to do anything. Although wireless sets for stay-behind teams reached Hong Kong in October, Communist advances in north China meant that they got no further. Under Communist rule, moreover, life became increasingly difficult and restricted for regular diplomats and SIS alike. At the end of March 1949, reviewing 'the situation in Tientsin since the Liberation', the head of station's assistant noted how the new regime had instructed that, apart from other limitations, all cable communications had now to 'be en clair and accompanied by a Chinese text'. The station at Urumchi, whose primary objective in February 1948 had been the 'penetration of Russian Central Asia', and whose station chief was a former medical missionary who planned to combine Bible-running with intelligence-gathering, was equally constrained after the Communists arrived in the late autumn of 1949, and not long after the SIS personnel were expelled.

SIS's problems in China have to be set in the context of the wider demands for intelligence from across the world placed on the Service by its customer departments, and the expectations which those customers had of what SIS could in fact do. This issue was raised by Orme Sargent early in 1948 when he wrote to Menzies complaining about the lack of warning the Foreign Office had received of recent disturbances in Kowloon (which had prompted an attack on the British consulate-general in Canton) and of unrest and violence in Baghdad. 'I must confess that I am a little perturbed', he wrote, 'to find that your organisation was unable to give us any warning of the course which events were likely to take recently in Kowloon and Baghdad.' Evidently alluding to the Communist political challenge in Western Europe, Sargent was 'anxious about the supply of secret intelligence because in the coming months we may well be faced with developments of a far-reaching nature throughout Europe, particularly in Italy and France'. Menzies replied reassuringly about France and Italy, where he thought the supply of intelligence was well covered. As for the particular cases of Kowloon and Baghdad, he quite reasonably argued to Sargent that it did not fall 'within the scope of Secret Intelligence, with its limited resources in peace, to provide a running forecast of specific outbreaks, even when spontaneous combustion is intensified by arson'. The 'task of Secret Intelligence', he argued, 'is to amplify the general warnings of H.M. Representatives and to attempt to penetrate the hostile elements sufficiently to procure fore-knowledge of their general plans'. He went on to explain why SIS had been unable to do more concerning the specific instances raised. He pointed out that in China his organisation was 'barely under way', and the seriousness of the Kowloon situation had presumably been reported on by MI5's local Defence Security Officer or consular officials. In Iraq, he admitted that the SIS representative had concentrated more on government sources than opposition contacts, but maintained (slightly lamely) that he had been quick to report when the riots started.[7]

Faced with the closing down of SIS's intelligence assets in China and increasingly insistent demands for information from customer departments, Ellis went out to Hong Kong to assess the situation and came to the conclusion that there was no alternative but to exploit the existing liaison with the Nationalist Chinese. Telegraphing to London early in 1949 he observed that SIS's 'China set-up' had been created in 1945 'as a long range project with no early demands on its productivity anticipated. Since then', he continued, 'events and fact-hungry departments have forced us to shorten range and speed up pace'. Currently, results were 'far too meagre', and if production was to be expanded he thought that 'orthodox methods' would have to be supplemented by an arrangement which Nationalist Chinese contacts had first suggested to the head of station at Nanking, at the end of 1948. The Chinese had proposed, for a payment of £3,000 per month (equivalent to £75,000 today), that they would make 'available all material, replying to special enquiries and undertaking specific tasks, maintaining and extending W/T and courier services'. They also offered, if needed, 'full collaboration' in breaking Communist codes, 'building up stay-behind network and co-operating in all efforts to penetrate Russian or Russian F.E. [Far East] occupied territory'.

In effect what was offered was a prefabricated intelligence service apparently able to provide precisely the kind of information and penetration that SIS's customers were demanding. Ellis recognised that the cost was high, but was so taken with the scheme that he suggested saving money elsewhere on the SIS budget by cutting the size of existing stations in China. Code-named 'Salvage', the proposal was adopted, and in spite of misgivings in some quarters an officer, posted to Hong Kong with the new designation China Area Co-ordinator, was authorised 'to pay what we must' to keep the scheme going. Salvage began well. A plethora of reports, mostly of detailed Communist troop dispositions, were well received by customers. The War Office was 'definitely in favour of continuing this information. Several reports have received "A" crits,' cabled London in May 1949. A Chinese-manned tactical radio network was allegedly set up (at SIS expense) linking Hong Kong with posts in southern mainland China. When a written agreement was negotiated with the Nationalists, the Chinese contrived to include a guarantee of immunity from interference by the Hong Kong government for a Salvage headquarters in Hong Kong. The implications of this became apparent when in September 1949 the police made a number of arrests which confirmed that the Kuomintang were using Hong Kong as a base for undeclared intelligence and sabotage operations, a revelation that badly damaged SIS's relations with the local authorities.

By this stage, too, doubts about Salvage reporting had arisen. R.1, the Political Requirements Section in Broadway, minuted in August 'that information supplied so far by Salvage on important political and strategic issues has been quite unreliable and looks rather as if it was bogus'. Further concerns were expressed about the lack of source details, the frequent reflection of the reports in Hong Kong newspaper articles and the continued flow of tactical information despite the fall of Canton to the Communists in October 1949 and the consequent disintegration of the radio network. Only the sustained appetite for military intelligence from the armed service customers, and their continued assessment of Salvage reports as of 'great value', kept the scheme going. At the end of 1949, moreover, Britain's future relations generally with the Nationalist Chinese were uncertain. In November London warned the Chief Controller Pacific in Singapore that the government was about to recognise the Communist Chinese People's Republic, leaving him with the prospect that, if the Communists conquered Formosa (Taiwan) too, as seemed very likely, he might not only have to withdraw the station which had been specially opened there for Salvage work but also prepare a stay-behind scheme for the island. The writer of this telegram hoped that the warning would 'enable you to handle Salvage sources in such a way as to ensure their continued support even on Formosan affairs'. It was a tall order, and small wonder that the message ended 'Good luck'.

In August 1947 an SIS station was opened in Japan as part of the United Kingdom Liaison Mission to the United States Supreme Commander Allied Powers (SCAP), General Douglas MacArthur. The individual chosen to head the station was a Canadian academic, who had been born and reared in Japan. He had been running a Japanese-language school for the Canadian army, and was described as 'a brisk, intelligent type of individual, much more "human" than the usual professor'. This officer who had no previous intelligence experience, underwent the two-month 'Combined General and Tradecraft Course' in London before travelling out to Japan to take up a university post, and his considered reflections on the course throw light on both the syllabus taught and the specific problems of intelligence work in Japan. He noted that the material presented in the training course was 'necessarily based chiefly on the successful operation of stations in Europe'. While 'certain principles such as decentralization for security, training and running of agents, investigation, carding and classification of sources and certain techniques such as are involved in the presentation of reports' were 'universally applicable', there was 'a mass of technical detail' which applied 'only partially' or 'not at all' to Japan. The inability of a Caucasian to 'fade into the local background' was an obvious example. In 'every area studied in the Course there were either natives friendly to Great Britain or well-disposed non-natives who could be contacted and who could function inconspicuously'. This did not apply in Japan.

A further difficulty was that the United States military administration had forbidden intelligence work of any kind, even by allies. The

SECRET.

M.I.6. Special Question.

No. M/809

Date 2.10.47.

Country CHINA.

Originator M.I.2b.

There have been indications recently of Chinese activity on the borders of BURMA and FRENCH INDOCHINA and information is required on the following points:-

a) What is the Order of Battle of the Chinese Forces on the China/Burma Frontier?

b) What is the Order of Battle of the Chinese Forces on the China/FIC Frontier?

c) What other forces could be made available quickly as reinforcements from the neighbouring provinces, e.g. KWEICHOW ?

Note. 1. In any reply please differentiate between

a) Chinese National Forces, and
b) Local Forces.

2. Wherever possible, unit locations and Commanders' names are required.

Note: Please complete the attached cancellation slip and return it to M.I.6A when you consider that your Question has either been satisfactorily answered or has become redundant.

A typical Military Intelligence questionnaire for SIS, indicating the kind of information customer departments wanted in the postwar years.

prospective head of station felt that there had been 'a tendency through-out the Course to underestimate the Americans', but while they might be 'amateurs on the European stage', they had 'studied the Pacific area very thoroughly' and could not 'safely be regarded as clumsy amateurs in any part of the Far East where they operated in the past or are operating today'. This made 'the task of carrying on clandestine illegal operations under the noses of the local administration very much more difficult than it would seem to be in any European or Mid-Eastern area with the possible exception of Russia'. As for the recruitment of agents, he observed that 'in the European area apparently there are everywhere per-sons who are willing to work for pay and who are completely venal so far as their own countries are concerned'. This, he asserted, was not the case in Japan. It was true, however, that 'Chinese, Koreans and possibly White Russians could be employed on this basis', though only with 'ex-treme safeguards', as such people, he claimed, were 'completely unreli-able and unprincipled'. In the case of the Japanese, he hazarded that a 'combination of ideological motives with adequate payment' might be a possibility. He finally reflected (and this was accepted in Broadway) that success would be possible only through very slow and careful 'ground-work', allowing that it might take 'two to three years' before any substan-tial results were obtained.

The head of station was absolutely right about the difficulties facing SIS operations in Japan, and the slowness with which any kind of net-work might be built up. It proved impracticable, moreover, for him to act as head of station while carrying a full load as a university professor, so another Service representative was more conventionally installed in the British mission in Tokyo. While he was directed to collect intelli-gence from China, Korea and, if offered, the Soviet Far Eastern territo-ries, the main priority was Communist activities in Japan itself. During 1949 the Tokyo head of station reported a general lack of progress in the region, blaming this on a combination of the Americans having bagged the best available local sources, a shortage of Japanese-speaking Unofficial Assistants and the demands of cover work.[8] In late 1948 George Blake was sent to head a new station in Seoul with instructions to target north-east China, as well as Communist activities in Korea. Blake, the son of a naturalised British father (originally from Istanbul) and a Dutch mother, had served in the Dutch resistance movement and the Royal Navy before joining SIS in 1944. By the end of 1949 he had made little headway. Shortly after the outbreak of the Korean War he was captured by the North Koreans and subsequently recruited as a Soviet spy.[9]

One Asian country in which SIS achieved success was Burma, where a station was opened in late 1947, shortly before the country became an independent republic and left the British Commonwealth. Both the head of station, Edward James, and his assistant had gained wartime intelligence experience with the British Fourteenth 'Forgotten' Army during the Burma campaign, and they were able to bring their specialist knowledge of the region and local contacts to the task. The main objective was penetration of Communist organisations in the country, particularly the pro-USSR Red Flag and the pro-China White Flag parties. An agent with friends in the police was able to acquire periodic Special Branch summaries, and another source was involved in liaison between the Karen nationalist movement and the Red Flag party. The information obtained was discussed with an MI5 Security Liaison Officer, a specialist in international Communism who was later integrated into the SIS station, and the resulting casework produced what SIS afterwards claimed was 'the deepest penetration of any national communist party in the world'. In Burma, too, SIS was able to provide valuable information about the ethnic minority Karens, whose guerrilla insurgency campaign in the late 1940s threatened to bring down the Rangoon government. In February 1949 the Karen leader Saw Ba U Gyi told the SIS representative himself that his people were 'fighting for their very existence', and SIS delivered a number of reports on the strength and disposition of Karen forces in the late summer of 1949 which Military Intelligence in the War Office warmly welcomed and graded 'A' for accuracy.[10]

Penetrating 'Sovbloc'

When in April 1946 Frank Roberts, the British minister in Moscow, enquired about policy relating to covert operations, it was confirmed that there was 'no change in the present position as regards Soviet Union under whom no secret service activities of any kind are conducted'.[11] Three years later a production conference in Broadway noted the continuing ban on 'clandestine operations of any kind on Moscow'. During

1946, however, the Foreign Office's restriction on work within the Soviet Union began to cause frustrations within SIS. In August the Director of Production circulated a paper to the Regional Controllers about stepping up operations in this area. 'In view of the paucity of information on the principal target, and the troubled nature of our political relations', he asked if 'we should not be justified in taking greater risks to obtain information'. There were, he suggested, two sorts of risks, '(a) those which apply primarily to the agent, and (b) those which give rise to the possibilities of diplomatic complications'. He thought it 'obvious that if we were prepared to go the whole hog, we should obtain a great deal more information in a much shorter time'. By 'going the whole hog', he had in mind 'wartime' techniques, such as 'parachute operations, widespread use of wireless, possibly raids of safes in Consulates etc. etc.' This paper generated 'considerable discussion' at the next Regional Controllers' meeting (on 2 September) when it was agreed that 'a more forward policy might well pay dividends'. The Controller Northern Area, Harry Carr, noted that the head of the Moscow station was not allowed to do any clandestine work, but he felt 'that potential lines existed there which might, without undue danger, be exploited if this restriction could be modified'. The representative in Helsinki was similarly prohibited from recruiting agents in Finland 'for despatch to Russia: here too he felt a more positive policy might show results'. He also thought that it might help if he could equip agents entering 'the Baltic territories' with radios, 'a practice which was still discouraged'. All the Controllers agreed that 'the possibilities of W/T in connection with the penetration of Russia and its Satellite States should be actively explored', and they also considered 'the possibility of disguising such sets as American, Polish or French'.

Dick Ellis, the Controller Production Research, had lots of ideas about 'burgling Russian Embassies and Consulates', instancing 'several operations of this nature which his organisation in the Americas had undertaken'. He said that any 'such operations should not be conducted by normal Stations' but that a separate organisation, 'somewhat on S.O. lines', should be 'established to undertake strong-arm and burglarious methods of producing intelligence'. He thought that 'a well conducted burglary might need some six months of preparation'. Sinclair, the VCSS, 'agreed that it might be well worth trying' but warned that 'Russian Embassies, etc, would prove hard nuts to crack and suggested that a start might be made on the Legations of Satellite Powers'. Other suggestions included 'planting Double-agents on the Russians, through the medium of British deserters (of which there are a number)', and also the possibility 'that a suitable cover for strong-arm methods might be found in the formation of an anti-Communist League, with headquarters in, say, Switzerland'.

Papers were prepared on the possibilities of wireless and the use of burglary against the Soviet target for a Regional Controllers' conference on 7 October. By looking realistically at the costs and benefits, they deflated some of the enthusiasm of the previous month. Despite the most careful disguising of wireless sets, and transmitting signals through cut-out stations in neutral countries, if an agent were 'caught "red-handed" there was little doubt that he would ultimately be "broken" and the greatest care would have to be taken if British complicity was not to be revealed'. As for the delivery of agents and radio sets, it was felt that in practical terms this might not be very difficult, but that the air force were unlikely to agree to any operation involving a 'long distance flight over Russia or Russian occupied territory in Service aircraft'. The 'picking up of agents', moreover, 'presented a far more difficult problem', as 'more elaborate ground organisation' would be necessary. Jack Easton, the ACSS, an airman himself, thought, however, that RAF co-operation might be possible 'for dropping agents a few miles inside hostile frontiers. Arrangements might be made to do this on the assumption that . . . faulty navigation or adverse weather [could] take aircraft a short way off their right courses'. Thus 'we might be able to drop men and material just within the frontiers of such places as Russian occupied Germany, Russia itself, the Ukraine, Poland and possibly Lithuania'. These reflections were seriously hedged about with qualifications and well-founded worries that other government departments might both disapprove and fail to offer any assistance.

The same tone suffused the discussion of burglary. While it might be a 'short cut to obtaining valuable information', the 'basic snag was that if ever responsibility for the crime were fixed on S.I.S. it might give rise to a diplomatic incident out of all proportion to the value of the information received'. The only justification for planning an operation of the sort was that 'the results would be outstandingly important and the risk had been reduced to a minimum', in which case it 'would almost inevitably involve the presence of inside sources and if these existed there would be no need for burglary at all in the ordinary sense of the word'. While agreeing with this, Ellis (now Controller Far East) thought that an operation might be 'so technically perfect' that the burglary need never be discovered. He confirmed this by describing two burglary operations he claimed to have organised during the war where 'two Embassies had been penetrated and highly satisfactory results obtained'. Despite this example, the conclusion drawn was notably conditional: 'burglary was almost certainly not worth attempting if the person burgled realised that burglary had been committed'. If it could be done 'so that this was not known', an operation might, 'after careful weighing up of the risks', be justified, but only 'in certain cases'. Above all, 'inside assistance was most necessary'.

The ban on SIS work in the Soviet Union was understood to refer to operations run within the country itself, for example by the Moscow station. There was a less stringent restriction on operations aimed at penetrating the USSR and the Soviet bloc from neighbouring countries, including those employing members of disaffected national minorities. When a new officer took over the Stockholm station in late June 1945 he was told his main task was to work against the Soviet Union which was 'now permissible . . . in all countries except the U.S.S.R. itself', this being defined as including 'the late Baltic States' and 'Poland east of the Curzon line'. At this stage he was merely to 'try to obtain contacts with a view to penetrating Russia should this be allowed at a later date'. In November London informed him that it was 'now permitted to penetrate Russia from perimeter'. The following spring an updated directive from London emphasised preparations for penetrating the Soviet Union, and instructed that 'immediate priority' should be given to 'the proposed expeditions to Baltic States' which, if successful, 'may well be the foundation for a permanent channel for physical penetration of Russia'. The officer was told to explore 'every possibility of physical entrance by our agents into Russia and her spheres of influence'. He was able to pick up some of the Baltic contacts which the wartime Helsinki station-in-exile had used (with mixed results) to gather intelligence on German targets. But by the late 1940s the intensely nationalist and anti-Russian groups from whom penetration agents might be recruited also wanted weapons, medicines and other practical assistance for active resistance operations against the Russians who had occupied their countries in August 1940. Matters were complicated by the fact that Swedish intelligence had also been running cross-Baltic operations during the war in co-operation with some of the same refugee organisations, and continued to do so in the postwar period.

Some (but by no means all) of this activity formed the basis of formal liaison between the Swedish and British services. In late 1947 the Swedes asked whether SIS could help them obtain a German E-boat (motor torpedo boat) for their operations. Vessels were available in Germany, and fortuitously a former German naval officer with wartime experience of secret operations into the Baltic states offered his services to SIS the following year. With 'informal clearance' from the Foreign Office, Menzies gave his approval for a boat and crew to be supplied for use by both the Swedish Intelligence Service and SIS. The boat was used for a Swedish operation in May 1949 and in October SIS infiltrated two trained Latvian émigrés who 'claimed to have the possibility of making contact . . . with some patriots who supported groups of Partisans living in the Latvian forests'. That SIS's Baltic operations depended on such émigré assurances illustrates the immense difficulty faced by any Western intelligence organisation seeking to penetrate the Soviet Union, and the consequent risks individuals (from intelligence chiefs to agents themselves) were prepared to take in the early days of the Cold War. As it happened, the Soviets had themselves penetrated most of the émigré groups, as well as some of the intelligence services, and most of the operations launched with such high hopes against the Soviet bloc in the late 1940s ended in disaster within a very few years.

The 'Climber' operations on the Soviet southern flank were no exception. 'Climber I' in 1948 had been designed to infiltrate two Georgians 'with an intelligence brief' into Soviet Georgia, but the unfortunate men had died on the frontier in obscure circumstances. 'Climber II' in August 1949 aimed to insert two further Georgians into the Soviet Union from mountainous north-east Turkey. In the spring of 1949 two émigrés, one apparently in his late forties and the other in his early thirties, were recruited in France and brought to England for training. They were given a special tradecraft course, with particular emphasis on secret writing, and two weeks' physical 'hardening-up' walking on Dartmoor. Here the only reported problem concerned their military clothing, which made them conspicuous among locals and holidaymakers. Next time, their trainer recommended that 'when eating in cafes or local farmhouses grey flannel trousers, light coloured shirts and sports jackets would have been better dress'. This snag was accentuated because the younger man 'refused to shave for days on end and at times he must have been considered as anything from a Moroccan Arab to an escaped convict'. But they finished the course satisfactorily, and travelled to Istanbul under false passports, posing as proprietors of a yoghurt factory in South America visiting Turkey 'to discuss various unspecified plans for improving and extending their business'.

The two men were met in Istanbul by Kim Philby, the head of station, who had arranged co-operation from members of the local security services and the local émigré Georgian community. The original plan had been for the Climber party, who were provided with Turkish army uniforms, to establish themselves close to the frontier. Here Philby and the SIS case-officer for the operation, 'disguised as Turkish sentries with fixed bayonets', were 'to carry out a normal frontier patrol and thereby observe the best route for the Climbers to take'. Once over the border, the Georgians, who had local contacts on the Soviet side, were to 'abandon and bury their Turkish kit and appear as ordinary local Russians'. For this operation their task was then 'to proceed to watch for contacts, safe-houses, letter-boxes and generally start to build up the nucleus of an organisation which can be used in the future'. It was estimated that this might take up to six months, after which one of the Georgians would return to report on the organisation which had been formed and 'also pass over, we hope, a massive weight of frontier intelligence, local living conditions, and possibly industrial intelligence, etc.'. Despite the very detailed scheme which had been prepared, the planners recognised that the arrangements for the frontier operation itself were 'naturally very fluid and Philby must be left to make ad hoc decisions according to the information available at the time'.

In the event, the Climbers refused to fall in with the SIS plan and at a very late stage proposed a more modest scheme whereby they would cross the frontier with local guides and remain in the USSR for only five weeks or so, during which they 'would establish contacts and obtain information on living conditions for the following summer when they would return and carry on the work of building up an organisation and obtaining intelligence'. This was something of a fait accompli and, 'although surprised', Philby agreed to the revised plan. While he remained in Istanbul, the Climbers, accompanied by their case-officer, headed for

Erzerum in eastern Turkey. From there the party took three days, by car, jeep and eventually an eight-hour horseback ride over 8,000-foot mountain passes, to reach a base camp two hours' walk or so from the frontier. During the final approach the older Georgian, who was badly affected by the altitude, collapsed and could go no further. Afterwards it was reckoned that he was nearer sixty years old than the forty-seven he had claimed to be. But, escorted by two guides, the younger man went on and crossed the frontier without further mishap. Just over two weeks later the Georgian reappeared in Turkey and with his older colleague was flown back to Britain where they were thoroughly debriefed during the autumn. All seemed to have gone well, until on his way back to the border the Georgian had encountered a Soviet patrol, from which he escaped after (he claimed) shooting two soldiers. In Georgia he had made contact with anti-Russian resistance groups. He reported extensively on frontier defences and living conditions in the region. There were also descriptions of naval installations along the Black Sea coast and sightings of several Soviet submarines. Although details of some hydroelectric power stations were taken to be broadly accurate, output figures from aircraft factories in Georgia were dismissed as 'nonsense', as was a reported tank factory in Tiflis.

While the actual intelligence product was relatively modest, Climber II was adjudged to have been a success, and a useful basis for further such ventures to penetrate the Soviet Union. But aspects of the operation were dangerously insecure. Even if (as was assumed long afterwards) Kim Philby had passed on details of Climber to his masters in Moscow, the fact that the operation was staged jointly with Turkish security personnel, that the village from where the actual penetration was launched (and where five local guides were engaged) was a regular base for border crossings, and that the presence of both Climbers in Turkey was well known among gossipy émigré Georgian groups in both Paris and Istanbul, all provided vulnerable points for the watchful Soviet authorities to learn about the mission. A senior Georgian in Paris (who from the start had been included in SIS's planning and knew about the border-crossing) reported that fellow émigrés were 'convinced that [the] Climbers had been on a special mission' to Turkey. He believed that these rumours had originated from Istanbul and 'somebody must have written from there to a friend' in Paris. The Climbers themselves did not help matters by arriving back in London 'with their suitcases bulging with every sort of Turkish delicacy clearly revealing their country of origin', which they were proposing to give their friends in Paris. They also had 'a large number of secondhand female garments which they were conveying from mutual friends' in Istanbul for émigrés in Paris. Before their original departure, moreover, they had apparently 'told several of their friends' in Paris that they were going to Istanbul.

Operation 'Valuable', a scheme for the penetration of Albania, was also being planned in 1948–9, and provides an example of covert action actively supported by Bevin and Attlee. Albania, where Enver Hoxha (whose anti-German resistance forces had been supplied by SOE) had led a Communist regime since the end of the war, was regarded as a good target for the kind of pressure – 'all possible means short of war' – which the British Chiefs of Staff in September 1948 envisaged bringing to bear in the developing Cold War. There was continuing unrest in Albania itself, as Hoxha's government sought to enforce its rule, and Albanian émigré groups in Italy, Greece and Turkey provided a reservoir of potential recruits for anti-Communist operations of one sort or another. Tito's breach with the Soviet Union in June 1948 had left Albania isolated and, geographically at least, it looked like a good place to begin chipping away at the Eastern bloc. Albania's other neighbour, Greece, too, might be disposed to support any action as Communist Greek rebels based in Albania had been making incursions across the frontier. In November 1948 the Foreign Office's Russia Committee, which had been set up in April 1946 to manage policy towards the Eastern bloc and on which the service Chiefs had just secured representation, decided to explore the possibility of operations against Albania.[12]

Kenneth Cohen in SIS was willing to take up the baton. Albania, he reflected in December 1948, would be 'a happy choice' for a response 'to the Russian campaign in kind, either by S.O. or quasi-S.O. activities'. The 'primitive political and economic state of the country' provided 'an opening of promoting tribal unrest'. There was the opportunity to weaken 'the support now being given to the rebels in Greece' and there would be a particularly low risk 'of causing an embarrassing situation' for the British government since Britain did not currently have diplomatic relations with Albania. Cohen, apparently, had an agent ready and willing to go and proposed that he could be dropped in during January 1949. Once in Albania he could assess the potential for special operations there. But when Menzies proposed this, Orme Sargent pressed him to produce a further paper on the possibilities in Albania. The task was given to Richard Brooman-White, a very well-regarded officer who had been an 'exceptional' head of station in Istanbul for a year before being brought back to Head Office to be Deputy Chief Controller Mediterranean. Heading his first draft, 'It is more blessed to give than to receive', Brooman-White devised a plan with two objectives: to relieve the pressure on Greece by guerrilla operations aimed at Greek rebel bases in southern Albania and fomenting 'insurrection in other areas of the country'; and to 'endeavour to undermine the Communist position in the weakest of the orbit countries', possibly producing 'repercussions in the satellite bloc which could in turn be followed up and exploited'. Methods envisaged included sending armed bands or fighting patrols across the frontier, sea landings and parachute drops from Italy or Greece. Since the Chiefs of Staff favoured working with the Americans, and as Menzies worried that the Americans might 'be planning on similar lines', Brooman-White inserted a note about the necessity for co-ordination, since 'two great powers cannot operate independently in small countries such as Greece and Albania'.

Although the SIS plan was more ambitious than the Foreign Office felt able to contemplate at that stage, it met with a constructive response. Ivor Porter, an ex-SOE officer working in the Foreign Office's Southern Department, prepared a 'counter-plan' on similar lines, but laying more emphasis on intelligence-gathering, while recruiting Albanians for subsequent operations. Sargent thought that this was 'the most we can hope to do in Albania and derive satisfactory results'. He stressed to Menzies the importance of setting up a good intelligence network in the country before attempting any operations, and told him that Bevin would want to be assured that the 'conditions in Albania' were 'sufficiently favourable to justify us in expecting a reasonable degree of success'. While Menzies welcomed the Foreign Office proposals, he observed that the nature of Albania and its people was 'such that no adequate estimate of resistance potentialities can be made purely by Intelligence methods – that is to say, it would not suffice to put in a few agents solely to form opinion on public feeling or transmit verbal assurances given by tribal chiefs'. The 'only way' to see whether there was 'any substance behind their words' was 'by more direct methods of probing and by testing local preparedness to take action on the smallest possible scale'. If such testing 'provided a satisfactory reaction', 'we would then move on to the next stage'. Clearly anxious to ensure that the government was aware of the consequences of embarking on any kind of action in Albania, Menzies also warned that it was 'not worth incurring the effort and possible loss of life entailed by the preliminary operations, unless we are prepared to follow them up by striking as hard as possible at any sensitive point we may find'. This might, he added, 'involve fairly extensive supply operations at a later date'.[13]

Sir William Strang (Sargent's successor as Permanent Under-Secretary in the Foreign Office) put the scheme up to Bevin (and, on Bevin's request, to Attlee) for approval, and on 28 April 1949 Strang wrote to Menzies conveying the Foreign Secretary's approval to 'set up an intelligence system in Southern Albania' to test local preparedness for action and, if the outcome of this was 'encouraging', to 'infiltrate instructors in modern guerrilla warfare, in order to recruit, arm, feed, clothe and train anti-Communist supporters for military operations against Greek rebel bases and lines of communication'. The 'practicability for extending operations to Northern Albania and to insurrectionary purposes' was left 'for further examination' in the 'light of the progress achieved'. Consultations in Washington revealed that the Central Intelligence Agency (which had been created in 1947) also had plans for Albania, similar to the British, 'though on a rather broader basis'. The State Department and CIA proposed joining forces to mount operations, with a combined Policy Committee directing the project. Although there were worries about the 'grandiose' nature of the American plans, and the extent of their involvement with dissident Albanian exiles, SIS agreed that co-operation was necessary, 'and that our original scheme should be regarded as the first phase in a joint operation', though an immediate effect of American participation was to widen the scope of the initial reconnaissance to include the infiltration of parties into central and northern Albania as well as the south. In practice some co-ordination with the Americans was unavoidable if the British operation was to succeed. Even in October 1949, John Teague in Broadway noted 'evidence of lines being crossed and the work of certain individuals for S.I.S. being hampered through American intervention and interest in the refugee Committees'. In the Foreign Office, moreover, it was argued that there was more chance of keeping some control over the Americans by working with them, and 'it would always be possible for us to decline participation in any later activity which went beyond what we should think desirable'.[14]

With the green light from the Foreign Office, SIS began serious work on the scheme, contacting dissident Albanians in Greece and Italy and making plans for a main base at Malta and a forward one in Corfu (for which it was accepted there would have to be some liaison with the Greek authorities). Training began in Malta at the beginning of August and in the early autumn twenty-nine southern Albanians in six parties were landed by boat along the Albanian coast near Corfu. Meanwhile (though getting the dissident Albanian émigré groups to agree proved very difficult) an Anglo-American-sponsored Committee for Free Albania was launched in Paris on 26 August, to provide the umbrella the Americans particularly desired for anti-Communist operations in Albania itself. Of the six SIS parties, one was wiped out and by the end of 1949 the fate of another was 'unknown'. Three parties, 'having become the object of intense interest to the Security Authorities', withdrew to Greece in less than four weeks, but the sixth 'successfully maintained itself for over 2 months'. Having 'failed to find winter quarters', however, 'and being also much harried by the now fully alerted Albanian Police', it also withdrew to Greece in early December. Before the fate of all the groups had become fully clear, one Foreign Office official optimistically concluded that the fact 'that at least four of these small and lightly armed parties, carrying comparatively heavy wireless equipment', had 'received sufficient help from the local population to enable them to survive for a number of weeks and to traverse this most difficult area', was 'a favourable indication of the state of affairs in the country'.[15]

Reflecting on the operation, SIS concluded that while there was evidence of 'resentment against the Communist regime', and that the loyalty of the police and army was 'doubtful', it had been 'clearly demonstrated that security is in practice almost impossible to maintain in operations of this type in Albania'. A report of leakages about the operation noted that there were widespread indications among émigré groups in Italy and Greece that something was up and that the British were recruiting Albanians from a refugee camp in Bari. At the beginning of July the Russian head of the Albanian counter-espionage service was reported as believing that the British were running agents from a base at Corfu. A representative of the

Italian Foreign Office revealed in a conversation in late September that he knew the British were 'training Albanians in Malta', but did not know 'whether the Americans had a hand in the scheme'. A report in December 1949 stated that members of the 'National Committee for Albania' had shown 'a complete lack of discretion in their letters to political followers in Italy, Turkey, Syria, Egypt and France'. The 'most serious result of this lack of security was that the Albanian Government was evidently aware of the imminent arrival of the parties some two months before they were actually infiltrated'. The parties that withdrew to Greece, moreover, 'talked freely to the Greek officials who interrogated them', thus jeopardising any future operations organised along similar lines.

The results of Operation Valuable in 1949 were not sufficiently positive to support moving on to the second stage, and 'the tentative project for encouraging active revolt against the Hoxha regime by introducing a shock force of trained Albanian guerrillas in 1950' was abandoned. The Foreign Secretary ruled that future British participation would be limited to 'continued support of the Committee for Free Albania', propaganda, economic warfare and 'recruitment of a small reserve force of Albanians for use as may become necessary'. Within the limitations, however, of these decisions (which left the door open for future agent operations in Albania), 'every assistance' was 'to be given to whatever further operations the Americans themselves decide to carry out in furtherance of the common purpose', which, at the end of 1949, were 'expected to be revealed in the near future'.

A special intelligence relationship?

Liaison with foreign intelligence agencies – those of close allies as well as those of less friendly states – has formed an essential part of SIS's work from almost the very beginning. Co-operation with the Allied United Nations against the Axis powers during the Second World War, and within the Western Alliance from the later 1940s, was particularly important. In many cases close wartime relationships – with Norway and the Low Countries, for example – underscored much friendly co-operation in the postwar years, some of which was formalised within the North Atlantic Treaty Organisation system after its foundation in April 1949.

In other instances the perceived (and growing) threat apparently posed by the Soviet Union prompted some national intelligence and security organisations in countries which had been neutral during the war (such as Sweden) to forge closer ties with corresponding British agencies than hitherto. Commonwealth countries, too, like Canada and Australia, began to be treated by Britain more on the basis of formal international equality than had been the case before, when their unquestioning loyalty had largely been assumed. In November 1947 a production conference in Broadway heard that representatives 'were keen on extending our relations with the Dominions', and were particularly interested in 'facilities, such as cover posts and the use of [diplomatic] bags'. The Dominions could also supply prospective agents and safe havens where defectors could be hidden away.

But the closest and most mutually productive relations of all were with the United States and they drew on the extensive (if not entirely untroubled) wartime relationships which had been established between the Office of Strategic Services (OSS), SIS, SOE and signals intelligence organisations on both sides. In March 1946 SIS summed up liaison with the United States as operating on four levels. First was secret intelligence liaison through Dunderdale's Special Liaison Controllerate and the London office of the American Strategic Services Unit which had taken over intelligence responsibilities following the abolition of OSS in October 1945. This liaison included exchange of reports, of which in 1945–6 the numerical balance was much in SIS's favour, with 4,403 being received as against 2,063 supplied. Well over half the SIS reports were on political subjects and most of the material dealt with Europe, though on Menzies's instructions comparatively little information was passed concerning the USSR. There was a similar exchange of secret intelligence material through a member of the SIS Washington station. SIS's counter-intelligence branch R.5 (formerly Section V) had a separate liaison in London with the American X2, which also had a separate link with MI5, mostly dealing with Communist matters. Finally, there was some local liaison between stations in the field. None of this was co-ordinated in any way and the view in Broadway was that 'somebody in this office ought to be responsible for co-ordinating our world-wide policy towards O.S.S. [sic] and the details of our exchanges with them'. But there were also some concerns, as it was thought that American agencies had a tendency towards leakage, which meant that SIS had to be 'especially careful about passing to the Americans the very information they themselves most want to have, namely that connected with the U.S.S.R.'.

In April 1946 Dick Ellis reported that the United States Chief of Secret Intelligence had stressed 'the importance of the intelligence received' through liaison with SIS. A recent British report had been rated 'by MIS [the Military Intelligence Service] as the most valuable single piece of Russian Order of Battle information it had received'. But there were also some reservations on the American side. When Ellis went to the USA the same month for talks with General John Magruder, head of the Strategic Services Unit, he learned that some people in Washington objected to 'having any direct contact with Allied Intelligence Services, on the grounds that they might be tempted to influence U.S. policy by making available information in such a form as to produce that effect'. On the whole, however, these concerns had been overcome, 'the advantages on technical and practical grounds outweighing the alleged objections raised by the more suspicious and politically-minded members of the committees'. Ellis found, nevertheless, that 'as a reaction against the rather loose and publicity-minded tendencies of O.S.S., there is an extremely cautious, official atmosphere about S.S.U.'; he put this down to the new staff being 'New England types who are notoriously not addicted to display or loquacity'. The following month the American Admiral William D. Leahy, President Truman's personal representative on the National Intelligence Authority (NIA) which had been formed to co-ordinate all federal foreign intelligence activities, came to England and confirmed a keen willingness to continue close Anglo-American intelligence relations. At a meeting with the Director-General of MI5, Sir Percy Sillitoe, Leahy 'thanked M.I.5 and all British Intelligence Services for their close and, to the United States, very profitable co-operation during the war', and said that he 'planned to demand at the next meeting of the NIA that the United States do everything possible to have this cooperation continued'.

From its formation in 1947 the Central Intelligence Agency began to develop increasingly close relations with SIS, a process reinforced by wider liaisons within the Western Alliance, which in turn were influenced by the emerging Cold War with the Soviet Union and its allies. In April 1948, Jack Easton, the Assistant Chief of SIS, visited Washington for three days of discussions with CIA colleagues, covering a wide range of topics, including the handling of defectors, potential deception operations, signals intelligence, special operations and propaganda. Easton explained to the Americans, for example, that the Foreign Office intended to set up a committee to handle propaganda somewhat on the lines of the wartime Political Warfare Executive, and he revealed that SIS had been considering how far 'black propaganda' operations could be taken in peacetime without their getting into 'physical action'. As regards special operations, Easton reported that SIS had taken over 'a small part of the old SOE' and was now 'an integrated organisation for intelligence and special operations'. He urged that SIS and the CIA should keep in touch over special operations in order not to duplicate efforts or cross lines.

At the end of his visit Easton secured CIA agreement to a joint CIA–SIS conference which was held in London six months later, attended by a high-powered team from the CIA, including the Director, Rear Admiral Roscoe Hillenkoetter. Reflecting the very real apprehensions about the likelihood of serious conflict with the Soviet Union, and demonstrating that liaison was not just a theoretical matter, this became known as the London Conference on War Planning, though in fact the topics covered went well beyond those simply connected with open hostilities. Shortly before the conference started Easton gave an oral briefing to SIS staff about the development of SIS's thinking on co-operation with the Americans, stressing that in a future war the Americans would be 'in the war from the outset and would be the predominant Allied country'. A shared assumption of the closest possible co-operation underpinned the discussions and much of the conference business was devoted to detailed practical matters, such as joint arrangements for handling tactical intelligence at theatre headquarters level, stay-behind projects, special operations planning, common training and how to deal 'with the French in peace and war'. It was hoped that this potentially fraught matter of relations with the French (if the experience of the Second World War was anything to go by) would be covered by the proposed formation of a Western Union Clandestine Committee, through which wider Allied liaison could be handled, under the auspices of the Western European Union collective self-defence treaty signed by the United Kingdom, France and the Benelux countries in March 1948. All in all, however, Anglo-American agreement at this conference formed the basis for long-term SIS–CIA liaison, including the work of organising what later became the Allied

Clandestine Committee of NATO, which dealt with the co-ordination of stay-behind matters, secret intelligence collection and special operations in the event of a future war in Europe.

Although the conclusions of the London conference embodied a very high level of agreement between the CIA and SIS, back in Washington there were concerns that too close a relationship with the British might jeopardise American autonomy in the event of a serious international crisis. In October 1948 Peter Dwyer, an SIS officer who handled liaison with both the CIA and the FBI in Washington, reported one CIA officer conceding that while they (the Americans) had 'relied heavily on us during the war', they now felt that the CIA 'must stand on its own two feet or get out of the business'. Dwyer considered that once the CIA had 'demonstrated to their own satisfaction that they can plan and achieve on their own what they have set out to do, they will be ready for a much closer coordination with us. In other words,' he continued, 'the local boy is determined to make good on his own.' 'Exactly what I have repeatedly said,' noted Menzies in the margin of Dwyer's report.

There were few such concerns on the British side, where there was a general recognition of the importance of the closest possible Anglo-American co-operation. When in March 1949 Hillenkoetter asked Menzies to send someone to Washington specifically to discuss special operations, both Menzies's Principal Staff Officer, and William Hayter, of the Services' Liaison Department at the Foreign Office, went over. Their 'line of thought' for the discussions sketched out two possible fields of Cold War action: 'the defensive one of protecting the rest of the world from Communist domination, and the offensive one of successively detaching those countries which have already been subjugated'. In an agenda suggested by Menzies, the two SIS representatives included 'Elimination of competitive action in Peace, especially where Stay-Behind plans are concerned', citing Norway and Belgium as examples where there had been line-crossing, as well as Greece and Turkey, and Albania, where Operation Valuable was already being planned. In Washington Menzies's staff officer found 'the tenor of the negotiations' had been 'extremely cordial' and they had 'broadly reached agreement on most of the main heads', although there were 'still differences over timing'. At the same time as the SIS visit, Maurice Oldfield of SIS's R.5 section was over meeting the CIA and the FBI (and later the Canadian services) for wide-ranging discussions on matters of common counter-intelligence interest. Again the atmosphere was friendly and co-operative, and Oldfield 'found a gratifying fund of goodwill for our Service'.

The British visits to Washington in May 1949 did much to cement relations between SIS and the CIA. 'From our standpoint,' wrote Hillenkoetter to Menzies on 20 June, 'the series of discussions with Messers. Hayter, [Menzies's Principal Staff Officer] and Oldfield was eminently satisfactory.' A wide measure of agreement was reached and it confirmed the CIA director's view 'of the necessity for a close working relationship between our services, particularly with regard to our relatively new responsibilities on the operations side'. Menzies replied in kind on 4 July: 'I deeply appreciated your letter . . . mainly because your reactions so fully endorse my own, but also for its cordial tone, which augurs well for our joint undertakings . . . No doubt', he continued, 'snags will arise, but I am confident that our firm realisation of a common purpose and a common gain will enable us to iron them out.' Menzies went on to suggest that a common approach could apply to 'other aspects of our joint campaign; e.g., to the intelligence support for our current operations and our future plans, and, in due course, to our use of propaganda'. The 'close working relationship' between SIS and the CIA, to which Hillenkoetter referred, was to become a crucial component in the extremely important Anglo-American strategic and military alliance which continued (despite the occasional wobble) for many years to come. Born of mutual self-interest, and perhaps even mutual self-preservation, the 'special intelligence relationship' remained a central feature of the foreign policy of successive British governments, lasting, indeed, for a long time after the end of the Cold War during which it was forged.

PART SEVEN

CONCLUSION

22

SIS: leadership and performance over the first forty years

The history of the British Secret Intelligence Service is far more than that of individual personalities, but any assessment of the Service's performance over its first forty years has to take into account the specific contributions of the first three Chiefs: Mansfield Cumming, Hugh Sinclair and Stewart Menzies. For thirty of those forty years, from 1909 to 1939, the small size of the Service put a special premium on the role of individual officers, especially the Chief. This was so in the testing, early days when Cumming was not much more than a one-man band, and also during the First World War when he had to fend off the predatory attentions of the Admiralty and War Office. But it was also true for Sinclair during the interwar years, when the independent existence of the tiny cash-starved Service continued to be threatened, and customer departments made increasingly unrealistic demands of it. From 1939 to 1949 Menzies's situation was rather different. After a difficult start, SIS established itself as an integral and valued part of the British war machine, not least (but also not only) because of the increasingly valuable signals intelligence emanating from Bletchley Park. Although the Service was challenged in some areas by the activities of SOE, its survival as an autonomous agency was never threatened in the way it had been during the First World War and immediately after. So secure was its independence that with sustained Foreign Office backing Menzies was able to see off Field Marshal Montgomery's scheme in 1947 for the Ministry of Defence to take over responsibility for the Service. So it was, that by 1949, in keeping with the crucially influential recommendations of the 1944 Bland Report (and as interpreted by Menzies's own 1945 postwar planning committee), SIS had emerged in a recognisably modern professional form, institutionally equipped, moreover, to survive and flourish for very many more years.

Mansfield Cumming and the establishment of the Service

We do not know if Mansfield Cumming was the only possible contender to head the foreign section of the new Secret Service Bureau in 1909, or whether the Director of Naval Intelligence sounded out other people in the month between the decision of the Committee of Imperial Defence on 24 July to form the Bureau and the letter he wrote to Cumming on 10 August saying he had 'something good' to offer. So far as the history of the Secret Intelligence Service is concerned, however, Cumming was an inspired choice. Not only did he grasp the essentials of secret service work from the very beginning, but he proved to be sufficiently robust and independent-minded to ensure the continued autonomy of his fledgling Service, especially during the First World War. His appointment was crucial to the early development of the Service. Plucked from the relative obscurity of studying harbour defences in Southampton, he adopted a rather different and calculated anonymity, turning himself into a kind of identikit spymaster: mysterious, secretive, engrossed by what became known as tradecraft – secret writing, disguise, cover and the like. Belying his Mr Punch-like appearance, moreover, Cumming was a strikingly modern figure, a workaholic fascinated by the latest technology, in love with fast cars and possessor of an early pilot's licence.

By August 1914 the Foreign Section of the Secret Service Bureau which Mansfield Cumming had created was already recognisably the forebear of the Secret Intelligence Service it was to become. The basic shape of the organisation, its priorities and working practices, the fastidious concern for security and the ethos of professionalism imbued by Cumming were all to survive throughout the Service's first forty years. Cumming also put his stamp on the organisation in other ways. He was the original 'C', signing himself thus from almost the very beginning. The earliest document with a 'C' signature in the archives is a memorandum to Admiral Bethell of 10 January 1910, and since Cumming's time all subsequent Chiefs have used the designation. From Cumming, too, came the practice whereby the Chief of the Service writes in green ink, the earliest use of which occurs in handwritten notes on a paper of 9 May 1910. The practice of writing in green was a naval tradition, by which officers in charge of branches or sections used it to indicate their superior status. John Fisher, First Sea Lord 1904–10 and 1914–15, for example, wrote with a characteristic green pencil.[1] Cumming, therefore, may have adopted it as much to confirm his autonomy vis-à-vis other naval officers as for any other purpose. That it might have been for external status reasons is rather confirmed by the fact that he did not consistently use green ink for his diary until January 1916. Whatever the rationale, his successors as Chief continue the practice to the present day.

Cumming habitually worked long hours. In August 1910 the Director of Military Operations, George Macdonogh (himself a notoriously hard worker), told him he was 'going on leave next week for a week or two. I said I did not see my way to get away at all, and he remarked that the work must be rather a tie. I wonder', confided Cumming to his diary, 'if any of them suspect how many hours a day I have to work? I reckon it 9.30 am to 11.30 pm, with 2 hours off, say 12 hours, but I get a very short Saturday afternoon and no Sunday. It is bound to continue for a year or two, but after that should settle down.' This was an optimistic prediction indeed, though in 1910 Cumming could hardly have anticipated the unrelenting responsibilities he would have to carry during the First World War. Sampling his diary entries for holiday periods gives a flavour of the extent to which he could not (or, of course, *would* not) let go of his duties. He worked all day in London on Good Friday 1915, travelled to France on the following day, and over the Easter weekend had meetings in Amiens and Paris. He 'worked late' on Christmas Eve 1916 (a Sunday), and on 25 December noted in his diary 'all day in office'. 'Rather quiet,' he added, 'not many staff about,' though 'Colonel Kell called & had a long yarn with me.' On August Bank Holiday 1917 (6 August) he was again in France, at a conference with Sir Douglas Haig's intelligence chief, General Charteris, following which he went on a tour along the British front line.

Cumming's achievements during the First World War are all the more remarkable considering the physical and personal loss from his devastating car accident of October 1914. He was by no means the only person to suffer thus during the war. The Prime Minister himself, Herbert Asquith, lost his eldest son Raymond in the Battle of the Somme in 1916. In a curious parallel to Cumming, George Macdonogh, while head of Army Intelligence at the British headquarters in France, was briefly incapacitated by a broken collarbone sustained in a car accident in September 1914, and during the following June lost to illness his seven-year-old only son, 'in whom all his hopes were centred', a blow which, Macdonogh's intelligence colleague Walter Kirke observed, 'he bore with admirable stoicism characteristic of the man'.[2] Stoicism, the default British reaction to such dreadful circumstances, was Cumming's response, too, as encapsulated by the terse entry, 'Poor old Ally died,' in his diary the day after the accident. It is difficult to estimate what the emotional impact of blows like this might have been, especially (as in Cumming's case) when combined with the draining physical toll of losing part of a limb, but the fact that, aged fifty-five, he was back to work at his office in London within about six weeks testifies to very considerable powers of resilience and fortitude.

It was clear from the start that Cumming was his own man, as demonstrated by his insistence in 1909 on continuing with the Southampton boom-defence work alongside running the new Secret Service Bureau. While Admiral Bethell wanted him to assume the Bureau responsibilities on a full-time basis, Cumming, although evidently attracted by the new commission and ultimately prepared to accede to Bethell's requirements, held out until he got permission to carry on in Southampton. This represented quite a commitment, as the records of the Boom Defence Experiments Committee confirm, and Cumming remained involved with the work from 1909 at least until the spring of 1914.[3] Although he was a naval officer and his appointment had originally come from the Director of Naval Intelligence (DNI), Cumming strikingly demonstrated his continuing independent-mindedness in May 1913 when he publicly disagreed with Bethell's successor as DNI, Captain Jackson, over the appointment of Captain Roy Regnart to be his 'branch agent' in Brussels. During the First World War, he was able to balance his obligations to the Admiralty and War Office, and ensure the support of the Foreign Office, sufficiently deftly to maintain his own (and his Bureau's) independence.

His wartime colleague Frank Stagg recalled long afterwards that '"C" always used to boast that, as he had three masters, he had not got one at all as he could always set the other two against any objector.' But this was not just a matter of playing one master off against another for short-term administrative convenience. Cumming had a clear strategic vision for his

Secret Service Bureau, and his determination to secure the organisation permanently on an interdepartmental and autonomous basis was embodied in the vitally important 'charter' he secured from Sir Arthur Nicolson on 17 November 1915, establishing that Cumming, as the 'Chief of the Secret Service', would have 'sole control', not only of 'all espionage and counter-espionage agents abroad' but also, crucially (subject to Foreign Office supervision), of 'all matters connected with the expenditure of Secret Service funds'. So important and fundamental was this document that, when the situation of SIS was being discussed in 1940, Stewart Menzies carefully copied it to the Permanent Secretary at the Treasury, Sir Horace Wilson.[4]

While the sailor Cumming's fending-off of military attentions during the First World War is understandable enough, his handling of the strong-willed, interventionist and unbiddable wartime DNI, Blinker Hall, is surely more remarkable. Despite his naval background, once he had taken on the secret service work Cumming clearly conceived his Bureau to be an interdepartmental organisation, which, while substantially (and at times primarily) serving naval and military needs, also had a distinctly civilian, 'political' role to play. Cumming clearly resented Hall's evident belief that he and his outfit were more or less an integral part of the Naval Intelligence empire, simply being at the DNI's beck and call (as illustrated, for example, with deployments in Spain). So difficult at one stage did relations between Hall and Cumming become that in September 1917 George Macdonogh (by then Director of Military Intelligence) 'hinted definitely [to Cumming] that if sacked by Navy he would take me on with pleasure'. But Cumming's continual desire, as he noted in January 1915 at a time of inter-service tension over intelligence arrangements for Russia, was to 'avoid friction between Army & Navy', and, despite occasional rows with both military and naval authorities, he generally succeeded in this aim.

A large part of Cumming's success stemmed from his cheerful and equable personality. Whatever professional disagreements he may have had with fellow officers, he always seems to have been able to maintain good relationships on a personal level, regularly socialising, for example, with both Macdonogh and Kirke, despite their repeated attempts to get the army to take control of his organisation. Cumming was very warmly regarded within the Bureau itself, as memoir recollections of him consistently testify. 'We all loved him to a man,' wrote Edward Knoblock, a playwright who had worked under Compton Mackenzie in Greece and later served at Head Office in London. 'He did us all most endless kindnesses, as not only the men but the girls who worked for him will remember to this day.'[5] The writer Valentine Williams identified Cumming's 'salient characteristic' as 'gentleness', and recalled 'he had nerves of steel . . . his phlegm was unshatterable. In the darkest moments, it was a tonic to his staff to see him at his desk, calm, affable, humorous, unafraid.'[6] At first encounter, Sir Paul Dukes reported that Cumming 'appeared very severe'; his speech was abrupt, and 'woe betide the unfortunate individual who ever incurred his ire!'. But 'the stern countenance could melt into the kindliest of smiles, and the softened eyes and lips revealed a heart that was big and generous'.[7] Cumming's boyish enthusiasm for gadgets and the latest technical inventions struck many a chord, and one (male) colleague indulgently noted his 'naughty side': a penchant for Edwardian pornography. 'With great mystery he would invite one to his office and take out of a secret drawer in his desk an illustrated portfolio of *Le Nu au Salon*' containing various 'tempting' reproductions. It was considered 'a great privilege to be shown these pictures while the old man enlarged on the beauty of the "female form divine"'.[8]

The love – it does not seem too strong a word in the circumstances – and affection which his staff felt for Cumming surely enhanced his reputation in the wider Whitehall world. Since he ran a happy – and tight – ship, his Foreign Office masters could be confident that he was a reliable and competent holder of a nationally important job which, if badly handled, could have disastrous consequences. Had the Foreign Office mandarins Nicolson, Hardinge and Crowe *not* been convinced that Cumming was a safe pair of hands, they would not, in their turn, have willingly backed him up when the independent survival of the nascent SIS was at stake. This was as true in the immediate postwar years as it had been during the war, when Cumming's preparedness to step down if his work was found to be unsatisfactory reflected the strength of his situation, as well as a winning (if perhaps slightly disingenuous) modesty about his own indispensability. But the evident confidence that he had been doing a good job was confirmed by Hardinge in February 1919 when he assured Lord Curzon not only that it was essential 'that the control of secret service operations in foreign countries should be in the hands of the Foreign

Office', but that the government had also had 'been extremely fortunate in securing the services of the present Chief'. The conferring of a knighthood on Cumming in July 1919 – a KCMG, in the prestigious Order of St Michael and St George, normally reserved for ambassadors, colonial governors and the like – was a very clear public recognition of the high esteem in which he was held.

A further important factor working to Cumming's benefit was the restricted view he took of what the Secret Service Bureau should actually do. There is no suggestion in the surviving documentation that he ever saw the function of his organisation as being more than the collection and distribution of information, as requested by other government departments. At no stage did he seek to offer policy advice, or even very much to analyse or manipulate the information gathered by his officers and agents. For him, the Bureau was simply an expert organisation, designed to respond as best it could to the requirements of customer departments. And, unlike some others in the intelligence world – Colonel French during the war, Basil Thomson immediately after, and even Cumming's successor, Hugh Sinclair, in the interwar years – he never showed any tendency towards empire-building.[9] When the Bureau grew, it did so organically and in response to customer demand. Cumming's institutional ambition was not in the slightest acquisitive (which could have made him enemies), but consistently protective, vigorously defending his organisation from the threatened depredations of other departments. His obsession, moreover, with secrecy (the 'first, last and most necessary essential') had a beneficial and self-effacing effect. By consistently maintaining as low a profile as possible, neither he nor his organisation appeared to threaten anyone else.

A final, and extremely significant, feature of Cumming's time as Chief is the shrewd political judgment he demonstrated in the face of the 1919 War Office proposal to amalgamate his department and MI5, at a time when ministers and officials alike were gripped by fears that Red Revolution might engulf the United Kingdom. Everything in Cumming's class and career background would have disposed him towards diehard right-wing political attitudes, militantly opposed to the threat of the Labour movement and socialism (let alone that of Communism). But what is remarkable about Cumming, in contrast to other toilers in the intelligence vineyard, such as Hall (a Conservative MP from 1918 to

1923), Thomson and Sinclair (certainly when he was Director of Naval Intelligence), who were prepared at times to let their right-wing political views supersede the obligations of constitutional government, is that, whatever his private political opinions, he carefully and wisely distanced himself and his organisation from domestic British politics. He saw clearly, as his successor Stewart Menzies was also to do twenty-five years later, the absolute necessity of keeping domestic and foreign intelligence work separate. Anticipating the possibility of a Labour government, and managing to do so in an admirably unhysterical way, Cumming asserted that combining his organisation with MI5 and getting involved in secret service against domestic political targets could jeopardise the effectiveness of foreign intelligence work by prompting public and parliamentary attacks on the intelligence machine as a whole. As with his passion for motor cars, speedboats and aeroplanes, Cumming, a nineteenth-century Victorian with a lively twentieth-century interest in technological advances, may have been more prepared to accept political change than many of his contemporaries. Or he may simply have appreciated that the active espousal of anti-left-wing politics could damage the work of his beloved Bureau. Whatever the reason, his decision to distance the Bureau from domestic security and intelligence work was absolutely sound.

Mansfield Cumming's achievement over the first fourteen years of the Secret Intelligence Service was not the creation of a perfect British foreign intelligence organisation. The Secret Service Bureau created in October 1909 was established to meet a specific short-term challenge to Britain from imperial Germany. It was a classic, pragmatic British fix, decided in rather a hurry and certainly without much, if any, thought about the longer-term future. The appointment of the linguist Vernon Kell to run the domestic side, while the monoglot Cumming was given the responsibility for foreign intelligence, which could have been disastrous, merely reflected the immediate preoccupations of their respective service departments. While the War Office was particularly worried about the vulnerability of home defence, the Admiralty, as always, had its eyes on a wider horizon. At the start Cumming and Kell were simply told to get on with the work, taking on the motley collection of existing covert sources the service ministries had haphazardly employed up to that point. Neither man was given much of a brief, nor were they asked to prepare any sort of business plan, or even to consider how Britain's security and intelligence requirements could best be arranged. If they had, the subsequent history of SIS and MI5 might have been very different. The 1925 Secret Service Committee (agreeing with Sinclair) had 'no hesitation' in stating that if they had been called upon to organise one from scratch, they would not have adopted 'the existing system as our model', but would have endeavoured 'to create a single department'. The 'heterogeneous interests, liaisons, traditions and responsibilities of the different services, however, had resulted in a system which, while it was not believed to be ideal, worked sufficiently well not to be replaced'. Successive proposals to create 'a single department' repeatedly came up against the objection that it might not bring any improvement, and (as observed in 1925) might well be 'an actual failure'. Here, again, the pragmatic British approach was to the fore, with root-and-branch reform based on some theoretical ideal being rejected in favour of an adequately working, if admittedly imperfect, system.

But there was more to it than that. In the first place, a residual bias against centralised and unified British security and intelligence arrangements also appears to have reinforced decisions not to move in that direction. This was certainly the case regarding Basil Thomson's ambitions to create a powerful domestic security agency in 1919–21. Second, considerations of the personalities involved, and the individuals who might head any consolidated organisation – certainly Thomson, but also Sinclair in the mid-1920s – also had a bearing on the decision-making process. Ministers and officials shied away from concentrating power in the hands of ostensibly ambitious men. Third, however desirable amalgamation might be from a bureaucratic point of view – it being seen as no more than a kind of administrative tidying up – there were strong arguments against it from the intelligence-processing perspective. Not only (as Cumming appreciated) could the conflation of domestic and foreign work bring political risks, but the concentration of all the British government's intelligence eggs into one super-agency basket through which all information would be supplied could undermine the extent to which customer departments were able to analyse and evaluate the material, rudimentary though that process was before the Joint Intelligence Committee system became established from the late 1930s. As the Director of Military Intelligence shrewdly put it in 1925, the existence of different organisations had 'the advantage of the check which [they] . . . automatically provided on each other's results'.

From the early months of the First World War until almost the end of his time as Chief, Cumming was repeatedly faced by powerful departmental interests (especially, though by no means solely, the War Office) trying to take control of his Bureau, or at the very least chip away at its operations. It is a testament to his success that, unlike Kell's MI5 or Thomson's Directorate of Intelligence, MI1(c)/SIS was never threatened with outright abolition, but, on the other hand, it was subject only to a series of take over bids. In these circumstances, Cumming's extraordinary feat was to create, nurture and protect a covert foreign intelligence-gathering organisation, with an established autonomous existence under the supportive stewardship of the Foreign Office, of sufficient status and reputation that by the early 1920s no one could imagine the British government doing without it.

Hugh Sinclair and the interwar years

When Mansfield Cumming died suddenly in June 1923, Hugh Sinclair had already been designated as his successor. While it had generally been assumed that another naval officer was the most appropriate person for the position, the appointment of the higher-ranking Sinclair also confirmed the degree to which the status of the Service had risen since its inception in 1909. Although Sinclair had plans for changes – in November 1923 he told Sir Eyre Crowe of the Foreign Office that he wanted 'to undertake a certain re-organisation' to make the Service 'more efficient' and 'provide a basis for a war organisation' – he in fact did little to change the Head Office structure which Cumming had introduced in 1919, with a Production side, responsible for the overseas deployment of the Service, and a Circulation (later Requirements) side, providing the link with the customer departments. As much for reasons of economy as anything else, in 1923–4 there was some contraction in the number of sections on each side, but the fundamental shape of the organisation was retained. For similar practical reasons, and as the overall size of the Service contracted, Cumming's Regional Inspector system, with deputies allocated to coordinate work overseas, also withered away. While the prevailing shortage of money through most of the 1920s and 1930s severely circumscribed the activities of the Service, Sinclair certainly wanted to expand his overseas operations, as confirmed by his sending of Valentine Vivian in 1927 to investigate intelligence possibilities in the Middle East and the resulting extensive (though still-born) scheme which Vivian drew up.

At home, Sinclair, with Foreign Office backing, evidently nursed ambitions to lead a unified British security and intelligence organisation. In 1925 Nevile Bland thought 'that unified direction was the ideal towards which we ought to work' and in 1927 Sir William Tyrrell, the Permanent Under-Secretary, told Sinclair that he 'never missed an opportunity' of pressing the case for a single organisation. Sinclair himself told the Secret Service Committee in 1927 that SIS, MI5 and Special Branch should be amalgamated. But, whatever theoretical case there may have been for a single agency, the fact that Sinclair himself was by far the most eligible candidate to head it seems to have had the potential to alarm and antagonise colleagues in other parts of the security and intelligence community. In this respect the views of Sir John Burnett-Stuart, the Director of Military Operations and Intelligence, as expressed to the Secret Service Committee in 1925 are extremely revealing. Burnett-Stuart expansively declared that SIS had 'improved enormously' under Sinclair. Since there is no corroborative evidence for this assertion, it is unclear in what particular ways matters had 'improved', though the evidence from 1923 when Sinclair's assumption of control over the Government Code and Cypher School was approved by the armed service Directors of Intelligence suggests that, as a former Director of Intelligence himself, he was thought to be sympathetic to the armed forces' specific intelligence needs. Nevertheless, despite his praise for Sinclair, Burnett-Stuart was quite opposed to any amalgamation as he 'would hesitate to put too much power into the hands of so energetic and capable an officer as "C"'.

Sinclair was pre-eminently a team captain within SIS, not in the wider Whitehall universe, and when he sought to expand his own and his agency's reach, he found that the very qualities which made him such a good commanding officer tended to work against him. His strengths as a leader – charisma, decision and dynamism – which engendered a fierce loyalty on the part of subordinates, together with his inclination to press ahead with ventures without perhaps fully anticipating all the possible consequences, at times led him and SIS into crossing existing Whitehall boundaries and trespassing into the territory of other departments. Spotting and seizing an opportunity to work against Communist

subversion in Great Britain (which also suited Sinclair's evident political predilections) had characteristics of a fine battlefield commander,
admirable perhaps in wartime when swift and decisive action could be
more important than any theoretical bureaucratic constraints, but risky
indeed in peacetime when the potential political costs of such action
needed to be taken carefully into account. And doing so without consulting or informing other interested parties was no way to win friends, as
is amply illustrated by the irritation of Sir Wyndham Childs, Assistant
Commissioner at Scotland Yard, in 1924 at the time of the Zinoviev
Letter affair on discovering that SIS had been running a domestic agent.
Where political matters were concerned, indeed, Sinclair was markedly
less fastidious than Cumming, and, as illustrated in his relations with
Sir John Anderson, Permanent Under-Secretary at the Home Office, not
at all so concerned about the distinction between domestic and foreign
intelligence-gathering.

In Anderson Sinclair came up against a seasoned Whitehall operator who was so well placed and bureaucratically adept (as well as being
evidently unsympathetic to Sinclair's empire-building tendencies) that
he was never going to outflank him. In the departmental representation on successive Secret Service Committees, the three constant figures
were Anderson (Home Office), Fisher (Treasury) and Hankey (Cabinet
Office), as well as successive Foreign Office Permanent Under-Secretaries.
While Sir Warren Fisher tended to back Sinclair and the Foreign Office
view, Sir Maurice Hankey tended to side with Anderson, especially when
the issue of interdepartmental responsibility for security and intelligence
came up. Hankey's insistence in 1925 that an undivided line of account-
ability to a specific government department, such as the Foreign Office or
the Home Office, was more important than any sort of joint arrangement
for a unified intelligence organisation may well have been coloured by
memories of the unsatisfactory division of control between War Office,
Admiralty and Foreign Office which had bedevilled Cumming's Bureau
in the First World War. Whatever his thinking, neither he nor Anderson,
although content to leave SIS under Foreign Office supervision, was prepared to support an amalgamated intelligence organisation with Sinclair
at its head.

During the deliberations of the 1925 Secret Service Committee
Anderson had questioned Sinclair about SIS's activities within the United

Kingdom and quite clearly expressed his concern over the issue. Perhaps Sinclair's political antennae were insufficiently sensitive to pick up the message, or perhaps he simply chose to ignore the implicit warning in Anderson's attitude. Either way, he made a serious mistake. The 1931 dispute with Special Branch over the running of agents in the United Kingdom was a case in point. While the Secret Service Committee essentially took Sinclair's side and primarily put the matter down to a personality clash, describing the policeman Colonel Carter as 'temperamentally incapable of taking a broad view or of seeing that all three organisations [SIS, MI5 and Special Branch] were really working for the same cause',[10] it is clear that both Carter and Special Branch had a case. Apart from Carter's alleged left-leaning politics (as identified by the politically right-wing Maxwell Knight and which may simply have reflected the policeman's anxiety to be politically even-handed), and beyond Sinclair's claims of the practical necessity of SIS operating within the United Kingdom, SIS had no formal brief to run agents at home. Carter, moreover, was not alone in resenting and opposing SIS's expanding domestic work, as he was backed up by the Metropolitan Police Assistant Commissioner Trevor Bigham. The continuation of domestic work, and the expansion of the Casuals, led directly to the embarrassing (for Sinclair) meeting in January 1931 when he was carpeted by Anderson, and following which, far from any unified organisation being created, SIS's remit was restricted, it was stripped of the Casuals, and MI5, as the Security Service, was given expanded responsibilities for domestic British counter-intelligence. One consequence, indeed, of Sinclair's persevering with SIS domestic operations was finally to torpedo any chance of the unified intelligence organisation he had so desired.

Of the first three Chiefs of SIS, Sinclair demonstrated the greatest tendency to cross the fine line between legitimate intelligence work, providing the government with clandestinely acquired information, as well as a political and military early-warning system, and becoming politically engaged in the policy-making process. During the Zinoviev Letter affair both Sinclair and his dynamic subordinate Desmond Morton (whom Sinclair loyally supported) asserted the genuineness of the letter rather more categorically than the evidence allowed. In part this was to protect the reputation of the Service, but it also reinforced a clearly anti-Labour political agenda. At the time of the Munich Crisis, Sinclair (in this instance supporting Malcolm Woollcombe) willingly supplied advice which broadly backed up the appeasement policy pursued by the Chamberlain government, and there are other indications in 1938–9 that politicians increasingly turned to him for policy advice. This may reflect the sheer intractability of the problems facing the government, underlying a tendency to seek advice from whatever quarter, as much as an increasing willingness on Sinclair's part to step into a greater advisory role than hitherto.

Sinclair had a reputation as a terrific bon vivant. Two scrapbooks of memorabilia preserved in the National Maritime Museum record a heroic number of fine dinners and other social events which he attended between the wars. He hosted a dinner at the Savoy Hotel in August 1928 for colleagues, including Menzies, Woollcombe, Russell and Maw of SIS and Denniston, Fetterlein and Hooper of GC&CS. Another dinner at the Savoy, on 18 August 1938, may throw light on those whom Sinclair regarded as his closest allies and associates. Sir Robert Vansittart and Nevile Bland of the Foreign Office attended, as did Sir Herbert Creedy (Permanent Under-Secretary at the War Office) and General John Dill (a former Director of Military Operations and Intelligence, and a future Chief of the Imperial General Staff). Sir Vernon Kell, Blinker Hall and Stewart Menzies (the only other SIS officer) were there, while Sir Warren Fisher and Sir Maurice Hankey had been invited, but were unable to attend. The six-course meal was accompanied by a selection of marvellous wines, including Château Haut Brion 1924, Fonseca Port 1912 and Grand Champagne Cognac from 1865. No wonder Admiral Sir Percy Noble (recently Fourth Sea Lord, and about to take over as Commander-in-Chief, China Station) wrote afterwards to thank Sinclair for 'the best dinner I have eaten for years'.[11]

Although Warren Fisher (Permanent Secretary to the Treasury and Head of the Civil Service, 1919–39) seems to have been a close confidant – his biographer says that he and Sinclair saw a lot of each other in the 1930s[12] – even he could do little to improve the parlous financial position of the Service between the wars. Sinclair's *cri de coeur* about finance in October 1935, when he complained that SIS had been 'constantly hampered' by lack of funds since 1919, had some effect, but the question remains, during his dozen years as Chief up to then, whether he might himself have done more to secure the Service's finances on a better basis. The

conflation of Service work within the Passport Control organisation, settled under Cumming just after the end of the war, certainly provided the
Service with both cover and a regular source of income. But the arrangement also had considerable disadvantages. The maintenance of a Passport
Control Office in any particular country depended on the prevailing visa
requirements between that country and the United Kingdom, a matter
over which SIS had little control. In 1928 a proposal to abolish the use of
visas for Finland highlighted this problem, and although it was decided
to retain their use in this case, Sinclair was moved to review the existing system. He noted that the 'essential demands' of a secret intelligence
service abroad had 'to some extent' been met by the Passport Control system, which provided more or less secure cover for representatives abroad
as well as a safe, rapid and regular means of communication with Head
Office. Asserting that business and journalistic cover was unworkable,
Sinclair argued that, without Passport Control Offices, some other cover
would have to be provided, such as placing at SIS's disposal a diplomatic
or consular post at the necessary places. Other countries' secret services,
he said, used not only armed forces attachés, but also members of their
Diplomatic Corps. There was, furthermore, a financial cost and, if the
Passport Control system were abolished, an additional £30,000 would
have to be found to cover the salaries of SIS representatives. This was a
major stumbling block, and the Foreign Office, moreover, were extremely
reluctant to offer diplomatic cover, so the system remained unchanged.

After 1928, Sinclair appears to have made no further efforts to raise
the question of the Passport Control system and SIS's relationship with
it. Even though the PCO cover became increasingly thin, he seems not
to have been too bothered by this, as indicated by his apparently untroubled admission in 1934 that 'the activities of our Passport Control
Officers all over the world are perfectly well known'. A more fundamental
problem arising from the system was its inflexibility, since to a very considerable extent SIS's overseas representation was tied to countries with
which Britain had visa agreements. If – or rather when – SIS's priorities
changed, it could prove difficult to transfer resources to other locations.
Sudden demands for increased intelligence from the Mediterranean in
the mid-1930s provoked by Mussolini's expansionist foreign policy, for
example, produced a situation where operations in Malta were expanded
and restricted turn and turn about, as funding was made available or

withdrawn. Apparently for the most part content to work within the PCO system, Sinclair seems to have begun to think strategically about overseas operations only when he set up the Z Organisation in 1936, which, as it turned out, was too late and too hastily assembled to be of much long-term use.

During the 1920s and into the 1930s there was a manifest national, and SIS, over-emphasis on the revolutionary threat from the Bolsheviks. The challenge was real, but not as dangerous to the stability of the United Kingdom as it was perceived to be, though potentially more dangerous to some parts of the empire which had begun to entertain thoughts of independence. Despite White Russian fabrications and operational difficulties, SIS's coverage of the revolutionary activities of the Comintern was reasonably good, that of other aspects of Soviet policy much less so. From the later 1920s, however, the Service began to learn from its experience of covering these targets and much improved its ability to analyse and assess the intelligence it gathered. During the 1930s attention was directed far too late to the coinciding threats posed by German rearmament and the rise of the Nazis. There were national political and psychological inhibitions external to SIS which in part account for this, as there was little or no relevant tasking from the main customer departments. Clearly reflecting his naval background, Sinclair's own perceptions of the chief threats to British interests – Italy in the Mediterranean and Japan in the East – reflected the prevailing concerns of the Admiralty for most of the interwar period. It took the Admiralty a lot longer than the Air Ministry, for example, to see Germany as a significant (let alone the most important) potential enemy. In this respect Sinclair and SIS were simply reflecting the priorities of (at least) one of their main customer departments. SIS's supply of information about political developments within Europe was also hampered by the low status and mistrust accorded to the Service by British diplomats. Combined with the embargo on operating against host countries these were disincentives to SIS coverage of local political developments, except where (as with Bolshevism) common cause could be made with local liaison services. The one liaison partner in the 1930s, France, where significant common cause was established against Germany certainly produced some intelligence benefits but it also led to an over-reliance on French reporting.

For SIS the years between the wars were ones of gradual professional development, from the rather successful MI1(c) military, mainly tactical and *de visu* intelligence service of the First World War into a Service which was still learning how to set about covering the needs of its political and economic customers, as well as those of the armed services. Desmond Morton's efforts to improve the grading of reports, the creation of Sections V and VI, and the flurry of developments in the late 1930s, especially those concerning GC&CS and on the technical side under Gambier-Parry, were very positive features. While a fair proportion of officers possessed useful qualities, such as a knowledge of languages, of foreign countries and of human beings, a degree of dedication and courage, and, with luck, a measure of native ingenuity, the Service was held back, both culturally and financially, by inefficient and damaging habits of poor recruitment and remuneration, and the almost total absence of systematic training in operational skills. Many of its officers were thus inevitably 'second-raters', a problem that continued into the Second World War, as Frank Foley observed from Turkey in March 1942. The management gap between the relatively tiny Head Office and the field was deep, spanned only by a few outstanding individuals. Leadership from the top was remarkably good, though overburdened with detail and the need to improve the Service's relations with its masters and customers. Delegation was poor. It took the violent stimulus of the Second World War, with the enormous expansion of the Service which accompanied it, finally to set it on the road to true professionalism.

Stewart Menzies and SIS during the Second World War and after

Any assessment of the wartime performance of the Service must take into account Menzies's role as Chief for all but the first two months of the conflict. In an environment (especially once Churchill became Prime Minister) where officials perceived to be inadequate were regularly replaced, Menzies was a great survivor. From November 1939 to the end of the war SIS had only one Chief, while its sister services MI5 and SOE both had three. Writing in the late 1960s, the distinguished historian Hugh Trevor-Roper, a wartime member of the Service, though admiring Menzies personally, described him as 'a bad judge of men' who 'drew his personal advisers from a painfully limited social circle' and never 'really understood the war in which he was engaged'.[13] Bill Cavendish-Bentinck, wartime chairman of the Joint Intelligence Sub-Committee, told his biographer in the 1980s that Menzies became Chief merely because he was next in line, that 'he would not have held the job for more than a year if it had not been for Bletchley', and that 'he was not a very strong man and not a very intelligent one'.[14] The career SIS officer John Bruce Lockhart asserted that Menzies 'didn't know much about spying but had a good instinct for Whitehall politics'. Nevertheless, he was a canny bureaucratic operator and impressed those who mattered. Edward Beddington, who served as Deputy Director/Army in SIS from March 1942 until mid-1944 (and was himself no fool), worried about giving his entire allegiance to Menzies, and agreed to do so only on condition that he retained a right of direct access to the Chief of the Imperial General Staff, Sir Alan Brooke. In his private memoirs (written in the late 1950s), Beddington recorded that he had known Menzies 'as a young officer in World War I and did not trust him very far. He would, I thought, if he could do so at times pull wool over my eyes,' but 'would be much less inclined to do so if he knew that I had the right of access to the C.I.G.S., which would also confirm to him that I had two Masters'.[15]

Menzies also forged a close relationship with Sir Alexander Cadogan, the Permanent Under-Secretary at the Foreign Office, who, although occasionally exasperated by his loquacity at their regular chats, was a powerful ally. This was demonstrated by sustained support throughout the war for SIS's continued institutional autonomy (if under broad Foreign Office control); the categorical assumption from at least 1942 that SOE would only be a temporary, wartime organisation; and the securing of the long-term postwar existence of SIS that was embedded in the conclusions of the Bland Report. There is evidence of Menzies's personal strengths in the memoirs of close colleagues. Forty years after having been posted to SIS in May 1942 to improve liaison with the Foreign Office, Patrick Reilly recalled that he 'very quickly became devoted to Menzies . . . No-one', he claimed, 'could work closely without feeling for him real respect and great affection.' With experience as Menzies's personal assistant for fourteen months, Reilly acknowledged that he 'had no gift or liking for organisation and administration' and observed that he was 'never able to impose himself' upon his mutually antagonistic chief assistants Dansey and Vivian. Yet he judged that Menzies had 'considerable flair' for intelligence work and, above all, 'was a fundamentally honest man in a position of great potential power where a dishonest one might have been disastrous'.[16]

It was not unusual in wartime Britain for men and women to work with little respite, but Menzies, like Cumming, seems to have been unusually committed to his job. His appointment diaries (which survive for all the war years except 1941) reveal no breaks longer than the occasional long weekend over the whole war. In August 1941 he made a special application for 'Privacy Telephone Equipment' – a scrambler phone – to be installed at his home. 'Without being able to talk freely to my office from my home,' he explained, 'I am virtually prevented from taking more than twenty-four hours leave, and now that the war has lasted nearly two years, I do feel occasionally the need for a little longer relaxation.' Robert Cecil, Menzies's personal assistant in 1943–5, asserted that he 'rarely left his desk during the war'. Partly this was to be available if a summons came from Churchill, which could happen at any time of the day or night. Cadogan noted an occasion in November 1942 when Churchill, 'overexcited', sent for Menzies at 11.00 p.m., then said Menzies looked tired and had better go to bed. Menzies 'admitted that he was, and would', but at 2.15 a.m. Churchill 'rang him up to ask a quite unnecessary question – and then apologised!'.[17] The unremitting wartime workload was shared throughout the Service. Patrick Reilly noted that Menzies's private office was 'staffed by two splendid women, Miss Pettigrew and Miss Jones, loyal discreet, working impossible hours'. The former was 'large and formidable', the latter 'smaller, better looking, elegant and gentle . . . Though they worked for several years in the same room they always called each other Miss Pettigrew and Miss Jones.'[18]

Menzies scarcely left London during the war and it does not seem at all likely (despite Cecil's explicit assertion and a story told by Frederick Winterbotham, both long after the war) that Menzies 'paid a short visit to the liberated Algiers' late in 1942. Winterbotham's story has plausible circumstantial detail. He says that, when Menzies heard that his 'old opposite number' Georges Ronin had escaped from occupied France, he flew out to Algiers to meet him. 'Colonel Rivet and Georges Ronin', continued Winterbotham, 'gave Stewart Menzies and me a splendid lunch on the sun-drenched roof of a little house in Algiers. With the coffee came the news that [Admiral] Darlan had been shot in his house a few hundred yards away.' Darlan was killed on Christmas Eve, but although there are no entries for 24 or 25 December, Menzies's diary shows appointments in London for dinner on 23 December and an engagement in the Cabinet War Room at 10.15 on the morning of 26 December. Rivet makes no mention of any Christmas Eve engagement with Menzies (or anyone else) in his diary, though he does mention lunch with Winterbotham 'and other English officers' on 12 December.[19] As to Ronin's presence in Algiers, Paul Paillole stated in his memoirs that he and Ronin arrived in England on 19 December 1942, and were met at Broadway by Menzies, and also that the two men met André Dewavrin in London on 27 December. An SIS telegram confirms that Ronin was in London on 27 December and was scheduled to fly to Gibraltar two days later. There is no indication in the Algiers station signals of any visit by the Chief and, finally, a surviving SIS staff member who was in Algiers in 1942–3 (albeit interviewed long afterwards) had no recollection whatsoever of any visit by Menzies. From the available evidence, the only foreign trips that Menzies made during the war were to Naples and Paris in October and Brussels in December 1944.[20]

The fact that SIS survived the Second World War at all has been ascribed primarily to the supremely and perhaps incalculably valuable work of the Government Code and Cypher School (GC&CS): the breaking of the codes and the precious Ultra signals intelligence which hugely informed Allied policy and operations during the war. Since GC&CS came under SIS's management, and its product was distributed through SIS channels (and, in the case of the Prime Minister, frequently by Menzies in person), the argument is that SIS, not itself a very competent or successful intelligence agency, rode on the back of Bletchley Park's achievements to a position by the end of the war of complacent and virtually invulnerable superiority.[21] This happy situation, it is argued, meant that SIS remained nominally in charge of Government Communications Headquarters (as GC&CS became known in 1946) for another decade; that it was able to ensure the abolition of its apparent rival SOE; and that, with the backing of the Foreign Office, it was able to fend off proposals for a unified British secret service and any attempts by the armed service departments to take it over. All these things came to pass, but it would be naive to assume that the emergence and survival of SIS after the end of the war can be ascribed solely to the golden goose of Bletchley Park. For

Menzies, it was not simply a case of carrying the sigint golden eggs to the Prime Minister. The goose had to be cared for as well, and it is clear that without the combination (eventually) of a light-touch superintendence over the internal organisation of GC&CS with a readiness to represent its interests vis-à-vis other government departments and to provide essential administrative and technical support (the latter from Gambier-Parry's inestimable Section VIII), the signals intelligence organisation could not have functioned as marvellously as in the end it did.

This is not to say that the relationship between SIS and its signals intelligence stepchild was wholly untroubled during the war, but, whatever the difficulties and frustrations the code-breakers and their colleagues may have experienced with Broadway's management, it is clear that from a very early stage Menzies (as Sinclair had been before him) was very well aware of the importance of GC&CS, devoting resources to it (not least Bletchley Park itself) and allowing it to expand with exponential rapidity over the first eighteen months of the war. (It might be remarked, moreover, that the unsystematic, chaotic style of recruitment, based on personal contacts and school and university networks which served GC&CS so well, was precisely the kind of thing which has been criticised in the case of SIS.) Menzies fought off two attempts from the armed services to wrest control of GC&CS from SIS, in the spring of 1941 and the winter of 1941–2. Both were principally instigated from the Directorate of Military Intelligence but Menzies successfully argued that the interservice nature of GC&CS's work (analogous to that of SIS itself) made the direct involvement of any individual armed service impracticable.[22]

While Menzies was nominally Director of GC&CS, Alastair Denniston, an Olympic field hockey player who had worked in the Admiralty's codebreaking Room 40 during the First World War, had been its operational head since the School's establishment in 1919. By the beginning of the war its administration was carried out by officers in Broadway with advice from a Joint Committee of Control composed of representatives from SIS and GC&CS. But this cumbersome system broke down under the enormous pressures of wartime demands and sudden growth. In October 1941, some weeks after Menzies had shown Churchill around Bletchley Park, four cryptanalysts wrote directly to the Prime Minister telling him of serious delays in their work due to staff shortages. 'As we are a very small section with numerically trivial requirements,' they wrote, 'it is very difficult to bring home to the authorities finally responsible either the importance of what is done here or the urgent necessity of dealing promptly with our requests.' The need was mostly for additional female clerical personnel, though they reported that 'some of the skilled male staff' who had so far 'been exempt from military service' were 'now liable to be called up'. The cryptanalysts claimed that they did 'not know who or what' was responsible for their 'difficulties', but they specifically exempted Commander Edward Travis (Denniston's deputy), who had 'all along done his utmost to help us in every possible way'. Churchill responded immediately with instructions marked 'action this day' that the cryptanalysts were to 'have all they want on extreme priority', and on 18 November Menzies reported that every possible measure was being taken.[23]

In December 1941, responding to a renewed attempt by the War Office to assert control over GC&CS, the Chiefs of Staff asked the 'Y' Committee (which comprised Menzies and the three service Directors of Intelligence) to look into the administration of signals intelligence. The following February Menzies implemented a series of reforms which finally 'inaugurated a period of continued improvement'. Diplomatic and commercial cryptanalysis was taken away from Bletchley Park and relocated in London under Commander Denniston, as Deputy Director (C), while the much more extensive armed forces work remained in place under Travis who, as Deputy Director (S), was given sole responsibility for all the work at Bletchley Park, subject only to control by Menzies and the Y Board on which Travis himself sat as GC&CS's representative. In February 1944 Travis was formally appointed Director of GC&CS (including responsibility for diplomatic and commercial work), with Menzies as Director-General.[24] From early in the war Menzies had been under sustained pressure to sort out the administration (and thus enhance the productivity) of all the work under his control. While he may not have responded as quickly as some critics desired (especially those in the armed services Directorates of Intelligence), when he did act he did so both decisively and, on the whole, effectively. Menzies's demotion of Denniston and replacement by Travis reflected an unsentimentality when it came to making tough decisions about the competence of longstanding colleagues, and was of a piece with his treatment of Valentine Vivian, when he was demoted from DCSS to be just a Deputy Director in March 1943, and of Rex Howard in September 1943, when Air Commodore

Peake was brought in above him to take over the Service's administration.

Neither Menzies nor SIS was perfect, but Trevor-Roper's claim that SIS, which at the end of the war 'remained totally unreformed', was 'unimportant' and 'an irrelevancy' to the Allied war effort[25] is simply preposterous. Admittedly starting from a low base, perhaps exemplified above all by the grievous damage and embarrassment of the Venlo incident, SIS made a significant and major contribution to victory in 1945. Menzies's stewardship of the signals intelligence effort is but one aspect of this. SIS's prewar liaison contacts with foreign intelligence services, consolidated and expanded with Allied governments-in-exile, as well as its exploitation of Vichy sources and the burgeoning Anglo-American relationship, produced enormous intelligence benefits. In neutral countries, and powerfully informed by the benefits of Ultra, SIS gained a stranglehold on the enemy's intelligence services and it was able to contribute markedly to the Allies' extremely successful deception operations. While intelligence returns in some areas (for example the Far East) were poor for most of the war, SIS networks made a major contribution to intelligence on V-weapons, to coast-watching in north-west Europe, to train-watching in the Low Countries and to the collection of the intelligence which so abundantly informed the D-Day landings and subsequent advance on Germany. In the Mediterranean theatre, there were significant achievements in Tunisia, and the Bari station was markedly productive over the last two years of the war. All this was underpinned by the admirable technical expertise of Section VIII, providing the secure communications without which both intelligence-gathering and its dissemination would indeed have been (to borrow Trevor-Roper's words) 'an irrelevancy'.

During the discussions about the postwar organisation of SIS in the Bland Report and after, Menzies's contributions reveal him to have had more in common with Cumming than with Sinclair. Writing to Peter Loxley after having been shown an early draft of Bland, Menzies evinced no inclination whatsoever towards the creation of a unified security and intelligence organisation. A 'complete amalgamation of effort', he observed, 'may prove to be neither practicable nor desirable'. In response to Loxley's concerns about the potential political leanings of the Service, Menzies insisted on a remarkable manifesto of political neutrality being included in the final report. He believed 'it to be of great importance that the S.I.S. should avoid incurring any suspicion that it is the instrument of

any particular political creed in this country' and that any targeting of political groups, whether 'Nazis, Communists [or] Anarchists', should specifically have to be confirmed by SIS's Foreign Office political masters. A
quarter of a century on, there is a clear echo here of Cumming's concern
that the Service might become identified with any one specific political
party. Though (as with Cumming) we know nothing of Menzies's personal political opinions, bearing in mind his own privileged social background and upbringing they are unlikely to have been very left of centre.
He would, however, certainly have remembered the trouble Sinclair got
into with domestic British intelligence operations, if not also the slightly
equivocal political role the Service had played during the Zinoviev Letter
affair, and on the evidence had learned from it, like Cumming displaying
a commendable and fastidious political judgment.

One of the clear measures of SIS's success over its first forty years was
its sheer institutional survival. This is not a trivial matter. It had to endure
in a kind of Whitehall Darwinian jungle, where the survival of the fittest
was the order of the day. This constantly varying environment, where priorities, policies, politics and personalities were continually changing, was
populated by very clever and ambitious people, as well as by very ambitious and powerful institutions. That SIS (with essential Foreign Office
backing) saw off repeated attempts to take it over is testimony at the very
least to the absence of any feasible alternative and at the best to a job well
done. The nature of SIS's survival, and its standing, is usefully encapsulated in discussions about the appointment of the fourth Chief in 1949 when
the Foreign Office began to think about a possible successor to Menzies.

'The present incumbent has done well,' observed William Hayter (head
of the Services Liaison Department) in April 1949. 'But he has held the
appointment for about 10 years now, and it is perhaps time that there was
a new approach to the questions involved, which it must be remembered
now include secret operations as well as secret intelligence.' Menzies's
approaching sixtieth birthday (in January 1950) 'would perhaps provide
an appropriate moment for making the change'. Reflecting on possible
candidates, Hayter felt it important to stress 'that this must not be a case
of "jobs for the boys". The appointment', he wrote, 'is too important for
that. In our present military weakness we are more than ever dependent
on efficient intelligence, and this is undoubtedly the most important post
in the whole intelligence organisation.' But where was the best man to be

found? While Hayter expected that the armed services 'may be expected to produce a long list' of candidates, he did not consider that any current member of SIS was 'suitable for appointment as its Head'. In particular, he did not think General Sinclair (the Vice Chief) should be appointed. Although he had 'done excellent work in re-organising the administration of the Service', he thought him 'rigid and unimaginative, and I think a Secret Service run by him would be wonderfully organised and never find anything out'. Sinclair, indeed, was the only internal candidate. Hayter reported that Menzies himself recognised that apart from him 'there is no one now in the service whose name should be considered'.

Only two individuals struck Hayter as really strong candidates. Cavendish-Bentinck he thought 'outstanding'. He 'probably knows more about the organisation than anyone not actually a member of it'; he had 'won the confidence of the Chiefs of Staff'; and he had 'exactly the right type of mind for the appointment'. But however well qualified he was, appointing Cavendish-Bentinck to a senior official position, let alone one as sensitive as Chief of SIS, could be problematic. In 1947, when he had been ambassador-elect to Brazil, he had been involved in a widely publicised divorce, during which he had 'given frank evidence' admitting 'adultery with a series of mistresses, with three of whom he had lived for various periods, and, in addition, at least three extra-marital adventures of an isolated character', following which he had resigned from the Diplomatic Service. Evidently alluding to this, Hayter reflected that it might be 'considered that matters irrelevant to his real qualifications will make him unacceptable'. Hayter's other possible nominee was 'Mr. White of the Security Service', the 'outstanding member of M.I.5 in every way'. For reasons which Hayter did 'not fully understand', it appeared 'far from certain' that Dick White would 'eventually become Head of that organisation'. He had 'all the qualities required for Head of the Secret Service, and his appointment might do something to put a stop to the endless bickering between the two organisations'.[26] Hayter was not quite right about White's future, though he was prescient all the same: in 1953 White became Director-General of MI5, and in 1956 was appointed Chief of SIS (which he remained until 1968), becoming the only person to have held both positions.

Although Caccia endorsed Hayter's recommendation of Cavendish-Bentinck – 'For this kind of job there is usually only one obvious candidate and in this case we are quite clear that Mr. Bentinck is that person' – when the Permanent Under-Secretary, Sir William Strang, raised the matter with the Foreign Secretary, Bevin 'asked that he should not be pressed to consider Mr. Cavendish-Bentinck'. He was also quite opposed to recruiting anyone from the armed services to head SIS, an opinion which 'applied equally to M.I.5'. Despite this, when Hayter formally drew up a list of possible candidates for Strang, he included White, a senior naval officer, three diplomats and a couple of outsiders, including Peter Fleming (the writer Ian Fleming's elder brother), who had served in SOE. Once again, Hayter asserted that there was 'no suitable candidate in the organisation, though "C" himself believes that General Sinclair, his present deputy, is qualified to succeed him. I do not agree with him.' Having discussed the matter with the Prime Minister, Bevin told Strang that Attlee had raised the possibility of an inquiry 'into the whole of our intelligence services i.e. naval, military and air intelligence, C's organisation and M.I.5', but he 'had not yet made up his mind'. In the meantime, concluded Bevin, 'it might be better to leave C where he was for another year or so'.[27] Menzies remained in post until July 1952 when he was, after all, succeed by John Sinclair.

The discussion about a possible new Chief reveals how, after forty years of existence, senior politicians and officials viewed SIS in its wider governmental context. No one contradicted Hayter's assertion that the job was 'the most important post in the whole intelligence organisation' and even though Hayter had also noted that GCHQ was 'now for all practical purposes entirely independent of the Secret Service', there was not the slightest suggestion (even in the aftermath of its immense wartime achievements) that signals intelligence had priority over SIS's human intelligence responsibilities. Bevin's determination that the armed services should not continue to have a monopoly of the top job reflected a widely held Foreign Office opinion that the Service was an interdepartmental organisation. It also perhaps embodied a desire for SIS to be primarily a civilian service, and certainly under overall Foreign Office control. Having from the very beginning beaten off successive armed service department attempts to take over SIS, the Foreign Office was not now going to relax its hold on the appointment of the Chief.

Over its first forty years, at least so far as the Directors of Naval and Military Intelligence were concerned, the Service moved from being an integrated, though publicly deniable, part of their empires (and one staffed by serving or retired members of the armed services) to its recognisably modern situation as a distinctly civilian and autonomous agency under the overall supervision of the Foreign Office. Indeed, the transition from a naval and military agency to a civilian one is illustrated by the fact that the first four Chiefs were all serving officers at the time of their appointment – two sailors and two soldiers in turn – but all the Chiefs thereafter (though they may have spent time in the armed services) have been civilians. In 1949, moreover, the involvement of the Prime Minister in the discussions also reflected the high national importance of SIS and its leadership. It was evidently not a decision the Foreign Secretary could take unilaterally. And Attlee's suggestion for yet another review, revealing a concern that matters could still be improved in the intelligence community, further emphasises the crucial significance which the government at the highest level invested in the intelligence function as a whole. This was particularly so in the postwar years when economic weakness, relative military decline and the rise of significant superpower challenges from the USA and USSR put a special premium on intelligence performance – one area, perhaps, where the United Kingdom might still yet lead the world. Central to this was the Secret Intelligence Service, which by 1949 had become a valued and permanent British institution.

Menzies was fond of reminding his Foreign Office masters that both Colonel Walter Nicolai (Germany's First World War Military Intelligence chief) and Vladimir Orloff of Russia, 'who in the past were considered the two greatest authorities on secret service work', both 'demanded forty years as the minimum period required for the establishment of a really efficient secret intelligence service'.[28] So it appears to have been for SIS. In 1949 Sir Stewart Menzies, with a staff of over two thousand at home and overseas,[29] had come a long way from Commander Mansfield Cumming sitting alone in his new office in October 1909 wondering what he might do. But the task facing them was essentially the same: Cumming, Sinclair, Menzies, and their colleagues, had the duty, indeed the privilege, of covertly and discreetly informing the British government about the threats and challenges posed to the United Kingdom's worldwide national interests. That the United Kingdom as a leading democratic state survived two world wars and numerous peacetime crises over the first half of the twentieth century must in part be ascribed to the success of its intelligence community, of which SIS formed (and forms) a major part. That SIS itself survived as a permanent and increasingly professional intelligence agency (though by no means perfect, and not without weaknesses and failure) further testifies to its resilience, responsiveness and *esprit de corps*.

Notes

PREFACE

1 The signals intelligence side is extensively covered in Hinsley, *British Intelligence in the Second World War*. I have in general aimed to avoid covering the same ground of this work and also that of Michael Goodman's forthcoming Official History of the Joint Intelligence Committee.

2 See FCO Historical Branch, "'My Purdah Lady'", for an outline account.

3 For useful examinations of attaché work, see Seligmann, *Spies in Uniform*, and Seligmann (ed.), *Naval Intelligence from Germany*.

4 Harker to Vivian, 14 Mar. 1935 (TNA, KV 2/1588). I am grateful to Phil Tomaselli for this reference.

5 Admiral Alexander Bethell to Cumming, 10 Aug. 1909, an image of which may be seen on the SIS website: http://www.mi6gov.uk/output/the-bethell-letter.hmtl (accessed 20 Jan. 2010).

6 See Hinsley, *British Intelligence in the Second World War*.

CHAPTER 1: THE BEGINNINGS OF THE SERVICE

1 The most important single source for the early history of SIS is Mansfield Cumming's diary, which he began to write up specifically as a record of his office work shortly after being appointed to the Secret Service Bureau. The earliest period covered by the diary, from August 1909 to January 1914 (but with substantial gaps, especially in 1911–13), exists only in a photocopy of a typescript apparently typed by Cumming himself.

2 Kennedy, *Rise and Fall of the Great Powers*; Howard, *Continental Commitment*.

3 For a review of the German threat in its various manifestations, and the British popular and official response, see Andrew, *Defence of the Realm*, 3–52; and Hiley, 'Failure of British counter-espionage'.

4 Andrew, *Defence of the Realm*, 5–6; Andrew, *Secret Service*, 31–3; Jeffery, *Sir Henry Wilson*, 75, 90, 100–3; Hiley, 'Failure of British espionage'.

5 Report and proceedings of CID sub-committee, Oct. 1909; conclusions of sub-committee, Apr. 1909 (TNA, CAB 16/8 and 16/232).

6 CID 103rd meeting, 24 July 1909 (TNA, CAB 2/2); Edmonds, 'Memoirs', ch. 20, p. 5 (Edmonds papers); memo regarding the formation of a Secret Service Bureau (TNA, KV 1/3).

7 The indispensable biographical source for Cumming is Judd, *The Quest for C.*; Cumming service record (TNA, ADM 196/20). For the Motor Yacht Club, see *The Times*, 14 Apr. 1908 and Guttridge, *Royal Motor Yacht Club*.

8 Grahame-White, *At the Wheel*, 122.

9 Bethell to Cumming, 10 Aug. 1909 (reproduced at http://www.mi6gov.uk/output/the-bethell-letter.hmtl (accessed 20 Jan. 2010)).

10 Tariff Reform, the replacement of Free Trade with national tariff barriers, had been adopted

by Germany in the late nineteenth century. We are grateful to Nicholas Hiley for cracking Cumming's code.

11 Kell diary 15–17 Nov. 1910 (TNA, KV 1/10).

12 Secret Service Bureau, minutes of meeting, 23 May 1911 (TNA, FO 1093/25).

13 Ibid., 23 Nov. 1911 (ibid.); *The Times*, 21 July; Wilson diary, 26 July 1911 (Wilson papers).

14 *The Times*, 1 and 5 Feb. 1912; note by Reginald Drake, 25 July 1947 (IWM, Payne-Best papers, SPB 3); petition by Stewart, Mar. 1914, and note by DMO, 25 May 1914 (TNA, WO 374/65422).

15 Wilson diary, 12, 18–19 Sept. 1911; Hiley, 'Failure of British espionage', 881–3; Secret Service Bureau, minutes of meeting, 23 Nov. 1911 (TNA, FO 1093/25).

16 Secret Service Bureau, minutes of meeting, 8 Nov. 1912 and 7 May 1913 (TNA, FO 1093/25).

17 Ibid., 7 May 1913.

18 For 'Willie' Clarkson, see McLaren, 'Smoke and mirrors'.

19 Spiers, who changed the spelling of his surname to Spears in 1918, was a liaison officer with General de Gaulle during the Second World War.

20 Some of Rotter's intelligence logbooks have survived in TNA, ADM 137, e.g. 137/3880; Hiley, 'Failure of British espionage', 887–8.

CHAPTER 2: STATUS, ORGANISATION AND EXPERTISE

1 Historical Sketch of the Directorate of Military Intelligence, 1914–18 (TNA, WO 32/10776).

2 Callwell to Henry Wilson, 30 Sept. 1914 (Wilson papers, HHW 2/75/9); draft telegram, 4 Oct. 1914 (TNA, WO 339/7419) (I am most grateful to Phil Tomaselli for drawing this document to my attention); Kirke to wife, 3 Oct. 1914 (Kirke papers (IWM), WMK 2, folder I). The best source for military intelligence on the Western Front is Beach, 'British Intelligence and the German Army'.

3 Mackenzie, *Greek Memories*, 90–1; Cumming service record (TNA, ADM 196/20).

4 Cumming service record (TNA, ADM 196/20); Kirke to wife, 12 Oct. 1914 (Kirke papers (IWM), WMK 2, folder I); Callwell to Wilson, 10 Dec. 1914 (Wilson papers, HHW 2/75/21).

5 Historical Sketch, 1914–18 (TNA, WO 32/10776).

6 Ibid.

7 Ibid.

8 Kirke diary, 29 Nov.–10 Dec. 1915 (Kirke papers (IWM), 82/28/1); Scheme for Reorganisation of S.S., Dec. 1915 (TS carbon copy) (Kirke papers (ICM), acc. no. 262).

9 For Merton see Hartley and Gabor, 'Thomas Ralph Merton'.

10 MI1(c) air reports, 21–22 March 1918 (SHD (Terre), 16N1298, vol. 22).

11 *The Times*, 15 Oct. 1929.

12 In January 1917 Browning also successfully put Cumming up for election to the Garrick Club – a favourite of theatrical men (information from Mr Marcus Risdell, Curator and Librarian of the Club).

13 According to a letter from Macdonogh to the DID, 12 Nov. 1917, the War Office had similar concerns.

14 For Dansey's early life, see Read and Fisher, *Colonel Z*.

15 Hoare, *Fourth Seal*, 31.

16 Kirke diary, 22 June, 11 Oct. 1915 (Kirke papers (IWM), 82/28/1).

17 Hartley and Gabor, 'Thomas Ralph Merton', 425.

18 Norman Thwaites to Wiseman, 1 Oct. 1918 (Wiseman papers, box 6, folder 175).

CHAPTER 3: OPERATIONS IN THE WEST

1 Maxse to FO, 19 Aug.; minute by Eyre Crowe, 21 Aug. 1914 (TNA, FO 371/2054).

2 See Tinsley's naval service record (TNA, ADM 340/136); for his employment and expulsion, see papers in TNA, FO 368/537–8; Kirke diary, 29 Nov. 1915 (Kirke papers (IWM), 82/28/1); memoir, part 2, p. 150 (Kirkpatrick papers, 79/50/1); memoir, p. 23, and extract from letters to Walter Leschander, n.d. (Payne Best papers (ICM), acc. no. 1239); Landau, *All's Fair*, 46–7.

3 Kirke diary, 29 Nov. 1915 (Kirke papers (IWM), 82/28/1); for Cameron see Winter, *Winter's Tale*, 184–221.

4 Kirke diary, 19 Mar. 1915 (Kirke papers (IWM), 82/28/1).

5 Memoir, part 1, p. 59 (Kirkpatrick papers, 79/50/1); Kirke diary, 29 Nov. 1915 (Kirke papers (IWM), 82/28/1).

6 History of Intelligence (B), B.E.F., France, Jan. 1917 to Apr. 1919, by Col. R. Drake (TNA, WO 106/45); Andrew, *Defence of the Realm*, 73–5.

7 History of Intelligence (B) by Col. Drake (TNA, WO 106/45).

8 For Oppenheim see Landau, *Spreading the Spy Net*, 37–8.

9 History of Intelligence (B) by Col. Drake (TNA, WO 106/45); History of British Secret Service in Holland in World War I, Aug. 1914–Feb. 1917 by M. R. K. Burge (TNA, WO 106/6189).

10 See Kirke diary, 30 May, 9–10 June, 23 July, 17 Aug. 1916 (Kirke papers (IWM), 82/28/1); Landau, *All's Fair*, 44, 46, 53; *The Times*, 21 Dec. 1916.

11 Landau, *All's Fair*, 43–4.

12 History of British Secret Service in Holland (TNA, WO 106/6189).

13 Landau, *All's Fair*, 108–12; Landau, *Secrets of the White Lady*, 47–57; 'B.149' to M. St Lambert, 7 July 1917 (Dewé papers, vol. 2); Decock, 'La Dame Blanche', 65–72, 101–7, 122–37; Proctor, *Female Intelligence*, 75–98 provides an excellent short account.

14 Proctor, *Female Intelligence*, 81–7; *London Gazette*, 29 Aug. 1919; La Dame Blanche papers, Box 1, folder 4(a/b); Landau, *Secrets of the White Lady*, 141–51.

15 Memoir, part 2, pp. 128–35 (Kirkpatrick papers, 79/50/1); Landau, *All's Fair*, 50–1; Landau, *Secrets of the White Lady*, 65–79.

16 'There is no doubt at this critical moment you represent the most abundant Allied intelligence source and that the results you are achieving are of inestimable value' ('Service anglais' to 'Service d'Observation anglais', 21 Jan. 1918, quoted in Decock, 'La Dame Blanche', 149).

17 For the Bureau Central Interallié see Cockerill, *What Fools We Were*, 41–2; and Mersey, *A Picture of Life*, 276–96. Various British CX reports (from Athens and Copenhagen in Dec. 1915) survive in the French records of the Bureau (see SHD (Terre), 7N1018).

18 Calculations from British intelligence reports in SHD (Terre), 16N1291–1300 (29 vols). Judd says that 'the CX prefix had staying power, surviving in later SIS vocabulary in a number of ways' (Judd, *Quest for C*, 333).

19 MI1(c) reports, 6, 8, 16 June 1917 (SHD (Terre), 16N1291, vol. 4); Newbolt, *Naval Operations*, v, 241–65; Jones, *War in the Air: Appendices*, 50.

20 Landau, *All's Fair*, 143–9; Rotterdam to London, 14 Mar. and 27 June 1916, enclosing reports from R.16 (TNA, ADM 223/637, which contains additional commendations by Naval Intelligence Staff).

21　'Service anglais' to 'Service d'Observation anglais', 21 July 1918 (Dewé papers, vol. 1); memoir, part 2, p. 150 (Kirkpatrick papers, 79/50/1).

22　Beach, 'British Intelligence and the German Army', 239–66.

23　*London Gazette*, 29 Aug., 12 Sept. 1919; *The Times*, 28, 31 Jan., 2 Feb. 1920.

24　D.1 report, 12 Nov. 1915; D.10 report, 8 May 1916 (TNA, MUN 4/518 and 4/3587); D.2 reports, 20, 23 Mar. 1915, 3 Jan. 1918; D.5 report, 12 Oct. 1917; D.62 report, 11 Apr. 1918 (SHD (Terre), 16N1291, 1295–6, 1298, vols 1, 11, 17, 24).

25　S.50 reports, 20 Apr., 10 May 1917; N.20 report, 3 Jan.; S.8 report, 4 Feb. 1918 (SHD (Terre), 16N1291, vol. 1; 1292, vol. 4; 1296, vol. 17; 1297, vol. 19).

26　Kirke diary, 25 Feb.–3 Mar., 22–23 Mar., 3, 10 Apr., 20, 22 June, 14 July 1915 (Kirke papers (IWM), 82/28/1).

27　*New York Times*, 28 Nov. 1915.

28　Kirke diary, 10 Jan. 1916 (Kirke papers (IWM), 82/28/1); Andrew, *Secret Service*, 146–53; Maugham, *Partial View*, 115–16.

29　Kirke diary, 23 Mar., 29 Nov. 1915 (Kirke papers (IWM), 82/28/1).

30　Ibid., 3 Dec. 1915 (ibid.).

31　Intelligence reports in SHD (Terre), 16N1291–1300.

32　For MI5 stations in Italy and the USA, see Andrew, *Defence of the Realm*, 104–6.

33　Economic Conditions (Enemy Countries), summaries nos 15–17, covering 23 June–20 July 1917 (SHD (Terre), 16N1292, vols 5–6); H. Llewellyn Smith to David Lloyd George (Minister of Munitions), 6 Aug. 1915 and attached note (TNA, MUN 4/3586); 'German Munitions Output' file (MUN 4/3262); report from D.1, 12 Nov. 1915 (MUN 4/3586); report from S.1, 12 Nov. 1916 (MUN 4/3587); report from Tiger, 27 Oct. 1916 (MUN 4/3262).

34　Stagg to Hoare, 11 May 1916 (Templewood papers, II.1.39).

CHAPTER 4: WORKING FURTHER AFIELD

1　There are general accounts of British intelligence in Russia, 1914–17 (on which I have drawn in this and succeeding paragraphs) in Macdonogh to General Sir Henry Wilson, 14 Jan. 1917 (Wilson papers, HHW 3/12/59); and History of the British Intelligence Organisation in Russia, 1914–Feb. 1917 (TNA, WO 106/6190). For a useful overall assessment, see Neilson, '"Joy rides"?'

2　Callwell to Wilson, 11 Dec. 1914 (Wilson papers, HHW 2/75/22).

3　History of the British Intelligence Organisation in Russia, 1914–Feb. 1917 (TNA, WO 106/6190).

4　Buchanan to FO, 20 Dec. 1914 (TNA, FO 371/2446/156).

5　*The Times*, 13, 16, 23 Aug. 1952.

6　Kirke diary, 7 Feb. 1916 (Kirke papers (IWM), 82/28/1); Cumming to Samuel Hoare, 12 May 1916 (Templewood papers, II.1.40).

7　Baird to Hoare, 13 Feb. (Templewood papers, II.1.36); Cumming to Hoare, 11 May 1916 (Templewood papers, II.1.38); Hoare's entertaining account is in his memoir, *Fourth Seal*.

8　Instructions for the Agent in charge of the Mission to Petrograd, n.d. [c. 11 May 1916], Cumming to Hoare, 12 May 1916 (Templewood papers, II.1.40–1); Hoare, *Fourth Seal*, 53, 57.

9　British Intelligence Mission, note by Hoare, 5 Feb. 1917 (Wilson papers, HHW 3/12/7).

10　Ibid.

11　Cumming to Hoare, 28 Apr.; 'Weekly Notes No. 2', 26 Dec.; Hoare to 'C', 30 Dec. 1916;

Hoare to Browning, 1 Jan.; 'The death of Rasputin', 1/2 Jan. 1917 (Templewood papers, II.1.15–16, 37, 47–9).

12 Hoare, *Fourth Seal*, 206; Jeffery, *Sir Henry Wilson*, 186–7; Secret Service in Russia, 20 Mar. 1917 (Templewood papers, II.2.2).

13 For speculation about the circumstances of Trotsky's detention, see Spence, 'Interrupted journey'.

14 See Popplewell, *Intelligence and Imperial Defence*, 147–64, a pioneering study of early British intelligence operations. There is some evidence of pre-Cumming secret service operations in the USA during 1914–15 (when the Pinkerton Detective Agency was hired to watch ports, print pamphlets and pay informants) in TNA, FO 1093/60.

15 Wiseman army service file (TNA, WO 339/21491); Murray, *Master and Brother*, 153; Fowler, *British–American Relations*, 16–18.

16 Gaunt, *Yield of the Years*, provides an only sporadically reliable account; Thwaites army service file (TNA, WO 339/19912); Thwaites, *Velvet and Vinegar*, 119–20, 131–43; US immigration details from passenger database at www.ellisisland.org (accessed 19 Feb. 2009). For an overview, see Spence, 'Englishmen in New York'.

17 Memo apparently by Wiseman, 28 Mar.; memo on scope and activities of MI1(c) in New York, 27 Apr.; Wiseman to Cumming, 6 Sept.; 'New York Office, Section V', n.d. (*c.* Oct.); list of salaries, 29 Jan. 1918 (Wiseman papers, box 6, folders 171; 173–5; 177).

18 Wiseman to Guy Standing (Head Office), 4 Apr. 1916; Wiseman to Cumming, 6 Sept.; Thwaites to Wiseman, 22 Nov. 1918 (Wiseman papers, box 6, folders 160, 171; box 3, folder 84); Thwaites, *Velvet and Vinegar*, 153–5.

19 Bruce Lockhart, 'Sir William Wiseman Bart – agent of influence'; Andrew, *For the President's Eyes Only*, 37–60.

20 House diary, 17 Dec. 1916, 15 Jan. 1917; House to Wilson, 26 Jan. 1917 (House papers, diary vols 4–5; box 121, folder 4272).

21 Willert, *Road to Safety*, 52; Spring Rice to Wiseman, 12 Feb. 1917 (Wiseman papers, box 3, folder 81).

22 Hankey diary, 1 Feb. 1916 (Hankey papers, HNKY 1/1); Freeman, 'The Zimmermann telegram revisited'.

23 House diary, 23 Feb.; 7 Mar. (House papers, diary vol. 5); Wiseman to Spring Rice, 6 Mar. (Wiseman papers, box 3, folder 81); 'Relations between the United States and Great Britain', endorsed by House, 8 Mar. (House papers, box 123, folder 4324); the 'Relations between the United States and Great Britain' paper was communicated to Britain in Spring Rice to FO, 8 Mar. 1917 (and circulated to the King, the Cabinet and other senior individuals) (Balfour papers, Add. 49740, fols 96–8).

24 See Fowler, *British–American Relations*.

25 Balfour to Spring Rice, 7 Apr. 1917 (TNA, FO 115/2317).

26 Memo by Wiseman, 16 Apr. 1917 (ibid.); 'Russia' [18 May], and 'Russian affairs', 26 May 1917, by Wiseman (Wiseman papers, box 10, folder 255); Wiseman to Sir Eric Drummond (private secretary to Foreign Secretary), 16, 20 June, and replies 19, 26 June 1917 (Wiseman papers, box 10, folder 255).

27 18 July 1917, receipt for $21,000 signed by Maugham (Wiseman papers, box 10, folder 256).

28 Fowler, *British–American Relations*, 113–18; 'Intelligence and propaganda work in Russia July–Dec. 1917', 19 Jan. 1918; summary by Wiseman of reports received from agent in Petrograd, 11 Sept. 1917 (Wiseman papers, box 10, folders 261 and 257).

29 Jeffreys-Jones, *American Espionage*, 96–101; Andrew, *Defence of the Realm*, 105–6; Balfour to Wiseman, 19 Dec. 1917; Wiseman to Charles S. Ascherson and reply, 13 Feb. and 3 Mar. 1918 (Wiseman papers, box 1, folders 6 and 4).

30 House diary, 18 Dec. (House papers, diary, vol. 5); Wiseman to Churchill, 10 Mar. 1919 (NARA, MID 11013-7-1); Fowler, *British–American Relations*, 221–35.

31 Accounts and correspondence concerning the Constantinople Quays Co. will be found in TNA, FO 1093/37–40. See also Hamilton, 'Dockside diplomacy'.

32 Hankey diary, 4 Mar. 1915 (Hankey papers, HNKY 1/1); James, *Eyes of the Navy*, 60–4.

33 Conference of Admirals in Malta, 2–9 Mar. 1916 (TNA, ADM 137/499).

34 'Orders' by Cumming, 3 July; Macdonogh to Hoare, 29 Dec. 1917; Hoare to Macdonogh, 3 Jan.; 'Measures undertaken to start military espionage in Austria and Turkey', 30 Apr. 1918 (Templewood papers, III.1.49, 68; III.2.5; III.3.38).

35 'Contrespionage and espionage in Italy', 1 Aug. 1918 (Templewood papers, III.4.29).

36 Cumming to Mackenzie, 8 Feb. 1917 (Mackenzie papers; Works I/Aegean Memories folder, fol. 265B). This account of work in the Eastern Mediterranean draws on the Mackenzie memoirs cited, as well as his *My Life and Times: Octave Four* and *Octave Five*.

37 'Organisation of the EMSIB' (1921 report) (TNA, KV 1/17).

38 Mackenzie to Cumming, 9 Mar.; to Sir Francis Elliot, 9 May; Proposed transfer of so-called passport records, note by Mackenzie, n.d. [July]; Cumming to Mackenzie, 23 July, 25 Nov. 1917 (Mackenzie papers; Works I/Aegean Memories folder, fol. 316; 573, pp. 28 & 42; folder Recip. Cull–Cz).

39 See Mackenzie to Cumming, 16 and 30 Mar. 1917 (Mackenzie papers; Works I/Aegean Memories folder, fols 333 and 370).

40 Mackenzie to Cumming, 10 July 1917 (Mackenzie papers; Works I/Aegean Memories folder, fols 742–3).

41 Geneva tel., 26 Oct. 1917 (SHD (Terre), 16N1295, vol. 13); Moberly, *Campaign in Mesopotamia*, iv, chs 37–9.

42 Kirke diary, 17 Apr. 1915 (Kirke papers (IWM), 82/28/1); 'memo on the advisability of maintaining in existence after the war Col. Samson's Secret service bureau' and Clayton to Cumming, 29 Nov. 1916 (Sudan Archive, SAD 693/10/84 and 694/3/71).

43 Sheffy, 'British Intelligence and the Middle East', 37–52; Sheffy, *British Military Intelligence*, ch. 5; Aaronsohn's relations with EMSIB are detailed in his diary, see the published version: Efrati (ed.), *Yoman Aharon Aharonson*.

44 Popplewell, *Intelligence and Imperial Defence*, ch. 13.

45 For Reilly, see Andrew Cook's admirably thorough study, *Ace of Spies*.

46 Lockhart's account is in his *Memoirs of a British Agent*.

47 Dukes vividly recounted his recruitment by SIS in his memoir, *Story of 'ST 25'*, 28–36. For British policy towards Russia, see Ullman, *Anglo-Soviet Relations*.

Chapter 5: The emergence of SIS

1 Mackenzie, *Greek Memories*, 411–12; Mackenzie, *My Life and Times: Octave Five*, 110.

2 The postwar situation and government responses are discussed in Jeffery, *British Army and the Crisis of Empire*; Jeffery and Hennessy, *States of Emergency*.

3 Andrew, *Defence of the Realm*, 106–9.

4 Memo by Long, 16 Jan., and by Shortt, 23 Jan. 1919 (TNA, CAB 127/356).

5 Cabinet minutes, 24 Jan. 1919 (TNA, CAB 23/9/WC519).

6 Report of Secret Service Committee, Feb. 1919 (TNA, CAB 127/356); for MI5's relations

with Thomson, see Andrew, *Defence of the Realm*, 116–20, and for a general discussion of the intelligence reorganisation debate, see Madeira, 'British official and Intelligence responses to Soviet subversion', parts I and II.

7 Crowe to Bland, 17 Nov. 1920 (Bland papers, BLND 9/2, part 1).

8 Wiseman to Thwaites, 23 Apr. 1919 (Wiseman papers, box 6, folder 176); Cumming to Mackenzie, 1 May [1919] (Mackenzie papers, folder Recip. Cull–Cz).

9 Vernon Kell also proposed using passport control work to help fund MI5 operations; see 'Proposed Scheme for Post-War Organization', May 1919, enc. with Kell to Haldane Porter, 28 Aug. 1919 (TNA, HO 45/19966).

10 For a thoughtful discussion of what may be deduced from the published Secret Service Vote, see O'Halpin, 'Financing British intelligence'.

11 'Scheme for the re-organisation and co-ordination of Intelligence', n.d., enc. with Basil Thomson to Walter Long, 18 Nov. 1918 (Long papers, 947/672); Report of Secret Service Committee, Feb. 1919 (TNA, CAB 127/356).

12 War Cabinet meetings, 5 and 15 Aug. 1919 (TNA, CAB 23/15/606A and 616A). For the impact of this review on defence spending generally, see Howard, *Continental Commitment*, 74–8.

13 Churchill to Prime Minister and others, 19 Mar. 1920, enc. memo on Reduction of estimates for Secret Services (Lloyd George papers, F/9/2/16).

14 Minute by Niemeyer, 21 Feb.; Crowe to Fisher, 24 May; Report of Cabinet committee, 27 July 1921 (TNA, CAB 127/357); Cabinet minutes, 22 Mar. 1921 (TNA, CAB 23/24/14(21)).

15 Secret Service Committee, 1st and 3rd meetings, 27 May and 2 June 1921 (TNA, CAB 127/355): War Office memo on Army requirements from Secret Service, 1 June 1921 (TNA, CAB 127/356).

16 Report of Secret Service Committee, 27 July 1921 (TNA, CAB 127/357); Thomson to Sinclair, 1 Nov. 1921 (Sinclair papers, MS 81/091, scrapbook vol. 1).

17 Treasury memo, n.d. [Jan. 1922] (TNA, CAB 127/358).

18 Note on the Secret Service by S. of S. for War, n.d. [Jan. 1922] (TNA, CAB 127/360); Secret Service Committee, 1st meeting, 4 Mar. 1922 (TNA, CAB 127/359).

19 Conference of ministers, 20 Feb. 1922 (TNA, CAB 127/356); Secret Service Committee, 1st–3rd meetings, 4, 24 and 27 Mar. 1922 (TNA, CAB 127/359).

20 Report of Secret Service Committee, 4 Apr. 1922 (TNA, CAB 127/356).

21 'Actual expenditure' in 1921–2 was £195,000 (Foreign Office: £145,000); and in 1924–5, £162,000 (Foreign Office: £137,000) (Cabinet Office papers).

22 'S.I.S. (Constantinople Branch) Summary of Intelligence Reports for week ending 16 Dec. 1920' (TNA, FO 406/45, p. 40).

23 A colour reproduction of this document was used for the endpapers of Judd, *Quest for C*.

24 Sykes service record, including minute by Rear Admiral Rushbrooke, 26 Mar. 1946 (TNA, ADM 340/424).

25 For Morton see Gill Bennett's definitive study, *Churchill's Man of Mystery*.

26 Wiseman to Thwaites, 20 Jan. 1919 (Wiseman papers, box 3, folder 84).

27 Notes by Robert Woollcombe, n.d. (Woollcombe papers).

28 Secret Service Committee, 1st meeting, 4 Mar. 1922 (TNA, CAB 127/359).

29 Mackenzie, *Ægean Memories*, 394.

30 Cumming to Hoare, 24 Jan. [1923] (Templewood papers, V.1).

31 Sinclair service record (TNA, ADM 196/43).

32 Hall to Sinclair, 18 Dec. 1918 and 14 Jan. 1919 (Sinclair papers MS 81/091, scrapbook vol. 1).
33 Lee (First Lord of the Admiralty) to Sinclair, 31 May 1921; and Admiralty to Sinclair, 17 May 1923 (Sinclair papers MS 81/091, scrapbook vol. 1).
34 *The Times*, 16 June 1923; Williams, *World of Action*, 338–9.
35 Andrew, *Secret Service*, 295; Pinero, *Gay Lord Quex*, 11, 15, 75.
36 *The Times*, 6 Nov. 1939; 'The Annual Submarine Dinner, 1921' (Sinclair papers MS 81/091, scrapbook vol. 1).

Chapter 6: From Boche to Bolsheviks

1 Wilson diary, 10 Nov. 1918 (Wilson papers); Tyrrell to Austen Chamberlain, 6 Dec. 1926 (*DBFP*, ser. 1A, vol. ii, no. 319).
2 Reduction of estimates for Secret Services, memo by Churchill, 19 Mar. 1920 (Lloyd George papers, F/9/2/16).
3 Richard Ullman's magisterial *Anglo-Soviet Relations* remains the best single treatment of this complex history.
4 Lockhart to Gregory (FO), 2 May 1919 (TNA, FO 371/4017); for Ransome, see Brogan, *Arthur Ransome*.
5 Dukes, *Story of 'ST 25'*, 31–2; 'Affairs in Russia', report by ST/25, 30 Apr. 1919 (quoted in *Story of 'ST 25'*, 360–74).
6 Agar's own account is in *Baltic Episode*; Dukes's *Story of 'ST 25'* differs in some details.
7 Quoted in Agar, *Baltic Episode*, 82.
8 Ferguson, *Operation Kronstadt* provides a fictionalised narrative of these events, with a shrewd commentary on operational matters.
9 There is an account of this episode in Bennett, *Churchill's Man of Mystery*, 43–4.
10 Note by Walford Selby (FO), 5 Mar. 1919 (TNA, FO 371/3962). Twelve of Reilly's despatches survive in this file.
11 Crowe to Curzon, 28 Dec. 1921 (Gilbert, *Churchill*, iv, companion part iii, pp. 1703–4).
12 There are accounts of the Trust, Savinkov and Reilly's fate in Spence, *Boris Savinkov*, and Cook, *Ace of Spies*.
13 For MI5's debriefing of Krivitsky, see Andrew, *Defence of the* Realm, 264–8.
14 Report of interdepartmental committee, Aug. 1921 (IOR, L/P&S/886); Foreign Office Confidential Print 11861, 'Violations of the Russian Trade Agreement', 1921 (some of these papers are also printed in *DBFP*, 1st ser., vol. xx).
15 'Classification of reports', c. 10 May 1922 (Lloyd George papers, F/26/1/30).
16 Bennett, *Churchill's Man of Mystery*, 44–5.
17 Nicholson (under the pseudonym John Whitwell) wrote a lively memoir, *British Agent*, published in 1966.
18 Landau, *All's Fair*, 227–34.
19 Foley army service record (TNA, WO 374/24816); see also Smith, *Foley*.
20 Eastern summary no. 1034, 6 Jan. 1923 (IOR, L/P&J/12/116, which also contains much additional SIS reporting during the Lausanne conference); Rumbold to Lancelot Oliphant (FO), 18 July 1923 (Rumbold papers, MS Rumbold, dep. 31, fols 246–7). For a discussion of intelligence at the Lausanne conference, see Jeffery and Sharp, 'Lord Curzon and secret intelligence'.
21 Menzies–Lainey correspondence, Mar.–July 1925 and May–Aug. 1926 (SHD (Terre), 7NN2248, dr 1034; and 7NN3270, dr 6).
22 For notes of Dunderdale's service, see TNA, ADM 337/128 and 137/2296. Examples of his reports survive in ADM 137/1735 and 1752–3; Lycett, *Ian Fleming*, 112, 114, 223.

23 The IPI file on Bajanov ('Bazhanov') is in IOR, L/P&J/12/359; *Sunday Telegraph*, 19, 26 Sept. and 3 Oct. 1976; see also Bazhanov, *Bazhanov and the Damnation of Stalin*.

24 Lycett, *Ian Fleming*, 31–8.

25 The challenges to British imperial interests in the region are covered in Jeffery, *British Army and the Crisis of Empire*.

26 Cumming to Sir Malcolm Seton (India Office), 2 Feb. (IOR, L/MIL/7/18813); Woollcombe (SIS) to Bland, 2 Oct. 1922 (TNA, FO 371/9945). For an overview, see Ferris, "'Far too dangerous a gamble'".

27 Ferris, "'Far too dangerous a gamble'"; SIS Eastern Summary no. 1031, 6 Jan. 1923 (IOR, L/P&J/12/127).

CHAPTER 7: DOMESTIC MATTERS

1 Secret Service Committee report, 1 Dec. 1925 (TNA, FO 1093/69).

2 Note on 'control of interception', n.d. [*c*. 1924] (TNA, WO 32/4897).

3 History of MI1(b) (TNA, HW 7/35).

4 Curzon to Walter Long (First Lord of the Admiralty), 24 Mar.; minute by Sinclair, 28 Mar.; minutes of conference held at the FO, 29 Apr. 1919 (TNA, ADM 1/8637/55).

5 'Code and Cypher School', memo by Lord Curzon (C.P. 3105), 3 July 1921 (Curzon papers, Mss Eur. F.112/302). This important memorandum is reproduced in full in Jeffery, 'Government Code and Cypher School'.

6 Curzon to Lee, 25 Apr.; and reply 23 May; minute by Lee, 2 May 1921 (TNA, ADM 1/8637/55 and HW 3/38). Details of the transfer are in TNA, FO 366/800.

7 Report of Inter-Service Directorate Committee, 9 Apr. 1923; note on 'control of interception', n.d. [*c*. 1924] (TNA, WO 32/4897).

8 Diary of Sir Henry Wilson, 17–18, 31 Aug., 1 Sept. 1920 (Wilson papers); Churchill to Curzon, 28 Aug. 1920 (Curzon papers, Mss Eur. F. 112/215); *The Times*, 19 Aug. 1920; Andrew, 'British Secret Service'; and Jeffery, 'British military intelligence'.

9 Ferris, 'Road to Bletchley Park', 67–8; for Robert Vansittart's use of signals intelligence material, see Ferris, "'Indulged in all too little'", 133–6.

10 Sinclair to Crowe, 3 Nov. 1923 (TNA, FO 1093/66).

11 Denniston, 'Government Code and Cypher School', 49.

12 For Stott, see Bennett, *Churchill's Man of Mystery*, 75–7.

13 Morris, *Portrait of a Radical*, 164; Wedgwood, *Memoirs of a Fighting Life*, 186.

14 I have drawn on Gill Bennett's careful and definitive study, *'A most extraordinary and mysterious business'*, for the following account.

15 *The Times*, 25 Oct. 1924.

16 For Morton's role, see Bennett, *Churchill's Man of Mystery*, 79–85.

17 SIS to Gregory (FO), 9 Oct. 1924 (TNA, FO 371/10478).

18 Bagot report 1970 (quoted in Bennett, *'A most extraordinary and mysterious business'*, 37).

19 Minute by Crowe, 15 Oct. 1924 (*DBFP*, 1st ser., xxv, 434).

20 Bennett, *'A most extraordinary and mysterious business'*, 73–4.

21 Jones, *Whitehall Diary*, i, 299–300; Cabinet minutes, 31 Oct. 1924 (TNA, CAB 23/48/57(24)).

22 Letter from Robert Woollcombe, *The Times*, 18 Oct. 1977.

23 Cabinet minutes, 4 Nov. 1924 (TNA, CAB 23/48/58(24)).

24 Cabinet minutes, 12 and 19 Nov. 1924 (TNA, CAB 23/49/59 and 60(24)).

25 This memorandum and its context is lucidly discussed in Bennett, 'A most extraordinary and mysterious business', 81–3.

26 Kenneth Lyon to Derby, 20 Nov. 1924 (Derby papers, 920 DER (17) 29/7).

27 Bennett, Churchill's Man of Mystery, 317.

28 Note by Baldwin, 10 Feb. (TNA, FO 1093/67); Secret Service Committee, 1st and 2nd meetings, 26 Feb. and 2 Mar. 1925 (TNA, FO 1093/68).

29 Sinclair to Nevile Bland (secretary to the committee), 18 Mar. (TNA, FO 1093/67); Secret Service Committee, 6th and 7th meetings, 17 and 19 Mar. 1925 (TNA, FO 1093/68).

30 Secret Service Committee, 8th and 10th meetings, 24 Mar. and 15 June; note by Hankey, 27 Mar. 1925 (TNA, FO 1093/67–8).

31 Secret Service Committee report, 1 Dec. 1925 (TNA, FO 1093/69).

32 Andrew, Secret Service, 316; James (ed.), Memoirs of a Conservative, 381–2.

33 Secret Service Committee, 2nd, 6th and 8th meetings, 2, 17 and 24 Mar. 1925 (TNA, FO 1093/67–8).

34 Secret Service Committee, 1st and 2nd meetings, 11 and 22 Mar. 1927 (TNA, FO 1093/71).

35 Note, 31 Mar. 1927 (TNA, KV 3/15).

36 Memo by Sinclair, 28 June 1927 (TNA, FO 1093/73). There is an excellent account of the Arcos raid in Bennett, Churchill's Man of Mystery, 94–106.

37 Andrew, Defence of the Realm, 154–6.

38 Sinclair to Tyrrell, 26 May; memo by Sinclair, 28 June 1927 (TNA, FO 1093/73); Secret Service Committee, 3rd and 4th meetings, 24 and 30 June 1927 (TNA, FO 1093/71).

39 The Macartney case is fully covered in Bennett, Churchill's Man of Mystery, 107–16. For Soviet work against British targets between 1917 and 1929 see Madeira, 'British official and Intelligence responses to Soviet subversion', and Madeira, 'Moscow's interwar infiltration'.

40 Bennett, Churchill's Man of Mystery, 136–49.

41 Undated note re Edwardes; note by Harker, 1 Aug. 1928 (TNA, KV 2/1016 and 2/989).

42 Minute by 'WHP', 5 Aug. 1925; note of telephone conversation with Maj. Morton, 19 Mar. 1926 (TNA, KV 2/2317).

43 Andrew, Defence of the Realm, 123–4.

44 Secret Service Committee 1931, notes of meetings (27 Apr., 11 and 22 June) (TNA, FO 1093/74).

45 Ibid.

46 Curry, Security Service, 102.

47 Thwaites to Wiseman, 22 Mar. 1919 (Wiseman papers, box 3, folder 85).

48 Another version of this story is in Williams, World of Action, 338.

49 Maugham, Ashenden, vii (Author's Preface).

50 Ibid., ix.

51 'Ashenden', Times Literary Supplement, 12 Apr. 1928.

52 Dukes, Red Dusk and the Morrow, vi, 4–5, 10; Tatler, 2 Apr. 1930, p. 35 (the series ran until 21 May).

53 Dukes, Story of 'ST 25', 35.

54 Mackenzie, First Athenian Memories, 75, 344.

55 Daily Telegraph, 27 Oct. 1932. Bywater wrote his own memoir (with H. C. Ferraby), Strange Intelligence, published in 1934.

56 Memo by J. A. Harker, 27 Oct. 1932 (TNA, KV 2/1271).

57 Mackenzie, My Life and Times: Octave Seven, 84–5; Mackenzie, Ægean Memories, 316; The Times, 8 Dec. 1932.

58 Draft proof of Major Valentine Patrick Terrel Vivian, n.d. (TNA, CRIM 1/630).

59 Mackenzie, *My Life and Times: Octave Seven*, 89–94; *The Times*, 25 Nov. 1932.

60 *The Times*, 13 Jan. 1933; Mackenzie, *Ægean Memories*, vii.

61 Mackenzie, *Water on the Brain*, 7, 16, 52–3, 85, 88–9.

62 Landau, *All's Fair*, preface.

63 Landau, *Spreading the Spy Net*, 29; Landau, *All's Fair*, 42–3.

Chapter 8: Existing on a shoestring

1 'Foreign Secret Service Finances', 6 Dec. 1929, forwarded by Nevile Bland to the Treasury (TNA, CAB 127/367).

2 Secret Service Vote (TNA, T 160/787).

3 Secret Service Committee, 2nd meeting, 24 Mar. 1922 (TNA, CAB 127/359).

4 In 1932 $100 was worth approximately £28.50. By 1934 this had fallen to approximately £20.

5 'British espionage in the U.S.', 15 Feb. 1921 (NARA, MID 9944-A-178).

6 Polk Diary, 16 Mar. 1920 (Polk papers, HM47 microfilm); Jeffreys-Jones, *American Espionage*, 129–30.

7 It is impossible to verify this as the report itself has not survived.

8 Lovestone later moved politically to the right and became a fervent anti-Communist.

9 Liddell to Borum, 20 Oct.; Hickerson to Herschel V. Johnson (US embassy London), 9 Nov. 1937 (NARA, RG84, box 1A, file 800B).

10 For the British end of this case, see TNA, KV 2/193–4. See also Andrew, *Defence of the Realm*, 210.

11 'Liaison with the United States Government Intelligence organisations', memo by Capt. Liddell, Mar.–Apr. 1938 (Vansittart papers, VNST II 2/21).

12 For Rutland, see Best, 'Intelligence, diplomacy and the Japanese threat', 86–8.

13 The context of British interests and intelligence in the region is ably explored in Best, *British Intelligence and the Japanese Challenge*, and Best, '"We are virtually at war with Russia"'.

14 Reduction of estimates for Secret Services, memo by Churchill, 19 Mar. 1920 (Lloyd George papers, F/9/2/16).

15 Best, *British Intelligence and the Japanese Challenge*, 51–3.

16 'The Noulens case', report by Vivian, 7 Mar. 1932 (TNA, FO 1093/97). See also Baxter, 'Secret Intelligence Service and the case of Hilaire Noulens'.

17 Diary of Capt. Malcolm Kennedy, 18 Sept. 1931 (Sheffield University Library, available online: http://www.sheffield.ac.uk/library/libdocs/kennedy_diaries.pdf (accessed 28 Aug. 2009)).

18 For the wider context of the Tait report [*c.* Apr. 1934], see Best, *British Intelligence and the Japanese Challenge*, 110–15.

19 The Mask decrypts of Comintern messages are in TNA, HW 17.

20 See Andrew, *Defence of the Realm*, 158–9.

21 See, for example, *Time* (Canadian edition), 25 Jan. (p. 31); *Le Petit Journal*, 7 fév.; *Ottawa Citizen*, 4 Feb. 1954.

22 For the family background, see Lympany, *Moura*.

23 For the divorce, see TNA, J 77/3691/9612.

24 *The Times*, 2 Aug. 1941. For the murder trial, see TNA, ASSI 26/310.

25 See correspondence in TNA, FO 366/966.

26 See 'Misappropriation of immigration deposits by E A Dalton', 1 Oct. 1936 (TNA, CO 733/322/8).

27 Note on the work of the Irish Section of the Security Service 1939–1945, Jan. 1946 (TNA, KV 4/9). See also O'Halpin (ed.), *MI5 and Ireland*, 20.

28 See O'Halpin, *Spying on Ireland*.

CHAPTER 9: APPROACHING WAR

1   Howard, *Continental Commitment*, 117. This work is an indispensable guide to British defence policy between the wars.

2   There is no reply from the French on file.

3   For Pollard's background, see Macklin, 'Major Hugh Pollard'.

4   The French side of the relationship is reliably covered in Forcade, *La République secrète*.

5   Paillole, *Services spéciaux*, 80–1.

6   Compte-rendu de visite de Menzies, 19 et 20 oct. 1937 (SHD (Terre), 7NN2701, dr 216).

7   Menzies to Rivet, July 1938, quoted in Aubin, 'Contre-espionnage', 263.

8   Compte-rendu de Mission à Londres, 30 jan.–1 fév. 1939 (SHD (Terre), 7NN2502, dr 250).

9   Papers relating to this case are in SHD (Terre), 7NN2425, dr 43180. See also Forcade, *La République secrète*, 221–6.

10 Porch, 'French intelligence and the fall of France', 37; Strong, *Intelligence at the Top*, 57–8; Hinsley, *British Intelligence*, i, 115.

11 See Hinsley, *British Intelligence*, i, appendix 1, 487–95; and the revised account in ibid., iii, part 2, appendix 30, 945–59.

12 Bertrand, *Enigma*, 60–1; see also Jan Stanisław Ciechanowski and Jacek Tebinka, 'Cryptographic cooperation – Enigma', in Stirling et al., *Intelligence Co-operation*, 442–62.

13 Hinsley, 'British intelligence in the Second World War', 218.

14 Winterbotham's account of this is in his book *Nazi Connection*, 44–96. De Ropp told his own story of spying for the British in a series of articles in the *Daily Mail*, 28 Oct.–1 Nov. 1957.

15 Summary of secret information regarding German policy and rearmament received from Dec. 1934 to Mar. 1935 [draft?], 4 Mar. 1935 (TNA, FO 371/18844 (endorsed with comments by Winterbotham and Sinclair, dated 8 Mar.)); Phipps to Simon, 25 Mar., enc. naval attaché despatch of 19 Mar. 1935 (TNA, FO 371/18860); German Naval Construction, 22 July 1936 (TNA, CAB 4/24, CID 1252-B); 'Germany: submarine construction', 8 Apr. 1936 (ICF/118) (TNA, CAB 104/29). For the Industrial Intelligence Centre, see pp. 313–14 below. See also Wark, 'Baltic myths and submarine bogeys', 66–7. This article illuminatingly discusses Admiralty use of secret intelligence in the 1930s.

16 Koutrik was employed by MI5 in 1940–1. See Andrew, *Defence of the Realm*, 245–6.

17 Benton, 'ISOS years', 365.

18 See, for example, Smith, *Foley*; and 'Documents relating to the work of Frank Foley' (FCO Historians' brochure, 2004) (http://www.fco.gov.uk/en/about-us/publications-and-documents/historians1/documents-from-archives/frank-foley/ (accessed 11 Jan. 2010)).

19 CSS tel. to Berlin, 9 Mar. 1939 (reproduced in 'Documents relating to the work of Frank Foley').

20 Cadogan diary, 3 Sept 1938 (Cadogan papers, ACAD 1/7).

21 Germany and Colonies, 3 Feb. 1938 (Woollcombe papers). On the same day the Cabinet Committee on Foreign Policy (which Chamberlain chaired) discussed a similar plan (*DBFP*, 2nd ser., xix, no. 488).

22 Sinclair was wrong about this, as Hitler did not approve plans for the invasion of Czechoslovakia until 30 May. See Andrew, *Secret Service*, 392–4. For a valuably sustained assessment of

British intelligence relating to Hitler personally, see Winter, 'British Intelligence'.

23 'What should we do?', 18 Sept. 1938 (TNA, FO 371/21659).

24 Moravec's version is in his memoir, *Master of Spies*, ch. 12.

25 'Germany: factors, aims, methods, etc', enc. with Sinclair to Jebb, 21 Dec. 1938 (TNA, FO 1093/86); Cabinet Committee on Foreign Policy, 'Possible German Intentions', memo by the Foreign Secretary, 19 Jan. 1939 (FP(36)74) (TNA, CAB 27/627).

26 Cabinet minutes, 30 Mar. (TNA, CAB 23/98/16(39)); FO tel. to Berlin and Rome, 9 May and 'Bogus Cabinet decision', 7 July 1939 (TNA, FO 1093/87).

27 Darwin diary, 22 Aug.; Darwin to Sibyl Darwin, 23 Aug. 1939 (Darwin papers, 62/218/1, box 1).

28 The history of the Industrial Intelligence Centre, and Morton's part in it, is very reliably covered in Bennett, *Churchill's Man of Mystery*, 135–75.

29 Undated note, with Vivian to Medlicott (APOC), 13 Aug. 1931 (BP Archive, arc Ref 129910).

30 Sinclair to Crowe, 17 May; minute by Hankey, 21 May 1932 (TNA, CAB 127/371).

31 Cohen, TS memoir, 1900–84 (Cohen papers).

32 Ibid.

33 For Stephenson's links with SIS (and Desmond Morton), see Bennett, *Churchill's Man of Mystery*, 218–20.

34 Denniston, 'Government Code and Cypher School', 52; Andrew, 'F. H. Hinsley and the Cambridge moles', 34.

35 Property transfer documents from Land Registry (Leicester Office), Bletchley Park, Title no. BM677; Sinclair's will, 4 Nov. 1938.

36 Denniston, 'Government Code and Cypher School', 68.

37 For Section D and origins of SOE, see Seaman (ed.), *Special Operations Executive*.

38 Compte-rendu de Mission à Londres, 30 jan.–1 fév. 1939 (SHD (Terre), 7NN2502, dr 250).

39 Hinsley, *British Intelligence*, i, 28–30.

CHAPTER 10: KEEPING AFLOAT

1 Darwin diary (Darwin papers, 62/218/1, box 1).

2 This notice was eventually circulated on 5 Oct.

3 The circulation list appended to this message did not include Poland, while Germany was crossed off.

4 According to the death certificate, Sinclair died of 'I(a) Exhaustion, (b) Malignant Tumour of the spleen [and] II Broncho-pneumonia'.

5 *The Times*, 8 Nov. 1939; Darwin diary, 4 Nov. 1939 (1939 (Darwin papers, 62/218/1, box 1); Cadogan diary, 30–31 Oct., 4 Nov. 1939 (Cadogan papers, ACAD 1/8); Sinclair to Cadogan (and copies to Wilson and Ironside), 3 Nov. 1939 (PUSD papers, FCO).

6 Wilson to Cadogan, 7 Nov.; Cadogan to Sir R. Carter (Admiralty), Sir P. J. Grigg (War Office) and Sir A. Street (Air Ministry), 9 Nov.; Grigg to Cadogan, 14 Nov.; Kingsley Wood (Air Minister) to Halifax, [13] Nov.; Churchill to Cadogan, 18 Nov. (PUSD papers, FCO; a typescript copy of this letter dated 19 Nov. is in the Churchill papers, CHAR 19/2A, fols 102–3); Cadogan diary, 19 Nov. 1939 (Cadogan papers, ACAD 1/8).

7 *The Times*, 30 June 1945; note by Cadogan, 22 Nov. 1939 (PUSD papers, FCO).

8 Note by Cadogan, n.d. (PUSD papers, FCO); Cadogan diary, 16 Nov. 1939 (Cadogan papers, ACAD 1/8). For Dansey's alleged ambitions, see Read and Fisher, *Colonel Z*, 195–200.

9 Cadogan diary, 27–28 Nov. (Cadogan papers, ACAD 1/8); note by Halifax, 29 Nov. (PUSD papers, FCO); John Darwin diary, 1 and 2 Dec. 1939 (Darwin papers, 62/218/1, box 1).

10 Liddell diary, 24 Nov. 1939 (TNA, KV 4/185).

11 For the crucial Polish role in informing British efforts to crack German codes, see Hinsley, *British Intelligence*, ii, part 2, 945–59.

12 Roskill, *War at Sea*, i, 100.

13 Roskill, *Hankey: Man of Secrets*, ii, 447.

14 'Summary of evidence supplied to Lord Hankey', n.d.; Godfrey to Hankey, 2 Feb. (PUSD papers, FCO).

15 'Sources of information', memo by NID, 2 Feb. 1940 (ibid.).

16 Though he can scarcely have been unaware of Buss's criticisms of SIS, Menzies told Guy Liddell of MI5 that he thought Buss was 'sound though perhaps not very convincing in his general manner' (Liddell diary, 23 Feb. 1940, TNA, KV 4/185).

17 By this Godfrey meant all intelligence material gathered from wireless sources. See the discussion of definitions in Hinsley, *British Intelligence*, i, 20–1.

18 'The Secret Services. Inquiry by the Minister without Portfolio. First report', 11 Mar.; Menzies to Jebb, 14 Feb. 1940 (TNA, CAB 127/376).

19 This was from the interception and assessment of German 'use of radio aids for navigation and low-grade tactical transmissions for such things as weather and reconnaissance reports' (see Hinsley, *British Intelligence*, i, 107–8).

20 Ibid., 91–2.

21 Hoare to Hankey and reply, 23 and 24 Apr.; Hankey to Menzies, 24 Apr. 1940 (TNA, CAB 127/375 (files retained by Cabinet Office)).

22 Hankey to Hoare, 24 Apr. 1940. (ibid.).

23 Hankey to Horace Wilson, 29 Apr.; Wilson to H. L. Ismay, 1 May 1940 (ibid.). The wartime development of the JIC will be covered in Michael Goodman's forthcoming Official History.

24 Blake, 'How Churchill became Prime Minister', 273. For Morton's position generally, see Bennett, *Churchill's Man of Mystery*, chs 10–11.

25 First meeting of Secret Service Committee, 3 June 1940 (PUSD papers, FCO).

26 Henry Hopkinson (private secretary to PUS) to Cadogan, 9 Aug. 1940 (ibid.).

27 Minute by Eric Seal, 28 Sept. 1940 (TNA, PREM 4/80/3); Dalton diary, 29 Apr. 1941 (Dalton papers, DALTON/1/24). In Oct. 1940 Menzies stopped regularly sending Morton specific reports, providing him thereafter only with political and military weekly summaries.

28 Hinsley, *British Intelligence*, i, 156.

29 Menzies to Hopkinson, 2 Oct. 1940 (PUSD papers, FCO).

30 Minute by Cadogan, 7 Oct.; Bridges to Hopkinson (in which he quotes Ismay's views), 10 Oct. 1940 (ibid.).

31 Cadogan to Bridges, 14 Oct. 1940 (ibid.).

32 Bridges to Cadogan, 13 Dec.; minute by Hopkinson, 14 Dec. 1940 (ibid.).

33 Second meeting of Secret Service Committee, 19 Mar. 1941 (ibid.).

34 Jebb to Cadogan, 13 June 1940 (ibid.).

35 Dalton, *Fateful Years*, 366. The formation of SOE is reliably covered in Seaman (ed.), *Special Operations Executive*.

36 This memo was endorsed by Menzies and Nelson on 4 May.

37 Memo by Dansey, 11 May 1943 (PUSD papers, FCO).

38 Selborne to Eden, 31 Mar. 1942, enclosing notes by Nelson and Jebb (ibid.).

39 Memo by Selborne, 22 Apr. (TNA, CAB 66/23, WP(42)170); Menzies to Peter Loxley

(Foreign Office), 27 Apr.; unsigned note [probably by Loxley] to Cadogan, 13 May 1942 (PUSD papers, FCO); 'S.O.E. and S.I.S. co-ordination', memo by Joint Planning Staff (final version), 15 May 1941 (TNA, CAB 84/45, JP(42)502).

40 Petrie to Lord Swinton, 30 Jan. 1941, quoted in GC&CS, 'Secret Service Sigint', vol. 1 (TNA, HW 43/6).

41 Ibid.

42 There is a marvellously vivid and detailed account of Section VIII's activities in Pidgeon, *Secret Wireless War*.

43 See Vivian to Menzies, 6 Jan. 1941 (reproduced in Cecil, '"C"'s war', 184–7).

44 For Slocum see Richards, *Secret Flotillas*, i, ch. 3.

45 Cadogan to Menzies and Service Directors of Intelligence, 10 Feb. 1942 (TNA, ADM 223/851).

46 Cadogan to Menzies, 3 July 1945 (PUSD papers, FCO); Cecil, '"C"'s war', 180; Reilly TS memoir (Reilly papers, Ms Eng. c. 6875).

47 Beddington, 'Memoirs', p. 276 (Beddington papers).

48 Cadogan (FO) to Menzies, 10 Feb. 1942, quoted in memo by DDMI(F), 7 Jan. 1945 (PUSD papers, FCO).

49 Biographical information on Kendall from 'The adventurous senator', *People* (Sydney, NSW), vol. 3, no. 21 (17 Dec. 1952), 38–41.

50 SIS evinced renewed interest in Ramsay in 1947, when his foreign-language skills might have been more useful. But he proved to be a recidivist and to 'great disappointment' it was learned that he was 'in Leeds Prison and will be there until 1950. I am afraid, therefore,' continued the file note, 'that we cannot consider him further. I had so very much hoped that he had changed his ways of life and could be of some use to his country.' Ramsay/Ramensky became something of a popular hero in Scotland, and has an entry in the *Oxford Dictionary of National Biography*.

Chapter 11: The European theatre

1 *The Times*, 4 Mar. and 21 Sept. 1939. There is a vivid participant account of the retreat in Wilkinson and Bright Astley, *Gubbins and SOE*, 41–5.

2 Margaret Reid and Leif C. Holstead, 'April 1940: A War Diary', 100–1 (Reid papers, MS 708/3). Foley's signals were circulated quite widely in London; see TNA, WO 106/6100 and FO 371/24834.

3 Jones recounted his wartime intelligence experiences in *Most Secret War* and *Reflections on Intelligence*.

4 The intensity of Swedish vigilance, both during the war and after, is illustrated by the detailed surveillance reports in 'Underrättelstjänst och sabotage: Brittisk underrättelstjänst [Intelligence and sabotage: British intelligence service]', vols 16 and 17, *c.* 1939–50 (Swedish Krigsarkivet).

5 For the Swedish security context, see Denham, *Inside the Nazi Ring* and McKay, *From Information to Intrigue*.

6 Mallet to Jebb (FO), 12 May 1940 (PUSD papers, FCO). The Rickman affair may be followed in Cruickshank, *SOE in Scandinavia*.

7 For Szymańska, see Garliński, *Swiss Corridor*, 84–92, which is in part based on interviews with Szymańska in 1979. Garliński's narrative does not consistently match the evidence in the SIS archives.

8 Hinsley, *British Intelligence*, i, 56–7.

9 Best provided his own account in *The Venlo Incident*.

10 Because rationing applied to clothes, SIS had to arrange a special issue of clothing coupons for the agent to purchase the evening dress. See also Hazelhoff, *Soldier of Orange*, 100–16.

11 For SOE see Foot, *SOE in the Low Countries*.

12 See, for example, Service Clarence reports nos 1–45 (Feb. 1941–May 1942) (Service Clarence papers, box 1).

13 The Belgian side is reliably covered in Debruyne, *Guerre secrète*.

14 Richards, *Secret Flotillas*, i, 13–15, 32–61. Mme de Gaulle, in fact, had already managed to escape.

15 Menzies to Hopkinson (FO), 2 Apr. 1941 (PUSD papers, FCO).

16 De Young de la Marck, 'De Gaulle, Colonel Passy and British intelligence'. For a dramatically reconstructed account, see Fourcade, *L'Arche de Noé*.

17 Hinsley, *British Intelligence*, ii, 248–9.

18 Polish intelligence work in Occupied Europe is very extensively covered in Stirling *et al.* (eds), *Intelligence Co-operation*.

19 There is background information about A.54 in Moravec, *Master of Spies*.

20 Templewood, *Ambassador on Special Mission*, 132–3; for an account of Hillgarth's role, in the context of naval attachés generally, see McLachlan, *Room 39*, 186–207.

21 Hoare to Eden, 27 July, and to Cadogan, 8 Aug; Eden to Hoare, 4 Aug. 1941 (PUSD papers, FCO).

22 *Daily Telegraph*, 14 Aug. 1941; minutes by J. M. Addis and Menzies, 15 Aug. 1941 (PUSD papers, FCO).

23 Madrid to FO, 18 Oct. 1941 (PUSD papers, FCO). For Clarke, see Howard, *British Intelligence*, v, pp. xi–xii, 33; Holt, *Deceivers*; and Mure, *Master of Deception*.

24 Menzies to Loxley (FO), 13 Nov.; Hoare to Cadogan, 8 Dec. 1941; Hoare to Cadogan, 6 Jan.; minutes by Roger Makins and Peter Loxley, 8 Jan.; Cadogan to Hoare, 9 Jan. 1942 (PUSD papers, FCO).

25 Menzies to Cavendish-Bentinck, Loxley (two letters), 9 Mar., 19 Apr. and 21 Dec.; FO and Madrid tels, May–June 1942 (PUSD papers, FCO). See also Erskine, 'Eavesdropping on "Bodden"'.

26 Johns's version of events is in his memoir, *Within Two Cloaks*, 67–116.

27 Foot and Langley, *MI9*, 43. My account of MI9 is substantially based on this work, in which the authors were unable to reveal the true extent of SIS's involvement with the organisation.

CHAPTER 12: FROM BUDAPEST TO BAGHDAD

1 The agent, for whom three months' payment of £200 per month was authorised in July 1939, ran at least eight sub-agents.

2 For the situation and British policy generally in the region see Barker, *British Policy in South-East Europe*.

3 Memo by Lord Hankey, 24 May 1940 (TNA, CAB 127/375 (files retained in Cabinet Office)); Rendel to Cadogan, 11 Feb. 1940 (PUSD papers, FCO).

4 In 1942 the agent was awarded an honorary MBE, and in 1944 a DSO.

5 Hinsley, *British Intelligence*, i, 368–73. For the coup, see Onslow, 'Britain and the Belgrade *coup*'.

6 'German offensive plans' by 'M.W.', 31 Dec. 1940 (PUSD papers, FCO). For the discussions about German intentions, see Hinsley, *British Intelligence*, i, ch. 11.

7 For the diplomatic context, see Woodward, *British Foreign Policy*, 12–15.

8 Despite these views, Hugessen was not beyond asking Gibson in Dec. 1943 if he could find a job in SIS for his daughter.

9 For Polish intelligence work in the Middle East and Central Asia, see Stirling *et al.* (eds), *Intelligence Co-operation*, chs 39–41.

10 Biographical information on Mounier from 'Order of the Liberation website' www.ordredelaliberation.fr (accessed 4 Oct. 2007).

11 For the LRDG see National Archives, *Special Forces in the Desert War* and Shelly, 'British Intelligence in the Middle East', 95–8.

12 For security organisation in the Middle East, see Hinsley and Simkins, *British Intelligence*, iv, 149–53.

13 See, for example, Menzies to Peter Loxley (FO), copies to Morton, 9, 11 and 19 May 1942 (PUSD papers, FCO).

14 *The Times*, 6 May 1941.

CHAPTER 13: WEST AND EAST

1 Stephenson has been the subject of much speculative writing. For a forensic assessment of the literature, see Naftali, 'Intrepid's last deception', and Thomas Troy's commentary thereon in *Wild Bill and Intrepid*, esp. 192–201.

2 Bennett, *Churchill's Man of Mystery*, 193–4, 218–20 and 253–7, reliably traces Stephenson's gradual incorporation into SIS. Troy, *Wild Bill and Intrepid* is also well researched, though there is no evidence in the SIS archives that Stephenson was ever known by the code-name Intrepid.

3 Federal Bureau of Investigation, 'British Intelligence Service in the United States (Running Memorandum)', 1 Jan. 1947 (Freedom of Information Act Release, 2009), p. 1.

4 Menzies to Jebb, 3 June 1940 (PUSD papers, FCO).

5 Menzies to Jebb, 21 June 1940 (ibid.).

6 Lothian to Halifax (Foreign Secretary), 10 and 11 July (TNA, FO 371/24237); note by Admiral Godfrey (DNI), 2 Aug. 1940 (TNA, ADM 223/84).

7 Seven months later Menzies asserted that it was Donovan who had made the 'fifty pats on the back' remark (Menzies to Hopkinson (FO), 2 Apr. 1941 (PUSD papers, FCO)).

8 Menzies to Hopkinson (FO), 30 Oct.; to Beaumont-Nesbitt (DMI), 22 Nov.; and to Churchill, 29 Nov. 1940; Churchill minute, n.d.; unsigned minute, n.d. (ibid.).

9 Menzies to Churchill, 26 Feb., and Churchill minute, 27 Feb. (TNA, HW 1/2); Menzies to Hopkinson, 2 Apr. 1941 (PUSD papers, FCO).

10 'History of the S.I.S. Division' (FBI internal history, 3 vols) (NARA, RG 65, WW2 FBI HQ files, box 17).

11 Details of the arrangements for Donovan's trip are in TNA, FO 371/26194; and Eden to Sir M. Lampson (Cairo) and Sir M. Plairet (Athens), 24 Dec. 1940 (TNA, FO 371/24263).

12 Troy, *Wild Bill and Intrepid*, 74–5.

13 Godfrey, 'Memoirs', vol. 5, part 1, 132–7 (Godfrey papers, MSS 319).

14 Quoted in Stafford, *Roosevelt & Churchill*, 213.

15 Report on visit to U.S.A., 30 Sept. to 11 Oct. 1941, by F. T. Davies, 15 Oct. 1941 (PUSD papers, FCO).

16 These events were rather more vividly described by Cynthia herself (written with the help of Montgomery Hyde) in *France Dimanche*, nos 899 and 900, 14 and 21 Nov. 1963. Hyde's book *The Quiet Canadian* draws extensively on the BSC History and includes pictures of the Vichy cyphers.

17 For the *Graf Spee* action and ocean warfare in 1940 see Roskill, *War at Sea*, i, chs 7 and 14.
18 The company concerned did not (alas) trade in vacuum cleaners.
19 A microfilm copy of the letter was supplied to the embassy by an Associated Press journalist; see Rio embassy to Washington, 12 Nov. 1941 (NARA, M1515 Brazil microfilms, reel 71).
20 The wartime context and intelligence challenges in the Far East are very well covered in Aldrich, *Intelligence and the War against Japan*.
21 *The Times*, 23 Sept. 1940.
22 'S.I.S. in the Far East', 15 July 1940 (TNA, ADM 223/496).

CHAPTER 14: THE TIDE TURNS

1 Peter Koch de Gooreynd (PA to CSS) to Peter Loxley, 3 Jan. 1944 (PUSD papers, FCO).
2 Menzies to Harold Caccia (FO), 20 Mar. 1946 (ibid.). The DGER was the newly created postwar Direction Générale des Études et Recherches.
3 Cecil, '"C"'s war', 180.
4 Peake was a director of his family colliery business and also of Lloyds Bank (of which he was later chairman). For Foley's concerns see above p. 419.
5 Cecil, '"C"'s war', 177.
6 Training Sheet for Per Ingebrightsen, Apr. 1943 (Norges Hjemmefront Museum, Oslo, FO II/8.5 Daec 0002 Diverse).
7 Menzies to Cadogan, 2 Nov. 1944 (PUSD papers, FCO).
8 Cecil, 'Five of Six at war', 348 (which draws on information made available to Cecil by Cowgill himself).
9 Hinsley and Simkins, *British Intelligence*, iv, 132–7, covers this and other aspects of SIS–MI5 relations.
10 Petrie to Menzies (with attachment), 17 Apr., and reply, 11 May 1942 (TNA, KV 4/120). For the internal organisation of MI5 during the Second World War, see Andrew, *Defence of the Realm*, Section C.
11 Cecil, 'Five of Six at war', 347; Hinsley and Simkins, *British Intelligence*, iv, 137.
12 Hinsley, *British Intelligence*, ii, 18–19.
13 Biographical information on Coggia from 'Order of the Liberation website' www.ordredela-liberation.fr (accessed 4 Oct. 2007). For Jones in captivity, see Bethge, *Dietrich Bonhoeffer*, 850–1; Wood (ed.), *Detour*, 103–4 and plate 13; and Pringle, *Colditz Last Stop*, 146–9.
14 Verstraete is identified as an SIS agent in Richards, *Secret Flotillas*, ii, 205, 366, 381.
15 Paillole, *Services spéciaux*, 429–34.
16 For Bowlby's prediction, see above p. 425.
17 The sports equipment arrived towards the end of December 1943.
18 The circumstances of Costa Lawrence's death are disputed, as noted in Nigel Clive's engrossing memoir, *A Greek Experience*.
19 See Baxter, 'Sir Hughe Knatchbull-Hugessen' and 'Forgeries and spies'.
20 Howard, *British Intelligence*, v, 49–50; see also Hinsley and Simkins, *British Intelligence*, iv, 211–12.
21 The Heinkel He-177 Griffon heavy bomber was, in fact, a spectacular German design failure.

CHAPTER 15: FROM SWITZERLAND TO NORMANDY

1 'Information received from Source JX/Knopf from Feb. 1942 to Apr. 1943' (TNA, WO 208/4309). For German counter-intelligence efforts against Choynacki, see Laqueur and Breitman, *Breaking the Silence*, 174–7.

2 Gisevius's version of events is in his memoir, *To the Bitter End*, for which Allen Dulles wrote an introduction.

3 Hinsley and Simkins, *British Intelligence*, iv, 200–1; see also McKay, 'Krämer case'. The MI5 side of things can be followed in TNA, KV 2/144–57.

4 See Thomas, 'Norway's role in British wartime intelligence', 124–6. Original SIS ship watchers' reports have survived in Norway. See, for example, Jan.–July 1943 in Norges Hjemmefront Museum, Oslo, FO II/8.6 N-RAP, box 17.

5 Olsen wrote a memoir of his activities, *Two Eggs on my Plate*.

6 Mackenzie, *Secret History of SOE*, 299–300.

7 For examples of other SIS work against German air defences see Hinsley, *British Intelligence*, ii, 248–52.

8 See, for example, Service Clarence reports nos 56–142, Aug. 1942–Mar. 1944 (Service Clarence papers, boxes 2–5).

9 For Ascension generally, see Pidgeon, *Secret Wireless War*.

10 'No path of flowers leads to glory' (from Lafontaine's *Fables*, x, 14).

11 Rémy, *Livre du courage*, ii, 60–2, gives a French perspective.

12 Fourcade's account is in her memoir, *L'Arche de Noé*, 339–452.

13 Lubicz's network is reported to have grown to 1,500 members during 1944 (see Stirling *et al.* (eds), *Intelligence Co-operation*, 242).

14 For the Polish involvement see ibid., 221–3. Czerniawski was also known as 'Armand Walenty' (see TNA, KV 2/72–3).

15 See also Rygor's memoirs, Rygor Słowikowski, *In the Secret Service*, 213.

16 For a further account of V-weapons intelligence, see Hinsley, *British Intelligence*, iii, part 1, 357–414.

17 For the threat from long-range weapons and the Allied response, see Collier, *Defence of the United Kingdom*, 331–421.

18 The intelligence situation during the planning stage and up to D-Day is described in Hinsley, *British Intelligence*, iii, part 2, 10–101.

19 Ibid., ii, 12–13, and iii, part 2, 11–12, 753–5. The Martian reports are in TNA, WO 219/1933–42.

20 See, for example, TNA, WO 208/4312, for MI14 appreciations from 1 Jan. to 11 June 1944. For pre-Mar. 1944 'Summary of MI14 indications files', see TNA, WO 208/4307–12.

21 'Ossex' teams served in the American sector, 'Brissex' in the British.

22 Foot, *SOE in France*, 366.

23 Loxley to Peter Koch de Gooreynd (PA to CSS), 17 Apr. and 7 May, and reply 19 Apr. 1944 (PUSD papers, FCO).

24 Menzies to Loxley, 11 May; minute by Cavendish-Bentinck, 13 May; Thomas Bromley (FO) to Charles Peake (British Political Officer at SHAEF), 16 May 1944 (ibid.).

25 For SCUs, see Pidgeon, *Secret Wireless War*, 67–70.

CHAPTER 16: VICTORY IN EUROPE

1 See, for example, Service Clarence reports nos 131–59 (Jan.–July 1944) (Service Clarence papers, boxes 5–6).

2 Documents from the War Crimes Group's inconclusive investigation of Chamier's fate are in TNA, WO 309/248.

3 Directive for British Section of Allied Control Commission in Finland, 12 Oct. 1944 (TNA, FO 371/43196). See also Magill, *Tasavalta tulikokeessa*, 112.

4   For Krämer see above pp.514–15.
5   For developments in Yugoslavia see Hinsley, *British Intelligence*, iii, part 1, 137–62.
6   Smith, *Sharing Secrets with Stalin*, 41–3. This book is excellent for Anglo-Soviet intelligence relations generally.
7   Menzies to Churchill, 17 July 1941 (TNA, HW 1/14). See also, Hinsley, *British Intelligence*, ii, 59–66.
8   Kitchen, 'SOE's man in Moscow'.
9   It is possible (though there is no indication in the documents that this was suspected by SIS) that these reports were provided with the knowledge of the NKVD.
10 Vivian to Loxley, and reply, 13 and 20 Oct; minute by Sargent, 18 Oct. 1943 (PUSD papers, FCO).
11 Thomas Bromley (FO) to Arnold-Forster (SIS), 8 Sept. 1944 (ibid.).
12 For Garbo, see Howard, *British Intelligence*, v, esp. appendix 2, 231–41.
13 For Ustinov's relations with women, see Ustinov, *Klop*, e.g. 174 and 178.
14 Cholmondeley was one of the brains behind the famous Operation 'Mincemeat' deception scheme in 1942 (Howard, *British Intelligence*, v, 89).
15 'Technische/Luftwaffe' was the Abwehr division devoted to aircraft industry intelligence.

Chapter 17: Asia and the end of the war

1   Publicised in the London *Evening Standard*, 16 Mar. 1942.
2   The provenance and significance of these signals was raised during the US inquiry into the Pearl Harbor disaster.
3   For the Japanese offensive against Thailand and Malaya, see Kirby, *War against Japan*, i, ch. 12.
4   Wilkinson War Journal, 7 Jan. 1943 (Wilkinson papers, WILK 1/1). For Wilkinson, see also Thorne, 'MacArthur, Australia and the British'.
5   Note by Wilkinson, 15 Oct. 1943 (Wilkinson papers, WILK 3/2/1).
6   Thorne, 'MacArthur, Australia and the British', part I, 53 n. 1.
7   Cross, *Red Jungle* provides a personal account.
8   For SOE's intelligence work see Aldrich, *Intelligence and the War against Japan*, 281–4, and for SOE generally see Cruickshank, *SOE in the Far East*.
9   Wilkinson War Journal, 9 July 1943 (Wilkinson papers, WILK 1/2 (closed)).
10 Beddington, 'Memoirs', p. 291 (Beddington papers).
11 For a general review of air operations, see 'Brief history of clandestine air operations in the South East Asia theatre of war', 1 June 1942–31 Aug. 1944; and 'Air operations for clandestine organisations', 1 June 1944–31 May 1945 (TNA, AIR 23/1950).
12 Garnons-Williams to Bowden-Smith and Mackenzie, 16 and 28 Apr. 1945 (TNA, HS 1/304); Aldrich, *Intelligence and the War against Japan*, 220–31.
13 'Co-ordination of British organisations in China', 3 Apr. 1945 (TNA, CAB 81/128, JIC(45)111(O)(final)).

Chapter 18: Postwar planning

1   Duff Cooper to Churchill & reply, 23 Mar. and 4 Apr. 1943 (PUSD papers, FCO).
2   'SOE and SIS co-ordination', 15 May 1942 (TNA, CAB 121/305A, JP(42)502).
3   G. C. Vickers and Capel-Dunn to Cavendish-Bentinck, 24 and 26 May 1943 (PUSD papers, FCO).
4   Diary of Sir Alan Lascelles, 3 Feb. 1945 (quoted in Hart-Davis (ed.), *King's Counsellor*, 291); *The Times*, 8, 9 Feb. 1945.

5 Draft memo by Loxley, n.d. (*c.* June 1943) (PUSD papers, FCO).

6 Minute by Loxley, 30 Aug. 1943 (ibid.).

7 Bland to Cadogan, 13 Oct.; minute by Loxley, 7 Apr. 1944 (ibid.). Ivone Kirkpatrick was also originally included on the committee but because he was unable to attend meetings did not participate.

8 Bland to Cadogan, 13 Oct. 1944 (ibid.).

9 Bland Report (ibid.).

10 At this point on one copy of the report a marginal note by a Foreign Office official reads: 'Most important, otherwise the S.I.S. man abroad will concentrate on what is easy & amusing' (ibid.).

11 Dansey to Loxley, enc. memo, 11 June 1944 (ibid.).

12 Bland Report, unrevised draft (ibid.).

13 Chiefs of Staff memo, 27 May 1945, COS(45)360 (TNA, CAB 80/94 (files retained in Cabinet Office)).

14 Cavendish-Bentinck to Loxley, 15 Apr.; Loxley to Leeper, 27 June 1944 (PUSD papers, FCO).

15 Minute by Menzies, 2 Nov. 1944 (ibid.).

16 Loxley to Menzies, 20 Oct. 1943 (ibid.).

17 Marginal note by Bland on copy of Menzies's minute of 2 Nov. (ibid.).

18 Loxley to Cadogan, 8 Nov. 1944 (ibid.).

19 Draft amendments to report of Bland committee, 7 Dec. 1944 (ibid.).

20 In the final version the phrase 'should always bear in mind . . . should therefore only engage' was recast as: 'should always bear in mind that political ideologies should not be investigated for their own sake alone; and that the S.I.S. should therefore only engage' (TNA, CAB 163/4 (files retained in Cabinet Office)).

21 DMI and DNI to Cavendish-Bentinck, 16 Feb. and 30 Jan. 1945 (ibid.).

22 DMI to Cavendish-Bentinck, 16 Feb. 1945 (ibid.). Sinclair based his remarks on Edward Beddington's comments on the Bland Report: 'the expansion of S.I.S. took place in this war at an impossibly late date, mostly in 1942' (Beddington to Sinclair, 7 Jan. 1945 (PUSD papers, FCO)).

23 DNI to Cavendish-Bentinck, 30 Jan. 1945 (TNA, CAB 163/4 (files retained in Cabinet Office)).

24 'The Intelligence Machine', 10 Jan. 1945 (TNA, CAB 163/6).

CHAPTER 19: ADJUSTING TO PEACE

1 Findlater Stewart report, 27 Nov. 1945 (Cabinet Office papers).

2 From January 1948 the Joint Intelligence Sub-Committee was renamed the Joint Intelligence Committee.

3 Caccia to Sir A. Cadogan, 29 Jan. 1946 (PUSD papers, FCO).

4 Caccia to Sir Orme Sargent, 25 Feb. 1946 (ibid.).

5 Cavendish-Bentinck to Cadogan, 25 June; minutes by Cadogan, Bevin and Attlee, 14, 21, 23 Aug. and 5 Sept.; 'Directive to Special Operations Executive', 10 Nov., COS(45)643(O) annex; minute by Sargent, 28 Nov. 1945 (ibid.).

6 Menzies to Caccia, 30 Jan.; minute by Caccia, 2 Feb.; circular FO telegram, 25 Mar. 1946 (ibid.).

7 Cabinet Office notes on costs of the Secret Service (Cabinet Office papers).

8 COS Committee, 30 Apr. 1947, COS(47) 59th meeting (TNA, DEFE 4/4).

9 Minute by A. V. Alexander, 30 June 1947, COS(47)135(O) (ibid., 5/5).

10 Forty-six meetings of the Regional Controllers were held between 26 Nov. 1945 and 15 Jan. 1947.

11 Sixty-four meetings of the VCSS's Production Conference were held between 21 Jan. 1947 and 6 Dec. 1949. The minutes of these meetings were routinely marked: 'To be destroyed after action taken'. On 2 Mar. 1948 PSO (?Principal Staff Officer) requested that all agenda and minutes of the conferences 'up till end of 1947 should be destroyed and destruction certificates should be rendered'.

12 As follows: R.1 Political; R.2 Air; R.3 Naval; R.4 Military; R.5 Counter-Intelligence; R.6 Economic; R.7 Scientific (from 1948); R.8 Scientific (to 1948), then Liaison; R.9 Co-ordinating (1946–8).

13 Hayter to Sargent, 13 Jan.; Menzies to Hayter, 30 Jan 1947 (PUSD papers, FCO).

14 Sillitoe to Bridges, 11 Nov.; minute by Donaldson, 8 Dec. 1948 (Cabinet Office papers).

15 Notes by Bridges and Donaldson, 23 Dec. 1948 (ibid.).

16 Strang to Menzies, 28 July; Sillitoe to Menzies, 9 Sept. and reply, 28 Sept. 1949 (ibid.).

17 Menzies to Hayter, 17 Apr. 1947 (PUSD papers, FCO).

18 Menzies to Hayter, 17 Jan., enc. memo on 'Future Indian intelligence liaison'; minute by Halford, 22 Jan. 1947 (ibid.).

19 'Future Indian intelligence liaison', by Monteath; Monteath to Bridges, 6 Mar.; Shone to Hayter, n.d. [May]; Menzies to Hayter, 21 June 1947 (ibid.).

20 Posts in the Diplomatic and Consular Services were restricted to men until 1946, and a bar on married women was enforced in the Foreign Office up to 1972 (see McCarthy, 'Petticoat diplomacy').

21 Bland Report, 12 Oct. 1944 (PUSD papers, FCO).

22 Minute by Bridges, 14 Oct. 1946 (Cabinet Office papers).

CHAPTER 20: DEPLOYMENT AND OPERATIONS IN EUROPE

1 Requirements from SIS, 20 June 1946, JIC(46)57(O)Revise (TNA, CAB 81/133 (files retained in Cabinet Office)); Russia committee meeting, 9 Oct. 1947 (TNA, FO 371/66372); Bevin minute, 25 Nov. 1947, CM(47)90 (TNA, CAB 128/10).

2 A restaurant survives to this day at 8 Rue Tournefort.

3 The BEM (British Empire Medal) was a lower grade yet than the MBE.

4 Bland Report, 12 Oct. 1944 (PUSD papers, FCO).

5 Maj. A. E. E. Reade (War Crimes Unit) to Military Department, Judge Advocate-General, 19 Mar. 1948 (TNA, WO 309/248). Some of the results of Kopkow's interrogation are in his MI5 file, TNA, KV 2/1500–1.

6 New York to London telegrams, 9 and 10 Sept. 1945 (PUSD papers, FCO).

7 Moscow to London: Venona decrypt of 1 Feb. 1965 (www.nsa.gov/venona/releases/17_Sept_1945_R5_m5_p1.gif (accessed 27 June 2008)); FO minutes, Sept. 1945 (PUSD papers, FCO).

8 Minutes by Cadogan, 11 and 19 Sept.; brief by Makins, 21 Sept. 1945 (PUSD papers, FCO). For the Council of Foreign Ministers meeting, see Documents on British Policy Overseas, ser. 1, vol.ii.

9 New York–London telegrams, 11–13 Sept. 1945; minutes by Cadogan and Bevin, 27 and 28 Sept. 1945 (PUSD papers, FCO).

10 'One cannot make an intelligence service with a parish priest.' Menzies to Caccia, 8 Mar. 1946 (ibid.).

11 Caccia to Menzies, 12 Mar. 1946 (ibid.).

12 'Revised directive to Special Operations', 18 Feb. 1946, COS(46)50(O) (TNA, CAB 80/99); FO circular tel., 25 Mar. 1946 (PUSD papers, FCO); Slessor to Sir James Robb (Vice Chief of the Air Staff), 21 Jan. 1948 (TNA, AIR 75/116, JCS 37). For Slessor, see Aldrich, *Hidden Hand*, 145–6.

13 See History of SOE's German Directorate (TNA, HS 7/145–8). On ME42 and Bonzos, see TNA, HS 6/689–90, and Rigden, *How to be a Spy*, 10.

14 Report by Lewis, 1 July 1946 (USA, NARA, RG226, 214/4/29). For the long-term tasking of the Control Commission, see Donnison, *Civil Affairs*, 195.

15 Foreign Office minutes, Apr.–May, Sargent to Menzies and reply (with Hayter minute), 14 and 16 June 1948 (PUSD papers, FCO).

16 Minutes by Garvey and Hayter, 7 and 11 Nov. 1947 (ibid.).

17 Minute by Speaight and Cavendish-Bentinck, 7 and 9 Oct. 1944 (ibid.).

18 Minutes by Loxley and Cadogan, 10, 13 and 20 Oct.; Cadogan to Menzies, 18 Oct.; Cohen (for Menzies) to Bromley (FO), 24 Dec. 1944; Duff Cooper to Cadogan, 17 Oct. 1945 (ibid.).

19 Minute by Halford, 17 June; Hayter to Manzies, 28 June 1948 (ibid.).

20 HO minutes and Paris–London correspondence, 7 May–21 June 1948 (ibid.).

21 See, for example, 'Underrättstjänst och sabotage: Brittisk underrättstjänst' (Intelligence and sabotage: British intelligence service), vols 16 and 17 (Krigsarkivet, Swedish National Archives).

22 Aspects of Communist activity in late 1940s Norway, and their ramifications in Britain, are explored in Insall, 'Relationship between the British and Norwegian Labour parties from 1945 to 1951'.

23 For the Norwegian side, see Riste, *Norwegian Intelligence Service*, 1–33.

Chapter 21: A worldwide Service

1 Andrew, *Defence of the Realm*, 352–66; Walton, 'British Intelligence and the Mandate of Palestine'.

2 For a cool and painstaking study of the problem, see Liebreich, *Britain's Naval and Political Reaction to the Illegal Immigration of Jews to Palestine*.

3 Menzies to Hayter, 19 Dec. 1946, enclosing 'Proposals for action' (PUSD papers, FCO).

4 Hayter to Menzies, 24 Feb. 1947 (ibid.).

5 For press coverage of the affair, see *The Times*, 19, 21 July, and *New York Times*, 21–22, 30 July 1947.

6 *The Times*, 28 July, 8 Oct. and 16 Nov. 1948.

7 Corres. between Sargent and Menzies, Jan.–Feb. 1948 (PUSD papers, FCO).

8 The general context in the region is admirably covered in Baxter, *Great Power Struggle in East Asia*.

9 For Blake, see Andrew, *Defence of the Realm*, 488–91.

10 CX reports and War Office minutes, Feb.–Sept. 1949 (War Office papers retained in Ministry of Defence).

11 Moscow to London and reply, 2 and 5 Apr. 1946 (PUSD papers, FCO).

12 Russia committee meeting, 25 Nov. 1948 (TNA, FO 371/71687, RC(48)16). The context of British policy-making on special operations against Communist states is usefully outlined in Aldrich, *Hidden Hand*, ch. 6.

13 'Communist action in Albania', memo by I. F. Porter, 3 Feb.; Sargent to Menzies, 18 Feb.;

Menzies to Sir William Strang (FO), 4 Mar. 1949 (PUSD papers, FCO).

14 Strang to Menzies, 28 Apr.; FO minutes, May; 'Albanian plan', 16 June; report on Operation Valuable, Dec. 1949 (ibid.).

15 Minute by A. Rumbold, 15 Nov. 1949 (ibid.).

CHAPTER 22: SIS: LEADERSHIP AND PERFORMANCE OVER THE FIRST FORTY YEARS

1 Churchill, *World Crisis*, 406.

2 *The Times*, 2 June 1915; Walter Kirke, 'Lieut.-Gen. Sir George M. W. Macdonogh' (*c.* July 1947) (Kirke papers (IWM), WMK 12, folder VI).

3 The relevant records are in TNA, ADM 116/1265/B.

4 Menzies to Wilson, 6 Sept. 1940 (PUSD papers, FCO).

5 Knoblock, *Round the Room*, 257.

6 Williams, *World of Action*, 335–6.

7 Dukes, *Story of 'ST 25'*, 35.

8 Knoblock, *Round the Room*, 257. From 1910 to 1914 eight issues a year of *Le Nu au Salon par Georges Normandy* (continuing a series initiated by the French poet Armande Silvestre in the 1880s) were published in Paris, containing reproductions of 'tasteful' pictures and sculptures of nude women, few of them by artists of the first rank.

9 A couple of entries in Walter Kirke's diary, at a time when Cumming felt keenly under assault from the military authorities, are the only suggestions that he might have been out for 'self aggrandisement' (27 May and 23 July 1916, quotation from 27 May) (Kirke papers (IWM), 82/28/1).

10 Secret Service Committee 1931, notes of meetings (27 Apr., 11 and 22 June) (TNA, FO 1093/74).

11 Menu cards and associated papers, 16 Aug. 1928 and 18 July 1935; Noble to Sinclair, 19 July 1935 (Sinclair papers MS 81/091, scrapbook vol. 1).

12 O'Halpin, *Head of the Civil Service*, 95.

13 Trevor-Roper, *Philby Affair*, 72.

14 Howarth, *Intelligence Chief Extraordinary*, p. 115.

15 Beddington, 'Memoirs', p. 276 (Beddington papers).

16 TS memoirs, fols 207–9 (Reilly papers, MS. Eng. c. 6918).

17 Cadogan diary, 5 Nov. 1942 (Cadogan papers, ACAD 1/11).

18 TS memoirs, fol. 213 (Reilly papers, MS. Eng. c. 6918).

19 Rivet diary, 12–24 Dec. 1942, quoted in Rivet, *Carnets secrets 1936–1944*.

20 Cecil, '"C"'s war', 181; Cadogan diary, 7 Dec. 1944 (Cadogan papers, ACAD 1/11); Winterbotham, *Ultra Secret*, p. 99); Paillole, *Services spéciaux*, 429–34.

21 This argument is advanced (for example) in Trevor-Roper, *Philby Affair*, 73–4.

22 The 1941–2 organisation of GC&CS is covered in Hinsley, *British Intelligence*, i, 271–4; ii, 21–7.

23 A. M. Turing *et al.* to Churchill, 21 Oct.; minutes by Churchill and Ismay, 22 Oct. and 19 Nov. 1941 (TNA, HW 1/155). Documents in the SIS archive show Menzies himself (before the code-breakers' letter to Churchill) appealing to higher authority to secure priority equipment and accommodation for Bletchley Park.

24 Hinsley, *British Intelligence*, iii, part 1, 461. Menzies's reorganisation was (curiously) drafted on the back of a racehorse sales catalogue dated 9 Sept. 1926 (TNA, HW 14/27).

25 Trevor-Roper, *Philby Affair*, 73.

26 Minute by Hayter, 30 Apr. 1949 (PUSD papers, FCO).
27 Minutes by Caccia, Aubrey Halford, Hayter and Strang, 2, 17 May, 5, 7, 8 and 14 July 1949 (ibid.).
28 He quoted this in a memo of 14 Feb. 1940.
29 670 officers; 900 'secretaries and clerks'; 800 'others'.

Bibliography

Public archives

(a) United Kingdom
India Office Records (IOR), British Library.
United Kingdom National Archives (TNA), Kew, England, coded as follows:
   ADM: Admiralty
   AIR: Air Ministry
   ASSI: Assizes records
   CAB: Cabinet Office
   CO: Colonial Office
   CRIM: Central Criminal Court
   DEFE: Ministry of Defence
   FO: Foreign Office
   HO: Home Office
   HS: Special Operations Executive
   HW: Government Communications Headquarters
   J: Supreme Court of Judicature
   KV: Security Service
   MUN: Ministry of Munitions
   PREM: Prime Minister's Office
   T: Treasury
   WO: War Office

(b) Foreign
Krigsarkivet, Swedish National Archives, Stockholm.
Norges Hjemmefront Museum, Oslo.
Service Historique de la Défense, fonds de l'Armée de Terre (SHD (Terre)), Château de Vincennes,
   France.
United States National Archives (NARA), College Park, Maryland.

Private papers and other collections

Balfour papers (British Library).
Beddington papers (Liddell Hart Centre for Military Archives, King's College London).
Bland papers (Churchill Archives Centre, Cambridge).
BP Archive (University of Warwick).

Cadogan papers (Churchill Archives Centre, Cambridge).

Churchill papers (Churchill Archives Centre, Cambridge).

Cohen papers (in private hands).

Curzon papers (India Office Records, British Library).

Dalton papers (London School of Economics).

Darwin papers (Imperial War Museum).

Derby papers (Liverpool Record Office).

Dewé papers (Archives famille Dewé se rapportant à Walthère Dewé), CEGES (Centre d'Études et de Documentation Guerre et Sociétés contemporaines), Brussels.

Edmonds papers (Liddell Hart Centre for Military Archives, King's College London).

Godfrey papers, including 'The Naval Memoirs of Admiral J. H. Godfrey' (8 vols, typescript) (Royal Naval Museum, Portsmouth, MSS 319) [Another copy in Churchill Archives Centre, Cambridge].

House papers (Yale University Library).

Kirke papers (Imperial War Museum (IWM) and Intelligence Corps Museum (ICM)).

Kirkpatrick papers (Imperial War Museum).

La Dame Blanche papers (Imperial War Museum).

Lloyd George papers (Parliamentary Archives).

Long papers (Wiltshire Record Office).

Mackenzie papers (Harry Ransom Humanities Research Center, University of Texas at Austin).

Payne Best papers (Imperial War Museum (IWM) and Intelligence Corps Museum (ICM)).

Polk papers (Yale University Library).

Reid papers: Letters and Papers of Margaret Grant Reid (Leeds University Library).

Reilly papers (Bodleian Library, Oxford).

Rumbold papers (Bodleian Library, Oxford).

Service Clarence papers (Imperial War Museum).

Sinclair papers (National Maritime Museum).

Sudan Archive (University of Durham).

Templewood (Sir Samuel Hoare) papers (Cambridge University Library).

Vansittart papers (Churchill Archives Centre, Cambridge).

Wilkinson papers (Churchill Archives Centre, Cambridge).

Wilson papers (Imperial War Museum).

Wiseman papers (Yale University Library).

Woollcombe papers (in private hands).

Printed primary sources

Documents on British Foreign Policy

Documents on British Policy Overseas

Published works and theses

Agar, Augustus, *Baltic Episode: A Classic of Secret Service in Russian Waters* (London, 1963).

Aldrich, Richard J., *The Hidden Hand: Britain, America and Cold War Secret Intelligence (London, 2001)*.

— *Intelligence and the War against Japan: Britain, America and the Politics of Secret Service* (Cambridge, 2000).

Andrew, Christopher, 'The British Secret Service and Anglo-Soviet relations in the 1920s, Part I: From the trade negotiations to the Zinoviev Letter', *Historical Journal*, 20/3 (1977), 673–706.

— *The Defence of the Realm: The Authorized History of MI5* (London, 2009) [published in the USA as *Defend the Realm*].

— 'F. H. Hinsley and the Cambridge moles: two patterns of intelligence recruitment', in Richard Langhorne (ed.), *Diplomacy and Intelligence during the Second World War: Essays in Honour of F. H. Hinsley* (Cambridge, 1985), 22–40.

— *For the President's Eyes Only: Secret Intelligence and the American Presidency from Washington to Bush* (London, 1995).

— *Secret Service: The Making of the British Intelligence Community* (London, 1985) [published in the USA as *Her Majesty's Secret Service: The Making of the British Intelligence Community*].

— and Dilks, David (eds), *The Missing Dimension: Governments and Intelligence Communities in the Twentieth Century* (London, 1984).

— and Noakes, Jeremy (eds), *Intelligence and International Relations, 1900–1945* (Exeter, 1987).

Aubin, Chantal, 'Contre-espionnage et sécurité intérieure pendant les années 1930: structures, défis et réponses', in Frédéric Guelton et Abdil Bicer (eds), *Naissance et évolution du renseignement dans l'espace européen (1870–1940)* (Vincennes, 2006), 247–76.

Barker, Elisabeth, *British Policy in South-East Europe in the Second World War* (London, 1976).

Baxter, Christopher, 'Forgeries and spies: the Foreign Office and the "Cicero" case', *Intelligence and National Security*, 23/6 (Dec. 2008), 807–26.

— *The Great Power Struggle in East Asia, 1944–50: Britain, America and Post-War Rivalry* (Basingstoke, 2009).

— 'The Secret Intelligence Service and the case of Hilaire Noulens', in FCO Historians, *Records*, 54–64.

— 'Sir Hughe Knatchbull-Hugessen and Turkish neutrality, 1942–1944', in Christopher Baxter and Andrew Stewart (eds), *Diplomats at War: British and Commonwealth Diplomacy in Wartime* (Leiden, 2008), 253–74.

Bazhanov, Boris, *Bazhanov and the Damnation of Stalin,* ed. David W. Doyle (Athens, Ohio, 1990).

Beach, James, 'British Intelligence and the German Army, 1914–1918' (PhD thesis, London University, 2005).

Bennett, Gill, *'A most extraordinary and mysterious business': The Zinoviev Letter of 1924* (London, 1999).

— *Churchill's Man of Mystery: Desmond Morton and the World of Intelligence* (London, 2006).

Benton, Kenneth, 'The ISOS years: Madrid 1941–3', *Journal of Contemporary History*, 30/3 (July 1995), 355–410.

Bertrand, Gustave, *Enigma ou la plus grande énigme de la guerre 1939–1945* (Paris, 1973).

Best, Antony, *British Intelligence and the Japanese Challenge in Asia, 1914–1941* (Basingstoke, 2002).

— 'Intelligence, diplomacy and the Japanese threat to British interests, 1914–41', *Intelligence and National Security*, 17/1 (March 2002), 85–100.

— '"We are virtually at war with Russia": Britain and the Soviet menace in East Asia, 1923–40' (forthcoming).

Best, S. Payne, *The Venlo Incident* (London, n.d. [1950]).

Bethge, Eberhard, *Dietrich Bonhoeffer: A Biography* (London, 1970).

Blake, Robert, 'How Churchill became Prime Minister', in Robert Blake and Roger Louis (eds), *Churchill* (Oxford, 1993), 257–90.

Blishen, A. O., 'Sir Stewart Graham Menzies', 'Sir Richard Gambier-Parry' and 'Valentine Patrick Terrell Vivian', in *Oxford Dictionary of National Biography* (online version at www.oxforddnb. com, accessed 11 Mar. 2010).

Brogan, Hugh, *The Life of Arthur Ransome* (London, 1984).

Bruce Lockhart, John, 'Sir William Wiseman Bart – agent of influence', *RUSI Journal*, 134/2 (Summer 1989), 63–7.

Bruce Lockhart, R. H., *Memoirs of a British Agent* (London, 1932).

Bywater, Hector C., and Ferraby, H. C., *Strange Intelligence: Memoirs of Naval Secret Service* (London, 1934).

Cecil, Robert, '"C"'s war', *Intelligence and National Security*, 1/2 (May 1986), 170–88.

— 'Five of Six at war: Section V of MI6', *Intelligence and National Security*, 9/2 (April 1994), 345–53.

Churchill, Winston, *The World Crisis, 1911–1914* (London, 1923).

Ciechanowski, Jan Stanisław, and Tebinka, Jacek, 'Cryptographic cooperation – Enigma', in Stirling et al., *Intelligence Co-operation*, 442–62.

Clive, Nigel, *A Greek Experience 1943–1948* (London, 1985).

Cockerill, Sir George, *What Fools We Were* (London, n.d. [1944]).

Collier, Basil, *The Defence of the United Kingdom* (London, 1957).

Cook, Andrew, *Ace of Spies: The True Story of Sidney Reilly* (2nd edn, London, 2004).

Cross, John, *Red Jungle* (London, 1957).

Cruickshank, Charles, *SOE in the Far East* (Oxford, 1983).

— *SOE in Scandinavia* (Oxford, 1986).

Curry, John, *The Security Service, 1908–1945: The Official History* (London, 1999).

Dalton, Hugh, *The Fateful Years: Memoirs, 1931–1945* (London, 1957).

Debruyne, Emmanuel, *La Guerre secrète des espions belges, 1940–1944* (Brussels, 2008).

Decock, Pierre, 'La Dame Blanche: un réseau de renseignements de la grande guerre 1916–1918' (PhD thesis, Université Libre de Bruxelles, 1981).

Denham, Henry, *Inside the Nazi Ring: A Naval Attaché in Sweden 1940–1945* (London, 1964).

Denniston, A. G., 'The Government Code and Cypher School between the wars', *Intelligence and National Security*, 1/1 (Jan. 1986), 48–70.

de Young de la Marck, David, 'De Gaulle, Colonel Passy and British intelligence, 1940–42', *Intelligence and National Security*, 18/1 (Spring 2003), 21–40.

Donnison, F. S. V., *Civil Affairs and Military Government North West Europe, 1944–1946* (London, 1961).

Dukes, Sir Paul, *Red Dusk and the Morrow: Adventures and Investigations in Soviet Russia* (London, 1922).

— *The Story of 'ST 25'* (London, 1938).

Efrati, Yoram (ed.), *Yoman Aharon Aharonson 1916–1919* (Tel Aviv, 1970).

Erskine, Ralph, 'Eavesdropping on "Bodden": ISOS v. the Abwehr in the Straits of Gibraltar', *Intelligence and National Security*, 12/3 (July 1997), 110–29.

FCO Historians, *The Records of the Permanent Under-Secretary's Department: Liaison between the Foreign Office and British Secret Intelligence, 1873–1939* (London, 2005).

FCO Historical Branch, '"My Purdah Lady": The Foreign Office and the Secret Vote 1782–1909' (*FCO History Notes*, no. 7, 1994).

Ferguson, Harry, *Operation Kronstadt* (London, 2008).

Ferris, John, '"Far too dangerous a gamble"? British intelligence and policy during the Chanak Crisis', in Erik Goldstein and B. J. C. McKercher (eds), *Power and Stability: British Foreign Policy, 1865–1965* (London, 2003), 139–84.

— '"Indulged in all too little"? Vansittart, intelligence and appeasement', *Diplomacy and Statecraft*, 6/1 (Mar. 1995), 122–75.

— 'The road to Bletchley Park: the British experience with signals intelligence, 1892–1945', *Intelligence and National Security*, 17/1 (March 2002), 53–84.

Foot, M. R. D., *SOE in France* (London, 1966).

— *SOE in the Low Countries* (London, 2001).

— and Langley, J. M., *MI9: The British Secret Service that Fostered Escape and Evasion 1939–1945 and its American Counterpart* (London, 1979).

Forcade, Olivier, *La République secrète: histoire des services spéciaux français de 1918 à 1939* (Paris, 2008).

Fourcade, Marie-Madeleine, *L'Arche de Noé* (Paris, 1968); English translation, *Noah's Ark* (London, 1973).

Fowler, W. B., *British–American Relations 1917–1918: The Role of Sir William Wiseman* (Princeton, NJ, 1969).

Freeman, Peter, 'The Zimmermann Telegram revisited: a reconciliation of the primary sources', *Cryptologia*, 30/2 (2006), 98–150.

Garliński, Józef, *The Swiss Corridor: Espionage Networks in Switzerland during World War II* (London, 1981).

Gaunt, Guy, *The Yield of the Years: A Story of Adventure Afloat and Ashore* (London, 1940).

Gilbert, Martin, *Winston S. Churchill*, iv, companion part 3 (London, 1977).

Gisevius, Hans Bernd, *To the Bitter End* (London, 1948).

Goodman, Michael, *Official History of the Joint Intelligence Committee* (forthcoming).

Grahame-White, Montague, *At the Wheel Ashore and Afloat* (London, n.d. [1935]).

Guttridge, Roger, *The Royal Motor Yacht Club: The First 100 Years, 1905–2005* (Poole, Dorset, n.d. [2005]).

Hamilton, Keith, 'Dockside diplomacy: the Foreign Office and the Constantinople Quays Company', in FCO Historians, *Records*, 19–26.

Hart-Davis, Duff (ed.), *King's Counsellor. Abdication and War: The Diaries of Sir Alan Lascelles* (London, 2006).

Hartley, Harold, and Gabor, D., 'Thomas Ralph Merton', *Biographical Memoirs of Fellows of the Royal Society*, vol. 16 (Nov. 1970), 421–40.

Hazelhoff, Erik, *Soldier of Orange* (London, 1972).

Hiley, Nicholas, 'The failure of British counter-espionage against Germany, 1907–14', *Historical Journal*, 28/4 (Dec. 1985), 835–62.

— 'The failure of British espionage against Germany, 1907–14', *Historical Journal*, 26/4 (Dec. 1983), 867–89.

Hinsley, F. H., *British Intelligence in the Second World War: Its Influence on Strategy and Operations*, 3 vols (London, 1979–88).

— 'British intelligence in the Second World War', in Andrew and Noakes (eds), *Intelligence and International Relations*, 209–18.

— and Simkins, C. A. G., *British Intelligence in the Second World War*, iv, *Security and Counter Intelligence* (London, 1990).

Hoare, Samuel, *The Fourth Seal: The End of a Russian Chapter* (London, 1930).

Holt, Thaddeus, *The Deceivers: Allied Military Deception in the Second World War* (London, 2004).

Howard, Michael, *British Intelligence in the Second World War*, v, *Strategic Deception* (London, 1990).

— *The Continental Commitment: The Dilemma of British Defence Policy in the Era of Two World Wars* (Harmondsworth, 1974).

Howarth, Patrick, *Intelligence Chief Extraordinary: The Life of the Ninth Duke of Portland* (London, 1986).

Hyde, H. Montgomery, *The Quiet Canadian: The Secret Service Story of Sir William Stephenson* (London, 1962).

Insall, A. J. G., 'The relationship between the British and Norwegian Labour parties from 1945 to 1951' (PhD thesis, London University, 2007).

James, Robert Rhodes (ed.), *Memoirs of a Conservative: J. C. C. Davidson's Memoirs and Papers, 1910–37* (London, 1969).

James, Sir William, *The Eyes of the Navy: A Biographical Study of Admiral Sir Reginald Hall* (London, 1955).

Jeffery, Keith, *The British Army and the Crisis of Empire, 1918-22* (Manchester, 1984).

— *Field Marshal Sir Henry Wilson: A Political Soldier* (Oxford, 2006).

— 'British military intelligence following World War I', in K. G. Robertson (ed.), *British and American Approaches to Intelligence* (London, 1987), 55–84.

— 'The Government Code and Cypher School: a memorandum by Lord Curzon', *Intelligence and National Security*, 1/3 (Sept. 1986), 454–8.

— and Hennessy, Peter, *States of Emergency: British Governments and Strikebreaking since 1919* (London, 1983).

— and Sharp, Alan, 'Lord Curzon and secret intelligence', in Andrew and Noakes (eds), *Intelligence and International Relations*, 103–26.

Jeffreys-Jones, Rhodri, *American Espionage: From Secret Service to CIA* (London, 1977).

Johns, Philip, *Within Two Cloaks: Missions with SIS and SOE* (London, 1979).

Jones, H. A., *The War in the Air: Appendices* (Oxford, 1937).

Jones, R. V., *Most Secret War* (London, 1978).

— *Reflections on Intelligence* (London, 1989).

Jones, Thomas, *Whitehall Diary*, ed. Keith Middlemas, i, *1916–1925* (London, 1969).

Judd, Alan, *The Quest for C: Mansfield Cumming and the Founding of the Secret Service* (London, 1999).

Kahn, David, *The Codebreakers: The Story of Secret Writing* (London, 1966).

Kennedy, Paul, *The Rise and Fall of the Great Powers: Economic Change and Military Conflict from 1500 to 2000* (London, pbk edn, 1989).

Kirby, S. Woodburn, *The War against Japan*, i, *The Loss of Singapore* (London, 1957).

Kitchen, Martin, 'SOE's man in Moscow', *Intelligence and National Security*, 12/3 (July 1997), 95–109.

Knoblock, Edward, *Round the Room* (London, 1939).

Landau, Henry, *All's Fair: The Story of the British Secret Service behind the German Lines* (New York, 1934).

— *Secrets of the White Lady* (New York, 1935).

— *Spreading the Spy Net: The Story of a British Spy Director* (London, n.d. [1938]).

Laqueur, Walter, and Breitman, Richard, *Breaking the Silence: The Secret Mission of Eduard Schulte, who Brought the World News of the Final Solution* (London, 1986).

Liebreich, Fritz, *Britain's Naval and Political Reaction to the Illegal Immigration of Jews to Palestine, 1945–1948* (London, 2005).

Lycett, Andrew, *Ian Fleming* (London, pbk edn, 1996).

Lympany, Moura, *Moura: Her Autobiography* (London, 1991).

McCarthy, Helen, 'Petticoat diplomacy: the admission of women to the British Foreign Service, c. 1919–1946', *Twentieth Century British History*, 20/3 (2009), 285–321.

McKay, C. G., *From Information to Intrigue* (London, 1993).

— 'The Krämer case: a study in three dimensions', *Intelligence and National Security*, 4/2 (April 1989), 268–94.

Mackenzie, Compton, *Ægean Memories* (London, 1940).
— *First Athenian Memories* (London, 1931).
— *Greek Memories* (London, 1932).
— *My Life and Times: Octave Four, 1907–1915* (London, 1965); *Octave Five, 1915–1923* (London, 1966); *Octave Seven, 1931–1938* (London, 1968).
— *Water on the Brain* (London, 1933).
Mackenzie, W. J. M., *The Secret History of SOE: The Special Operations Executive 1940–1945* (London, 2000).
Macklin, Graham D., 'Major Hugh Pollard, MI6, and the Spanish Civil War', *Historical Journal*, 49/1 (2006), 277–80.
McLachlan, Donald, *Room 39: Naval Intelligence in Action, 1939–45* (London, 1968).
McLaren, Angus, 'Smoke and mirrors: Willie Clarkson and the role of disguises in inter-war England', *Journal of Social History*, 40/3 (Spring 2007), 597–618.
Madeira, Victor, 'British official and Intelligence responses to Soviet subversion against the United Kingdom, 1917–1929' (PhD thesis, Cambridge University, 2009).
— 'Moscow's interwar infiltration of British Intelligence, 1919–1929', *Historical Journal*, 46/4 (2003), 915–33.
Magill, J. H., *Tasavalta tulikokeessa* (Mikkeli, Finland, 1981).
Maugham, W. Somerset, *Ashenden, or the British Agent* (London, 1928).
— *The Partial View* (London, 1954)
— *The Summing Up* (London, 1938).
Mersey, Viscount, *A Picture of Life 1872–1940* (London, 1941).
Moberly, F. J., *The Campaign in Mesopotamia, 1914–1918*, 4 vols (London, 1923–7).
Moravec, Frantisek, *Master of Spies: The Memoirs of General Frantisek Moravec* (London, 1975).
Morris, A. J. A., *C. P. Trevelyan, 1870–1958: Portrait of a Radical* (Belfast, 1977).
Mure, David, *Master of Deception: Tangled Webs in London and the Middle East* (London, 1980).
Murray, Arthur C., *Master and Brother: Murrays of Elibank* (London, 1945).
Naftali, Timothy J., 'Intrepid's last deception: documenting the career of Sir William Stephenson', *Intelligence and National Security*, 8/3 (July 1993), 72–99.
National Archives, *Special Forces in the Desert War, 1940–1943* (Kew, 2001).
Neilson, Keith, '"Joy rides"?: British intelligence and propaganda in Russia, 1914–1917', *Historical Journal*, 24/4 (1981), 885–906.
Newbolt, Henry, *Naval Operations*, v, *From April 1917, to the End of the War* (London, 1931).
O'Halpin, Eunan, 'Financing British intelligence: the evidence up to 1945', in K. G. Robertson (ed.), *British and American Approaches to Intelligence* (Basingstoke, 1987), 187–217.
— *Head of the Civil Service: A Study of Sir Warren Fisher* (London, 1989).
— *Spying on Ireland: British Intelligence and Irish Neutrality during the Second World War* (Oxford, 2008).
— (ed.), *MI5 and Ireland, 1939–1945: The Official History* (Dublin, 2003).
Olsen, Oluf Reed, *Two Eggs on my Plate* (London, 1952).
Onslow, Sue, 'Britain and the Belgrade *coup* of 27 March 1941 revisited', *Electronic Journal of International History*, no. 8 (March 2005) (www.history.ac.uk/ejournal/Onslow.pdf) (accessed 9 July 2007).
Paillole, Paul, *Services spéciaux: 1935–1945* (Paris, 1975).
Pidgeon, Geoffrey, *The Secret Wireless War* (rev. repr., St Leonards-on-Sea, Sussex, 2006).
Pinero, Arthur W., *The Gay Lord Quex* (London, 1899).
Popplewell, Richard J., *Intelligence and Imperial Defence: British Intelligence and the Defence of the Indian Empire, 1904–1924* (London, 1995).

Porch, Douglas, 'French intelligence and the fall of France', *Intelligence and National Security*, 4/1 (Jan. 1989), 28–58.

Pringle, Jack, *Colditz Last Stop: Six Escapes Remembered* (London, 1988).

Proctor, Tammy M., *Female Intelligence: Women and Espionage in the First World War* (London, 2003).

Read, Anthony, and Fisher, David, *Colonel Z: The Life and Times of a Master of Spies* (London, 1984).

'Rémy' [Gilbert Renault], *Le Livre du courage et de la peur*, 3 vols (Paris, 1945–7).

Richards, Brooks, *Secret Flotillas*, 2 vols: i, *Clandestine Sea Operations to Brittany, 1940–1944*; ii, *Clandestine Sea Operations in the Mediterranean, North Africa and the Adriatic, 1940–1944* (both London, 2004).

Rigden Denis, *How to be a Spy: The World War II SOE Training Manual* (Toronto, 2004).

Riste, Olav, *The Norwegian Intelligence Service, 1945–1970* (London, 1999).

Rivet, Géneral Louis, *Carnets secrets du chef des services spéciaux 1936–1944*, ed. Olivier Forcade and Sébastien Laurent (Paris, 2010).

Roskill, Stephen, *Hankey: Man of Secrets*, 3 vols (London, 1970–4)

— *The War at Sea 1939–1945*, 3 vols (London, 1954–61).

Rygor Słowikowski, Mieczysław Z., *In the Secret Service: The Lighting of the Torch* (London, 1988).

Seaman, Mark (ed.), *Special Operations Executive: A New Instrument of War* (London, 2006).

Seligmann, Matthew S., *Spies in Uniform; British Military and Naval Intelligence on the Eve of the First World War* (Oxford, 2006).

— (ed.), *Naval Intelligence from Germany: The Reports of the British Naval Attachés in Berlin, 1906–1914* (Aldershot, Hants, 2007).

Sheffy, Yigal, 'British Intelligence and the Middle East, 1900–1918: how much do we know?', *Intelligence and National Security*, 17/1 (March 2002), 37–52.

— *British Military Intelligence in the Palestine Campaign, 1914–1918* (London, 1998).

Shelly, Adam, 'British Intelligence in the Middle East, 1939–1946' (PhD thesis, Cambridge University, 2007).

Smith, Bradley F., *Sharing Secrets with Stalin: How the Allies Traded Intelligence, 1941–1945* (Lawrence, Kan., 1996).

Smith, Michael, *Foley: The Spy Who Saved 10,000 Jews* (London, 1999).

Spence, Richard B., *Boris Savinkov: Renegade on the Left* (Boulder, Colo., 1991).

— 'Englishmen in New York: the SIS American Station, 1915–21', *Intelligence and National Security*, 19/3 (Autumn 2004), 511–37.

— 'Interrupted journey: British intelligence and the arrest of Leon Trotskii, April 1917', *Revolutionary Russia*, 13/1 (June 2000), 1–28.

Stafford, David, *Roosevelt & Churchill: Men of Secrets* (London, 1999).

Stirling, Tessa, Nałęcz, Daria, and Dubicki, Tadeusz (eds), *Intelligence Co-operation between Poland and Great Britain during World War II*, 2 vols: i, *The Report of the Anglo-Polish Historical Committee* (London, 2005); ii, *Documents*, ed. Jan Stanisław Ciechanowski (Warsaw, 2005).

Strong, Kenneth, *Intelligence at the Top: The Recollections of an Intelligence Officer* (London, 1968).

Templewood, Viscount (Sir Samuel Hoare), *Ambassador on Special Mission* (London, 1946).

Thomas, Edward, 'Norway's role in British wartime intelligence', in Patrick Salmon (ed.), *Britain and Norway in the Second World War* (London, 1995), 121–8.

Thorne, Christopher, 'MacArthur, Australia and the British, 1942–1943: the secret journal of MacArthur's British Liaison Officer' (Parts I and II), in *Australian Outlook*, 29/1 and 2 (April and Aug. 1975), 53–67 and 197–210.

Thwaites, Norman, *Velvet and Vinegar* (London, 1932).

Trevor-Roper, Hugh, *The Philby Affair: Espionage, Treason, and Secret Services* (London, 1968).

Troy, Thomas F., *Wild Bill and Intrepid: Donovan, Stephenson and the Origins of the CIA* (London, 1996).

Ullman, R. H., *Anglo-Soviet Relations, 1917–1921*, 3 vols (London, 1961–72).

Ustinov, Nadia Benois, *Klop and the Ustinov Family* (London, 1973).

Walton, Calder, 'British Intelligence and the Mandate of Palestine: threats to British national security immediately after the Second World War', *Intelligence and National Security*, 23/4 (Aug. 2008), 435–62.

Wark, Wesley, 'Baltic myths and submarine bogeys: British naval intelligence and Nazi Germany 1933–1939', *Journal of Strategic Studies*, 6/1 (1983), 60–81.

Wedgwood, Josiah C., *Memoirs of a Fighting Life* (London, 1941).

'Whitwell, John' [Leslie Nicholson], *British Agent* (London, 1966).

Wilkinson, Peter, and Bright Astley, Joan, *Gubbins and SOE* (London, 1993)

Willert, Sir Arthur, *The Road to Safety: A Study in Anglo-American Relations* (London, 1952).

Williams, Valentine, *The World of Action* (London, 1938).

Winter, Ormonde, *Winter's Tale: An Autobiography* (London, 1955).

Winter, P. R. J, 'British Intelligence, Adolf Hitler and the German High Command, 1939–1945' (PhD thesis, Cambridge University, 2009).

Winterbotham, Frederick William, *The Nazi Connection* (London, 1978).

— *The Ultra Secret* (London, 1974).

Wood, J. E. R. (ed.), *Detour: The Story of Oflag IVC* (London, 1946).

Woodward, Sir Llewellyn, *British Foreign Policy in the Second World War* (rev. repr., London, 1972).

Index